COMPLEX HUMAN BEHAVIOR

A series of volumes edited by
Leon Festinger and Stanley Schachter

COGNITIVE ORGANIZATION
AND CHANGE:
AN INFORMATION PROCESSING APPROACH

COGNITIVE ORGANIZATION AND CHANGE: AN INFORMATION PROCESSING APPROACH

BY ROBERT S. WYER, JR.

UNIVERSITY OF ILLINOIS AT CHAMPAIGN-URBANA

 LAWRENCE ERLBAUM ASSOCIATES, PUBLISHERS
1974   Potomac, Maryland

DISTRIBUTED BY THE HALSTED PRESS DIVISION OF

JOHN WILEY & SONS
New York   Toronto   London   Sydney

Lawrence Erlbaum Associates, Publishers
12736 Lincolnshire Drive
Potomac, Maryland 20854

Distributed solely by Halsted Press Division
John Wiley & Sons, Inc., New York

Library of Congress Cataloging in Publication Data

Wyer, Robert S.
    Cognitive organization and change.

    (Complex human behavior)
    1.   Cognition.   2.   Attitude (Psychology)   3.   Atti-
tude change.   4.   Human information processing.
I.   Title.
BF311.W87   153   74-12312
ISBN 0-470-96899-0

Printed in the United States of America

CONTENTS

v

Preface

This book grew out of a graduate course in cognitive organization and change that I taught during my tenure at the University of Illinois at Chicago Circle. Two primary objectives of the course are reflected in this book: first, to provide a general conceptual framework for critically and systematically analyzing research and theory on attitude and opinion change; second, to stimulate research on fundamental problems, related to these phenomena, that are made salient as a result of this analysis.

As the preceding comments suggest, the orientation of this book is not eclectic. On the other hand, its perspective is not so parochial that the typical reader will be uncomfortable with the approach taken and with the interpretations given to the phenomena being considered. In progressing through the volume, one will find that nearly all of the theoretical and empirical issues pervading current research and theory in attitude and opinion change are discussed, although often in a different context, and from a different point of view, than is common in this area. Attention is focused upon the way in which information affects cognitions (beliefs and attitudes) about the objects to which it pertains, and the manner in which these cognitions are reported to others. Four basic issues related to these processes are considered in some detail: (a) the manner in which previously formed cognitions are organized and interrelated, and the effect that information bearing directly upon one cognition has upon others; (b) the factors that affect the reception of new information, and the tendency to accept this information as valid; (c) the manner in which several different pieces of information, presented in combination, are used in arriving at judgments of objects; and (d) the factors that affect the language used to communicate these judgments to other persons. In the course of this discussion, we will attempt to develop a general conceptual orientation that will be helpful in (a) identifying and evaluating the assumptions underlying alternative theoretical formulations of belief and attitude formation and change, (b) interpreting existing data bearing upon these phenomena, and (c) generating many new hypotheses concerning them. In many instances, quantitative descriptions of the processes being considered are proposed; these descriptions suggest ways of predicting the magnitude of attitude and belief change in many situations, and also have value as "diagnostic" tools in isolating the relative contributions of factors that account for these changes.

Many groups and individuals have contributed in different ways to the preparation of this volume. A major portion of the manuscript was completed while I was visiting psychologist at the MRC Social and Applied Psychology Unit, University of Sheffield, England, on sabbatical leave from the University of Illinois. I am grateful to the Unit, and particularly to its director, Dr. Peter B. Warr, for assistance during this phase of the project. The preparation of the manuscript, and virtually all of the research I have done which bears upon the issues discussed (some of which is reported here for the first time), was supported by National Science Foundation grants GS 1356, GS 2291, GS 29241, and GS 39938. Without this support, the book would not have been possible.

Three individuals — Robert P. Abelson, Norman H. Anderson, and William J. McGuire — have had a major impact upon my work over the course of the past several years; this influence has been both through direct criticism of my work and through the inspiration provided by their own outstanding contributions to research and theory in cognitive organization and information integration. Two other colleagues, Harry F. Gollob and Harry S. Upshaw, have also been major sources of stimulation and criticism. The influence of these persons, and my indebtedness to them, will be readily apparent to readers of this book.

Other persons' contributions are less obvious, but no less strongly felt. Among these is Isadore Farber, whose remarkable analytical and critical ability has made him an invaluable professional colleague, and whose confidence in me at an early stage of my professional career, along with that of Glenn Terrell, has had a personal value inexpressible in words. O. J. Harvey and William A. Scott, with whom I worked as a graduate student, not only stimulated my substantive interests in cognitive social psychology but, in combination, provided a blend of innovativeness and methodological and conceptual rigor that I have strived to maintain.

Several colleagues have made detailed criticisms of this manuscript. I am particularly indebted to Charles L. Gruder, Reid Hastie, and Harry Gollob, each of whom made extensive and perceptive comments on major sections, and to Harry Upshaw and Steven J. Sherman, who provided equally valuable criticisms of individual chapters. Still other colleagues, whose identities are not know to me, have had less direct but important influences upon the ideas contained in this volume through their reviews of my work for publication in professional journals. These criticisms, not always favorable, have been of great value, and my sincere appreciation to these "anonymous" colleagues is gratefully acknowledged.

Perhaps the largest debt of gratitude is owed those who, as undergraduate and graduate students, assisted in the design and conceptualization of the research upon which much of this book is based. While a complete list of these persons is impossible, particularly important contributions were made by Marti Bazell, Marshall Dermer, Lee Goldberg, Thomas Gronek, Marilyn Henninger, Edward Kepka, John Lyon, Linda Oyer, Steven Polen, Hugh Rehm, Daniel Romer, Nancy Rosen, Sandra Schwartz, and Stanley Watson.

Finally, I want to express very sincere appreciation to the staff of Lawrence Erlbaum Associates, whose expenditures of time and effort on behalf of this book have been far beyond the call of duty, and with whom it has been a genuine pleasure to work.

Robert S. Wyer, Jr.

May 1974

1
MAN AS AN INFORMATION PROCESSOR: AN APPROACH TO THE INTERPRETATION OF BEHAVIOR

This book is about the manner in which beliefs and attitudes are developed and modified. More fundamentally, it is concerned with how information about persons, objects, or events is used in arriving at and reporting judgments of these stimuli. This information may be contained in written or oral communications about the stimulus to be judged. It may also be provided by more subtle aspects of the situation in which the judgment is made. For example, a person who administers an opinion questionnaire may convey the impression that he personally agrees with the statements contained in it. Or, a person who offers someone money to perform a task may give the impression that he personally considers the task to be important. Such impressions, correct or not, may affect the judgments reported in a given situation.

Another source of information is a person's behavior when in contact with the object to be judged. For example, a child who observes someone scream upon seeing a snake may infer that snakes are harmful. Studies of the acquisition of behavior and attitudes through observational learning (for a summary, see Bandura & Walters, 1963) demonstrate the potency of this information. In some circumstances, one's *own* behavior, like the behavior of others, may provide information about a stimulus. Bem (1967) has suggested that people typically do not make definite judgments of a stimulus until they are asked to do so; once they are asked, their own recent behavior toward the stimulus may provide cues as to what these judgments should be. Thus, if a person has picked up a snake and fondled it, and he is subsequently asked to judge the pleasantness of snakes, he may reason: "Persons who fondle snakes typically regard them as pleasant. I have fondled a snake; therefore, I must regard snakes as pleasant." Bem's general hypothesis can be applied in situations where the stimulus being judged is the judge himself. It suggests, for example, that a person's judgment that he is not very hungry may at times be the *result* of a decision to go without lunch rather than a *determinant* of this decision.

The "judgment" referred to above can also be of several types. One type of judgment is probabilistic; that is, one may estimate the likelihood that an object has a particular attribute, or that a certain statement about an object is true. Judgments may also be in terms of the *amount* of an attribute possessed by an object (for example, the intelligence of a college professor, or the favorableness of one's own feelings toward Communism). As we shall see, these two types of judgments are theoretically quite similar, and the processes underlying them may differ primarily in complexity. However, each has certain unique properties that make it useful in understanding particular judgmental phenomena.

I. MAN AS AN INFORMATION PROCESSOR

To convey the general philosophical approach to understanding cognitive processes we will take in this book, it may be helpful to draw an analogy between the human "information processor" and the computer, its electronic counterpart. Each processor is capable of receiving information, operating upon it according to certain rules, storing the results of these operations in memory, altering the contents of certain areas of memory to which new information is relevant, and ultimately reporting the results of these operations in a form that is implicitly or explicitly specified by a "user." The user of a human information processor may be the investigator in a psychological experiment, the teacher of a large lecture course, or simply a participant in an informal social interaction.

Several aspects of an information processor must be understood if it is to be used effectively and if its output is to be correctly interpreted:

1. The structure and organization of memory—the laws that govern the organization and storage of information in memory and the relations among the contents of different memory locations.

2. Information acquisition—the rules governing the reception of information, or "inputs"; limitations upon the amount of information that can be accommodated, and the rate at which it can be assimilated; successive vs. simultaneous input of information; time-sharing capabilities (that is, the capacity to receive and process two different and unrelated bodies of information simultaneously); priority decisions in times of overload.

3. Integration and processing of information—the logical and arithmetic operations used in generating solutions to problems of interest to the user; the processes of modifying the contents of memory locations in response to new information.

4. Language translation rules—the transformation of input information into "machine language," that is, into a form that can be processed by internal procedures available to the central processor; retranslation of problem solutions into a form that is understandable and acceptable to the user. (Since the form of the input information and the form of the output requested by the user may differ, the translation rules involved may also differ.)

The general analogy between electronic information processors and human processors seems appropriate. However, there is of course an important distinction. The rules and operations involved in the processing of information by a computer are all imposed by the designer of the machine. In the case of the human processor, these rules and operations are not known *a priori*. The objective of the psychologist is to discover the nature of these rules and operations and to use them to predict the output resulting from certain sets of input information.

In the preceding analogy, the role of motivation is well-hidden. One does not usually attribute "motivation" to a computer, at least as the term is commonly used (cf. Cofer & Appley, 1964). In one sense, however, computers *are* motivated; that is, they use information to attain certain specific objectives (generally, to solve particular problems of interest to the user). In this sense, the user gives motivation or incentive to the processor through the program he selects to analyze his data. In many instances, the objective of a human information processor (or *subject*, since he is the focus of attention throughout this book) is also specified by the user. In a psychological experiment, for example, the subject comes to the situation with the implicit expectation that his services are required to help the experimenter test a particular hypothesis, or to investigate a particular problem. While instructions are given concerning the general nature of the task to be performed, the specific problem to be solved (that is, the experimenter's hypothesis) is often not stated, or at least is incompletely described. The subject must therefore use whatever additional information is provided him to interpret the nature of the problem and to determine which "program" he should call from memory and use to generate an acceptable solution (in other words, what he should do in order to generate outputs that will adequately answer the question investigated by the experimenter). Then, he must report these solutions in a form that the user will regard as acceptable.

Readers will recognize this notion as a restatement of Orne's (1962) hypothesis that subjects are influenced by demand characteristics of the experimental situation. It draws attention to the fact that subjects in an experiment may simply be trying to behave as they think they are expected to behave by the person with whom they are interacting. Although this conclusion has little theoretical significance, it is not without interest. It emphasizes that an understanding of a subject's responses in an experimental situation requires a careful analysis of (*a*) the information provided the subject, both directly or indirectly, about the experimental task and (*b*) the inferences the subject is likely to draw from information concerning the experimenter's objectives and expectancies.

Of course, the behavior *ostensibly* considered most acceptable by an experimenter may not be the behavior he would *actually* like to have occur. For example, suppose an experimenter indicates that a test he is administering measures intellectual ability. The experimenter may be interested in selecting low-ability subjects to participate in a later experiment and thus would prefer subjects to generate "incorrect" responses. However, in the absence of an explicit statement to the contrary, a subject is likely to infer that the experimenter's objective is to see how many "correct" answers he can produce and therefore will generate as many responses of this type as possible.

The preceding analysis is perhaps somewhat oversimplified, since it suggests that there is only one "user" of the human information processor at any given time. In fact, there may be several different users (for example, other participants in the experiment, or persons outside the experimental situation to whom the subject may communicate his activities and their results). If the outputs considered acceptable by these users differ, it could be difficult to predict *a priori* which user would determine the "program" used by the subject, and thus which outputs will be generated. Fortunately, in practice this problem may not be as serious as it seems. Milgram (1965a, 1965b) has obtained impressive evidence to suggest that when the expectancies ostensibly held for a subject by an experimenter conflict with those presumably held for him by others outside the experimental situation, the former most often determine the subject's behavior. In these studies, unpaid volunteer subjects were asked to "teach" a stooge to perform a task by administering a shock whenever the stooge made an error. The subjects used had no connection the university at which the study took place and were in no way responsible to the experimenter. As the experiment progressed, the "learner" made frequent errors according to a prearranged schedule. After each error, the amount of shock administered was increased. (The stooge was placed in a room out of sight of the subject, and of course actually received no shocks at all.) Despite loud moaning and protesting by the stooge that he had a "heart condition," many subjects continued to administer shocks up to the maximum level (450 volts) and required only mild verbal pressure by the experimenter to do so. In fact, the average amount of shock administered by a sample of 40 subjects was 368 volts. In contrast, when the experimental situation was described to control (nonparticipating) subjects, they generally regarded the experiment as "immoral" and predicted on the average that they would be willing to administer only 135 volts of shock. Similar predictions about subjects' behavior were made by a group of experienced clinical psychologists to whom the experiment was described (Milgram, 1965b). These data suggest that the tendency to comply with the wishes of the investigator in a psychological experiment is far stronger than researchers often assume. Since nonparticipants clearly disapproved of shocking the "learner," Milgram's findings also suggest that behavior in an experiment is more influenced by the immediate demands of the situation than by expectancies held for subjects by others outside this situation.

II. GENERAL IMPLICATIONS FOR RESEARCH

The approach outlined above has some quite specific implications for research on attitude and belief processes, as we shall attempt to demonstrate in the chapters to follow. More generally, the orientation we are proposing focuses upon (a) the type of information provided the subject in a particular social situation about the objectives he is expected to attain and the means of attaining them, and (b) the subject's capacity to receive and process information in the situation. This orientation may potentially help to clarify many social psychological phenomena studied in the laboratory. To support this assertion, some examples may be helpful.

A. Experimenter Effects upon Information Processing

The point we have made—that subjects often use the information provided in an experiment to infer the nature of the experimenter's expectations, and then respond in a way that conforms to these expectancies—may seem obvious. However, it is overlooked in many studies that are designed to investigate more central theoretical issues. Thus the results of these experiments are often difficult to interpret. To provide some examples of this, and also to show the distinction between an "information processing" interpretation of behavior and alternative theoretical interpretations, let us consider some representative experiments in the area of attitude and opinion change. In each case, we will first describe relevant aspects of the experiment and the theoretical issue it was designed to investigate, and will then reinterpret the experiment and the results obtained from an information processing point of view.

1. Sampson and Insko (1964). Sampson and Insko designed an interesting study to test certain implications of cognitive-consistency theory. According to this theory, inconsistencies among beliefs and attitudes are aversive and therefore tend to be eliminated. In the situation studied by Sampson and Insko, a state of consistency was defined as one in which a subject's (P's) belief about an object (X) was either similar to that of another (O) who was liked, or dissimilar to that of a disliked O. They tested the hypothesis that when P receives information that his cognitions about O and X are inconsistent, he will change his belief about X to regain consistency.

To test their hypothesis, the authors constructed an interaction situation in which a confederate (O) behaved toward P in a way that was intended to induce P either to like him or to dislike him. Under Liking conditions, O behaved toward P in a friendly and cooperative manner on a group achievement task, attributed favorable characteristics to him, and presented himself as similar to P in social and cultural background and in general attitudes and values. Under Disliking conditions, O behaved uncooperatively on the group task, blamed P for the failure to complete it successfully, attributed negative characteristics to P, and presented himself as dissimilar to P in background, attitudes, and values. After the manipulation of liking had been administered, P and O were asked to make judgments of the distance moved by a point of light (X) in a standard autokinetic situation. This task was described as a projective test of personality; subjects were told that persons who made similar estimates of X were similar in their underlying personality structure. Upon learning of P's initial estimates, O made judgments that were either very similar to P's or very dissimilar to P's. As predicted, when P found that his judgments of X were different from those of a liked O, he changed them to make them more similar to O's; on the other hand, when P found that his judgments were the same as those of a disliked O, he changed them to make them different from O's.

Although the results of this study support Sampson and Insko's theoretical position, an alternative interpretation is possible. Assume that P's primary objective in the study was to respond in a manner expected of him by the experimenter, and that he used the information provided him to determine the nature of these expectancies. Note that the manipulation of P's liking for O, although it was undoubtedly successful, also provided ostensibly objective information to P that O was either similar to him in background and values (under Liking conditions) or dissimilar to him (under Disliking conditions). P was also told that the autokinetic task was a measure of similarity in personality. If P inferred that the experimenter regarded the instrument as valid, he may have responded in a way that the experimenter would consider "correct," that is, in a way that ostensibly reflected the actual similarity between P and O, independently of P's personal liking for O. This would also account for the results obtained.

Here, and in the remaining studies we will discuss, it is important to bear in mind that the original interpretation of the results given by the authors may indeed be valid. The mere existence of an alternative explanation of a phenomenon obviously does not indicate that the original interpretation is incorrect. It is much easier to generate *post hoc* hypotheses for obtained results than to construct studies that successfully test the validity of *a priori* hypothesis. The studies being described here are presented primarily to demonstrate an information processing approach to understanding social phenomena and not to destroy other interpretations.

2. Walters, Marshall, and Shooter (1960). These authors also used an autokinetic task to test an hypothesis stemming from a social-learning formulation of behavior. When a subject has been deprived of social contact for a brief period of time, he learns relatively more quickly when social approval is given for a "correct" response. This finding had originally been interpreted as evidence that deprivation of social stimulation increases the value of this type of stimulation, much as going without eating increases the reinforcement value of food (cf. Gewirtz & Baer, 1958). However, Walters et al. argued that the increased effectiveness of social reinforcement under deprivation conditions is not due to the absence of social contact *per se*, but rather is due to an increase in general arousal that often accompanies social isolation. This arousal increases sensitivity to cues elicited by the reinforcing agent, and therefore previously conditioned responses are made to these cues. Walters et al. hypothesized that if social deprivation and arousal were manipulated independently, only the latter variable would affect responsiveness to a social reinforcer.

In the experiment, college subjects, run individually, were initially exposed to the autokinetic situation and were asked to estimate the distance moved by the point of light over a series of trials. Then, subjects run under *high arousal* conditions were administered a test that purportedly measured their intelligence and general ability. Subjects run under *low arousal* conditions were asked to indicate their aesthetic preference for each of a set of stimuli and were told that there were no right or wrong answers. It was assumed that subjects would be more concerned about their performance in the first condition than in the second, and that therefore their arousal would be greater. To manipulate social deprivation, half of the subjects under each arousal condition performed the task in the presence of the experimenter, while the remaining subjects performed the task with the experimenter out of the room.

After the above test had been completed, the autokinetic task was readministered. Before beginning, each subject was told that his initial judgments had generally been too low, and that on the present series of trials the experimenter would indicate whether he had responded within an acceptable range of the correct judgment by saying "right." The experimenter then began to "reinforce" responses that were equal to or greater than the subject's largest response on previous trials, and this continued until a criterion of three consecutive responses as large as that on earlier trials was reached. As predicted, subjects under high arousal conditions reached criterion in fewer trials, and made generally larger estimates, than did subjects under low arousal conditions, while the manipulation of social isolation had no significant effects.

To interpret the study within an information-processing framework, consider what information is provided subjects concerning the experimenter's objective. Subjects who are asked to take an intelligence test may infer that the experimenter is interested in measuring their ability to perform well, or to generate correct answers. They may assume that this objective also applies to the autokinetic task, during which the experimenter, in effect, gives them detailed information about how to generate "right" answers. In contrast, subjects who are initially administered the preference task are told explicitly that there are no right or wrong answers, and thus may infer that the experimenter is interested in their personal opinions, and not in the objective accuracy of their responses. If this inference is also assumed to generalize to the autokinetic situation, these subjects may be inclined to report their actual judgments of the distance moved by the light, regardless of information provided them concerning the "correct" distance. To this extent, reinforcement would have less effect upon these subjects than upon those administered the intelligence test, as the authors found. The presense or absence of the experimenter while the subjects perform the intelligence (or preference) test conveys little if any information concerning the type of response in which the experimenter is interested, and thus should have no effect upon subjects' judgments. (If anything, the experimenter would appear to be more concerned about subjects' performance when he remains in the room during the task than when he leaves. It is therefore worth noting that nonisolated subjects made nonsignificantly larger estimates, and were conditioned nonsignificantly more rapidly, than isolated subjects.) In summary, an information-processing formulation could also account for the results obtained by Walters et al.

Incidentally, an information-processing orientation makes salient other questions about the nature of the effects observed in studies where subjects are asked to make judgments of physical stimuli. As we have noted, one function of the information processor (be it a human subject or a computer) is to translate internally coded information into a form that is acceptable to the user. In judgmental tasks of the sort constructed by Walters et al., it is often unclear whether experimental manipulations affect the subjective judgments of the stimuli presented, or simply the language used to report these judgments. These alternative possibilities cannot be distinguished in the study described above. However, it seems likely that social reinforcement of the nature administered by Walters et al. did not affect subjects' actual perceptions of the distances the light moved, but rather affected the numbers they assigned to these distances. That is, after being told that their estimates were too low, subjects may have inferred that the rule they had been using to label their subjective judgments was incorrect, and thus they may have added a constant to their original responses. While the distinction between subjective judgments and verbal reports may be obvious, it often proves to be an important one in interpreting research on social judgment and attitude change. This issue will be discussed more fully in Chapter 3.

3. Aronson and Mills (1959). Aronson and Mills tested an implication of cognitive-dissonance theory for the effect of severe initiations upon subsequent liking for a group. The essentials of this theory, which are discussed in detail in Chapter 11, can be summarized briefly. When a person decides to engage in a particular activity, certain cognitions are consonant with this decision (that is, they imply that the decision was correct) while others are dissonant (they imply that the decision was incorrect). Dissonance is aversive and thus tends to be reduced by changing one or more of the cognitions involved. In the situation constructed by Aronson and Mills, subjects decided whether or not to join a discussion group. A liking for the group was assumed to be consonant with the decision to join, while the severity of the initiation required in order to join was assumed to be dissonant. One way of reducing the proportion of dissonance with the decision to join is to increase the amount of consonance, that is, to increase one's liking for the group. Based upon this reasoning, Aronson and Mills predicted that liking for the group would be greater among subjects who were required to undergo a severe initiation in order to join than among those who underwent a milder, and thus less dissonance-arousing, initiation.

To test this hypothesis, the authors recruited female volunteers to join a discussion group on sex. In order to join, subjects were required to take an "embarrassment test." Under *severe initiation* conditions, subjects read aloud some fairly obscene sex-related words and also a vivid description of sexual activity. This task was assumed to be extremely embarrassing to the subjects involved. Under *mild initiation* conditions, subjects simply read a short list of rather innocuous sex-related words (e.g. "prostitute," "virgin," etc.). Subjects under *control* conditions were not exposed to any initiation. All subjects were then told that the group discussion had already begun and that they should therefore listen in on the discussion through earphones but not actively participate. They listened to a prerecorded, boring discussion of the sexual behavior of animals. Then they were asked to estimate how interesting the discussion had been. Results were as expected: Severely initiated subjects rated the discussion as more interesting than both controls and mildly initiated subjects.

Many alternative interpretations have been given to the results obtained in this interesting study (cf. Chapanis & Chapanis, 1964), several of which have subsequently been demonstrated to be incorrect (Gerard & Mathewson, 1966). An information-processing interpretation still seems plausible. The severity of the initiation may be an implicit indication to subjects of the importance the experimenter personally attaches to the discussion; a person who requires a severe initiation in order to join a group generally considers the group discussion to be more important and worthwhile than a person who imposes a less stringent criterion for admission. If this is the case, subjects under severe initiation conditions may have rated the discussion as more interesting, not because they personally believed it to be so, but because they inferred that the experimenter considered such a judgment more acceptable.

Results of a study by Schopler and Bateson (1962) provide indirect support for this interpretation. These authors replicated the severe-initiation and control conditions used by Aronson and Mills. In addition, they ran a third condition that was identical to the severe initiation condition except that, after subjects were initiated but before they heard the discussion, the experimenter "incidentally" remarked that he personally had found previous discussions to be "pretty dull" and that the present discussion "probably won't be at all exciting." Under this condition, subjects' ratings of the discussion were significantly less than those of severely initiated subjects who did not hear the experimenter's opinion, and did not differ appreciably from control subjects' ratings. This suggests that when the experimenter's opinions are made explicit, subjects conform to these opinions and use the quality of initiation as a cue only when direct information about the experimenter's expectations is not available. (Curiously, Schopler and Bateson apparently overlooked this interpretation of their data and discussed their results within a much more complicated social-power framework.)

4. Scott (1957, 1959). Scott performed a series of studies to test the hypothesis that social reinforcement for engaging in attitude-related behavior can produce attitude change. In the second study, pairs of subjects debated an issue before a panel of three judges (the experimenter, another professor, and a graduate student). After presenting their arguments and rebuttal, subjects were informed of who had won the debate. (The outcome of the debate was predetermined and therefore was independent of the actual quality of subjects' performances.) Scott found that winners changed their attitudes toward the position they had advocated significantly more than did losers, who did not differ from a control group that did not engage in the debate. Moreover, similar changes occurred regardless of whether subjects' initial attitudes had been in favor of or opposed to the position advocated. Scott's hypothesis was therefore supported.

In evaluating the extent to which the results described above are also interpretable within the information-processing framework proposed, it is important to note that the experimenter himself served as one of the judges in the debates being staged, and that he also had access to subjects' reports of their attitudes after the debates. Results therefore seem quite consistent with the assumption that subjects attempt to respond in a manner that they believe is acceptable to the experimenter. Winners were implicitly told that the experimenter (as well as others) approved of behavior associated with advocating a particular position. It is therefore not too surprising that on a subsequent questionnaire they would continue to advocate this position. As Scott himself observes, a better procedure would be to have the attitude questionnaire administered in a completely different experimental context by someone other than the experimenter. However, even this precaution might not eliminate the problem. Subjects who receive information that their advocacy of a position is approved by one person may infer that their endorsement of this position will also receive approval from others. Therefore, social "reinforcement" may have fairly widespread effects upon persons' behavior in a variety of social contexts.

While Scott found that reward increases attitude change, other studies have found attitude change to be related *negatively* to the amount of monetary incentive given to advocate a position in which one does not believe (Brehm & Cohen, 1962; Festinger & Carlsmith, 1959). Although several attempts have been made to account for these opposite findings (McGuire) 1968a; Rosenberg, 1965; Wallace, 1966; Zajonc, 1968), none seems completely satisfactory. A resolution of the dilemma is suggested by considering the informational properties of the incentive used in the studies supporting each hypothesis. In studies that show positive relations between reward and attitude change, such as Scott's, reward is typically given *after* the attitude-related behavior has occurred, ostensibly as a consequence of superior performance. In these cases, as noted above, the reward may provide information that the opinions expressed and the behavior of advocating them will receive approval from others; the tendency to express these opinions in the future may therefore increase. In studies that show negative relations between reward and attitude change, the incentive is typically offered before engaging in the attitude-related behavior, as an inducement to engage in the behavior, and is *not* contingent upon the quality of one's performance. In these studies, the reward offered may convey the information that the behavior is regarded by the experimenter as difficult or unpleasant, and that the subject is not expected to want to perform the activity requested. An experiment reported by Linder, Cooper, and Jones (1967) is interesting to consider in this context. Subjects received either high ($2.50) or low ($.50) pay to write an essay. Under "free-decision" conditions, subjects were offered the pay as an "incentive" for writing the essay, before they agreed to do so. Under "no choice" conditions, subjects were not told of the pay they would receive until after they had implicitly agreed to write the essay. It seems reasonable that in the first condition, subjects are apt to infer that the amount of pay offered reflects the strength of the experimenter's belief that they are unwilling to write the essay, presumably because they are opposed to the position to be advocated. In the second condition, however, subjects may be more apt to infer that the amount of pay reflects the experimenter's approval of the position to be advocated. Therefore, if subjects respond in a manner they believe is expected of them, the attitudes of "free-decision" subjects should be more favorable under low pay conditions, while those of "no choice" subjects should be more favorable under high pay conditions. Linder et al.'s results are consistent with this hypothesis.

The above distinction between the informational properties of the reward given subjects in the two types of experiments described may not be as clear as the above analysis seems to imply. Reward given as an inducement to advocate a given position may conceivably convey *both* the impression that the subject himself is not expected to support this position by the person offering the reward *and* the impression that the advocacy of this position is regarded favorably by others. Suppose that the person to whom the subject reports his attitude is not the same as the person who has rewarded him for counterattitudinal behavior, and has no apparent knowledge that the subject had engaged in this behavior. Under such conditions, the attempt by the subject to comply with the specific expectancies held for him by the source of the reward may be eliminated, while the attempt to respond in a manner believed to be generally approved by others may be retained. Rosenberg (1965) reported data consistent with this prediction. Specifically, he found a *positive* relation between attitude change and the reward given for counterattitudinal advocacy when subjects reported their attitudes to someone who ostensibly had no knowledge of their counterattitudinal behavior.

5. *Kiesler, Nisbett, and Zanna (1969).* These authors devised a study to test an implication of Bem's (1965) hypothesis that subjects infer their beliefs from observations of their own belief-related behavior. Subjects, run individually, were asked to deliver arguments against air pollution to passers-by in the street. At the same time, a confederate, posing as another subject, was asked to argue for auto safety. After the subject had committed himself to perform the task, the confederate also agreed to do so and gave one of two reasons for his decision. In one *(belief-relevant)* condition, he indicated that he wouldn't mind convincing people "about something he really believed in," and that this was "the important thing." In the second *(belief-irrelevant)* condition, he indicated that it would be good to be in a study that had scientific merit, and that this was "the important thing." The authors argued that subjects, having heard the reason given by the confederate for agreeing to perform the task, would interpret their *own* commitment to the task as an indication that they too were doing it for this reason. As predicted, subjects under belief-relevant conditions reported themselves to be more opposed to air pollution than subjects run under other experimental conditions, while not differing from other subjects in their attitudes toward the issue assigned to the confederate.

Although the authors' interpretation of their data is intriguing, an alternative interpretation is suggested if one assumes that the subject's objective in the experiment was to respond in a manner considered acceptable by the experimenter. In this study, unlike others we have discussed, the experimenter himself gave no indication of his opinions either about the issue to be discussed or about why a subject should agree to perform the task. (At least, these cues did not differ over experimental conditions.) In this case, information about what is appropriate for the subject to say and do is provided by the stooge. In one condition, the confederate conveyed the impression that it is acceptable to advocate an opinion publicly only if one believes in it. In the other condition, he conveyed the impression that it is acceptable to advocate an opinion regardless of one's personal view. The findings reported by Kiesler et al. may not have resulted from differences in how the subject actually interpreted the implications of his behavioral commitment for his attitude, but rather from differences in the apparent acceptability of *reporting* beliefs that are inconsistent with one's public statements.

In fairness to Kiesler et al., it should be noted that other aspects of their data may call this alternative interpretation into question. The confederate who agrees to support auto safety because he believes in it is also providing information that it is desirable to express this belief. Thus, if subjects were complying with cues provided by the confederate concerning what was likely to be acceptable to the experimenter, they should have also manifested relatively more favorable attitudes toward auto safety under this condition than when the confederate did not indicate his personal belief. However, this difference, although in the direction expected from this line of reasoning, was not significant.

The preceding examples indicate the primary distinction between an information-processing orientation and other approaches to understanding social phenomena. In each of the first three studies described above, behavior was assumed by the experimenters to result from a state of internal arousal which was created either by the coexistence of inconsistent cognitions or by fear. In contrast, an arousal construct is not central to an information-processing approach. The emphasis of this approach is upon the type and amount of information provided a subject about the objective of the user (in most cases, the experimenter), and the way in which information is assimilated and operated upon to generate outputs that will attain this objective.

B. Influences upon the Capacity to Receive and Process Information

In addition to focussing attention upon the type of information provided a subject, an information-processing orientation suggests the need to consider the effects of (a) differences in the *amount* of information the subject is required to receive at any given time and (b) the complexity of the cognitive "rules" required to process the information adequately. A subject is limited in the amount of information he can assimilate and process at one time. When the informational demands upon him exceed these limits, the subject may attend only to that subset of the information presented that appears relevant to his objectives (that is, the objectives of the "program" he is using). Second, he may use different, more simple rules for integrating the information than he would if more time were available to operate upon it, or if there were less information to process.

There are many specific implications of these assumptions, several of which we will consider in detail in later chapters of this book. However, some more general implications may be worth noting at this time.

1. Effects of Situational and Individual Difference Variables. The ability of a subject to receive information, and to process it once it is received, may be limited in part by situational factors that prevent him from performing these operations. For example, if the information is presented in the context of other, distracting material, or if the subject is required to perform other, unrelated tasks while the information is presented, not only may his reception of the information be impaired, but he may be less able to integrate it effectively with other information he has stored in memory. In fact, the effects of "distraction" upon information processing have been studied fairly extensively, and we shall consider research bearing upon them in Chapter 7. If these effects can be understood, they may have important general implications. It is conceivable that many situational and individual-difference variables determine the impact of new information upon beliefs and attitudes, because of their mediating influence upon the reception and integration of this information. To give but one example, subjects who are emotionally aroused may be less likely to receive and integrate new information than less aroused subjects. Conceivably, the effectiveness of fear-arousing communications (cf. Janis, 1967; Leventhal, 1970) is due to the distracting effects of fear upon information processing, and not to motivational factors *per se*. A similar argument has in fact been suggested by McGuire (1968b).

Individual-difference variables may of course not only affect the subject's ability to receive and process information, but also his tendency to do so. This tendency may be affected by the relevance of the information to the ostensible objectives of the person to whom he is communicating (the experimenter). For example, if a subject believes that the objective of the experimenter is to determine how well persons can recall or understand the information presented, he may process information differently than if he believes that the experimenter is interested in his judgment of the validity of this information (or, alternatively, whether he agrees with its implications). The effects of such variations in experimental objectives have not been fully explored (for one example, see McGuire & Papageorgis, 1962). Also, if the information is relevant to other objectives of the subject outside the immediate experimental situation (e.g., maintenance of good health, discussions with other persons about contemporary issues of interest to him), he may process it differently than if it is on a topic of little interest to him. These possibilities are considered more fully in Chapter 7 where we discuss information reception and acceptance in some detail.

2. Effects of Amount and Type of Information. We have argued that when the information-processing demands upon a subject are substantial, he may resort to simpler rules in order to assimilate information. This general hypothesis has several implications for research on information integration. As an example, consider a typical impression-formation task in which a subject is asked to estimate his liking for a person described by a set of adjectives (cf. Anderson, 1962, 1965a; Wyer, 1969b, 1973a). In such a situation, the subject must integrate the information into an overall impression of the person described, estimate subjectively the favorableness of this impression, and finally report it in an unfamiliar language provided him by the experimenter (e.g., a series of numbers along a response scale). Several different "rules" have been postulated to govern information integration processes, which we will describe and evaluate in Chapter 9. The general hypothesis described above has implications for these processes.

For example, the simplicity of the rule used to integrate information in an impression-formation task should increase with the amount of *information* the subject is required to process and should decrease with amount of *time* he is given to process it. It is interesting to note in this regard that subjects are often required to process larger sets of information (four or more pieces) in studies that tend to support additive models of information integration (e.g., Anderson, 1965a, 1968b) than in studies that tend not to support such models (e.g., Sidowski & Anderson, 1967; Wyer, 1974a; Wyer & Dermer, 1968; Wyer & Watson, 1969). Moreover, in some studies, the time given subjects to form an impression and report their evaluations is typically well-controlled; in others, subjects are given as much time as they wish to perform the judgmental task. The different results obtained in these studies could be attributable to differences in the amount of information presented, and the time available to assimilate it, upon the complexity of the integration rule used.

The difficulty of processing a given set of information may depend in part upon characteristics of the information itself. For example, if the adjectives used to describe a stimulus person seldom occur together, a subject may have more difficulty in integrating them than if they are commonly associated. Similar difficulties may be encountered if the information presented is simply hard to understand. To this extent, a subject may be relatively more likely to resort to a simple strategy for processing "inconsistent" information than for processing consistent information. One such strategy may simply be to disregard certain pieces of the information (cf. Anderson & Jacobson, 1965; Wyer, 1970a). Or, he may not attempt to integrate the information but rather may consider the implications of each piece separately and then combine these implications according to a simple mechanical procedure. In either event, the rule used in processing inconsistent (or hard to understand) information may differ from that used to process more consistent (or easily interpretable) information. If this is the case, attempts to identify a single information-processing rule that governs the integration of all types of information may prove frustrating.

Finally, it is conceivable that the rules used by subjects to process information change as the type of information being considered, and the integration task itself, becomes more familiar. It is difficult *a priori* to predict the nature of such changes. Consider again the impression-formation task, in which subjects are typically asked to evaluate a large number of different persons sequentially. It is conceivable that on initial trials when the task is unfamiliar, the information-processing demands upon subjects are excessive, and therefore simpler rules are used than on later trials, after the task has become easier. On the other hand, one could as easily argue that subjects become less interested in the experiment as it progresses and thus resort to simpler rules that do not require much cognitive effort. In any event, these possibilities emphasize the need not only to control for the order of presenting stimuli in impression-formation tasks (which is typically done), but also to investigate systematically the possible differences in information integration over trials (which is typically *not* done).

III. A PREVIEW OF THINGS TO COME

In this book we will consider three general issues—the organization of concepts and cognitions, the reception and acceptance of information, and the integration of new information and its effects upon new and existing cognitions. In the next two chapters of this section we will try to provide a general conceptual framework for interpreting attitudes and beliefs and the manner in which these cognitions are reported; this framework will be used for discussing much of the theory and research considered in the chapters to follow. In the second section, concerned with cognitive organization, different theoretical formulations of the manner in which beliefs and attitudes are interrelated will be discussed and compared, and the research bearing upon the validity of these formulations will be evaluated. In the third section, concerned with the reception and integration of new information, we will first consider general factors that affect the acceptance or rejection of new information, borrowing heavily from McGuire's (1968b) two-factor model of persuadability. Then, we will discuss specific characteristics of information that determine the magnitude of its influence when presented both separately and in combination with other information. Various formulations of the manner in which information is combined to affect inferences about social stimuli will be considered in detail, drawing upon theory and research on both impression formation and cognitive-consistency processes. In this context, the effects of persons' own behavior upon their beliefs and attitudes will be discussed. Finally, an approach to the study of complex social-inference phenomena will be described.

In progressing through the volume, the reader will note that nearly all of the theoretical and empirical issues pervading the current research and theory on attitude and opinion change and social-evaluation processes are touched upon, although often in a different context from that in which they are usually considered. However, despite its scope, the book is not intended to be *the* definitive work on attitude and belief formation and change. Rather, its purpose is to suggest an approach to studying these processes that is both analytic and heuristic. The discerning reader will undoubtedly note several theoretical and empirical holes that must be filled before there is a complete understanding of the phenomena being discussed. He may also be disturbed by a failure to cover adequately some of the research relevant to these phenomena. These deficiencies, however, are hopefully offset by the heuristic value of the book. The approach to be taken will clarify several assumptions underlying current theoretical formulations of attitude and belief processes and will generate several new hypotheses concerning the nature of these processes. In many instances, quantitative descriptions of the processes being considered are proposed. Inevitably, portions of the discussion will simply consist of the presentation of old ideas in a new dressing. However, it is hoped that a sufficient number of fresh insights into cognitive behavior will be provided to stimulate the reader and entice him to perform some of the research required to answer the many questions raised.

2
THE NATURE OF COGNITIONS—
JUDGMENTS, BELIEFS
AND ATTITUDES

Before we begin to discuss the effects of information upon judgments of stimuli and the relations among these judgments, it will be necessary to define more precisely what is meant by such terms as "judgment," "belief," and "attitude," and to provide a general description of the role of these cognitions in inference processes.

The approach we will take assumes that stimuli are interpreted by assigning them to various cognitive *categories* or classes. A category is considered to be no more than a symbol that is used to represent one or more internal or external stimuli (objects, events, ideas, verbal statements, etc.) in memory. A stimulus is a member of a category if it is referred to by such a symbol.

A stimulus is assigned to a certain category on the basis of its membership in one or a combination of other categories. For example, an object may be assigned to the category "tree" if it belongs to each of the categories "wooden," "leafy," "growing in the ground," "tall," etc. Or, an object may be labeled "likeable" if it is a member of the categories "friendly," "dependable," "honest," and perhaps others. These latter categories are often referred to as *attributes* of the object. The distinction between an attribute and a category is of course an artificial one; a particular symbol may refer to either an attribute or a category, depending upon how it is used. For example, "honest" would be considered an attribute if it is a criterion for membership in the category "likeable." However, "honest" is itself a category with attributes that serve as criteria for assigning objects to it (e.g., "returns lost money," "doesn't cheat on exams," etc.), while "likeable" could be considered an attribute of less abstract categories such as "John Smith," "hippies," and others. The two terms are used only for convenience, to distinguish between a given category and others that are used as criteria for membership in it.

The set of attributes used as criteria for membership in a given category may be conjunctive, disjunctive, or both. For example, a stimulus may be assigned to a category X either if it has attribute A or if it has both attributes B and C. If "either A or both B and C" is a necessary and sufficient condition for membership in X, the rule for assigning an element to X could be represented by the logical expression

$$A \cup (B \cap C) \supset X$$

In this case the expression $A \cup (B \cap C)$ serves as the *definition* of the category X. To give a concrete example, a "strike" in baseball might be defined as either a pitch that the batter swings at and either misses (A) or hits in foul territory (B), or a pitch that passes the batter in the area above home plate (C), above the batter's knees (D) and below his armpits (E); that is,

$$A \cup B \cup (C \cap D \cap E) \supset \text{strike}.$$

I. JUDGMENT, PERCEPTION, AND MISPERCEPTION

The attributes that serve as criteria for membership in a given category may differ from subject to subject. Moreover, if the element of experience to be classified possesses a large number of attributes, different subjects may attend to different subsets of these attributes. Thus two persons may often assign the same stimulus to different categories. For present purposes, the *judgment* of a stimulus and the *perception* of a stimulus will both be considered equivalent to the assignment of the stimulus to a cognitive category. In other contexts, a distinction is often made between judgments and perception. For example, perception is often used only to refer to judgments of objects made in the presence of these objects. However, whether the stimulus being judged is physically present or is an image recalled from memory is generally incidental to the issues we will discuss in this book.

It will often be more important to distinguish between the subject's *judgment* (or perception) of a stimulus and his *report* of this judgment in a language acceptable to the person with whom he is communicating. In many psychological experiments, the subject is given a set of *response* categories and must decide how to use them in reporting his assignment of elements to the *cognitive* categories comprising his cognitive "structure," or memory. Of course, cognitive categories and response categories may be referred to by the same symbol. "Tree" may be one such category. The distinction is most important when either the labels attached to cognitive categories are unfamiliar to the user (the person being communicated to), or the response categories provided by the user are unfamiliar to the subject. The first case often occurs when a subject is called upon to describe an object to a child or to the speaker of a foreign language. The latter case often occurs in psychological experiments where subjects are asked to indicate their judgments of objects along scales composed of categories with numerical labels. In both cases the subject, or communicator, must relabel the categories he would typically use to describe the object, so that the labels will meet the requirements of the person receiving the communication. Often the rules governing this translation are unclear.

From the above discussion it is apparent that judgment is closely tied to language. This is not to say that nonverbal categories do not exist. Such categories are predominant in the fields of music and art, where ideas are typically developed and communicated through modalities other than the spoken word. Although these ideas and experiences are often assigned verbal symbols, they can be organized and communicated without the use of these symbols. While the concern of this book is primarily with the assignment of elements to categories that have verbal (or numerical) labels, the existence of categories that do not have these labels should be noted.

A. Misperception

If information is available that a stimulus object possesses all of the attributes that comprise the definition of a given category, the object may be assigned to this category with complete certainty. Frequently, however, not all of the information required is available, and a subject is forced to make his judgments on the basis of only a subset of the defining attributes. In such an event, the subject may often assign the object to a different category than he would have if complete information had been available. Such errors of classification are often referred to as *misperceptions.*

At other times, complete information about the attributes of an object is available, but a subject nevertheless fails to attend to all of this information. This can occur for several reasons. One reason is that although a fairly large number of attributes may comprise the definition of a category, very reliable inferences can often be made on the basis of only a subset of these attributes. In such instances, the subject may typically attend to only this subset. For example, although "wooden" may be a defining attribute of "tree," we typically do not determine the composition of every object we judge to be a tree; instead, we classify objects as trees on the basis of a smaller number of attributes that have led to reliable judgments in the past. If one of these objects turned out to be made of cast iron, we would have committed a misperception.

Some excellent examples of misperception are reported in a classic study by Allport and Postman (1947). Subjects were presented with a drawing of a scene inside a subway. Some of the objects and persons portrayed differed in subtle ways from those that were familiar to subjects in everyday-life experience. When later asked to recall these objects, subjects tended to remember them, not as they actually were, but rather as they usually appeared outside the experimental situation. For instance, an advertisement containing the slogan "Smoke Lucky Rakes" was recalled as "Smoke Lucky Strikes." Such errors may be interpreted in the manner outlined above. At the time of the study, the words "Smoke Lucky" were strongly linked to

"Strikes," and subjects could generally attend only to the first part of the phrase in order to interpret it reliably.

Once an object has been assigned to a category, it may be assigned other attributes that are commonly possessed by category members, even though no information is directly available about them. For example, if an object has been classified as a tree on the basis of the attributes "leafy," "branches," and "growing in the ground," it may subsequently be assigned the attribute "wooden." Similarly, a person who has been classified as a "Republican" on the basis of the attributes "votes for Richard Nixon" and "supports Republican congressional candidates" may be assigned the attributes "conservative," "capitalist," and others that are considered to be typical of "Republicans." The tendency to infer an object's attributes from its category membership may vary with the category involved and also may vary over subjects. As pointed out previously, these inferences often may not be correct, particularly if the attributes to be inferred are not common to all members of the category. The tendency to assign a large number of attributes to an object on the basis of its membership in a single category is often referred to as *stereotyping*.

B. Probabilistic Inferences

When all of the information required to classify a stimulus is not known, a subject may not be completely certain that the stimulus belongs to the category being considered. The magnitude of his certainty may be located along a continuum of likelihood, or subjective probability. When the category involved contains at most one member (for example, the category "World War III"), this probability may simply represent the subject's degree of certainty that the member does (or will) exist. When the category contains several members, this probability may represent the subject's estimate of the proportion of stimuli similar to the one being judged that belong to the category.

It should be noted in this context that when information about a stimulus is limited, it may be assigned to a category not only on the basis of attributes comprising the definition of this category, but also on the basis of other attributes shared by some members of the category. Thus, under such conditions *any* attribute (or combination of attributes) of a stimulus could be used to infer its class membership. The subject's confidence that his classification is correct may correspond to the proportion of objects in the category who have the attribute(s) in question. For example, a subject who is told that a person is "dependable" may infer with a subjective probability of .40 that the person is "likeable," if he estimates that 40% of all "dependable" persons are "likeable."

II. THE NATURE OF BELIEFS AND ATTITUDES

A. Beliefs

We are now in a position to consider the nature of beliefs and attitudes as these terms will be used throughout this book. A *belief* is defined as the subjective probability associated (*a*) with membership of a stimulus in a given category or (*b*) with the relation between members of different categories. For example, the belief that there will be a Third World War may be interpreted as the subjective *unconditional* probability that a member of the category "Third World War" exists, while the belief that Tibetans are warlike may be the subjective *conditional* probability that an object belongs to the category "warlike," given that it belongs to the class "Tibetan." Alternatively, each could be interpreted as an estimate of the unconditional probability that the statement in question belongs to the category "True." If the second interpretation is accepted, beliefs in fairly complex statements can be easily described. For example, the belief that "if there is a food shortage, many Americans will starve" may be interpreted as the conditional probability that the statement "many Americans will starve" is in the category "True," given that the statement "there is a food shortage" is "True." However, some caution should be taken in treating these two interpretations as equivalent. A subject may estimate that 90% of Tibetans are warlike, and yet regard it as very unlikely that the statement "Tibetans are warlike" is universally true. Thus he may make quite different responses to a question concerning whether Tibetans are warlike, depending upon his interpretation of this question.

Statements in which different types of verbs are used can also be interpreted in one of the ways described above. For example, the statement "Communists support civil disorder" is equivalent in meaning to "Communists are supporters of civil disorder." Beliefs associated with this statement could be interpreted either as the subjective conditional probability of belonging to "supporters of civil disorder" given membership in "Communist," or as the unconditional probability that the statement is "True".

Jones and Gerard (1967), who have also considered the role of categorization processes in the study of attitudes and beliefs, distinguish between the classification of an object and beliefs about the object. In their analysis, beliefs pertain to relations between two categories, each of which is defined by a separate, independent set of attributes. Statements that refer to relations between a category and its defining attributes are not interpreted as belief statements. On this basis, the assertion "Italians are aggressive" would refer to a belief, since the categories "Italian" and "aggressive" are defined in terms of independent sets of attributes. However, "Italians are natives of Italy" would not be interpreted as a belief statement if "native of Italy" is a defining attribute of "Italian." The above distinction is somewhat fuzzy, as Jones and Gerard admit. Both of the above examples could be interpreted as statements of the relation between membership in one category and membership in a second. The primary difference between the statements is that the first is more likely to be universally true than is the second.

Fishbein (1963) has distinguished between beliefs *in* an object and beliefs *about* the object. In Fishbein's terms, the former refers to the likelihood that an object exists. A belief in God, or a belief that there will be a Third World War, are of this type. Beliefs about an object pertain to whether or not the object has certain attributes. The two previously cited statements about Italians are both examples of this type of belief. The proposed conceptualization includes beliefs of both types. In the terminology being proposed here, "beliefs in" are estimates of the likelihood that a particular category contains at least one member. "Beliefs about" are estimates of the likelihood that members of one category are members of a second. A possible distinction between these two types of beliefs is that the first is interpretable as a subjective unconditional probability, while the second is a subjective conditional probability. However, this distinction may not be important if both types of beliefs can be interpreted as estimates of the probability that the statement involved belongs to the category "True."

B. Attitudes

While our interpretation of beliefs is fairly consistent with the definitions proposed by other authors, our conceptualization of attitudes is less traditional. Historically, attitudes have been defined in terms of a feeling of favorableness or unfavorableness toward an object which mediates overt behavior toward that object. For example, Allport (1935) defined an attitude as "... a mental and neural state of readiness, organized through experience, exerting a directive or dynamic influence upon the individual's response to all objects and situations with which it is related [p. 798]." A typology of definitions of "attitude" has been suggested by McGuire (1968a).

Attitudes are often measured by asking subjects to estimate the favorableness of their feelings about an object along a bipolar evaluative ("good-bad") scale, or alternatively by determining their agreement with statements that vary in the favorableness of their implications for the object. Sophisticated scaling techniques have been developed in an effort to obtain reliable estimates of the degree of affect that an individual experiences toward an object (for a summary of relevant theory and methodology, see Edwards, 1957; Scott, 1968). Such techniques are, in effect, procedures for transforming "outputs" of a subject into a language that is acceptable to the user.

Fundamentally, however, a subject's reported attitude toward an object is interpretable in terms of his judgment of the object's membership in a cognitive category. To this extent, it is no different from a belief. For example, the attitude statement "Blacks are bad" concerns the relation between membership in the category "Black" and membership in the category "bad." The statement is no different in principle from the statements "Blacks are intelligent" and "Blacks are residents of Chicago's South Side," which also concern relations among different categories. There is no *a priori* reason to assume that the factors that affect judgments of category membership depend upon the nature of the categories involved. In fact, as we shall see in Chapter 4, similar laws appear to describe the relations among such judgments, regardless of whether the categories involved are evaluative or nonevaluative. In the following discussion, we will interpret both beliefs and attitudes as estimates of the likelihood that members of certain categories exist, or that members of one category belong to a second.

Many readers may be appalled by this apparently sterile conceptualization of an attitude. On one hand, it ignores completely the internal emotional or physiological state that is often assumed to accompany judgments that an object is good or bad. (For empirical support for this assumption, see Hess, 1965).) On the other hand, our conceptualization ignores any consideration of the implications of attitudes for overt behavior toward the attitude object. However, these omissions may be strengths rather than deficiencies, since they underscore the need to investigate empirically the relations between judgments of an object as desirable or undesirable (attitudes) and other types of responses to the object, and also the need to identify situational variables that affect these relations.

The interpretation of beliefs and attitudes as subjective probabilities suggests a useful notation for referring to these cognitions. Beliefs in the existence of a member of category A may be denoted simply as P_A. Conditional probabilities of membership in a category B, given membership in A, may be denoted $P_{B/A}$. This notation will be used frequently throughout the remainder of this book.

III. MEMBERSHIP IN ORDINAL CATEGORIES—
THE INTERPRETATION OF CATEGORY RATINGS

A. Theoretical Considerations

The preceding discussion has focused upon the membership of elements in nominal categories. In much of the research on social judgment, the subject is required to respond by placing stimulus objects along a bounded rating scale, or in other words, by assigning each of them to one of a specified set of ordered categories. Typically these categories are identified by numbers that represent relative quantities of the attribute being judged. In order to report his judgment, the subject must first equate the cognitive (judgmental) categories he uses to describe different quantities of the attributes with the numbered response categories provided him by the experimenter.

In some instances, no restriction is placed upon the number of response categories to which a subject can assign stimuli, or upon the labels he attaches to these categories. For example, in judging a physical stimulus, the subject may be allowed to use any number he thinks is most likely to correspond to the actual amount of the attribute being judged. However, in practice a subject under such conditions is apt to use only a small subset of the numerical labels available to him. To this extent, his response may not differ in many respects from those made along bounded category scales of the type described in the preceding paragraph. Thus, while the following discussion focuses upon judgments made along the latter type of scales, it may have more general implications.

A subject who is asked to report his judgment of an object along a scale may generally believe that the object belongs, with some probability, to several of the available response categories. This may be either because he is not completely certain of the underlying cognitive category to which the object belongs, or because he is uncertain of the relation between his cognitive categories and the response categories he is asked to use. In either case, his rating of the object may reflect his estimate of the most representative response category available for describing the object. This estimate (E_o) may conceivably be described in one of three ways:

1. the expected value, or *mean* of the distribution of subjective probabilities that the object belongs to each category; that is,

$$E_o = \Sigma\, P_i V_i \qquad (2.1)$$

where P_i is the subjective probability that the object belongs to the ith category $(i = 1, N)$, and V_i is the numerical value assigned to this category.

2. the *median* of the distribution of these subjective probabilities;

3. the *mode* of the distribution of these subjective probabilities; that is, the category to which the object is most likely to belong.

The first of these estimates, if empirically valid, is the most attractive, since the mean has mathematical properties that make it useful in quantitative formulations of cognitive organization. Moreover, Eq. (2.1) establishes a theoretical link between beliefs that an object belongs to a "nominal" category and magnitude judgments of the object along a category scale. Note that the subjective probability that an object belongs to a category X is interpretable as the expected value of the object along a two-category scale in which one response category, "member of X," is assigned the value of 1 and the second, "non-member of X," is assigned the value 0. Then,

$$E_o = P_{x'}(0) + P_x(1) = P_x,$$

where P_x and $P_{x'}$ are the beliefs that the object is and is not in X, respectively. It is interesting to speculate that the cognitive processes governing the two types of judgments are similar, differing only in the number of alternative categories to which the object can be assigned.

B. Empirical Evidence

What is the evidence supporting this interpretation of category ratings? The present author (Wyer, 1973a) designed a study to answer this question. Subjects were first presented 23 single personality adjectives and 35 adjective pairs with instructions to form an impression of a person described by each set and then to estimate how well they would like such a person by placing a check along an 11-category scale ranging from −5 (labeled "dislike very much") to +5 ("like very much"). After subjects had made all 58 ratings, they were presented the sets of adjectives again. This time, however, they were reminded that they would typically not like all persons described by a given set of adjectives equally well, since these persons might differ from one another with respect to other attributes that were relevant to liking. Then, when a set of adjectives was presented, subjects were told to imagine 100 persons who might be described by the set, and then to estimate how many of these persons they would be likely to place in each of the 11 categories comprising the rating scale.

For example, suppose the adjective presented was "intelligent." A typical subject's estimates of the number of persons in each of the scale categories might be distributed as follows:

$$: \frac{0}{-5} : \frac{0}{-4} : \frac{5}{-3} : \frac{5}{-2} : \frac{0}{-4} : \frac{10}{0} : \frac{15}{1} : \frac{25}{2} : \frac{20}{3} : \frac{10}{4} : \frac{10}{5}$$

Dislike   Like very
very much   much

The expected value of such a distribution can be easily calculated by first converting each frequency to a proportion of all persons who belong to the category and then applying Eq. (2.1). In this case, $E_o = .05(-3) + .05(-2) + .10(0) + .15(1) + \ldots + .10(5) = 1.90$.

The expected value of the distribution associated with each adjective set was determined for each subject separately. These values were then compared with the actual category ratings made by the subject during the first part of the experiment. The average correlation between the category ratings of the 58 stimuli and the expected values of the frequency distributions corresponding to these stimuli (calculated after converting correlations computed for each subject to Fisher's Z), was .885. The standard error of estimating category ratings from expected values, again calculated from data for each subject separately and averaged over subjects[1], was .504, or about half of a scale unit.

---

[1]The standard error of estimate was calculated using the formula

$$\sigma_c = \sqrt{\frac{\Sigma(O_i - P_i)^2}{n}}$$

where O_i and P_i are the obtained and predicted values of the ith category rating. The predicted values used were the actual values generated by Eq. (2.1), without the introduction of curve-fitting parameters estimated with the use of regression analyses.

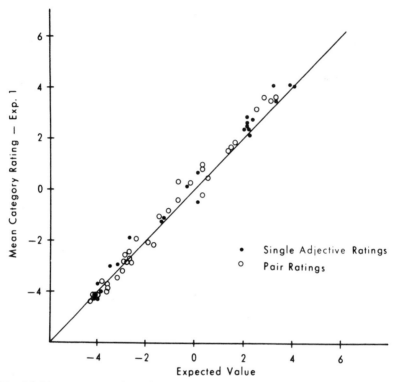

Fig. 2.1. Mean category ratings of stimulus persons as a function of mean predicted value, based upon Eq. (2.1) (reprinted from Wyer, 1973a).

The mean category rating of each stimulus set is plotted as a function of the mean predicted value of Fig. 2.1. The correlation between mean obtained and mean predicted values over the 58 stimuli was .997, and the standard error of estimating mean obtained from mean predicted values was .426. Moreover, the relation between obtained and predicted values appears linear.

To compare the accuracy of Eq. (2.1) with that of other measures of central tendency, the median and the mode of the distributions generated by each subject for each stimulus were determined. The correlation between actual ratings and predicted ratings based upon Eq. (2.1) was greater than the correlation between actual ratings and predicted ratings based upon the median for 35 of 42 subjects, and was greater than the correlation between actual ratings and predicted ratings based upon the mode for 39 of these subjects. The standard error of estimating actual ratings from Eq. (2.1) was less than the standard error of estimating these ratings from the median in 33 of 42 cases, and was less than the standard error of estimating them from the mode in 41 of these cases. Thus, of the three alternative predictors, the expected value is clearly the most accurate.

The relatively low accuracy of predictions based upon the mode is of particular importance in evaluating the support for the interpretation of category ratings being proposed. The task of generating frequency distributions in the study described above may have been tedious, and perhaps even confusing. It is therefore conceivable that subjects in generating each distribution *first* selected the response category they considered to be most likely to describe the type of object to be rated, assigned the largest number of objects to this category, and then unsystematically distributed them along the scale, simply to fulfill the demands of the experiment. If this occurred, the psychological meaningfulness of these distributions would be questionable. However, if this procedure had typically been used, the mode would generally have been the best predictor of subjects' actual category ratings. The fact that the mode was consistently inferior to the expected value therefore lends indirect support to the interpretation under consideration.

C. Uncertainty Associated with Category Judgments

A subject's estimate of the likelihood that an object belongs to a given category is clearly related to his certainty that the object is (or is not) a category member. However, this relation is not monotonic. A subject who assigns an object to the category "Tree" with a probability of 1.0 and a subject who assigns the object to "Tree" with a probability of 0 may both be completely confident that their judgment is correct. The greatest uncertainty may be expressed by a subject who believes with a subjective probability of .5 that the object is a "Tree", or in other words, who believes that the object is equally likely to belong to the two categories involved ("tree" and "non-tree").

This general principle is also applicable when the object can be placed in more than two possible categories. For example, if a subject believes that all objects are either "animal," "vegetable," or "mineral," he may be least confident of his assignment of an object to one of these categories if he believes that it is equally likely to belong to each (if the probability of membership in each is 1/3).

An index of the subjective uncertainty associated with a judgment is suggested by information theory (Attneave, 1959; Shannon & Weaver, 1949). If the probability that an object is a member of each of N categories is known, the uncertainty of its category membership is given by the equation

$$U_o = -\Sigma P_i \log_2 P_i \qquad (2.2)$$

where P_i is the probability that the object belongs to the ith category. According to this equation, uncertainty should be minimum if $P_i = 1$ when $i = k$ and $P_i = 0$ when $i \neq k$; in this case,

$$U_{o_{min}} = -(1)\log_2 1 = 0$$

TABLE 2.1

Uncertainty and Standard Deviations of Four
Hypothetical Probability Distributions

Probability distribution	Response categories					U_o	SD
	-2	-1	0	1	2		
A	0	0	0	1.0	0	0	0
B	.2	.2	.2	.2	.2	2.3	1.41
C	0	0	.5	.5	0	1.0	.71
D	.5	0	0	0	.5	1.0	2.00

It should be maximum when the probability of belonging to each of the N categories is the same $(= 1/N)$; then

$$U_{o_{max}} = N(-1/N) \log_2 (1/N) = \log_2 N$$

If the rating of an object along a scale of ordered categories is interpretable as the expected value of the underlying distribution of probabilities associated with membership in these categories, Eq. (2.2) could be used to predict the subjective uncertainty associated with such a rating. For example, the predicted uncertainty of the hypothetical distribution shown on page 00 would be

$$U_o = -.05 \log_2 .05 - .05 \log_2 .05 - .10 \log_2 .10 - \ldots$$

$$-.10 \log_2 .10 = 2.811$$

Equation (2.2) is insensitive to the ordinal positions of the categories into which objects are placed. Consider the probability distributions shown in Table 2.1, which pertain to ratings of objects along a 5-category scale from -2 to +2: Uncertainty is minimum in distribution A and is maximum in distribution B. Distributions C and D reflect equal uncertainty, despite the fact that the two categories in which objects are placed differ. Other more commonly used indexes of dispersion make different predictions. For example, the standard deviation of distribution A is lowest, followed by that of distributions C, B, and D. Thus these two measures would generate quite different predictions of subjective uncertainty.

Which index of dispersion is the more valid index of subjective uncertainty was investigated in a second experiment by the author (Wyer, 1973a). A second group of subjects was exposed to the same 58 sets of adjectives that had been used in the first experiment to obtain data on subjective frequency distributions. They first estimated how well they would like a person

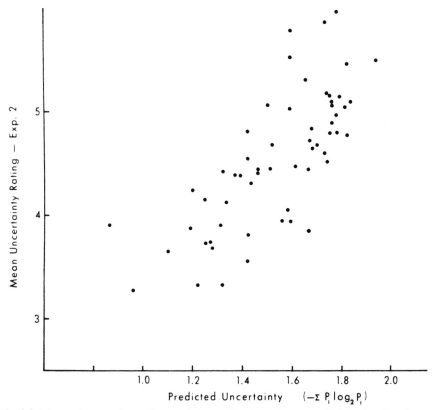

Fig. 2.2. Mean category ratings of uncertainty as a function of mean predicted value, based upon Eq. (2.2) (reprinted from Wyer, 1973a).

described by each adjective set along an 11-category scale identical to the ones used in Experiment 1; then, following this rating, they estimated how confident they were that their rating would prove to be accurate if they actually met the person described. These latter ratings, which were recorded along a scale from 0 (not at all confident) to 10 (extremely confident), were reverse scored so that higher numbers reflected greater uncertainty. The average of these ratings over subjects provided an estimate of the actual subjective uncertainty associated with ratings of each adjective set. The predicted uncertainty associated with these ratings was calculated by applying Eq. (2.2) to the distributions generated by each subject in Experiment 1. Estimates of actual subjective uncertainty are plotted as a function of mean predicted values in Fig. 2.2. The correlation between these sets of data is .740.

To compare the predictive effectiveness of Eq. (2.2) with that of other possible indexes of uncertainty, actual uncertainty estimates were also correlated over stimuli with (a) the mean standard deviation of the probability distributions generated by Experiment 1 subjects, and (b) the

TABLE 2.2

Intercorrelations of Alternative Indexes
of Uncertainty ($n = 58$)

Indexes	1	2	3	4 a	b
1. Actual uncertainty estimates (Experiment 2)	—	.74**	.69**	.43**	.39**
2. Information index of uncertainty		—	.93**	.51**	.22
3. Mean standard deviation of subjective frequency distribution			—	.45**	.20
4. Standard deviation of category ratings of stimuli over subjects					
a. Experiment 1				—	.58**
b. Experiment 2					—

*$p < .05$
**$p < .01$

standard deviation of category ratings of each stimulus by both Experiment 1
and Experiment 2 subjects. These data, shown in Table 2.2, indicate that the
information measure of uncertainty is a more accurate predictor of subjects'
actual uncertainty than is either of the other two indexes.

The low correlations involving the standard deviation of subjects' category
ratings are of incidental interest. This measure has sometimes been used as
an estimate of stimulus ambiguity (cf. Kaplan, 1971a). The data in Table 2.2
suggest that such an index is probably invalid. Intuitively, this conclusion
makes sense. A subject may individually be very confident of his rating of a
stimulus and yet may disagree substantially with other subjects about what
the rating should be.

D. Relation between Extremity of Response and Uncertainty

Equation (2.1) can predict an extreme category rating only when the object
being judged is very likely to be a member of the most extreme categories at
one end of the scale and very unlikely to be a member of the remaining
categories. Such a probability distribution would produce a low value of U_o.
Thus the uncertainty associated with extreme category ratings should

theoretically be lower than that associated with ratings near the center of the scale. This prediction is supported in the experiments described above. The mean predicted uncertainty, estimated from Eq. (2.2), is plotted in Fig. 2.3A as a function of the mean predicted category ratings, estimated from Eq. (2.1). Actual estimates of the uncertainty associated with stimulus ratings are plotted in Fig. 2.3B as a function of the actual category ratings made of these stimuli. In both cases, the predicted relation is apparent.

The role of subjective uncertainty will prove to be of substantial importance when we begin to consider the manner in which different pieces of information about an object are integrated and the relative influence of these pieces of information upon category ratings. For example, the less the uncertainty about a rating based upon a single piece of information, the greater the influence this piece of information may have when it is combined with others. We will return to this topic in Chapters 8 and 9.

E. General Implications for Attitude Change

The above interpretation of category ratings has general implications for an understanding of the dynamics of attitude change when such change is reported along a category scale. A change in a subject's rating of an object O along a scale presumably reflects a change in his estimate of the probability that O is a member of one or more of the scale categories available. For example, a subject who believes that O belongs to categories "2" and "4" each with a probability of .5 would theoretically evaluate the object as 3.0 along the scale provided him. If he now receives information implying that O is in category "−1," he may increase his belief that O is in this category, and correspondingly decrease his belief that O is in other categories. If the resultant subjective probabilities that O is in categories "−1," "2," and "4" become .2, .4, and .4 respectively, the subject's rating of O should decrease to 2.2.

Information that changes a subject's evaluation of an object may also affect his confidence in the accuracy of his evaluation. In the above example, the subject's initial uncertainty about his rating of O, estimated from Eq. (2.2), would theoretically be 1.00. After receiving the information implying that O is in "−1," his uncertainty about his new rating of O would be predicted to increase to 1.52. Such effects are not typically discussed in theory and research on attitude and opinion change but are an integral part of these phenomena.

It is conceivable that information about an object may affect a subject's uncertainty about his rating of the object but not affect the magnitude of this rating. For example, suppose in the above example the information presented was a "two-sided" communication that implied that O was either in category "1" or category "5." If the subjective probabilities that O belongs to these two categories increase by the same amount, the expected category rating of O might not change, while the uncertainty associated with this

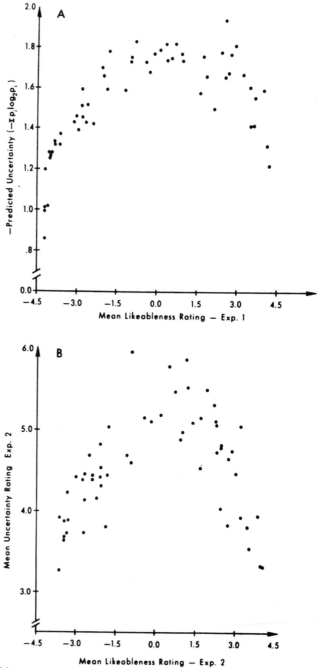

Fig. 2.3. Mean uncertainty about category ratings as a function of the magnitude of these ratings, based upon predicted values generated by Eqs. (2.1) and (2.2), and (b) subjects' actual estimates (adopted from Wyer, 1973a).

rating would increase. The proposed interpretation of category ratings thus suggests a more sensitive method of analyzing the effects of information than that traditionally used in studies of attitude and belief change.

The above examples are oversimplified, since the information provided about an object often does not specifically mention the rating scale category to which the object belongs. The recipient of the information may therefore assign its implications to each of several categories with some probability. Under these conditions, the effect of the information upon a subject's rating of O may be more difficult to describe, and may depend upon the nature of the conjunction of the probability distributions underlying (a) the subject's initial judgment of O (his "initial attitude") and (b) the position advocated by the communication. We shall consider this problem in more detail in Chapter 9.

3
EFFECTS OF RESPONSE LANGUAGE ON THE INTERPRETATION OF BELIEFS AND ATTITUDES

As we observed in Chapter 1, a subject who is asked to report his judgment of a stimulus is confronted with two tasks. First, he must assign the stimulus to a given cognitive category on the basis of the information available to him. Second, he must report this judgment in a language that is acceptable to the person with whom he is communicating. Differences between subjects in their responses to a stimulus, or changes in a given subject's responses to a stimulus over a period of time, may therefore be attributable either to differences in judgments of the stimulus (that is, in the cognitive categories to which the stimulus is assigned) or to differences in the relation between these judgments and the response categories used for communicating them. As a result, differences in ratings of a stimulus may often be difficult to interpret.

These difficulties are particularly acute when subjects are required to report their judgments in an unfamiliar language. For example, an American who is just learning to speak French may frequently describe stimuli by labels that differ markedly from those normally used by Frenchmen to describe them, and therefore he may communicate his experiences in a way that is either misunderstood by a French recipient or is not understood at all. A second case, and one to be discussed at length in this chapter, occurs when subjects are called upon to report their judgments of stimuli along a category scale. While the categories comprising such a scale are sometimes described by verbal labels, more often they are simply designated by numbers. Subjects who have seldom used such a scale may be quite uncertain about the meaning the experimenter assigns to the categories comprising it. When this occurs, subjects may differ substantially in their ratings of a given stimulus. Moreover, a given subject may change his ratings over time because he has changed his assumption about the realtion between rating scale categories and subjective cognitive categories relevant to the judgment being made. Assume that a subject P is asked to evaluate himself and places himself in the category +5 along a scale numbered from −7 (bad) to +7 (good). However, after receiving information that another (O) has rated him as +1 along this scale, P changes his self rating to +2. This could indicate that information about O's rating decreased P's belief that he (P) is a good person. But suppose that P inferred from the information that he had been interpreting the scale categories incorrectly, that is, that these categories pertain to greater amounts of subjective goodness than he had originally assumed. Then, the decrease in P's self-rating might only reflect a change in the language used by P to report his self-worth.

Effects upon the language used to report one's responses along a category scale have been the subject of intensive research and theory in the areas of psychophysics (Krantz & Campbell, 1961; Parducci, 1965) and social psychology (Ostrom & Upshaw, 1968; Upshaw, 1962, 1965, 1969). An extensive discussion of these effects and their theoretical underpinnings is beyond the scope of this book. In this chapter we will consider some of the factors that may affect the manner in which judgments are reported and will attempt to demonstrate the importance of taking these effects into account when interpreting research on attitude and belief processes.

I. DETERMINANTS AND EFFECTS OF RATING SCALE POSITION

When a subject is asked to report his judgment of a stimulus along a scale of numbered categories, how might he decide which category to use? One possibility is that he will try to position his response scale so that the center of the scale corresponds to the average subjective value of the stimuli he expects to judge. To this extent subjects who expect to evaluate stimuli with generally high values would make lower ratings of any given stimulus than would subjects who expect to evaluate stimuli with predominantly low values.

An alternative procedure for positioning one's response scale has been hypothesized by several investigators, including Johnson (1955), Parducci (1965), Upshaw (1962), and Volkman (1951). They speculate that a subject attempts to position his response scale so that the two most extreme response categories correspond to the most extreme values he would assign to stimuli of the particular type he is being asked to judge. Having done this, he equates each of the intermediate response categories with a certain range of judgments that lies within these extremes. While the nature of this equation is unclear, it is convenient for the time being to assume with Upshaw (1962) that the range of judgments assigned to each response category is the same. Once the rating scale categories and judgmental categories have been associated according to this procedure, the subject presumably assigns each stimulus to the response category corresponding to the judgment he has made of it.

To see the implications of this hypothesis, suppose that one subject, P_1, is told he will be asked to judge a series of weights along a scale from 1 to 10, and that these weights will range between 1 pound and 5 pounds. A second

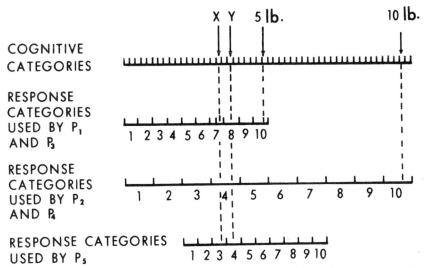

Fig. 3.1. Theoretical category ratings of stimuli X and Y by subjects whose response scale positions differ.

subject, P_2, is given similar instructions but is told that the weights will vary between 1 pound and 10 pounds. Assume that the judgments made of weights by P_1 and P_2 are similar. Nevertheless, the ratings they make of particular stimuli would differ. This is seen clearly in Fig. 3.1. The first line of this figure shows the locations of both subjects' judgments of the 5- and 10-pound stimuli along a continuum composed of ordered cognitive categories (subjective stimulus values), and also their judgments of two "test" stimuli, X and Y, along this continuum. If the preceding analysis is correct, P_1 will position his response scale so that the 5-pound weight falls in the most extreme category, while P_2 will position his scale so that the 10-pound weight falls in this category. The positions of these response scales are shown in the second and third lines of the diagram. Suppose that P_1 and P_2 are now both asked to rate X and Y. Although both subjects' judgments of these stimuli are the same, P_1 will assign X and Y to the response categories "7" and "8" respectively, while P_2 will assign both stimuli to "4." Moreover, although both P_1 and P_2 assign X and Y to different cognitive categories, and thus would agree that Y weighs more than X if asked to compare them directly, their category ratings suggest that P_1 believes Y is heavier than X but P_2 does not. More generally, the subject who considers the wider range of stimulus values, and thus has "larger" response categories, appears to differentiate less among the stimuli being rated. While this observation seems obvious, it will prove to be important as we shall see presently.

A. A Response Language Interpretation of Context Effects

In the above example, the range of stimuli to be judged was stated explicitly by the experimenter. When it is not made explicit, other cues may provide an indication of the range of stimulus values to which the response scale pertains. For example, if several stimuli are to be rated, the initial stimuli presented may suggest the range of stimulus values that subjects are expected to consider and thus may affect their ratings of subsequent stimuli. To illustrate this, consider three additional subjects, P_3, P_4, and P_5, who are not told about the nature of the stimuli they will be asked to rate. Assume that on initial trials P_3 is exposed to stimuli that range between 1 and 5 pounds, P_4 is shown stimuli that range between 1 and 10 pounds, and P_5 is exposed to stimuli that range between 3 and 7 pounds. Stimuli X and Y are then presented. If the initial range of stimuli presented affects the position of one's response scale in the manner suggested above, P_3 and P_4 will position their scales in a manner similar to those of P_1 and P_2, respectively, and therefore their ratings of X and Y will be similar to those made by the first two subjects. P_5 will position his response scale so that the 3- and 7-pound weights lie in categories "1" and "10," as shown in Fig. 3.1, and will rate X and Y as "3" and "4," respectively. The comparison of predicted ratings by P_3 and P_5 suggests that the larger the value of the initial stimuli presented, the lower will be the ratings of the subsequent stimuli.

It is of course conceivable that the range of stimuli a subject has previously experienced affects his criteria for assigning objects to underlying cognitive categories, and thus affects the range of stimuli he will assign to these categories as well as to the response categories with which they are equated. This possibility and its theoretical implications have been considered in detail by Upshaw (1969). It may therefore be incorrect to assume that context effects of the sort described above are attributable *only* to differences in response language. However, the fact remains that response language differences may often contribute substantially to the magnitude of effects observed in research on social and psychophysical judgment. While not denying the possible effects of context on underlying judgments, we shall concentrate in this chapter upon context effects on response language alone.

In this regard, the prediction that the rating of a stimulus will be related inversely to the objective values of the context stimuli preceding it is consistent with the "contrast" effects reported in many studies of social judgment (for summaries of this research, see Sherif & Hovland, 1961, and Upshaw, 1969). Such effects have often been attributed to perceptual causes. However, according to the present interpretation the effects may not necessarily be the result of differences in the underlying judgments of stimuli when presented in different contexts, but rather they may be attributable to differences in the language used to report these judgments.

Effects of Previous Experience. A subject's choice of language may also be affected by his experience, before he enters the experimental situation, with the particular stimuli to be rated. Suppose P_1 is asked to judge the weight of a steel brick along a scale from 1 to 10, while P_2 is asked to estimate the weight of a bag of feathers along a similar scale. Since steel bricks typically weigh more than feathers, P_1 may position his response scale to include higher stimulus values, and also a broader range of values, than P_2. As a result, a 5-pound stimulus may be assigned to a lower category (rated as less heavy) by P_1 than by P_2. Moreover, P_1 may differentiate relatively less among his ratings of stimuli that objectively weigh the same as those considered by P_2, even though he and P_2 make similar subjective judgments of these stimuli.

The effect of past experience on response language may be particularly pronounced when the judgments to be reported are evaluative, since subjects are more likely to differ from one another in the quality of stimuli they typically encounter in their everyday lives. For example, a life-time resident of Iowa City, Iowa is likely to rate his first view of the Rocky Mountains higher along a response scale of attractiveness than is a life-time resident of Interlaken, Switzerland. Or, a resident of an impoverished area of Chicago's South Side is apt to rate the quality of a given dwelling higher along such a scale than would a resident of an upper-middle-class northern suburb. Moreover, a subject may differentiate less among his ratings of scenery and residences if he has had a broad range of experiences with these types of stimuli than if his experiences have been relatively limited. This latter prediction may seem counterintuitive. It could reasonably be argued that the more experienced, and thus more knowledgeable, subject is apt to be more sensitive to subtle details of the stimuli he experiences, and thus better able to differentiate among them. However, both hypotheses could be valid. The second hypothesis pertains to distinctions among subjective judgments of stimuli, whereas the first pertains to differences in the *reports* of these judgments along a bounded category scale.

B. Effects of One's Own Attitude on Social Judgments

An interesting application of the above formulation of response language effects upon category ratings was made by Upshaw (1962) in a study of the relation between one's own attitude and the judgment of opinion statements related to this attitude. In an earlier study, Hovland and Sherif (1952) found that subjects who themselves had extremely favorable attitudes toward Negroes rated opinion statements as less favorable toward Negroes than did subjects whose own attitudes were relatively neutral. In addition, the subjects with extreme attitudes showed less tendency to differentiate among their ratings of these stimuli. Hovland and Sherif attributed their results to tendencies for subjects with extreme attitudes to distort their perception of attitude-related material (see Sherif & Hovland, 1961, for an elaboration of their argument). However, Upshaw argued that these results could also be explained if subjects who are asked to rate a series of opinion statements position their response scales in a manner that includes not only the range of values of the stimuli they expect to rate, but also the values of their own attitudes. What are the implications of this? Suppose three subjects P_1, P_2,

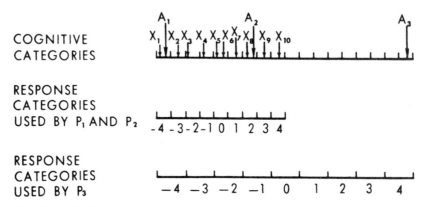

Fig. 3.2. Subjective stimulus judgments and response scale positions of persons (P_1, P_2, and P_3) differing in own attitude (A_1, A_2, and A_3, respectively).

and P_3 are asked to rate the favorableness of a series of ten opinion statements, X_1–X_{10}, toward a particular issue. Assume that all three subjects' judgments of these stimuli, and also their own attitudes (A_1, A_2, and A_3, respectively) are positioned as shown along the continuum at the top of Fig. 3.2. Since A_1 and A_2 are both within the range of the ten stimuli to be judged, X_1 and X_{10} determine the positions of the two extreme response categories used by both P_1 and P_2. However, since A_3 is substantially more extreme than any of the stimulus items, the value of this attitude, rather than the value of X_{10}, determines the position of the most favorable response category used by P_3. The hypothetical position of each subject's rating scale, and his ratings of stimuli along this scale, are shown in Fig. 3.2. As indicated in this figure, Upshaw's formulation implies that P_1 and P_2 should report their judgments of the ten stimuli similarly; however, P_3's ratings of the stimuli should be more unfavorable, and also less differentiated, than ratings made by P_1 and P_2. This in effect is what Hovland and Sherif found.

An important implication of the above analysis is that contrast effects should occur only when a subject's own attitude is outside the range of the stimuli to be judged. As long as his own attitude is within this range, its position should not affect judgments of stimuli. This prediction would not be made by the formulation proposed by Sherif and Hovland.

To test the validity of his interpretation, Upshaw asked subjects with Pro (favorable), Neutral, and Anti (unfavorable) attitudes toward Negroes to rate one of the three series of opinion statements by placing them in 11 ordered categories. Series 1 contained statements conveying a wide range of feelings toward Negroes. This range was assumed to be sufficiently broad to include the attitudes of all three groups of subjects. Series 2 contained identical items, except that statements conveying very unfavorable attitudes were omitted; the range of favorableness covered by this series was assumed to include the attitudes of Pro and Neutral subjects but not those of Anti subjects. Series 3 was identical to Series 1, except that favorable statements

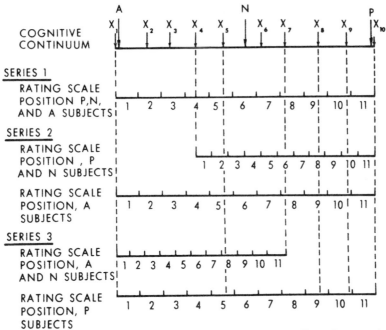

Fig. 3.3. Response scale positions and stimulus ratings by subjects differing in own attitude and in the stimulus series they are asked to judge (based upon Upshaw, 1962, p. 90).

were omitted; the range of item values in this series was assumed to include the attitudes of Neutral and Anti subjects but not those of Pro subjects.

To predict differences in subjects' item ratings as a function of their own attitudes and the stimulus series they received, first assume that the values of ten stimulus items $(X_1 - X_{10})$ and the attitudes of Pro, Neutral, and Anti subjects (P, N, and A) are positioned as shown on the first line of Fig. 3.3. Suppose that Series 1 contains all ten stimuli, that Series 2 contains only stimuli $X_4 - X_{10}$, and that Series 3 contains only $X_1 - X_7$. Since P, N, and A are all within the range of the items in Series 1, the position of the response scale used by subjects to rate these stimuli should be the same, regardless of subjects' own attitudes. The omission of unfavorable items in Series 2 should not affect the positions of Anti subjects' rating scales, since these subjects' own attitudes are near the position of the most unfavorable stimulus item (X_1). However, the range of items covered by Pro and Neutral subjects' scales should decrease. Similarly, the omission of favorable items from Series 3 should not affect the positions of Pro subjects' scales but should affect the positions of the scales used by Anti and Neutral subjects. The theoretical positions of the response scales used under each experimental condition are shown in Fig. 3.3.

The effects of stimulus series and subjects' own attitudes can now be predicted from Fig. 3.3 by selecting an item common to all three stimulus series and projecting it upon the hypothetical response scales used under

TABLE 3.1

Predicted and Obtained Item Ratings as a Function of
Stimulus Series and Initial Attitude

Ratings	Anti	Neutral	Pro
A. Predicted ratings of item X_s			
Series 1 (all items)	5	5	5
Series 2 (unfavorable items ommitted)	5	2	2
Series 3 (favorable items ommitted)	8	8	5
B. Obtained ratings			
1. Modscale items			
Series 1	6.15	6.23	5.87
Series 2	6.61	5.89	5.40
Series 3	6.64	6.63	5.83
2. Moderately anti items			
Series 1	3.98	3.26	3.19
Series 2	3.75	2.93	2.53
Series 3	4.33	3.73	2.93

each condition. For example, predicted ratings of item X_s are shown in Table 3.1(A). The relative ratings of other common items should be similar.

To compare the actual ratings made by subjects under different conditions, Upshaw selected two sets of common items, labeled "midscale" and "moderately anti." The mean ratings of these items as a function of own attitude and stimulus series are shown in Table 3.1(B). These results only partially support predictions. As expected, when asked to judge Series 2 stimuli, Anti subjects rated items more positively than did Pro and Neutral subjects, while Pro and Neutral subjects did not differ greatly in their ratings; when exposed to Series 3, Pro subjects rated items more negatively than did

Anti and Neutral subjects, while the latter two groups did not differ as much in their response. Moreover, Pro subjects rated items in Series 3 about the same as they rated these items in Series 1, while Anti and Neutral subjects rated items in Series 3 somewhat more positively than they rated them in Series 1. However, Anti subjects' ratings of Series 2 items were similar to their ratings of identical Series 1 items only when the items were moderately unfavorable; their ratings of midscale items in Series 2 were not only more favorable than their ratings of these items in Series 1, but were as favorable as their ratings of these items in Series 3. These latter results are clearly contradictory to predictions.

Upshaw's model also has some difficulty accounting for the fact that subjects exposed to Series 1 rated items less favorably as their own attitude became more favorable. However, this finding may not necessarily indicate that his formulation is wrong, but only that it is incomplete. It is conceivable that, independently of the process described above for positioning one's response scale, a tendency exists for subjects to use the midpoint of the response scale to represent the average value of the stimuli they expect to judge, and to assign individual stimuli to response categories that are above or below this origin according to their deviation from this average. If one's own attitude functions as a stimulus, the average stimulus judgment, and hence the position of the scale origin, would increase with the favorableness of this attitude, and individual stimulus ratings, defined in relation to this origin, would decrease. This could account for the negative relation between stimulus ratings and own attitude among subjects exposed to Series 1 stimuli. However, a second obvious implication of this hypothesis is that, controlling for subjects' own attitudes, common items should be rated most favorably in Series 3 (in which the average stimulus item is relatively unfavorable) and least favorably in Series 2 (in which the average item is relatively favorable). This was not consistently the case in Upshaw's experiment. The relative contributions of the two factors hypothesized to affect rating scale position, and the conditions under which each factor is most influential, need further study. Nevertheless, as Upshaw notes, no alternative formulation of judgment does a better job of accounting for his data than the one he has proposed. Despite the difficulties in interpreting aspects of his data, his study provides evidence that a process similar to the one described above underlies subjects' use of response scales in reporting their judgments. More recent research (e.g., Ostrom, 1966; Upshaw, 1965) provides additional support for the existence of such a process.

It may be of interest to consider the preceding analysis of "response language" effects in the context of the interpretation of category ratings proposed in Chapter 2. In that chapter, we hypothesized that the rating of a stimulus reflects the expected value of an underlying distribution of subjective probabilities that the stimulus belongs to the response categories available. Moreover, the subjective uncertainty associated with the rating is theoretically a function of the dispersion of this distribution. In general, as the range of stimuli assigned to each response category increases, the subjective probability associated with a given stimulus rating becomes distributed over fewer categories, and the uncertainty associated with this rating, defined by Eq. (2.2), becomes less.[1] Therefore, factors that theoretically affect the range of stimuli assigned to each response category should also affect uncertainty. For example, the uncertainty associated with ratings of any given stimulus along a response scale should be less when it is embedded in a wide range of stimuli than when it is embedded in a narrow range of stimuli. Similarly, the uncertainty associated with ratings of a given stimulus should be less among subjects who have had a wide range of experiences with stimuli of this type, prior to performing the judgmental task. Finally, if subjects with extreme views are likely to hold attitudes with values outside the range of stimuli being judged, and therefore are apt to use broad response categories, they should be relatively more confident of their judgments of attitude-relevant stimuli than are subjects with more moderate views.

C.   Effects of an Increase in Stimulus Range

In the preceding examples we have usually considered only cases in which the stimuli rated by a subject are within the range of those he has previously experienced or that he expects to receive. Some additional considerations arise when a subject is exposed to a stimulus that is more extreme than any he has experienced in the past. For example, suppose P has previously experienced eight stimuli $(X_1 - X_8)$ and has assigned them the values shown in the first line of Fig. 3.4. If asked to rate these stimuli along a scale from -4 to $+4$, he would presumably position his response scale as shown in line 2. Suppose that P is now exposed to a new stimulus, X_9, that has a more extreme value than any he has previously experienced. This should lead him to reposition his response scale as shown in the third line of the figure. As a consequence of this repositioning, P's ratings of $X_1 - X_8$ should become more negative. This makes intuitive sense. Suppose the stimuli involved are opinion statements concerning U.S. defense and military expenditures, rated along a scale of conservatism/liberalism. Presumably, after hearing a point of view expressed (X_9) that is much more liberal than any he has previously known, P will rate other opinions as more conservative.

---

[1]To give a simplifying example, assume that P believes a stimulus to be in each of four adjacent categories with equal probability $(P_i = .25)$. If his response scale is positioned so that each response category corresponds to a single cognitive category, the uncertainty associated with his rating of the stimulus would be predicted from Eq. 2.2 to be $4(-\frac{1}{4} \log_2 \frac{1}{4}) = 2.0$. On the other hand, if his scale is positioned so that each response category includes two adjacent cognitive categories, the subjective probability that the stimulus belongs to each response category would be .5, and the uncertainty associated with the rating would be $2(-\frac{1}{2} \log_2 \frac{1}{2}) = 1.0$.

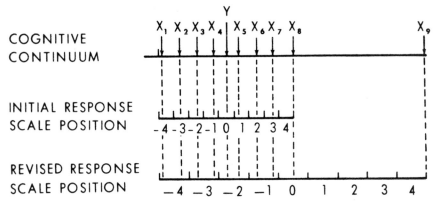

Fig. 3.4. Theoretical response scale positions and stimulus ratings before and after exposure to a stimulus (X_9) outside the range of one's previous experience.

A case of special interest is one in which P himself advocates a position that is within the original set of stimuli. Suppose, for example, that P intially considers his attitude to be neutral, or "moderate." Such an attitude would presumably be located at point Y, the middle of the range of other opinions. If now P is exposed to X_9, the location of his opinion along the repositioned response scale would appear to decrease; that is, P would rate himself as more conservative. This of course assumes that P is committed to his original opinion. It is conceivable that P is less committed to his actual opinion about the issue than to the manner in which he presents himself to others. That is, P may wish to describe himself as "moderate," or as middle-of-the-road. However, in order to do so along the revised response scale, P would have to change his opinion to a position near X_8. This interpretation suggests that although very extreme views may be rejected, exposure to these views may positively affect the opinions of subjects who are more committed to describing themselves by certain verbal labels than to the point of view represented by these labels.

The above example is particularly interesting since it suggests an instance in which a subject will change his underlying attitude toward an issue without changing his *report* of this attitude. Alternatively, if he maintains his underlying attitude, his reported attitude will change away from the position advocated in the information presented. Still other circumstances might arise in which a subject will change his reported attitude toward the position advocated by another (O) without changing his underlying judgment of the attitude object. This is most likely when new information about the position advocated by O is itself presented in terms of a response along the rating scale. Recall the example given at the beginning of this chapter, in which P has evaluated himself as +5 along a rating scale from −7 to +7 but subsequently receives information that O has rated him as only +1 along this scale. We suggested that a subsequent change in P's self-rating might not reflect a decrease in his judgment of his personal worth but rather may indicate a shift in the position of his response scale in relation to the cognitive categories he uses to judge with. Note that if such a shift in scale position occurs, P's ratings of *all* objects along the response scale would be affected. Evidence that negative evaluation by a source decreases ratings both of oneself and the source (Harvey, 1962; Harvey, Kelley, & Shapiro, 1957) is interesting to consider in this light. However, ratings of persons and objects that are in no way associated with P and O should also be affected. Indeed, knowledge of the magnitude of change in ratings of such "irrelevant" stimuli may help one to separate the effects of information upon underlying judgments of objects from its effects upon the language used to report them.

D. Effects of Unequal Response Categories

A simplifying assumption underlying the preceding analysis has been that the response categories used by subjects are equal in size, that is, that each category pertains to an equal range of judgments. In actuality this may not be true. Indeed, it is because of the questionable validity of this assumption that scaling methods such as successive intervals and paired comparison are often preferred to the method of equal appearing intervals (Edwards, 1957; Thurstone, 1959). When these techniques are applied, it is usually found that response categories increase in size as they become more extreme. Difficulties may therefore arise when comparing the magnitude of change in ratings of stimuli at different points along the response scale. To take an extreme case, suppose that judgments of a set of attitude statements are positioned as shown along the continuum at the top of Fig. 3.5, and that along this continuum, equal distances reflect equal differences in judged favorableness. These attitude statements are mapped onto the response scale shown in the second line, which is drawn so that response categories increase in size as they become more extreme. Consider two persons, P_1 and P_2, whose initial attitudes are located near statements X_4 and X_7, respectively; these attitudes would fall in response categories 1 and 4. Now suppose information is presented that leads P_1 to change his attitude to the position of X_2, and P_2 to change his opinion to the position of X_5; these attitudes would correspond to category ratings of -3 and $+2$. The magnitudes of these changes are equal in subjective (judgmental) units of favorableness. However, P_1's reported attitude changes by four response categories, while P_2's attitude changes by only two categories. In other words, the more extreme initial attitude would appear more resistant to change. This resistance, which is theoretically predicted (Osgood & Tannenbaum, 1955) and empirically found (Hovland, Harvey, & Sherif, 1957), could at least partially be an artifact of the erroneous assumption that rating scale categories pertain to equal ranges of judgments.

Another phenomenon that is subject to reinterpretation along similar lines is also reported by Hovland et al. (1957). These authors hypothesized on

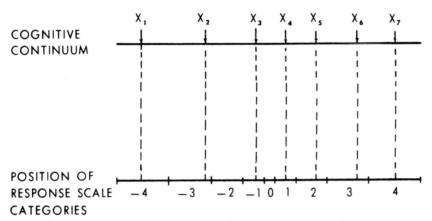

Fig. 3.5. Subjective judgments and responses along a scale composed of unequal response categories.

theoretical grounds that subjects with extreme attitudes accept a narrower range of attitude statements, and reject a wider range of statements, than do subjects with more neutral attitudes. To test this hypothesis, subjects in a "dry" Southern state were given eight statements that were fairly evenly distributed in their values along a category rating scale pertaining to the favorableness of selling and using alcohol. They first indicated the statement with which they agreed most (the position of their "own attitude"). Then, they indicated other statements that they "did not really object to" and also statements that they did object to. As predicted, subjects with extreme attitudes accepted fewer statements and rejected more statements than did those with more neutral attitudes. However, this could occur if extreme and neutral subjects actually have equal "latitudes of acceptance and rejection" when defined in judgmental units, but extreme response categories are larger in terms of these units than are moderate ones. A given range of favorableness near the center of the response scale would then include more rating scale categories, and thus more statements, than the same range near an extreme of the response scale, and the number of statements accepted by subjects whose own attitudes lie within the former range would therefore be greater. While this interpretation is not necessarily any more valid than the one originally proposed by Hovland, Harvey, & Sherif, the nature of the response language used by subjects in reporting their judgments must be taken into account before a clear interpretation can be made of their data.

II. ADDITIONAL DETERMINANTS OF RESPONSE LANGUAGE DIFFERENCES

A. The "Frequency Principle"

When subjects are asked to rate a large number of stimuli along a scale, their responses may be affected in part by assumptions they make about the manner in which the objective values of these stimuli are distributed over the scale categories available. Parducci (1965) has argued that subjects often assume that each response category should be used with equal frequency, and that they consequently attempt to distribute their ratings of stimuli evenly over those categories. If this assumption is made, subjects' ratings of stimuli may often depend not only upon the range of stimuli to be rated, but also upon the distribution of these stimuli with respect to the attribute being judged. For example, a given stimulus would be assigned to a more extreme response category if the distribution of values of the stimuli accompanying it is normal than if this distribution is rectangular. Moreover, a given stimulus would be assigned to a more positive response category if the distribution of context stimulus values is positively skewed than if it is either rectangular or negatively skewed. Since the mean value of the stimuli presented would be more negative in the first case than in the second or third, application of the "equal-frequency" assumption would produce an apparent "contrast" effect. While this effect is similar in some respects to that predicted on the basis of differences in rating scale position as described earlier in this chapter, Parducci (1965) has been able to isolate the relative influence of each factor upon the response categories to which stimuli are assigned.

Since the theoretical contribution of these two effects of response language, and the means of distinguishing them, are discussed in detail by Parducci (1965) they will not be elaborated here. It is reasonable to assume that the tendency to employ the frequency principle is partially a function of the implicit assumptions made by subjects concerning the expectancies held for them by the experimenter. To this extent, its effects may be minimized by appropriate instructions to subjects before their ratings are made.

B. Individual Differences in Response Style

Any psychologist who has collected data by asking subjects to report their judgments along a series of rating scales has become immediately and often painfully aware of substantial individual differences in response style. That is, some subjects use only a small number of available categories, while others tend to spread their responses over the entire set of categories. Some subjects use only the most extreme categories in reporting their responses, while others concentrate their responses near the center of the scale. These stylistic differences could occur independently of the manner in which the rating scale is positioned in relation to the subjective judgments being made.

1. Generalization of Response Style Over Stimulus Domains. The psychological significance of differences in response style is unclear. Some authors (e.g., Harvey, Hunt, & Schroder, 1961; White, Alter, & Rardin, 1965) assume that the tendency to use few and extreme response categories indicates a lack of cognitive differentiation and therefore has quite broad implications for conceptual and personality functioning. Indeed, the generalization of this tendency over stimulus domains has been demonstrated. Glixman (1965) selected statements of each of three types: descriptions of objects, references to oneself, and attitude statements about nuclear war. In each case, he asked subjects to sort the statements into groups, with no restrictions placed upon the maximum or minimum number of groups used. He found consistently positive correlations between the number of groups used to classify statements in one domain and the number used to classify statements in other domains.

In a study more directly related to the use of rating scale categories (Wyer, 1969a), we first asked subjects to estimate the favorableness of 80 personality-trait adjectives along a scale from −10 to +10. On the basis of their ratings in this domain (Domain 1), we selected subjects whose responses over items had either a high (S) or low (s) standard deviation and either a high (D) or low (d) index of dispersion.[2] The first measure was used as an index of the extremity of category ratings; the second, as an index of the tendency to use all categories with equal frequency. (Thus, subjects whose responses had a high standard deviation and low index of dispersion were those who used few and extreme categories in reporting their judgments.) Subjects representing each of the four combinations of response characteristics (SD, Sd, sD, and sd) in Domain 1 returned three weeks later to participate in a second, ostensibly unrelated study in which they estimated their agreement with each of 20 opinion statements about Negroes (Domain 2) and also judged the favorableness toward Negroes of the attitude conveyed by each of a different set of 20 statements (Domain 3). These responses were also made along a scale from −10 to +10. The percentage of responses in each of the 21 categories made by each group of subjects in each domain is shown in Fig. 3.6. Differences in the index of dispersion of responses in Domain 1 generalized to responses in both Domain 2 ($p < .10$) and Domain 3, but the standard deviaiton of responses in Domain 1 generalized only to responses in Domain 3. Nevertheless, the similarity of the response characteristics over domains is fairly striking, particularly since a period of three weeks had elapsed between responses in Domain 1 and those in the other two domains.

However, general differences in the response characteristics described above do not necessarily imply general differences in the judgments underlying responses or in the relation of judgmental categories to response categories. Pettigrew (1958) constructed a measure of "category width" which theoretically identifies individual differences in the general tendency to

---

[2]The formula for calculating the index of dispersion (for a derivation, see Hammond & Householder, 1962) is

$$D = \frac{h(n^2 - \Sigma n_i^2)}{n^2 (h - 1)}$$

where h = the number of possible categories that can be used for recording responses, n = the total number of responses, and n_i = the number of responses in the ith category.

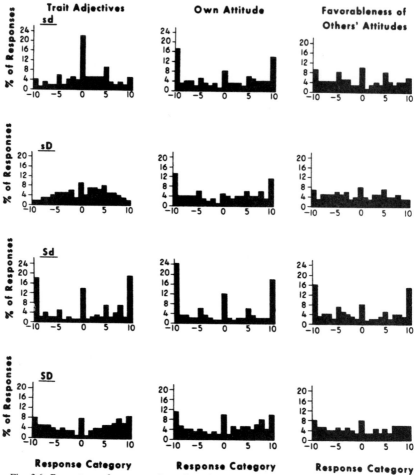

Fig. 3.6. Percentage of responses in each scale category, determined in three domains, as a function of response style characteristics defined in Domain 1 (test adjectives) (reprinted from Wyer, 1969a, p. 107).

believe that stimuli can have a wide range of values. This measure should theoretically be related to the range of stimulus values that subjects include in each response category. Although Murdoch (1965) found that the measure was related to the standard deviation of stimulus ratings in some domains, it was related to neither of the characteristics considered in our study. In some instances, the tendency to use few and extreme rating scale categories may simply reflect a strategy of responding on a particular type of measuring instrument that has little psychological significance. Subjects who are bored with the experiment may respond with little thought and thus may use few categories (cf. Hinckley, 1932), while subjects who are more concerned about reporting their opinions accurately may make finer distinctions. Similar factors may affect the extremity of responses. If this is the case, an assumption often made in attitude research may sometimes be incorrect. That is, subjects who appear to have extreme attitudes by virtue of their use of extreme response categories may not be the most "involved" with the issue to which the attitude pertains, but rather they may be the *least* involved in the experiment.

2. *Implications for Social Judgment.* Individual differences in response style may be relatively unimportant when comparisons are made between groups of randomly selected subjects. They may be more necessary to take into account when subjects are placed in groups on the basis of one set of ratings and are subsequently compared in terms of a second set of ratings. Consider, for example, a study by Manis (1961) on the effects of one's own attitude on the judgments of attitude-related messages. In this experiment, subjects were classified as either favorable, neutral, or unfavorable toward fraternities on the basis of self-reports of their attitudes along a category scale. Subjects of each type then estimated the favorableness toward fraternities of each of several opinion statements. These estimates were also reported along a category scale. Manis's predictions about the effects of own attitude on judgments of attitude-related messages were based upon an assumption that subjects reduce tension generated by communications advocating positions different from their own by distorting their interpretations of these communications. He argued that if a communication advocates a position that is only slightly different from one's own attitude, it tends to be displaced toward this attitude, or assimilated, while if the message endorses a position that is very dissimilar to one's own attitude, it is rejected and thus is interpreted as even more discrepant from this attitude. Thus, pro-fraternity subjects should "assimilate" pro-fraternity messages (judge them as relatively more favorable) and "contrast" anti-fraternity message (judge them as more unfavorable), while anti-fraternity subjects should contrast pro-fraternity messages (judge them as more favorable) and assimilate anti-fraternity messages (judge them as more unfavorable). In support of this hypothesis, Manis found that both pro-fraternity and anti-fraternity subjects rated pro messages as more favorable to fraternities, and anti messages as more unfavorable to them, than did subjects whose own attitudes were relatively neutral.

However, an alternative interpretation of Manis's results is possible. Suppose subjects differ in their tendency to use extreme categories in reporting both their own attitudes and their judgments of attitude-related messages. Subjects who generally use extreme categories would then appear to have more extreme attitudes (and thus are more likely to be classified as either pro-fraternity or anti-fraternity) than subjects who use categories near the center of the scale. The former subjects would also rate pro-fraternity messages as more pro, and anti-fraternity messages as more anti, than would subjects who do not use extreme categories. Thus, Manis's findings could be the result of consistencies in response style over content domains, and not of the factors he assumed to be operating.

Some evidence supporting this possibility was obtained by Wyer (1969a) in the study described previously. In this study, ratings of statements about Negroes were analyzed as a function of subjects' own attitudes toward Negroes. Subjects with extremely favorable attitudes toward Negroes rated anti-Negro statements as more anti-Negro, and pro-Negro statements as more pro-Negro, than the mean ratings of these statements, replicating Manis's findings. Subjects with the least favorable attitudes toward Negroes rated anti-Negro statements as less anti, and pro-Negro statements as less pro, than the mean. However, since these latter subjects were typically not *anti*-Negro, but rather were relatively neutral (as inferred from the normative scale values of the items they agreed with), these findings are also consistent with predictions based upon "assimilation-contrast" theory. Overall, differences in own attitude accounted for 7.1% of the variance in item ratings.

A second analysis was then performed in which the response style characteristics of subjects, inferred from subjects' ratings in Domain 1 (personality adjectives), were controlled. The extremity of ratings of attitude statements increased with the standard deviation of adjective ratings and decreased with the index of dispersion of these ratings. Altogether, interactions of response style characteristics with item favorableness accounted for 10.6% of the total variance in item ratings. However, the interaction of own attitude and item favorableness was not significant ($p <$ .10) and accounted for only 2.7% of the total variance. In other words, when response style variables and own attitude were not confounded, only the former variables accounted for a significant proportion of variance in the ratings of attitude-relevant communications.

III. CONCLUDING REMARKS

In this chapter we have pointed out the need to distinguish between differences in beliefs and attitudes and differences in the language used to communicate them, and we have tried to provide some insight into factors that may affect response language. The reader is referred to Parducci (1965), Ostrom and Upshaw (1968), and Upshaw (1965, 1969) for a more extensive and rigorous discussion of these issues and their implications for theory and research on social judgment. In the chapters that follow, we shall be discussing much research on the factors that produce changes in attitudes and beliefs. To simplify this discussion, we will generally not distinguish between judgmental categories and response categories. Nevertheless, in evaluating this research, it may often be important to keep in mind that the changes observed under various conditions could conceivably result, not from changes in underlying judgments of the stimulus objects involved, but rather from changes in the manner of reporting these judgments to the experimenter.

II
COGNITIVE ORGANIZATION

Two general types of research on cognitive organization have been conducted. One is concerned with the manner in which relatively small subsets of cognitions are interrelated, and with the laws that govern these relations. The second has focused upon the determinants and effects of more general characteristics of cognitive structure (the degree of differentiation and integration of concepts, their relative centrality, and others). Although study of the latter characteristics (cf. Bieri, 1961; Harvey, Hunt, & Schroder, 1961; Kelly, 1955; Rokeach, 1960; Scott, 1963, 1965) has proceeded fairly independently of research and theory of the first type described, the two avenues of investigation are obviously related. If the laws that govern the organization of small sets of cognitions are understood, the determinants and effects of more general structural characteristics may be more easily predicted and interpreted. The next few chapters will therefore concentrate upon the nature of these laws.

Theoretical formulations of the manner in which cognitions are interrelated have usually been based upon an assumption that subjects organize their beliefs and attitudes in ways that are internally consistent. Indeed, a recent sourcebook (Abelson, Aronson, McGuire, Newcomb, Rosenberg, & Tannenbaum, 1968) contains contributions from over eighty prominent psychologists, nearly every one with a somewhat different theoretical perspective to which the construct of cognitive consistency is directly or indirectly relevant. Although there is general agreement that consistency plays a role in organizational processes, there is less agreement about the criteria for determining whether a given set of cognitions is consistent. It is, in fact, somewhat unclear whether "consistency" is in the eye of the beholder (typically the experimenter), of the person who actually possesses the cognitions, or both. In Chapter 1, we likened a subject to a computer that processes information according to rules and procedures specified by the user. A computer would be regarded as inconsistent if its outputs are not those expected by the user, given his knowledge of the inputs to the computer and the rules governing its operation. The human subject may likewise be regarded as inconsistent if his outputs differ from those that the "user" (the person to whom the subject is communicating) expects on the basis of his knowledge of the inputs to the subject and the assumptions he makes about how the subject "operates." In this case, however, the user's judgment that the subject is inconsistent either could result from the subject's failure to apply the rules that typically govern his cognitive functioning, or it could be due to an incorrect assumption by the user about what these rules are. It is conceivable that the rules of cognitive organization differ substantially over subjects, and that what is "inconsistent" to one may not be so to another. If this is the case, the role of consistency in cognitive organization would be extremely difficult to determine.

Fortunately, there appears to be some similarity in the combinations of cognitions that different subjects believe to be "consistent" or "inconsistent." Consider the following sets of statements made by a hypothetical person P.

1. "O is my best friend"; "O despises me."
2. "I strongly favor civil rights legislation"; "I intend to vote for Senator O"; "O is unalterably opposed to civil rights legislation."
3. "Smoking causes lung cancer"; "I am afraid of getting cancer"; "I smoke."
4. "I love Janet"; "Janet is going to mary John"; "I love John."

If we heard P make the statements contained in any one of these sets, and if we had no additional information about the reasons he did so, we might label P as "inconsistent." However, what criteria have we used in making this judgment? The criteria may be difficult to state explicitly and, moreover, may differ over the four sets of statements. We have learned to recognize and label quite different combinations of statements as "consistent" or "inconsistent" without adopting any single set of criteria that applies universally. In other words, "inconsistent" is a category with a disjunctive definition.

The point of view outlined above has been formalized by Abelson and his colleagues (Abelson, 1968, 1973; Abelson & Reich, 1969). They propose that persons construct *implicational molecules,* or sets of propositions about the relations among fairly general cognitive categories. The nature of these molecules depends upon the combination of general categories involved. Cognitions about specific members of these categories are "consistent" if the relations they describe are those specified in an implicational molecule relating the categories. For example, suppose that a molecule consists of the statements: "Boy loves girl," "Girl loves another boy," and "Boy dislikes the other boy." Then, a set of cognitions about P (a member of "boy"), Janet (a member of "girl"), and John (a member of "other boy") would be judged consistent or inconsistent, depending upon whether these elements were related in the ways described in the molecule. Abelson and Reich have used this approach in developing a computer simulation of social inference processes and receptivity to information. We shall return to their interesting work in Chapter 12.

Although no single law may govern the organization of all cognitions, the number of such laws may be fairly small. If laws of organization can be expressed in precise terms, "inconsistency" in specific instances may be defined in terms of differences between the actual relations among cognitions and those implied by these laws. On the surface, this reasoning may seem fallacious. If a law fails to hold under certain conditions, this could well mean that it is either invalid or incomplete. However, a vast number of cognitions typically comprise the memory of a human subject. When new information is presented, substantial time may be required for its effects to "filter down" to all of the cognitions to which the information is directly or indirectly relevant (McGuire, 1968a). Moreover, although cognitions are logically related, they may seldom be considered in combination, and thus the organizational processes governing their relation may not be invoked.

The preceding discussion makes salient the difficulty of assessing the validity of a hypothetical law of cognitive organization. Three criteria have been employed in research performed to date. One criterion is simply whether the relations among cognitions to which the law theoretically pertains are accurately described by the law. For example, consider the simple law

$$A \times B = C$$

where A, B, and C are three cognitions. If quantitative indices of these cognitions are available, one criterion might simply be whether the product of A and B is equal in magnitude to C. However, this criterion alone is inadequate for two reasons. First, if the equation is not accurate, this does not necessarily mean that subjects do not apply the rule in organizing their cognitions; it may simply reflect a temporary inconsistency among cognitions which exists because subjects have rarely considered them in combination. Second, if the law *does* describe the relation among the three cognitions accurately, this does not necessarily indicate that subjects actively organize their cognitions in the manner implied by the law. For example, A, B, and C could have been acquired independently as a result of information bearing upon each cognition separately, and their relation may somewhat fortuitously be that described by the above equation. (For instance, suppose that A, B, and C are the beliefs, or subjective probabilities, that a person has blonde hair, that a person is intelligent, and that a person both has blonde hair and is intelligent, respectively, and that each belief is acquired as a result of previous experience the subject has had with the type of persons involved. Then, if blonde hair and intelligence are independent, the equation $A \times B = C$ might describe the relations among these beliefs even though the subject has never actually considered the beliefs in relation to one another.) Thus, while the quantitative accuracy of a hypothetical law of cognitive organization is suggestive, it alone is not a sufficient criterion for the validity of the law.

A second criterion is whether a change in one of a set of cognitions affects others in a manner implied by a law hypothesized to govern their organization. For example, if A, B, and C are related in the manner implied by the equation $A \times B = C$, a change in A should affect C; moreover, the magnitude of this effect should be greater when B is large than when B is small. Unfortunately, problems also arise in applying this criterion. If a hypothetical law of organization accurately predicts the magnitude of change in one cognition that results from change in another, this would provide quite strong evidence that subjects are indeed applying the law. However, if the actual change is *not* of the magnitude predicted, this does not necessarily mean that the law is *not* valid. It may simply indicate that insufficient time has elapsed for the effect of change in one cognition to filter down to the other cognitions that are related to it. Note also that the effect of change in one cognition may be distributed over several cognitions and not restricted to a single one. For instance, if a change in A is induced, this might not only affect C, but also B; thus, the change in C would not be of the magnitude expected if this cognition alone were affected by the change in A.

The third criterion, although not frequently used, may be the most satisfactory. As we noted above, cognitions may be inconsistent because they have not recently been considered in combination. However, once inconsistent cognitions are made salient to a subject in close temporal proximity to one another, he should modify one or more of them in a manner implied by the laws governing his cognitive organization, and thus the accuracy of these laws in describing the relation among his cognitions should increase. Such an increase in consistency was originally hypothesized by McGuire (1960), who labelled it the "Socratic effect." *The occurrence of the Socratic effect is a necessary implication of the assumption that cognitions are organized according to specifiable laws.* If this assumption is correct, and if subjects do *not* modify salient cognitions that are inconsistent according to a particular hypothetical law of cognitive organization, one must conclude that this law is invalid. Thus, of the three criteria for assessing the validity of a law of cognitive organization, the occurrence of a Socratic effect may be the most critical.

Before turning in more detail to the question of how subjects organize their cognitions, the question of *why* they do is worth considering briefly. Several theorists (Festinger, 1957; Heider, 1958) hypothesize that cognitive inconsistencies are inherently unpleasant, and that the awareness of such inconsistencies gives rise to motivation to eliminate them. However, from the point of view we are espousing in this book, it is unnecessary to postulate such an aversive motivational state. The organization of cognitive material according to certain rules is a function of the human information processor, much as the organization of analogous material is a function of a computer.

While certain types of cognitive inconsistencies may empirically be accompanied by unpleasant emotional states, there is no *a priori* need to assume that the resolution of such inconsistencies is stimulated by this unpleasantness. And, in fact, as we shall show in Chapter 5, and again in Chapter 11, there is little evidence to support the contention that inconsistency *per se* gives rise to aversive emotional reactions.

In the next three chapters a number of alternative theories of cognitive organization will be presented. Similarities and differences in the implications of these formulations will be identified, and research bearing upon their validity will be discussed and evaluated. This research will have two main foci—the extent to which either existing or newly-formed cognitions are interrelated according to hypothetical laws of cognitive organization, and the extent to which change in one cognition affects others in ways specified by these laws. When the theoretical formulation being considered assumes that inconsistency among cognitions is aversive, research bearing upon this assumption will also be considered.

Many laws of cognitive organization could also describe the manner in which information about certain relations among stimuli is used to infer other relations among these stimuli. It of course is quite possible that the laws governing the organization of existing cognitions are the same as those that govern inference processes. However, it is not necessarily the case. For example, a subject who does not know Bob's and Joe's feelings toward one another may predict that they like one another on the basis of information that they agree that marijuana should be legalized. However, the same subject may nevertheless believe that two other persons, Sam and George, dislike one another intensely, despite their agreement on the issue in question, and may report all these beliefs without feeling that there is any degree of inconsistency among them. At the risk of some redundancy, several of the rules hypothesized to govern the organization of concepts will be discussed again, but from a different perspective, in Section III, where we will consider the dynamics of social inference and information integration in some detail.

4
SUBJECTIVE PROBABILITY MODELS OF COGNITIVE ORGANIZATION

In Chapter 2, beliefs and attitudes were both interpreted as subjective estimates of the likelihood that a stimulus belongs to one or more cognitive categories. According to this interpretation, the laws of cognitive organization are those that govern relations among subjective probabilities. This immediately raises an interesting possibility: Are the relations among subjective probabilities similar to the relations among objective probabilities? If this were the case, quantitative statements of the relations among beliefs and attitudes could be derived by simply applying the laws of mathematical probability theory.

Upon first consideration, the hypothesis that subjective probabilities are related according to the laws of mathematical probability may seem implausible. However, the *general* relations predicted by mathematical probability theory seem intuitively to correspond to those that govern beliefs. For example, a subject who believes that one of two events is unlikely to occur will probably belive that *both* events in combination are even more unlikely to occur, but that the likelihood of one *or* the other *or* both occurring is somewhat greater than the likelihood of either considered independently. Or, if a subject believes that event B depends upon the occurrence of A (that is, if $P_{B/A} \neq P_{B/A'}$), a change in his belief about A will have greater effect upon his belief about B than if he considers B to be independent of A. These "common sense" predictions would probably be supported regardless of whether the relations among beliefs conform exactly to the laws of probability theory. The question is whether more precise statements of the relations among subjects' beliefs and attitudes can be made by applying these laws.

What, then, is the evidence that relations among subjective probabilities are predictable from the laws relating objective probabilities? Rigorous tests of this hypothesis have been limited. In this chapter we will summarize some of the research bearing upon this hypothesis and will evaluate its implications for the processes of organizing attitudes and beliefs.

I. TESTS OF THE RELATIONS AMONG SUBJECTIVE PROBABILITIES

One of the first series of experiments to investigate the hypothesis in question was performed by Peterson, Ulehla, Miller, Bourne, and Stilson (1965). These authors were concerned with the validity of the following equation:

$$P_A P_{B/A} = P_B P_{A/B} \qquad (4.1)$$

where P_A and P_B are the probabilities that A and B will occur, $P_{B/A}$ is the conditional probability that B will occur if A occurs, and $P_{A/B}$ is the conditional probability of A given B. If the variables in the equation pertain to the actual probabilities of the events involved, the equation would be a tautology; both sides of the equation are equal to P_{AB}, or the probability that both A and B will occur. However, if the variables in the equation refer to subjects' *estimates* of these probabilities, the validity of the equation is an empirical question. To test its validity, Peterson et al. first asked subjects to estimate how many persons out of 100 had each of 20 attributes. Then, they told subjects to assume that 100 persons actually had each of these attributes in turn, and to estimate how many of these persons would also have each of the other 19. These frequencies, converted to proportions, were used to estimate probabilities relevant to the test of Eq. (4.1) for each of the 190 possible pairs of adjectives constructed. The two products comprising Eq. (4.1) were calculated for each adjective pair and were then correlated over pairs for each subject separately. The average of these correlations over 12 subjects was .67. This relationship was nearly as strong as could be expected, given the reliability of the data. (The average test–retest correlation of subjects' estimates of the probabilities involved was only .72.) In other experiments reported, Peterson et al. obtained further correlational support for the validity of Eq. (4.1) in describing the relations among subjective probabilities of experimentally manipulated events (for example, outcomes of different tosses of a set of dice).

Although Peterson et al.'s data are suggestive, their correlational analyses do not indicate the extent to which exact quantitative statements of the relations among subjective probabilities can be made by applying mathematical probability laws. Tests of a modification of Eq. (4.1), commonly known as Bayes theorem, bear more directly upon the question. In effect, Bayes theorem is Eq. (4.1) rewritten in the form

$$P_{B/A} = \frac{P_B P_{A/B}}{P_A} \qquad (4.2)$$

This equation has been applied in several studies of decision making processes under conditions of subjective uncertainty (cf. Edwards, 1968; Slovic & Lichtenstein, 1971). It is of particular interest since it can theoretically predict changes in beliefs associated with B as a result of information about the occurrence of an event A. Specifically, if one knows a subject's belief that A will occur, his belief that A will occur given that B is true, and his initial belief that B is true, one can predict the change in his belief about B produced by information that A has actually occurred $(P_{B/A} - P_B)$. Since this formulation is more relevant to information integration than to cognitive organization, a detailed discussion of its implications for cognitive processes and the data bearing upon its validity will be postposed until Chapter 11. In general, Eq. (4.2) appears to overestimate subjects' actual beliefs following the presentation of new information. That is, subjects are more "conservative" in their judgments than the formulation predicts. This could be evidence against the general hypothesis that relations among subjective probability conform to the laws of mathematical probability theory. On the other hand, most tests of Eq. (4.2) have employed decision-making situations in which the accuracy of subjects' predictions can be objectively verified by the experimenter. Under such conditions, subjects may be hesitant to report extreme beliefs, since to do so and to be shown subsequently to be wrong would be embarrassing. This would be particularly likely if subjects infer that the experimenter is interested in their ability to generate correct predictions. Such cautiousness would affect subjects' reports of their beliefs but would not necessarily affect the beliefs themselves. If the "conservatism" observed in applications of Bayes's theorem to human decision-making is a result of this factor, these tests alone would not necessarily invalidate Eq. (4.2) as an accurate description of the relations among subjective probabilities.

Several other direct tests of the accuracy of mathematical probability laws in describing the relations among beliefs and attitudes have been reported by the present author and his colleagues (Rosen & Wyer, 1972; Wyer, 1970c, 1972, 1973a, 1973c; Wyer & Goldberg, 1970). Since their data bear upon a number of different types of relations, the validity of each relation will be discussed separately.

A. Estimation of Conjunctive Probabilities

One of the simplest laws of mathematical probability theory is the equation:

$$P_{AB} = P_A P_{B/A} \qquad (4.3)$$

Two studies were performed to investigate the accuracy of this equation. Wyer and Goldberg (1970) selected 15 pairs of statements about events that were not of great importance to the subjects used in the research (e.g., "Russia will win the 1972 Olympics," "I can recite the alphabet backwards without error," etc.). For each pair of statements (A and B), 40 introductory psychology students estimated the likelihood that A was true (P_A), that B was true (P_B), that if A was true, B was true $(P_{B/A})$, that both A and B were true (P_{AB}), and that either A or B or both were true $(P_{A \cup B})$. Items pertaining to these probabilties were distributed randomly throughout a 75-item questionnaire. Both in this and other studies reported in this chapter, estimates were made along an 11-point scale ranging from 0 (extremely unlikely) to 10 (extremely likely) and were subsequently converted to units of subjective probability by dividing them by 10. Obtained and predicted estimates of P_{AB} were calculated for each subject separately and then averaged over subjects. These data are plotted in Fig. 4.1(A). Although predicted values of P_{AB} substantially underestimated obtained values, the amount of this underestimate was fairly constant. A regression analysis of data in Fig. 4.1(A) yielded the equation:

$$P_{AB} = 1.00P_A P_{B/A} + .16.$$

This equation accounted for 71% of the variance in P_{AB}.

A later study by Wyer (1970c) produced comparable results. In this study, subjects read paragraphs about nine hypothetical situations and estimated the likelihood that various statements about the persons involved in each situation were true. Two paragraphs were constructed for each situation, and these were intended to affect subjects' estimates in different ways. Judgments were made after reading each paragraph. Mean obtained values of P_{AB} are plotted as a function of mean predicted values based upon Eq. (4.3) in Fig. 4.1(B). Predicted values of P_{AB} again underestimated obtained values. A regression analysis of the data in Fig. 4.1(B) yielded the equation:

$$P_{AB} = .86P_A P_{B/A} + .18.$$

This equation accounted for 91% of the variance in P_{AB}.

The psychological significance of the intercept parameter required to produce an accurate estimate of P_{AB} is not clear. The need for this parameter is particularly confusing since, as we shall see, other equations that require direct or indirect estimates of P_{AB} describe the relations among subjective probabilities accurately without requiring the introduction of *ad hoc* curve-fitting parameters.

B. Estimation of Disjunctive Probabilities

Data obtained in the two studies described above allowed the test of a second relation implied by probability theory:

$$P_{A \cup B} = P_A + P_B - P_{AB} \qquad (4.4)$$

where $P_{A \cup B}$ is the probability that either A or B or both is true, and P_A, P_B, and P_{AB} are defined in the manner described previously. Mean obtained values of $P_{A \cup B}$ in Wyer and Goldberg's experiment are plotted as a function of predicted values in Fig. 4.2. Similar data obtained in the second experiment are presented in Fig. 4.3. The standard error of estimating

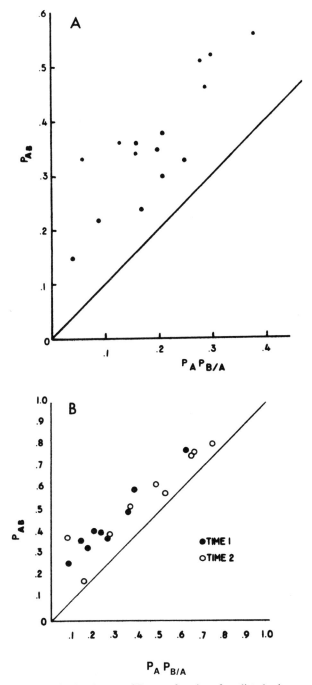

Fig. 4.1. Mean obtained estimates of P_{AB} as a function of predicted values; reprinted from (a) Wyer and Goldberg (1970, p. 103) and (b) Wyer (1970c, p. 566).

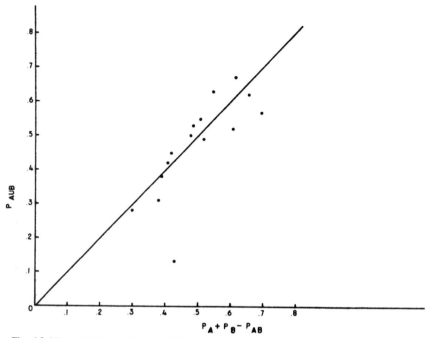

Fig. 4.2. Mean obtained estimates of $P_{A \cup B}$ as a function of mean predicted values (reprinted from Wyer & Goldberg, 1970, p. 105).

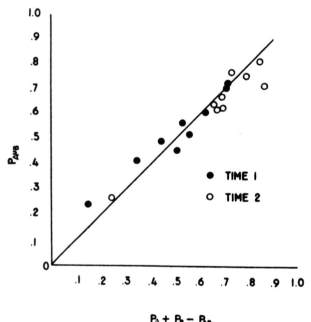

Fig. 4.3. Mean obtained estimates of $P_{A \cup B}$ as a function of mean predicted values; (reprinted from Wyer, 1970c, p. 567).

obtained values from predicted values was .095 in the first experiment and .057 in the second experiment. Thus Eq. (4.4) appears to describe quite accurately the relations among the beliefs involved. Note that subjects' estimates of P_{AB}, which were not accurately predicted from Eq. (4.3), nevertheless produce an accurate fit when entered into Eq. (4.4).

C. Prediction of Similarities Between Persons

A more complex hypothetical relation among subjective probabilities was used by Wyer and Goldberg (1970) to predict the likelihood that two persons are similar with respect to an attribute, given that they are liked, disliked, or regarded neutrally. Assume that a person can be placed into one of three categories: liked (L), disliked (D), and neutral (N). One's beliefs that a liked person possesses or does not possess a certain attribute A can be represented by the conditional probabilities $P_{A/L}$ and $P_{A'/L}$ ($= 1-P_{A/L}$), respectively. The probability that two randomly selected liked persons both possess A is theoretically equal to the quantity $P_{A/L}^2$, and the probability that both do not possess A is equal to the quantity $P_{A'/L}^2$. Therefore, the probability that two liked persons are similar with respect to A ($P_{S/LL}$) should be

$$P_{S/LL} = P_{A/L}^2 + P_{A'/L}^2. \qquad (4.5a)$$

Similarly,

$$P_{S/DD} = P_{A/D}^2 + P_{A'/D}^2 \qquad (4.5b)$$

$$P_{S/NN} = P_{A/N}^2 + P_{A'/N}^2 \qquad (4.5c)$$

and

$$P_{S/LD} = P_{A/L}P_{A/D} + P_{A'/L}P_{A'/D} \qquad (4.5d)$$

where $P_{S/DD}$, $P_{S/NN}$, and $P_{S/LD}$ are the probabilities that two persons are similar with respect to A, given that both are disliked, that both are regarded neutrally, and that one is liked while the other is disliked.

To explore the accuracy of these equations in describing the relations among the beliefs involved, eight attributes were selected. Subjects made estimates corresponding to the various components of Eq. (4.5) along 11-point scales similar to those used in the studies previously described. Figure 4.4 shows the mean obtained estimates of similarity as a function of mean predicted values for each of the four pairs of persons considered. The standard error of estimating obtained values from predicted values was .095, or about one scale unit. Deviations from prediction were not systematic, except in the case of $P_{S/DD}$; although predicted beliefs that two disliked persons are similar were linearly related to actual beliefs over the eight attributes for which data were available, they consistently overestimated these beliefs.

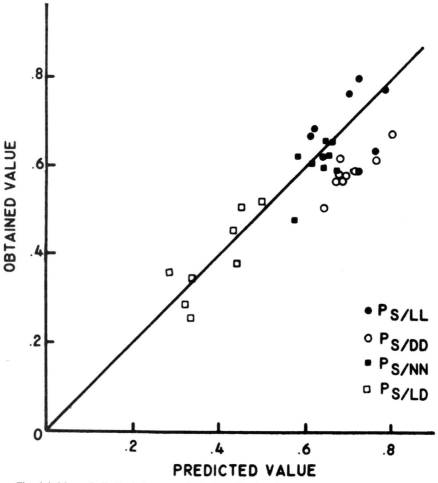

Fig. 4.4. Mean similarity judgments of liked, disliked and neutrally regarded persons as a function of mean predicted values based upon Eq. (4.5) (reprinted from Wyer & Goldberg, 1970, p. 107).

D. Syllogistic Inferences

The relation tested most extensively by the author and his colleagues is the following mathematical tautology:

$$P_B = P_A P_{B/A} + P_{A'} P_{B/A'} \qquad (4.6)$$

where P_B, P_A, and $P_{B/A}$ are as defined previously, $P_{A'}$ ($= 1 - P_A$) is the probability that A does not occur (or is not true), and $P_{B/A'}$ is the conditional probability of B, given that A does not occur (or is not true)[1]. This equation is

---

[1]This equation can be derived by partitioning P_B into two components, P_{AB} and $P_{A'B'}$ and then applying Eq. (4.3) to each component.

particularly interesting since it can be used to predict the effect that beliefs in one statement may have upon beliefs in another. Equation 4.6 is very similar to McGuire's (1960) model of cognitive organization. McGuire hypothesized that

$$P_B = P_A P_{B/A} + P_k$$

where P_B is one's belief in the conclusion of a logical syllogism of the form "A," "if A, then B," "B," the quantity $P_A P_{B/A}$ is the conjunctive probability that the premises of the syllogism are true, and P_k is the probability that B is true for reasons other than those contained in the two premises. Equation 4.6 is thus simply an extension of McGuire's formulation which provides an exact estimate of P_k.[2]

Several studies have been performed to determine the validity of this equation and to explore its generality over different content domains. In one study, described briefly above (Wyer, 1970c), subjects read two paragraphs about each of nine different hypothetical situations. Each set of paragraphs was relevant to a different pair of belief statements (A and B). Their content was such that both the subjective estimates of $P_{B/A}$ and $P_{B/A'}$, and the difference between these probabilities, varied systematically over the nine situations. The first paragraph describing each situation implied that A was unlikely to be true, while the second paragraph implied that A was very likely to be true. However, no information was given in either paragraph that bore directly upon the likelihood that B was true. After reading each paragraph, subjects estimated the likelihood that B was true (P_B) and then made estimates corresponding to $P_A, P_{B/A}$, and $P_{B/A'}$. Predicted and obtained values of P_B were calculated for each subject separately and then averaged over subjects for each situation. These data are plotted in Fig. 4.5. The standard error of estimating P_B from Eq. (4.6) was .029 after reading the first paragraph pertaining to each situation, .042 after reading the second paragraph, and .036 overall.

In an earlier study (Wyer & Goldberg, 1970), Eq. (4.6) was applied to relations among beliefs formed prior to the experiment. Subjects participated in two sessions one week apart. In the first session, they reported their beliefs in the truth of 50 statements, five of which pertained to each of ten syllogisms of the form "A," "If A, then "B," "B." These estimates corresponded to the five probabilities in Eq. (4.6). (In this study, estimates of $P_{A'}$ were obtained directly and were not assumed equal to the quantity $1-P_A$.) In each case A and B pertained to a contemporary social issue (for example, "Drug companies charge excessive prices for the pills they produce," and "The size

---

[2]It may be noted that this estimate of P_k is not independent of beliefs associated with the premises; and increase in P_A would decrease the value of P_k. This relation was not assumed by McGuire in developing his formulation. The different implications of Eq. (4.6) and McGuire's model are compared in more detail by Wyer and Goldberg (1970).

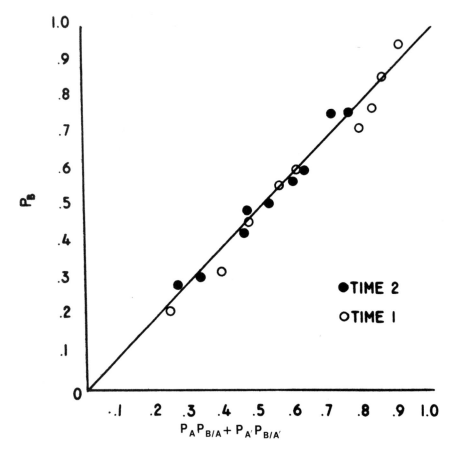

Fig. 4.5. Mean obtained estimates of P_B as a function of mean predicted values based upon Eq. (4.6)—newly formed beliefs (reprinted from Wyer, 1970c, p. 564).

of drug companies' profits should be placed under the control of the federal government"). In the second session, subjects read a series of persuasive communications that either supported, opposed, or where irrelevant to the validity of statement A in five of the ten syllogisms, and then made new estimates of the same beliefs they had reported in session 1.

There were two stimulus replications of this design. Mean obtained values of P_B are shown in Fig. 4.6 as a function of mean predicted values in each experimental session. In the first session, standard errors of estimating P_B from Eq. (4.6) were .037 and .034 for Replications 1 and 2, respectively; in the second session, these errors were .024 and .040.

While the fit of Eq. (4.6) appears quite good in the two experiments described above, these experiments do not provide an adequate statistical test of goodness of fit and do not enable systematic discrepancies from prediction to be identified. What is more important, they do not conclusively

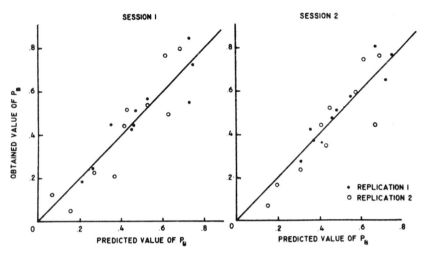

Fig. 4.6. Mean obtained values of P_B as a function of mean predicted values based upon Eq. (4.6)—previously formed beliefs (reprinted from Wyer & Goldberg, 1970, p. 110).

demonstrate that the beliefs comprising Eq. (4.6) combine subjectively in the manner implied by this equation; such a demonstration is of course essential if the model is to be accepted as a valid description of the psychological processes of cognitive organization to which it theoretically pertains. A procedure for investigating these issues is suggested by functional measurement theory (Anderson, 1970), which we will discuss in more detail in Chapter 9. Suppose P_A, $P_{B/A}$, and $P_{B/A'}$ are all manipulated independently over three levels, and that subjects estimate P_B based upon each combination of these variables. If an analysis of variance is performed on these estimates as a function of the three manipulated variables, and if Eq. (4.6) is valid, the following should occur:

1. P_B should be a significant positive function of both $P_{B/A}$ and $P_{B/A'}$ but should not necessarily be related to P_A.

2. The interaction of P_A and $P_{B/A}$ should be significant. However, the effect of $P_{B/A}$ at each level of P_A should differ by a constant (a positive function of P_A). Statistically, this means that the interaction should be concentrated in a single degree of freedom corresponding to the linear $\times$ linear (bilinear) component, and the residual should be nonsignificant (for an elaboration of the basis for this prediction, see Anderson, 1970).

3. The interaction of P_A and $P_{B/A'}$ should be significant and of a form similar to the interaction of P_A and $P_{B/A}$. (In this case, the effect of $P_{B/A'}$ should be an *inverse* function of P_A.) Again, the interaction should be concentrated in the bilinear component, and the residual should be nonsignificant.

4. The interaction of $P_{B/A}$ and $P_{B/A'}$, and the triple interaction of the conditionals and P_A, should be nonsignificant.

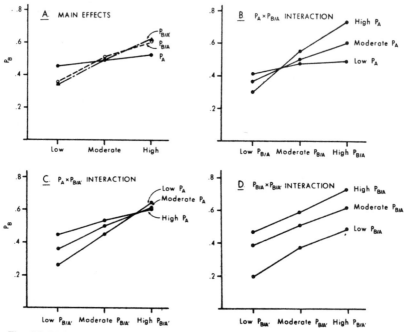

Fig. 4.7. Main effects and interactions pertaining to estimates of P_B as a function of empirically manipulated values of P_A, $P_{B/A}$, and $P_{B/A'}$ (reprinted from Wyer, 1974b).

To explore these possibilities, the author (Wyer, 1974b) asked subjects to estimate the likelihood that a particular person possessed a hypothetical attribute B (P_B) on the basis of information about the likelihood that people in general possessed a gene A (P_A) and the likelihood that people who possessed the gene did and did not possess the attribute ($P_{B/A}$ and $P_{B/A'}$, respectively). Twenty-seven different sets of information were constructed, which represented all combinations of three levels of P_A (high, moderate, and low), three similar levels of $P_{B/A}$, and three levels of $P_{B/A'}$. These levels were communicated to subjects by the verbal labels *usually, sometimes,* and *rarely.* Each set of information was presented in the following form:

People *usually* (*sometimes, rarely*) have gene *x*.

People who have *x usually* (*sometimes, rarely*) have attribute *X*.

People who do *not* have *x usually* (*sometimes, rarely*) have attribute *X*.

After reading each set of information, subjects estimated, the likelihood that a particular person possessed the attribute (P_B), possessed the gene (P_A), possessed the attribute *if* he possessed the gene ($P_{B/A}$), and possessed the attribute if he did *not* possess the gene ($P_{B/A'}$). As in previous studies, these estimates were made along a 0–10 scale, and were subsequently divided by 10 to convert them to units of probability.

Data pertaining to the four predictions described above are shown in Fig. 4.7. P_B increased significantly with both $P_{B/A}$ and $P_{B/A'}$, as expected. More important, the expected interactions of P_A with $P_{B/A}$ and P_A with $P_{B/A'}$ were both significant and of the nature implied by the model. Further analyses revealed that each interaction was concentrated in its bilinear component ($p < .001$), with the residual being nonsignificant ($p > .25$). The triple interaction of P_A, $P_{B/A}$, and $P_{B/A'}$ just reached significance ($p < .05$); this interaction (Fig. 4.7D) appears due to a single deviant point, occurring when both conditional probabilities were low. Considered in totality, the results provide good support for the hypothesis that the beliefs comprising Eq. (4.6) combine subjectively to affect P_B in the manner implied by the equation.

An indication of the quantitative accuracy of the model in this experiment is shown in Fig. 4.8, in which mean obtained values of P_B are plotted as a function of mean predicted values. The standard error of estimating mean obtained from mean predicted values was .048. To investigate systematic differences between predicted and obtained values, "obtained vs. predicted" was introduced as a "dummy" variable in an analysis of variance of P_B as a function of P_A, $P_{B/A}$, and $P_{B/A'}$. If errors in predicting P_B from Eq. (4.6) are unsystematic, all main effects and interactions involving the dummy variable should be nonsignificant. In fact, only one such effect, a triple interaction of the dummy variable, P_A, and $P_{B/A'}$, was significant. This interaction indicated that when $P_{B/A'}$ was low, the model underestimated P_B by more when P_A was low than when it was high; however, when $P_{B/A'}$ was high, the model underestimated P_B by less (or overestimated it more) when P_A was high than when it was low. These discrepancies, which were small in all cases, could be reduced by assigning $P_{B/A'}$ a weight that is inversely proportional to its scale value; this would increase the contribution of the second term of Eq. (4.6) when $P_{B/A'}$ is low and reduce its contribution when $P_{B/A'}$ is high. (This differential weighting would apply only to $P_{B/A'}$; no interactions involving the dummy variable and $P_{B/A}$ were significant.) These data are of theoretical significance, since they suggest that subjective probabilities may not combine exactly in the same manner implied by Eq. (4.6). However, since the discrepancies are small, the increase in consistency obtained through differential weighting of $P_{B/A'}$ may not be sufficient to offset the practical advantages of generating quantitative descriptions of the relations among cognitions without the use of *ad hoc* parameters, determined on the basis of curve-fitting procedures.

E. Implications for Social Evaluation Processes

A modification of Eq. (4.6) may be used to describe the relation between beliefs that a person O has a certain attribute and beliefs that O is liked. Consider the equation:

$$P_L = P_X P_{L/X} + P_{X'} P_{L/X'} \qquad (4.7)$$

where P_L is the probability that O is liked, P_X and $P_{X'}$ are the probabilities

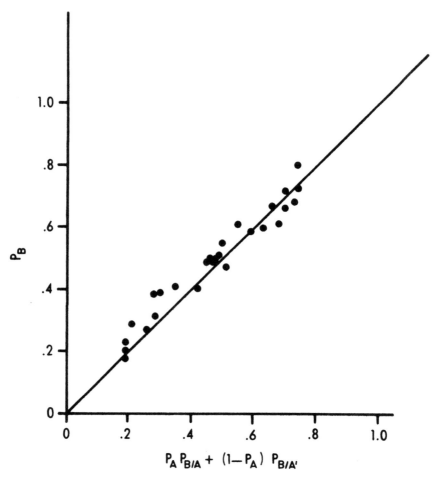

Fig. 4.8. Mean obtained estimates of P_B as a function of predicted values based upon Eq. (4.6) (reprinted from Wyer, 1974b).

that O does and does not possess an attribute X, and $P_{L/X}$ and $P_{L/X'}$ are the conditional probabilities of liking a person who does and does not have X, respectively. The validity of this equation was investigated in two studies, one in which O was a fictitious person, and a second in which O was either the subject himself or another participant in the experiment. In the first study (Wyer, 1973c) subjects read sets of two paragraphs about four different persons, each set pertaining to a different attribute (X). The attributes selected were either favorable ($P_{L/X} > P_{L/X'}$) or unfavorable ($P_{L/X} < P_{L/X'}$), as inferred from normative data. One paragraph in each pair established a high value of P_X, while the other implied a low value. (For example, in one instance, in which X was the attribute "honest," one paragraph described a situation in which O found and returned a wallet containing a substantial

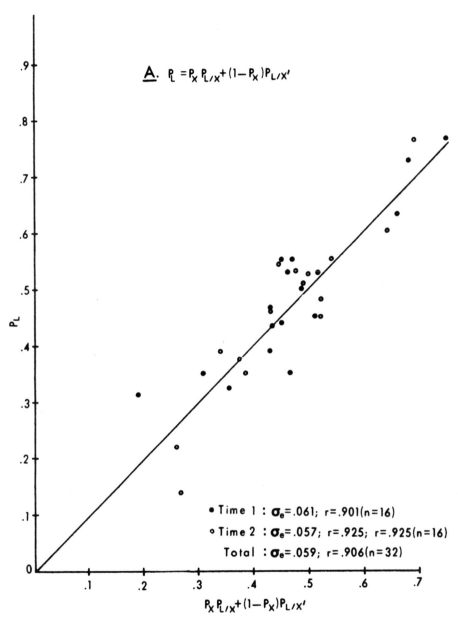

Fig. 4.9. Mean obtained estimates of P_L as a function of mean predicted values, based upon Eq. (4.7) (reprinted from Wyer, 1973c).

amount of money, while the other described a situation in which O stole an examination from a faculty member's office.) The two paragraphs pertaining to each attribute were presented to subjects in counterbalanced order with instructions after reading each paragraph to estimate, along a scale from 0 to 10, how likely it was that they would like the person described (P_L) and then the other probabilities comprising the right side of Eq. (4.7). Mean obtained values of P_L based upon each attribute are plotted in Fig. 4.9 as a function of mean predicted values under each order condition, and for each of two stimulus replications, both after reading the first paragraph pertaining to X (Time 1) and after reading the second (Time 2). The fit of Eq. (4.7), which did not significantly depend upon the favorableness of X, is not as good as that of Eq. (4.6) when the probabilities of hypothetical events were estimated (see Fig. 4.6). Nevertheless, it is sufficient to suggest that the model is potentially applicable to social evaluation processes.

In the study described above, the information about O pertained primarily to a single attribute. However, judgments of a person's likeableness are typically a function of beliefs about several different attributes. The set of beliefs that bear indirectly upon likeableness judgments is apt to be large and highly interconnected. For example, information that pertains most directly to an attribute X may affect beliefs that O has a second, unmentioned attribute Y, and these latter beliefs are also related to likeableness. These relations should theoretically be described by the equations:

$$P_Y = P_X P_{Y/X} + P_{X'} P_{Y/X'}$$

and

$$P_L = P_Y P_{L/Y} + P_Y P_{L/Y'}.$$

To investigate the accuracy of the proposed model in describing such relations, all subjects in the preceding study were also asked after reading each paragraph to estimate the likelihood that O was intelligent (P_I) and sarcastic (P_S), and in addition to estimate the various conditional probabilities necessary to test the two general equations described above ($P_{L/I}$, $P_{L/I'}$, $P_{I/X}$, $P_{I/X'}$, etc.). Mean obtained estimates of P_I and P_S are plotted in Figs. 4.10A and 4.10B as a function of mean predicted values based upon beliefs about X. Obtained estimates of P_L are plotted as a function of predicted values based upon beliefs about intelligence and sarcasm in Figs. 4.8C and 4.8D. Relations involving beliefs about attributes other than X were not described as accurately as the relation between beliefs about O's likeableness and beliefs about X. These inaccuracies may result in part from the time required for the information to "filter down" to all cognitions upon which it bears. Subjects in this study were always asked to estimate their liking for O before making other judgments. This ordering may have given them the impression that their principal task was to infer O's likeableness from information about X, and as a result, cognitions relevant to this inference may have been organized first. It is interesting to speculate that accuracy would have been greater if more time had elapsed between the presentation of information about X and subjects' reports of their judgments.

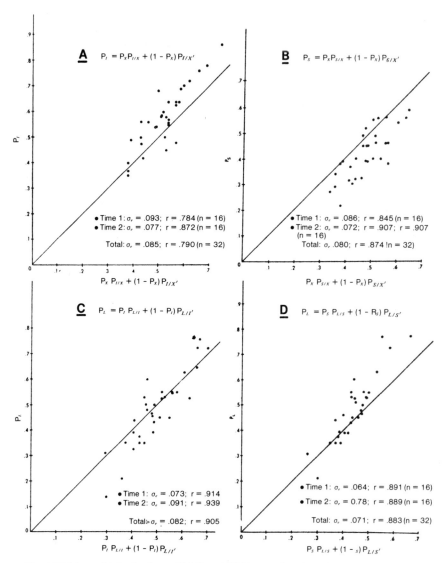

Fig. 4.10. Mean obtained values of (a) P_I and (b) P_S as a function of mean predicted values; mean obtained values of P_L as a function of mean predicted values based upon beliefs about (a) intelligence and (b) sarcasm (reprinted from Wyer, 1973c).

In a second study (Wyer, 1972), Eq. (4.7) was applied to the relations among beliefs about actual persons. Each subject (P) briefly described a personal characteristic of himself to another (O) and then reported his beliefs that he and O were similar with respect to this characteristic, that he would like O, and that O like him (in this study, X was defined as "similar with respect to [the characteristic P described]"). These beliefs were reported both before and after P received bogus feedback that O believed them to be either very similar or very similar with respect to the characteristic. Equation 4.7 described the relations among these beliefs much less accurately in this study than in the study in which hypothetical persons were evaluated. Specifically, the standard errors of estimating P_L, based upon grouped data, were on the order of .125, while correlations between predicted and obtained values ranged between .53 and .62. These data, like those reported by Wyer and Goldberg, suggest that the probability model is less accurate when describing beliefs about real objects and events than beliefs about fictitious ones.

II. EFFECTS OF CHANGE IN ONE COGNITION UPON OTHERS

One indication of whether Eq. (4.6) is a valid description of cognitive organization is whether it can predict accurately the effects of change in one cognition upon others. For example, a change in the belief that A is true should have predictable effects upon the belief that B is true. In general,

$$\Delta P_B = \Delta(P_A P_{B/A} + P_{A'} P_{B/A'}).\qquad(4.8a)$$

If P_A changes by an amount ΔP_A while $P_{B/A}$ and $P_{B/A'}$ are unaffected, this equation simplifies. Specifically, if $P_{A'} = 1-P_A$ so that $\Delta P_{A'} = -\Delta P_A$ then

$$\Delta P_B = \Delta P_A (P_{B/A} - P_{B/A'}).\qquad(4.8b)$$

Equation 4.8b shows that the magnitude and direction of change in P_B produced by a given change in P_A depend upon the difference between one's belief that B is true if A is true and one's belief that B is true even if A is *not* true. The difference between $P_{B/A}$ and $P_{B/A'}$ is an estimate of the relevance of beliefs in A to beliefs in B.

Data from all four studies described above bear upon the predictive effectiveness of Eq. (4.8). In Wyer's (1970c) study, in which subjects estimated the likelihood of nine hypothetical events on the basis of information presented in the experiment, the second paragraph about each situation increased P_A while leaving $P_{B/A}$ and $P_{B/A'}$ relatively unaffected. The mean obtained change in P_B after reading this paragraph is plotted in Fig. 4.11 as a function of the mean change predicted by Eq. (4.8a). Changes in P_B were predicted quite accurately; the standard error of estimating ΔP_B from Eq. (4.8a), based upon the data in Fig. 4.9, was .051. Moreover, the change in P_B was related positively to the difference between $P_{B/A}$ and $P_{B/A'}$ as Eq. (4.8b) would predict.

In Wyer and Goldberg's (1970) study, in which beliefs about current events and contemporary social issues were investigated, changes in P_B were less accurately predicted. In this study, an attempt was made to change subjects' previously existing beliefs in A through persuasive communications. Mean changes in P_B are shown as a function of predicted changes in Fig. 4.12 for each of two stimulus replications. These data are hardly as impressive as those described in Fig. 4.9; the standard error of estimating ΔP_B from Eq.

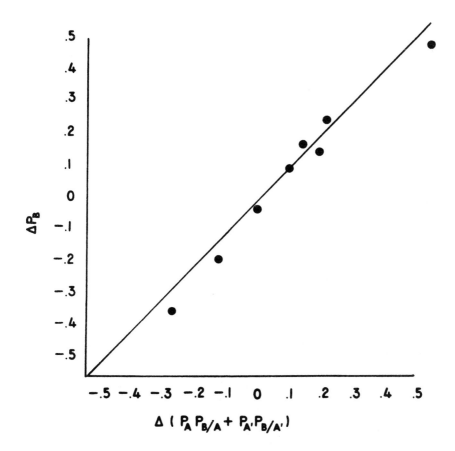

Fig. 4.11. Mean obtained changes in newly formed beliefs (ΔP_B) as a function of mean predicted values based upon Eq. (4.8a) (reprinted from Wyer, 1970c, p. 564).

(4.8a) in this case was .107. There may be both methodological and theoretical reasons for this relatively low accuracy. First, the changes in P_A induced by the persuasive communications were generally small; we were apparently very poor propagandists. Second, the difference between $P_{B/A}$ and $P_{B/A'}$ was not systematically varied and in several instances may also have been small. Each of these factors could reduce both obtained and predicted changes in P_B and increase the sensitivity of the relation between these variables to errors of measurement. Finally, as noted in the introduction to this section, cognitive reorganization may proceed slowly, particularly when the beliefs involved are firmly embedded in one's cognitive structure. Since subjects reported their beliefs immediately after they read the persuasive communications, the effects of these communications may not have had time to filter down to beliefs remotely associated with those to which they directly pertained.

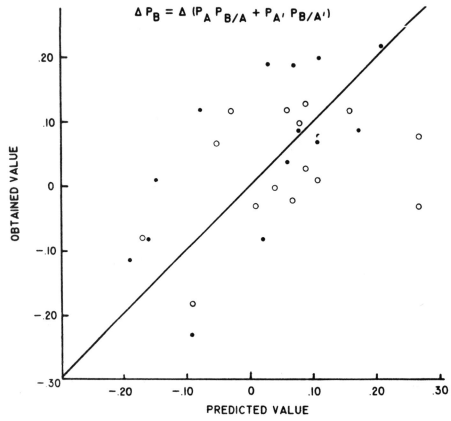

Fig. 4.12. Mean obtained changes in previously formed beliefs (ΔP_B) as a function of mean predicted values (reprinted from Wyer & Goldberg, 1970, p. 111).

Changes in subjects' beliefs that hypothetical persons were liked following information designed to change their beliefs that these persons possessed an attribute X (Wyer, 1973c) are plotted in Fig. 4.13 as a function of predicted changes based upon beliefs about X, about intelligence, and about sarcasm. In each case, these changes were quite accurately predicted. Actual changes in beliefs that *real* persons (the subject himself or another) are liked following information intended to change P_X (Wyer, 1972) were less accurately predicted (Fig. 4.14); however, much of this inaccuracy seems attributable to two deviant points and therefore may not be too serious.

If Eq. (4.6) is a valid description of the manner in which cognitions are organized, it is conceivable that change in P_A may affect not only P_B but also other cognitions comprising this equation (e.g., $P_{B/A}$ or $P_{B/A'}$). In fact, Wyer (1970c) found that estimates of $P_{B/A}$ and $P_{B/A'}$ both increased as a result of information affecting P_A; these changes, which were not in themselves of sufficient magnitude to account for the obtained changes in P_B, were most pronounced when either $P_{B/A}$ was initially high or $P_{B/A'}$ was initially low.

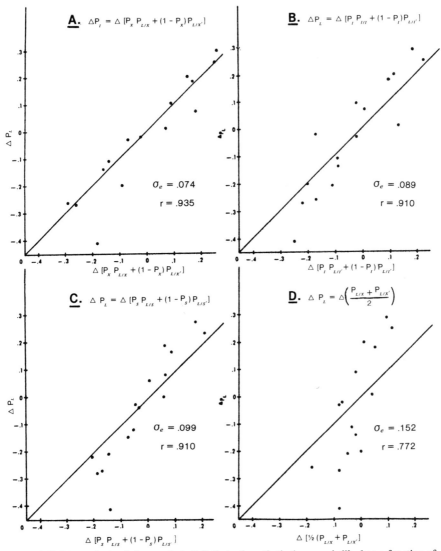

Fig. 4.13. Mean obtained changes in beliefs that a hypothetical person is liked as a function of predicted changes based upon beliefs about (a) X, (b) intelligence, (c) sarcasm, and (d) the average of $P_{L/X}$ and $P_{L/X'}$ (reprinted from Wyer, 1973c).

However, an earlier study by McFarland and Thistlethwaite (1970), in which relations among previously formed beliefs were investigated, did not obtain evidence for such changes. In their study, beliefs in both P_A and $P_{B/A}$ were independently manipulated through persuasive communications. Although changes in these beliefs each appeared to affect P_B, changes in beliefs in one premise had no effect upon beliefs in the other. These results are not necessarily inconsistent with ours. There is nothing in the formulation being

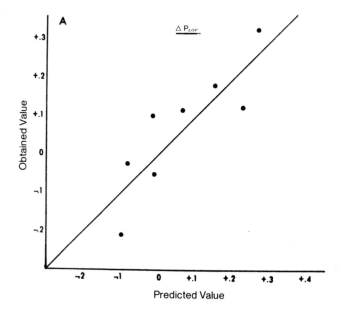

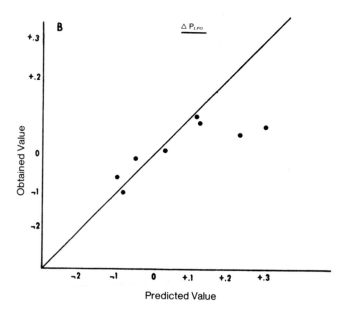

Fig. 4.14. Mean obtained changes in P's belief (a) that O likes him ($\triangle P_{LOP}$) and (b) that he likes O ($\triangle P_{LPO}$) as a function of predicted values (reprinted from Wyer, 1972, p. 282).

proposed to indicate the relative magnitudes of change in each component of Eq. (4.6) following change in P_A. It is possible that in McFarland and Thistlethwaite's study the effects of changes in beliefs in premises were completely absorbed by changes in beliefs in the conclusion, while in our study the effects of change in P_A were distributed over beliefs in both the conclusion and the other premise. The reason for such a difference between the two studies is unclear. Perhaps the effects of change in previously formed, deep-rooted beliefs are more concentrated than the effects of changes in newly established beliefs to which the subject is not particularly committed. Further research is required on this question.

III. PREDICTION OF RELATIONS AMONG CATEGORY RATINGS

The above formulation may seem to have limited implications for traditional research in attitude change, since in this research attitudes are usually inferred from evaluations of objects along a bipolar category rating scale and not from probability estimates. However, if the interpretation of category ratings as subjective expected values is valid, an extension of Eq. (4.6) can theoretically be applied to relations among category ratings. Equation (4.6) implies that the subjective probability that an object O is in category i along a category scale is given by the equation:

$$P_i = P_X P_{i/x} + P_{x'} P_{i/x'}$$

where X is some attribute. However, from Eq. (2.1), the evaluation of O along the scale (E_O) is described by the equation:

$$E_O = \Sigma\, P_i V_i$$

where V_i is the numerical value assigned to the ith scale category. By substituting the expression for P_i into this equation and rearranging terms,

$$E_O = \Sigma\, (P_X P_{i/x} + P_{x'} P_{i/x'})\, V_i$$

$$= P_X \Sigma\, P_{i/x}\, V_i + P_{x'} \Sigma\, P_{i/x'}\, V_i$$

The summation in the first term of the above expression is theoretically the evaluation of an object that is known to possess X, while the summation in the second term is the evaluation of an object that does not have X. Thus,

$$E_O = P_X E_{O/x} + P_{x'} E_{O/x'} \tag{4.10a}$$

where $E_{O/x}$ and $E_{O/x}'$ are the evaluations of an object with X and an object without X, respectively. If information is presented that affects the belief that O possesses X by an amount ΔP_X but leaves $E_{O/x}$ and $E_{O/x}'$ unchanged, the effect of this information upon E_O would be:

$$\Delta E_O = \Delta P_X\, (E_{O/x} - E_{O/x'}). \tag{4.10b}$$

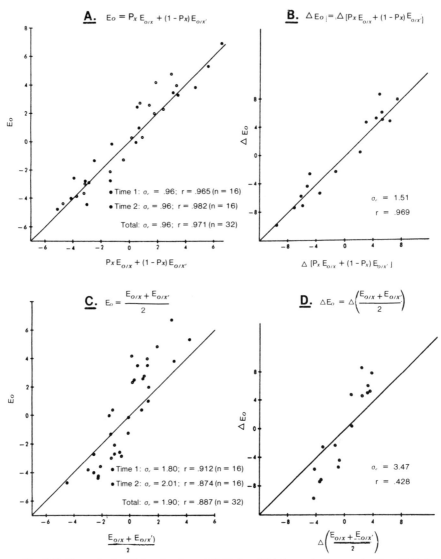

Fig. 4.15. Mean obtained (a) evaluations of O (E_O) and (b) change in these evaluations (ΔE_O) as a function of mean predicted values based upon Eq. (4.10) and, for purposes of comparison, as a function of the mean of the "conditional" evaluations (reprinted from Wyer, 1973a).

To investigate the predictive accuracy of this formulation, the author performed a study (Wyer, 1973b) analogous to that in which the probability of liking hypothetical persons was predicted (see p. 74). In the present study, however, subjects after reading each paragraph pertaining to X indicated how much they would like O along a 21-category scale from −10 (dislike very much) to +10 (like very much). Estimates of how well they would like a person known to possess X $(E_{O/x})$ and not to possess X $(E_{O/x'})$ were obtained in a similar manner. Mean obtained values of E_o and ΔE_o for each set of stimulus materials used in the study are plotted in Fig. 4.15 as a function of mean predicted values based upon Eq. (4.10). The fit of the equation is quite good, particularly in light of the fact that this fit is obtained without the introduction of *ad hoc* curve-fitting parameters. Further research is of course required to test the generalization of Eq. (4.10) over different content domains, and to determine its accuracy in situations in which real objects and events are evaluated. however, this equation may prove to be very useful in generating quantitative predictions of attitude change. For example, it could theoretically be used to predict the effect of change in a subject's belief that marijuana is harmless (P_x) upon his "attitude" toward the legalization of marijuana (E_o).

It is of interest to note the similarity of Eq. (4.10a) to Fishbein's (1963) summative model of cognitive organization and information integration. We will consider the extent of this similarity in more detail in Chapter 6.

IV. SOURCES OF COGNITIVE INCONSISTENCY

There are sufficient discrepancies from predictions based upon the hypothesis that subjective probabilities obey the laws of mathematical probability theory to suggest either that the generality of this hypothesis is limited or that additional factors must be introduced to account for these discrepancies. If the hypothesis is valid, then deviations from the laws of probability may reflect temporary cognitive inconsistencies among the cognitions involved. Such inconsistencies could occur for several reasons. One reason, suggested earlier, is simply that in a cognitive system composed of a vast number of beliefs and attitudes, certain cognitions may never be considered in relation to one another unless they are made salient to the subject in close temporal contiguity (Abelson & Rosenberg, 1958; McGuire, 1960, 1968b). This may not normally occur, unless the subject recalls these cognitions from memory in order to decide (*a*) how he should respond in a new situation or (*b*) how he should attain some objective to which the cognitions are relevant. However, beliefs may also become salient as a result of a request to report them publicly in close proximity to one another. In any event, once related beliefs are made salient, the laws governing their organization should be applied to them, and inconsistencies among them should be reduced.

The elimination of inconsistencies may often be a complex and time-consuming process. A change in a belief that increases its consistency with one set of cognitions could decrease its consistency with a second set. The larger the number of relations in which a cognition is involved, the more likely it is that inconsistencies will exist among certain of these relations, and the more difficult it is to eliminate these inconsistencies. The indication that changes in newly formed beliefs that are minimally related to others can be predicted more accurately than changes in previously formed, more deep-rooted beliefs (cf. Wyer, 1970c, 1972; Wyer & Goldberg, 1970) indirectly supports this argument.

The sorts of inconsistencies that exist among a set of cognitions are often unpredictable and may be interpreted as "random cognitive error." However, certain factors may produce systematic inconsistencies that depend upon the nature of the beliefs involved and the conditions under which they are reported. The "conservatism bias" observed in tests of Bayes theorem may be the result of one such factor. A second source of inconsistency may be "wishful thinking" (McGuire, 1960). That is, subjects may tend to believe that statements they would like to be true are indeed more probable, other things being equal, than statements they would like not to be true.

Evidence of wishful thinking was first reported by McGuire (1960). He constructed a series of syllogisms of the form "A," "If A, then B," "B," and obtained estimates both of the likelihood that each statement in these syllogisms was true and of how desirable it would be *if* the statement were true. He then calculated for each syllogism the difference between the subjective probability that the conclusion was true and the product of the subjective probabilities that the two premises were true (the quantity $P_B - P_A P_{B/A}$). He found that this difference was substantially greater when the desirability of the conclusion of the syllogism was relatively high (that is, greater than the average desirability of the premises) than when it was low.

If Eq. (4.6) is a valid description of the theoretical relation among beliefs, the effect of wishful thinking may often be more difficult to predict than McGuire's study suggests. For example, assume that the effects of wishful thinking upon a belief is a constant proportion of the desirability of the event or relation to which the belief pertains. Then, the reported belief in A, P_A, could be described by the equation $P_A = P_{A_t} + kD_{A'}$ where P_{A_t} is the subject's "true" or unbiased belief, D_A is the desirability of A, and k is a proportionality constant. Reported beliefs in other statements could be represented similarly. If wishful thinking affects each belief in Eq. (4.6), this equation could then be rewritten as

$$P_{B_t} + kD_B = (P_{A_t} + kD_A)(P_{B/A_t} + kD_{B/A}) + (P_{A'_t} + kD_{A'})(P_{B/A'_t} + kD_{B/A'})$$

$$= P_{A_t}P_{B/A_t} + P_{A'_t}P_{B/A'_t} + k(P_{B/A_t}D_A + P_{A_t}D_{B/A} + P_{B/A'_t}D_{A'}$$

$$+ P_{A'_t}D_{B/A'}) + k^2(D_A D_{B/A} + D_{A'}D_{B/A'})$$

Since theoretically $P_{B_t} = P_{A_t}P_{B/A_t} + P_{A'_t}P_{B/A'_t}$, these terms can be eliminated from the above equation, and it can be shown that the reported belief in the conclusion is theoretically greater than the value predicted by Eq. (4.6) if

$$D_B > (P_{B/A_t}D_A + P_{A_t}D_{D/A} + P_{B/A'_t}D_{A'} + P_{A'_t}D_{B/A'})$$

$$+ k(D_A D_{B/A} + D_{A'}D_{B/A'})$$

and is less than the predicted value if D_B is less than this quantity. The above expression can be somewhat simplified, and the constant k eliminated, by rearranging terms and substituting reported values of the conditional probabilities for the unbiased values:

$$D_B > D_A P_{B/A} + D_{A'} P_{B/A'} + P_{A_t} D_{B/A} + P_{A'} D_{B/A'}$$

It is clear from this equation that both the magnitude and the direction of inconsistencies produced by wishful thinking depend not only upon the relative desirability of the beliefs involved but also upon the strength of these beliefs. Thus, although wishful thinking may affect the accuracy of Eq. (4.6) in describing the relations among beliefs, the magnitude and direction of these effects are often difficult to predict *a priori*.

V. THE "SOCRATIC EFFECT"

As we have noted, if certain hypothetical laws describe the manner in which a subject organizes his cognitions, deviations from these laws (inconsistency) should decrease in magnitude once the cognitions involved are made salient to the subject in close temporal contiguity. If this "Socratic effect" does not occur, it would indicate either that the subject does not actively organize his cognitions in *any* way whatsoever, or that the particular laws hypothesized to describe his organizational processes are invalid. One implication of this line of reasoning is that if subjects are asked to report a set of hypothetically related beliefs on a questionnaire, and are then readministered the same questionnaire at a later time, their beliefs will show greater consistency during the second administration than they showed during the first.

Substantial support has, in fact, been obtained for the existence of the Socratic effect when subjective probability models are used to describe cognitive organization. McGuire (1960) found that the effects of wishful thinking significantly decreased when subjects were readministered the same questionnaire one week after completing it for the first time. Other evidence for the effect has been obtained by Dillehay, Insko, and Smith (1966)[3] and by Watts and Holt (1970). These studies, like McGuire's, did not employ a precise index of inconsistency but interpreted decreases in effects attributed to wishful thinking as changes in the direction of greater consistency. However, Wyer and Goldberg (1970) used the standard error of estimating P_B from Eq. (4.6) as a measure of inconsistency and found that for each of 10 sets of statements this error was less during a second administration of the belief questionnaire than during the first administration one week earlier.

The Socratic effect is robust and does not appear to be an artifact of the somewhat contrived experimental conditions in which it is measured. Rosen

---

[3]While the effects obtained in Dillehay et al.'s study are not statistically significant, they are generally in the direction expected.

and Wyer (1972) tested three different hypotheses concerning the reasons for the effect. First, they hypothesized that when subjects are asked to report their beliefs about contemporary social issues on a questionnaire, they are not initially aware that the questionnaire items are related and therefore respond to them independently. However, when they receive the questionnaire a second time, they begin with an awareness that the belief items are associated, consider them in relation to one another, and try to appear consistent in their responses to them. If this is true, inconsistencies among the beliefs reported during the first administration of the questionnaire should be reduced, and the Socratic effect should be decreased, by informing subjects before they complete the form the first time that the questionnaire items are related. Rosen and Wyer tested this hypothesis, using the absolute discrepancy between predicted and obtained values of P_B in Eq. (4.6) as an index of inconsistency. Although the Socratic effect occurred, its magnitude was not significantly affected by increasing subjects' awareness during the first session that belief items in the questionnaire were related. Nor was its magnitude affected by explicit information from the experimenter that consistency among beliefs either was or was not an indication of intelligence and personal adjustment. These latter findings suggest that the increase in consistency observed in this study did not result from subjects' attempts to respond in a manner that they believed to be socially desirable.

A second hypothesis was suggested by the possibility that deviations from the relation described by Eq. (4.6) result from inaccuracies in reporting beliefs rather than from inconsistencies among the beliefs themselves. Inaccuracies may occur primarily when subjects have not had a chance to think carefully about their beliefs, and to recall belief-relevant information, before communicating them. These inaccuracies may be particularly large when subjects complete a belief questionnaire for the first time. However, by the time they complete the form a second time, subjects have had more opportunity to reflect upon their beliefs and to recall additional information pertaining to them; their later responses may therefore be closer approximations of their "true" beliefs and may appear more consistent. If this reasoning is valid, the initial consistency of subjects' responses should be greater, and the magnitude of the Socratic effect should be less, when subjects have ample opportunity to recall belief-relevant information before they receive the questionnaire the first time. To test this hypothesis, Rosen and Wyer gave subjects ten minutes to write down as much factual information as they could that was relevant to proposition B in one of the sets comprising the belief questionnaire. Contrary to predictions, this had no effect upon either the initial consistency of beliefs related to B or the increase in their consistency over time.

A third hypothesis was that the effect was simply due to increased practice in completing the type of questionnaire being administered. When subjects are asked to report their beliefs along a set of unfamiliar rating scales and under unfamiliar conditions, they may tend to make "clerical" errors. Once they have become more familiar with the questionnaire and the experimental situation, they may make fewer errors, and the consistency of their responses may therefore increase. If this is the case, however, an increase in consistency over experimental sessions should be detected even when items in the questionnaire given during the second session pertain to completely different beliefs than do those contained in the first questionnaire. Contrary to this hypothesis, Rosen and Wyer found that while beliefs reported by subjects who received the same form in both sessions became more consistent in the second session, beliefs of subjects who received different forms in the two sessions were actually *less* consistent in the second session. Thus, a "practice" hypothesis must also be rejected.

A final possible explanation of the Socratic effects obtained by Wyer and his colleagues is suggested by the fact that the predictive accuracy of Eq. (4.6) necessarily increases if all probabilities comprising this equation regress toward .50. Thus, if subjects become more conservative in their estimates over sessions, this could produce an artifactual increase in the consistency of these estimates. However, Rosen and Wyer found no evidence of such regression effects in their study. The decrease in consistency over sessions among subjects who were administered different questionnaire forms would also be difficult to explain on the basis of such a generalized regression effect.

The failure to support alternative explanations of the Socratic effect provides indirect support for McGuire's original hypothesis that subjects organize their cognitions consistently and perform "cognitive work" in order to reduce any inconsistencies among these cognitions once they have been made salient. Moreover, this work occurs in the absence of external pressure to perform it. The effect might seem intuitively to depend upon the importance of the issues to which the cognitions pertain. That is, subjects would seem more likely to perform the cognitive work required to reorganize their cognitions if they are concerned about the issues to which the cognitions pertain than if they are not. However, this does not appear to be the case. In a later study (Wyer, 1974c), the author presented sets of belief statements that were similar in form to those used by Rosen and Wyer but varied in the importance of the issue to which they alluded. (This manipulation was validated by subjects' postexperiment estimates of how concerned they were about the issue described by statement B in each set.) Contrary to expectations, the Socratic effect was equally pronounced when the issues were of concern to subjects and when they were of relatively little concern. Moreover, its magnitude did not depend upon whether the belief conveyed by statement B was evaluative (e.g., "The legalization of marijuana is desirable") or nonevaluative ("The structure of the family will change drastically by the end of the century"). These latter data provide indirect support for the hypothesis that simply the awareness of inconsistent beliefs, regardless of the nature of these beliefs, is sufficient to stimulate cognitive reorganization.

The tests of the Socratic effect described above pertained to a particular law of cognitive organization described by Eq. (4.6). However, there is some evidence that it generalizes to other laws implied by the general hypothesis that relations among cognitions are described by the law of mathematical probability. Rosen and Wyer obtained independent estimates of P_A and $P_{A'}$ and found that the absolute discrepancy between $P_{A'}$ and $(1 - P_A)$ decreased over time. Moreover, inconsistency among the beliefs comprising Eq. (4.6) also decreased over time, even when the effects of inconsistency between P_A and $P_{A'}$ were eliminated. In addition, Wyer (1974c) found that the Socratic effect also occurred when inconsistency was defined on the basis of Eq. (4.3) and Eq. (4.4). These results add support for the subjective probability approach to cognitive organization proposed in this chapter. Whether the Socratic effect applies equally well to other formulations is a question we will consider in later chapters.

There may nevertheless be certain limitations to the generalization of the Socratic effect. For example, Watts and Holt (1970) found that the Socratic effect was greater when subjects expected to communicate their beliefs to others after the second administration of the questionnaire than when they were told they would receive new belief-relevant information after reporting their beliefs in the second session. Subjects who expect to receive such information may postpone their attempts to eliminate inconsistencies among their beliefs until this information is received and assimilated.

VI. CONCLUDING REMARKS

A. Evaluation of the Approach

What can be concluded concerning the validity of the hypothesis that relations among beliefs and attitudes conform to the laws of mathematical probability theory? The evidence, based upon functional measurement analyses, that beliefs do combine subjectively in the manner implied by Eq. (4.6), in combination with evidence that accurate quantitative descriptions of the relations among several different types of cognitions can frequently be obtained by applying these laws, is encouraging. This accuracy is particularly impressive in light of the fact that *ad hoc* curve-fitting parameters are generally not essential to produce a good fit. (While some small systematic deviations from prediction are apparent, no alternative approach to the study of cognitive organization has been as successful in this regard, as we shall see in the chapters that follow.)

There are undoubtedly limits to the generality of this hypothesis. For example, the failure of Eq. (4.3) to generate accurate quantitative predictions of conjunctive probabilities (P_{AB}) suggests that the laws of mathematical probability may not strictly apply in this case. Moreover, these laws describe the relations among newly formed beliefs and attitudes much more accurately than they describe the relations among previously formed cognitions about real objects and events. However, this latter limitation may be of more practical than theoretical concern. The most important evidence for the validity of the approach to cognitive organization described in this chapter is the strong and consistent finding that the predictive accuracy of laws based upon mathematical probability theory increases over time, once the relevant cognitions are made salient to subjects. This finding is a necessary implication of the assumption that these laws provide valid descriptions of the manner in which cognitions are organized.

B. Directions for Future Research

1. Further Tests of the Model. Unfortunately, to date there have been few direct attempts to tie the probability relations being tested to the underlying psychological processes they are assumed to describe. The one attempt to do this by applying functional measurement procedures (Wyer, 1974b) showed that the beliefs to which Eq. (4.6) pertains appear to combine subjectively in the manner implied by this equation. However, this is not to say that *all* sets of beliefs combine in the manner suggested by mathematical probability laws. The application of functional measurement techniques to other hypothetical relations, such as that described by Eq. (4.3), may help greatly to clarify the nature of the processes to which they pertain, and to circumscribe more carefully the conditions in which mathematical probability laws are valid descriptions of the relations among subjective probabilities.

The accuracy of many of the probabilistic equations considered in this chapter is particularly surprising because of the apparent complexity of the relations they describe. Since a subject's capacity to process large amounts of information is limited, one would expect that the more complex the hypothetical equation describing the relations among beliefs, the less likely it is that the equation will hold. Although "complexity" is somewhat difficult to define precisely, it may depend upon such factors as the number of beliefs in the equation, the number of different objects to which they pertain, the number of probabilities in each term of the equation, and the number of terms. The accuracy of probability laws should be investigated as a function of these factors.

2. General Implications for Belief and Opinion Change. In instances in which predictions of the relations among cognitions are relatively inaccurate, obtained values of beliefs are often highly correlated with predicted values. Thus, despite the failure for the laws of probability to generate precise quantitative descriptions of the relations among cognitions in some cases, these laws may be sufficiently close approximations of these relations to suggest more general hypotheses concerning the manner in which cognitions are organized and the way in which change in one cognition will affect others. As we shall see in the chapters that follow, the application of these laws to several specific phenomena related to belief and attitude organization and change can provide new theoretical insights into the nature of these phenomena and the conditions under which they may occur. Thus the heuristic value of the approach may be considerable.

To provide an example of the usefulness of this approach in generating nonquantitative predictions of attitude and belief change, suppose a subject believes that C is true either if both X and Y are true or for reasons (K) unrelated to X and Y. That is,

$$(X \cap Y) \cup K \supset C$$

The probability that C is true should equal the probability that both X and Y, or K, or both are true, that is,

$$P_C = P_{(X \cap Y) \cup K}$$

If beliefs associated with X, Y, and K are independent, the above equation may be rewritten:

$$P_C = P_X P_Y + P_K (1 - P_X P_Y)$$

$$= P_K + P_X P_Y (1 - P_K)$$

Now, suppose that information is presented that changes the subject's belief that X is true by an amount ΔP_X, leaving his beliefs in Y or in K unaffected. This should produce a change in P_C of ΔP_C. Substituting the revised beliefs into the preceding equation:

$$P_C + \Delta P_C = P_K + (P_X + \Delta P_X) P_Y (1 - P_K)$$

Solving for ΔP_C and simplifying:

$$\Delta P_C = P_Y \Delta P_X (1 - P_K) \tag{4.11}$$

The implications of this equation are not profound but are of theoretical importance. First, a given change in P_X should have less effect upon P_C when P_K is large, or in other words when C is likely to be true for reasons other than $X \cap Y$. More generally, when there are many different reasons to believe that C is true, information pertaining to any particular belief related to C will have less influence.

Second, a given change in P_X should have greater effect upon P_C when P_Y is large than when it is small. Therefore, suppose in the above example that a propagandist must choose between providing information that will increase P_X by an amount ΔP_X and information that will produce an equal increase in P_Y ($\Delta P_Y = \Delta P_X$). Then, the propagandist would be more successful in changing a subject's belief about C if he presents information supporting the statement $(X$ or $Y)$ that the subject initially believes is the less likely to be true.

Both of the above predictions are intuitively plausible, and perhaps neither is very exciting. The point, however, is that the application of mathematical probability laws to these questions generates hypotheses that are testable with traditional experimental procedures, and may be empirically valid, regardless of the accuracy of these laws in generating precise quantitative descriptions of the relations among the beliefs involved.

3. Individual Differences in Cognitive Functioning. The probability models described in this chapter may conceivably be used to identify more precisely the factors that contribute to individual differences in belief and opinion change. For example, suppose that two persons, A and B, both receive information about their possession of a personality attribute X. After receiving this information, A changes his self-evaluation (P_L) but B does not. What could account for this difference? According to Eq. (4.7), at least three factors could contribute. First, A may have believed the information, and thus have changed his estimate of P_X, while B did not. Second, both A and B may have believed the information, but B may consider X to be irrelevant to his self-evaluation (that is, $P_{L/X} = P_{L/X'}$); alternatively B may *initially* have considered X to be relevant but may have decreased his belief in its relevance *after* receiving information about it. Finally, A and B may both have believed the information, and may believe that X is equally relevant to their self-evaluations, but B, unlike A, may not process information in the manner implied by Eq. (4.7). To this extent, the equation should describe B's cognitive organization less accurately than A's; furthermore, its inaccuracy may increase after B has received information about X.

If A and B were to differ in one or more of the ways described above, these differences may be reflected by other differences between them. For example, differences in the tendency to change P_X may be correlated with differences in gullibility, intelligence, extremity of initial beliefs, etc. The relevance of X to self-evaluations may vary with sex or social role. The greatest interest may be in factors that predict differences in the tendency to organize cognitions in the manner implied by the equation, independently of the above considerations. If the information about X is unfavorable, differences in the tendency to change self-evaluations in the manner implied by Eq. (4.7) may interpreted as differences in the tendency to "compartmentalize," or dissociate specific types of beliefs from one another (cf. Wyer & Polsky, 1972). Alternatively, they may reflect more general differences between subjects in the manner in which they process information. It is interesting to speculate that the differences in cognitive functioning that characterize certain pathological "disorders of thought" (cf. Coleman, 1964) are reflected by differences in the descriptive accuracy of equations such as those considered in this chapter.

C. Generalization to Larger Sets of Information

While the discussion in this chapter has been limited to relations among small sets of beliefs, the approach described can of course be applied to larger sets. For example, consider the following statements:

A. Americans are capitalists.
B. Capitalists are religious.
C. Religious persons do not exploit the poor.
D. Capitalists exploit the poor.
K. Americans exploit the poor for reasons other than those implied by "A"–"D".
E. Americans exploit the poor.

What is the relation of a subject's beliefs in statements A, B, C, D, and K to his belief that E is true? Suppose that the subject believes E to be true if

1. both A and B are true and C is false, or
2. both A and D are true, or
3. K is true.

That is,

$$(A \cap B \cap C') \cap (A \cap D) \cup K \supset E$$

According to the laws of probability, the belief that E is true (P_E) is equal to the belief that the expression on the left is true. If A, B, C, D, and K are independent, then the equivalent probabilities simplify to the following expression:

$$P_E = P_K + P_{K'} P_A (P_D + P_{D'} P_B P_{C'})$$

Suppose that information is presented that changes P_D by an amount ΔP_D, leaving beliefs in A, B, C, and K unchanged. The consequent change in P_E would be predicted to be

$$\Delta P_E = \Delta P_D [P_A P_{K'} (1 - P_B P_{C'})].$$

VII. APPENDIX: A METHODOLOGICAL NOTE

The reader who wishes to apply the approach described in this chapter may often have difficulty in developing probability equations from inference rules such as those described above, unless he is very familiar with probability theory. However, these equations may be generated quite simply through the use of modified Venn diagrams. Assume that A and A' refer to the occurrence and nonoccurrence of one event, and that B and B' refer to the occurrence and nonoccurrence of a second event. The conjunctive probability associated with each combination of outcomes (A and B, A and B', etc.) may be represented in the following diagram, where the conjunctive probabilities of the events described by the row and column are given in the square where they intersect:

	B	B'
A	P_{AB}	$P_{AB'}$
A'	$P_{A'B}$	$P_{A'B'}$

Note that the sum of the probabilities in the cells comprising any given row or column is equal to the probability of the event to which the row or column pertains. For example, $P_A = P_{AB} + P_{AB'}$; $P_{B'} = P_{AB'} + P_{A'B'}$; etc. Moreover, the sum of all four products is unity.

Now suppose that a subject believes that an event X will occur if either A or B occurs, that is, $A \cup B \supset X$. The instances in which either A or B occurs may be represented by the cells containing a 1 in the diagram below:

	B	B'
A	1	1
A'	1	

Now, the probability that A or B occurs is the sum of the conjunctive probabilities associated with these three cells, that is,

$$P_X = P_{A \cup B} = P_{AB} + P_{AB'} + P_{A'B}$$

If A and B are independent, $P_X = P_A P_B + P_A P_{B'} + P_{A'} P_B$. However, this sum can be expressed more simply. Since both cells in the first row are involved, and the sum of the probabilities in this row is P_A, an alternative expression is,

$$P_{A \cup B} = P_A + P_{A'B} = P_A + P_{A'} P_{B'}$$

Or, since both cells in the first column are involved, and the sum of these probabilities is P_B,

$$P_{A \cup B} = P_B + P_{AB'} = P_B + P_{A'} P_{B'}$$

In other words, $P_{A \cup B}$ can be estimated by any expression that includes the cells designated by "1" once and only once. Still another estimate of $P_{A \cup B}$ may be obtained by determining the probability associated with all cells that do not contain a "1" and subtracting this from the sum of the probabilities of all cells, or 1.0; that is,

$$P_{A \cup B} = 1 - P_{A'B'} = 1 - P_{A'} P_{B'}$$

Finally, note that if the cells pertaining to P_A and those pertaining to P_B are summed, the cell pertaining to P_{AB} is counted twice. If this redundancy is eliminated by subtraction, a fourth expression for the sum of the three cells containing a "1," or $P_{A \cup B}$, is derived:

$$P_{A \cup B} = P_A + P_B - P_{AB}$$

$$= P_A + P_B - P_A P_B$$

This equation is identical to Eq. (4.4).

The above technique is useful in determining the equivalence of various probability statements. For example, to persons unfamiliar with probability theory, the fact that

$$P_A + P_{A'} P_B = P_B + P_A P_{B'} = 1 - P_{A'} P_{B'} = P_A + P_B - P_A P_B$$

may not be intuitively obvious. However, its primary value in the present context comes when one wishes to obtain a probability associated with a belief derived from more complex logical rules. For example, suppose a subject believes that an event X will occur if either C is true, or if D is false and either A or B is true, or if A, B, and C are all false; that is,

$$C \cup [D' \cap (A \cup B)] \cup (A' \cap B' \cap C') \supset X$$

A somewhat more complex table might be constructed to describe four statements, any one of which could be true or not:

	B		B'		
A	1				C'
	1	1	1	1	C
A'	1	1	1	1	
	1		1	1	C'
	D'	D		D'	

In this diagram, each cell is contained in two columns and two rows. However, as in the earlier case, each cell corresponds to the combination of events described by the rows and columns in which it is combined. For example, the upper right-hand cell corresponds to the conjunction of events A, B', C' and D'; the probability of occurrence of this combination of events is $P_{AB'C'D'}$ or, if the events are independent, $P_A P_{B'} P_{C'} P_{D'}$.

To determine the probability that X is true in the above example, first place a "1" in all cells that pertain to C; then do likewise in all cells that pertain to both D' and A, to both D' and B, and to A', B', and C' in combination. These cells are indicated in the above diagram. The probability of X is therefore the sum of the probabilities associated with these cells. These cells include all those corresponding to D', plus all those corresponding to both C and D in combination, plus the cell corresponding to A', B', C', and D in combination. Therefore, one expression for P_x might be:

$$PX = P_{D'} + P_{CD} + P_{AB'C'D}$$

An alternative expression would be:

$$PX = P_{D'} + P_{C'D'} + P_{A'B'C'D}$$

Both of the above expressions are equivalent and are obtained by summing the conjunctive probabilities of the cells marked "1" in the above diagram and making sure that each is involved once and only once.

Thus it becomes fairly easy to derive theoretical statements describing fairly complex relations among cognitions. The empirical validity of these statements is of course another question.

5
BALANCE MODELS OF
COGNITIVE ORGANIZATION

Several theoretical formulations of cognitive organization pertain primarily to cognitions about one object's feelings or affect for another (for example, "John loves Mary" and "I oppose capital punishment"). According to these formulations, cognitions are organized so that the relations they describe are "affectively" consistent according to certain specified criteria. The most frequently studied of these criteria are derived from cognitive balance theory (Heider, 1946, 1958). Although this theory (like many) was originally postulated on the basis of "common sense" intuitions about the relations among beliefs and attitudes, it has become increasingly formalized, modified, and extended since its inception (e.g., Abelson & Rosenberg, 1958; Cartwright & Harary, 1956; Newcomb, 1968; Phillips, 1967; Taylor, 1970; Wellens & Thistlethwaite, 1971; Wiest, 1965).

The principles of cognitive balance are well-known. However, suprisingly little attention has been given, either theoretically or empirically, to the more fundamental cognitive processes that underlie these principles. From the point of view we are proposing in this book, balance theory has several implications for (a) the rules used by subjects in assigning objects to cognitive categories and in inferring attributes of these objects from their category memberships, and (b) the functional equivalence of various relations among cognitive categories. In this chapter, we will discuss certain of these implications. Then we will describe and evaluate representative research that bears upon the validity of balance theory in describing the way in which cognitions are interrelated.

I. THE INTERPRETATION OF A BALANCED STATE

A. A Comparison of Sentiment and Unit Relations

Heider (1958) defines two types of relations among cognitive elements:
1. *sentiment* relations—relations conveying feeling or affect of one

element toward another (for example, "I like John," or "Mary opposes American involvement in Southeast Asia".)

2. *unit* relations—associations of two objects on the basis of "belonging," that is, group membership, ownership, etc. (e.g., "Philip is the son of Pete," "Mark Twain is the author of *Tom Sawyer*," "John is a Communist," etc.).

The distinction between unit relations and sentiment relations is not as clear as the above definitions seem to indicate. Sentiment relations also form psychological units between the elements to which they pertain. If a person believes that John loves Mary, he may think of John and Mary as a "unit" at least as frequently as he might if John and Mary were cousins. Moreover, note that the statements "John likes Mary" and "John is a Mary-liker" are equivalent. The latter statement is similar in form to "John is a Communist" and could easily be considered to be a *unit* relation according to the criteria outlined above.

Indeed, Heider initially assumed that the processes of organizing sentiment and unit relations are similar. He assigned positive (p) valences both to favorable sentiment relations between elements and to unit relations between these elements, and assigned negative (n) valences both to unfavorable sentiment relations and to the absence of unit relations. The assumption that the absence of a unit relation is functionally equivalent to an unfavorable sentiment relation is generally invalid, as several theorists (e.g., Cartwright & Harary, 1956) point out, as Jordan (1953) has found empirically, and as Heider himself later recognized (1958, p. 204). One reason for this is suggested by the interpretation of both sentiment and unit relations as relations between membership in one category and membership in another. Cognitions about positive unit relations and positive sentiment relations may function similarly because the two object-categories involved in these relations have common members. For instance, if a subject believes that Communists are probably likers of Communism, the two cognitions "John is a Communist" and "John is a liker of Communism" should play similar roles in his cognitive system. In contrast, the categories "non-Communist" and "Communist-disliker" may have fewer members in common; while dislikers of Communism may typically be non-Communists, non-Communists are less apt to dislike Communism; they could be indifferent to Communism or may not even have heard of it. To this extent, a cognition about the absence of a unit relation between two elements ("John is not a Communist") and a cognition about a negative sentiment relation ("John dislikes Communism") may function differently.

In their formalization of balance theory, Cartwright and Harary (1956) assume that the absence of a unit relation is functionally equivalent to no relation at all. However, the legitimacy of this assumption depends upon the inclusiveness of the object categories involved. It seems reasonable to hypothesize that, in general, as an object category becomes more inclusive, the less likely it is that positive unit relations involving this category function as positive sentiment relations, and the more likely it is that negative unit relations involving the category function as negative sentiment relations. Thus in the preceding example the fact that John is a Communist would be less apt to imply that John is a liker of Communism if 99% of the world's population were Communist than if only a small proportion of the population were Communist; alternatively, the fact that John is not a Communist would be more apt to imply that John dislikes Communism under the former conditions than under the latter.

B. Heiderian Balance

Heider was primarily concerned with sets of relations involving three elements, one of which was typically the subject himself (P). He proposed (1946, p. 107) that if two elements are positively associated through either a unit or a sentiment relation, P will have similar feelings about them; that is, he will either like both or dislike both. Moreover, if P has similar sentiments toward two elements, he will tend to associate them; that is, he will judge them as "belonging" to one another, as similar, or as having positive feelings toward one another. On the other hand, if P's sentiments toward two elements differ, he will cognitively "segregate" them; that is, he will not respond to them as a unit and will tend to believe that their sentiments toward one another are unfavorable.

If positive and negative valences are assigned to the relations in each set described above, the number of n relations in each set is even (either 2 or 0). Based upon this observation, Heider proposed that *any* system of relations among three elements could be considered balanced if the number of negative relations in the set was even. This principle could also apply to two-element systems. That is, a system containing only elements A and B would be balanced if A's relations to B and B's relations to A are either both p or both n. Thus the sets of relations ["John loves (p) Mary," "Mary loves (p) John"] and ["John dislikes (n) Nixon," "John dislikes (n) Republicans," "Nixon is (p) a Republican"] are balanced, while the set ["John likes (p) Americans," "John supports (p) communism," Americans hate (n) communism"] is imbalanced.

Using graph theory, Cartwright and Harary (1956) extended balance principles to cover sets of relations among more than three elements. They assumed that the absence of a unit relation indicated no relation at all among the elements involved, rather than an n relation. They then defined a state of balance as one in which every closed path connecting all or a subset of the elements contained an even number of n relations. For example, consider the following statements:

I admired John F. Kennedy.
Kennedy was the enemy of big business.
I oppose big business.
Big business exploits the poor.

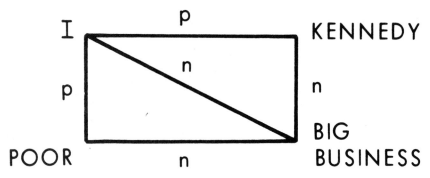

Fig. 5.1. Hypothetical balance diagram of relations between I, Kennedy, the poor, and big business.

I support the interests of the poor.

Kennedy was not poor.

The last of these statements conveys the absence of a unit relation between the two elements "Kennedy" and "Poor"; thus these elements would not be directly connected. The other relations would be represented as shown in Fig. 5.1. Although this diagram contains three n relations, there is an even number of n relations in each closed path connecting the elements (that is, "I-Kennedy-big business-I." "I-big business-poor-I," and "I-Kennedy-big business-poor-I"). Thus the set of cognitions is balanced.[1]

C. Symbolic Psycho-logic

A second extension of balance theory, which has nearly identical implications to Cartwright and Harary's, is found in Abelson and Rosenberg's (1958) statement of the principles of symbolic psycho-logic. These theorists were concerned primarily with sentiment relations, which they classified as positive (p), negative (n), or neutral (o), depending upon the affective tone of the relation described. A fourth type of relation, ambivalence (a), was interpreted as the conjunction of a p and an n relation between the same two elements (e.g., A like (p) B *and* A dislike (n) B. Abelson and Rosenberg postulate the following rules of psycho-logic:

1. XrY implies ẎrX, where r is any one of the relations p, n, or o; e.g., "John likes Mary" implies "Mary likes John."

2. XpY and YpZ imply XpZ; e.g., "I like John" and "John likes Mary" imply "I like Mary."

3. XnY and YnZ imply XpZ; e.g., "I dislike John" and "John dislikes Mary" imply "I like Mary."

---

[1]It can be shown that a system is balanced if each path in a subset that covers each relation at least once contains an even number of negative signs. Thus, in this example, the third path described need not be considered, since the first two paths in combination include all five relations.

4. XpY and YnZ (or XnY and YpZ) imply XnZ; e.g., "I like John" and "John dislikes Mary" (or "I dislike John" and "John likes Mary") imply "I dislike Mary."

5. XoY and YrZ (or XrY and YoZ) imply XoZ; e.g., "I am indifferent to John" and "John likes Mary" (or "I like John" and "John is indifferent to Mary") imply "I am indifferent to Mary."

From these fundamental relations, others may be derived. For example, XnY and XnZ imply YpZ, since XnY implies YnX, and YnX and XnZ imply YpZ. Moreover, XpY and YnZ and XpW imply WnZ, since XpW implies WpX, XpY and YnZ imply XnZ, and WpX and XnZ imply WnZ.

The group of relations implied by each of Rules 1-4 would meet the criterion for balance proposed by Cartwright and Harary; that is, each group contains an even number of n relations. Since Cartwright and Harary did not consider neutral sentiment relations in their formulations, Rule 5 is unique to psycho-logic. On the other hand, psycho-logic, unlike Cartwright and Harary's formulation, does not take into account the effects of unit relations. This latter omission is easily overcome. Denote a positive unit relation by u and the absence of a unit relation by u'. Then, the following additional rules, if added to those proposed by Abelson and Rosenberg, could accommodate the effects of unit relations implied by graph theory:

6. XrY and YuZ (or XuY and YrZ) imply XrZ, where r is either u, p, o, or n; e.g., "I like John" and "John is a Communist" implies "I like Communists"; alternatively, "I am a Communist" and "Communists dislike rock-and-roll" imply "I dislike rock-and-roll."

7. XrY and $Yu'Z$ (or $Xu'Y$ and YrZ) implies either XpZ or XoZ or XnZ, where r is either u, p, o, or n; e.g., the cognitions "I like John" and "John is not a Communist" have no implications whatsoever for my sentiment toward Communists.

D. Determination of Balance in Complex Systems

Abelson and Rosenberg developed a procedure for applying psycho-logic to large systems of interrelated cognitions. Consider the set of relations shown graphically in Fig. 5.1. These relations may be summarized in the following matrix:

	A	B	C	D
A. I		p	n	p
B. Kennedy			n	u'
C. big business				n
D. poor				

Abelson and Rosenberg postulate that the set of relations contained in such a matrix is balanced if none of the relations described is n or if the matrix can be transformed into one with no n relations through successive transformations of row and column elements. A transformation is made by replacing an element (i.e., a cognitive category) by its opposite, and then "reversing" the sign of its relation with each of the other elements in the row and column to which it pertains. For example, suppose element C as denoted in the third row and third column of the above matrix is replaced by C' (not-C) and the relations in which it is involved reversed (in this case, changed from n to p). This would result in the transformed matrix:

	A	B	C'	D
A		p	p	p
B			p	u'
C'				p
D				

Since this transformed matrix contains no n relations, it, and consequently the original matrix of relations, is balanced. More complex systems may require more than one transformation to achieve a matrix with no n relations. Each successive transformation is assumed to describe a set of relations equivalent to the original.

The criterion for balance is whether, indeed, such a matrix with no n relations can be obtained. If, regardless of the number of transformations, all n relations cannot be eliminated, then the system is imbalanced.

The comparability of this model to the original formulation proposed by Heider and extended by Cartwright and Harary becomes obvious by referring to the diagram in Fig. 5.1. In such a diagram, each element is necessarily involved in two and only two relations in *any single loop*. Suppose, following Abelson and Rosenberg's procedure, we replace an element by its negation (e.g., "Kennedy" by "not-Kennedy," or "big business" by "not big business") and reverse the signs of all relations in which the element is involved. In doing so, we have changed two relations in each loop, and thus we have changed the n relations in the loop by an even number. Consequently, if a loop initially contains an odd number of n relations, or is imbalanced, transformations of the sort proposed by Abelson and Rosenberg will not be able to decrease this number below one. However, if a loop contains an even number of n relations, or is balanced, such transformations could decrease this number to zero.

The usefulness of Abelson and Rosenberg's procedure for determining balance increases with the size and complexity of the cognitive system to which it is applied. The procedure can easily be programmed on a computer. It has an advantage over the graph-theoretical approach taken by Cartwright and Harary in that when the system is imbalanced, it can be used more easily to identify the minimum number of cognitions that must be changed in order to produce balance. Abelson and Rosenberg hypothesize that when a system is not balanced, subjects will tend to balance it in the way that requires the fewest changes in their beliefs. Thus, the procedure they propose can be used to predict differences in the difficulty of balancing different sets of cognitions; also, to predict which specific cognitions in these sets are most likely to change.

E. Assumptions of Balance and Psycho-logic

Some explicit and implicit assumptions underlying Abelson and Rosenberg's procedure are worth noting. One assumption is that the relations between any two elements are reciprocal (that is, if XrY, then YrX, where r is a given type of relation). A second assumption is that each element has a positive relation with itself (that is, XpX). Given these assumptions, the matrix of original relations considered in the above example would be

	A	B	C	D
A	p	p	n	p
B	p	p	n	u'
C	n	n	p	n
D	p	u'	n	p

and the revised matrix, after replacing C by C', would be:

	A	B	C'	D
A	p	p	p	p
B	p	p	p	u'
C'	p	p	p	p
D	p	u'	p	p

(Since the relation between C and itself changes twice, once when row relations are reversed and once when column relations are reversed, it remains positive.) While the validity of the above two assumptions is an empirical question, neither seems theoretically necessary. Although systems containing the relations XpY and YnX can never be balanced according to the criteria proposed by Abelson and Rosenberg, a system containing the relations XpY and YoX *could* be balanced according to these criteria. There are intuitively several conditions in which it would make more sense to allow for this type of nonreciprocity. For example, John may favor equal opportunities for women and yet believe that such opportunities will not benefit him personally in any way. Or, John may admire the late John F. Kennedy but believe that Kennedy did not know him, and thus did not have any particularly positive regard for him.

The assumption of a p relation between each element and itself is also not essential. An o relation could also be assumed without affecting any conclusions based upon the procedure. Incidentally, the assumption of either a p or an o relation between each element and itself does not eliminate the possibility that a subject may have unfavorable feelings about himself. This case can be handled if a distinction is made between the subject as evaluator (P) and the subject as an object of evaluation. Suppose that P has the following cognitions:

> I despise myself.
> I like John.
> John despises me.

These cognitions could be represented in the following matrix, where missing relations are assumed to be o.

	A	B	C
A. I	p	n	p
B. self	o	p	o
C. John	o	n	p

The set of relations is then balanced, since the replacement of B by B′ would result in the matrix:

	A	B′	C
A	p	p	p
B′	o	p	o
C	o	p	p

Other, unstated assumptions underlying Abelson and Rosenberg's procedure may be more noteworthy, since they have implications for the cognitive processes underlying the procedure. These assumptions pertain to the functional equivalence of certain types of beliefs. Suppose that objects are members of either A or A′ and of either B or B′. Then, the transformation procedure assumes that the following sets of beliefs about sentiment relations are functionally equivalent:

$$ApB = AnB' = A'nB = A'pB' \qquad (5.1a)$$
$$AnB = ApB' = A'pB = A'nB' \qquad (5.1b)$$
$$AoB = AoB' = A'oB = A'oB' \qquad (5.1c)$$

Equation 5.1a would imply, for example, that the statements "Americans support capitalism," "Americans oppose non-capitalism," "non-Americans oppose capitalism," and "non-Americans support non-capitalism" are functionally equivalent. Eq. (5.1c) would imply that the statements "Americans are indifferent to problems of the poor," "Americans are indifferent to things that are not problems of the poor," "non-Americans are indifferent to problems of the poor," and "non-Americans are indifferent to things that are not problems of the poor" function similarly. An implication of psycho-logic, and perhaps of balance theory in general, is that subjects treat these sets of statements as equivalent, or at least that if they believe one statement in a set, they tend also to believe the others.

The above equations of course apply only to sentiment relations. If the opposite of a positive unit relation is interpreted as no relation rather than as an n relation, then positive unit (u) relations in a matrix such as that described above would not be converted into n relations as a result of transformations of the nature proposed by Abelson and Rosenberg, but rather into u' relations. This would imply:

$$AuB = Au'B' = A'u'B = A'uB' \qquad (5.1d)$$

For example, "Americans are capitalists," "Americans are not non-capitalists," "non-Americans are not capitalists," and "non-Americans are non-capitalists" are functionally equivalent. Note that Eq. (5.1d) is similar to Eq. (5.1a) except that p and n relations are replaced by u and u' relations. However, although u relations, like p relations, contribute to the balance of a system of cognitions, u' relations, unlike n relations, have no effect upon the balance of the system.

Several of the equivalences described in Eqs. (5.1a)-(d) are not logically valid. Nevertheless, they could describe the assumptions actually made by subjects in organizing their cognitions. Unfortunately, little information is available concerning this possibility. Do, in fact, subjects who believe that A is indifferent to B also tend to believe that A is indifferent to B' and that A' is indifferent to B? Are subjects who believe that A opposes B also likely to believe that nonmembers of A support B and that nonmembers of A oppose nomembers of B? An understanding of the limitations of balance theory and the conditions under which it applies may ultimately require an answer to these questions.

F. Definition of Balance

We are finally in a position to define (or redefine) a state of cognitive balance:

A system of relations among cognitive elements is balanced if none of the relations is negative (n) or if the system can be transformed to an equivalent system containing no negative relations by applying Eq. (5.1a)-(1d).

What does this mean psychologically? Note that in an imbalanced system there always is at least one instance in which two elements have different affective relations with a third, that is, in which A and B disagree in their judgment of a third element C. Alternatively, a balanced system is always equivalent to one in which no such disagreements exist. Considered in this light, one implication of balance theory is that cognitive elements are organized into groups that agree with one another, or at least do not disagree, in their beliefs about every other element. In other words, agreement is the critical factor. This interpretation suggests that the organization of cognitions is based upon a view of the world through rose-colored glasses.

In the preceding discussion we have ignored an assumption of balance theory that imbalanced sets of cognitions create tension, and that attempts to decrease imbalance are motivated by the desire to eliminate these unpleasant cognitive states. This assumption is not necessary in order to postulate the balance principle as a rule of cognitive organization. Note that an imbalanced set of relations that pertains to actual persons may often reflect the fact that two of the parties involved differ in their opinions about the third. Such a disagreement may conceivably create antagonism between the disagreeing parties and thus lead to an unpleasant *social* situation. Whether *cognitions* about such a situation are unpleasant to the person holding them is of course something else again. We shall reconsider this issue later in this chapter when research on the judged pleasantness of balanced and imbalanced structures is discussed.

II. A QUANTITATIVE DESCRIPTION OF BALANCED SYSTEMS

There have been surprisingly few attempts to describe quantitatively the relations among beliefs and attitudes implied by the principles of balance and psycho-logic. The congruity principle proposed by Osgood and Tannenbaum (1955) states that a set of relations between two persons (P and O) and an object (X) is consistent if the valences of the relations (p or n) are in balance *and* if the absolute magnitude of P's affective relation to O is equal to the absolute magnitude of P's affective relation to X. Despite its apparent similarity to the principles of cognitive balance, this principle is basically an extension of Osgood, Suci, and Tannenbaum's (1957) formulation of the manner in which different pieces of information about an object combine to affect evaluations of the object. We will discuss congruity theory in more detail in Chapter 6.

The approach described in Chapter 4 can theoretically be applied to the sorts of relations among cognitions with which Heider was initially concerned, and also to the more complex relations implied by the laws of psycho-logic. For example, the affective relations among two persons A and B and an object O can be described by the equation:

$$P_L = P_{S_O} P_{L/S_O} + P_{S'_O} P_{L/S'_O} \tag{5.2}$$

where P_L is the probability that A likes B, P_{S_O} and $P_{S'_O}$ are the probabilities that A and B are similar or dissimilar in their attitudes toward O, and P_{L/S_O} and P_{L/S'_O} are the conditional probabilities that one person likes another, given that they are similar or dissimilar in their attitudes toward O. Note that in this case, S_O is essentially the attribute "similar in attitude toward O" and thus is analogous to X in Eq. (4.7). S_O could of course refer to the similarity of A's and B's unit relations to O (e.g., the similarity of their socio-economic backgrounds) as well as to the similarity of their sentiment relations to O.

The accuracy of Eq. (5.2) in describing the relations among cognitions of this type was investigated by Wyer (1972) in a study described in Chapter 4.

Each subject (A) described to another (B) a certain one of his characteristics (typically, his attitude toward an object or issue, such as "communism" or "morality"). Estimates relevant to Eq. (5.2) were obtained from A both immediately after he had given this description of himself, and again after he had received feedback from B that they were either very similar or very dissimilar to one another in the characteristic A had described. As noted in Chapter 4, Eq. (5.2) was only moderately effective in predicting A's belief that he liked B, and also that B liked him, as a function of his belief that he and B were similar. Although predicted values were correlated with obtained values, they generally underestimated actual ratings. However, with the exception of two deviant points, *changes* in A's beliefs as a results of feedback were predicted quite accurately (see Fig. 4.12).

A. Theoretical and Empirical Contingencies in the Applicability of Balance Theory

Equation 5.2 suggests certain limitations to the conditions under which balance theory applies. The difference between P_{L/S_O} and P_{L/S'_O} is interpretable as the relevance of S_O to liking. If $P_{L/S_O} > P_{L/S'_O}$ as in Wyer's (1972) study, Eq. (5.2) would predict a positive relation between P_L and P_{S_O}; that is, A should like B more to the extent that A's and B's attitudes toward O are similar. This is exactly what balance theory predicts. However, suppose $P_{L/S_O} = P_{L/S'_O}$, or in other words, similarity in attitude toward the object is completely irrelevant to liking. Then, Eq. (5.2) implies that P_L should not vary with $P_{S'_O}$ or in other words, that A's liking of B should not depend upon his belief that B is similar to him in attitude toward O.

Some indirect support for this prediction was obtained in a study by Zajonc and Burnstein (1965). Subjects were asked to learn balanced and imbalanced sets of relations involving two persons and an object (either the concept of "integration" or *Newsweek*). If cognitions are organized according to the principle of cognitive balance, sets of balanced relations should be easier to learn and remember than imbalanced sets of relations. Zajonc and Burnstein found this to be true only when the object was "integration"; when the object was *Newsweek*, balanced and imbalanced sets were equally difficult to learn. If similarity in attitudes toward integration is more relevant to liking than is similarity in attitudes toward *Newsweek*, Zajonc and Burnstein's findings are consistent with predictions based upon Eq. (5.2), although they are difficult to explain on the basis of balance theory alone.

The case in which $P_{L/S_O} < P_{L/S'_O}$ is also worth considering. In such an event, P_L and P_{S_O} should be related negatively according to Eq. (5.2); that is, subjects who believe they are similar in their attitudes toward O should be *less* apt to like one another than subjects who believe they have different attitudes toward O. In practice, these conditions may arise infrequently. (One such condition might occur when A and B are of the opposite sex, and O is the

TABLE 5.1

Obtained and Predicted Beliefs about the Similarity of
Liked and Disliked Persons

Estimates	Two liked persons	Two disliked persons	Two neutrally regarded persons	One liked and one disliked person
Obtained	.70	.59	.61	.39
Predicted	.69	.70	.63	.39

attribute "desire for sexual relations with men"; another might arise when A and B are males and O is a particular female.) However, they are of theoretical interest since the rules of cognitive organization implied by Eq. (5.2) and those implied by balance theory make directly opposite predictions in these instances.

A second attempt to quantify the relations implied by balance theory also suggests some limitations upon the generality of balance theory. Using Eq. (4.5), Wyer and Goldberg (1970) calculated the predicted and obtained estimates of the likelihood that two persons were similar with respect to each of eight characteristics, given that (a) both were liked, (b) both were disliked, (c) both were regarded neutrally, and (d) one was liked and the other was disliked. Balance theory would not predict differences between the similarity of two liked persons and that of two disliked persons. However, persons who are equally well-liked should be rated as more similar to one another than should persons who differ in likeableness. Since relations involving neutrally regarded persons are neither balanced nor imbalanced, regardless of the degree of similarity between these persons, beliefs that such persons are similar should fall between beliefs that two liked (or two disliked) persons are similar and beliefs that one liked and one disliked person are similar.

The mean predicted and mean obtained estimates of the likelihood that different pairs of persons were similar are given in Table 5.1. Predicted similarity ratings based upon Eq. (4.5) were completely in accord with predictions based upon balance theory. However, contrary to predictions of both theoretical formulations, actual estimates of the similarity between two disliked persons were substantially lower than estimates of the similarity between two liked persons, and they did not differ appreciably from estimates of the likelihood that two neutrally regarded persons are similar. The reason for this is unclear. Conceivably, "likeable" is defined by a conjunction of attributes, each of which is necessary for inclusion in the category; thus two liked persons, who necessarily share this set of attributes, are believed to be similar. However, "dislikeable" may have a disjunctive definition; any one of several different attributes may be sufficient (but not necessary) for inclusion in the category. Thus, two disliked persons may be less likely to have specific attributes in common than two liked persons. While this interpretation is intuitively plausible, it of course would not account for the relatively poor predictive accuracy of Eq. (4.5), which should theoretically not depend upon such factors.

B. Quantification of the Laws of Psycho-logic

If subjective probabilities obey the laws of mathematical probability theory, the relations implied by the rules of psycho-logic may be described quantitatively. Rules 2-5 on page ___ can be rewritten as follows:

$$(ApB \cap BpC) \cup (AnB \cap BnC) \supset ApC \qquad (5.3a)$$
$$(ApB \cap BnC) \cup (AnB \cap BpC) \supset AnC \qquad (5.3b)$$
$$AoB \cup BoC \supset AoC \qquad (5.3c)$$

If beliefs about A's relation to B are independent of beliefs about B's relation to C, and if p, n, and o relations between the same two elements cannot coexist, these relations may be described probabilistically:

$$P_{ApC} = P_{ApB} P_{BpC} + P_{AnB} P_{BnC} \qquad (5.4a)$$
$$P_{AnC} = P_{ApB} P_{BnC} + P_{AnB} P_{BpC} \qquad (5.4b)$$
$$P_{AoC} = P_{AoB} + P_{BoC} - P_{AoB} P_{BoC} \qquad (5.4c)$$

Note that these equations would not be strictly valid unless the relations involving A and B and those involving B and C are the *only* ones that bear upon the relation between A and C. In practice, this is generally not the case; other sets of statements, if true, also imply a certain type of relation between A and C. This complicates matters greatly. For example, consider the effects of the common relation of A and C to a fourth element D. Equations analogous to Eqs. (5.3a-c) could be written involving these relations. According to Abelson and Rosenberg, ApC is believed if at least one of the two sets of "premises" implies the relation according to the rules of psycho-logic and *neither* set implies a negative relation. The probability statement describing this condition would be:

$$P_{ApC} = (P_{ApB}P_{BpC} + P_{AnC}P_{BnC})(P_{ApD}P_{DpC} + P_{AnD}P_{DnC} + P_{AoD} + P_{DoC} - P_{AoD}P_{DoC})$$
$$+ (P_{AoB} + P_{BoC} - P_{AoB}P_{BoC})(P_{ApD}P_{DpC} + P_{AnD}P_{DnC})$$

Thus, the rules of psycho-logic generate extremely complex expressions for quantitatively describing the relations among beliefs and attitudes.

C. Measurement of Consistency

If the entire set of cognitions that pertains to a given belief could be identified, a probabilistic equation could be written to describe their theoretical relations to one another. The accuracy of this equation in describing these relations would theoretically be an index of the degree of consistency among the cognitions involved. Unfortunately, the near impossibility of circumscribing the entire set of beliefs to be included in such an equation precludes the use of this index. An indirect estimate of the degree of consistency among beliefs associated with a given relation may nevertheless be obtained. Assume that the probabilities P_{ApC}, P_{AnC}, and P_{AoC} are denoted P_p, P_n, and P_o, respectively. If B is the only other element to which A and C are related, the conditions that imply the three possible relations between A and C are mutually exclusive [see Eqs. (5.3)-(c)] and thus

$$P_p + P_n + P_o = 1.$$

However, suppose that A and C are both related to a fourth element, D. Then, the conditions that imply each type of relation between A and C are not necessarily mutually exclusive; the implication of A's and C's relations to D may differ from the implication of their relations to B. When this occurs, Abelson and Rosenberg postulate an ambivalent (*a*) relation between A and C. This relation is, in effect, the coexistence of two different sentiment relations between these two elements. A state of ambivalence is theoretically equivalent to a state of inconsistency, or imbalance,[2] and thus, if the principles of psycho-logic are valid, should be eliminated through cognitive reorganization.

While ambivalence is hard to assess directly, Wyer and Goldberg (1970) have pointed out that when ambivalence exists, the above equation should be modified as follows:

$$P_p + P_o + P_n - P_a = 1,$$

where P_a is the probability of an ambivalent relation between A and B, or the probability of the conjunction of two or more of the possible sentiment relations between these elements (that is, $P_{p \cap n}$). More simply, the degree of ambivalence of a relation between A and B would be indicated by the extent to which $P_a > 0$, or

$$P_p + P_o + P_n > 1.$$

If the laws of psycho-logic are valid descriptions of the manner in which a set of cognitions is organized, conditions that make these cognitions salient

---

[2]For example, an ambivalent relation between A and C would occur if a subject held the cognitions ApB and BpC (which imply ApC) and also the cognitions ApD and DnC (which imply AnC). However, this set of relations is imbalanced, since the closed path A-B-C-D-A contains an odd number of *n* relations.

should affect beliefs that bear upon P_p, P_n, and P_o in a way that reduces the discrepancy between the sum of these probabilities and unity. In other words, the "Socratic effect" would be indicated by a decrease in this discrepancy over time.

D. Some Conceptual Problems

In Chapter 2 we noted that beliefs associated with statements of the form "A is B" can be interpreted either as unconditional probabilities that the statement is a member of the category "True" or as conditional probabilities that members of category A are members of category B. The similarity between predictions based upon balance theory and those based upon the assumption that subjective probabilities obey the laws of mathematical probability may depend upon which of these interpretations is the more valid. Consider the unit relations "Cops are sadists" (CuS) and "Sadists are insane" (SuI), which in combination imply the unit relation "Cops are insane" (CuI). According to balance theory, if these were the only existing cognitions involving the three elements, $CuS \cap SuI \supset CuI$, and therefore, $P_{CuI} = P_{CuS \cup SuI}$. However, if the beliefs associated with the three statements are interpreted as conditional probabilities ($P_{S/C}$, $P_{I/S}$, and $P_{I/C}$, respectively), the equation relating these beliefs according to probability theory would be:

$$P_{I/C} = P_{S/C}P_{I/SC} + P_{S'/C}P_{I/S'C}$$

where $P_{I/SC}$ is the conditional probability of belonging to I, given membership in *both* S and C, $P_{S'/C}$ is the probability of not belonging to S, given membership in C, and $P_{I/S'C}$ is the probability of belonging to I, given membership in C but not S.

Differences in the effects of these alternative interpretations become more striking when statements about sentiment relations are involved. Consider the statements "Cops hate hippies" (CnH) and "Hippies like drugs" (HpD) which, according to the rules of psycho-logic, imply "Cops hate drugs" (CnD). However, if the three statements are equivalent to "Cops are hippy-haters," "Hippies are drug-likers," and "Cops are drug-haters," beliefs in the three statements could be interpreted as the conditional probabilities $P_{hippy-hater/cop}$, $\bar{P}_{drug-liker/hippy}$, and $P_{drug-hater/cop}$, respectively. Unless some assumptions are made concerning the relation between membership in the category "hippy" and membership in the category "hippy-hater," and between membership in "drug-liker" and membership in "drug-hater," there would be no way at all of relating these beliefs according to the laws of probability theory.

III. EMPIRICAL TESTS OF BALANCE THEORY

What is the evidence that cognitions are organized according to the laws of balance and psycho-logic? Much of the research generated by balance theory has focused upon the utility of balance principles in predicting inferences about persons and objects, based upon information presented about them. That is, subjects are given information about certain relations among a set of cognitive elements and are asked to predict the remaining relation. The rules governing such inferences are not necessarily similar to those governing the organization of cognitions, as we have pointed out previously. Since the manner in which information combines to affect judgments is considered in detail in Section III of this book, research bearing upon the implications of balance theory for these judgmental processes will be discussed at that time (see Chapter 10).

One indication of the validity of balance principles in describing cognitive organization is the extent to which relations among previously formed cognitions conform to these principles. A second is the extent to which sets of new cognitions about the relations among unfamiliar objects tend to be organized in a balanced manner. Third, if an imbalanced set of beliefs is made salient to a subject, or if a change in one belief temporarily creates imbalance, there should be a subsequent change in one or more of the cognitions involved, to eliminate the imbalance. A corollary of this latter hypothesis stems from the assumption of balance theory that cognitions are organized consistently because inconsistency is aversive. If this is true, imbalanced sets of cognitions should be judged to be more unpleasant than balanced sets.

Although the implications of balance theory are conceptually clear, it has proved difficult to test these implications adequately. Let us turn to some of the relevant research and attempt to evaluate the support it provides for the hypothesis that balance principles govern cognitive organization.

A. Relations among Existing Cognitions

Balance theory is sometimes applied in sociometric studies of subjects' choices of others as friends or coworkers, and their perceptions of others' choices. For example, Kogan and Tagiuri (1958) asked naval enlisted personnel first to indicate the three crew members they would most like to spend a liberty with, and then to predict the three choices made by each other crew member. Analogous data were obtained about the three persons with whom each member would least like to go on liberty. The sentiment relations among each combination of three persons in the crew could be inferred from these data. A relation between two persons was assumed to be positive (or negative) if *either* person chose the other as most (or least) desirable. (Certain sets of relations were neither balanced nor imbalanced, since neither of two persons had chosen the other as either most or least desirable.) Kogan and Tagiuri compared the actual frequency of occurrence of different types of triads to the frequency with which these combinations of relations would occur by chance. Balanced triads, consisting of three p relations or of one p and two n relations, occurred more frequently than expected, while imbalanced triads (one n and two p relations) occurred less often than expected. These differences were significant regardless of whether the triads were based upon subjects' actual choices or upon their predictions of other members' choices. In one sense, these data are not surprising. Certainly one would rather take liberty with persons who get along well with one another than with persons who do not. P's perception that A and B like one another, as well as his personal liking for both A and B, may be a criterion for choosing A and B as company. The most interesting finding may therefore be the greater than chance probability of triads consisting of n relations between P and both A and B and a p relation between A and B. That is, if P disliked both A and B, he tended to believe that A liked B, and A did in fact tend to choose B as company under these conditions. This finding, predicted by balance theory, is not as easily explained on the basis of "common sense". Kogan and Tagiuri also found that subjects' perception of one another's choices were balanced significantly more frequently than their actual choices. This suggests that subjects' tendencies to form balanced sets of beliefs were not simply a reflection of the actual relations among the persons involved.

While Kogan and Tagiuri's findings are suggestive, Davol (1959) pointed out a methodological problem with their study which resulted from the fact that balance could occur in several different ways among the same three elements. For example, a triad consisting of P, O, and Q was considered balanced if (a) either P chose O or O chose P, (b) either P chose Q or Q chose P, and (c) either O chose Q or Q chose O. This procedure artifactually increased the number of balanced sets of relations reported. In analyzing the actual sociometric ratings of dormitory residents, Davol considered only mutually positive or mutually negative relations among the persons involved. He found that when one subject's (P's) relations with two others (O and Q) were both mutually positive, the relation between O and Q was mutually positive significantly more often than it was negative, as balance theory would predict. However, when P's relations with O and Q were both mutually negative, the relation between O and Q was significantly more likely to be negative than to be positive, contrary to balance theory predictions. When P's relations to O and Q were mutually positive and mutually negative, respectively, the third relation was more often negative than positive, but the difference was not significant. In the latter case, most of the relations between O and Q were not mutual.

While the results of Davol's study would not be predicted by balance theory, the data reported were based upon actual relations between the persons involved, not perceived relations. Thus the conclusion that they invalidate balance theory should be treated with caution. In fact, Davol's findings could simply be attributed to the fact that some persons are popular, and thus are generally liked by others, while some are generally unpopular, and thus are generally disliked. P's liking of O and Q may be an indication of O's and Q's general popularity. Thus, when P likes O and Q, both O and Q

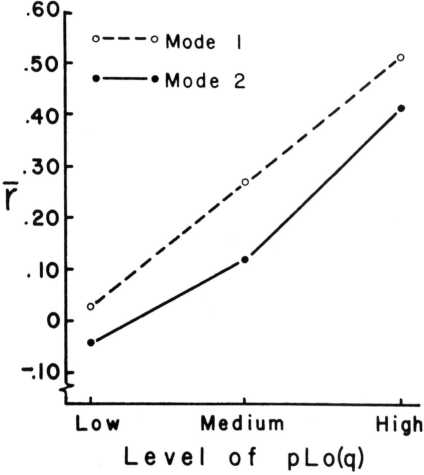

Fig. 5.2. Mean *r* at each of three levels of pLo (Mode 1) and pLq (Mode 2) (reprinted from Wiest, 1965, p. 10).

may be popular, and therefore each may be apt to like the other. When P dislikes both O and Q, both O and Q may be unpopular, and therefore each may be apt to dislike the other. When P likes O and dislikes Q, O may be popular and Q unpopular; therefore, Q may like O while O dislikes Q. These *post hoc* hypotheses are in complete agreement with Davol's findings.

Wiest (1965) performed one of the most sophisticated tests of balance theory, with the use of sociometric procedures. His study is of additional interest since it takes into account the intensity of relations as well as their direction. Consider again a triad of persons P, O, and Q. Wiest reasoned that the correlation between P's liking for Q and P's estimate of O's liking for Q should depend upon the magnitude of P's liking for O. That is, when P likes O, the correlation between the other two relations should be positive; when P dislikes O, this correlation should be negative; and when P feels neutrally toward O, the other two relations should be uncorrelated.

To test these hypothesis, Wiest obtained sociometric ratings from elementary and junior high school subjects. Subjects' predictions of others' ratings were also obtained. Two analyses of these data are of particular interest. In one ("Mode 1"), Wiest correlated P's liking for Q (pLq) and his estimates of O's liking for Q (oLq) at three levels of P's liking for O (pLo): positive, neutral, and negative. In the second ("Mode 2"), he correlated pLo and oLq at three levels of pLq. These correlations, averaged over subjects, are plotted in Fig. 5.2.

These data provide equivocal support for balance theory. The correlation between two of the relations is a positive function of the third relation, as predicted. However, when the third relation is negative, the other two relations are not negatively correlated; rather, they are not correlated at all.

What do Wiest's data imply about the manner in which cognitions about other persons are organized? First, note from Fig. 5.2 that oLq was more positively correlated with pLq than with pLo. In other words, the tendency to believe that another person's ratings are similar to one's own is generally greater than the tendency to believe that liked persons like others. Data pertaining to Mode 1 indicate that P's tendency to project his own evaluations of persons onto others (or alternatively, his tendency to conform to evaluations he expects others to make) is greater when the persons being rated are liked than when they are disliked. Finally, data pertaining to Mode 2 suggest that P's liking for O is related to O's regard for persons he himself likes but is not related to O's regard for those he personally dislikes.

All three studies cited above are consistent in finding that sets of three positive relations tend to occur more frequently than would be expected by chance. However, when at least one of the relations is negative, other relations do not consistently conform to those predicted by balance theory. Data from these studies may nevertheless be useful in developing a general understanding of why persons like others and what sorts of inferences are made about liked persons. But more about this later.

B. Organization of New Cognitions

Several tests of balance theory have considered the manner in which subjects organize new cognitions about unfamiliar persons and objects. Since such cognitions are formed only on the basis of information provided in the experiment, their organization is unlikely to be greatly affected by previously formed beliefs and attitudes unknown to the experimenter. For this reason, the operation of balance principles should be more easily detected under such conditions. In fact, however, research on the organization of newly formed cognitions shows that balance principles apply only under limited

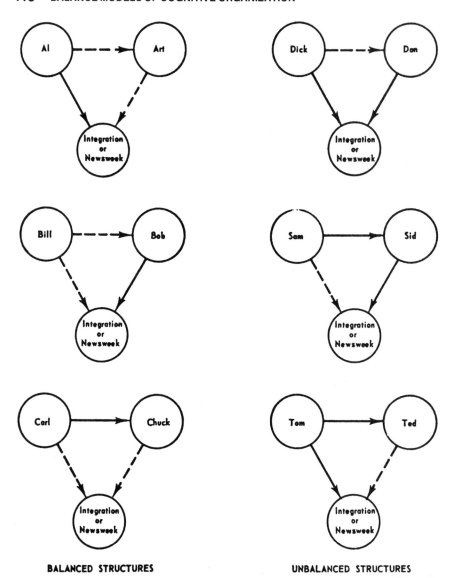

BALANCED STRUCTURES   **UNBALANCED STRUCTURES**

Fig. 5.3. Balanced and imbalanced triads of relations presented by Zajonc and Burnstein (reprinted from Zajonc & Burnstein, 1965, p. 155).

conditions, and that they typically have less influence than other principles that govern the manner in which new information is assimilated.

For example, consider the study by Zajonc and Burnstein (1965) mentioned briefly earlier in this chapter. These authors argued that if cognitions are organized according to the rules of balance, balanced sets of relations should be easier to learn and remember than imbalanced sets, and errors in recalling relations should be more likely to produce balance rather than to produce imbalance in the sets in which they are contained. To test these hypotheses, they constructed six types of triads consisting of two persons and an object X (either "integration" or *Newsweek*). These triads are shown in Fig. 5.3. The 18 relations comprising these triads were presented in random order. In each case, subjects were given the names of two elements and were asked to predict whether the relation between them would be positive (liking or approval) or negative (disliking or disapproval). After making each prediction, they were told the actual relation. The 18 relations were presented for each of 10 successive trials.

Compelling support for balance theory was not obtained in this study. When the object used in the triads was "integration," there were fewer errors in recalling relations in balanced triads than those in imbalanced ones. However, when the issue involved was *Newsweek*, the accuracy of recall was not a function of the degree of balance. The reason for this contingency has already been discussed (see page 109). In addition, n relations in imbalanced triads were recalled less accurately than p relations in these triads, while p and n relations in balanced triads were recalled with equal accuracy.

Two factors other than balance may in combination account for many of Zajonc and Burnstein's results. One is a *positivity bias,* or a tendency to recall relations as favorable regardless of other relations in the triad. The second is a *similarity bias,* or a tendency to recall the three relations comprising the triad as similar (either all positive or all negative). In Zajonc and Burnstein's study, this latter bias may be reflected in a tendency to recall relations as similar to the one that is predominant in the triad in which it is contained. In other words, relations may be recalled as p in imbalanced triads (which consist of one n and two p relations) and as n in balanced triads (which consist of one p and two n relations). Now, suppose that similarity and positivity biases have additive effects. Then, when triads are imbalanced, both biases would produce errors in recalling n relations, and so these relations should be recalled much less accurately than p relations. When triads are balanced, however, a positivity bias would produce errors in the recall of n relations, while a similarity bias would produce errors in the recall of p relations. These effects may cancel, leading to no appreciable difference in the accuracy of recalling p and n relations. Zajonc and Burnstein's data are consistent with both predictions.

Later studies by Zajonc and his colleagues provide further evidence for the existence of positivity and similarity biases. Zajonc and Sherman (1967), using the same learning paradigm employed by Zajonc and Burnstein, constructed sets of relations among three persons. Two relations were either p or n sentiment relations and one was a negative unit (u') relation (e.g., "A does not know B"). Three types of triads were considered: pnu', ppu', and nnu'. The authors expected that subjects would have difficulty in recalling the u' relation in each triad and were interested in whether errors in recalling these relations would produce balance or imbalance. According to a balance principle, u' relations should be recalled as n in pnu' triads, as p in ppu' triads, and as p in nnu' triads. If a similarity bias is operating, however, u' relations should be recalled as p and n with roughly equal frequency in pnu' triads, as p in ppu' triads, and as n in nnu' triads. Zajonc and Sherman's data are more consistent with the latter set of predictions. Specifically, in pnu' triads, u' relations were recalled as p an average of 2.47 times and as n an average of 2.33 times. In ppu' triads, they were recalled more frequently as p ($M = 2.79$) than as n ($M = 1.54$), while in nnu' triads they were recalled more frequently as n ($M = 2.85$) than as p ($M = 1.72$).

The most detailed investigation of balance theory with the use of learning paradigm was performed by Rubin and Zajonc (1969). Subjects were required to learn the relations in eight different triads consisting of two persons, P and O, and an object X. Four of the triads ($ppp, pnn, npn,$ and nnp) were balanced, and four ($nnn, npp, pnp,$ and ppn) were unbalanced. Three different objects were considered: "integration," "Larry," and "me." Several results of this study are notworthy:

1. Balanced structures were learned no more easily than unbalanced structures, regardless of the object involved. Thus, Zajonc and Burnstein's (1965) finding that balanced structures were learned more easily when the issue involved was "integration" was not replicated. Perhaps integration was of less concern to subjects at the time this study was run than to subjects in the earlier study.

2. Ease of learning depended significantly upon the nature of X. When X was "integration," relations between P and O were learned more easily than P's and O's attitudes toward X. When X was "Larry," all three relations were learned with equal facility. When X was "me," attitudes toward X were learned more easily than attitudes between P and O. In combination, these results imply that relations involving oneself are learned most easily, followed by relations among persons other than oneself, and then by relations involving issues and inanimate objects. These relations conceivably differ along a dimension of personal relevance. To this extent, results suggest the conclusion that relations are learned more easily if they are more personally relevant.

3. When the relation between P and O was positive, balanced triads were learned more easily than imbalanced ones; when P's relation to O was negative, there was no difference in the ease of learning balanced and imbalanced triads. Note that when P's relation to O is positive, balanced triads are those in which P and O agree in their attitudes toward X. Thus these data suggest that agreement about X is a relevant factor in organizing cognitions only when P likes O. This hypothesis has also been proposed by Newcomb (1968).

4. Positive relations were recalled more easily than negative relations, providing further evidence for a "positivity" bias. However, any given relation was more likely to be recalled as *p* if one of the other two relations in the triad was *p* than if this same relation was *n*. This finding is of particular interest. It suggests, for example, that if P is believed to like O, he is believed more apt to like X than to dislike X, independent of O's relation to X. This tendency to generalize a person's sentiments over different objects was interpreted by Rubin and Zajonc as a *friendliness bias,* that is, a belief that persons who like one thing tend to like another. On the other hand, if P is believed to like X, O is believed more likely to like X than to dislike it. This generalization of sentiments toward an object across different sources was interpreted as a *popularity bias,* that is, a tendency to believe that an object liked by one person is liked by a second. These two biases contributed more to differences in the learning of relations in Rubin and Zajonc's study than did a bias toward "balance."

Some caution should be taken in generalizing the results of studies such as Zajonc's to relations among existing cognitions, particularly to those in which the subject himself is an element. For example, Rubin and Zajonc's data suggest that there should be a positive correlation between P's liking for X and his belief that O likes X, regardless of P's liking for O. On the other hand, recall that in Wiest's (1965) study, where P was the subject himself and O and X were actual acquaintances, this correlation was much greater when P liked O than when he did not. A "popularity" bias may be most apparent when the persons and objects being related are unfamiliar and when the subject's own attitudes are not involved.

If a general tendency exists to report relations among elements as positive, regardless of their context, balanced sets of relations would occur more frequently than imbalanced sets by chance alone. To see this by way of an example, suppose the unconditional probability of occurrence of a *p* relation between two elements is .8, and an *n* relation is .2. Then, the probability that each basic type of triads will occur by chance is:

three *p* relations (*ppp*)	.512
two *p*, one *n* (*ppn, pnp, npp*)	.384
two *n*, one *p* (*pnn, npn, nnp*)	.096
three *n* (*nnn*)	.008

The chance probability of a balanced triad (three *p* relations, or one *p* and two *n* relations) is .608, while the chance probability of an imbalanced triad is .392.

Wyer and Lyon (1970) circumvented this problem by calculating chance probabilities of occurrence of relations among persons and objects in a manner similar to that described above and then determining whether the actual likelihood of occurence of different combinations of these relations differed from these chance probabilities. They constructed hypothetical situations involving either three persons (POO), two persons and an object (POX) or one person and two objects (PXX). The description of the situations did not allude in any way to the type of sentiment or unit relations among the elements. Subjects were presented a situation, and were then asked to consider each pair of elements in turn and to indicate which of three statements was the most likely to describe the relation between them. These statements conveyed either positive (*p*), negative (*n*), or neutral (*o*) affect between the elements, as inferred from normative data. The order of presenting each pair of elements was counterbalanced. Thus, the unconditional probability of inferring each type of relation between a pair of elements could be estimated by the proportion of subjects selecting this relation when the two elements involved were presented first. The unconditional probability of assigning an *n* relation was consistently lower than that of assigning a *p* or an *o* relation, suggesting that *n* relations tend to be avoided. However, the chance probability of assigning a *p* relation was greater than that of assigning an *o* relation only when both elements in the relation were persons.

There are 27 possible combinations of *p, o,* and *n* relations. The chance probability of occurrence of each combination was estimated by the product of the unconditional probabilities of occurrence of the three relations involved. This estimate was then compared to the actual probability that a single subject selected the set of relations in combination.[3] To assess the relative contributions of similarity and balance principles, four sets of relations are particularly useful to consider: sets of similar relations that are either balanced (*ppp*) or imbalanced (*nnn*) and sets of dissimilar relations that are either balanced (*pnn, npn, nnp*) or imbalanced (*ppn, pnp, npp*). Expected (chance) and actual probabilities of occurrence of these sets of relations are presented in Table 5.2 for each configuration of elements and each stimulus replication. Four aspects of these data are particularly relevant:

1. Sets of three *p* relations occurred more frequently than expected by chance at all six combinations of stimulus replication and type of configuration. This would be predicted by both balance and similarity principles.

2. Sets of three *n* relations occurred significantly more frequently than chance in five of six cases. This finding is consistent with the similarity principle but not with the balance principle.

3. Sets of one *p* and two *n* relations occurred more frequently than chance in five of six cases. This finding is consistent with the balance principle but not with the similarity principle.

---

[3]The expected and obtained probabilities are not strictly independent, since data used to calculate unconditional probabilities were also used to calculate conjunctive probabilities. This dependence is not serious, however. While an extremely high probability of inferring a given combination of relations implies a high unconditional probability of inferring each of the relations in a triad, the reverse is not true. If anything, the effect of this dependence artificially decreased the difference between chance probabilities and actual probabilities.

TABLE 5.2

Obtained and Expected Probabilities of Occurrence of
Relations Differing in Similarity and Degree of Balance

Relations	Replication 1			Replication 2		
	POO	POX	PXX	POO	POX	PXX
Balanced and similar (ppp)						
Obtained	.337*	.063*	.042*	.337*	.200*	.084*
Expected	.085	.007	.001	.118	.007	.002
Imbalanced and similar (nnn)						
Obtained	.021*	.000	.032*	.042*	.021*	.032*
Expected	.002	.000	.002	.002	.000	.002
Balanced and dissimilar (nnp, npn, pnn)						
Obtained	.042	.063*	.032*	.021	.032*	.032
Expected	.024	.020	.006	.027	.002	.007
Imbalanced and dissimilar (npp, pnp, ppn)						
Obtained	.042*	.011	.011	.042*	.053	.021
Expected	.093	.066	.006	.109	.027	.005
Total, balanced						
Obtained	.379	.126	.074	.358	.232	.116
Expected	.109	.207	.007	.145	.079	.009
Total, imbalanced						
Obtained	.063	.011	.043	.084	.074	.053
Expected	.095	.066	.008	.111	.027	.005
Total, similar						
Obtained	.385	.063	.074	.379	.221	.116
Expected	.087	.007	.003	.120	.077	.004
Total, dissimilar						
Obtained	.084	.074	.043	.063	.085	.053
Expected	.117	.086	.012	.136	.029	.012

* Differs from expected value; $p < .05$, two-tailed.

4. Sets of one *n* and two *p* relations did not consistently occur either more or less frequently than chance. This finding is contradictory to both balance and similarity principles.

Although both similarity and balance principles may sometimes underlie the organization of the types of cognitions used in this study, their applicability is far from universal. Sets of relations that were *either* balanced or similar were formed more frequently than expected by chance, but sets that were both imbalanced and dissimilar were not formed less frequently than expected. Similarity seems to be a somewhat more important principle than balance. (In this regard, sets of three *o* relations also occurred more frequently than expected by chance.)

Summary and evaluation. Despite some evidence that balanced sets of cognitions occur more frequently than expected by chance, the research reported in this section, considered as a whole, casts considerable doubt upon the general validity of the hypothesis that balance is an important principle underlying the organization and retention of new cognitions. Zajonc's work has been invaluable in identifying several other principles that may independently or in combination contribute to cognitive organization: *positivity* (the assumption that sentiments among cognitive elements are favorable), *similarity* (the assumption that all sentiment relations among a set of elements are the same), *friendliness* (the assumption that a given person has similar sentiments toward all objects he encounters), *popularity* (the assumption that a given object is evaluated similarly by all persons), and *agreement* (the assumption that persons agree in the evaluation of an object).[4] These principles in combination could account for nearly all of the instances in which balance theory appears to be supported. However, in some instances these principles may be in conflict. Unfortunately, at this writing little evidence is available concerning whether under such conditions they have equal influence or whether certain principles have priority over others. We shall reconsider this question when we discuss social inference processes in Chapter 10.

C. Unpleasantness of Balanced and Imbalanced Structures

A common assumption made in applying balance theory is that imbalanced sets of cognitions are aversive or unpleasant to the person

---

[4]The popularity and agreement principles are of course quite similar. However, the first pertains to a general characteristic of the object being evaluated, while the second pertains to a characteristic of the persons who perform the evaluation. Rubin and Zajonc's studies suggest that while the effect of popularity is independent of other relations among elements, agreement is more likely to be inferred only when the parties involved are assumed to like one another. Subjects who believe that P likes X may tend to believe that O likes X either because P likes O and therefore agrees with O, or because X is generally likeable. Thus, when P likes O, both agreement and popularity principles may operate, but when P dislikes O, only the popularity principle is involved.

TABLE 5.3

Predicted Pleasantness as a Function of Liking and Agreement

Liking/disliking	P and O agree about X	P and O disagree about X
P and O like one another	very pleasant	very unpleasant
P and O dislike one another	slightly unpleasant	moderately unpleasant

possessing them, and that cognitive reorganization is stimulated by the desire to eliminate this aversive state of affairs. Much of the research stemming from cognitive balance theory has therefore been devoted to an understanding of the type of situations that subjects will describe as unpleasant, either for themselves or for others. Theoretically, situations that describe balanced sets of relations among persons or objects should be reported as pleasanter than situations that describe imbalanced sets.

Evidence bearing upon the hypothesis is often difficult to interpret because unpleasantness resulting from the inconsistency among cognitions about a situation is confounded with unpleasantness resulting from social or interpersonal conflict among the participants in the situation. Consider a set of relations between two persons (P and O) and an object (X). If a naive subject were asked to list the factors that affect the pleasantness of a situation in which these persons were placed, he might identify intuitively at least two: the degree of liking of P and O for one another, and the extent of these persons' agreement about X. The latter may be most relevant if P and O must arrive at some decision about X, or if disagreement about X is likely to lead to a heated argument. It is also reasonable to expect that the effects of these two factors are not independent. An argument between friends may conceivably lead to greater unpleasantness or emotional upset in the situation than an argument among persons who do not know one another or who expect to have little to do with each other outside the immediate situation in which they find themselves. Thus the effects of agreement about X may be greater when P and O like one another than when they do not. Predictions based upon this "social conflict" hypothesis are summarized in Table 5.3. This table describes two main effects, liking and agreement, and also an interaction of these variables. Cognitive balance theory would also predict an interaction of liking and agreement. However, the nature of this interaction would differ from the one described in Table 5.3 in one important way: When P and O dislike one another, the situation should be judged as *more* pleasant when P and O disagree than when they agree.

Although the contributions of the variables described above can usually be isolated in studies of the determinants of judged pleasantness, the nature of these contributions is often obscured in the analyses reported. For example, Gerard and Fleischer (1967) asked subjects to read eight stories, each involving a main character (P), another person (O), and a third person, object, or event (X). Each story provided information concerning P's liking for O and P's and O's attitudes toward X. All eight combinations of *P* and *n* relations among P, O, and X were represented. Following each story, subjects rated the described situations along a scale ranging from "uneasy" to "pleasant." Gerard and Fleischer analyzed their data as a function of P's attitude toward O (P*p*O or P*n*O) and degree of balance (balanced or imbalanced). Mean pleasantness as a function of these variables is described in Table 5.4.

Analyses of these results yielded a significant interaction but no main effects. At first glance, these data are difficult to interpret, since they suggest that balanced sets of relations are more pleasant than imbalanced ones only when P's attitude toward O is unfavorable. The results become less mystifying, however, when one realizes that the interaction obtained above is, in essence, the main effect of similarity between P's and O's attitudes toward X. (That is, P and O agree when the structure is balanced and P*p*O and when the structure is imbalanced and P*n*O, and disagree under under the other two conditions.) These data may be rearranged as shown in Table 5.5.

Considered in this way, Gerard and Fleischer's data indicate that pleasantness is a positive function of the amount of agreement between P and O about X but does not depend upon P's liking for O. Degree of balance (indicated by the interaction of liking and agreement) has no effect whatsoever upon judged pleasantness.

TABLE 5.4

Mean Pleasantness as a Function of Liking and Degree of Balance
(Gerard & Fleischer, 1967)

Liking/disliking	Balanced	Imbalanced	M
P*p*O	4.01	3.51	3.76
P*n*O	2.85	3.99	3.42
M	3.43	3.75	

TABLE 5.5

Mean Pleasantness as a Function of Liking and Agreement
(Gerard & Fleischer, 1967)

Liking/disliking	Agreement of P and O About X		M
	Agree	Disagree	
PpO	4.01	3.51	3.76
PnO	3.99	2.85	3.42
M	4.00	3.18	—

Data from a parallel study by Gerard and Fleischer (1967) are also of interest. In this study, subjects read the same group of stories used in the experiment described above and then were asked to recall certain details of the stories (the titles, names of the main characters, and the plot). One point was given for each item recalled. Analyses of recall scores as a function of P's liking for O and story structure (balanced vs. imbalanced) yielded a significant interaction of these variables but no main effects. However, if these data are reorganized in the manner described above, they indicate that stories in which P and O disagreed about X were recalled better ($M = 2.52$) than stories in which P and O agreed ($M = 2.24$), while neither P's liking for O nor degree of balance had a significant effect. The fact that situations where persons disagreed were both rated as less pleasant and were recalled better suggests that stories that describe social conflict, although more aversive to the participants in the situation, are more interesting to subjects who read about these situations and are therefore better remembered. In any event, degree of balance *per se* is not a relevant factor underlying either recall or judged pleasantness.

While Gerard and Fleischer's data provide support for only one of the "intuitive" predictions made above, results of other studies are more consistent with these predictions. Zajonc (1968) has summarized the results of several studies in which unpleasantness ratings were made of situations involving two persons and an object. In two sets of data reported by Hershkowitz (1954), one set reported by Jordan (1953), and four of five sets reported by Rodrigues (1966), results conformed to those intuitively expected; that is, judged pleasantness increased with agreement between P and O regardless of P's liking for O, but the increase was greater when P liked O than when he did not. More simply, these studies typically showed that situations in which P both liked O and agreed with O about X were rated as much more pleasant than situations in which P either disliked O or disagreed with O about X, while the judged pleasantness of the remaining three combinations of liking and agreement did not greatly differ from one another.

The main evidence cited by Zajonc that contradicts "intuitive" predictions was obtained in an unpublished study by Steiner and Spaulding (1966). These authors found in four different samples that when P disliked O, situations where P and O disagreed were rated as more pleasant than situations in which P and O agreed, as predicted by balance theory. The difference between this study and other investigations is unclear.

Newcomb's (1968) reformulation of the conditions under which balance theory applies is worth considering in the context of the data summarized by Zajonc. Newcomb argued that in triads consisting of two persons P and O and an object X, balance theory is applicable only when the relation between P and O is positive. Thus Newcomb is essentially taking cognizance of the fact that agreement has greater effect upon pleasantness ratings when the relation between P and O is positive than when it is negative, as the results summarized by Zajonc tend to show.

A corollary of the hypothesis that imbalanced sets of relations are unpleasant is that such relations are unstable, or are likely to change. Data reported by Wyer and Lyon (1970) bear upon this prediction. Using the stimulus materials described earlier in this chapter, we first collected normative estimates of the stability of situations in which only one of the three relations comprising each triad was described. These relations conveyed either p, o, or n sentiments between the pairs of elements involved. Then, "experimental" subjects were presented each relation in the context of information about the quality of the other two relations in the triad and asked to estimate the stability of the situation described by the entire set of relations. These contexts consisted of all nine possible combinations of the favorableness of the two relations involved (pp, po, pn, op, oo, on, np, no, and nn). The contribution of the context to estimates of the stability of each relation was determined by subtracting the normative rating of the relation from ratings of the relation in the context of others.

If imbalance is aversive, situations in which it occurs should be less stable (more likely to change) than *non*balanced situations (those with at least one o relation among the elements involved). If balanced states are attractive, situations in which balanced cognitions occur should be more stable than nonbalanced situations. However, Wyer and Lyon found that balanced situations containing a given relation were rated as more stable than nonbalanced ones containing the same relation in only 19 of 36 cases. On the other hand, imbalanced situations containing a given relation were rated as less stable than nonbalanced ones containing this relation in only 18 of 36 cases. In other words, not only were balanced situations not particularly attractive, but imbalanced states were not particularly aversive. Other types of comparisons are consistent with this conclusion. Pooled over all configurations, balanced states consisting of three p relations and of one p

and two *n* relations were rated as only slightly more stable than the mean rating of the relations involved when considered individually under control conditions (+.59 and +.24, respectively). Ratings of imbalanced triads consisting of three *n* relations also did not differ appreciably from control ratings (*M* = +.39). Imbalanced situations containing one *n* and two *p* relations were rated as fairly unstable, relative to control conditions (*M* = –1.49). However, note that in such triads, P either disliked O or disagreed with O about the desirability of X. Thus this result is consistent with the hypothesis that *social* conflict is the primary determinant of judged unpleasantness rather than cognitive imbalance *per se*.

The only consistent support for balance theory in Wyer and Lyon's study occurred when one of the two context relations was positive and the other was negative. Under this condition, stability estimates decreased as the favorableness of the third relation increased. Under other context conditions, the extent to which stability estimates conformed to predictions of balance theory depended substantially upon whether the elements in the triad were persons or objects, and whether specific relations among these elements were positive or negative. Thus, the stability of situations is clearly not a simple function of the balance of the relations among the persons and objects involved in these situations.

If situations are judged as unpleasant because of the social conflict that potentially exists in them, then subjects should believe it to be desirable to change the specific relations that produce this conflict. Evidence supporting this hypothesis was obtained by Rodrigues (1967). Subjects considered each of eight hypothetical combinations of positive and negative relations among themselves (P), another (O), and an issue (X), and then indicated their willingness to change their belief about each of the relations involved. P indicated greater willingness to change his liking for O when he initially disliked O than when he initially liked him, regardless of whether O agreed or disagreed with him about X. He indicated greater willingness to change his belief about O's attitude toward X when O initially disagreed with him than when O initially agreed with him, regardless of whether or not he liked O. Finally, P expressed greater willingness to change his own opinion about X when a liked O disagreed with him than under other combinations of liking and agreement. In other words, subjects appeared to regard it as more desirable to like O than to dislike him, and to have O agree with them than to have him disagree with them, but were willing to change their own opinions in order to reduce conflict only when O was liked. As with Wyer and Lyon's study, balance theory is not very useful in either predicting these results or in explaining them after the fact.

D. The "Socratic Effect"

We have argued that if balance principles govern cognitive organization, cognitions should become more balanced once they are made salient in close temporal contiguity. Two studies were performed by the author (Wyer, 1974) to investigate this possibility. In the first study, eight sets of four elements were constructed. Each set consisted of the subject himself (P), two other persons (O_1 and O_2), and an issue (X). The issues selected varied in their subjective importance to the subjects run in the study (British undergraduate students); moreover, in each case O_1 was someone who was likely to be concerned about X, while O_2 was less obviously concerned about it. (For example, in one case X was "British entry into the Common Market," O_1 was "Harold Wilson," and O_2 was "Mick Jagger.") In each of two experimental sessions one week apart, subjects reported their feelings toward each of the other elements in each set, O_1's feelings toward O_2 and X, and O_2's feelings toward O_1 and X. Responses to these items, which were distributed randomly throughout a questionnaire, were recorded along category scales ranging from –5 (very unfavorable) to +5 (very favorable) and were subsequently rescored as +1, 0, or –1, depending upon whether they were greater than, equal to, or less than zero along the scale.

The data collected in this study provided information pertaining to six different triads of elements within each 4-element set, that is, PO_1X, PO_2X, PO_1O_2, PO_2O_1, O_1O_2X, and O_2O_1X. (According to this notation, the order of the elements reflects the direction of the sentiment relations involved; for example, the triad O_1O_2X, pertains to O_1's feelings about O_2 and X and O_2's feelings about X.) The product of the values assigned to the three relations comprising each triad was used as an index of the degree of balance of the triad. If cognitions become more balanced over time once they are made salient, this product should become more positive over experimental sessions. In fact, however, the average balance of triads considered in this study was not significantly greater in session 2 $(M = .165)$ than in session 1 $(M = .106$; $F = 2.15$; $df = 1/23$; $p > .10)$. Moreover, the chance in degree of balance over time did not depend upon whether or not the subject himself was one of the elements of the triad, or whether the issue was important to him.

To supplement the analyses described above, the numbers of balanced and imbalanced triads were determined for each subject and analyzed separately as a function of experimental session and the type of elements comprising the triad. In neither analysis was the effect of session significant; that is, the number of balanced triads did not increase over sessions, nor did the number of imbalanced triads decrease.

As we noted on page 112, the set of cognitions pertaining to a particular relation between two elements may be imbalanced if the sum of the subjective probabilities of a positive (p), neutral (o), and negative (n) relation between the elements exceeds unity, or if $P_p + P_o + P_n > 1$. Thus a second indication of the existence of the Socratic effect is the extent to which the sum of these probabilities decreases over experimental sessions once the cognitions involved become salient. To explore this possibility, a second study was performed with stimulus materials similar to those described above. In this study, however, three different items were constructed for each pair of elements, one pertaining to each of the three sentiment relations between them.[5] Subjects in each of two sessions were presented randomly ordered statements describing the 168 relations (three relations for each of the seven pairs of elements comprising each 4-element set) and estimated the likelihood that each statement was true along a scale from 0 (not at all likely) to 10 (extremely likely). These estimates were subsequently divided by 10 to convert them to units of subjective probability. Pooled over element pairs, the quantity $P_p + P_o + P_n$ was greater than unity in session 1 ($M = 1.269$), indicating some degree of "ambivalence" as conceptualized by Abelson and Rosenberg (see page 102). However, this sum did not decrease appreciably in session 2 ($M = 1.257$). Nor were any of the individual probabilities comprising this sum less in session 2 (.494, .348, and .415 for P_p, P_o, and P_n, respectively) than in session 1 (.490, .365, and .410). In addition, changes in inconsistency over time did not reliably depend on the type of elements involved in the relations considered. Thus, this study also provides no evidence that subjects modify their cognitions in a manner implied by balance theory, once these cognitions are made salient.

The data described above raise serious questions about the validity of balance principles of cognitive organization. However, note that if p, o, and n relations are mutually exclusive, and if cognitive organization is generally described by the law of subjective probability, the *absolute* difference between the quantity $(P_p + P_o + P_n)$ and unity should decrease over experimental sessions. Supplementary analyses of the data obtained in the second study described above revealed that this difference was in fact less in Session 2 ($M = .295$) than in session 1 ($M = .327$; $F = 7.03$; $df = 1/24$; $p < .01$); the magnitude of this effect did not depend upon either the importance of X or the particular pair of elements comprising the relation. Therefore, the results of this study, while they do not support balance theory, are consistent with the subjective probability formulation proposed in Chapter 4.

E. Effects of Change in One Cognition Upon Others

If cognitions are organized according to certain general rules, externally induced changes in one of these cognitions should affect others in a manner implied by these rules. Thus, if sentiment and unit relations are organized in a manner implied by balance theory, then a change in one of a set of relations (from p to n or from n to p) should produce a change in the sign of one or more of the remaining relations. This general hypothesis is obviously of great practical as well as theoretical interest, since it suggests that evaluations of an

---

[5] Sentiments toward O_1 and O_2 were described by the phrases "have high personal regard for" (p), "feel neither positively nor negatively toward" (o), and "have low personal regard for" (n). Corresponding sentiments toward X were described by the phrases "favors," "neither favors nor opposes," and "opposes."

object can be modified indirectly by changing attitudes toward persons who are believed to like or dislike the object. Moreover, the basis for the sentiments involved is theoretically irrelevant. Thus, suppose that P likes O, is personally in favor of withdrawing U.S. troops from Southeast Asia, and believes that O is also in favor of troop withdrawal. According to balance theory, P's attitude toward troop withdrawal could be changed by presenting information that O is immoral, that he dislikes P, or that he has other attributes which would lead P to dislike him, even if these attributes are quite irrelevant to the issue at hand or to the likelihood that O's opinion is correct.

While balance theory predicts changes in the direction of sentiment relations, most studies of attitude change report only changes in magnitude. It is usually assumed that a change in magnitude toward the position predicted by balance theory provides support for the theory. This is not necessarily true unless the change is of sufficient magnitude to reverse the sign of the sentiment relation involved. Of course, if several relations are involved, and not all subjects change the same relation in order to produce balance, the *average* change in any one relation many not appear to be of this magnitude. Moreover, it may take time for the effects of new information to filter down to beliefs to which the information does not directly pertain (McGuire, 1960). Nevertheless, this possible interpretative difficulty should be kept in mind in evaluating the research to be discussed in the pages that follow.

1. The Principle of Least Effort. Changes in specific cognitions are often difficult to predict from balance theory because there are typically multiple ways of eliminating imbalance. For example, imbalance among the relations ApB, BpC, AnC could be eliminated by changing any one of the three relations, or by changing all three simultaneously. The theory is not precise as to which alternative will be used in any given instance. In recognition of this problem, Abelson and Rosenberg (1958) made two hypotheses concerning which of a set of relations will change in order to produce balance. First, a set of cognitions will tend to be balanced in a manner that implies a desirable state of affairs for the subject. Thus, imbalance among the cognitions "I dislike Joe," "Joe has money," and "I like money" is less likely to produce a change in the second or third cognitions than a change in the first, particularly if an implication of changing my relationship with Joe is that I stand a good chance of being given some of his money. Second, imbalance will be eliminated in a way that requires the fewest number of changes in previously formed cognitions. In the above example, therefore, a change in only one of the cognitions would be predicted rather than a change in all three. For want of a better term, we will refer to this rule as the *principle of least cognitive effort.*

Some support for this principle was found in a study involving a fairly complex set of relations (Rosenberg & Abelson, 1960). Subjects were asked to play the role of the owner of a large department store. All subjects were

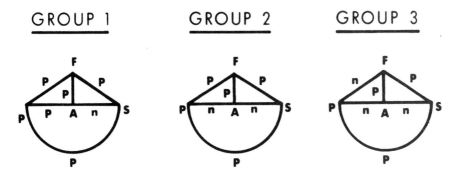

Fig. 5.4. Cognitions held by subjects in three situations constructed by Rosenberg and Abelson (1960).

initially given information to the effect that a high volume of sales is desirable (PpS), that displays of modern art decrease sales (AnS), that Fenwick (the manager of the rug department) plans to mount a modern art display (FpA), and that Fenwick has increased sales since becoming manager (F$_p$S). Then, one group of subjects was told that in their role of owner they were favorably disposed toward both modern art and Fenwick (PnA and PpF). A second group was told to assume a negative attitude toward modern art and a favorable attitude toward Fenwick (PnA and PpF). A third group was told to assume an unfavorable attitude toward both objects (PnA and PnF). The relations resulting from this information are shown for each group in Fig. 5.4. Note that while each set of relations is imbalanced, balanced could be gained in each case by changing a single cognition. Specifically, Group 1's cognitions could be balanced by changing the belief that modern art decreases sales; Group 2's, by changing the belief that Fenwick will mount a modern art display; and Group 3's, by changing the belief that Fenwick has increased sales since becoming manager.

After receiving one of the sets of information described above, each group of subjects evaluated the persuasiveness and accuracy of three communications: one arguing that modern art actually increased sales (ApS), another arguing that Fenwick did not actually plan to display modern art (FnA), and the third arguing that Fenwick had actually failed to increase sales in the past (FnS). Presumably, subjects should evaluate most favorably the communication which, if accepted, would allow them to attain a balanced set of cognitions by changing the fewest beliefs. That is, Group 1 should evaluate the communication implying ApS most highly; Group 2, the communication advocating FnA; and Group 3, the communication implying FnS. These predictions are clearly supported, as shown in Table 5.6.

Some additional comparisons are relevant to this general hypothesis. Assume that by virtue of P's role as store owner, his attitude toward sales (that is, PpS) is unchangeable. Then, if Group 1 subjects accepted the communication advocating FnA, one additional cognition (PpA) would have

TABLE 5.6

Mean Evaluation of Communications as a Function
of Communication Type and Experimental Group
(adapted from Rosenberg and Abelson, 1960)

Experimental group	Assertion advocated in communication		
	ApS	FnA	FnS
1	11.18	9.54	7.37
2	7.94	10.25	7.66
3	7.39	9.29	11.49

to be changed to produce balance. However, if they accepted the communication advocating FnS, two additional cognitions (PpF and PpA) would have to be changed to produce balance. Similarly, Group 3 subjects would have to change one additional cognition if they accepted the communication advocating FnA, and two additional cognitions if they accepted the communication advocating ApS. Therefore, the principle of least effort predicts that Group 1 will prefer the communication supporting FnA to the one supporting FnS, while Group 3 will prefer the communication supporting FnA to the one supporting ApS. These predictions are also supported by the results shown in Table 5.6.

The data described above do not pertain directly to the hypothesis that belief change is predictable from the principle of least effort. However, if the acceptance of a communication can be interpreted as an indication of the likelihood of changing the belief to which the message pertains, the results clearly support the principle and more generally support balance theory.

The principle of least effort is often hard to apply to previously formed cognitions, because all of the relations in which each cognitive element is involved are not known. Suppose that P has the cognitions "I like George" and "I oppose the war in Southeast Asia" and is told that George supports the war in Southeast Asia. A change in the cognition "I like George" to "I dislike George" might create imbalance among other sets of cognitions in which P's attitude toward George is involved (for example, "I favor civil rights legislation," "George favors civil rights legislation," "I dislike President Nixon," "George dislikes President Nixon," etc.). On the other hand, a change in the cognition "I oppose the war in Southeast Asia" might also create imbalance among several other cognitions (for example, "I like Mary," "Mary opposes the war in Southeast Asia," "I am opposed to killing people," "The war in Southeast Asia facilitates killing people," etc.).

Theoretically, P should change the cognition that will have the least effect upon other beliefs in his cognitive structure. Which cognition this is, however, if often unclear *a priori,* at least to the experimenter. In some instances, it may be "easiest" for P to deny the credibility of the new information (in this case, the information that George supports the war) and retain his original beliefs.

2. Changes in Evaluations of Self and Others. Many investigations of attitude change are basically studies of the manner in which different types of information are used to arrive at judgments about oneself and others. As such, they are more relevant to a discussion of social inference processes than to cognitive organization (see Chapter 10). Other studies, which are more clearly relevant to cognitive organization, and difficult to evaluate because of methodological deficiencies that allow alternative interpretations of the results obtained. Thus, there is a surprising scarcity of research on attitude change that bears directly and unequivocally upon the validity of balance principles in describing the manner in which cognitions are organized. A few representative studies will be described here.

The implications of balance theory for attitude change phenomena are often tested in a paradigm in which a person O is connected through an assertion to an object or issue X and the effect of this association upon P's evaluations of both O and X are observed. A particularly interesting application of this paradigm is when X is P's "self." A study by Harvey et al. (1957) provides an example of this application. Each subject (P) was paired with either a previous acquaintance or with someone he did not know (O). After briefly describing themselves to one another, P and O rated both themselves and the other along a series of bipolar scales. In a later experimental session, P received fictitious information that O had rated him much more unfavorably along these scales than he had rated himself. After receiving this feedback, P rerated both himself and O.

To apply balance theory to this study consider a triad consisting of P, O, and P's "self" (the object of both P's and O's evaluation). If one can assume that initially P has a positive attitude toward both himself and O, the triad resulting from O's derogation of P's "self" would be imbalanced:

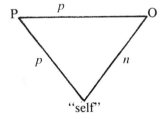

According to balance theory, any of several things could occur in order to regain balance: P could decrease his self-evaluation, he could develop an unfavorable attitude toward O, he could deny the credibility of the information that O evaluated his "self" unfavorably, or he could misinterpret O's evaluation as actually favorable. Harvey et al. found evidence for each of these tendencies. In general, P's attitude toward himself should be associated with a greater number of other cognitions than should his attitude toward O; thus, according to the principle of least effort, the former attitude should be relatively less likely to change than the latter. This was in fact the case.

The principle of least effort can also be applied in predicting the effect of differences in P's prior acquaintanceship with O. The greater P's familiarity with O, the more likely it is that the relation between P and O is linked to other attitudes and beliefs in P's cognitive structure. Changes in P's evaluation of O should therefore be less predominant and the other methods of regaining balance (devaluating oneself, denying or distorting O's rating) should be more predominant, when O is an acquaintance rather than a stranger. Harvey et al.'s data also support these predictions.

Effects of Shifts in Response Language. As we noted in Chapter 3, it is often difficult to distinguish between the effects of information upon a subject's actual beliefs and the effects of such information upon the language used by the subject to report these beliefs. In the present context, if O's rating of an object along a response scale deviates from P's own rating of the object, P may infer that he has been interpreting the scale categories incorrectly. He may therefore revise the position of his response scale in relation to the judgmental categories he uses to classify stimuli, so as to correspond more closely to the way in which the scale is apparently positioned by O. Such changes in response language would of course affect all objects along the response scale involved. The results obtained by Harvey et al. could be at least partially attributed to the effects of feedback from O upon response language rather than to the effect of this feedback upon underlying beliefs about oneself and O.

Some indirect evidence bearing upon this possibility is reported in a study by Steiner (1968) who investigated the effects of both positive and negative feedback. In this experiment, P initially took a battery of tests and then rated himself along a series of 15 semantic differentials. He also rated the "average person" along these scales. He was then told that the test scores would be analyzed by a senior undergraduate psychology student (O) who was described verbally by the experimenter, and P was then asked to estimate O's ability to rate P accurately. In a second experimental session, P received information that O's ratings of him along 10 of the semantic differentials were either three scale units higher (more favorable) or three units lower than his own original ratings long these scales. He then rerated himself and the "average person" along these scales and also reassessed O's ability.

Several aspects of the results of this study are of interest. Feedback about O's ratings affected P's self-ratings in the expected directions. However, changes in ratings due to positive feedback ($M = 1.71$) were greater than changes resulting from negative feedback ($M = 1.16$), despite the fact that feedback of each type was equally discrepant from P's original self-ratings. P's ratings of the "average person" also changed in the direction of the feedback about P. However, changes in these ratings were less when positive feedback was given ($M = .48$) than when negative feedback was given ($M = 1.01$). Steiner attributed these changes to "projection." On the other hand, since beliefs abou the "average person" have little direct relevance to O's beliefs about P, the change in "average person" ratings could also be attributed to shifts in the position of P's response scales resulting from the feedback about O's ratings. If this latter interpretation is valid, the actual change in P's underlying judgments under the two feedback conditions could be estimated by the difference between the change in his reported self-ratings and the change in his "average person" ratings. These revised scores suggest that positive feedback changed P's actual self-ratings by 1.23 units, while the effect of negative feedback upon these judgments was minimal (.15 units). In other words, only favorable information about P affected P's actual judgment of himself; unfavorable information simply changed the manner in which P used the response scales available to him and did not affect his underlying beliefs about himself.

Changes in ratings of O are also interesting to consider in this light. Steiner found that favorable feedback from O increased P's ratings of O by 1.36 units but, in contrast to the findings of Harvey et al., negative feedback did not affect P's ratings of O ($M = .06$). Note, however, that whereas ratings of O in Harvey et al.'s study were made along the same scales used in recording self-judgments, and to which feedback pertained, ratings of O in Steiner's study were made along scales different from those to which the feedback pertained. Steiner's results are therefore consistent with the conclusion that negative feedback about P affected only P's response language and was not interpreted by P as an unfavorable evaluation. Harvey et al.'s results may need to be interpreted in light of these findings.

e. *Effects of Unfavorable Self-Evaluations.* An implicit assumption underlying a balance interpretation of the studies described above is that a subject has a favorable attitude toward himself. If P's initial attitude toward "self" is negative, then an unfavorable evaluation of "self" by a liked O would produce a balanced triad and thus should not produce appreciable change in either P's self-evaluation or his attitude toward O. On the other hand, if O evaluates P's "self" favorably, this should produce imbalance and should lead either to an increase in P's self-evaluation or to a decrease in his evaluation of O. The possibility that derogation by another may increase the favorableness of one's attitude toward the other is intriguing. Although little research is available that bears directly on this question, Gerard (1965) found that information intended to decrease P's evaluation of himself led to favorable sentiments toward others who disagreed with P on an achievement task. This study, which pertains more directly to information integration processes than to cognitive organization, is discussed in greater detail in Chapter 10.

A study by Secord, Backman, and Eachus (1964) also pertains to the effects of feedback about oneself upon the evaluations of self and others, but it has a somewhat different focus from the experiments described previously. This study is of additional interest since it pertains to changes in unit relations. In this experiment, P first ranked 15 needs measured by the Edwards Personal Preference Schedule (EPPS) in terms of how characteristic these needs were of (a) himself, (b) his best friend of the same sex, and (c) a person of the same sex whom he disliked. P was then administered the EPPS. In a second session, P received false feedback about the "actual" rank order of his needs, as indicated by his scores on the EPPS. This order was the same as P's initial self-rankings except that a need initially low in P's rankings both of himself and his friend was elevated to the second position (thus indicating that this need was very characteristic of P). Following this feedback, P made new rankings of the needs in terms of how characteristic they were of him, his friend, and his enemy.

What would balance theory predict concerning changes in these rankings? The feedback to P presumably established a positive unit relation between P and a need X (PuX). When the other person rated (O) is a friend, PpO. Thus, according to balance principles, OuX; that is, there should be a positive unit relation between O and X. This is in fact what Secord et al. found; the position of the manipulated need in P's ratings of O significantly increased following information that P himself had the need. When O is an enemy, or PnO, predictions are somewhat less clear. This cognition in combination with PpX implied Ou'X, or in other words, that there is no necessary relation between O and X. Consistent with this prediction, no significant change occurred in the position of the manipulated need in ratings of disliked persons. It is unclear whether or not disliked persons were expected to have the manipulated needs in the first place. (If P's belief that O had X was already low, no change would be expected as a result of the feedback.) Despite this ambiguity, the results of Secord et al.'s experiment provide support for balance theory.

3. Changes in Judgments of Inanimate Objects. Perhaps the most interesting implication of balance theory for attitude change phenomena is that if P dislikes O, he will tend to adopt an opinion about a third object (X) that differs from O's opinion; in other words, P will change his judgment of X in a direction opposite to that advocated by a disliked O. A study by Sampson and Insko (1964), described in Chapter 1, did in fact show that when P presumably disliked O, he changed his judgments of an autokinetic stimulus away from O's judgments of the stimulus. As we have pointed out, their results can unfortunately be attributed to attempts by P to conform to the implicit expectations held for him by the experimenter. Additional evidence of this "boomerang" effect was obtained by Osgood and Tannenbaum (1955) in a study to be discussed in more detail in Chapter 6. In this study, subjects first evaluated a series of public figures (O) and social issues (X) and then received information that O either supported or opposed X. O and X were then reevaluated. When P initially disliked O but liked X, information that O also supported X decreased P's evaluation of X; moreover, when P initially disliked both O and X, information that O also disliked X increased P's rating of X. While these changes were not large (see Table 6.2), they were in the direction predicted by balance theory. Furthermore, note that in both conditions described above an alternative way for P to regain balance is to increase his evaluation of O. This also occurred.

IV. EVALUATION

In sum, the research summarized in this chapter provides quite limited support for the hypothesis that cognitive balance is an important principle underlying cognitive organization. There are a number of theoretical and empirical limitations to the conditions under which the principle seems to apply. Under those conditions in which it does accurately describe the relations among cognitions, there are often alternative explanations of these relations that have little if anything to do with cognitive balance *per se*. There appears to be little if any support for the hypothesis that imbalanced cognitive states are aversive and that this aversiveness gives rise to motivation to eliminate them. Moreover, when imbalanced sets of previously formed cognitions are made salient to subjects, there is no evidence that subjects actively reorganize these cognitions in order to decrease imbalance.

Although the results of several studies cited in this chapter are partially consistent with balance theory, they nevertheless raise several questions about the usefulness of the theory in accounting for attitude change phenomena in the situations described. For example, if a set of three cognitions is imbalanced, P should theoretically change only one of these cognitions; simultaneous changes in two of them would not eliminate imbalance. However, the studies cited above consistently report changes in P's sentiments toward both O and X following information relating O and X. To be consistent with balance theory, these data would have to be attributed to an artifact of averaging over subjects, and not to simultaneous changes in evaluations of O and X by each individual subject. Second, balance theory can predict changes in P's sentiments toward O and X only if O's relation to X is out of balance with these sentiments. Thus the theory cannot account for Steiner's finding that P's evaluations of O and X both changed following information that O's relation to X was in balance with these evaluations but was more extreme than P's relation to X.

Alternative formulations of cognitive organization can theoretically generate predictions of simultaneous changes in the judgments of O and X and also can account for changes under conditions in which the relations between O and X are in balance with P's relations to these elements. Two such formulations will be discussed in detail in the next chapter, along with a more intensive consideration of source effects upon attitude change.

The above comments do not necessarily imply that balance principles should be completely discarded. Rather, they suggest that the principles in their present form are overly general and simplified descriptions of the manner in which cognitions are organized. Perhaps a more fundamental understanding of the sorts of relations that subjects treat as equivalent in meaning, and the criteria they apply in determining the validity of statements relating cognitive elements, would suggest a revision of these principles which would be more useful in describing the cognitive processes to which the research considered in this chapter pertains. In this regard, the heuristic value of balance theory and the experiments performed to test its validity should not be minimized. The results of these experiments, while not strongly supporting the theory, suggest avenues for further investigation of the processes underlying the organization of cognitions. Future research should be devoted to the pursuit of the questions raised by these studies and not simply to repeated attempts to validate balance principles *per se*.

6
SUMMATIVE AND AVERAGING MODELS OF COGNITIVE ORGANIZATION

Two other general formulations of the manner in which cognitions are organized have generated considerable research on attitude formation and change. One model, proposed by Fishbein (1963), assumes that the evaluation of an object is the weighted *sum* of the evaluative implications of its attributes, while the other, proposed by Osgood and his colleagues (Osgood & Tannenbaum, 1955; Osgood et al., 1957), assumes that the evaluation of an object is a weighted *average* of these implications. Traditionally, these formulations have been applied less frequently to organizational processes *per se* than to the question of how different pieces of information combine to affect judgments. We will evaluate their implications for this question in Chapter 9, where we will consider more carefully the matter of whether information integration is a summative or an averaging process. However, the two models also have several implications for the manner in which beliefs and attitudes are interrelated and for the effect that change in one cognition has upon others. Unlike balance theory, they provide quantitative descriptions of the relations of cognitions to one another. Moreover, each is consistent in some ways with the general discussion of cognitive processes outlined in Chapter 2.

I. FISHBEIN'S SUMMATIVE MODEL

A. Theoretical Considerations

A summative model of cognitive organization has been proposed by Peak (1955) and Rosenberg (1960) as well as by Fishbein (1963). Since Fishbein's model has been the most frequently subjected to empirical test, it will be the focus of the present discussion. This formulation hypothetically describes the relation between a subject's attitude toward an object O, defined along a category scale, and his beliefs that O possesses certain attributes. Fishbein's distinction between beliefs and attitudes is reflected by the types of scales used to assess them. That is, beliefs about O are viewed as subjective estimates of the likelihood that O possesses certain characteristics or attributes; this assumption is consistent with the definition proposed in Chapter 2. Each attribute may be placed along an evaluative scale of favorableness or affect. Fishbein hypothesizes that the attitude toward O, as reported along this scale, is predictable from the sum of the independent evaluations of a set of attributes, each weighted by the belief that O possesses the attribute. That is,

$$A_o = \Sigma P_{ko}F_k \qquad (6.1)$$

where A_o is the evaluation of O along a scale of favorableness, F_k is the evaluation of the attribute k along this scale, and P_{ko} is the subjective probability that O possesses k.

While the form of Eq. (6.1) has intuitive appeal, its theoretical underpinnings are not completely clear. (For a discussion of the relationship of of this model to behavior theory, see Fishbein, 1967.) However, the equation is consistent in several respects with the description of categorization processes outlined in Chapter 2. At the risk of some injustice to Fishbein's own conceptualization of attitude and belief processes, let us consider his formulation from the general theoretical standpoint outlined in this book and in this way identify certain of the implicit assumptions that may underlie it.

To recapitulate briefly, an attribute of an object O is in effect a cognitive category into which O is placed. That is, the statement that O is "honest" is an assertion that O belongs to the category "honest objects." Suppose that members of the category "honest" are invariably members of a certain rating scale category. Then, if O is a member of the category "honest," it is necessarily a member of the rating scale category to which "honest objects" belong. In other words, if "honest objects" are known to be in the category "+4," and if O is known to be "honest," then O should be a member of the category "+4."

In general, however, objects are assigned to categories with less than complete certainty. If O is honest with a subjective probability of P_h, and if "honest" and "not honest" objects are in the ith rating scale category with the probabilities $P_{i/h}$ and $P_{i/h'}$, respectively, then the theoretical probability that O is in category i is given by the expression

$$P_i = P_h P_{i/h} + P_{h'} P_{i/h'}$$

Now if category ratings are interpretable as subjective expected values, as suggested in Chapter 2, an expression for the evaluation of O along a scale of M categories can be obtained by substituting the above expression for P_i in Eq. (2.1): That is:

$$A_o = \Sigma P_i V_i \tag{6.2}$$

$$= P_h \Sigma P_{i/h} V_i + P_h' \Sigma P_{i/h'} V_i$$

$$A_o = P_h F_h + P_h' F_h' \tag{6.3}$$

where F_h and F_h' are the category ratings of the attributes "honest" and "not honest" respectively.[1] Note that this equation would be identical to Fishbein's model if O is believed to possess two mutually exlusive attributes, "honest" and "not honestly," with probabilities P_h and P_h' respectively.

Now, consider a situation in which O is believed to possess one *but not more than one* of N attributes. Then, $\sum_{k=1}^{N} P_{ko} = 1$, where P_{ko} is the probability that O possesses attribute k. In this case, the probability that O belongs to category i, or P_i, is represented by the expression:

$$P_i = \sum_{k=1}^{N} P_{ko} P_{i/k}$$

Substituting this expression into Eq. (6.2):

$$A_o = \sum_{k=1}^{N} P_{ko} \sum_{k=1}^{M} P_{i/k} V_i$$

$$= \sum_{k=1}^{N} P_{ko} F_k \tag{6.4}$$

where F_k is the category rating of the kth attribute.

Although Eq. (6.1) and Eq. (6.4) are identical in form, there is one major difference between them. In Eq. (6.4), $\Sigma P_{ko} = 1$. In Eq. (6.1), however, this restriction is not made. Thus Fishbein's model can be derived from the general formulation of cognitive processes described in Chapter 2 if and only if the attributes of the object being evaluated are assumed to be mutually exclusive. In general, this assumption is obviously invalid; objects may possess several attributes ("honest," "intelligent," "friendly," etc.) simultaneously. It is of course possible in principle to derive expressions for evaluations based upon such attributes. For example, consider two attributes A and B. The probability that O belongs to scale category i is:

$$P_i = P_{A \cup B} P_{i/A \cup B} + P_{A'B'} P_{i/A'B'}$$

where $P_{A \cup B}$ is the probability that O possesses A or B or both, and $P_{A'B'}$ is the probability that O possesses neither A nor B. Since $P_{A \cup B} = P_A + P_B - P_{AB}$, where P_{AB} is the probability that O possesses both A and B, this equation may be expanded:

$$P_i = P_A P_{i/A} + P_B P_{i/B} - P_{AB} P_{i/AB} + P_{A'B'} P_{i/A'B'}$$

---

[1] Strictly speaking, F_h and F_h in Eq. (6.3) are the favorableness ratings of an object definitely known to be "honest" and "not honest," respectively, rather than the favorableness ratings of "honest" and "not honest" *per se*. Although these ratings may not always be identical, for purposes of the present analysis no distinction between them has been made.

Substituting this expression into Eq. (6.2) and substituting the appropriate favorableness ratings for the expected values obtained through this procedure:

$$A_o = P_A F_A + P_B F_B - P_{AB} F_{AB} + P_{A'B'} F_{A'B'} \tag{6.5}$$

where F_A, F_B, F_{AB}, and $F_{A'B'}$ are the favorableness ratings of A, of B, of A and B in combination, and of neither A nor B.

As stated, Fishbein's formulation includes only the first two terms of this expression. In other words, Eq. (6.1) takes into account instances in which O possesses both A and B *twice,* but it does not take into account at all the probability that O possesses neither of the attributes in question.

When more than two attributes are involved, the expression for A_o derived from the categorization formulation is more complex, but in general it can be written in the form

$$A_o = \Sigma P_{ko} F_k + C_{ko} \tag{6.6}$$

where C_{ko} is a composite of terms that pertain to sets of attributes. In this expression, $\Sigma P_{ko} > 1$ unless $C_{ko} = 0$. Thus, the theoretical formulation outlined in Chapter 2 implies that for Eq. (6.1) to be a complete description of the relations among the cognitions involved, C_{ko} must be irrelevant to the evaluation of O. That is, beliefs in the conjunctive occurrence of attributes must receive greater weight than would be expected on the basis of the interpretation of category ratings as subjective expected values, while the belief that O possesses none of the attributes considered has no effect at all upon the evaluation of O.

These assumptions may be unnecessary, however, if one is willing to accept Eq. (6.1) as an incomplete description of the relations among cognitions. In practice, only a subset of the attributes, assumed to be particularly relevant to the evaluation of O, is used in determining the predictive validity of Eq. (6.1). If the value of C_{ko} in Eq. (6.6) is positively correlated with $\Sigma P_{ko} F_{ko}$, or if its value is small in magnitude compared to this sum, the failure to take it into account would simply decrease the correlation between predicted and obtained values of A_o, and also decrease the likelihood of generating exact predictions of change in A_o as a function of change in beliefs about O's attributes. To this extent, correlational tests of the predictive accuracy of the model may be conservative.

B. Some Methodological Problems

Equation (6.1) is often difficult to apply and to test in specific situations. One problem arises when every attribute that is relevant to a subjects's evaluation of O is not known to the investigator, and thus sufficient information is not available for determining the accuracy of Eq. (6.1). A related problem is created by the fact that the probabilities associated with different attributes are not independent. As a result, information that affects the belief that O has one attribute (e.g. "intelligent") may affect beliefs that he has other relevant attributes (e.g. "educated," "creative," "talkative," etc.). These dependencies are implicit in the formulation but are not clearly specifiable *a priori*. These problems often make it difficult to construct an exact test of the fit of the model or to evaluate adequately the empirical support obtained for it.

On the other hand, correlations between predicted and obtained values of A_o are apt to be higher when the beliefs associated with different attributes are interrelated than when they are not. For example, assume that only M of these are known to the investigator. Then, Eq. (6.1) could be rewritten:

$$A_o = \sum_{k=1}^{M} P_{ko} F_k + \sum_{k=M+1}^{N} P_{ko} F_k$$
$$= A_{pred} + R_o$$

where A_{pred} is the value of A_o predicted by the investigator and R_o is the contribution to A_o of attributes unknown to the investigator. Suppose that the subject believes that attributes similar in favorableness (that is, similar in F_k) generally occur together and that attributes differing in favorableness tend not to occur together. Then, the greater the subjective probability that O possesses known attributes of a given affective quality, the more likely it is that he possesses unknown attributes of the same affective quality. If this reasoning is correct, there should be a positive correlation between A_{pred} and R_o. Moreover, A_o should be correlated nearly as positively with A_{pred} alone as with the sum of A_{pred} and R_o.

A third problem in generating a precise test of the accuracy of Eq. (6.1) stems from the fact that procedures for measuring P_{ko} and F_{ko} are not clear. The theoretical derivation of the model described at the beginning of this chapter suggests that P_{ko} should be defined along a scale from 0 to 1. However, the appropriate scale for measuring F_k is less obvious. Different predictions about the relative magnitudes of attitudes can be generated, depending upon the particular numerical values assigned to categories along this scale. As an example, assume that F_k is measured along a scale of 11 categories that in one case have been assigned values from −5 to +5 and in a second case have been assigned values from 0 to 10. Suppose that one object, O_1, is believed to possess attributes A and B with the probabilities .1 and .9, respectively, and that a second object, O_2, is believed to possess these attributes with probabilities of .3 and .5, respectively. In case 1, the values of P_{ko} and F_k and the predicted evaluations of the two objects might be as shown in Table 6.1(A).

In case 2, the favorableness ratings of A and B would presumably each be increased by 5 response units. These values and the predicted evaluations of O_1 and O_2 with this scaling procedure are shown in Table 6.1(B). In case 1, $A_{o1} < A_{o2}$, while in case 2, $A_{o1} > A_{o2}$. In other words, the conclusion concerning

TABLE 6.1

Predicted Evaluations of O_1 and O_2 Resulting from
Different Response Scales for Measuring F_k

Scales	O_1			O_2		
	P_{ko}	F_1	$P_{ko}F_k$	P_{ko}	F_k	$P_{ko}F_k$
A. Scale ranging from -5 to $+5$						
Attribute A	.1	5	.5	.3	5	1.5
Attribute B	.9	1	.9	.5	1	.5
Predicted evaluation			1.4			2.0
B. Scale ranging from 0 to 10						
Attribute A	.1	10	1.0	.3	10	3.0
Attribute B	.9	6	5.4	.5	6	3.0
Predicted evaluation			6.4			6.0

the relative favorableness of O_1 and O_2 depends upon the response language used by subjects to report their judgments.

Fishbein typically uses a standard set of 7-category bipolar semantic differentials to measure F_k. However, as we pointed out in Chapter 3, even if a standard response scale is provided for recording favorableness judgments, the relation of categories along this scale to underlying judgmental categories may vary over subjects and may also depend upon characteristics of the situation in which ratings are obtained. These factors may combine to decrease the overall predictive accuracy of Eq. (6.1) and may also lead to erroneous predictions about subjects' relative preferences for stimuli.

C. Empirical Tests

Tests of the validity of Fishbein's model for describing the organization of attitudes and beliefs have been primarily correlational in nature. In an early study, Fishbein (1963) selected 10 attributes that had been frequently associated with "Negro" in a free association task. Subjects evaluated each attribute along five 7-category evaluative (A) scales ("clean-dirty," "good-bad," etc.) and then estimated their beliefs that Negroes possessed each attribute along five 7-category belief (B) scales ("probable-improbable," "likely-unlikely," etc.). The first set of ratings, summed over the five scales, provided an estimate of F_k for each attribute, and the second set, summed, provided an index of P_{ko} for the attribute. Subjects also rated "Negro" along the five A scales; the sum of these ratings was used as an index of A_o. Predicted values of A_o, calculated for each subject separately on the basis of Eq. (6.1), were correlated .801 ($n = 50$; $p < .001$) with actual values of A_o. This value was higher than the correlations of A_o with the evaluative and belief components (i.e., ΣF_k and ΣP_{ko}) considered separately ($r = .468$ and .653, respectively). Thus, both components seem to contribute to the prediction of A_o.

In a later study, Fishbein (1965) applied Eq. (6.1) to the prediction of sociometric ratings in informal discussion groups. Four-person groups were formed, each with a designated leader. Each leader met with three different groups. Following each discussion, the leader estimated the likelihood that each group member engaged in a series of behaviors along the B scales described above. These behaviors had been normatively scaled in favorableness (F_k) before the experiment. The leader then evaluated each group member and also indicated the most and least preferred member of the group. Finally, after he had participated in all three discussions, the leader indicated his most and least preferred group. In each discussion group, the leader's attitude toward each group member was predicted from Eq. (6.1) on the basis of his beliefs about the member's behavior and the normative favorableness of this behavior. On the average, predicted and obtained ratings were correlated .753 over the 9 members rated by each leader. The high and low estimates of A_o within each group were accurate 64.3% of the time in predicting the leader's choices of the most and least preferred group members. Finally, the sum of the predicted values of A_o over the three members of each group was 89% accurate in predicting the most and least preferred group in which the leader participated.

The attributes and behaviors used to test Eq. (6.1) in the above studies were undoubtedly not a complete set of those that were relevant to the evaluations being made. Indeed, in Fishbein's (1963) study, the attributes were selected on the basis of the frequency with which they were used to describe Negroes rather than their relevance to liking. The accuracy of Eq. (6.1) might have been increased had the latter criterion been used. On the other hand, it may often not be necessary to use a large sample of attributes in generating predictions of A. Wyer (1970b) applied an extension of Fishbein's model in predicting the evaluations of persons occupying different social roles. Twenty bipolar attribute dimensions were each paired randomly with a different social role. (For example, one of the roles selected was "photographer," and poles of the dimension paired with it were "clean" and "dirty.") Data were then obtained for each role-attribute pairing to test the equation

$$A_o = P_t F_t + (1-P_t) F_{t'}$$

where A_o is the evaluation of a role occupant, F_t and $F_{t'}$ are the favorableness ratings of the attributes described by the positive and negative poles of the dimension paired with the role, and P_t is the probability that the role occupant is described by the positive pole of this dimension.[2] Averaged over subjects, predicted and obtained evaluations of A_o based upon this equation were correlated .748 over the 20 roles considered. In other words, over 55% of the variance in A_o was predicted from information about only two of O's attributes.

One reason for the success of the model in the above study may be that the contribution of attributes that were not considered in forming the predictor (R_o) was nevertheless correlated with the predictor (A_{pred}). This is more likely to occur when the attributes involved are personality characteristics than when other types of attributes are involved. This contingency is suggested in a recent application of Fishbein's model to the prediction of attitudes toward specific behavioral acts (Ajzen & Fishbein, 1972). Subjects read about four hypothetical situations. In each, a protagonist was confronted with a choice of whether or not to engage in a course of action, the outcome of which was uncertain. Subjects first estimated the likelihood that each course of action would succeed (P_s) and the desirability of success and failure $(F_s$ and $F_f)$. Then they estimated the desirability of undertaking the course of action described (A_{act}). This latter estimate was predicted from an equation of the form:

$$A_{act} = P_s F_s + (1 - P_s)F_f.$$

The correlation between obtained and predicted values based upon this equation depended upon the particular choice situation involved. The formulation was most accurate $(r = .814)$ in predicting attitudes toward investing in a project that would result in monetary gain if successful but financial loss if unsuccessful. It was least accurate $(r = .299)$ in predicting attitudes toward donating a kidney to one's brother which, if successful, would save his life. The authors attributed this low correlation to the fact that considerations independent of the success or failure of the transplant (for example, the effect of losing a kidney upon one's own health) entered into the decision but were not taken into account in the predictor equation. These

---

[2] Note the similarity of this equation to Eq. (6.4). If t' is assumed to indicate "not t," and if F_t and F_t' referred to the favorableness of a role occupant who possessed t and t', this equation would be a complete predictor of A_o according to the derivation of Fishbein's formulation described at the beginning of this chapter.

results suggest that accuracy in predicting A_o may indeed be limited when R_o is large and is not correlated with A_{pred}.

D. General Implications

Fishbein's formulation has been applied primarily to information integration processes, and we shall return to it again in that context. Unfortunately, its potential implications as a model of cognitive organization have not been fully investigated. While a construct of "consistency" is not explicit in this formulation, the assumption that Eq. (6.1) describes the relations among beliefs and attitudes has several implications similar to those of models considered in previous chapters. First, the relation described by Eq. (6.1) should show a Socratic effect; that is, the accuracy of the equation should increase once the beliefs and attitudes involved are made salient to subjects in close temporal proximity. Second, changes in any of the components of Eq. (6.1) should have predictable effects upon one or more of the other components. For example, if P changes his attitude toward O (A_o), this change should be accompanied by a change either in his beliefs that O has certain attributes or in his estimate of the favorableness of these attributes. Or, when information leads P to change his belief that O has a certain attribute and yet P does *not* change his overall attitude toward O, either the probability that O has other attributes, or the favorableness of these attributes, should theoretically change in a way that maintains the value of the right side of Eq. (6.1).

Since Fishbein's formulation pertains to the cognitions related to one's attitude toward a particular object, it is not necessarily inconsistent with the laws of cognitive balance, which concern the relations among cognitions about several different objects. In fact, Eq. (6.1) has implications for the processes underlying attitude and belief change that result from imbalanced states. As a simple example, consider the prediction from balance theory that if P believes that O likes him, he will tend to like O. Why should this be true? In terms of Fishbein's formulation, "likes P" may be an attribute that P regards as favorable. Alternatively, O's liking for P may imply that O has certain favorable attributes as "friendly," "helpful," etc.; the more probable it is that O has these attributes, the more favorably P should evaluate him. Suppose that P now receives information that O has derogated him in some way. This information may decrease P's belief that O has the attributes "likes P," "friendly," etc., and thus, according to Eq. (6.1), may decrease P's attitude toward O (A_o). Furthermore, information that O has derogated P may lead P to decrease his belief that he *personally* has certain favorable attributes (or increase his belief that he has unfavorable ones.) To this extent, the information would also decrease P's self-evaluation. This effect could also be predicted by balance theory. As noted in Chapter 5, balance theory cannot predict simultaneous changes in the direction of both P's attitude toward O and his attitude toward himself. According to Fishbein's formulation, however, such simultaneous changes in attitudes are theoretically possible. Of course, Eq. (6.1) does not *necessarily* imply that either attitude will become negative simply because P learns that O dislikes him. Whether or not this occurs depends upon P's belief that the object being evaluated (himself or O) has other favorable attributes relevant to liking that are not affected by O's judgment of P. In other words, Fishbein's model predicts changes in attitudes that are consistent in direction with those predicted by balance theory, but it does not require that these changes be of such a magnitude that balance is restored. To this extent, Eq. (6.1) may be more useful in describing the results of many studies of social evaluation processes than are the less flexible principles of balance theory and psychologic.

Another interesting configuration to consider from the standpoint of both Fishbein's model and balance theory is that in which P likes one person (A) and dislikes a second (B). According to balance theory, P should believe that A and B dislike one another. If Fishbein's model is valid, why would this be true? If P dislikes B, it is presumably because he believes with high probability that B has unfavorable attributes, and with low probability that B has favorable ones. P may assume that A's beliefs about B's attributes are similar to his own, and P therefore may expect A's attitude toward B, estimated by Eq. (6.1), to be similar to his. But why should P believe that B dislikes A, since P believes that A has favorable attributes with high probability? Equation (6.1) suggests two possibilities. First, P may believe that B disagrees with him about whether or not A has certain attributes relevant to liking. Second, he may believe that B disagrees with him about the favorableness of these attributes. On the other hand, if P assumes that B's judgments, like A's judgments, are similar to his own, he should believe that B likes A, contrary to predictions based upon balance theory. It is difficult *a priori* to predict which of these several assumptions will be made by P in any given instance; each may be made with some probability, depending upon the attributes involved. However, if this is the case, support for balance theory when P likes A and dislikes B should generally be greater when the third relation pertains to A's liking for B than when it pertains to B's liking for A. There is evidence to support this prediction. Newcomb (1968) has concluded from a survey of relevant literature that the relation between P's liking for an object and his belief that O likes it is less likely to conform to balance principles when P dislikes O than when P likes O. If the object involved is another person, this conclusion is effectively identical to that drawn from our analysis based upon Fishbein's model.

II. OSGOOD AND TANNENBAUM'S CONGRUITY MODEL

A. General Principles

The congruity model of cognitive organization and change proposed by Osgood and his colleagues (Osgood & Tannenbaum, 1955; Osgood, et al., 1957) has often been interpreted as an extension of cognitive balance theory that generates quantitative predictions of the effects of one cognition upon others. However, the assumptions upon which this theory is based and those underlying balance theory are quite different. Although it is not clearly stated by Osgood and Tannenbaum (1955), congruity theory fundamentally consists of two principles. One concerns the manner in which different attributes of an object combine to affect judgments of the object, and the second concerns the effect that the association of attributes may have upon the subsequent evaluations of these attributes. In their most general form, the principles may be stated as follows:

Principle 1. The evaluation of an object described by a collective of attributes is a composite of the evaluations based upon each attribute considered in isolation, with the more extreme (more polarized) components receiving the greater weight.

Principle 2. Once an attribute is associated with others in a collective, its evaluation becomes identical to the evaluation of the collective.

The above principles can theoretically be applied to any type of attribute. In practice, Principle 1 has been applied to the prediction of evaluations of objects described by various personality adjectives (L. Anderson & Fishbein, 1965; Osgood, et al., 1957) and social roles (Rokeach & Rothman, 1965). Principle 2 has typically been applied when a communication about an issue (*I*) is attributed to a particular person (S), and the effects of this association upon evaluations of both S and *I* are predicted. In such instances, the attributes associated are the name or description given to S (e.g., "Richard Nixon") and the opinion about *I* conveyed by the communication (e.g., "opposition to forced integration of public schools"). These attributes are presumably combined to form a collective evaluation in the general manner prescribed in Principle 1, and the subsequent evaluation of each attribute becomes identical to this collective evaluation.

The process by which the implications of different attributes combine to affect evaluations of the objects they describe is intentionally vague in our statement of Principle 1. The quantitative accuracy of congruity theory in predicting attitude change of course depends upon the ability to describe precisely the information integration process underlying this principle. On the other hand, an incorrect assumption about the nature of this process would not in itself invalidate the general principles of cognitive organization implied by congruity theory as we have stated them. In fact, several alternative formulations of information integration are potentially applicable

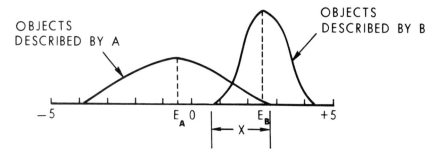

Fig. 6.1. Hypothetical distribution of objects described by A and B along a category scale from −5 to +5.

to Principle 1. Fishbein's model for describing the relation between evaluations of an object and evaluations of its attributes is among these. While integration processes will be discussed in detail in Chapters 8-10, one formulation, which is based upon the general description of categorization processes proposed in Chapter 2, may be worth mentioning briefly at this time.

Consider two attributes A and B. The evaluation of a representative object with each attribute along a response scale is theoretically the expected value of the subjective distribution of all objects with this attribute along the scale. Assume that these distributions and their expected values (E_A and E_B) are as shown in Fig. 6.1. Now a certain number of objects have both A and B, and thus are presumably common to both distributions; these objects lie somewhere within the range marked "X" in Fig. 6.1. Since the evaluation of an object with both A and B is presumably the expected value of the distribution of such objects along the scale, it therefore must lie somewhere within X. Two things are suggested by this analysis. First, the evaluation of objects possessing both A and B should generally (although not necessarily) lie between the evaluation based upon A alone and the evaluation based upon B alone. Second, the evaluation of objects with both A and B should be closer to the evaluation of the single attribute with the narrower underlying probability distribution. The uncertainty associated with ratings decreases as these ratings become more extreme (see Fig. 2.3). Therefore, ratings of an object described by two attributes should generally be closer to the more extreme of the two ratings based upon each attribute considered separately. This of course is what Principle 1 asserts.

Principle 2 follows if it is assumed that once two attributes are associated and the class of objects possessing both is circumscribed, objects with one attribute but not the other are disregarded when subsequently rating each attribute separately. Thus, in the above example, once A and B are associated, the evaluation of A would be predicted by the expected value of the distribution of objects with both A and B, ignoring objects with A but not B. This assumption might be plausible if subjects who are called upon to evaluate A consider only the subset of objects described by A that are salient to them at the time (in this case, those objects that also have B) when deciding upon the most representative value of this attribute.

B.   A Quantification of Congruity Principles

Osgood and his colleagues have proposed a means of quantifying the two principles described above. In effect, their proposal is a somewhat arbitrary hypothesis about the manner in which evaluations of objects are related to evaluations of their individual attributes. Specifically, Osgood et al. (1957) assume that the evaluation of objects with both A and B (E_{AB}) is an average of the evaluations of objects with A and objects with B $(E_A$ and $E_B)$, each weighted by its relative extremity, or degree of polarization. If E_A , E_B , and E_{AB} are defined in relation to a point of neutrality, or scale origin, and if $|E_A|$ and $|E_B|$ are the absolute values of E_A and E_B, respectively, E_{AB} would theoretically be predicted from the equation:

$$E_{AB} = \frac{|E_A|}{|E_A| + |E_B|} (E_A) + \frac{|E_B|}{|E_A| + |E_B|} (E_B) \qquad (6.7)$$

According to Principle 2, the subsequent evaluation of E_A and E_B should also be equal to E_{AB} and therefore should be predictable from Eq. (6.7). Expressions for the predicted changes in E_A and E_B $(\Delta E_A$ and $\Delta E_B)$ may be generated by simply subtracting their original values from E_{AB}; that is,

$$\Delta E_A = E_{AB} - E_A = \frac{|E_A|}{|E_A| + |E_B|} (E_A) + \frac{|E_B|}{|E_A| + |E_B|} (E_B) - E_A$$

$$= \frac{|E_A| (E_A) + |E_B| (E_B) - (|E_A| + |E_B|) E_A}{|E_A| + |E_B|}$$

$$= \frac{|E_B|}{|E_A| + |E_B|} (E_B - E_A) \qquad (6.8a)$$

and, by analogy,

$$\Delta E_B = \frac{|E_A|}{|E_A| + |E_B|} (E_A - E_B) \qquad (6.8b)$$

Thus, the predicted change in a given component evaluation is equal to the difference between the original evaluations of the components being associated, weighted by the relative extremity of the evaluation of the other component.

When congruity principles are applied to situations in which a source and an issue are associated, a special problem arises if the source opposes the issue or is *negatively* associated with it. However, as assumed by cognitive balance theory (see Chapter 5, p. 106), a negative association between A and B may be equivalent to a positive association between A and the antithesis of B, or B'. To this extent, the evaluation of B' may be equal in magnitude but opposite in direction to the evaluation of B; that is, $E_{B'} = -E_B$. Predicted changes in E_A and E_B when A and B are related negatively would then be determined by first generating a predicted evaluation of the collective of A and B' ($E_{AB'}$) and calculating the predicted changes in E_A and $E_{B'}$. These equations are identical to Eq. (6.8a) and Eq. (6.8b) with E_B replaced by $E_{B'}$. Since $E_{B'} = -E_B$ and $|E_{B'}| = |E_B|$, appropriate substitutions yield the expressions:

$$\Delta E_A = \frac{|E_B|}{|E_A| + |E_B|} (-E_B - E_A) \qquad (6.9a)$$

and

$$\Delta E_B = \frac{|E_A|}{|E_A| + |E_B|} (-E_A - E_B) \qquad (6.9b)$$

Although derived differently, Eqs. (6.8) and (6.9) are identical to those proposed by Osgood and Tannenbaum (1955) in applying congruity principles to attitude change phenomena.

The similarity between the implications of congruity theory and the implications of balance theory can be communicated most easily through an example. Consider a case in which P evaluates A and B as +3 and −1 respectively. He then receives a communication that A and B are associated positively. This produces an "imbalanced" state, as shown in the following diagram:

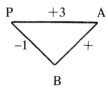

Applying the congruity principle, the evaluation of A and B in combination, and thus the evaluations of both A and B after they have been associated, is predicted from Eq. (6.7) to be:

$$E_{AB} = \frac{|3|}{|3| + |-1|} (3) + \frac{|-1|}{|3| + |-1|} (-1) = 2.0$$

The resultant state is balanced:

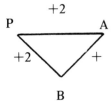

Note that the evaluation of A, the initially more polarized, changes relatively less.

If P had received information that A opposed B, or that A and B were negatively associated, the valences of the relations in the configuration would initially be balanced:

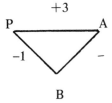

Nevertheless, according to the congruity principle, the evaluations of A and B would change. The final evaluations of each can be predicted by using Eqs. (6.9a - b), or alternatively by first determining the predicted evaluation of A and B′, letting $E_{B'} = -E_B = 1$; that is,

$$E_{AB'} = \frac{|3|}{|3| + |1|} (3) + \frac{|1|}{|3| + |1|} (1) = 2.5$$

Then the final evaluations of A and B′ would theoretically equal 2.5, the evaluation of B $(= E_{B'})$ would be –2.5, and the resulting configuration would be:

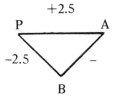

The above examples demonstrate one of the more interesting predictions of congruity theory. Note that the evaluation of the initially less polarized element (B) increases when B is associated positively with A and decreases when B is associated negatively with A. Since A is regarded favorably, this would intuitively be expected. However, the evaluation of the more polarized element (A) decreases regardless of whether the association between A and B is positive or negative. This prediction, if valid, has important practical, as well as theoretical, implications. For example, suppose that A is a politician and that B is a policy that people in his constituency regard as moderately favorable. What stand should A take with respect to this policy? If he is personally held in higher esteem than the policy, congruity theory predicts that he will lose favor *either* if he supports the policy or if he opposes it; his best strategy would be not to associate himself with the policy in any way whatsoever. On the other hand, a political opponent who either is regarded unfavorably or is generally unknown (and thus evaluated neutrally) would gain prestige by supporting this same policy.

Analogous considerations arise when evaluations of the policy are more highly polarized than the evaluations of persons who associate themselves with it. That is, if a policy is already regarded favorably, a person who is sincerely interested in having the policy adopted but who himself is held in only moderately high esteem by the public should theoretically neither publicly support nor oppose the policy, since the policy would lose favor if he becomes associated with it in any way at all.

C. Generalization of the Model

Although it has seldom been tried empirically, congruity principles can be applied to relations among more than two elements. For example, consider a set of three attributes A, B, and C, the evaluations of which are initially $+1$, -3, and $+5$, respectively. Suppose that these attributes all become positively associated. According to Principle 1, the evaluation of the collective E_{ABC} should be:

$$E_{ABC} = \frac{|1|}{|1| + |-3| + |5|} (1) + \frac{|-3|}{|1| + |-3| + |5|} (-3) + \frac{|5|}{|1| + |-3| + |5|} (5)$$

$$= 1.89$$

Thus, applying Principle 1, the predicted changes in evaluations of A, B, and C would be $+.89$, $+4.89$, and -3.11, respectively. This example is of additional interest since in this case the most extreme component does *not* change least. In other words, the hypothesis that more extreme evaluations are more resistant to change generally applies only to instances in which just two objects of evaluation are associated.

Analogous procedures can of course be used to predict changes in evaluations that occur when certain of the elements are negatively associated. For example, suppose that B and C are two public policies and that A is a source of two communications about these policies. Assume that the initial evaluations of A, B, and C are those given in the preceding example. Information is now received that A supports B but opposes C. To generate predictions, the negative relation between A and C would first need to be

TABLE 6.2

COLLECTIVE RATINGS AND CHANGES IN COMPONENT RATINGS PREDICTED BY CONGRUITY THEORY

E_A	E_B	E_{AB}	ΔE_A	ΔE_B
−3	−5	−4.25	−1.25	.75
−3	−4	−3.43	−.43	.57
−3	−3	−3.00	0	0
−3	−2	−2.60	.40	−.60
−3	−1	−2.50	.50	−1.50
−3	0	−3.00	0	−3.00
−3	1	−2.00	1.00	−3.00
−3	2	−1.00	2.00	−3.00
−3	3	0	3.00	−3.00
−3	4	1.00	4.00	−3.00
−3	5	2.00	5.00	−3.00

replaced by a positive relation between A and the antithesis of C, or C′. If this is done, and if $E_C' = -E_C$, the collective evaluation E_{ABC}' and thus the final evaluations of A, B, and C′, would be computed to be −3.67. The final evaluation of C ($= -E_C'$) would be +3.67. Therefore, the information about A's attitudes toward B and C would be predicted to decrease E_A, E_B, and E_C by 4.67 units, .67 units, and 1.33 units, respectively.

This extension of congruity theory, while applicable to source effects, may be of greater practical interest in research on interpersonal relations and social evaluation processes. For example, one could theoretically predict changes in evaluations of several persons as a result of information that all have become members of the same social group, or that some have become members of the group but others have been rejected for membership.[3]

D. Some Implications of the Weighting Procedure

The accuracy of congruity theory in generating quantitative predictions of change in evaluations should only be as good as its accuracy in predicting the manner in which information about objects combines to affect the evaluation of these objects. Unfortunately, tests of the predictive effectiveness of Eq. (6.7) as a model of information integration, discussed in greater detail in Chapter 9, have invariably been disappointing (cf. L. Anderson & Fishbein, 1965; Rokeach & Rothman, 1965; Wyer, 1969b, 1973a; Wyer & Watson,

---

[3] In this case, individual persons would function as "attributes" of the group.

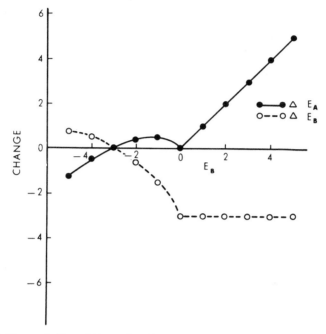

Fig. 6.2. Changes in E_A and E_B predicted by congruity theory as a function of the initial value of E_B, based upon data from Table 6.2.

1969). Equation 6.7 assumes that information integration is essentially an averaging process. The validity of this assumption is not completely clear, as we shall attempt to demonstrate in Chapter 9. However, assuming for the moment that an averaging process *is* involved, the question remains as to whether the particular criterion used in weighting each component is valid. Although more extreme components may have greater influence than less polarized ones, the assumption that their influence is directly proportional to their relative extremity is somewhat arbitrary. Moreover, this assumption leads to some unexpected predictions. Assume that the initial evaluation of A (E_A) is –3 along a scale from –5 to +5, and that A then becomes positively associated with a second object, B. The predicted changes in E_A and E_B are tabulated in Table 6.2 and are plotted as a function of E_B in Fig. 6.2

The complexity of these functions is intuitively surprising. For example, the change in E_A increases, decreases, and the increases again as the difference between the initial values of E_B and E_A become greater. Thus, an association between A and B has greater positive influence upon E_A when E_B is initially either favorable or slightly *un*favorable than when it is neutral. This prediction might be reasonable if a neutral evaluation of B implies complete lack of knowledge about B, while positive and negative evaluations both imply that the subject is somewhat familiar with B before learning about its relation to A. Information that A is associated with either a favorable or a mildly unfavorable element may imply that A has more favorable characteristics than those that led to its initial evaluation (–3), and therefore this evaluation may increase as Fig. 6.2 suggests. However, if subjects are unfamiliar with B, associating it with A may give them no useful information about A whatsoever, and thus may not affect E_A. While this interpretation seems plausible, the assumption that a neutral initial evaluation of B connotes lack of knowledge about B may often be unwarranted. If such an evaluation indicates either ambivalence or indifference, the above interpretation would not apply.

1. *Correction for Incredulity.* There is a second curious aspect of the predictions shown in Fig. 6.2. When initial evaluations of B are positive, changes in E_A are identical to the initial values of E_B while changes in E_B are the same regardless of the initial value of E_B. Neither of these predictions seems plausible. In fact, the prediction that change in E_B is independent of its initial value contradicts the general hypothesis that change in the evaluation of an element is inversely proportional to its relative extremity. Osgood and Tannenbaum recognize this problem in their model and consequently introduce an additional factor to bring predictions more into line with expectations. They argue that when the valences of the relations in a configuration are not in balance, subjects tend to disbelieve the communication about A's association with B, and that their incredulity leads to an attenuation of both $\triangle E_A$ and $\triangle E_B$. Incredulity, and thus the amount of the attenuation, is assumed to increase with the sum of the absolute magnitudes of E_A and E_B.[4] In Fig. 6.2, since the association between A and B is positive, a correction for incredulity would be applied when E_A and E_B are opposite in sign (that is, when $E_B < 0$). If this correction is made, the predicted change in E_B decreases as the initial value of E_B becomes more positive, as would intuitively be expected. Moreover, while the change in E_A becomes increasingly greater as the initial value of E_B increases, the *rate* of change becomes less as the initial value of E_B becomes more positive.

2. *A Response Language Interpretation of Unequal Weighting.* While the correction for incredulity may help to bring predicted changes into line with obtained changes, it should be noted that both of the problems described above arise only because of the peculiar characteristics of the somewhat arbitrary weighting procedure described in Eq. (6.7) for predicting collective evaluations. An alternative model, in which the weight of a component increases with its extremity but is not expressible as a simple function of its relative polarization, might perhaps eliminate the discontinuities in the functions described in Fig. 6.2, and the theoretical problems that arise because of them. To provide but one example, reconsider the possibility

---

[4] Specifically, Osgood and Tannenbaum propose that the correction for incredulity is estimated by the quantity $a (E_A{}^2 + b) (E_B{}^2 + E_B)$, where a and b are empirically determined constants.

TABLE 6.3

Collective Ratings and Changes in Component Ratings
Predicted by Alternative Formulation of Principle 1

Rating scale values		Judgmental units		Collective evaluation		ΔE_A	ΔE_B
E_A	E_B	E_A	E_B	Judg-mental units	Rating scale value		
−3	−5	−6	−15	−10.5	−4.1	−1.1	.90
−3	−4	−6	−10	−8	−3.5	−.5	.50
−3	−3	−6	−6	−6	−3.0	0	0
−3	−2	−6	−3	−4.5	−2.5	.5	−.50
−3	−1	−6	−1	−3.5	−2.16	.84	−1.16
−3	0	−6	0	−3	−2.0	1.00	−2.00
−3	1	−6	1	−2.5	−1.75	1.25	−2.75
−3	2	−6	3	−1.5	−1.25	1.75	−3.25
−3	3	−6	6	0	0	3.00	−3.00
−3	4	−6	10	2.0	1.5	4.50	−2.50
−3	5	−6	15	4.5	2.5	5.50	−2.50

suggested in Chapter 3 that the range of stimuli placed in each category along a rating scale increases with the extremity of the category; that is, extreme response categories include wider ranges of stimuli, defined in judgmental units, than do more neutral categories. Suppose for simplicity that the size of a rating scale category in judgmental units is equal to its numerical value in rating scale units. Rating scale values, positioned along a continum defined in judgmental units, would then be as shown below:

```
· · · · · · · · · · · · · · · · · · · · · · · · · · · · · · · ·
───────────────────────────────────────────────────────────────
−5        − 4        −3      −2  −1 0 1   2      3      4        5
```

Now assume further that when A and B are associated, the evaluation based upon these elements in combination is the simple average of the evaluations of A and B considered separately when these evaluations are defined in judgmental rather than rating scale units. To predict the ratings of A and B in combination, and the resultant changes in E_A and E_B, first determine the positions of E_A and E_B along a scale defined in units of judgment, compute the average of these values, and then find the position of this value along the rating scale. Let us apply this procedure to the preceding example, in which $E_A = -3$ in rating scale units and E_B varies between −5 and +5. Predicted

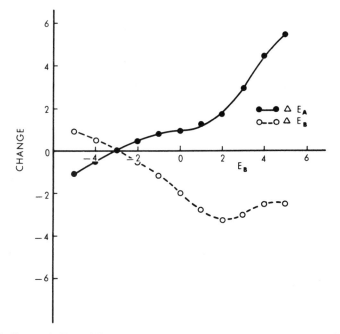

Fig. 6.3. Changes in E_A and E_B predicted by a response language formulation as a function of intitial value of E_B, based upon data from Table 6.3.

values of E_{AB}, ΔE_A, and ΔE_B, determined on the basis of the above assumptions, are tabulated and plotted as a function of the initial value of E_B in Table 6.3 and Fig. 6.3, respectively.

The specific assumptions underlying the derivation of these predicted values are undoubtedly invalid. However, the general procedure used in deriving these values generates predictions that often parallel those made on the basis of Eq. (6.7); at the same time, it eliminates some of the above mentioned problems resulting from the application of this equation. For example, the initially more polarized evaluation typically changes less. ΔE_A increases monotonically as E_B becomes more positive; thus the influence of B is a positive function of the extremity of its initial evaluation. Up to a point, E_B also changes more as its initial value becomes more positive. However, when E_B is initially more positive than E_A is negative, change in E_B is related negatively to its initial value. This latter tendency may be analogous to the effect of "incredulity" postulated by Osgood and Tannenbaum. Note, however, that it only occurs when E_B is as or more extreme than E_A. Also, the effect of incredulity upon change in E_A is not apparent.

E. Why Are Incongruities "Resolved"?

In fairness to Osgood and Tannenbaum (1955), it should be noted that their application of the congruity principle to the prediction of attitude change seems to be based upon quite different assumptions from those described above. They argue that when objects differing in their evaluative implications are associated, cognitive pressure is created to eliminate these differences. Incongruity, like imbalance, is apparently assumed to be an aversive cognitive state that gives rise to cognitive reorganization in order to eliminate the unpleasantness. It is further assumed that the source of the incongruity is a difference in the favorableness of the objects being associated.

At this point it may be worthwhile to consider more carefully why communications that associate objects differing in favorableness produce incongruent cognitive states. Intuitively, this would not seem always to be the case. If a subject evaluates social welfare positively and a reactionary senator negatively, information that the senator supports increased Medicare benefits would seem incongruous to him. However, he might regard this information as incongruous regardless of his personal attitudes toward the two objects involved. This would be true because reactionary senators typically oppose social welfare programs, and information that such a senator supports Medicare is logically inconsistent with previous inferences about the senator's beliefs and attitudes. On the other hand, suppose a highly regarded comedian tells a joke that according to some independent criterion is poor. Would incongruity result from such an association? Since even the best comedians often tell poor jokes, there is nothing really inconsistent about this association. In fact, the joke might even be regarded as *less* favorable if it is told by a generally good comedian than if it is told by a typically poor one. (Certainly many of us laugh at jokes told by colleagues at a party that would hardly elicit such a response if told in the same way by a professional comic.) Perhaps a difference between the evaluations of elements being associated is not a sufficient criterion for inconsistency.

Wyer and Schwartz (1969) performed a study to investigate this possibility. Subjects received a series of communications under instructions that each communication came from the same source. The communications in a given series were of one of four types: statements about Negroes, statements about social issues, cartoons, and photographs. Normative values of these communications had previously been obtained along a relevant evaluative scale (either favorableness toward Negroes, liberalness, funniness, or interest value, respectively). Subjects either received five positive communications followed by five negative ones, or five negative communications followed by five positive ones. They rated each communication as it was presented along the appropriate scale. At various points in the sequence, source evaluations were also made. The first set of communications produced the expected initial differences in source evaluations. The critical question was how the evaluation of a particular communication would be related to the quality of those that preceded it, and thus by implication to the evaluation of its source. Statements about Negroes and social issues were both evaluated more positively when their source was positive than when it was negative. This relation is of course what congruity theory predicts. However, cartoons and photographs were both evaluated *less* positively when their source was positive than when it was negative. This relation is directly contrary to predictions based upon congruity theory. Clearly an initial difference between source and object evaluations is not a sufficient condition for incongruities to be resolved in the manner predicted by Osgood and Tannenbaum. Based upon their findings, Wyer and Schwartz concluded that the resolution of evaluative incongruities results primarily from attempts to eliminate inconsistencies in meaning between the communication attributed to a source and previous information about the source that provided the basis for the initial evaluation of him. When inconsistencies in meaning do not exist, the source evaluation may provide a frame of reference, or comparison level, for evaluating the communications presented and thus may produce "contrast" effects of the sort described in Chapter 3. In any event, Wyer and Schwartz's results indicate an important contingency in the conditions under which congruity theory is applicable.

F. Empirical Support for Congruity Theory

Direct evidence for the validity of congruity principles in describing cognitive organization is surprisingly limited. Precise tests of the theory depend to some extent upon the accuracy of Eq. (6.7) as a model of information integration. As we have mentioned, this equation appears in fact to be a quite inaccurate predictor of the manner in which information combines to affect judgments (for details of the research bearing upon the validity of this equation, see Chapter 9). However, certain indications of the validity of the model in describing organizational processes can be gained that do not depend upon the accuracy of this equation. For example, Principle 2 implies that once cognitive elements are combined in a collective, each element acquires the value assigned to the collective as a whole. A second implication of this principle is that once two elements are associated, their evaluations become equal in absolute magnitude and either similar or opposite in direction, depending upon whether the association between them is positive or negative. This latter implication is of importance in determining whether cognitions that are hypothetically organized according to congruity principles exhibit a Socratic effect. That is, if Principle 2 governs cognitive organization, and if a set of related cognitions is made salient to a subject in temporal contiguity, the consistency of these cognitions should increase in a manner described by this principle. While there is not a great deal of evidence bearing upon the validity of these predictions, let us consider the support for each in turn.

1. *Effect of Collective Evaluations Upon Component Ratings.* Most of the evidence on whether evaluations of an element become similar to the overall

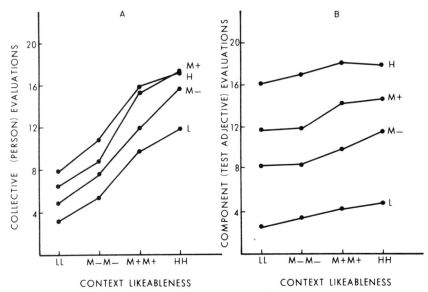

Fig. 6.4. Mean evaluations of (a) collectives (persons) and (b) components (test adjectives) as a function of the normative likeableness of the context adjectives (based upon data from Wyer & Dermer, 1968).

evaluation of the collective in which the element is contained comes from research on context effects in impression formation. In these studies subjects are typically asked first to make an evaluation of a person described by a set of personality adjectives, and then to evaluate the attribute described by one of these adjectives. If Principle 2 is valid, the evaluations of these attributes should be equal to the evaluations of the collective in which they are contained.

In one study of context effects (Wyer & Dermer, 1968), "test" adjectives at each of four levels of normative likeableness (H, M+, M−, and L, representing high, moderately high, moderately low, and low, respectively) were combined with two "context" adjectives at each of these likeableness levels (HH, M+M+, M−M−, and LL). Subjects rated a person described by each set of three adjectives along a scale from 0 (dislike very much) to 20 (like very much), and then evaluated the attribute described by the test adjective along an identical scale. Collective (person) ratings and component (test adjective) ratings are shown in Fig. 6.4 as a function of context likeableness and test adjective likeableness. Component ratings increased consistently as a function of the likeableness of the context adjectives accompanying them, replicating the results of previous studies of context effects (Anderson, 1966; Anderson & Lampel, 1965), and suggesting that component ratings are in fact displaced toward the ratings of the collectives in which they were contained. However, a comparison of Fig. 6.4a and 6.4b indicates that

TABLE 6.4

Collective Ratings and Test Adjective Ratings as a Function
of Context Range and Context Likeableness
(adapted from Wyer & Watson, 1969)

Ratings	Context likeableness	
	Low	High
A. Collective ratings		
Low range	−3.60	4.37
Moderate range	−3.91	5.78
High range	−4.89	5.06
B. Test adjective ratings		
Low range	−2.84	2.94
Moderate range	−3.83	3.66
High range	−3.77	3.49

component ratings are clearly not *equal in magnitude* to the collective ratings.

Wyer and Watson obtained collective and test adjective ratings under different instructional conditions and a somewhat different design. Specifically, subjects were not asked to evaluate persons. In fact, they were told that the adjectives in each set did not apply to a single person. They were nevertheless instructed to make a collective evaluation of the adjectives in each group and then to evaluate the test adjective. Adjective sets were constructed such that the average normative likeableness of the two context adjectives, and the range in likeableness of those two adjectives, varied independently. The same test adjectives were used at all levels of context range. Collective ratings and test adjective ratings, both made along a scale from −10 to +10, are shown in Table 6.4 as a function of the two experimental variables. These data provide only partial support for congruity theory. When context adjective evaluations were very high, the relations of both collective ratings and test adjective ratings to context range were curvilinear, reaching a maximum when the range was moderate. Moreover, in both cases the effect was greater when range increased from low to moderate than when it increased from moderate to high. When context evaluations were negative, however, the effects of context range upon collective and component ratings were not comparable. While collective ratings became substantially more negative as range increased from moderate to high, test adjective ratings became slightly more positive. Undue emphasis should perhaps not be placed upon this discrepancy, since it represents only one cell in the design and might be spurious. It may be more important that, as in Wyer and Dermer's study, component ratings, while related to collective evaluations, were not identical to these evaluations. Thus Principle 2 appears to be invalid as stated. A more accurate statement might be that once objects are associated in a collective, the evaluation of each becomes a weighted function of the collective evaluation and the evaluation of the object before it is associated with others. This is in fact the interpretation given to context effects by Anderson (1966). Such a reformulation of Principle 2 would not be trivial but in fact would require a new conceptualization of a "congruent state." Specifically, it would imply that the evaluations of the various components being associated in the collective need not be equal in magnitude to be "congruent."

2. *Evidence for the Socratic Effect.* Congruity theory has traditionally been applied to cognitions about two persons (P and O) and an issue (X). Assume that P's evaluations of 0 and X are E_{PO} and E_{PX}, respectively. Then, when O's evaluation of X (E_{OX}) is positive, E_{PO} and E_{PX} are congruent when they are equal in both magnitude and direction (when $E_{PO} = E_{PX}$). When E_{OX} is negative, these cognitions are congruent when they are equal in magnitude and opposite in direction ($E_{PO} = -E_{PX}$). In each case, the inconsistency (*Inc*) between the two cognitions would be indicated by the absolute difference between the two values being compared; that is,

$$Inc = |E_{PO} - E_{PX}| \tag{6.10a}$$

when E_{OX} is positive, and

$$Inc = |E_{PO} + E_{PX}| \tag{6.10b}$$

when E_{OX} is negative. If subjects tend to organize their cognitions in the manner implied by Principle 2, *Inc* should be generally low and, moreover, should decrease once the cognitions involved are made salient to the subjects in temporal contiguity.

Some evidence bearing upon these hypotheses was obtained in a study by the author (Wyer, 1974c) described in Chapter 5 (p. 129). In each of two experimental sessions one week apart, subjects estimated the favorableness of the sentiments between pairs of elements in each of eight 4-element sets, each set consisting of the subject himself (P), two other persons (O_1 and O_2), and an issue (X). The importance of X varied over the sets of elements considered; moreover, in each set, X was expected to be of more concern to O_1 than to O_2. Four triads of relations pertaining to each 4-element set were of interest:

1. P's evaluations of O_1 and X, and O_1's evaluation of X;
2. P's evaluations of O_2 and X, and O_2's evaluation of X;

3. O_1's evaluations of O_2 and X, and O_2's evaluation of X;

4. O_2's evaluations of O_1 and X, and O_1's evaluation of X.

In each case, the inconsistency (*Inc*) between the first two evaluations was computed on the basis of Eq. (6.10a) or Eq. (6.10b), depending upon whether the third evaluation was positive or negative. Inconsistency was generally quite large in the first session of the experiment ($M = 2.30$ units along an 11-point scale) and did not decrease appreciably in the second session ($M = 2.15$). Further analyses indicated that the change in inconsistency over time did not depend upon either the set of relations comprising the triad or the importance of X. These data therefore do not support the hypothesis that subjects reorganize their cognitions according to congruity principles once the "incongruity" between them is made salient. (It is of course conceivable that beliefs were not in fact made salient to subjects in the questionnaire used in this study. However, the fact that the Socratic effect has been detected when subjective probability models of cognitive organization are applied to beliefs contained in questionnaires of similar length argues against this possibility.)

3. *Effects of Change in One Cognition Upon Others.* A related implication of congruity theory as formulated by Osgood and Tannenbaum is that if two previously unrelated cognitive elements are associated, the evaluations of these elements will change in the manner implied by Eqs. (6.8)-(6.9). One of the first and most rigorous tests of this hypothesis was performed by Tannenbaum (1956; see also Osgood & Tannenbaum, 1955). The stimuli used consisted of three sources ("Labor Leaders," "the Chicago Tribune," and "Robert Taft") and three issues ("legalized gambling," "abstract art," and "accelerated college programs"). These stimuli were selected on the basis of normative data indicating that positive, negative, and neutral evaluations of each were made with about equal frequency. Subjects initially rated all six objects along a series of 7-point semantic differentials. Five weeks later, they read newspaper articles each of which included either a positive or a negative assertion about one of the issues that was attributed to one of the sources. They then reevaluated both sources and issues along the same scales used in reporting their initial estimates.

The scales used for recording judgments ranged from -3 to $+3$ with an assumed origin at 0. Subjects were then classified according to whether their initial evaluations of each source (E_s) and each issue (E_i) were positive ($+$), neutral (0), or negative ($-$); thus, nine combinations of initial attitudes toward S and I were considered ($++$, $+0$, $+-$, $0+$, etc.). To determine predicted changes in E_s under $++$ conditions, Tannenbaum assumed that each of the nine combinations of positive valences ($+3$ and $+3$ for E_s and E_i respectively, $+3$ and $+2$, $+3$ and $+1$, $+2$ and $+3$, etc.) occurred with equal frequency, and he therefore averaged the nine predicted changes in E_s generated for these combinations by Eqs. (6.8)-(6.9) for positive and negative assertion conditions. Analogous procedures were used to generate predicted changes in E_s and E_i for the other eight combinations of initial evaluations.

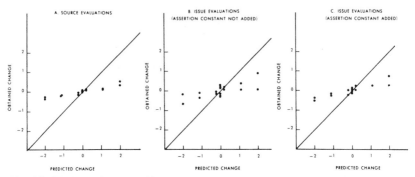

Fig. 6.5. Obtained changes in (a) source evaluations and issue evaluations (b) before and (c) after introducing the "assertion constant," as a function of predicted changes (based upon data from Osgood & Tannenbaum, 1955).

The correction for incredulity was applied when the valences of the relations involved were initially out of balance. Obtained changes in E_S and E_I under each condition were determined by averaging subjects' actual changes in their evaluations over appropriate stimulus sets and response scales. Both obtained and predicted values are tabulated for each set of conditions in Tables 6.4 and 6.5; obtained values are plotted as a function of predicted values in Fig. 6.5.[5]

Obtained changes in both E_S and E_I are both much less extreme than predicted changes. Moreover, while predicted and obtained changes in E_S are highly correlated ($r = .952$), predicted and obtained changes in E_I are less strongly related ($r = .738$). Note that in 17 of 18 cases the changes in E_I resulting from a given combination of initial attitudes is greater in magnitude than the change in E_S under corresponding conditions. For example, $\triangle E_I$ under + + conditions was .19 and −.33 when positive and negative assertions were used, respectively, while $\triangle E_S$ under these conditions was .09 and −.17; similarly, $\triangle E_I$ under + − conditions was .40 and −.14 when positive and negative assertions were used, while $\triangle E_S$ under − + conditions was .8 and −.12. On the average, $\triangle E_I$ in the direction advocated by the assertion was .17 greater than $\triangle E_S$ under comparable conditions. To eliminate the effect of this difference in determining the validity of congruity principles, Osgood and Tannenbaum subtracted an *assertion constant* of .17 from obtained changes in E_I when the assertion was positive, and they added this constant to obtained changes when the assertion was negative. These revised values are shown parenthetically in Table 6.5 and are plotted as a function of predicted values in Fig. 6.5C. While the overall correlation between predicted and obtained values is increased by introducing the assertion constant

---

[5] Obtained changes reported by Osgood and Tannenbaum are not in the same units as predicted values. To facilitate comparisons between obtained and predicted values, these data have been divided by 270. For the rationale for this procedure, see Osgood and Tannenbaum (1955).

TABLE 6.5

Obtained and Predicted Changes in E_s as a Function
of Initial Attitudes and Type of Assertion
(from Osgood & Tannenbaum, 1955)

Type of assertion/	Initial evaluation of I		
Initial evaluation of S	$+$	0	$-$
A. Postive assertion			
Initial evaluation of S			
$+$			
Predicted	.2	−.0	−1.1
Obtained	.09	.06	−.16
0			
Predicted	2.0	0	−2.0
Obtained	.56	.09	−.35
$-$			
Predicted	1.1	0	−.2
Obtained	.18	.05	−.03
B. Negative assertion			
Initial evaluation of S			
$+$			
Predicted	−1.1	0	.2
Obtained	−.17	−.00	.13
0			
Predicted	−2.0	0	2.0
Obtained	−.26	.06	.36
$-$			
Predicted	−.2	0	1.1
Obtained	−.2	0	1.1
Obtained	−.12	−.01	.13

($r = .899$), predictive accuracy is actually increased only when the initial
evaluation of S was neutral or negative; the predicted influence of positively
evaluated sources was invariably more pronounced than the obtained
influence without taking into account assertion effects, and this discrepancy
from prediction is even more apparent once the effects of the assertion *per se*
are eliminated.

TABLE 6.5

Obtained and Predicted Change in E_1 as a Function
of Initial Attitude and Type of Assertion
(from Osgood & Tannenbaum, 1955)

Type of assertion/ Initial evaluation of S	Initial evaluation of I		
	+	0	−
A. Positive assertion			
Initial evaluation of S			
+			
Predicted	.2	2.0	1.1
Obtained	.19 (.02)	.91 (.74)	.40 (.23)
0			
Predicted	0	0	0
Obtained	.14 (−.03)	.30 (.13)	.18 (.01)
−			
Predicted	−1.1	−2.0	−.2
Obtained	−.09 (−.26)	−.19 (−.36)	−.04 (−.21)
B. Negative assertion			
Initial evaluation of S			
+			
Predicted	−1.1	−2.0	−.2
Obtained	−.33 (−.16)	−.67 (−.50)	−.14 (.03)
0			
Predicted	0	0	0
Obtained	−.27 (−.10)	−.29 (−.12)	−.13 (.04)
−			
Predicted	.2	2.0	1.1
Obtained	.07 (.24)	.08 (.25)	.06 (.23)

Note: Numbers in parentheses indicate obtained changes after addition of the assertion constant.

The data reported by Osgood and Tannenbaum are not presented in sufficient detail to assess the accuracy of the model in generating exact quantitative predictions of attitude change. However, several comparisons bear upon the general validity of the model. For example, if a neutrally regarded object is associated with an object that is either favorably or unfavorably evaluated, the evaluation of the neutral object should become equal in magnitude to the evaluation of the non-neutral object, while the evaluation of the latter should not change. Only partial support was obtained for this prediction. When E_s was initially neutral and E_I was non-neutral, the absolute magnitude of $\triangle E_s$, averaged over conditions, was .38, while the average absolute magnitude of $\triangle E_I$ (after taking into account assertion effects) was .045. When E_I initially was neutral and E_s was non-neutral, the absolute magnitudes of $\triangle E_s$ and $\triangle E_I$ averaged .03 and .46, respectively. Thus, while the non-neutral evaluation did not change substantially, the change in the neutral evaluation was not nearly as great as the theory predicts (2.0).

A second implication of the theory is that the evaluation of an element will change more when its initial value is neutral than when it is either positive or negative. Results support this prediction. That is, at each of the six combinations of assertion type and initial evaluation of I, E_s changed most when it was initially neutral; similarly, at each of the six combinations of assertion type and initial evaluation of S, E_I changed most when it was initially neutral. To this extent, results are more consistent with predictions based upon Eq. (6.7) than with predictions of the alternative procedure for generating collective ratings, based upon the assumption of unequal scale categories (cf. Figs. 6.4 and 6.5).

The most intriguing prediction derived from congruity theory is that when the signs of the three relations in a configuration are initially balanced, the evaluation of the more polarized component will become less extreme. (For example, a very favorably evaluated object should become less favorable when it is associated positively with a moderately favorable object.) Although a rigorous test of this hypothesis was not made, supplementary data reported by Osgood and Tannenbaum (1955) are suggestive. Specifically, out of 38 cases where the initial values of E_s and E_I met the conditions necessary to test this hypothesis, changes were in the predicted direction in 21 cases and were in the opposite direction in only 2 cases, with 15 instances of no change.

Although other results reported by Osgood and Tannenbaum are consistent with congruity theory, they could be accounted for by alternative formulations of cognitive organization. In this regard, it is of interest to interpret the results obtained in Tannenbaum's study in terms of a model such as Fishbein's. In general, the latter model predicts that evaluations of an object (a) will increase with beliefs that the object possesses favorable attributes and (b) will decrease with beliefs that the object has unfavorable attributes. In Tannenbaum's study, S's assertion about I may have provided information about the attributes of both S and I. That is, when E_I is favorable, support for I may function as a favorable attribute, and opposition to I may function as an unfavorable attribute. When E_I is unfavorable, the opposite may be true. Similarly, the type of persons who support or oppose I may function as an attribute of I. Fishbein's model would therefore predict that when S supports I, E_s will increase with the favorableness of I, and E_I will increase with the favorableness of S. When S opposes I, these relations should be reversed. Similar predictions are made by congruity theory and are supported by Tannenbaum's results.

Fishbein's formulation might have more difficulty in predicting *a priori* the findings that neutral evaluations change more than either favorable or unfavorable evaluations. However, this finding is not necessarily contradictory to his formulation. According to Eq. (6.1), change in the evaluation of an object O should be proportional to change in beliefs that O has favorable or unfavorable attributes. The basic question is therefore whether beliefs about the attributes of a neutrally regarded O are more likely to change than beliefs about the attributes of an O that is either favorably or unfavorably regarded. The answer may be affirmative when a neutral evaluation reflects initial uncertainty about the attributes of the object involved. If O is already believed with high probability to have a particular attribute, new information confirming this belief will have relatively little effect. On the other hand, if O is believed not to possess the attribute, information that he has it may be discounted as invalid. Thus, in neither case may the effect of the information be as great as when initial beliefs about O's attributes are relatively weak.

While Osgood and Tannenbaum (1955) do not report the effect of differences in the initial magnitudes of E_s and E_I, other analyses of the same data, reported by Tannenbaum (1956), indicate as expected that more extreme initial evaluations were more resistant to change. On the other hand, the change in E_I in the direction of the assertion was an increasing monotonic function of E_s. Although this finding is intuitively not surprising, it is somewhat at odds with congruity theory, which predicts that if the initial evaluation of one element is moderately polarized, the relation between change in this evaluation and the initial evaluation of the other element should be *non*monotonic (see Fig. 6.4). Tannenbaum's data actually appear more consistent with predictions based upon the assumption of unequal rating scale categories (see Fig. 6.5).

While in Tannenbaum's study predicted changes were consistently more extreme than obtained changes, in other situations predicted changes may be less than those that actually occur. For example, in a study by Norris (1965), subjects evaluated both the United States Public Health Service and one of four medical practices (chest X-rays, use of penicillin, tooth brushing, or regular medical check-ups). Then they read a communication attributed to USPHS that opposed the practice. In seven of eight different experimental groups, the change in evaluation of the practice was greater than that predicted from Eq. (6.9). However, Norris did not take into account the effects of the "assertion constant." This constant, if added, presumably would have increased predictive accuracy.

F. General Applications of Congruity Theory to Source Effects

The data described above raise questions about the validity of the specific quantification of the congruity principles proposed by Osgood and Tannenbaum. However, at a nonquantitative level these principles may nevertheless be quite useful, since they predict the direction and relative magnitude of changes in several cognitions simultaneously, and thus can be applied to attitude change processes in fairly complex situations. Research on the influence of source characteristics upon communication effectiveness supports the validity of this assertion. For example, consider again the study by Harvey et al. (1957), described in Chapter 5. In this experiment, subjects received information that either a stranger or an acquaintance had evaluated them less favorably than they had originally evaluated themselves. They then reevaluated both themselves and the source. Under the conditions in which this study was run, it seems reasonable to assume that the acquaintance was initially evaluated favorably by subjects, while the initial evaluation of the stranger was relatively neutral. If this is the case, congruity theory would predict that evaluations of the source will decrease relatively more when he is a stranger than when he is an acquaintance, while evaluations of oneself (the "issue") will decrease more when the source is an acquaintance than when he is a stranger. The results obtained are consistent with these predictions.

An interesting extension of this interpretation of Harvey et al.'s findings is supported in a study by Weiss (1957). To recapitulate, Harvey et al. found (and congruity theory predicts) that a negative association between a source S and a positively regarded issue (I) will decrease E_I more when E_S is initially very favorable than when it is less so. However, congruity theory also predicts that E_S can be increased by associating S with an issue that the subject (P) evaluates favorably. These two effects in combination imply that S will have more influence upon P's evaluation of one issue (I_1) after he has become associated positively with a second issue (I_2) that P favors. To test this hypothesis, Weiss asked subjects to read an article opposing fluoridation (I_1) which ostensibly had been taken from the *New York Daily Worker*, a presumably unfavorable source (S). Before reading this article, however, subjects received a second communication of one of three types: (*a*) an article from the *Daily Worker* favoring academic freedom $(I_2$, a concept favored by $P)$, (*b*) a nonpolitical article from the *Daily Worker*, on an issue evaluated neutrally by P, or (*c*) an article from the *New York Times* favoring academic freedom. Type (*a*) communications were expected to increase P's evaluation of S, and therefore to increase the impact of the message opposing flouridation, while Types (*b*) and (*c*) were not expected to have any effect. In fact, subjects decreased their evaluations of flouridation under all three conditions, but decreased them significantly more when they had read Type (*a*) messages than when they had received other types.

The experiments described so far have dealt with the effects of an association between two elements upon evaluations of these elements. A corollary of Principle 2 is that if two elements are already associated, change in the evaluation of one of them should predictably affect evaluations of the other. For example, information that increases the evaluation of an issue I should also increase the evaluation of a source who is associated positively with it, decrease the evaluation of a source who is associated negatively with it, and have no effect upon the evaluation of a source who is unrelated to it. Information that decreases the evaluation of I should have the opposite effects upon evaluations of these sources. These hypotheses were investigated by Tannenbaum and Gengel (1966). Subjects first evaluated three psychologists (S_1, S_2, and S_3) and also the concept of teaching machines (I). They then received communications, ostensibly drawn from an American Psychological Association sponsored symposium on teaching machines, which indicated that S_1 favored teaching machines, S_2 was indifferent to them, and S_3 opposed them. Finally, they received a persuasive communication that either supported or opposed teaching machines. The three sources and I were then reevaluated. Subjects were divided into those whose evaluations of I increased following the persuasive communication and those whose evaluations of I decreased after receiving this message. Changes in evaluations of each source by each group of subjects are shown in Table 6.6. Unexpectedly, both groups of subjects substantially increased their ratings of S_2. Tannenbaum and Gengel point out that a general increase in evaluations of all three sources may have resulted from information that they had participated on an ostensibly prestigeful professional panel. If this is the case, obtained charges in E_{S2} might be interpreted as a baseline for comparing changes in evaluations of the other two sources. The results of this study would then strongly support congruity theory. Relative to changes in E_{S2}, subjects who increased their evaluations of I increased their evaluation of S_1 by 1.51 units and decreased their evaluation of S_3 by 2.82 units; on the other hand, subjects who decreased their evaluations of I decreased their evaluation of S_1 by 3.77 units and increased their rating of S_3 by 1.36 units.

Let us recapitulate the implications of the last two studies described above. Tannenbaum and Gengel showed that changes in the evaluation of an issue (I_1) produce changes in the evaluation of a source (S) who is associated with this issue. Weiss demonstrated that the association of S with one issue (I_1) can affect the influence of S's statements about a second issue (I_2). The next logical step would be to show that changes in the evaluation of I_1 will produce predictable changes in the evaluation of I_2 by virtue of the common association of these issues with S. Consider four conditions:

1. S is associated positively with both I_1 and I_2 (in the terminology of psycho-logic, SpI_1 and SpI_2).
2. S is associated positively with I_1 and negatively with I_2 (SpI_1 and SnI_2).
3. S is associated negatively with I_1 and positively with I_2 (SnI_1 and SpI_2).
4. S is associated negatively with both I_1 and I_2 (SnI_1 and SnI_2).

Now, assume that E_{I1} increases. According to congruity theory, this should

TABLE 6.6

Mean Attitude Change toward Sources Favoring (L+),
Neutral toward (Lo), and Opposed to (L–) Concept
as a Function of Concept Favorableness
(adapted from Tannenbaum & Gengel, 1966, p. 302)

| | Source | | | |
Concept manipulation	L+(S₁)	Lo(S₂)	L–(S₃)	Marginals
Positive	5.49	3.98	1.16	3.54
Negative	–.25	3.52	4.88	2.72
Marginals	2.62	3.75	3.02	

produce an increase in E_{I2} under condition 1, but a decrease in E_{I2} under condition 2. Similarly, a decrease in E_S should produce a decrease in E_{I2} under condition 3 and an increase in E_{I2} under condition 4. Thus, an increase in E_{I1} should produce an increase in E_{I2} under conditions 1 and 4 and a decrease in E_{I2} under conditions 2 and 3. A decrease in E_{I1} should have the opposite effects.[6]

Tannenbaum (1966) obtained impressive support for these complex hypotheses. Subjects first received one of four types of information about a relatively neutral source's evaluation of two concepts: teaching machines (I_1) and Spence learning theory (I_2). Each type of information established one of the four pairs of associations described above. Subjects then read a persuasive communication either supporting or opposing teaching machines. Changes in E_S and E_{I2} under each of the four conditions are shown in Table 6.7. In all cases, results are consistent with predictions. Since they could also be predicted by other formulations of cognitive organization (see Footnote 6), these data of course do not provide conclusive evidence of the validity of congruity theory. Nevertheless, this and the other studies described above clearly demonstrate the usefulness of the theory in generating predictions in this area of research.

---

[6] These predictions, which may be somewhat hard to follow on the basis of congruity theory, are more easily seen by applying the principles of psycho-logic. For example, suppose that P's evaluation of I_1 becomes positive; that is, PpI_1. Then, in condition 1,

$$PpI_1 \cap SpI_1 \cap SpI_2 \supset PpS \cap SpI_2 \supset PpI_2$$

Similarly, in condition 2,

$$PpI_1 \cap SpI_1 \cap SpI_2 \supset PpS \cap SnI_2 \supset PnI_2$$

Predictions under other conditions may be generated similarly. The two formulations are completely consistent in their predictions, and therefore the evidence to be reported may be interpreted as support for either formulation.

TABLE 6.7

Mean Attitude Change toward Source (E_s) and Learning Theory (E_{l2})
as a Function of Favorableness of Teaching Machines (E_{l1})
and Associations between Source and Concepts
(adapted from Tannenbaum, 1966, pp. 496-497)

Evaluation of I_1	Association between source and concepts			
	SpI_1, SpI_2	SpI_1, SnI_2	SnI_1, SpI_2	SnI_1, SnI_2
A. ΔE_s				
E_{l1} positive	+4.96	+4.72	−2.52	−2.96
E_{l1} negative	−3.96	−3.00	+3.76	+3.32
B. ΔE_{l2}				
E_{l2} positive	+2.84	−1.92	− .76	+1.56
E_{l2} negative	−2.72	+ .60	+2.12	−2.52

G. Effects of Information Content — Determinants of the "Assertion Constant"

In their closing remarks, Osgood and Tannenbaum (1955) point out that several factors other than congruity may determine the effect of a communication from a source upon judgments of both the source and the issue to which the message pertains. However, if congruity principles or a modification of them are to be useful in generating accurate quantitative predictions of the attitude change, these factors must be identified and their effects must be clearly understood.

When a source is associated with an issue through a communication, the evaluation of the issue may be affected not only by characteristics of the source but also by characteristics of the information contained in the communication (that is, by the quality of the arguments presented, the extremity of the position advocated, the literary style in which the message is written, etc.) The effects of these characteristics are implicitly taken into account by the "assertion constant." For example, the magnitude of this constant is presumably greater when the arguments presented are more persuasive. Several characteristics of information that may determine the magnitude of its influence are discussed in detail in Chapter 8. However, since a general understanding of the determinants and effects of the assertion constant is necessary in order to evaluate the usefulness of congruity theory as a formulation of cognitive organization, certain considerations are worth mentioning at this time.

Two assumptions made by Osgood and Tannenbaum in postulating an assertion constant are of particular importance. First, the constant was applied only to the evaluation of the issue about which the assertion is made. This decision was based upon the finding that evaluations of the issue changed *relatively* more in the direction of the assertion than did changes in source evaluations under analogous conditions. However, this finding does not necessarily preclude the possibility that the quality of the assertion affects the evaluations of both the source and issue; it indicates only that the assertion affects E_I more than it affects E_S. If the assertion is embedded in a communication, factors such as writing style and the quality of the arguments presented may affect the recipient's beliefs that S has attributes such as "intelligent," "logical," "persuasive," etc. If this occurs, E_S should be affected as well as E_I. Unfortunately, this possibility has not been determined empirically.

A second assumption made by Osgood and Tannenbaum is that the "assertion constant" is in fact a constant. This assumption implies that the effects predicted by congruity theory and those attributable to information content are independent and additive. Strong and perhaps surprising support for this assumption was obtained in an important study by Tannenbaum (1967). Four different persuasive communications were constructed for use in this study, two of which $(I+)$ supported the concept of teaching machines and two of which $(I-)$ opposed this concept. Two sources were also selected, one of which was favorable $(S+)$ and the other of which was unfavorable $(S-)$. After making initial evaluations of the issue, subjects received two communications, one attributed to $S+$ and the other attributed to $S-$. Four different pairs of messages were considered:

1. $S+I+$ and $S-I-$ (that is, a communication supporting I from a favorable source, and a communication opposing I from an unfavorable source)
2. $S+I-$ and $S-I+$
3. $S+I+$ and $S-I+$
4. $S+I-$ and $S-I-$

After receiving one of these pairs of communications, subjects reevaluated I. The mean change in E_I under each condition is shown in Table 6.8.

There are several ways of looking at these data. Note that according to congruity theory, $S+I+$ and $S-I-$ communications should both increase E_I while $S+I-$ and $S-I+$ should both decrease E_I. For convenience, denote the magnitude of these effects as C+ and C−, respectively. In addition, the information content of $S+I+$ and $S-I+$ communications should both increase E_I while the content of $S+I-$ and $S-I-$ messages should both decrease E_I. Denote these effects as Inf+ and Inf−, respectively. Now, if the effects of congruity and information content are independent and additive, the change produced by each of the four pairs of communications should be

TABLE 6.8

Predicted and Obtained Change in Evaluations of *I* Under
Each Communication Condition (from Tannenbaum, 1967)

Communication pair	Predicted change	Obtained change
1. S+I+ and S–I–	C+ + Inf+ + C+ + Inf–	+5.36
2. S+I– and S–I+	C– + Inf– + C– + Inf+	–4.16
3. S+I+ and S–I+	C+ +Inf+ + C– + Inf+	+2.30
4. S+I– and S–I–	C– + Inf– + C+ + Inf–	–2.42

the sum of their individual contributions. These sums are also shown in Table 6.8. Note that the sum of the predicted effects of Pairs 1 and 2 (that is, 2C+ + 2C– + 2Inf+ + 2Inf–) is equal to the sum of the predicted effects of Pairs 3 and 4. The actual magnitudes of these sums are 1.20 and –.12, respectively. While Tannenbaum does not test this difference statistically, it is undoubtedly not significant. Thus, the assumption that source and content effects are additive is supported by these data.

Other comparisons are worth noting. For example, the theoretical difference between the effects of Pairs 1 and 2 (2C+ – 2C–) is twice the effect of congruity, independent of content effects. This difference is 9.52. On the other hand, the difference between the effects of Pairs 3 and 4 (2Inf+ – 2Inf–) is twice the effect of content, independent of congruity effects. This difference is 4.72. In other words, congruity effects were twice as great as content effects in this study. Caution should obviously be taken in generalizing these results, since the effect of content varies with the quality of the particular communications presented. However, the magnitude of the source effect obtained in this study is impressive.

1. *Permanence of Source Effects.* Source effects may nevertheless be much less permanent than the effects of information content. In an early study by Hovland and Weiss (1951), subjects read articles about four different topics. Each article was attributed either to a highly credible source or to a relatively unreliable source. (For example, the high and low credibility sources of communications about the "future of movie theatres" were *Fortune* magazine and the writer of a syndicated movie gossip column, respectively.) Subjects who had initially indicated their opinion on each topic in a questionnaire administered five days before the experiment reported their opinions again after receiving the communications, and still a third time four weeks later. As predicted, communications from highly credible sources had initially more positive influence upon subjects' opinions than did those from low credibility sources. However, the influence of communications from high

credibility sources decreased over the four week period following their presentation, while the influence of communications from low credibility sources actually increased over this period! Why should these changes occur?

One plausible explanation of Hovland and Weiss's findings is based in part upon the assumption that source and content effects are independent. Suppose that over a period of time the source of a communication is forgotten but the content of the communication remains in memory. Then, judgments made some time after the communication was presented should be a function primarily of information content, the effects of the source having been dissipated. Since source effects presumably add to content effects when the source is favorable but subtract from content effects when the source is unfavorable, the decrease in source effects over time could account for the changes observed by Hovland and Weiss. This interpretation was investigated by Kelman and Hovland (1953). Their study was basically similar to Hovland and Weiss's except that in the second experimental session, half of the subjects under each source credibility condition were reminded of the source of the original communication before their opinions were reassessed. The initial effects of source credibility were retained among these subjects but were not apparent among subjects who were not reminded of the source. These results provide indirect support for the hypothesis that source effects and information effects are often additive, but that source effects, while initially strong, are much less permanent than information effects.

2. Contingencies in the Independence of Source and Information Effects. The conclusion that source and content effects are independent, if generally valid, is of methodological importance. It implies that the influence of specific characteristics of the information presented about an object can be studied independently of the effects of cognitive reorganization as implied by congruity principles. Unfortunately, the generality of this conclusion may be limited. One characteristic of message content, not considered in Tannenbaum's study, is the discrepancy between the position advocated in the information and that held by the subject. The effects of differences in this discrepancy appear to be highly contingent upon characteristics of the source. It should be noted of course that the magnitude of such a discrepancy depends both upon the characteristics of the communication and upon the recipient's initial position. Indeed, some studies have attempted to vary discrepancy by varying the extremity of subjects' initial attitudes while holding the position of the communication constant. Under such conditions, congruity theory predicts that the greater the discrepancy (that is, the more extreme the subject's initial evaluation of the issue), the less effect the communication will have upon this evaluation. Results obtained are usually consistent with these predictions (cf. Hovland, Harvey, & Sherif, 1957).

If, on the other hand, discrepancy is a function of the position advocated in the communication, holding the initial evaluation of the issue constant, the effects of such a discrepancy are not predictable from congruity theory. It would be nice if these effects, like the effects of information content reported by Tannenbaum, simply added to the effects predicted by congruity theory, and thus could be incorporated into the assertion constant. This possibility is unlikely, however, since several studies have shown that the effect of communication discrepancy depends upon the initial evaluation of the source. For example, Bergin (1962) found that the attitude change produced by a communication from a very favorable source increased with the amount of the discrepancy between the position advocated and the subject's initial position. However the amount of change produced by a communication from an unfavorable source decreased as its position became further removed from the subject's. In another study, Aronson, Turner, and Carlsmith (1963) found that when the source was assumed to be "mildly credible," the relation between amount of attitude change and communication discrepancy was curvilinear. Perhaps attitude change first increases and then decreases as the communication becomes more discrepant from one's view, regardless of the source; however, the amount of discrepancy that produces maximum attitude change is a positive function of source prestige. In any event, the above findings imply that the magnitude of the "assertion constant" is in some cases a function of the initial attitude toward the source and, therefore, that source and content effects are not always as easily separable as Tannenbaum's study seems to suggest.

H. A Subjective Probability Formulation of Source and Information Effects: An Alternative to Congruity Theory

While congruity principles are clearly useful in generating hypotheses concerning source effects upon attitude change, other theoretical formulations can generate similar predictions. For example, most of the results obtained by Harvey et al. (1957), Weiss (1957), and Tannenbaum (1966) are consistent with the principles of cognitive balance and psycho-logic, as well as congruity theory, and can also be interpreted by applying a model such as Fishbein's. Moreover, the quantitative accuracy of the predictions based upon congruity theory is limited.

An alternative formulation of source effects, which has the added advantage of allowing a direct investigation of the extent to which these effects are independent of information content, is suggested by the subjective probability model proposed in Chapter 4. Assume that:

$$E_I = P_C E_{I/c} + (1 - P_C) E_{I/c'} \qquad (6.10)$$

where E_I is the evaluation of an issue or concept I, P_C is the belief that a communication from source S would support this position, and $E_{I/c}$ and $E_{I/c'}$ are the conditional evaluations of I, given that C does and does not support it. The difference between $E_{I/c}$ and $E_{I/c'}$ is an indication of source credibility, or the relevance of S's opinion to the evaluation of I.

1. *Separation of Source and Information Effects.* To demonstrate the use of this formulation, first suppose that a communication supporting I is presented and is attributed to S. The effect of this communication upon E_I should be predictable from changes in beliefs comprising the right side of Eq. (6.10). If source and information effects are indeed independent, the magnitude of their contributions can be identified. To the extent that communication content affects beliefs independently of the source of this communication, it should have equal effects upon both $E_{I/C}$ and $E_{I/C'}$ while leaving the difference between the conditionals (that is, source credibility) unaffected. An index of this "information" effect ($\Delta E_{I,\;Inf}$) would be the mean change in these conditionals,[7] that is,

$$\Delta E_{I,\;Inf} = \Delta (E_{I/\;C} + E_{I/C'})/2$$

The contribution of the source to change in E_I ($\Delta E_{I,s}$) would be estimated from the equation

$$\Delta E_{I,s} = \Delta P_C (E_{I/C} - E_{I/C'}).$$

(This change would of course be positive when $E_{I/C} > E_{I/C'}$ and negative when $E_{I/C} < E_{I/C'}$) The overall change in E_I would simply be the sum of these two effects (see footnote 7).

The results reported by Hovland and his colleagues are worth considering in this context. These authors argue that after a period of time has elapsed, the source becomes dissociated from the communication content. This may be indicated by a regression of the value of P_C toward .5. This regression

---

[7] In general,

$$E_I + \Delta E_I = (P_C + \Delta P_C)\,(E_{I/C} + \Delta E_{I/C})$$

$$+ (1 - P_C - \Delta P_C)\,(E_{I/C'} + \Delta E_{I/C'}).$$

It can be shown by rearranging terms that

$$\Delta E_I = \Delta P_C(E_{I/C} - E_{I/C'}) + \Delta P_C\,(\Delta E_{I/C} - \Delta E_{I/C'})$$

$$+ P_C\,\Delta E_{I/C} + (1 - P_C)\,\Delta E_{I/C'}.$$

If source and information effects are independent, $\Delta E_{I/C'} = \Delta E_{I/C'}$ and therefore the second term on the right side of this equation is 0. Moreover, if this is true,

$$P_C\,\Delta E_{I/C} + (1 - P_C)\Delta E_{I/C} = \Delta E_{I/C} = \Delta E_{I/C} = \Delta E_{I/C} + E_{I/C'})/2.$$

Thus,

$$\Delta E_I = \Delta P_C\,(E_{IC} - E_{I/C'}) + \Delta(E_{IC} + E_{IC'})/2$$

$$= \Delta E_{I,s} + \Delta E_{I,\;Inf}$$

as these terms are defined in the text.

would produce a corresponding regression of E_I toward the average of $E_{I/C}$ and $E_{I/C'}$, or toward the evaluation of I induced by communication content alone. Note that the change in E_I would be negative when $E_{I/C} > E_{I/C'}$ (when S is high in credibility), but positive when $E_{I/C} < E_{I/C'}$ (S is low in credibility). This is of course what Hovland et al. found. However, it is important to bear in mind that to obtain the apparent increase in opinion change over time, S must in fact be viewed as "negatively credible"; that is, I must be evaluated less favorably when S supports it than when he does not. Sources of this nature may be difficult to find in practice. It is more often the case that low credibility sources are simply unreliable, and therefore $E_{I/C} = E_{I/C'}$. Under this condition no change in E_I would be expected over time.

If source and information effects are *not* independent, the preceding analyses would not be strictly valid. However, the extent of their independence may be investigated directly. Suppose that a communication containing either strong or weak arguments in support of X is attributed to either a high or a low credibility source. It is conceivable that the judgment of the source's credibility is affected by the quality of the arguments in the communication attributed to him as well as by the description of him provided by the experimenter. To this extent, the communication content should affect the difference between $E_{I/C}$ and $E_{I/C'}$ as well as the average of these two conditional evaluations. It is also conceivable that source characteristics affect judgments of the quality of the arguments presented, and therefore affect the contribution of communication content. To this extent, the manipulation of source credibility should affect the average of $E_{I/C}$ and $E_{I/C'}$ as well as the difference between them. The proposed model allows one to investigate systematically the validity of the assumption that source and information effects are independent, but automatically takes any nonindependence into account in generating quantitative predictions of opinion change.

2. *Other Implications for Congruity Resolution Phenomena.* Congruity theory has been of particular interest because of its ability to predict simultaneous changes in evaluations of both a source and a concept, following receipt of a communication associating them. The probability model may also be used to describe this phenomena, and to clarify the conditions in which it will occur.

Suppose again that we present a communication that associates a source S with a concept X. In general, the change in evaluation of X would be given by the equation

$$\Delta E_I = \Delta [P_C E_{I/C} + (1 - P_C) E_{I/C'}] \tag{6.11}$$

where the terms are as defined previously. Change in the evaluation of S would be described by the equation

$$\Delta E_S = \Delta [P_C E_{S/C} + (1 - P_C) E_{S/C'}] \tag{6.12}$$

where E_I is the evaluation of S, and $E_{S/C}$ and $E_{S/C'}$ are the conditional evaluations of S given that a communication from him does and does not advocate a particular position regarding I. Note that if a communication generally has greater effect upon judgments of an issue than upon judgments of the source (Osgood & Tannenbaum, 1955), the difference betwen $E_{I/C}$ and $E_{I/C'}$ should be greater than the difference between $E_{S/C}$ and $E_{S/C'}$.

The effects of factors such as incredulity and the assertion constant are automatically taken into account in Eqs. (6.11)-(6.12). If the quality of the communication affects the magnitude of the assertion constant, this effect should be reflected by changes in $E_{I/C}$ and $E_{I/C'}$ after one reads the communication. If the communication is treated with incredulity, either for reasons suggested by Osgood and Tannenbaum or because the message is simply too extreme to be believed, this should be reflected by a smaller change in P_C. Thus the existence of these effects does not necessarily decrease the possibility that Eqs. (6.11)-(6.12) describe source effects accurately.

A central hypothesis of congruity theory, that more extreme initial evaluations are less likely to change, is less obviously predictable from these equations. However, consider the conditions under which an initially extreme value of E_I would occur. First, assume that the subject is not very familiar with S. In such an event, his initial estimate of P_C (his belief that a communication from S would support I) is likely to be fairly moderate, and therefore $P_C = P_{C'}$. To this extent, an extremely high (or low) initial value of E_I could theoretically occur only if $E_{I/C}$ and $E_{I/C'}$ are *both* high (or both low), and thus are fairly equal in both magnitude and direction. But under these conditions, a change in P_C should not substantially affect E_I.[8] Thus this reasoning implies that extreme initial values of E_I (and, by analogy, of E_S) are unlikely to change appreciably, as congruity theory predicts. However, it does *not* imply that moderate initial evaluations *will* change substantially, since it is not necessary that $E_{I/C}$ and $E_{I/C'}$ differ greatly under these conditions.

An initially extreme value of E_I could also occur if $E_{I/C}$ is extremely positive and P_C is initially very high. This would imply that S is both credible and is believed to advocate an evaluation of I ($E_{I/C}$) that is similar to the subject's personal evaluation (E_I). Under such conditions, the initial evaluation of S is likely to be positive. In this case, a communication from S opposing I might have a substantial effect upon P_C, and thus upon E_I. However, this change is also consistent with congruity theory, which of course predicts that an extreme attitude towards an issue *will* change substantially if it is opposed by a source toward whom attitudes are just as strong.

Regardless of their quantitative accuracy, Eqs. (6.11)-(6.12) are of heuristic value, since they help to identify more general questions about the funda-

---

[8] If $E_{I/C}$ and $E_{I/C'}$ are minimally affected by the communication itself, $\Delta E_I = \Delta P_C (E_{I/C} - E_{I/C'})$. Thus, changes in E_I produced by a given change in P_C is a function of the difference in magnitude between $E_{I/C}$ and $E_{I/C'}$.

mental processes underlying source effects than does congruity theory. For example, consider Weiss's study, which showed that source effects upon P's attitude toward one concept (I_1) were increased by associating S with a position on a second issue (I_2) that P favored. Why should this occur? According to Eq. (6.10), there are at least two possibilities. First, a communication associating S and I_2 may increase P's belief that S is a reliable source and therefore increases the difference between $E_{n/c}$ and $E_{n/c'}$. Second, the belief that S advocates a particular position regarding I_1 (that is, P_c) may change more when S has previously been found to agree with P about I_2. This might be true if P tends to pay more attention to communications from sources he believes generally agree with him. The relative validity of these explanations seems worth investigating regardless of the quantitative accuracy of Eq. (6.11).

Harvey et al.'s study is also worth reconsidering from this general point of view. These authors found that negative ratings by an acquaintance decreased P's self evaluation (E) more, but affected the source evaluation (E) less, than similar ratings by a stranger. Furthermore, P was more apt to deny the credibility of ratings by an acquaintance. How might these differences be reflected in Eqs. (6.11) - (6.12)? The relatively greater tendency to deny the credibility of ratings made by acquaintances suggests that P_c changed less under acquaintance conditions. While this could account for the relatively smaller change in E_s when S was an acquaintance, it would also imply less change in E_I under this condition, contrary to the results obtained. However, it seems reasonable to suppose that an acquaintance's evaluation of P is regarded as more relevant to P's self-evaluation than is a stranger's evaluation. If this is so, the difference in the "conditional" issue evaluations ($E_{I/c} - E_{I/c'}$) would be relatively greater when S is an acquaintance. This difference in relevance may be sufficient to produce a greater change in E_I under these conditions, even though the change in P_c is less. In any event, the subjective probability formulation being proposed provides a possible mechanism for describing and interpreting these effects and their relations within a single theoretical framework.

I. Summary and Evaluations

Congruity theory consists of two basic principles. One pertains to the manner in which information about an object combines to affect evaluations of the object, and the second pertains to the relation between the evaluation of an object and subsequent evaluations of its attributes. The quantification of these principles proposed by Osgood and his colleagues has not been very successful in generating accurate predictions of attitude change. Moreover, inconsistency among cognitions as defined by congruity principles does not decrease over time once these cognitions are made salient. These findings call into question the validity of the hypothesis that subjects actively organize their cognitions in the manner implied by these principles.

At a nonquantitative level, however, congruity principles are useful in predicting the direction and relative magnitude of simultaneous changes in more than one cognition. Unfortunately, research performed to date has seldom provided critical tests of the theory, and thus the results of this research are also consistent with several alternative formulations of cognitive organization.

Tests of congruity theory as a formulation of attitude change have been generally restricted to a consideration of the effects of associating a source and an attitude object through an assertion. The formulation should apply equally well, and perhaps better, to changes in evaluations of objects that are associated in other ways. (For example, one should be able to predict changes in evaluations of two persons as a result of information that both are members of the same political organization, that they are relatives, etc. Predictions of these effects should not require the introduction of factors such as the "assertion constant.") Moreover, the theory can be generalized to predict the simultaneous change in more than two elements as a result of information that these elements are associated. These possibilities would be worth exploring.

III
THE RECEPTION, ACCEPTANCE AND INTEGRATION OF INFORMATION

In evaluating the support for theoretical formulations of cognitive organization we considered several studies of the effects of change in one cognition upon other related cognitions. In this research, change in the first cognition was usually induced by the information contained in a verbal communication. The factors that determine the magnitude of such a communication's influence upon cognitions to which it directly pertains have thus far been largely ignored. For new information about an object to influence beliefs about the object, it must first be received and understood and must then be accepted as valid. Three classes of variables may affect reception and acceptance: characteristics of the situation in which the information is presented, characteristics of the recipient of the information (individual difference variables), and characteristics of the information itself. In the first chapter in this section we will be concerned primarily with the effects of the first two classes of variables. In subsequent chapters, we will focus on characteristics of the information presented, how such characteristics determine the magnitude of the information's influence, and rules that govern the manner in which different pieces of information combine to affect judgments.

7
THE RECEPTION AND ACCEPTANCE
OF INFORMATION

Before new information can affect judgments of an object to which it applies, it must first be received and comprehended, and then must be accepted as valid. The reception and acceptance of information may depend in part upon characteristics of the information itself (its clarity, its internal consistency, etc.), the effects of which are discussed in Chapter 9. However, these processes may also depend upon characteristics of the situation in which the information is presented and upon characteristics of the receiver. A large number of situational and individual difference variables undoubtedly affect reception and acceptance, and a complete discussion of their effects is beyond the scope of this book. However, the influence of many of these variables may be described and interpreted within a fairly simple conceptual framework. In this chapter, we will outline an approach to analyzing reception and acceptance processes and will apply the approach to some representative bodies of research on attitude and opinion change.

I. A CONCEPTUAL FRAMEWORK

The basic ideas contained in this chapter, like those pervading many other chapters of this book, have been inspired by the work of William McGuire. Many readers will undoubtedly recognize the formulation to be proposed here as similar in its assumptions and implications to McGuire's (1968b) theory of persuadability. It differs from McGuire's theory primarily (a) in that the factors assumed to determine the influence of a communication are expressed probabilistically and (b) in its account of the effects of experimental "demand" characteristics.

The probability that a subject is influenced by a given communication (P_I) is predictable from the equation:

$$P_I = P_R \, P_{I/R} + P_{R'} P_{I/R'}, \tag{7.1}$$

where P_R is the probability of receiving and comprehending the communication, and $P_{I/R}$ and $P_{I/R}{}'$ are the probabilities of being influenced by the communication, given that one does and does not receive it, respectively.[1, 2] For simplicity, let $P_{I/R} = P_Y$, where P_Y is the probability of yielding to the communication given that it is received. This probability may be estimated from the equation

$$P_Y = P_{CA} P_{Y/CA} + P_{CA'} P_{Y/CA'} \qquad (7.2)$$

where P_{CA} and P_{CA}' are the probabilities that the arguments contained in the communication are and are not successfully refuted through counterarguing, and $P_{Y/CA}$ and $P_{Y/CA}'$ are the probabilities of yielding if the contents of the communication are and are not refuted. Substituting this expression into Eq. (7.1),

$$P_I = P_R (P_{CA} P_{Y/CA} + P_{CA'} P_{Y/CA'}) + P_{R'}P_{I/R'}. \qquad (7.3)$$

While the above equation appears complex, its general implications are clear. That is, the probability that a communication will have influence (P_I) is a multiplicative function of (a) the probability that it is received and understood, (b) the probability that the arguments contained in it are discredited, and (c) the extent to which yielding is contingent upon the validity of the arguments contained in the communication (the difference between $P_{Y/CA}$ and $P_{Y/CA}'$). According to this formulation, situational and individual difference variables affect the impact of a persuasive communication because of their influence upon one or more of the components of Eq. (7.3).

A. The Role of P_R and P_{CA}

The combined effects of P_R and P_{CA} are of both theoretical and practical importance. To clarify the nature of these effects, assume for the present that a subject is not influenced by a communication he does not receive ($P_{I/R'} = 0$). Assume further that a subject will always accept the position advocated by a communication when he personally does not refute the arguments contained in it ($P_{Y/CA'} = 1$) and will never adopt this position when he does refute these arguments effectively ($P_{Y/CA} = 0$). Then, Eq. (7.3) reduces to

$$P_I = P_R P_{CA'} = P_R(1 - P_{CA}) \qquad (7.4)$$

This equation implies that two factors, one of which affects message reception and the other of which affects the persuasiveness of the arguments in the message, will have multiplicative, and thus interactive, effects upon the

---

[1] Note that, unlike similar equations used to describe cognitive organization, the components of this equation refer to objective probabilities and not subjective probabilities. Thus, the equation necessarily provides an accurate description of the processes to which it pertains.

[2] Here, and elsewhere in this chapter, an understanding of the contents of the communication is considered to be part of "reception."

communication's influence. Often, however, a single factor may have similar effects upon both reception and counterarguing. In such cases, the effect of the communication may be difficult to predict unless the values of P_R and P_{CA} are known. For example, assume that the likelihood of receiving a communication and the likelihood of refuting the arguments contained in it are both moderate; that is, $P_R = P_{CA} = .5$. Then from Eq. (7.4), $P_I = .25$. Now compare this condition to one in which the probabilities of receiving the communication and of refuting it are both low (e.g., $P_R = P_{CA} = .2$) and also to one in which these probabilities are both high ($P_R = P_{CA} = .8$). In each of these latter conditions, Eq. (7.4) predicts that $P_I = .16$. In other words, relative to "control" conditions, the impact of the communication will be reduced by factors that *either* increase or decrease the probability of both receiving a communication and refuting its contents. There are numerous implications of this general hypothesis which we shall consider presently. To give but one example, P_R and P_{CA} may both increase with the general intelligence of a recipient, and also with his knowledge of the issue to which the message pertains. To this extent, subjects who are very intelligent and those who are very unintelligent will both be less influenced by a given communication than will moderately intelligent subjects. Similarly, very informed and very uninformed subjects will be influenced less than those who are moderately informed about the issue at hand.

Another implication of the above analysis is that situational factors that simultaneously affect P_R and P_{CA} may not have detectable effects upon the influence of the information presented unless individual differences in these probabilities are controlled. For example, suppose that both P_R and P_{CA} are .8 for subjects of high ability who are asked to pay complete attention to a message, but that they decrease to .5 when the attention of these subjects is distracted. Assume that the corresponding probabilities for low ability subjects are both .5 and both .2, respectively. On the basis of Eq. (7.4), the likelihood that high ability subjects are influenced should increase from .16 to .25 as their attention decreases, while the likelihood that low ability subjects are influenced should decrease from .15 to .16. Thus, averaged over ability levels, the situational variables affecting attention would appear to have no effect upon the influence of the communication.

B. The Role of $P_{Y/CA}$, $P_{Y/CA'}$ and $P_{I/R'}$

In the preceding analysis we have assumed that $P_{I/R'} = 0$, $P_{Y/CA} = 0$, and $P_{Y/CA'} = 1$. While it is reasonable to assume that in general $P_{Y/CA} < P_{Y/CA'}$, the magnitude of this inequality, and thus the effect of reception and counterarguing upon the impact of a communication, may vary. This difference may depend in part upon the relevance of the arguments in the communication to the position being advocated. It may also depend upon situational factors, and upon characteristics of the recipient himself, that induce him either to agree publicly with the implications of a communication, despite his belief that the arguments presented are weak, or to disagree publicly with the position advocated, even when he does not or cannot refute the arguments presented. For example, a subject who receives a persuasive communication may sometimes believe that the person presenting the message (e.g., the experimenter) agrees with the position advocated and would like him to do so as well. Differences in the attempts to comply with such expectancies would presumably be reflected by differences in $P_{Y/CA}$. In other conditions, a subject may believe that he would be considered wishy-washy, and thus be evaluated negatively, if he were to conform to the position advocated, and thus he may not be overtly influenced despite the fact that he cannot refute the arguments presented. In still other cases, a subject may believe that the arguments presented are probably weak and easily refuted, even though he personally has not tried to refute them. The effect of differences in the strength of these latter beliefs would be indicated by differences in $P_{Y/CA'}$.

$P_{Y/CA}$ and $P_{Y/CA'}$ should be distinguished from $P_{I/R'}$, or the likelihood of being influenced given that the contents of a communication are not received. While it may seem intuitively reasonable to assume that $P_{I/R'} = 0$, it is conceivable that situational factors produce systematic changes in opinions for reasons that are independent of the communication being presented. For example, there is some evidence, to be discussed later in this chapter, that subjects who expect to receive a communication change their opinion toward the position they expect will be advocated in the message—in *anticipation* of receiving it. Differences in the magnitude of such changes would presumably be reflected by differences in $P_{I/R'}$. We will consider research and theory bearing on these questions when we discuss "forewarning" effects later in this chapter.

2. Measurement of Mediating Variables

The usefulness of Eq. (7.3) in describing attitude change processes ultimately depends upon the availability of adequate indices of the variables comprising this equation. Differences in P_R may conceivably be reflected by differences in the ability to recall the content of the communication after it is presented. However, the recall of factual material may be an insufficient index of of P_R if, as we have proposed (footnote 2), the comprehension of the material and its implications is also considered to be a necessary condition for "reception." While a measure of P_{CA} is somewhat less obvious, one index of this quantity, proposed by Osterhouse and Brock (1970), may be the number of counterarguments a subject can generate within a given period of time after receiving the message. (The use of this index is based upon the assumption that if the subject has effectively refuted the arguments contained in a communication during the course of its presentation, he should subsequently be able to list more counterarguments than if he has received the message without trying to refute its contents, or if he has tried but been unable to do so.) This measure is not ideal, since it does not provide an indication of the *effectiveness* of the counterarguments generated (or, more important, how effective the subject *himself* believes they are). Moreover, it does not distinguish between general arguments against the proposition and arguments against the specific points made in the message being presented. The incorporation of qualitative differences in counterarguments into Osterhouse and Brock's measure would provide a more valid estimate of P_{CA} as we have defined it.

The value of $P_{I/R'}$ in any given situation is often difficult to predict *a priori*. In principle, this fact should not create serious problems for the formulation we have proposed, since the value can be inferred from changes in the beliefs of "control" subjects who, though undergoing the same procedure and initial instructions as "experimental" subjects, do not receive the communication. Unfortunately, however, such "control" subjects have seldom been run in experiments performed to date.

Direct measures of $P_{Y/CA}$ and $P_{Y/CA'}$ are more difficult to obtain. However, Eq. (7.3) is necessarily a mathematically valid description of the relations among the probabilities involved (see footnote 1). Thus, if valid measures of P_{CA}, P_R, and $P_{I/R'}$ can be obtained, situational differences in the impact of a persuasive communication that are not predictable from observed differences in these probabilities must necessarily be attributable to differences in the two conditional probabilities.

Since measures of the variables described above have typically not been obtained in experiments on communication effectiveness, an application of Eq. (7.3) to this research is necessarily speculative. Nevertheless, the equation may help to identify the possible processes that underlie attitude change in these studies and to assess the generalizability of these processes. To demonstrate the validity of this assertion, let us consider in the context of the framework we have proposed four representative areas of research on communication effectiveness. These areas concern the effects of distraction, the influence of fear-arousing communications, the determinants of resistance to persuasion, and the effects of forewarning.

II. EFFECTS OF DISTRACTION

A. General Considerations

Equation (7.3) implies that factors that simultaneously decrease the reception and comprehension of a communication and the tendency to refute it will first increase the influence of the information but then, beyond a certain point, will decrease the influence of this information. Among the more obvious factors of this sort are those that distract the subject from concentrating on the contents of the communication as it is presented. Since a fair amount of research has been performed on the effects of distraction

TABLE 7.1

P_R, P_{CA} and P_I as a Function of Distraction (X)

Assuming $P_I = P_R(1 - P_{CA})$

Instance and variable		Level of distraction												
		X_0	X_1	X_2	X_3	X_4	X_5	X_6	X_7	X_8	X_9	X_{10}	X_{11}	X_{12}
A. Case 1: $P_R = P_{CA} = 1$ at X_0	P_R	1	1	1	.9	.8	.7	.6	.5	.4	.3	.2	.1	0
	P_{CA}	1	1	1	.9	.8	.7	.6	.5	.4	.3	.2	.1	0
	P_I	0	0	0	.09	.16	.21	.24	.25	.24	.21	.16	.09	0
B. Case 2: $P_R = 1$, $P_{CA} = .5$ at X_0	P_R	1	1	1	.9	.8	.7	.6	.5	.4	.3	.2	.1	0
	P_{CA}	.5	.5	.5	.4	.3	.2	.1	0	0	0	0	0	0
	P_I	.5	.5	.5	.54	.56	.56	.54	.5	.4	.3	.2	.1	0
C. Case 3: $P_R = P_{CA} = .5$ at X_0	P_R	.5	.5	.5	.4	.3	.2	.1	0	0	0	0	0	0
	P_{CA}	.5	.5	.5	.4	.3	.2	.1	0	0	0	0	0	0
	P_I	.25	.25	.25	.24	.21	.16	.09	0	0	0	0	0	0

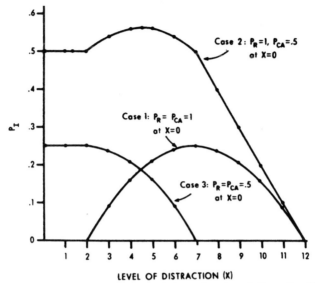

Fig. 7.1. Probability of being influenced (P_I) as a function of distraction (X) for each case shown in Table 7.1.

upon communication influence, the nature of these effects, and some contingencies in their occurrence, are worth analyzing in terms of Eq. (7.3).

Consider some distracting factor X which can vary over several levels. In Case 1, assume that in the absence of X the probabilities of receiving the communication and refuting its contents effectively are both unit ($P_R = P_{CA} = 1$) and that low levels of X do not appreciably affect these probabilities. However, beyond a certain level, X_2, X has a negative effect upon both P_R and P_{CA}. In case 2, assume that X has similar effects upon P_R and P_{CA} but that the initial likelihood of refuting the communication is low ($= .5$). In case 3, assume that X has similar effects but that P_R and P_{CA} are both initially low ($= .5$). Finally, assume for simplicity that in all three cases $P_{Y/CA} = 0$ and $P_{Y/CA'} = 1$. Then, hypothetical values of P_R and P_{CA}, and the values of P_I predicted by Eq. (7.4), are shown in Table 7.1 as a function of X. P_I is shown graphically as a function of X in Fig. 7.1. Note that the level of X that produces the maximum influence (P_I) increases with the *initial* values of P_R and P_{CA} (i.e., the values at X_0). Moreover, conditions can be constructed in which distraction should theoretically either increase the influence of a communication, decrease its influence, or have no effect upon its influence, depending upon the initial levels of P_R and P_{CA} that happen to be involved. These initial levels may be affected by at least three types of variables: characteristics of the communication itself, characteristics of the receiver, and characteristics of the situation (for example, instructional set). To provide some examples of these effects, let us turn to some of the recent research on distraction effects and consider it in the context of the formulation described above.

B. Research on Distraction Effects

Effects of communication characteristics. Suppose an experimenter wishes to consider the effects of a distracting stimulus (X) upon the impact of a particular communication. To do this, he compares the influence of the message when presented in the absence of any distraction (X_0) to its influence when accompanied by a moderately high level of interference (X_7). From Fig. 7.1 it is clear that the magnitude and direction of the effect observed may depend upon factors other than X that affect P_R and P_{CA}. For example, if the communication is easy to understand but contains weak arguments, Case 1 may apply, and hence an increase in its influence would occur as distraction increases. However, if the communication is easy to understand but contains arguments that are difficult to refute, Case 2 may apply, and no effect of distraction would be observed. Finally, if the communication is hard to understand but contains cogent arguments, Case 3 may apply, and distraction would decrease the impact of the communication. In fact, results of a study by Regan and Cheng (1973) support two of these predictions. Subjects heard messages that were either simple (described by the authors as "easily understood but not very convincing" or complex ("difficult to understand, but convincing if understood") under two distraction conditions. (In this study, distraction was manipulated by accompanying the communication with music played at either high or low volume.) Consistent with the preceding analysis, distraction increased the influence of the simple message but decreased the impact of the complex one.

Effects of individual differences. The initial levels of P_R and P_{CA} may also be influenced by characteristics of the recipient of the communication. For example, consider the effect of general intelligence. Presumably the ability to comprehend and to counterargue effectively both increase with intelligence. Suppose that for bright subjects, $P_R = P_{CA} = 1$ in the absence of distraction, while for unintelligent subjects, $P_R = P_{CA} = .5$ under these conditions. Thus, bright subjects are representative of Case 1, and unintelligent subjects, of Case 3. To this extent, a level of distraction equal to X_7 in Table 7.1 should increase a communication's influence upon intelligent subjects but should decrease its influence upon unintelligent ones.

A perhaps more interesting individual difference variable, which may differentially affect P_R and P_{CA}, is the initial attitude toward the position advocated in the communication. Subjects who strongly disagree with the position being advocated may be more inclined to counterargue than subjects who are indifferent to or in favor of the position. Thus, the former subjects may be representative of Case 1, while the latter may be representative of Case 2 (that is, P_R may be high, but P_{CA} relatively low). To this extent, a level of distraction equal to X_7 should increase the effect of a communication upon subjects who disagree with the position advocated, but should have little effect upon the communication's impact upon subjects who do not disagree with this position.

The first direct test of distraction effects, by Festiner and Maccoby (1964), provides some support for the above hypothesis. Both fraternity members (presumably in favor of fraternities) and nonmembers (neutral or opposed to fraternities) listened to a tape-recorded speech attacking the fraternity system. The speech was accompanied by a visual stimulus that was either highly distracting (a humorous silent film satirizing the Jackson Pollack style of art) or minimally distracting (a film of the speaker). Subjects then reported their personal attitudes toward fraternities. As expected, distraction increased the influence of the message upon opinions of fraternity members; however, its influence upon nonmembers was equally great at both distraction levels.

The magnitude and direction of the distraction effects predicted above obviously depend upon the particular levels of distraction selected. They may also depend upon situational, message, and individual difference variables that affect P_R and P_{CA} in the absence of distraction. For this reason, it is not very surprising that other studies have not consistently replicated Festinger and Maccoby's findings. For example, in a study by Haaland and Venkatesan (1968), subjects listened to a communication about lowering the voting age as they watched either a distracting or a nondistracting film. In this study, distraction *decreased* the influence of the communication. The authors attributed this "reversal" to poorer message reception in their study than in Festinger and Maccoby's. This relatively low reception in their study resulted because the levels of distraction compared by Haaland and Venkatesan were greater than those used by Festinger and Maccoby, or because the arguments contained in their persuasive communication were cogent but difficult to understand. (In the latter event, Case 3 would apply rather than Case 1.)

Effect of instructional set. The importance of instructional set upon the initial levels of P_R and P_{CA}, and thus its effect upon communication influence, is suggested in a study by Zimbardo, Snyder, Thomas, Gold, and Gurwitz (1970). Subjects listened to a message while performing a distracting number-summation task. In *message set* conditions, greater importance was attached to understanding the message than to performing the number task, while in *number set* conditions the relative importance of the two activities was ostensibly reversed. It seems reasonable to assume that number-set instructions decreased the likelihood that subjects received and counterargued the communication, even in the absence of distraction, and that this condition was similar to Case 3 as described in Table 7.1c. (Supplementary data indicated that the message was in fact recalled relatively less well under this condition.) In contrast, the message-set condition is more similar to Case 1. Therefore, if the distraction resulting from number summation is at about X_7 in Table 7.1, distraction should increase the influence of the communication under message-set conditions but should decrease its effectiveness under number-set conditions. This, in effect, is what Zimbardo et al. found.

The preceding interpretation of Zimbardo et al.'s results is somewhat tenuous, since subjects under message-set conditions reported spending no less time counterarguing than subjects under no-distraction (control) conditions. However, the proportion of time spent counterarguing may not be an adequate index of P_{CA}, which refers to the likelihood that the arguments contained in the communication are in fact refuted. Perhaps distraction does not decrease subjects' *attempts* to counterargue but only decreases their success in this endeavor. In a more recent study by Osterhouse and Brock (1970), the amount of counterarguing was measured by asking subjects, after they had received the message and reported their attitudes, to write down their "thoughts and ideas" about the position advocated. The number of counterarguments contained in this list was assumed to reflect the number of counterarguments made against the communication at the time it was presented. Consistent with expectations, the number of arguments listed decreased as distraction increased, while the acceptance of the position advocated became greater.

III. EFFECTS OF FEAR-AROUSING COMMUNICATIONS

A. General Considerations

Theory and data on the effects of fear-arousing communications have evolved largely from two separate and extensive programs of research conducted by Leventhal (1970) and by Janis (1967). In this research, subjects typically receive, in more or less vivid (fear-arousing) terms, both information describing a danger and information about how to avoid the danger. For example, subjects may be shown pictures describing the consequences of lung cancer, accompanied by information to the effect that the likelihood of getting lung cancer can be reduced by not smoking cigarettes. Subjects' acceptance of the latter information (e.g., their belief in the proposition that smoking causes lung cancer) is then investigated as a function of the intensity of the fear-provoking material.

The theoretical positions of Janis and Leventhal are well-developed in the two articles cited above, and a reiteration of their positions is unnecessary in the present context. However, an alternative interpretation of the effects of fear-arousing communications is suggested by the preceding analysis of distraction effects. That is, fear conceivably affects the acceptance of a communication, not because of its motivational properties *per se*, but because the arousal it generates functions as internal "noise," which distracts subjects either from comprehending the contents of the communication or from counterarguing it effectively. In other words, it decreases P_R and/or P_{CA}. This hypothesis, which is similar to that suggested by McGuire (1968b), has some interesting implications. For example, if P_R and P_{CA} both decrease as the amount of fear increases, the effect of increasing fear upon the likelihood of being influenced by a communication

(P_I) should be nonmonotonic; the communication's influence should increase up to a point as fear increases, but it should decrease as fear becomes still more extreme.

According to a distraction interpretation, the level of fear that produces the maximum influence depends in part upon the levels of P_R and P_{CA} in the absence of fear. As either or both of these initial probabilities decrease, a smaller amount of fear is required to produce the maximum influence or, alternatively, the more likely it is that any given amount of fear will reduce rather than increase communication effectiveness. This has interesting implications. For example, it is reasonable to assume that the initial levels of P_R and P_{CA} are higher for subjects with high intellectual ability than for subjects with low ability. If this assumption is valid, the likelihood that high ability subjects are influenced by a communication should increase up to a point with the amount of fear evoked by the descriptive material accompanying it (see Case 1, Table 7.1), while the likelihood that low ability subjects will be influenced may decrease with the intensity of the fear-provoking material (Case 3). Other variables that may affect the initial levels of P_R and P_{CA}, and thus may affect both the magnitude and the direction of the influence of fear-provoking material, will be considered as they become relevant in the research to be discussed.

B. Research on the Effects of Fear-Arousing Messages

A vast amount of research has been performed on the effectiveness of fear-arousing communications, and many apparently conflicting results have been obtained. We will consider only a few representative studies to demonstrate the applicability of the proposed formulation to the issues upon which this research focuses.

1. *Evidence for a Nonmonotonic Effect of Arousal.* The data most obviously consistent with the preceding formulation were collected in an early study by Janis and Feshback (1953). Subjects whose responses to a questionnaire suggested that they were either high or low in chronic anxiety received a message advocating the adoption of a new dental hygiene practice. This message was accompanied by material assumed to arouse either high or low fear. (Highly fear-provoking material consisted in part of a series of slides slowing unpleasant mouth diseases and severe tooth decay.) Attitudes toward accepting the recommendation to adopt the hygiene practices were assessed both before and after the communication. On the basis of the assumption that emotional arousal is distracting, and therefore decreases both P_R and P_{CA}, what results might be expected? Suppose the internal and external sources of arousal (chronic anxiety level and the communication content) have additive effects upon the arousal experienced by subjects. Then, P_R and P_{CA} should both be relatively high (and P_I low) among low anxiety subjects exposed to a mild fear-arousing communication, and they should both be low

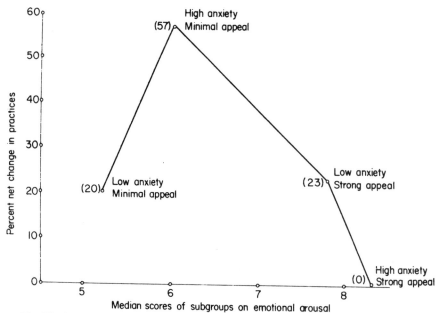

Fig. 7.2. Acceptance of recommendations as a function of chronic anxiety and fear-arousing communication content (reprinted from Janis, 1967, p. 194).

(and P_I *again* low) among high anxiety subjects exposed to a high fear-arousing message. The remaining two groups of subjects should have intermediate levels of arousal, resulting in moderate values of P_R and P_{CA} and a relatively high value of P_I. Data reported by Janis and Feshbach, shown in Figure 7.2, are consistent with this interpretation.

A validation of the above interpretation of Janis and Feshbach's results requires an independent indication of the effects of the fear-provoking material upon reception and counterarguing. In a later study, Janis and Milholland (1954) found that more fear-relevant material, but *less* persuasive material (material supporting the recommendation being made), was recalled in high fear-arousing messages than in low fear-arousing messages. While this is consistent with our interpretation of Janis and Feshbach's findings, Leventhal (1970) has pointed out that the high-fear messages constructed by Janis and Milholland were longer than the low-fear messages, primarily because of differences in the amount of fear-provoking material presented. It is conceivable that persuasive material is less likely to be recalled when it is embedded in a large amount of irrelevant material, regardless of whether the latter material is fear-provoking. Duke (1967) found that the content of persuasive messages similar to those used by Janis was recalled as poorly when the slides accompanying them were blank as when they contained fear-provoking material. This finding suggests that the fear-arousing component of the communication may indeeed by distracting, and thus may reduce P_R and P_{CA}, but that this distraction is not mediated by fear *per se*.

Janis (1967) reviewed several additional studies (Berkowitz & Cottingham, 1960; Goldstein, 1959; Niles, 1964) that he interpreted as evidence for a nonmonotonic relation between fear arousal and communication effectiveness. Based upon the assumption that individual difference variables (e.g., vulnerability) and communication variables (fear-provoking content) have additive effects upon the fear experienced while the communication is presented, Janis ordered the experimental conditions in several studies according to the total amount of fear generated by them. The influence of the communications presented under these conditions appeared to increase and then to decrease as the assumed level of fear became greater. Leventhal (1970) noted that if experimental conditions in the same studies are reordered on the basis of subjects' self-reports of their fear, this relation disappears. However, self-reports may not be reliable indications of the actual fear experienced. This would be particularly true if, as Leventhal himself hypothesizes, subjects engage in "defensive denial" of danger when they feel unable to cope with it directly. Defensive denial should be manifested not only in a resistance to accept the implications of the factual content of the message, but also in an unwillingness to acknowledge that the fear-provoking material was anxiety-arousing. Thus, Leventhal's reanalysis of Janis' reanalysis of the results of the studies cited is not a critical argument against the existence of a nonmonotonic relation between fear and communication effectiveness.

2. *Effect of Communication Relevance.* The results of Janis and Feshbach's experiment emphasize the need to take into account factors in addition to the content of the communication that affect P_R and P_{CA}. Another such factor may be the personal relevance of the communication to the recipient, or alternatively, the recipient's belief that he is personally vulnerable to the danger described. The effect of relevance is somewhat difficult to predict *a priori*. It seems reasonable to assume that subjects are less likely to try to refute the contents of a communication that is not personally relevant, and that P_{CA} is probably low under such conditions. However, the effect of relevance upon reception (P_R), and its interaction with the intensity of the fear-provoking content of the communication, are less clear. An early study by Berkowitz and Cottingham (1960) is useful to consider in this context. Subjects, who were classified into high and low relevance groups on the basis of how often they used automobiles, received a communication advocating the use of safety belts. This message was accompanied either by statistical data and affectively neutral arguments (a "mild" appeal) or by more dramatic arguments and pictures of rather gory traffic accidents (a "strong" appeal). Before we consider the effects of these appeals upon subjects' attitudes toward the use of safety belts, supplementary data reported by the authors are worth noting. When the issue to which the message pertained was low in relevance, the subjects' reported interest in the message increased with the intensity of the appeal,

but their acknowledged discomfort was not affected. This finding suggests that the "fear-arousing" material was not distracting to these subjects; rather, it may have increased P_R while not appreciably affecting P_{CA}. To this extent, Eq. (7.4) predicts that the impact of the communication should increase with the strength of the appeal. This in fact was what Berkowitz and Cottingham found. In contrast, when the communication was high in relevance, subjects reported both more interest and more discomfort as the intensity of the appeal increased. Conceivably the increase in interest and the distraction due to discomfort (arousal) have compensating effects upon P_R, and for that matter, upon P_{CA} as well. In such an event, differences in the effectiveness of the appeals upon these subjects are difficult to predict *a priori* from Eq. (7.4). In fact, Berkowitz and Cottingham found that the strength of the appeal had little apparent effect upon the attitudes of subjects to whom the message was relevant. This finding does not contradict the general formulation being proposed, although knowledge of P_R and P_{CA} under the conditions being compared would of course be necessary to interpret the result adequately.

3. *Effects of Self Esteem.* Many studies of individual differences in responding to fear-arousing communications bear directly or indirectly upon Leventhal's (1970) hypothesis that subjects who feel unable to cope with the danger implied by the communication will deny its implications, and therefore will be less influenced by strong appeals than by mild ones; in contrast, subjects who perceive themselves to be able to cope with the danger will be more influenced by strong appeals than by mild ones. Although it is based upon different assumptions, this hypothesis is reasonably consistent with a distraction interpretation of fear effects. Subjects who feel able to cope with the danger being described may be less aroused, and therefore less distracted, by any given amount or intensity of fear-provoking material. For example, "copers" may be representative of Case 1 (Table 7.1A) while "noncopers" are more representaitve of Case 3 (Table 7.1C). It is therefore likely that strong appeals will increase the communication's impact upon "copers" but will decrease its impact upon "noncopers." Results of a study by Dabbs and Leventhal (1966) indicated that high self-esteem subjects' attitudes toward taking a tetanus inoculation were more favorable when the recommendation to take the shots was accompanied by highly fear-provoking material than when it was accompanied by mildly fear-provoking material. However, low self-esteem subjects were slightly less influenced when the intensity or the fear content was high than when it was low. If a subject's self-esteem is an indication of his belief that he can "cope" with the danger described in the message (Dabbs, 1964), these results are fairly consistent with a distraction interpretation. However, other aspects of Dabbs and Leventhal's data are more difficult to explain. For example, relative to control conditions in which *no* fear-provoking material was presented, the mild appeal increased the impact of the message upon low self-esteem

subjects, as would be expected, but slightly decreased its impact upon subjects with high self-esteem. This decrease could not be predicted on the basis of the assumption that the fear-provoking material is distracting. Conceivably, high-esteem subjects are actually stimulated to counterargue more, and more effectively, when the fear-provoking material is mild than when it is nonexistent, and their internal state of arousal does not appreciably distract them from either receiving or counterarguing until the fear-provoking material is quite intense. However, in the absence of direct measures of P_R and P_{CA}, this interpretation must be regarded as *ad hoc* and very speculative.

A second study bearing upon the effects of self-esteem was reported by Leventhal and Trembly (1968). In this study, unlike those we have discussed previously, the content of the fear-provoking materials was held constant, but the method of presenting it was varied. Specifically, a film pertaining to automobile accidents was presented at either high intensity (a large picture accompanied by loud sound) or low intensity (a small picture accompanied by low sound). A control (low fear) group received no film at all. High-esteem subjects consistently increased their expressed desire to take the recommended safety precautions (for example, to drive slowly, to have their automobiles checked, etc.) as the intensity of the communication increased. In contrast, low-esteem subjects' judgments along these dimensions increased (relative to control conditions) when they received the low intensity message, but decreased as the intensity of the message became more extreme. While these results are more consistent with the distraction interpretation than those obtained by Dabbs and Leventhal, supplementary data reported in the former study are somewhat confusing. Specifically, high-esteem subjects reported feeling less fatigued after receiving the high intensity communication than after receiving the low intensity one; however, this difference was reversed in the case of low-esteem subjects. This suggests that low-esteem subjects were more aroused by the fear-provoking material than high-esteem subjects, as speculated above. However, it could also indicate that low-esteem subjects engaged in more cognitive work to counterargue the implications of the high fear-arousing communication than did either high-esteem subjects exposed to highly arousing appeals, or low-esteem subjects exposed to milder appeals. This interpretation would be inconsistent with the distraction interpretation, which assumes that P_{CA} decreases as the strength of the appeal increases. Perhaps subjects' *attempts* to counterargue increase with the strength of the appeal, but their *success* in this endeavor decreases. Note also that if P_R decreases with fear in the manner described in Table 7.1, a decrease in communication impact with increase in fear could of course be predicted regardless of the direction in which P_{CA} changes. Independent indexes of P_R and P_{CA} are again necessary to clarify these issues.

C. Concluding Remarks

The preceding review has not scratched the surface of the research on the effects of fear-arousing communications on attitudes. (For a more comprehensive review of this research, see Leventhal, 1970.) However, the review is sufficient to demonstrate that many if not all of the effects of fear-arousing communication, and contingencies of these effects upon individual difference variables, are potentially interpretable in terms of the effects of these variables upon the probabilities of receiving and comprehending a communication and of counterarguing it effectively. While some of the specific assumptions we have made concerning the effects of fear upon these probabilities may be incorrect, it is clear that direct measures of these variables would greatly clarify the phenomena discussed in this section. It is conceivable that in some instances the fear-arousing content of the communication may affect neither P_R nor P_{CA} but rather may affect the tendency to agree publicly with the recommendation being made (regardless of whether or not the message is refuted effectively), and thus may affect $P_{Y/CA}$ and $P_{Y/CA'}$. Certainly, strong appeals are more likely than mild appeals to give subjects the impression that the position being advocated is important to the source (the person or organization administering the materials). The effectiveness of the communication upon attitudes reported in the experimental session could be due in part to compliance with these expectancies. Differences between the effects of appeals on reported attitudes and the effects of these appeals on actual behavior (e.g., the extent to which subjects actually engage in the behavior recommended in the communication), noted by Leventhal (1970), suggest that this may be the case. An understanding of the effects of different fear-provoking materials upon P_R and P_{CA}, as well as upon P_I, might help to answer this question.

IV. DETERMINANTS OF RESISTANCE TO PERSUASION

To the extent that the influence of a communication is less when P_{CA} is high (when the arguments contained in the communication are effectively refuted), communication effectiveness should be decreased by factors that lead to successful counterarguing. This general hypothesis was the focus of McGuire's (1964) program of research on factors that induce resistance to persuasion. McGuire was primarily concerned with the type of information that decreases a subject's vulnerability to subsequent attacks upon his beliefs. The specific propositions considered by McGuire were cultural truisms (for example, "Everyone should brush his teeth after every meal if possible"). Although subjects typically believe such propositions to be unquestionably true, they have little factual basis for these beliefs. McGuire constructed persuasive communications that attacked these propositions and, in the absence of other information, substantially decreased subjects' beliefs that they were true. He reasoned that this influence was due primarily to the fact that since subjects had never before questioned the validity of the propositions, they were unprepared to refute the arguments contained in the attacks. He hypothesized that the effects of these attacks could be decreased by exposing subjects to information that would help them to defend against these arguments and by giving them practice in counterarguing.

A. Supportive versus Refutational Defenses

As an initial test of the general hypothesis described above, McGuire and Papageorgis (1961) compared the effectiveness of two types of defenses against the persuasive communication to be administered (the attack). One, a *supportive* defense, contained arguments supporting the proposition to be attacked, each argument accompanied by a paragraph substantiating it. The second, a *refutational* defense, contained arguments against the proposition, each argument followed by a paragraph refuting it. In some cases, these defenses were prepared by the experimenter and read by the subjects, while in other cases they were written by the subjects themselves. Two days after reading or writing their defense, subjects received the attack and then indicated their belief that the proposition was valid. These beliefs were compared to those of control subjects who had received no defense against the attack.

The relative effectiveness of the defenses described above may be predicted on the basis of their likely effects upon P_{CA}. First, consider defenses prepared by the experimenter. Such defenses should be effective to the extent that they provide information that helps subjects to refute the arguments contained in the subsequent attack. Supportive defenses do not directly pertain to arguments against the proposition to be attacked, and thus the information they provide should minimally affect the ability to refute these arguments. In contrast, refutational defenses both mention arguments against the proposition and refute these arguments. To the extent that the arguments refuted in these defenses are similar to those contained in the impending attack, this information is likely to increase P_{CA} and thus to reduce P_I.

Now consider defenses prepared by the subject himself. Such defenses provide no new information that will help the subject to counterargue, and so their effect, if any, may be primarily attributable to the practice they give the subject in refuting arguments against the proposition to be attacked. The preparation of refutational defenses undoubtedly provides more practice in counterarguing than does the preparation of supportive defenses and thus should lead to a greater increase in P_{CA}. Thus, in both cases, refutational defenses should be more effective than supportive defenses, regardless of whether they are read or are prepared by the subjects themselves.

McGuire and Papageorgis's findings support these predictions. Subjects who received supportive defenses were little affected by them, regardless of whether they were read or written; these subjects' final beliefs in the propostion $(M = 7.39$ along a 1-15 scale) did not differ appreciably from those of control subjects $(M = 6.64)$. However, refutational defenses enabled subjects to maintain much stronger post-attack beliefs $(M = 10.32)$ than did control subjects. Beliefs were better maintained when these defenses were read $(M = 11.32)$ than when they were written by the subjects themselves $(M = 9.32)$; this suggests that information about counterarguments prepared by others increases P_{CA} more than does practice in preparing one's own counterarguments. If subjects have never before questioned the validity of the truisms being attacked, and hence are unprepared to counterargue, their own rebuttals may be relatively inferior in quality and thus may be less effective defenses than those written by the experimenter.

B. Effects of Perceived Vulnerability to Attack

The likelihood that subjects are unable to counterargue effectively when they are initially asked to do so suggests a somewhat different interpretation of the effectiveness of refutational defenses. An argument against a proposition in which the subject believes may be effective because the subject becomes aware of an inconsistency between two or more of his cognitions (e.g., his belief in the proposition, and his beliefs in the arguments against it) and therefore changes one or more of these beliefs in a manner implied by the rules governing his cognitive organization. The dynamics of this reorganization, and the reasons for its occurrence, may be similar to those underlying the "Socratic effect." To the extent that reorganization involves change in beliefs in the arguments against the proposition, the "cognitive work" required to accomplish it should be facilitated by (a) providing the subject with new information that calls into question the validity of these arguments and (b) giving him the opportunity to recall previously formed beliefs that either support the proposition or imply that the arguments against it are invalid.

An important hypothesis proposed by McGuire is consistent with the reasoning outlined above. Specifically, he proposes that if a subject becomes aware that a strongly held belief is "vulnerable to attack" (or in our terms, that there is a possible inconsistency among his beliefs), he will be stimulated to bolster his defenses against subsequent attacks through cognitive reorganization. This has two interesting implications. First, simply the mention of arguments against a proposition may be sufficient to make the subject aware of his vulnerability to attack and therefore may stimulate him to bolster his defenses through cognitive reorganization. This reorganization may affect his beliefs in arguments, regardless of whether they are the same as or different from those actually refuted in the defense. Second, the more vulnerable the subject perceives himself (that is, the greater the inconsistency among his cognitions), the more likely he may be to perform cognitive work necessary to counterargue the subsequent attack effectively, and thus the more resistant to persuasion he may become. Several studies by McGuire and his colleagues bear upon these hypotheses. In one (Papageorgis & McGuire,

1961), subjects who read refutational defenses were resistant to persuasion even when the arguments contained in the defense differed from those in the impending attack. In a later study reported by McGuire (1964), subjects read defenses consisting of either two or four arguments, either none or two of which were actually refuted. Not surprisingly, resistance to the subsequent attack increased with the number of arguments refuted in the defense. However, resistance also increased with the number of arguments presented but *not* refuted. Both studies support the hypothesis that simply the awareness of arguments against the proposition is sufficient to stimulate the subject to prepare himself to defend against subsequent attacks upon this proposition. Moreover, the greater the number of such arguments (and thus the more aware he is of his vulnerability), the better he prepares himself.

If refutational defenses are effective because they lead the subject to bolster his defenses against attack, their effectiveness should increase up to a point with the amount of time he has to engage in this activity before the attack is presented. McGuire (1964) found that refutational defenses pertaining to different arguments from those contained in the attack were more effective when they were presented two days prior to the attack than when they were presented immediately before the attack. In contrast, refutational defenses against the same arguments contained in the impending attack were equally effective under both conditions. In the latter case, the increase in P_{CA} resulting from practice in counterarguing during the two days between defense and attack may have been offset by a reduction in the amount of relevant information in the defense which was recalled for use in counterarguing.

C. Information versus Practice Effects

The two factors underlying the effectiveness of refutational defenses—the information that they provide which helps the subject to counterargue, and the stimulation they give him to practice counterarguing—may sometimes be negatively correlated. To separate the effects of these factors, McGuire (1961) asked subjects either to read or to write refutational defenses against arguments that were either the same as or different from those in the impending attack. When a defense pertains to arguments that are the same as those contained in the later attack, its effectiveness may be due primarily to the specific information it provides concerning the means of refuting these arguments. Since defenses prepared by the experimenter are likely to be of higher quality than those prepared by the subject himself, the former should be more effective than the latter, as found in the earlier study by McGuire and Papageorgis (1961).

In contrast, when the refutational defenses pertain to arguments different from those contained in the attack, they may have an effect only insofar as they make the subject aware of his vulnerability to attack and thus stimulate him to prepare effective counterarguments during the interval between the defense and the impending attack. Again assuming that the defenses written by the subject himself are inferior in quality to those prepared by the experimenter, this vulnerability should be more apparent when defenses are written than when they are read. Thus, refutational defenses against arguments different from those in the attack should be *less* effective if they are read than if they are written by the subjects themselves. McGuire's (1961) results support both predictions. An interesting implication of the preceding analysis is that if a subject reads *weak* defenses against arguments not contained in the impending attack, he should become more aware of his vulnerability and thus should become *more* resistent to the attack than a subject who reads strong defenses against these arguments. This implication is worth investigating.

D. Conclusions

While the support for McGuire's interpretation of the factors that affect resistance to persuasion is impressive, this interpretation would be strengthened if more direct information were available on the effects of various defenses upon subjects' ability to counterargue effectively at the time they receive the attack. A measure of counterarguing ability similar to that proposed by Osterhouse and Brock and discussed earlier in this chapter may be useful in this regard. It is conceivable that refutational defenses may affect other components of Eq. (7.3) than P_{CA}. For example, evidence that certain arguments against the proposition can be refuted may increase subjects' beliefs that arguments in general are invalid, regardless of whether the subject himself attempts to refute them. This evidence may be obtained either from information provided by the experimenter (when defenses are read) or through the subject's personal experience in refuting the arguments presented (when defenses are written). To this extent, the decrease in P_I resulting from these defenses could be due to a decrease in $P_{Y/CA'}$ (the likelihood of yielding, given that the subject does not refute the arguments effectively) rather than to an increase in P_{CA}. While this interpretation would not account for McGuire's finding that resistance to persuasion increases with the number of arguments mentioned but not refuted in the defense, it could account for the general effectiveness of refutational defenses against arguments that differ from those contained in the attack. The relative effects of defenses upon P_{CA} and $P_{Y/CA'}$ may be worth exploring in further research in this area.

Some additional lines of research are suggested by considering the cognitive processes underlying the preparation of defenses in the context of the formulation of cognitive organization proposed in Chapter 4. Suppose that beliefs in two propositions, A and B, are related according to the equation

$$P_B = P_A P_{B/A} + (1 - P_A) P_{B/A'}$$

Then, to the extent that the preparation of defenses against attacks upon A decreases the change in P_A produced by these attacks, such defenses should also decrease the effect of an attack upon P_B. This decrement should be greater to the extent that $P_{B/A}$ differs in magnitude from $P_{B/A'}$. Thus the model suggests a method of predicting quantitatively the generalization of resistance to persuasion induced through the techniques considered by McGuire and others.

V. EFFECTS OF FOREWARNING

A. Warning Effects upon Counterarguing

McGuire's research on resistance to persuasion suggests that one's awareness that a belief is vulnerable to attack is sufficient to lead him to bolster his defenses against attacks on this belief and thus to reduce the effectiveness of such attacks. A corollary of this hypothesis is that simply warning a subject that his belief is likely to be attacked will decrease the effectiveness of the attack once it is presented.

Some support for this prediction was reported by Freedman and Sears (1965). These authors informed high school subjects under one condition that they were about to hear a speech on an unmentioned topic and that they should attempt to assess the speaker's personality. In a second condition, subjects were told that they were about to listen to a speech arguing that teen-age drivers were a menace and that they would subsequently be asked to give their own opinion on the issue. As expected, the communication had less influence upon subjects in the second condition than in the first. Moreover, the effectiveness of the warning in reducing the communication's influence increased with the time between its occurrence and the presentation of the persuasive message. This latter result suggests that forewarning is effective because it gives the subject an opportunity to prepare himself for counterarguing the attack effectively.

Additional support for this general hypothesis was obtained by McGuire and Papageorgis (1962). In this study, subjects were told that the purpose of the experiment was either to test their ability to think analytically or to test their susceptibility to influence. They were then either exposed to a supportive defense, a refutational defense, or no defense against a proposition of the type described in the preceding section. Information about the persuasive intent of the communication increased the effectiveness of the defensive materials (particularly the supportive defense) but had little if any effect upon the influence of the communication when given in the absence of defensive materials. The fact that warning in and of itself had no effect suggests that it functioned primarily to stimulate the subjects to assimilate the material contained in the defenses. Without exposure to those defenses, warned subjects may not have had sufficient time to prepare their own defenses adequately and thus were substantially influenced by the message, despite the warning. To the extent that forewarning increases the likelihood of counterarguing effectively against the persuasive communication (P_{CA}), this increase is apparently not the result of a more critical evaluation of the persuasive material while it is presented, but rather it is the result of cognitive work performed before the material is received.

B. Anticipatory Belief Change

While the preceding analysis of forewarning effects seems straightforward, it may be oversimplified. Information to a subject about the purpose of the experiment may suggest to him the nature of the responses the experimenter is likely to consider acceptable. To the extent that the subject attempts to comply with these "demands," differences in the influence of a persuasive communication (P_I) may result not from differences in P_R or P_{CA} but rather from differences in $P_{Y/CA}$ and $P_{Y/CA'}$ (the likelihood of yielding, given that arguments are and are not effectively refuted, respectively). Moreover, if the position to be advocated in the communication is made known to subjects, changes in their reported attitudes as a result of attempts to comply with implicit expectancies of the experimenter may conceivably occur even before the communication is actually presented. To this extent, differences in P_I would be attributable to differences in $P_{I/R'}$. Let us consider this latter possibility in more detail.

Informing the subject that the message he is about to receive is intended to persuade him may often suggest to him that the experimenter supports the position advocated in the communication and therefore would approve of his agreement with this position. On the other hand, the subject may infer that an indication that he has *changed* his opinions as a result of receiving the communication may be interpreted by the experimenter as a sign of guillibility or wishy-washiness and thus be considered undesirable. Confronted with these apparently competing expectancies, how is the subject likely to respond? One means of resolving the dilemma would be to report agreement with the position to be advocated *before* receiving the communication. In this way, the subject would be able to present himself as agreeing with the position to be advocated (and thus presumably with the opinion advocated by the experimenter) while at the same time not changing his belief as a result of the communication (and thus appearing to be firm in his beliefs and resistant to social pressure).

A formulation with similar implications was proposed by McGuire and Millman (1965). These authors argued that when subjects anticipate that they are apt to be persuaded by an impending communication, they become apprehensive that conformity to the opinion advocated may indicate that they are either gullible or wishy-washy. To avoid the loss of self-esteem resulting from such a self-perception, they may convince themselves that they already agree with the position advocated before the message is presented. Therefore, the primary difference between McGuire and Millman's formulation and the "demand" interpretation proposed here is that the former assumes that anticipatory belief change is stimulated by a desire to save face and maintain *self*-esteem, while the latter assumes that it results from a tendency to comply with the expectancies of the experimenter, and therefore to gain the *experimenter's* esteem.

Both formulations imply that situational factors that give the subject the impression that he is likely to be persuaded by an impending communication, but at the same time suggest it would be viewed unfavorably (either by the subject himself or by the experimenter) to appear too easily persuaded, will lead to anticipatory change in reported beliefs in the direction of the position to be advocated. Several studies bear upon this hypothesis. McGuire and Millman (1965) selected eight different issues. Four of these issues were interpreted as controversial and emotion-laden (e.g., the high likelihood of further Communist takeovers in Latin America, the difficulty of developing a cure for cancer, etc.), and the other four were assumed to be "technical" and less controversial (e.g., the growing shortage of animals for laboratory research, the abolition of the sales tax, etc.) [3]. Subjects were told that they would be asked to read passages written by skillful specialists advocating specified positions on certain of the issues described, and that after reading these communications they would be asked to give their own opinions about the issues. They were first given a sample of four of the eight issues to which the communications pertained (two emotional and two technical) and the positions to be advocated. They then read communications pertaining to two of these issues, as well as communications pertaining to two of the four issues that had not been mentioned in advance. Finally, they reported their personal opinions on all eight issues.

Several results of the above study bear upon the interpretations of forewarning effects described previously. First, communications were no less effective when subjects had been previously informed of the issues and positions than when they had not. This finding suggests that the warning had no effect upon P_{CA}. Since there was only a short period of time between the warning and the presentation of the persuasive message, and thus subjects did not have much time to bolster their defenses before receiving the attack, this finding is not surprising.

In contrast, subjects who were told the position to be advocated in the communication but did *not* actually receive the communication reported opinions that were significantly more in the direction of the opinion advocated than did subjects who were not forewarned. This supports the hypothesis that anticipatory belief change occurred as a result of the

---

[3] The ambiguity of the distinction between "technical" and "emotional" issues has been noted by Hendrick and Jones (1972). For example, it is hard to see why the abolition of the sales tax is more technical and/or less emotional than the difficulty of finding a cure for cancer.

warning *per se* and not as a result of the content of the communication. The effect of the forewarning was greater when the issues involved were "emotional" than when they were "technical." McGuire and Millman interpret their results as support for self-esteem theory. That is, if subjects are more concerned about "emotional" issues than about technical ones, they should anticipate more loss of self-esteem by conforming to communications about the former issues and therefore should engage in relatively more precommunication belief change. However, it also seems reasonable to suppose that subjects expect the experimenter to regard them as less wishy-washy if they are persuaded by communications on technical or factual matters than if they change their minds on emotional matters of personal relevance, and thus they may manifest relatively less anticipatory belief change for this reason. In this regard, it is worth noting that when persuasive communications were actually presented, those pertaining to technical issues had greater impact than those pertaining to emotional ones.

1. *Source Effects.* An additional variable considered by McGuire and Millman, source reputability, may potentially discriminate between the two alternative interpretations of forewarning effects. If the source is skillful and persuasive, self-esteem should be more threatened by conforming to him when he is disreputable than when he is reputable. On the other hand, subjects are likely to expect the experimenter to agree more with the position advocated by a reputable source than with that advocated by a disreputable one. Thus, a self-esteem interpretation would imply relatively greater anticipatory belief change when the source is disreputable, while a demand interpretation would imply relatively less.

In McGuire and Millman's experiment, sources were all allegedly highly skillful and persuasive but differed in their apparent reputability (some were members of a Presidential Advisory Committee, while others were persons convicted of "rather distasteful" crimes). In this study, the type of source had no effect upon anticipatory belief change. However, results of a later study (Papageorgis, 1967), in which source expertise and source reputability were manipulated independently, seem if anything to support a demand interpretation. Subjects were told that the study was intended to measure the opinion change resulting from listening to persuasive communications. They were then told they would hear a communication from a source that was either reputable (a deputy undersecretary of defense) or disreputable (the secretary of an extremely right-wing political organization) and was either skillful (an eloquent and persuasive speaker) or unskillful (a person whose talk consisted of a series of "unrehearsed, off-the-cuff comments to a reporter" lacking in organization and style of presentation). Subjects reported their opinions after receiving information about the issue and the position to be advocated by one of these sources, but before they received the actual communication. Anticipatory beliefs in the position to be advocated were greater when the source was described as either reputable or skillful than when he allegedly possessed neither of these attributes, and they were also greater than in a control condition in which no warning was given. The highly skillful, disreputable source, which should produce the greatest anticipatory change according to self-esteem theory, did not differ in its effects from the unskilled, reputable source, which should theoretically produce the least anticipatory change.

A later study (Deaux, 1972) is also directly relevant to this issue. In this experiment, anticipatory agreement with the view to be advocated by either a high prestige source (a college professor) or a low prestige source (an Appalachian high school student) was investigated as a function of experimentally manipulated self-esteem (feedback about the results of a personality test). Subjects agreed more with the high prestige source than with the low prestige source, but only if they had received unfavorable feedback about themselves. This finding was replicated in a second experiment which showed that the positive effect of source prestige under negative feedback occurred only among subjects whose *measured* self-esteem (inferred from self-reports) was fairly high. Under no condition, however, was anticipatory change appreciably greater when source prestige was low. These results, while contrary to the implications of a self-esteem formulation, are reasonably consistent with a demand compliance interpretation. Negative feedback may increase subjects' beliefs that they are likely to be evaluated unfavorably by the experimenter, and therefore such feedback may increase their attempts to comply with his wishes. Moreover, since high scores on a self-report measure of self-esteem may reflect strong tendencies to respond in a socially desirable fashion (and thus in a way that the experimenter considers desirable), it is also not surprising that source prestige effects were more pronounced among subjects who attained these scores.

2. *Effects of Expectancies to Receive a Persuasive Communication.* If forewarning changes subjects' reported beliefs in the direction of the view to be advocated because subjects infer that the experimenter prefers (or expects) them to adopt this position, these changes should occur even when subjects believe they will not actually receive the persuasive communication, but are only led to believe that it exists. In contrast, self-esteem theory would predict an effect only when subjects anticipate hearing and being persuaded by the subsequent talk. Papageorgis (1967) investigated this possibility by informing subjects in one condition of the opinion advocated in a tape-recorded speech but telling them that they would not hear the recording because it had been damaged in shipment. Despite the fact that subjects did not expect to hear the communication, their attitudes toward the position advocated in it were significantly more favorable than those of control subjects who were not forewarned and were nearly as favorable as those of subjects who anticipated receiving messages. While these results are consistent with the demand interpretation, they could be an artifact of Papageorgis's design. Subjects who were told that they would not hear the critical communication were

nevertheless informed that they *would* hear communications on other issues. Cooper and Jones (1970) argued that subjects may have been confused about which communications they would receive and which they would not, and thus the anticipatory change manifested in the "communication expected" conditions generalized to the "communication not expected" conditions. To obtain support for this argument, they replicated Papageorgis's experiment but added a condition in which subjects were warned of the positions advocated by various communications but were told they would hear *none* of them. In this condition, no anticipatory change in the direction advocated was observed. A second experiment by the same authors led to similar conclusions. These results are difficult to account for on the basis of a demand interpretation. It could perhaps be argued that when subjects are informed that the study is to measure opinion change, but that all of the communications to be used to induce opinion change were damaged and cannot be presented, they may infer that their participation in the experiment is not particularly important and that their responses will not actually be used by the experimenter. Thus, they may not bother to comply with the experimenter's expectancies. However, this *ad hoc* interpretation is not extremely convincing.

What conclusions can be drawn on the basis of the research summarized above? McGuire and Papageorgis's (1962) study indicates that one effect of forewarning about the position to be advocated in a persuasive communication is to stimulate subjects to prepare defenses against the anticipated attack and therefore to increase P_{CA}. However, another and perhaps competing effect is to increase the likelihood of agreeing with the position to be advocated, even in the absence of effective counterarguing. These may be detected even before the attack is presented. It is unclear whether these effects result from tendencies to comply with implicit expectancies or desires of the experimenter, or whether they result from attempts to maintain self-esteem in the face of an anticipated attack. Although problems for a demand interpretation are created by the evidence that awareness of the existence of a persuasive communication may be insufficient to induce anticipatory belief change unless subjects actually expect to receive the communication, the effects of differences in source credibility and prestige create equally serious problems for a self-esteem interpretation.

The possibly opposing effects of warning upon the likelihood of influence resulting from changes in P_{CA} and $P_{I/R'}$ may warrant further exploration. These effects may be independent if a demand interpretation of anticipatory belief changes is valid. However, this is less apt to be the case if a self-esteem interpretation is valid, since factors that increase the subject's ability to counterargue the impending attack effectively should decrease his expectancy to be influenced, and thus should decrease anticipatory belief change due to the threat of appearing gullible. This possibility could be investigated by varying the time interval between the forewarning and the mention of anticipated (precommunication) opinion change. P_{CA} presumably increases with the opportunity to bolster one's defenses and thus increases with the time between warning and attack (Freedman & Sears, 1965). Therefore, self-esteem theory would predict that $P_{I/R'}$, and therefore anticipatory belief change, should decrease as the interval between warning and attack increases. On the other hand, a demand interpretation would not predict such a decrease.

IV. SUMMARY

In this chapter we have discussed the impact of situational and individual difference variables upon communication effectiveness in terms of three processes: the reception and comprehension of the communication's content, the effective refutation of the content through counterarguing, and changes in one's attitude toward the position advocated for reasons unrelated to either reception or counterarguing. Unfortunately, since independent measures of these latter processes are typically unavailable, our interpretation of the research discussed has often been quite speculative. Nevertheless, it serves to demonstrate the potential theoretical and practical value of analyzing communication effectiveness in terms of these processes. If situational determinants of the various components of Eq. (7.3) can be identified, and if the magnitude of their effects on these components can be assessed, the impact of situational and individual difference variables on the influence of information about an object, and their interactive effects, can potentially be understood and predicted.

An equally important consideration is, of course, the characteristics of the communication's content itself. These characteristics determine the effects of the message on cognitions relevant to it. The next four chapters are devoted to this question.

8
CHARACTERISTICS OF INFORMATION
THAT AFFECT SOCIAL JUDGMENTS

In testing and applying the models of cognitive organization discussed earlier in this volume, a change in one cognition (B) was typically predicted as a function of the change in a second related cognition (A). An equally important question of course is how to predict the magnitude of change in A. In practice, this change is often induced by presenting a written or oral communication containing several arguments that intuitively are expected to be effective. Although these intuitions often turn out to be correct, we need a more precise understanding of the characteristics of a complex communication that determines its influence upon judgments. We also need to know how this information is processed by subjects in order to arrive at these judgments. In the next few chapters we will consider both of these questions in some detail.

Although a concern over characteristics of information that affect beliefs and opinions is not of recent vintage (cf. Hovland, Janis, & Kelley, 1953), there has been a rebirth of interest in the question in the context of theory and research on impression formation. In this research, subjects are usually asked to "form an impression" of a hypothetical person on the basis of a set of personality adjectives and then to estimate along a category scale how well they would expect to like such a person. These estimates are then analyzed as a function of certain characteristics of the adjectives upon which they are based.

The impression formation task described above seems far removed from social inference situations encountered outside the laboratory, and the information presented bears only slight resemblance to a "persuasive communication" of the sort typically used to induce opinion change. One may therefore question whether research employing this task has many implications for information integration phenomena in less contrived situations. However, the use of this task and content domain has many inherent advantages for studying these phenomena. These advantages become clear when we consider the problems of selecting different types of information, determining the characteristics of this information fairly precisely, and manipulating these characteristics systematically to determine their effects upon judgments. A very large pool of discrete pieces of information about the objects to be judged must be available. so that one can select those that vary systematically with respect to the characteristics being investigated. Moreover, subjects must not only understand the meaning of each individual piece of information but must generally agree about its characteristics. Few types of information meet these criteria as well as personality adjectives do. Anderson (1968c) has compiled a standard list of 555 different personality traits. One would be hard pressed to generate as large a pool of information of other types that affects the evaluations of a given class of objects so strongly.

It is of course conceivable that the effects of informational characteristics (favorableness, relevance, redundancy, inconsistency, etc.) upon judgments, and the process of integrating the implications of different pieces of information in order to arrive at these judgments, do not generalize over stimulus domains. However, if we can understand information integration phenomena in one domain, we may be in a better position to predict the extent of this generalization. Therefore, in this chapter we will discuss several factors that determine the influence of different pieces of information when presented both separately and in combination. Then, in Chapter 9, we will consider theoretical formulations that take certain of these factors into account in describing quantitatively the manner in which different pieces of information combine to affect judgments.

Before we become too immersed in this discussion, it may be well to note that the characteristics of the information we will consider are usually defined in terms of subjects' responses to this information. In effect, the relation between these informational characteristics and evaluations of an object described by the information is a relation between a subject's responses to the stimulus material in one context and his response to it in a second. By considering this relation, we are implicitly assuming that a subject's interpretation of information about an object, as inferred by the experimenter from his (or others') responses to it in a different context, affects the weight the subject attaches to it in arriving at an evaluative judgment of the object. A subject's interpretation may even affect the information integration procedure underlying the judgment. The research to be described below should be considered primarily in terms of its implications for these processes.

I. FAVORABLENESS AND IMPORTANCE

If a subject believes a given set of attributes to be desirable, he is likely to express positive regard for an object that has these attributes. However, although two attributes may be regarded as equally favorable, information that an object possesses one attribute may have different effects upon the evaluation of this object than information that it has the other. There are several possible reasons for this. The most intuitively obvious reason is that one attribute is more relevant to the judgment being made than the other. For example, suppose that a subject P defines the cognitive category "likeable" by the conjunction of attributes "kind, friendly, and sincere." Then, although he may consider "kind" and "beautiful" to be equally favorable, he may believe that a person described as "kind" is more apt to be "likeable" than a person described as "beautiful" and may therefore rate him more positively along a scale of likeableness.

A second reason why two equally favorable attributes have different effects is that while neither is itself a defining attribute of the cognitive category being considered, one is more strongly associated with defining attributes than is the second. Thus, in the above example, suppose that P considers "warm" and "beautiful" to be equally desirable. However, he believes that "warm" persons are more apt to be "kind, friendly, and sincere" than are "beautiful" persons. Then, in the absence of any other information, P may be more apt to judge a "warm" person as "likeable" than a "beautiful" person.

The definition of "likeable," and therefore the effect of information about a particular attribute upon judgments of likeableness, may depend upon the type of object being judged. For example, it may be more important to know whether or not a person is "kind" if she is a "mother" than if she is a "window-cleaner." To this extent, information about this attribute should have relatively greater effect upon evaluations of a mother than of a window-cleaner. Three studies support this hypothesis. Rokeach and Rothman (1965) paired adjectives with different social roles. One group of subjects evaluated a person described by each adjective-noun combination, while a second group of subjects estimated the relative importance they would attach to each piece of information (that is, the adjective or the noun) in determining whether or not they would like each stimulus person. Not surprisingly, the actual contribution of each component piece of information to the evaluation was predictable from independent estimates of its relative importance in the collective.

In a similar study (Wyer, 1970b), stimuli were constructed from eight pairs of social roles and, for each pair, an attribute dimension that was assumed to be relevant to one role but not the other. (For example, in one case the attribute dimension was "moral-immoral" and the roles were "priest" and "water-skier.") Subjects evaluated role occupants described by each pole of the attribute dimension paired with it (e.g., "moral priest," "immoral priest," "moral water-skier," etc.). The effect of information along a dimension upon evaluations of role occupants was inferred from the difference between the rating of an occupant described by the positive pole of dimension and the rating of an occupant described by the negative pole. In each of the eight cases considered, information had greater effect upon evaluations of persons occupying the role to which the attribute involved was more important. In a second experiment (Wyer, 1970b), analyses of data pertaining to a larger number of adjective-role combinations led to similar conclusions.

II. AMBIGUITY

The impact of information may also be affected by its ambiguity. A piece of information about an object is ambiguous if a subject is uncertain about its evaluative implications. This uncertainty may be indicated by the extent to which an object described by the information is believed to be in several different evaluative categories with equal probability. The information measure of subjective uncertainty proposed in Chapter 2 [Eq. (2.2)] may provide an index of ambiguity. It is reasonable to expect that ambiguous information has less influence upon judgments than information with clearer implications. In a study described in Chapter 2 (Wyer, 1973a), subjects estimated how well they would like (a) a person described by each of eight adjectives and (b) a person described by each of the 28 possible pairs formed from these adjectives. The relative influence of an adjective A upon evaluations based upon the pair was estimated from the expression $(E_{AB} - E_B)/(E_A - E_B)$, where E_A, E_B, and E_{AB} are the mean category ratings based upon A alone, B alone, and A and B in combination.[1] The average weight of each adjective was correlated $-.710$ ($p < .02$) with its ambiguity as defined by Eq. (2.2). Although the sample of adjectives considered is obviously too small to inspire confidence in the generality of this finding, the relation is suggestive.

The effects of ambiguity may interact with those of other informational characteristics. For example, an adjective that is inconsistent with other information about the object being described may be more apt to be discounted if it is ambiguous than if it is not. Alternatively, the interpretation of ambiguous information may be relatively more influenced by the context in which it is presented. These possibilities will be considered later in this chapter.

A. Negativity and Degree of Polarization

Osgood et al. (1957) hypothesize that information about highly polarized attributes (that is, attributes that are either very favorable or very unfavorable) will have more influence than information about moderately polarized attributes. In addition, adjectives that describe unfavorable attributes have more influence than adjectives that describe favorable ones

---

[1] This expression is obtained by solving for w in the equation $E_{AB} = wE_A + (1-w) E_B$, where w is the relative weight attached to E_A.

(Anderson, 1968b; Wyer, 1973a; Wyer and Watson, 1969). These findings could result from the fact that polarized information and unfavorable information are both relatively unambiguous and therefore receive more attention. The lower uncertainty associated with more extreme category ratings has been noted in Chapter 2. Moreover, using Eq. (2.2) to measure subjective uncertainty, the author (Wyer, 1973a) found that the uncertainty associated with ratings of 15 sets of favorable adjectives (mean favorableness = 2.55; mean uncertainty = 1.62) was significantly greater than that associated with ratings of 15 sets of equally polarized unfavorable adjectives (mean favorableness = −2.57; mean uncertainty = 1.48; $t = 3.22$; $p < .02$). A parallel analysis of subjects' actual estimates of their uncertainty produced comparable results. Why less uncertainty should be attached to ratings based upon unfavorable attributes is not completely clear. Perhaps a person is disliked if he possesses any one of several unfavorable attributes but is liked only if he has a number of favorable attributes in combination. That is, the possession of an unfavorable attribute may be a sufficient condition for disliking a person, while the possession of a favorable attribute may be necessary but not sufficient for liking him.

B. Source of Credibility and Prestige

Uncertainty about the implications of a piece of information may depend not only upon characteristics of the information itself but also upon the nature of its source. If the source is known to be unreliable, or is suspected of bias, a subject may have little confidence that the implications of the information are valid, and the influence of this information may therefore be decreased. Some evidence of this was obtained in an unpublished study by the author. Subjects estimated their liking for persons described by a pair of adjectives. Before making each rating they were told that the source of the information presented was either a very accurate judge of people, whose descriptions were similar to those of trained clinical psychologists nearly 95% of the time, or a relatively poor judge whose descriptions were similar to those of trained psychologists only slightly more often than chance. Each adjective pair was presented to some subjects under high credibility conditions and to others under low credibility conditions. Mean evaluations as a function of the average likeableness of the adjectives upon which they are based are shown in Fig. 8.1 under both credibility conditions. Evaluations based upon information from low credibility sources were consistently less extreme than those based upon information from high credibility sources. Note also that the ratio of the slopes of the functions contained under the two credibility conditions is fairly constant. This suggests that the probability that the information presented is valid and the favorableness of this information combine multiplicatively to affect evaluations. Such a conclusion would be consistent with Fishbein's (1963) model of cognitive organization [see Eq.

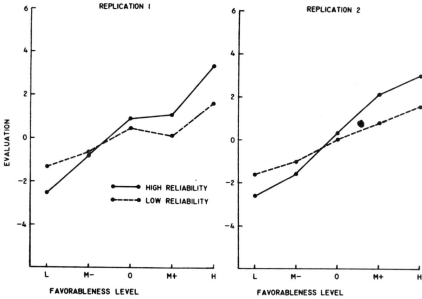

Fig. 8.1. Evaluations of persons as a function of the favorableness of the adjectives describing them and source reliability.

(6.1)]. However, other formulations could also account for these data, as we shall see in Chapter 9.

In the study described above, the source's credibility was based upon his ability or expertise. Research with other types of stimulus materials (e.g., Bergin, 1962) also indicates that the effect of a communication is greater when source expertise is high. The effect of differences in credibility resulting from other factors (e.g., bias, or vested interest in advocating a particular position) may be similar. In such cases, however, this effect may be more difficult to predict *a priori*. The objectivity attributed to a given source may depend both upon the type of issue to which the communication pertains and the particular position being advocated. For example, a convicted murderer may be attributed greater objectivity if he communicates information supporting capital punishment than if he communicates information favoring its abolition. Kelman and Hovland (1953) found that a persuasive message advocating leniency for juvenile criminals had greater effect when it was attributed to a judge than when it was attributed to an exconvict. However, suppose the message had advocated severe treatment of criminals. In this case, the judge might have been suspected of more bias than the exconvict, and the communication attributed to him might have had relatively less influence. We will return to this question in Chapters 10 and 11.

The influence of information may depend upon source characteristics other than credibility. One factor considered in previous chapters is the subject's liking for the source. In some instances, source favorableness may affect judgments of expertise and objectivity. However, Aronson and Golden (1962) found that prejudiced elementary school subjects were more influenced by a communication when it was attributed to a white engineer than when it was attributed to a Negro engineer, even though they believed that both sources were equally intelligent. This finding suggests that source favorableness has an effect independent of source credibility. A subject's belief that a source is likeable could conceivably affect the weight he attaches to information from the source, in much the same way as does his belief that the source is credible. On the other hand, Tannenbaum's (1967) study, described in Chapter 6, suggests that the effects of source favorableness and the effects of information content are additive rather than multiplicative. This matter requires further investigation.

III. NOVELTY

A. Theoretical Considerations

Information about an object is novel if it is unlikely to be contained in a communication about the object. The more novel a piece of information is, the greater influence it may have. In support of this general prediction, Feldman (1966) found that the "modifying capacity" of an adjective (an index of its influence upon the evaluations of objects described by it) was correlated −.50 with its log frequency in the Thorndike-Lorge word count. However, the precise nature of novelty effects, and the psychological reasons for their occurrence, are unclear from this study. For example, novel information may be considered to be more reliable, or more relevant to the evaluation, than information that is more commonly used to describe people. Or, it may simply be more informative, in that it more clearly distinguishes the person described from the typical person with whom subjects have contact. To this extent, the novelty of an adjective could determine its *absolute* influence in a collective, independent of the characteristics of the information presented with it. On the other hand, it is conceivable that the novelty of a piece of information may affect its salience and thus the *relative* attention paid to it when it is presented in combination with others. To this extent, the influence of an adjective would depend not only upon its own novelty but also upon the novelty of the other adjectives accompanying it.

If the novelty of an adjective determines the *absolute* magnitude of its influence, the evaluation of an object O based upon two adjectives A and B (E_O) would be described by the equation

$$E_O = n_A F_A + n_B F_B \tag{8.1}$$

where n_A and n_B are proportional to the novelty of A and B. According to this equation, the effect of differences in n_B depends upon the favorableness of B but not the favorableness of A.

The effects implied by Eq. (8.1) are consistent with those predicted by Fishbein's (1963) model of cognitive organization (see Chapter 6). To see this more clearly, assume that the initial probabilities that A and B describe O are P_A and P_B, respectively. Then, before information about A and B is presented,

$$E_O = P_A F_A + P_B F_B.$$

After information about B is presented, P_B increases to unity, and so

$$E_O = P_A F_A + F_B.$$

The effect of this information is therefore $(1-P_B)F_B$. That is, the lower the value of P_B, or the more novel the information that O has B, the greater will be the influence of this information. Moreover, the effect of differences in novelty should be greater when F_B is highly polarized (either very positive or very negative).

If, on the other hand, the novelty of an adjective determines the relative attention paid to it in the collective used to describe O, and thus affects its relative influence in the collective, E_O would be more appropriately described by the equation:

$$E_O = \frac{n_A F_A + n_B F_B}{n_A + n_B}. \tag{8.2}$$

Suppose that in one condition $n_B = n_A$, and in another condition $n_B = 2n_A$. The difference in E_{AB} under those two conditions can be shown to equal the quantity $(F_B - F_A)/6$. A critical comparison of the two formulations of novelty effects is therefore whether the magnitude of the effect of differences in n_B depends upon the favorableness of *both* B and A, or only upon the favorableness of B.

B. Measurement of Novelty

Since the normative data used to estimate novelty in this study were also used in measuring other informational characteristics to be discussed in this chapter (e.g., redundancy and inconsistency), the collection of these data may be worth describing in detail. Forty stimulus persons were selected. These persons were assumed to cover a wide range of likeableness and to be representative of the population of persons with whom subjects were familiar. Although a few of these stimuli were specifically named ("Josef Stalin," "John F. Kennedy," etc.) most were more generally described ("your high school English teacher," "the person you have met most recently that you would least like to know better," etc.). Each of 225 subjects was given two of these stimulus persons and asked to indicate on a check list which of 240 adjectives would describe each. These data can be used to calculate the proportion of times that any single adjective or combination of adjectives was

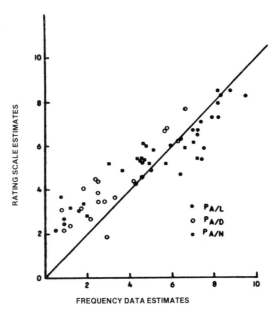

Fig. 8.2. Rating scale estimates of the probability that liked, disliked, and neutrally regarded persons possess A as a function of the proportion of stimulus persons ascribed A by a different group of subjects (reprinted from Wyer & Goldberg, 1970, p. 106).

used to describe a stimulus person. Such proportions were used to estimate the subjective probabilities that these sets of adjectives describe a person in the population of those with whom subjects were familiar.

The above procedure assumes that the proportion of persons who are assigned a certain attribute by a *group* of subjects reflects an *individual* subject's belief that a person possesses this attribute. Although evidence bearing directly upon this question is not available, data collected in another context (Wyer & Goldberg, 1970) suggest that this assumption may generally be valid. Two groups of subjects were run. Each subject in one group selected one person he liked, one person he disliked, and one person he regarded neutrally and then in each case indicated whether or not the person would be described by each of a set of 20 personality adjectives. The proportion of times that each adjective was applied to a given type of person was assumed to indicate the subjective conditional probability that this type of person possessed the attribute described by the adjective. Subjects in the second group were simply asked to form an impression of a liked, disliked, or neutrally regarded person and then to estimate, along a scale from 0 to 10, the likelihood that such a person would possess each of the 20 attributes. Each of those estimates, divided by 10 and averaged over subjects, provided a second index of the subjective probability that the type of person involved possessed each attribute. Mean rating scale estimates of the probabilities that liked, disliked, and neutrally regarded persons possess each attribute

TABLE 8.1

Evaluations as a Function of A Adjective Favorableness (F_A),
B Adjective Favorableness (F_B), and B Adjective Novelty (n_B)
(adapted from Wyer, 1970a, p. 123)

Favorableness of A adjective (F_A)		Favorableness of B adjective (F_B)				
		L	M–	O	M+	H
H	High n_B	−1.96	1.73	5.56	6.51	7.68
	Low n_B	−.59	2.60	5.04	6.51	7.15
M+	High n_B	−2.50	1.54	5.03	6.82	7.09
	Low n_B	−1.44	1.80	4.28	6.04	6.55
M–	High n_B	−6.55	−4.68	−3.59	−1.67	−.34
	Low n_B	−6.52	−5.06	−3.61	−1.36	−.34
L	High n_B	−6.92	−5.56	−3.94	−2.72	−2.29
	Low n_B	−6.75	−5.32	−4.67	−2.84	−2.94
M	High n_B	−4.84	−1.74	.77	2.26	3.04
	Low n_B	−3.83	−1.50	.26	2.09	2.61

($P_{A/L}$, $P_{A/D}$, and $P_{A/N}$, respectively) are plotted in Fig. 8.2 as a function of the proportion of such persons that were assigned the attribute by the first group of subjects. While the rating scale estimates of low probabilities tend to be greater than the actual proportions of times that attributes were assigned, the relation between these variables is sufficiently linear to support the assumption that frequency data can be used to approximate subjective probabilities.

C. Evidence for Novelty Effects

To investigate the nature of novelty effects, the author (Wyer, 1970a) assumed that the novelty of an adjective is inversely proportional to the probability it is used to describe a stimulus person, as inferred from the frequency data described above. Sets of two adjectives, A and B, that varied systematically in the favorableness of A (F_A), the favorableness of B (F_B), and the novelty of B (n_B) were selected. Subjects estimated their liking for persons described by each pair. Mean evaluations as a function of F_A, F_B, and n_B are shown in Table 8.1.

Evaluations based upon pairs containing novel B adjectives were consistently more polarized than evaluations based upon pairs containing equally favorable but less novel B adjectives. The effect of differences in novelty increased as F_B became more polarized, as expected. However, the effect of novelty did not significantly depend upon F_A. In other words, novel adjectives had greater influence, but the magnitude of their influence was independent of the type of adjectives accompanying them. Thus, of the two alternative interpretations of novelty effects considered in this section, the one underlying Eq. (8.1) seems to be the more appropriate.

Information may be more "novel" when describing some types of objects than others. For example, if priests are generally assumed to be moral, information that a priest is moral would be low in novelty and therefore should have little effect upon evaluations of the priest. On the other hand, information that a priest is immoral may be very "novel" and thus have substantial effect. To investigate such possibilities, Wyer (1970b) paired 20 different roles randomly with both the positive (t+) and negative (t−) poles of 20 attribute dimensions. Subjects evaluated an occupant of each role without any other information about him (E_o), an occupant of the role described by the positive pole of the dimension paired with it (E_{ot+}), and an occupant of the role described by the negative pole of the dimension (E_{ot-}).

The favorableness of the two poles of each dimension $(F_{t+}$ and $F_{t-})$ and the likelihood that an occupant of each role (O) possessed the positive pole of the dimension (P_{t+}) paired with the role were also estimated. Suppose for simplicity that t+ and t− are the only attributes relevant to the evaluation of O. According to Fishbein's model, the evaluation of O in the absence of definite information about his attributes would be

$$E_o = P_{t+} F_{t+} + (1-P_{t+})F_{t-}$$

If information is now presented that O possesses t+, $P_{t+} = 1$, and

$$E_{ot+} = F_{t+}.$$

the effect of information that O possesses t+ is then

$$E_{ot+} - E_o = F_{t+} - P_{t+}F_{t+} - (1-P_{t+})F_{t-}$$
$$= (1 - P_{t+}) (F_{t+} - F_{t-})$$

Similarly, if information is presented that O possesses t−, $P_{t+} = 0$, and therefore

$$E_{ot-} = F_{t-};$$

the effect of this information upon the evaluation of O is then

$$E_{ot-} - E_o = F_{t-} - P_{t+} F_{t+} - (1-P_{t+}) F_{t-}$$
$$= -P_{t+} (F_{t+} - F_{t-}).$$

Wyer correlated predicted and obtained values of the effects of adding information about both t+ and t−. These correlations over the 20 dimension-role pairings (.518 and .806, respectively) were highly significant in both cases. However, additional analysis indicated that while weighting the quantity $(F_{t+} - F_{t-})$ by P_{t+} significantly increased the predictability of differences between E_{ot-} and E_o, weighting this quantity by $(1 - P_{t+})$ did not increase the predictability of the difference between E_{ot+} and E_o. In other words, the effects of unfavorable information about social role occupants depended upon its novelty, but the effects of favorable information about them did not. The reason for this contingency, which was not apparent in the first (Wyer, 1970a) study described above, is unclear.

IV. REDUNDANCY

A. Theoretical Considerations

Two pieces of information are redundant if one can be inferred from the other. For example, two adjectives are redundant if an object described by one is believed to be described by the second with high probability. In such cases, the second adjective contributes little to one's knowledge about an object already described by the first. Put another way, the total amount of information conveyed by a set of highly redundant adjectives is less than that conveyed by an equal number of less redundant adjectives.

Redundant pieces of information about an object should have less effect upon evaluations of an object than nonredundant pieces. This hypothesis, like the hypothesized effect of novelty, is consistent with Fishbein's description of cognitive organization. Suppose for simplicity that a subject bases his evaluation of O upon two attributes A and B. If information about A alone is presented, the evaluation of O should be predicted by the expression

$$E_O = F_A + P_{B/A}F_B$$

where $P_{B/A}$ is the subjective conditional probability that a person described by A is described by B. If information is now given that O possesses B as well as A,

$$E_O = F_A + F_B .$$

The effect of adding this information is therefore equal to $(1 - P_{B/A})F_B$. This analysis has two implications. First, as B's redundancy with A increases (that is, as $P_{B/A}$ becomes greater), its effect upon E_O is less. Second, the effect of differences in B's redundancy increases with the absolute magnitude of F_B.

The theoretical similarity between the effects of redundancy and the effects of novelty is obvious. In both cases, information about an attribute of O is postulated to have less effect to the extent that O is believed to possess the attribute in the absence of this information. In effect, information about O is novel to the extent that its implications are not redundant with those of

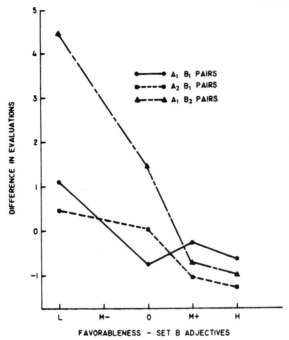

Fig. 8.3. Difference between evaluations of pairs containing set B adjectives high in redundancy and evaluations of pairs containing set B adjectives low in redundancy, as a function of the favorableness of set B adjectives (reprinted from Wyer, 1968, p. 246).

beliefs about O before any information about him is received. Thus, redundancy and novelty may be conceptually similar (if not identical) characteristics.

B. Empirical Evidence

Several investigations of redundancy effects have been reported (Dustin & Baldwin, 1966; Schmidt, 1969; Wyer, 1968; 1970a) with fairly similar results. Wyer (1968) defined the redundancy of one adjective (B) with another (A) as the conditional probability of B given A, as estimated on the basis of the normative probability data described previously.[2] Pairs of adjectives (A and B) were constructed in such a way that the normative favorableness of A and B (F_A and F_B) varied systematically over pairs. Moreover, half of the B adjectives selected were highly redundant with A adjectives, and the other half were much less redundant with A. B adjectives at each level of redundancy were matched in favorableness. Three stimulus replications were constructed. Subjects estimated (along a 21-category scale) how well they would like a person described by each pair of adjectives. The effect of redundancy was inferred from the difference between evaluations based upon A adjectives in com-

---

[2] $P_{B/A}$ can be estimated from these data by dividing the proportion of times a stimulus person was described by both A and B in combination (P_{AB}) by the proportion described by A (P_A).

TABLE 8.2

Mean Evaluations of Adjective Sets as a Function of Favorableness
Level and Information Redundancy
(reprinted from Wyer, 1960, p. 246)

Level of favorableness	Single adjective	Complete redundancy (identical)	High redundancy	Low redundancy
H	6.26	6.36	6.76	7.02
M+	2.04	1.48	1.62	2.20
O	−.61	−.97	−1.09	−1.24
L	−5.83	−6.26	−6.95	−7.04

bination with highly redundant B adjectives and evaluations based upon the same A adjectives in combination with less redundant B adjectives. If redundancy has the hypothesized effect, this difference should be related negatively to the favorableness of the B adjectives involved. These difference scores, averaged over subjects and levels of F_A, are plotted in Fig. 8.3 as a function of F_B. The magnitude of the redundancy effect varied over stimulus replications, but in all cases the effect was in the expected direction.

As a somewhat more direct test of redundancy effects, Wyer selected a subset of single adjectives and adjective pairs at each of four favorableness levels. These stimuli consisted of eight adjectives (two at each level of favorableness) each presented in isolation, each presented in a pair with itself (complete redundancy), each paired with a second equally favorable adjective associated with it with high probability (high redundancy), and each paired with an equally favorable adjective associated with it with low probability (low redundancy). Mean evaluations based upon these sets of adjectives are shown in Table 8.2. At each favorableness level, evaluations become more extreme as redundancy decreases. Moreover, the effect is greater when the adjectives involved are either very favorable or very unfavorable than at moderate levels of favorableness. However, evaluations based upon completely redundant (identical) adjectives were unexpectedly more extreme than those based upon single adjectives. Perhaps repetition increases the subjective probability that the information presented is credible and increases the extremity of evaluations for this reason. A similar interpretation of repetition effects has been suggested by L. Anderson and Fishbein (1965).

Some Definitional Problems. Since the conditional probability of B given A is not necessarily equal to the conditional probability of A given B, the index of redundancy used in the above study $(P_{B/A})$ requires the assumption that A is always considered before B. This assumption is clearly unjustified. Furthermore, it is difficult to apply the index used in this study to larger sets of information. However, these problems may be overcome. If A and B are independent, the likelihood that they are used in combination to describe an object (P_{AB}) is the product of the unconditional probabilities of their occurrence $(P_A P_B)$. Thus a measure of redundancy may be the extent to which the actual conjunctive probability of occurrence of A and B exceeds the product of the individual probabilities of their occurrence. A later study (Wyer, 1970a), in which positive values of the quantity $(P_{AB} - P_A P_B)$ were used as an index of redundancy, obtained results comparable to those of the study described above. A similar index can be applied to larger sets of information. There may also be problems with this measure. Note that the maximum possible value of P_{AB} depend upon the values of P_A and P_B. For example, if $P_A = P_B = .1$, the maximum redundancy according to this definition is .09, whereas if $P_A = P_B = .5$, the maximum redundancy is .25. Whether such a difference in redundancy has any empirical or theoretical significance is unclear. An alternative index might be the ratio of the conjunctive probability to the product of the unconditional probabilities, that is, $P_{AB}/P_A P_B$.

C. Generalization of Redundancy Effects

While the effects of redundancy have been investigated in a limited domain, it seems likely that the results obtained generalize to other types of information about other types of objects. For example, two opinion statements about an object would be redundant to the extent that a person who makes one statement is more likely to make the other than would be expected by chance. If this interpretation is correct, a person who makes two statements, each conveying a favorable opinion about an object, should be inferred to have a less extreme attitude toward the object if the statements are redundant than if they are not. Similarly, persuasive communications supporting a particular issue should be less influential if the statements contained in them are redundant than if they are relatively independent. For example, if the assertions "War leads to the killing of innocent people," "War prevents social and economic development," and "War leads to inflation" convey equally unfavorable opinions about war, and if subjects who believe the first tend also to believe the second but not necessarily the third, then a pair of persuasive communications arguing that the first and third statements are true should have a greater effect on a subject's evaluation of war than a pair of equally effective communications arguing that the first and second statements are true.

V.   INCONSISTENCY

Two pieces of information are inconsistent if both pieces in combination are unlikely to be valid. For example, two adjectives are inconsistent if a person described by one is unlikely to be described by the other. When two inconsistent adjectives are applied to the same person, the recipient of this information may typically regard one or both pieces of information as invalid. If the entire set of information is regarded as incredible, its influence should be decreased; that is, an evaluation based upon it should be less extreme than an evaluation based upon equally favorable but more consistent information. On the other hand, it is conceivable that when information is inconsistent, only part of it is rejected as incredible. In some circumstances, this could lead to a *more* extreme evaluation than would occur if the evaluation were based upon equally favorable but less inconsistent information. The problem, of course, is to predict which pieces of inconsistent information are discounted. Several factors have been investigated, including the proportion of consistent information, initial predispositions to evaluate objects favorably or unfavorably, the extremity and negativity of the scale values of the information, and the magnitude of the inconsistency in the information. Let us discuss the effects of these factors in turn.

A. Proportion of Consistent Information

Anderson and Jacobson (1965) constructed sets of three adjectives, one of which differed in its evaluative implication from the other two. For example, in the set *honest, considerate, gloomy,* the third adjective, which describes an unfavorable attribute, was assumed to be inconsistent with the other two. The adjectives contained in certain of the sets constructed (e.g., *honest, deceitful, gloomy*) were actually antonyms. Anderson and Jacobson argued that the "odd" adjective in each set would tend to be discounted, and thus the evaluation based upon the information presented would be more extreme. (For example, in the set *honest, deceitful, gloomy,* the first adjective should be given less weight, and thus the evaluation should be relatively more negative.) This hypothesis was tested under three instructional conditions. In Condition 1, subjects were told that the three adjectives in a set represented equally important aspects of the personality of the person being described. In Condition 2, they were told that all three adjectives might not be equally valid descriptions of the person. In Condition 3, they were explicitly told that one of the three adjectives in each set did not apply. Discounting was assumed to occur when the evaluation based upon all three adjectives deviated in the appropriate direction from the simple average of the evaluations based upon each adjective considered separately. According to this criterion, some discounting occurred under all three conditions. However, discounting was least in Condition 1 and greatest in Condition 3.

B. Effects of Initial Predisposition

Anderson and Jacobson's findings provided the basis for a study by Kaplan (1971b) of the effects of subjects' initial predispositions to evaluate persons favorably or unfavorably before receiving information about them. Kaplan argued that if one's predisposition functions as a piece of information, it should influence which adjectives in a set are discounted. For example, consider a set of two adjectives, one with favorable implications and the other with unfavorable implications. If subjects' initial predispositions function as a third piece of information, Anderson and Jacobson's findings imply that persons with favorable predispositions will discount the unfavorable adjective, while those with unfavorable predispositions will discount the favorable one. To test this hypothesis, Kaplan constructed sets of two or four adjectives, each containing an equal number of adjectives with high normative likeableness (H) ratings and adjectives with low normative (L) ratings. Differences in initial predispositions were inferred from tendencies to choose H or L adjectives as most likely to describe "persons in general." Subjects evaluated a person described by each set of adjectives under instructional conditions comparable to Conditions 1 and 2 in Anderson and Jacobson's study. When they were told that the adjectives might not be equally valid descriptions of the persons being evaluated (Condition 2), subjects with positive predispositions evaluated these persons more favorably than did similar subjects under control conditions (Condition 1), while subjects with negative predispositions evaluated these persons relatively less favorably.

One of the more curious results reported by Anderson and Jacobson, that unfavorable adjectives in the context of two favorable ones were discounted more than were favorable adjectives in the context of two unfavorable ones, can potentially be explained on the basis of Kaplan's findings. Suppose subjects typically have a predisposition to evaluate persons positively. Then, subjects who receive one unfavorable and two favorable adjectives would have the equivalent of one unfavorable and three favorable pieces of information and hence would discount the unfavorable one. However, subjects who receive one favorable and two unfavorable adjectives would have the equivalent of two pieces of information of each type and hence may discount the favorable and unfavorable adjectives with roughly equal probability. Anderson and Jacobson's findings are consistent with this interpretation.

C. Magnitude of Inconsistency, Extremity, and Negativity

Contrary to expectations, Anderson and Jacobson found that discounting was no greater when stimulus sets contained antonyms than when they contained adjectives that differed only in their evaluative implications. This finding is difficult to interpret. Conceivably, although the *semantic* inconsistency of the information combined in these sets differed, subjects may have believed that both sets were equally unlikely to describe a single person. A more precise index of the subjective inconsistency of a set of adjectives may be the difference between the conjunctive probability that these adjectives describe a person and the product of the unconditional probabilities that each adjective, considered independently, describes a person. For example, A and B would be inconsistent if $P_{AB} - P_A P_B < 0$. (Note that, to this extent, inconsistency and redundancy are opposite poles of a single continuum defined by the quantity $P_{AB} - P_A P_B$.)

To separate the effects of favorableness and inconsistency, Wyer (1970a) used the above index and paired favorable and unfavorable adjectives such that the *mean* favorableness of the adjectives comprising each pair was either very favorable (H), moderately favorable ($M+$), neutral (O), moderately unfavorable ($M-$), or very unfavorable (L). Adjectives in the pairs representing each favorableness level were either low (e.g. *punctual* and *belligerant*), moderate (*reckless* and *courteous*), or high (*pleasant* and *antisocial*) in inconsistency, as inferred from the same normative probability data used to estimate redundancy and novelty. Adjective pairs at each inconsistency level were matched in normative favorableness. Evaluations of persons described by these pairs were investigated as a function of the mean favorableness of the adjectives presented and their inconsistency. What results might be expected?

It seems reasonable to expect that as inconsistency increases, first only part of the information is discounted, but then, as inconsistency becomes extremely great, the entire set of information is rejected. The most ambiguous pieces of information may be discounted first. Adjective pairs in this study were constructed so that in H and $M+$ pairs the favorable adjective was more polarized than the unfavorable one, in $M-$ and L pairs the unfavorable adjective was the more polarized, and in O pairs the two adjectives were equally polarized. If ambiguity is an inverse function both of extremity and, to a lesser extent, of favorableness (see p. 221), the less extreme information should generally be the more ambiguous in pairs of unequally polarized adjectives, while the favorable piece should be the more ambiguous in pairs of equally polarized adjectives (O pairs). Therefore, if the above reasoning is correct, evaluations based upon H and $M+$ pairs should initially become more favorable as inconsistency increases, while evaluations based upon O, $M-$, and L pairs should become more unfavorable. However, when inconsistency becomes very great, and *both* adjectives in each pair are discounted, there should be a decrease in the extremity of ratings at all favorableness levels.

The results of Wyer's study, summarized in Table 8.3, generally support these hypotheses. Evaluations of H, $M-$, and L pairs became more extreme as inconsistency increased from low to moderate, implying that the less polarized adjective was discounted, but then became less extreme as inconsistency continued to increase, implying that the entire set of information was rejected. Evaluations of $M+$ and O pairs did not appreciably change as inconsistency increased from low to moderate; however, as

TABLE 8.3

Evaluations of Adjective Pairs as a Function of Mean
Favorableness Level and Inconsistency
(reprinted from Wyer, 1970a, p. 191)

| | Degree of inconsistency | | |
Favorableness level	Low	Moderate	High
H	2.59	2.92	1.85
M+	−.37	−.63	1.18
O	−1.13	−.78	−2.77
M−	−2.30	−3.19	−2.32
L	−2.64	−3.52	−3.09

inconsistency increased from moderate to high, these evaluations changed in the direction one would expect if the more ambiguous piece of information in each pair were discounted. Perhaps a greater amount of inconsistency was required to produce discounting at these favorableness levels. (Since a direct measure of information ambiguity was not used in this study, our interpretation of these results should be treated with some caution.)

D. Generalizability of Discounting Effects

Discounting may be most likely to occur when the validity of the information presented is more a matter of opinion than of fact. Since descriptions of a person's personality may depend greatly upon the biases of the judge and the particular circumstances in which he has observed the person being described, such information can easily be regarded as unreliable. In contrast, factual information about a person is likely to be regarded as invalid only if its source is believed to be an outright liar. Inconsistencies among this latter type of information may therefore be less apt to produce discounting, at least when its source is apparently the experimenter. A study by Himmelfarb and Senn (1969) provides some support for this hypothesis. Subjects estimated the social class of different stimulus persons on the basis of information about the person's occupation, his level of education, and his annual income. Each piece of information was assumed to imply either a high (H), moderately high (M), moderately low (M−), or low (L) social class. Inconsistencies were assumed when the information presented implied markedly different social classes. For example, a set of inconsistent information might have been "a tobacco laborer (L) with a 4th grade education (L) making $20,000 a year (H)." Stimulus sets were constructed in a manner analogous to the procedure used by Anderson and Jacobson. Analyses of the data provided no evidence of discounting. If anything, inconsistent information appeared to be *contrasted,* or given more weight, rather than discounted. In general, subjects' judgments of the social class of persons described by three pieces of information were remarkably close to the unweighted average of the judgments made on the basis of each piece presented separately. These data place an important limitation upon the generality of findings reported by Anderson and Jacobson, Kaplan, and Wyer.

VI. THE EFFECT OF CONTEXT ON THE INTERPRETATION OF INFORMATION

A. Theoretical Considerations

As we noted in Chapter 2, a subject's evaluation of an object along a response scale may reflect the expected value of the distribution of subjective probabilities that the object belongs to each of the scale categories. A subject's uncertainty about how to classify an object described by a single adjective may be due at least in part to the fact that this adjective has a variety of possible interpretations or meanings, each with a different evaluative implication. For example, "aggressive" could imply "malicious," "hostile," and "belligerent," which have unfavorable connotations. Alternatively, it could imply "hard-working," "assertive," "ambitious," and "willing to take initiative," which have favorable connotations. A subject who is asked to evaluate a person described as "aggressive" may not know which set of attributes is implied and therefore may not be confident that any particular rating of this person is valid.

In some instances the most appropriate interpretation of an adjective may be inferred from other information about the object it describes. For example, information that a "cruel" person is "aggressive" is more apt to convey hostility and belligerence than information that a "warm-hearted" person is "aggressive." One implication of this is that "aggressive" will be interpreted as a more favorable attribute if considered in the context of "warm-hearted" than if considered in the context of "cruel."

If the meaning of a piece of information depends upon its context, it may often be very difficult to predict *a priori* the effect that this information will have. An excellent example of this is provided in a study by Aronson, Willerman, and Floyd (1966). In this study, subjects listened to a tape-recorded interview of a candidate for a position in which knowledge and intelligence were important factors. In one condition the candidate appeared to be highly competent in responding to a series of questions designed to assess his knowledge, while in another condition he appeared to be very incompetent. After completing the interview, the candidate was given a cup of coffee. Half of the candidates at each level of competence were heard to spill their coffee over their "new suit," while the remainder drank their coffee without mishap. Subjects then estimated their liking for the candidate. Competent candidates were generally better liked than incompetent ones. However, information that the competent candidate spilled his coffee often increased his likeableness, while similar information about the incompetent candidate decreased his likeableness. Put another way, the behavioral attribute "spilled coffee over himself" had exactly opposite effects when presented in the context of the attribute "competent" as opposed to "incompetent." These results suggest that the behavioral attribute was interpreted differently in the two contexts and therefore had different evaluative implications. For example, in the context of "competent," it may have been interpreted as an indication of being "human," "down-to-earth," and "approachable," while in the context of "incompetent" it may have implied the attributes "clumsy" and "careless."

1. *A Change-of-Meaning Model of Context Effects.* The manner in which adjectives shift in meaning as a function of their context, originally postulated by Asch (1946), has been formulated more explicitly by Ostrom (1967) and applied to impression formation processes. Ostrom hypothesizes that when a subject is asked to evaluate the attribute described by an adjective presented in isolation, his evaluation is a composite (for example, an "average") of the implications of the alternative intepretations given to it. When the adjective is presented in the context of other information, however, the subject renders certain of its possible interpretations improbable and discounts them. His subsequent evaluation is then a composite of the implications of only those interpretations that remain. When an adjective is accompanied by information with generally favorable implications, interpretations with unfavorable connotations are the most likely to be rejected. The implications of the remaining interpretations, and thus the evaluation based upon the adjectives, should consequently be more favorable when the adjective is presented with favorable information than when it is presented alone or with unfavorable information.

The particular function relating the evaluation based upon a personality adjective to the evaluative implications of its possible interpretations is not stated by Ostrom. Fishbein's (1963) general model of cognitive organization may again be applicable. Assume that the evaluation of a personality adjective, like the evaluation of any other object, is a function of the favorableness of a set of implications, each weighted by the probability that the adjective has this implication; that is,

$$E_o = \Sigma P_{io} F_i$$

where in this case E_o is the evaluation based upon adjective O, F_i is the favorableness of the ith interpretation of O, and P_{io} is the probability that this interpretation is valid. When O is presented in a favorable context, the probabilities associated with favorable interpretations increase, and the probabilities associated with unfavorable interpretations decrease, producing an increase in E_O. When O is presented in an unfavorable context, these probabilities shift in the opposite directions, and hence E_O decreases.

2. *A Halo Effect Interpretation of Context Effects.* Evidence that the evaluation of an attribute described by a single adjective does increase with the favorableness of the information presented with it (its context) has been obtained repeatedly under a variety of conditions (Anderson, 1966, 1971a; Anderson & Lampel, 1965; Kaplan, 1971a; Wyer, 1974c; Wyer & Dermer, 1968; Wyer & Watson, 1969). However, there are other possible interpretations of this context effect than the change-of-meaning explanation proposed by Asch and by Ostrom. Anderson (1971a) has hypothesized that when subjects are called upon to evaluate a trait in the company of others, they respond not only to the trait itself but also to its context. The contribution of the context is viewed as a "generalized halo effect." In other words, some fraction of the overall favorableness of the object being evaluated generalizes to each of the individual attributes possessed by the object. If the "halo effect" is independent of the characteristics of the attribute being evaluated, the evaluation of an attribute in context may be predictable as a weighted linear function of the evaluation of the attribute when considered in isolation and the overall evaluation of the object possessing the attribute. Since the latter evaluation increases with the favorableness of the context adjectives, a halo effect as well as meaning shift could account for an increase in evaluations of single traits with the favorableness of adjectives accompanying them.

The two interpretations of context effects described above are not necessarily incompatible; it is conceivable that meaning shift and a halo effect occur simultaneously to different degrees, depending upon the particular conditions in which evaluations are made. However, an understanding of the extent to which meaning shift accounts for context effects, and under what conditions, is of considerable importance. If the interpretation of an adjective changes when it is presented with others, and if the magnitude of this change depends upon the particular combination of adjectives involved, then a precise description of the manner in which information about an object combines to affect judgments of the object may be very difficult to obtain. On the other hand, if each adjective retains its context-free meaning when it is combined with others, it may be possible to predict evaluations based upon several adjectives as a function of the evaluations based upon each adjective in isolation. Because of the importance of this issue for an understanding of information integration processes, the experimental evidence bearing upon it is worth detailed consideration.

B. Situational Determinants of Context Effects

The first rigorous investigations of context effects were performed by Anderson and his colleagues (Anderson, 1966; Anderson & Lampel, 1965). In the 1965 experiment, stimulus sets of three adjectives were constructed by combining a "test" adjective at two levels of likeableness (M+ and M−, according to the notation used in previous sections) with a pair of "context" adjectives at each of four levels of likeableness (*H*, *M*+, *M*−, and *L*). Two instructional conditions were run. In Condition P, subjects were told to assume that the adjectives in each set described a person, and they were asked to estimate how well they would like such a person before evaluating an "individual trait of the person" (the *test* trait). In Condition *W*, traits were considered individually rather than as a collective: Subjects were told to assume that the three adjectives in each set described different personality traits, and after reading each adjective aloud they were asked only to estimate how well they would like "the traits implied by the [test] adjective." Anderson found that evaluations increased with the likeableness of context traits (a positive context effect) under Condition *P* but not under Condition *W*. In a second study (Anderson, 1966), in which four levels of test trait likeableness were used, the context effect under Condition *P* was replicated.

If context effects are attributable to a generalized halo effect of the type hypothesized by Anderson, the magnitude of this effect should be directly proportional to the likeableness of the context traits. Moreover, the effect of context should be similar, regardless of the test adjectives involved; in other words, the interaction of test adjective likeableness and context likeableness should theoretically be zero. In Anderson and Lampel's (1965) study, this interaction was in fact not significant. In the second (Anderson, 1966) study, this interaction was significant but accounted for only 0.3% of the variance in test adjective ratings. Data relevant to this interaction (Fig. 8.4) indicate that context effects on test adjectives at all four levels of test adjective likeableness are parallel except for two deviant points (when the context was M− and the test adjective was either M− or M+). While these deviations could be attributable to idiosyncratic shifts in meaning of the test adjectives involved at these levels, the support these data provide for Anderson's hypothesis is impressive.

In a later study, Anderson (1971a) reported additional data that he interpreted as evidence against a change-of-meaning interpretation of context effects. In this study, two groups of subjects evaluated collective and test adjectives under instructions comparable to those used in Condition P of the earlier studies. However, half of the subjects wrote a brief paragraph about each stimulus person before rating him and the individual traits describing him. Anderson argued that providing this opportunity to integrate

TEST ADJECTIVE

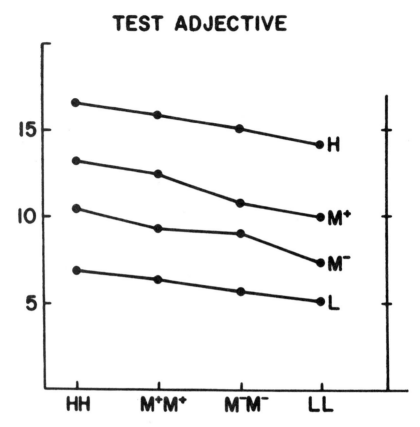

Fig. 8.4. Test adjective ratings as a function of context adjective likeableness (reprinted from Anderson, 1966, p. 279).

the information presented would increase the likelihood that the meanings of individual traits are affected by their contexts. Thus, if meaning shift contributes to context effects, these effects should be greater under this condition. However, Anderson found no greater context effects under this condition than when subjects were not given the opportunity to write paragraphs about the stimulus person described. It is of course possible that subjects integrated the information presented equally well under both experimental conditions, despite different opportunities to communicate the results of this integration in writing. Thus, while a significant difference in magnitude of the context effects obtained under the two conditions might support a change-of-meaning interpretation, the absence of such a difference does not necessarily contradict this interpretation. A more important finding in this study was that the critical interaction of test adjective likeableness and context likeableness was not significant under either experimental condition.

1. *Effects of Instructional Set.* If context effects are attributable to changes in meaning, the magnitude of these effects should be reduced by instructions that dissociate the traits in the collective or that decrease the degree of their interdependence. However, support for this hypothesis is equivocal. The author and his colleagues (Wyer & Dermer, 1968; Wyer & Watson, 1969) constructed several conditions in which adjectives in each set were rated as a collective but were otherwise minimally related. Specifically, Wyer and Dermer considered three conditions in addition to P and W:

W_C—subjects were told that the adjectives in each set did not apply to a single person, and that it would often be difficult to think of them as describing a single individual. When each set was presented, subjects estimated how well they would like the traits as a collective and then estimated their liking for the test trait.

P_D—subjects were told that the adjectives in each set described a person, but that many of the persons described had "disorganized" personalities and often behaved in inconsistent ways; the adjectives describing each stimulus person were contributed by different judges who had observed the person at different times and may have seen different aspects of his personality.

G—subjects were told that each adjective in a set described a different person; when each set was presented they first estimated how well they would like the *group* of persons, and then how well they would like the person described by the test adjective.

Wyer and Watson constructed two additional conditions in which subjects were asked to use a fairly mechanical procedure in arriving at collective ratings:

W_S—subjects were told that the adjectives in each set were unrelated and did not apply to a single person; when a set was presented, they were told to estimate the *sum* of the likeableness of the attributes described by "adding up" their estimates of how well they would like each separately; then, they were asked to record their evaluation of the test attribute alone.

W_A—Instructions were similar to those in Condition W_S; in this case, however, subjects were asked to estimate how well they liked the three traits described *on the average.* They were specifically instructed to estimate their liking for each trait and to report the average of these estimates before recording their evaluations of the test trait.

The stimuli used in these studies were three-adjective sets representing all combinations of four levels of context likeableness and four levels of test adjective likeableness. The context effects obtained in Conditions W_C, P_D, and G did not significantly differ from those obtained in Condition P, but they were significantly greater than those obtained in Condition W. However, context effects in Conditions W_S and W_A were significantly less than in Condition P, while not differing from those obtained in Condition W. In other words, instructions to form an overall impression of a collective of adjectives produced context effects upon component adjectives, even when these adjectives were minimally related (except by virtue of their physical juxtaposition in the collective). However, instructions to form the collective evaluation by combining component judgments according to a mechanical rule (e.g. adding or averaging) tended to eliminate the effect. While these latter data are not conclusive, they suggest that the process of information integration that produces context effects is not equivalent to that occurring when subjects are instructed simply to add or to average the implications of the information presented.

To confuse matters further, Wyer, unlike Anderson, obtained highly significant interactions of context likeableness and test adjective likeableness in each of his studies (for an example of one such interaction, see Fig. 6.4B). These interactions contradict the assumption that the rating of a test adjective is a simple linear function of its context-free evaluation and the evaluation of the collective in which it is contained. The reason for this important difference between the two sets of experiments is not completely clear. One possibility is that Anderson, unlike Wyer, exercised substantial control over the conditions under which ratings are made. For example, in Anderson's (1966) experiment, the time between stimulus presentation and subjects' ratings was carefully controlled. In more recent studies, Anderson (1971a) has instructed subjects run under Condition P that each adjective was contributed by a different acquaintance who knew the person well, that each adjective is accurate and equally important, that equal attention should be paid to each adjective, and that some inconsistencies occur because different acquaintances often see different aspects of the person's personality. In contrast, Wyer instructed subjects under Condition P simply to form an impression of a person described by the set of adjectives presented and then to estimate how well they would like such a person, without more explicit instructions about the source of the information or how it should be treated. Perhaps meaning shift is more likely to occur in this condition than in the more rigorously controlled conditions studied by Anderson.

Another possible reason for Anderson's failure to detect a significant test × context interaction is suggested by the procedures he has used to construct stimulus sets. Specifically, complex counterbalancing procedures are often used, so that within a given stimulus replication each of several different test adjectives at each likeableness level is paired with each of several context sets at each likeableness level. For example, in Anderson's (1971a) study, four different M+ and four different M− test adjectives were each combined with two different pairs of adjectives at each level of context likeableness. In analyzing evaluations based upon these stimuli, ratings pertaining to each combination of context likeableness and test likeableness were pooled over the eight different sets representing this combination. This pooling procedure may prevent the detection of idiosyncratic effects of context adjectives upon the meanings assigned to test adjectives and thus increase the likelihood of a nonsignificant test × context interaction. In Wyer's studies, each replication consisted of only one test adjective at each likeableness level combined with one context pair at each likeableness level. This procedure may increase the likelihood of detecting idiosyncratic effects such as those expected on the basis of a meaning shift interpretation of context effects.

2. *Some Direct Evidence for Changes in Meaning.* As we noted earlier, both meaning shift and a generalized halo effect could conceivably contribute independently to context effects, the contribution of each depending upon the particular instructional conditions used. Wyer (1974c) attempted to identify the relative contribution of each factor, in a study designed to provide a more direct test of Ostrom's formulation of meaning shift than the studies described above. If this formulation is valid, the meanings assigned to a test adjective should differ as a function of its context; moreover, the average of the evaluative implications of these interpretations should increase with context likeableness in a manner corresponding roughly to the increase in actual ratings of these test adjectives. Finally, to the extent that shifts in meaning contribute to context effects, these effects should be substantially reduced by eliminating from test adjective ratings any variance that is predictable from the evaluative implications of the meanings assigned to these adjectives.

To investigate these hypotheses, we first obtained preliminary data on the alternative interpretations of several personality adjectives by asking subjects to list as many possible words or phrases that each adjective could mean if it were used to describe a person. From these adjectives, two were selected at each of three levels of normative likeableness ($M+$, O, and $M-$). At least 15 meanings, differing in the favorableness of their implications, had been generated for each of these adjectives. (As an example, one of the $M+$ adjectives selected, *agreeable,* was assigned the meanings: warm, agreeing with everyone on everything, wishy-washy, cowardly, conceding, bending easily, congenial, amenable, likeable, pleasant, conformist, personable, persuadable, obliging, and sociable.) A second group of subjects was then presented these 90 "meanings" in random order with instructions to estimate how well they would like a person described by each word or phrase. Estimates were made along a 21-point scale from -10 to $+10$. The average rating of each meaning was taken as the normative value of its likeableness.

Stimuli for the main experiment consisted of test adjectives each combined with a pair of context adjectives at each of four likeableness levels (H, $M+$, $M-$, and L). The experiment was run in two parts. In Part A, subjects first evaluated each collective along a 21-point scale similar to that described above, and then evaluated the test adjective along the scale. These ratings were made under one of three conditions. In Condition P_w, instructions were similar to those used previously by Wyer under Condition P; that is, subjects were told simply to form an impression of the person described by the collective, to estimate their liking for such a person, and then to evaluate one of his traits, designated by the experimenter (the test trait). In Condition

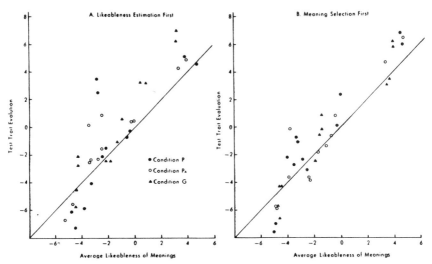

Fig. 8.5. Test adjective ratings as a function of the average likeableness of the meanings assigned to them.

P_{And}, more explicit instructions were given about how to treat the information; these instructions were comparable to those used by Anderson (1971a) and described on page 242. In the third condition, G, subjects were told to assume that each adjective described a different person and to evaluate the three persons as a group before estimating their liking for the person described by the test trait.

In Part B, subjects were first reminded that an adjective could be interpreted in different ways, depending upon the circumstances in which it was used. Then, after instructions relevant to the particular condition being run (P_W, P_{And}, or G), they were presented with each set of adjectives and asked to indicate all words or phrases in an appropriate list of 15 alternatives that might be possible interpretations of the test adjective. The average normative likeableness of the "meanings" selected was used as a predictor of the actual evaluation of the adjective in the context in which it occurred.

The order of performing Parts A and B was counterbalanced. Mean test adjective evaluations under each instructional condition are plotted as a function of mean predicted values in Fig. 8.5. Actual evaluations were both more positive and more extreme than predicted values but were highly correlated with these values (averaged over subjects, $r = .917$ when the meaning selection task was performed before likeableness estimates were made, and $r = .825$ when likeableness estimation was performed first; moreover, mean $r > .625$ under every instructional condition.)

Actual and predicted test adjective ratings under each combination of instructions and task order are shown in Fig. 8.6 as a function of context likeableness. Context effects were more pronounced when meaning selection

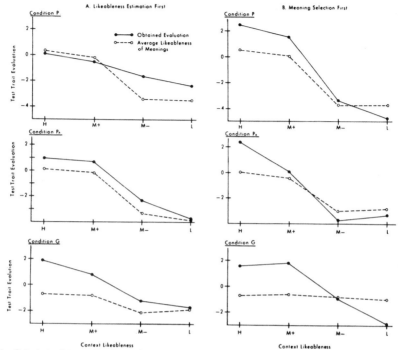

Fig. 8.6. Actual test adjective ratings, and the average likeableness of the meanings assigned to them (predicted ratings), as a function of context likeableness, instructional set, and task order (reprinted from Wyer, 1974c).

was performed first, suggesting that the meaning selection task produced an artificial inflation of these effects. Perhaps the task created the impression that subjects were expected by the experimenter to vary their ratings as a function of their context, and subjects tended to comply with this expectation. Context effects on the average likeableness of the meanings selected were nearly identical under both task order conditions.

Data in Fig. 8.6 show that when likeableness estimates were made first, context effects on actual and predicted test adjective evaluations were nearly identical in Condition P_{And}. However, actual evaluations were less strongly affected by context than were predicted ratings in Condition P_W, but were more strongly affected than predicted ratings in Condition G. Statistical analyses support these conclusions. For example, an analysis of the residual test adjective ratings (obtained by eliminating, through use of regression procedures, the proportion of variance in these ratings that could be provided from variance in meaning) indicated a nonsignificant context effect in Condition P_{And}, a significant negative context effect in Condition P_W, and a significant positive context effect in Condition G.

Unfortunately, the interpretation of this study is not completely unequivocal. For example, it can be argued that differences in the meanings assigned to each test adjective in context, like differences in the evaluation of the test adjective, were the result of a generalized halo effect of the sort hypothesized by Anderson. The study fails to demonstrate conclusively that subjects based their selections only upon their altered interpretations of the test adjective and did not respond directly to the context adjectives. These latter responses could conceivably have occurred despite explicit instructions to select words and phrases that were possible interpretations of the test adjective. However, note that if the meanings assigned to test adjectives in context and the evaluations of these adjectives in context are both influenced by a generalized halo effect, the relative magnitude of these influences should be similar in each instructional condition. The fact that predictions based upon the meanings assigned to test adjectives are differentially accurate over the three conditions would be difficult to explain on the basis of a generalized halo effect *alone*.

To the extent that the meanings assigned to test adjectives in the above study are not themselves attributable to halo effects of the type hypothesized by Anderson, what conclusions are suggested? First, under conditions similar to those used by Anderson (1971a), changes in meaning can completely account for context effects. Second, the smaller context effect under P_W than under P_{And} suggests that in the former condition context likeableness has two opposing effects, one of which, a contrast effect, is eliminated by the more detailed instructions used by Anderson. Finally, the fact that the context effect in Condition G was greater than that predicted suggests that under this condition, but *not* when adjectives described a single person, context effects may be partially attributable to a generalized halo effect. That is, liking for a person may in part be a function of the quality of his associates, independent of the personal characteristics implied by adjectives specifically describing him. (The nature of one's associates may function as an attribute, and therefore may affect how well he is liked, in much the same manner as his other attributes.) This interpretation would not be clearly applicable when both test and context adjectives are applied to the same person, as in Conditions P_W and P_{And}.

If the above interpretation of our results is valid, these results must be reconciled with evidence that context effects occur under a variety of instructional conditions designed to dissociate context and test adjectives. Perhaps, contrary to the expectations of Wyer and Dermer, simply the juxtaposition of adjectives on a slide is often sufficient to affect their meanings in a way that will produce context effects, provided these adjectives are rated as a collective. On the other hand, instructions to combine the evaluative implications of different adjectives according to a mechanical rule (such as adding or averaging) may decrease shifts in meaning and thus reduce context effects.

C. Informational Determinants of Context Effects

Let us now consider characteristics of the information presented that may determine the magnitude of these effects. Three factors have been investigated: the amount of context information presented, the ambiguity of the test information, and the inconsistency between the test information and the context information. Evidence that context effects depend upon these factors bears indirectly upon the validity of Ostrom's and Anderson's interpretations of these effects.

1. *Amount of Context Information.* According to Ostrom's formulation of meaning shift, interpretations of test information that are rendered unlikely by the context information are discounted. This should produce a change in the evaluation of the test information, which is theoretically a composite of the implications of the remaining interpretations. It seems reasonable to hypothesize that the greater the number of pieces of equally favorable information comprising the context, the more likely it is that implications of test information that differ in favorableness from those of the context information will be discounted. Therefore, context effect should increase with the number of pieces of equally polarized information comprising the context. Support for this prediction has been obtained by both Anderson (1971a) and Kaplan (1971a). Although both of these researchers interpret their findings as contradictory to a change-of-meaning interpretation, they seem entirely consistent with Ostrom's formulation. Incidentally, Ostrom's interpretation implies that test and context information will have reciprocal effects upon one another's meaning. Thus, when context and test adjectives are equally favorable, evaluations of both test and context adjectives should increase. Ostrom (1967) himself has found support for this hypothesis.

2. *Ambiguity of Test Information.* It seems intuitively reasonable to expect that the more ambiguous a piece of information, or alternatively the wider the range of its possible evaluative implications, the more likely it is that its interpretations will be affected by context information. To this extent, context effects should be greater when the test information is more ambiguous. This prediction would *not* be made on the basis of Anderson's formulation of context effects; according to this formulation, the contribution of context likeableness to test adjective evaluations does not depend upon characteristics of the test information itself.

To investigate this hypothesis, the author (Wyer, 1974c) selected test adjectives from a pool for which subjects had generated frequency distributions of persons described by them, and thus which could be classified as high and low in ambiguity as defined by Eq. (2.2). Test adjectives at three levels of normative likeableness ($M+$, O, and $M-$) and two levels of ambiguity were each combined with pairs of context adjectives representing four likeableness levels (H, $M+$, $M-$, and L). Subjects rated each collective of three adjectives, and then the test adjective, under instructional conditions

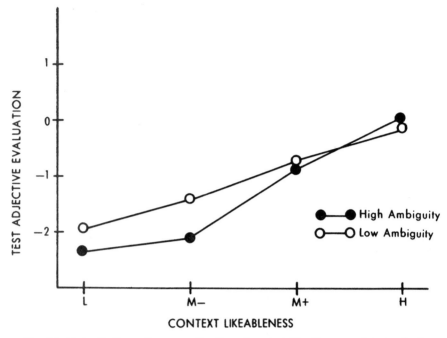

Fig. 8.7. Test adjective ratings as a function of context likeableness and test adjective ambiguity (reprinted from Wyer, 1974c).

P_W, P_{And}, and G, as described on page 241. Test adjective ratings, pooled over instructional conditions, are shown in Fig. 8.7 as a function of context likeableness and test adjective likeableness. Test adjective ratings increased with context likeableness as expected ($F = 47.55$; $df = 3/99$; $p < .001$). The magnitude of this increase did not depend upon instructional set but was significantly greater when the ambiguity of test adjectives was high than when it was low ($F = 5.05$; $df = 3/99$; $p < .01$).

The results described above could be attributed to a generalized halo effect if the ratings of collectives containing highly ambiguous test adjectives were relatively more similar to the normative context ratings than were the ratings of collectives containing equally favorable but less ambiguous test adjectives. However, this was not the case. Although analyses of collective ratings yielded a significant interaction of context likeableness and test adjective ambiguity, this interaction, displayed in Fig. 8.8, is not attributable to the fact that collective ratings were displaced more toward the favorableness of context adjectives when the text adjectives were more ambiguous. Thus, of the two alternative interpretations of context effects considered in this section, the change-of-meaning interpretation is more consistent with the results of this experiment.

Other Studies of Ambiguity Effects. It is important to note that earlier investigations (Kaplan, 1971a; Wyer & Watson, 1969) failed to obtain

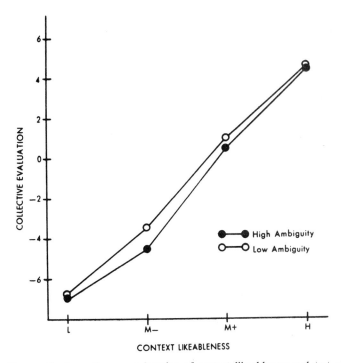

Fig. 8.8. Mean collective ratings as a function of context likeableness and test adjective ambiguity (reprinted from Wyer, 1974c).

convincing evidence for the contingency of context effects upon test adjective ambiguity. It seems likely, however, that these failures were due in part to an inadequate measure of ambiguity. For example, Kaplan (1971a) used the standard deviation of subjects' ratings of a trait in isolation as an index of ambiguity and found that differences in this characteristic did not relate to differences in context effects. However, as we pointed out in Chapter 2, the fact that subjects disagree about the favorableness of an attribute does not necessarily indicate that any particular subject is uncertain about his evaluation of the attribute. The low correlation between the standard deviation of attribute ratings over subjects and the mean subjective un- certainty expressed by subjects about these ratings (Table 2.2) supports this contention. While Kaplan reports evidence that the index he used is significantly related to the test-retest reliability of individual subjects' ratings of the attributes involved, the magnitude of this relationship is not reported and is probably quite low.

Wyer and Watson (1969) assumed that the range of meanings that an adjective could have was indicated by the difference between the most (M) and the least (L) a person described by the adjective would be liked. However, they found that the range of evaluations an adjective could generate above the normative rating based upon the adjective (M–X) was correlated negatively with the range of evaluations it could generate below its normative rating (X–L). Since this finding indicated that it was inappropriate to combine these indices into a single estimate of range of meaning (that is, M–L), the effect of differences in each range measure was considered separately. In investigating these effects, test adjectives differing in the range of their implications (M–X or X–L) were matched in normative likeableness (X). As expected, context effects were relatively greater on adjectives that had a wide range of possible evaluative implications below their normative likeableness (that is, adjectives high in X–L). However, contrary to expectations, context effects were related *negatively* to the range of implications that adjectives could have above their normative likeableness. In light of the negative correlation between M–X and X–L, both findings could indicate that context effects are a positive function of the range of evaluative implications an adjective can have below its normative likeableness. This hypothesis could be investigated more systematically with the measure of ambiguity defined by Eq. (2.2).

3. *Inconsistency Between Test and Context Information.* Meaning shift hypothetically occurs because interpretations of the test information which contradict implications of the context information are discounted. If this is true, meaning shift should be more likely, and context effects greater, when context and test information are inconsistent. A rigorous test of this hypothesis requires a precise index of inconsistency, which can be varied independently of differences in the normative favorableness of the test and context information. Although such a test has not been made, an experiment performed by Wyer and Schwartz (1969) in a different content domain is indirectly relevant. In this study, discussed in more detail in Chapter 6, subjects rated a (test) communication along an evaluative dimension after receiving previous (context) communications from the same source. Four types of communications were considered: attitude statements about Negroes, statements conveying liberal or conservative beliefs about various social issues (child-rearing practices, social welfare, foreign aid, sexual relations, etc.), cartoons of different degrees of "funniness," and photographs differing in interest value. Statements conveying different attitudes towards Negroes were expected to be most inconsistent in meaning (and thus to show the most positive context effects), followed by statements about social issues conveying different degrees of liberalism, and then by cartoons and photographs differing in quality. In each case, subjects first received a set of communications that were either all "positive" or all "negative" along the appropriate dimension and then rated the test communication along the dimension. In accord with predictions, there was a significant positive context effect on judgments of statements about Negroes, a nonsignificant but positive effect on judgments of statements about social issues, a nonsignificant but negative effect on judgments of cartoons, and a significant negative effect on judgments of photographs.

The results described above apply only to conditions in which context and test communications are attributed to the same source. When these communications come from different sources, there is no obvious reason to discount implications of test communications that are inconsistent with implications of the context communications, and therefore a positive context effect might not be expected. Wyer and Schwartz found that context effects under such conditions were significantly negative in three of the four content domains but unexpectedly remained positive when statements about Negroes were judged.

Wyer and Schwartz's data suggest that context information has two opposing effects. One, a "contrast" effect, may be due to shifts in response scale position toward the value of the context (see Chapter 3). The second, an "assimilation" effect, may be due to an attempt to resolve inconsistencies in the meaning of the communications. The latter effect may override the contrast effect when inconsistency is high. This conclusion is consistent with results obtained in Condition P_w of Wyer's (1974c) study, where a negative context effect was detected after variance attributed to changes in meaning was eliminated. Finally, Wyer and Schwartz's data suggest that if information is highly inconsistent, meaning shift may occur even when the information does not concern just one person. This interpretation indirectly supports the possibility that meaning shift accounts for context effects under conditions such as W_c, in which the stimulus adjectives are not related in any way except by virtue of their presence in the same stimulus set.

D. Concluding Remarks

Considered in its totality, the research described in this section seems most consistent with a meaning shift interpretation of context effects. On the other hand, an alternative hypothesis, that the influence of context information is attributable to a generalized halo effect, cannot be completely rejected. Research cited as evidence against a meaning shift interpretation has often employed both procedures of analysis and instructions that may artifactually decrease the likelihood of detecting the effects of meaning shift. In less contrived situations, such as the one investigated by Aronson et al. (1966), meaning shift may be much more likely. However, proponents of a meaning shift interpretation have not unequivocally demonstrated the validity of their position. As we have noted, the validity of models of information integration that describe collective evaluations as an additive function of the evaluations based upon each component considered in isolation may depend upon whether or not components do change their meaning in different contexts. The somewhat equivocal evidence concerning this possibility must be kept in mind when considering such models.

VII.   ORDER OF PRESENTATION

Of the characteristics of information that determine its influence, the sequence in which information is presented may have the greatest practical importance. Do the first pieces of information presented have the greater influence (a *primacy* effect) or are later pieces more influential (a *recency* effect)? The answer to this question is not simple; it depends upon the type of information involved, beliefs the subject has formed before he is exposed to the information, and even the grammatical context in which the information is embedded.

To determine the magnitude of primacy or recency effects, a typical procedure is to present favorable (H) and unfavorable (L) information about an object in both possible orders (HL and LH) and compare the evaluations of the object under these two conditions. A greater evaluation under HL than under LH conditions provides evidence for a primacy effect, while a relatively greater evaluation under LH conditions indicates a recency effect.

Order effects have been attributed to several different factors. Since studies of these effects typically bear upon the contribution of different combinations of these factors, it may be advisable to consider the theoretical influence of each factor in turn before embarking upon a discussion of these studies.

A.   Theoretical Determinants of Order Effects

1. *Meaning shift.* When information has several possible interpretations, each with a different evaluative implication, the first piece of information in a sequence may provide a context for interpreting later pieces. Consequently, the favorableness of information may be interpreted as similar to that of the information that precedes it. If this occurs, judgments based upon an entire set of information should be relatively more similar to the evaluative implications of the first pieces of information than to those of the later pieces, producing an apparent *primacy* effect. This hypothesis has been suggested by Asch (1946) and more recently by Chalmers (1969). Results obtained by Wyer and Schwartz (1969) suggest that meaning shifts of this sort are more likely, and therefore that primacy effects will be more pronounced, when the information presented is inconsistent.

2. *Discounting.* When the information presented is inconsistent, certain pieces may be discounted, or given less weight. Whether the first or the last pieces of information are more likely to be discounted is somewhat difficult to predict *a priori*. If subjects typically assume that the first information presented is regarded by the communicator as more important than subsequent information, they may give it greater weight, and *primacy* effects will occur. If the later-occurring information seems inconsistent with the earlier information there may be an even greater tendency to disregard it, and primacy effects may be increased.

3. *Grammatical context.* When information is presented in a sentence, the importance attached to it by the communicator may be suggested by its grammatical structure as well as its serial position. For example, a subject may infer that "stupid" is regarded as more important by a person who describes O as "honest but stupid" than by a person who describes him as "stupid but honest." In other words, information following "but" may receive greater weight, and *recency* effects may occur. When the same information is connected by "and," this may not be the case. Again, the tendency to discount one piece of information or the other should depend upon the consistency of this information.

4. *Contrast effects.* The initial stimuli in a series may provide a frame of reference, or comparison level, for judging subsequent stimuli. To this extent, information will be judged as *less* favorable when it is preceded by favorable information than when it is preceded by unfavorable information. Evaluations of an object should consequently be more negative when information about it is presented in an *HL* rather than an *LH* sequence, or a *recency* effect should be evident.[3]

5. *Forgetting.* When the communications are lengthy, or when a long period of time elapses between their presentations, the first information may be forgotten, and the evaluation of the object involved may therefore depend primarily upon the implications of the final information. That is, there may be a *recency* effect which becomes greater as the time between presentations of the first and last information increases.

6. *Attention decrement.* Subjects may not pay equal attention to all pieces of information presented. However, it may be difficult to predict *a priori* whether greater attention will be paid to the first or last information. If subjects are bored with the judgmental task or have no interest in the information presented, they may be inclined to make premature judgments on the basis of the first information presented without bothering to read or assimilate the later information. This would produce a *primacy* effect. On the other hand, if new information is redundant with previous information about the object, or if its implications are consistent with one's initial beliefs about the object, it may generally be of little interest and therefore may not receive much attention unless the recipient suspects that the validity of his initial beliefs is in question. This latter hypothesis implies that information supporting one's initial beliefs will have less effect if it is presented before

---

[3]To see this, assume that the favorableness of H and L information when each is presented in isolation is +3 and −3 respectively. Assume further that the judgment of H information is increased by one unit (to +4) when it is preceded by L information, while the judgment of L information decreases by one unit (to −4) when it is preceded by H information. Then, the sum of the favorableness judgments of information presented in an HL sequence would be +3 + (−4) = −1, while the total favorableness of the same information presented in an LH sequence would be −3 + (+4) = +1.

information refuting these beliefs than if it is presented after refutational information. This should produce a *recency* effect.[4]

Let us now evaluate the implications of research on order effects for the various hypotheses described above.

B. Empirical Investigations of Order Effects

1. *Effects of Prior Commitment.* Our preceding discussion suggests that the direction of order effects may depend in part upon whether subjects are committed to an opinion about the object to be judged before they receive information about it. Some evidence bearing upon this contingency was reported by McGuire and Papageorgis (1961) in a study that was not designed to test order effects *per se*. Subjects received communications arguing against an assertion that they initially believed to be unquestionably true (for example, "It's a good idea to brush your teeth after every meal"). In some cases, the attacking communication was preceded by a message supporting the validity of the assertion, while in other cases only the attack was presented. The initial supportive messages had no effect whatsoever upon subjects' final beliefs in the assertions; that is, attacking communications had the same influence regardless of whether or not a supporting communication had preceded them. These data support the hypothesis that subjects do not attend to the content of an initial communication supporting their own view. While a condition in which the supportive communication followed the attacking communication was not run, it seems likely that the supporting message would have had at least some influence in this case, and hence that a recency effect would have been detected.

More direct evidence for a recency effect was obtained in an early study by Cromwell (1950). He presented two communications, one supporting national medical care and the second opposing it, in both possible orders, and found that such aid was more favorably evaluated when the supporting communication was presented last. If it can be assumed that Cromwell's subjects typically had strong initial opinions about the desirability of federal medical assistance, these data are consistent with the hypothesis in question. In an even earlier study by Lund (1925), using issues that were particularly

---

[4]This recency effect should occur regardless of one's initial attitude, so long as this attitude is not neutral. To see this, assume that the effects of H and L information are $+3$ and -3 respectively if attention is paid to them, and that the effect of decreased attention to them, occurring when information consistent with one's initial judgment is presented first, is 1 unit. Then, if a subject has an initially favorable attitude, the effect of information presented in an HL sequence would be $+2 + (-3) = -1$; in an LH sequence, it would be $-3 + (+3) = 0$. If a subject has an initially unfavorable attitude, the effect of the HL sequence should be $+3 + (-3) = 0$, and of the LH sequence, $-2 + (+3) = +1$. Thus in each case, the HL sequence leads to the less favorable final evaluation.

relevant at the time the study was performed, evaluations of these issues were *less* favorable when supporting communications were presented last. However, these two studies differed in a very important respect. In Lund's study, but not in Cromwell's, subjects reported their opinion after receiving the first part of the message as well as after the second. There is evidence that public commitment to a point of view decreases the effects of subsequent information opposing this view (Deutsch & Gerard, 1955; Hovland, Campbell, & Brock, 1957). Therefore, Lund's procedure may have reduced the influence of the second communication presented and prevented the detection of recency effects.

The recency effect obtained by Cromwell could conceivably be attributable to factors other than attention decrement. For example, subjects may have paid equal attention to both parts of the communication but may have been more willing to accept a refutational communication as valid when it was preceded by a supportive one. (This would occur if a supportive communication increases subjects' beliefs that the source is credible.) However, McGuire and Papageorgis's finding that an initial supportive communication neither increased nor decreased the effectiveness of a subsequent refutational message argues against this alternative interpretation.

When subjects do *not* have strong initial opinions about the objects they are asked to evaluate, different considerations arise. Evidence that primacy effects occur when information is presented about hypothetical persons has frequently been found by Anderson and his colleagues. Anderson and Barrios (1961) presented to subjects one of four sets of six adjectives: (*a*) *HL*—three *H* adjectives followed by three *L* adjectives; (*b*) *LH*—three *L* adjectives followed by three *H* adjectives; (*c*) *GD*—six adjectives varying in favorableness, ordered such that favorableness decreased with serial position; or (*d*) *GA*—six adjectives varying in favorableness, ordered such that favorableness increased with serial position. Adjectives in each set were read to subjects by the experimenter. Strong evidence of primacy effects was found in comparing evaluations based upon *HL* and *LH* sets composed of the same six adjectives, and also in comparing GD and GA sets formed from the same adjectives.

A more rigorous investigation of order effects was subsequently performed (Anderson, 1965b) in which sets of either six or nine adjectives were presented, and the positions of the L and H adjectives contained in these sets were systematically manipulated. For example, adjectives in a set consisting of three L and three H adjectives (that is, a 3L3H set) were presented in four different orders: LLLHHH, HLLLHH, HHLLLH, and HHHLLL. The position of the L adjectives in 3L6H sets and the position of the H adjectives in both 3H3L and 3H6L sets were varied similarly. Evaluations based upon the information presented were related negatively to the ordinal position of H adjectives in 3H3L and 3H6L sets and were related positively to the ordinal position of L adjectives in 3L3H and 3L6H sets.

2. *Meaning Shift, Discounting, and Attention Decrement.* The primacy effects in the two studies described above could be due to either meaning shift, discounting, or attention decrement. How can these alternative interpretations be tested? One method might be to insure that subjects pay equal attention to each piece of information presented. If primacy effects are eliminated under such conditions, this would argue against a meaning shift interpretation and would support an attention decrement interpretation. Anderson and Hubert (1963) did in fact find that primacy effects were greatly attenuated when subjects were asked to recall each adjective before making their evaluations. Subsequently, Hendrick and Costantini (1970) found that primacy effects were eliminated when subjects were asked to pronounce each adjective as it was presented but were quite apparent when subjects listened passively to this information. Both of these studies support the attention decrement hypothesis.

Indirect evidence against a meaning shift interpretation of order effects was reported by Anderson and Norman (1964). In this experiment judgments were made of four different types of stimuli. As usual, primacy effects were detected when evaluations were made of persons described by sets of three H and three L adjectives. However, they were also obtained when evaluations were made of meals consisting of three desirable and three undesirable foods. Since the type of information presented in the latter domain would be unlikely to be assigned different meanings in different contexts, the primacy effect obtained in this case is probably attributable to other factors. A possible ambiguity in the interpretation of Anderson and Norman's data arises from the fact that primacy effect did not occur in two other domains (where subjects either evaluated (*a*) a newspaper containing headlines of high and low interest value or (*b*) a hypothetical week in their lives, on the basis of descriptions of three desirable and three undesirable events occurring during the week). Anderson and Norman point out that the pieces of information in the latter two domains were short sentences, rather than single words as in the case of personality adjectives and foods. When the stimulus materials are more lengthy, and thus more time elapses between the first and last piece of information presented, the initial information may be forgotten, or at least may be less salient; consequently, the more recent information may have greater effect.

The above studies do not bear directly on the validity of a discounting interpretation of primacy effects. However, since discounting should occur primarily when there is inconsistency among the pieces of information presented, the primacy effect obtained when subjects rated meals composed of different foods suggests that discounting is not sufficient to account for these effects. A more direct test of a discounting interpretation was performed by Hendrick and Costantini (1970). Subjects evaluated persons described by sets of three H and three L adjectives that varied in their inconsistency. (The inconsistency of H and L adjectives in a given set was inferred from control subjects' estimates of the likelihood that a person described by the H adjectives would also be described by the L adjectives.) Significant primacy effects occurred, the magnitude of which did not depend upon the degree of inconsistency. These results argue against the discounting hypothesis and, by default, provide further support for an attention decrement interpretation.

3. *Effects of Forgetting.* In each of the experiments described above, information was presented sequentially, with a short interval (about 3 seconds) after each piece. As more time elapsed between the first and last pieces of information presented, the first information is more likely to be forgotten, producing a recency effect. While this hypothesis has not been tested in the domain of impression formation, a study by Miller and Campbell (1959) is directly relevant. These authors assumed that the rate at which material is forgotten is a decreasing exponential function of the time elapsed since its presentation (Ebbinghaus, 1913). That is, a much greater amount of information is forgotten during the period of time immediately after its presentation than during later periods. Miller and Campbell gave subjects two communications about a court case, one favoring the plaintiff and the other favoring the defendant, and asked them to estimate the degree to which each party was at fault. In addition to varying presentation order, the authors systematically varied the time intervals between presentation of the first communication, presentation of the second, and subjects' judgments. Under conditions comparable to those used in other studies of order effects (where presentation of the two communications and subjects' judgments occurred immediately after one another), neither primacy nor recency effects were detected. (This finding is consistent with evidence, reported by Anderson and Norman, that primacy effects are attenuated when the pieces of information presented are fairly lengthy.) In a second condition, in which one week separated the presentation of the two communications and judgments were made immediately after the second communication was received, a strong recency effect occurred. In a third condition, in which a week separated the two communications and an additional week separated the second communication and subjects' judgments, the recency effect was eliminated. The first and second communications should both be recalled well in the first condition, while both should be recalled poorly in the third condition; however, in the second condition, only the most recent communication may be remembered well. Thus these findings are consistent with the hypothesis that subjects' judgments at any given time are a function of the total amount of recalled information that is relevant to these judgments.

Perhaps the most interesting finding reported by Miller and Campbell occurred in a fourth condition in which subjects received the second communication immediately after the first but did not report their judgments until a week later. Under this condition a strong primacy effect occurred.

Since the two communications should be remembered about equally well under this condition, particularly after the lapse of a week, the primacy effect must be attributable to other factors. Miller and Campbell suggest that the first piece of information presented about an object has a higher probability of being believed than later pieces, and therefore has greater influence under conditions which all pieces of information are remembered about equally well. Unfortunately, this reasoning would also imply a primacy effect when evaluations were made immediately after both communications were presented, but such an effect was not apparent.

4. *The Effect of Grammatical Context.* Since no evidence of either meaning shift or discounting was obtained in the series of studies described above, it is tempting to conclude that these factors are irrelevant to the prediction of order effects. Such a conclusion may have limited generality. In the majority of the studies of order effects cited above (and for that matter, in most of the studies described in this chapter), the information presented was simply a list of personality adjectives. In contrast, in more informal situations, similar information is usually conveyed in the context of a sentence (for example, "Bob is intelligent and aggressive," "Mary is beautiful but dumb," etc.). In an exploratory investigation of order effects under such conditions, the author (Wyer, 1973b) selected either consistent or, inconsistent pairs of H and L adjectives from the stimulus materials used by Hendrick and Costantini (1970). The same set of adjectives was used in forming consistent and inconsistent pairs so that idiosyncratic effects of the individual adjectives involved could be controlled. In addition to order of presentation, Wyer varied the grammatical context in which the adjectives occurred. Under "And" conditions, adjectives were presented in the form of "X is ____ and ____," with instructions to estimate the likeableness of X. Under "But" conditions, the adjectives were presented in the form "X is ____ but ____." In a control condition, the adjectives were simply presented side by side, with instructions to estimate the likeableness of a person described by them.

To control for between-group differences in the evaluations of component adjectives, evaluations based upon each adjective considered separately were also obtained. The average of each subject's evaluations based upon the two adjectives in each pair presented separately was then subtracted from his evaluation based upon the adjectives in combination. These differences, averaged over subjects, are shown in Table 8.4 as a function of the experimental vairables considered. A recency effect was evident under all three instructional conditions. Under control conditions, the magnitude of this effect did not depend upon the inconsistency between the adjectives involved. Connecting adjectives by "and" and placing them in a sentence increased primacy effects when these adjectives were inconsistent but increased recency effects when they were consistent. In contrast, connecting

TABLE 8.4

Difference between Collective Evaluation and Average
Component Evaluation as a Function of Grammatical
Context, Inconsistency, and Presentation Order
(reprinted from Wyer, 1973b, p. 48)

Context condition	Consistent sets			Inconsistent sets		
	HL order	LH order	Difference (LH–HL)	HL order	LH order	Difference (LH–HL)
Control	−1.22	− .46	.76	−1.36	− .61	.75
And	−1.32	− .30	1.02	− .99	− .82	.17
But	− .33	.23	.56	−1.21	− .06	1.15

adjectives by "but" increased recency effects when they were inconsistent but increased primacy effects when they were consistent.

The recency effect observed when adjectives were not presented in a sentence may seem contradictory to the primacy effects obtained in previous studies. However, in the earlier studies, sets of six or nine adjectives were generally used. The decrease in attention that seems to produce primacy effects in these studies may not be detected when smaller sets of information are involved.

The effects of connecting adjectives by "and" are interesting to consider in light of Wyer and Schwartz's (1969) study of context effects. These authors found that evaluations of individual pieces of information were displaced toward the favorableness of the information preceding it only when the information being judged was inconsistent in meaning with the context information. When the information being judged was consistent with the information preceding it, evaluations based upon it were displaced away from the favorableness of the context. Similar effects may have occurred under "And" conditions of the present experiment. That is, when the two adjectives presented were inconsistent, the favorableness of the second may have been displaced toward that of the first; if this occurred, the overall evaluation based upon the pair of adjectives would also shift toward the favorableness of the first adjective presented, producing a primacy effect. When the adjectives were consistent, however, the evaluation of the second adjective may have been displaced away from that of the first; the overall judgment based upon the revised component evaluations would then be relatively closer to the judgment of the second adjective presented, producing a recency effect.

Connecting information by "but" might intuitively be expected to increase the emphasis upon the second piece of information. However, the results described in Table 8.4 provide evidence of this only when the adjectives involved were inconsistent. In this case, the first adjective may have been discounted. However, when the information was consistent, "but" seems to have increased the relative importance of the first piece of information. For example, if "beautiful" and "dumb" are consistent, a description of Mary as "beautiful but dumb" may convey to the subject that beauty is a more critical characteristic than intelligence, while a description of her as "dumb but beautiful" may create the opposite impression.

The above interpretation is admittedly speculative. Other, perhaps more parsimonious interpretations are plausible. One, suggested to the author by Seymour Rosenberg [5], is based upon the possibility that the relative influence of adjectives connected by a conjunction depends in part upon whether the use of the conjunction is consistent with common usage. In everyday conversation, "and" is typically used to connect semantically consistent pieces of information, while "but" is most often used to connect information with at least partially inconsistent implications. As Table 8.4 indicates, recency effects were substantially greater when conjunctions were used in a conventional rather than an atypical way. The unconventional use of a conjunction may produce a tendency to discount the second piece of information presented. On the other hand, the conventional use of a conjunction may actually increase the emphasis placed upon the later-occurring information (relative to conditions in which the information is simply listed).

The merits of these alternative interpretations of our results require further investigation. In any event, these results indicate that order effects are not as simply explained as previous studies suggest. It seems reasonable to conclude that primacy effects often occur because less attention is paid to the later pieces of information present. However, when information is presented in a manner similar to everyday conversation, both meaning shift and discounting may also occur to different degrees, depending upon the inconsistency of the information and its grammatical context. Perhaps when information is not presented in a grammatical context, some subjects respond to it as if it were connected by "and" and others as if it were connected by "but." In this regard, it is interesting to note that differences due to inconsistency were not detected under the control conditions of our study, but that the recency effect obtained under these conditions was nearly identical to the simple average of the effects obtained under "And" and "But" conditions.

---

[5] Personal communication.

VIII. SUMMARY

In this chapter we have identified several different characteristics of information that affect the magnitude of its influence. While certain of these effects are quite straightforward and predictable, others are interrelated and often complex. On the basis of the evidence presented in this chapter, the following conclusions seem justified: The effect of information may depend not only upon its favorableness but also upon its relevance to the evaluation being made. The relevance of information, and therefore its influence, may vary with the type of object being evaluated. The influence of information may decrease if subjects are uncertain about its implications, either because it comes from an unreliable source or because it is ambiguous. Information about attributes that are not typically used to describe objects has greater effect than information about less novel attributes. Information about attributes that are highly redundant (that is, attributes that are associated with high probability) is less influential than information about less strongly related but equally favorable attributes. When information is inconsistent, part or all of the information may be discounted; which piece is discounted may depend upon its ambiguity, upon the order in which it is presented, and, if it is presented in a sentence, upon its grammatical context. Any given piece of information may have a variety of interpretations, and there is some, although equivocal, evidence that the interpretation made of it in any given instance varies with the type of information accompanying it. This variation may be more pronounced when the information is ambiguous, or when it is inconsistent with the context information. Differences in the interpretation of a piece of information when presented in different contexts may produce apparent differences in this information's effects in these contexts. When a large amount of information is presented about an unfamiliar object, relatively less attention is paid to later pieces of information, and thus the first information presented has relatively greater impact. However, when subjects have already formed definite opinions about the object to which the information is relevant, they may pay little attention to information that supports their original opinions, unless it is preceded by information attacking these opinions. Finally, when information about an object is presented in sentences, factors in addition to attention decrement may need to be taken into account in predicting the relative influence of this information.

9
MATHEMATICAL MODELS OF INFORMATION INTEGRATION

In Chapter 8 we described several factors that determine the effects of different pieces of information upon judgments of an object. In light of the large number of such factors and the complexity of their effects, it may seem unrealistic to try to formulate accurate quantitative descriptions of the manner in which information is integrated. This would appear particularly true of formulations that describe the effect of several pieces of information in combination as a linear function of the effects of each piece considered separately, and of models that take into account only the favorableness of the information presented. However, such models are often surprisingly effective. In this chapter we will describe several different mathematical formulations of information integration and will evaluate the empirical support for each. Before we embark upon this discussion, however, it may be worthwhile to consider the psychological implications of each general type of formulation to be considered and attempt to identify the fundamental assumptions about information integration processes that underlie it.

I. GENERAL INTERPRETATIONS OF INTEGRATION PROCESSES

A. Summative and Averaging Interpretations

The vast majority of information integration models proposed in recent years describe evaluations based upon several pieces of information as a function of either the sum or the average of the evaluative implications of each piece of information considered separately. While summative and averaging models are mathematically similar, these models have quite different implications for the procedure subjects use to arrive at judgments and the assumptions they make in adopting this procedure. Some illustrative examples may help to clarify the nature of these differences.

First, suppose a subject P is asked to estimate the material wealth of a person O based upon information that he owns a penthouse, an apartment building, and a chain of restaurants. It seems reasonable to expect that P will base his estimate of O's wealth upon the total value of the objects O owns. His judgment could therefore be predicted by summing his estimates of the values of each piece of property considered separately. Judgments of other characteristics of O may be arrived at through similar procedures. Suppose P is asked to evaluate O based upon information that he is friendly, intelligent, and reliable. These attributes each have a certain degree of favorableness, and thus they may contribute independently to an estimate of O's total "goodness" in much the same way that each object owned by O contributes to an estimate of his total wealth. To this extent, the information integration process used by P would be *summative*.

Now consider a somewhat different situation. Suppose P is told that two different judges have evaluated O as $+3$ and $+5$ along a category scale and is then asked to make his own evaluation of O. If he believes that each judge's evaluation is equally accurate, he may infer that the judgment most likely to be correct lies somewhere between the two judges' evaluations (that is, about $+4$). Similarly, suppose that P is told that O has been described by one judge as "dependable" and by another as "honest." He may assume that the adjective selected by each judge is the one the judge believes to be the *most representative* description of O's overall personality. In such a case, he may infer that each judge's description of O is an indirect indication of the judge's evaluation of O, and therefore he may combine the evaluative implications of these descriptions in much the same way as if he were given more direct information about each judge's evaluation. To this extent, the information integration procedure used by the subject would appear to be *averaging*.

The process of arriving at a judgment based upon several pieces of information, and therefore the appropriateness of a summative or averaging model for describing this process, may depend largely upon the type of judgment to be made, the type of stimuli to be judged, and the particular experimental conditions involved. To give a rather trivial example, compare (a) the task of judging the economic well-being of a family, based upon information about the income of each individual member of the family, and (b) the task of judging the economic well-being of a particular area of Chicago on the basis of information about the income of each individual resident. Subjects who perform the first task are likely to assume that each individual member contributes independently to the support of his family and therefore may treat the *total* family income as the best index of the family's economic status. Subjects who perform the second task are likely to assume that the economic level of the area is best indicated by the most representative income of residents in the area, and thus they may attempt to assess the *average* income. Such effects, should they occur, would be hardly more surprising than the effects of specific instructions to sum the implications of the various pieces of information in one case and to average them in a second; the only difference is that in the first task, the appropriate integration rule is inferred on the basis of previous experience with the type of task and the materials presented rather than from explicit instructions given by the experimenter.

Similar situational differences may arise in research on impression formation. First, consider a situation in which subjects are told that O has been described by a single judge as "honest, dependable and stupid," and are then asked to evaluate such a person. Compare this situation with a second in which subjects are told that O has been described differently by three independent judges; specifically, that one judge has described him as "honest," another as "dependable," and the third as "stupid." In the latter situation, subjects are further told to treat each description of O as equally important in arrriving at an evaluation of him. In the second situation it seems possible if not probable that a subject will assume that each judge has described O by the adjective he believes to be most characteristic of O, and that the evaluative implications of the adjective selected by each judge provide an indication of that judge's estimate of O's likeableness. The subject may therefore be more likely to average the independent evaluative implications of the three adjectives in this situation than in the first situation described, where it is clear that all three adjectives *in combination* describe O.

B. A Concept Identification Interpretation

A third formulation of information integration to be discussed in this chapter is based upon quite different assumptions about the processes involved than either a summative or an averaging model assumes. This formulation is suggested by the description of judgmental processes outlined in Chapter 2. Let us recapitulate briefly. Suppose a subject is asked to place O in one of a set of ordered categories. In order to assign O to one of these categories with complete certainty, the subject would require information about each of the attributes that in combination serve as criteria for membership in the category. When only a few of O's attributes are known to the subject, he may believe that O could belong with some probability to any of several categories. His evaluation of O may indicate his estimate of the most representative category to which O belongs and therefore may be predicted from the expected value of the distribution of subjective probabilities that O belongs to each of the categories involved. Now, as more information about O's attributes becomes available, certain of these probabilities are likely to change. These changes may often affect the expected value of the distribution of the probabilities and thus may affect the particular category to which O is assigned. Considered in this light, the process of evaluating an object is similar to that involved in a "concept identification" task, where a subject must identify on the basis of limited information, the category to which an object belongs. This identification process differs fundamentally from that assumed to underlie additive models of information integration. That is, rather than summing or averaging the separate implications of different pieces of information to arrive at a category rating, the subject is using this information to circumscribe the set of categories he believes to be most representative of this set.

1. *General Implications for Mathematical Models of Integration Processes.* If the above interpretation is valid, is it possible to predict exactly the evaluation based upon several pieces of information from the evaluations based upon each piece of information separately? The answer is probably "no." The subjective probability distribution underlying category ratings based upon several pieces of information is theoretically the *conjunction* of the distributions underlying ratings based upon each piece presented separately. However, the nature of this conjunction cannot be determined from the expected values of the component distributions alone. Thus it is impossible to predict perfectly the magnitude of collective evaluations from the component evaluations.

This same conclusion can be demonstrated mathematically. Evaluations based upon adjective A, adjective B, and A and B in combination (E_A, E_B, and E_{AB}, respectively) are theoretically described by the following equations:

$$E_A = \Sigma P_{i/A} V_i,$$
$$E_B = \Sigma P_{i/B} V_i,$$

and
$$E_{AB} = \Sigma P_{i/AB} V_i,$$

where V_i is the value of the ith scale category and $P_{i/A}$, $P_{i/B}$, and $P_{i/AB}$ are the subjective conditional probabilities of membership in the ith category given A, given B, and given A and B in conjunction. If E_{AB} is a predictable additive function of E_A and E_B, then for all i, $P_{i/AB}$ should be a predictable additive function of $P_{i/A}$ and $P_{i/B}$. If subjective probabilities obey the laws of probability theory, however, this is not the case; rather,

$$P_{i/AB} = \frac{P_A P_{i/A} P_{B/iA}}{P_{AB}} = \frac{P_B P_{i/B} P_{A/iB}}{P_{AB}}$$

where P_A is the subjective probability that an object of the type being judged would be described by A, P_{AB} is the probability that such an object would be described by both A and B, $P_{B/iA}$ is the probability that an object is described by B given that it is described by A and is in category i, etc. Since these probabilities cannot be inferred from the values of E_A and E_B, this equation suggests that collective evaluations cannot generally be predicted from component ratings alone.

2. *Implications for an Averaging Model.* It may be worth noting that although a summative model would not be consistent with the interpretation of category ratings as subjective expected values under any conditions, an

averaging model *would* be consistent with this interpretation if subjects treat the adjectives describing O as *mutually exclusive* and assign a value to O that best represents the collective of objects described by one, but no more than one, of these adjectives. To see this, assume that the evaluations of an object described by A alone (E_A) and by B alone (E_B) are represented by the expressions

$$E_A = \Sigma P_{i/A} V_i = \frac{\Sigma n_{iA}}{n_A} V_i$$

and

$$E_B = \Sigma P_{i/B} V_i = \frac{\Sigma n_{iB}}{n_B} V_i$$

where n_A and n_B are the total numbers of objects described by the adjectives A and B, respectively, and n_{iA} and n_{iB} are the numbers of objects described by A and B that are also in the ith rating scale category. Suppose that a subject who is asked to evaluate an object described by A and B first constructs a superordinate category C composed of persons who are A or B but not both. The category rating of persons in C would be

$$E_C = \Sigma P_{i/C} V_i = \frac{\Sigma n_{iC}}{n_C} V_i .$$

But if A and B are mutually exclusive, $n_{iC} = n_{iA} + n_{iB}$ and $n_C = n_A + n_B$; therefore,

$$E_C = \Sigma \frac{n_{iA} + n_{iB}}{n_A + n_B} V_i = \frac{\Sigma n_{iA}}{n_A + n_B} V_i + \frac{\Sigma n_{iB}}{n_A + n_B} V_i .$$

Since $\Sigma n_{iA} V_i = n_A E_A$, and $\Sigma n_{iB} V_i = n_B E_B$, appropriate substitutions yield the expression

$$E_C = \frac{n_A}{n_A + n_B} E_A + \frac{n_B}{n_A + n_B} E_B = w E_A + (1-w) E_B .$$

In other words, according to this formulation, the evaluation of an object described by A *or* B but *not both* is a weighted average of the evaluations based upon A and B separately, while the evaluation of an object described by *both* A and B is not. An implication of this analysis is that weighted average models are more applicable when subjects are predisposed to arrive at evaluations by considering the category values implied by each adjective separately and then weighting these values, rather than by considering objects described by the *conjunction* of these adjectives. This conclusion is consistent with the earlier, more intuitive analysis of the conditions under which subjects are apt to use an averaging procedure in arriving at judgments based upon several pieces of information.

Even if additive models can theoretically provide only approximate descriptions of information integration processes, they are still worthy of very serious consideration. There are at least two somewhat different criteria for evaluating a mathematical model of information integration. One is whether the mathematical procedures used to predict component ratings from collective ratings correspond to the cognitive processes to which the model theoretically pertains, and whether the parameters of the model have psychological significance. The second criterion is simply whether the model predicts collective ratings accurately. It is of course unlikely that formulations based upon entirely different assumptions can describe integration processes with complete accuracy. Therefore, if a particular model fits perfectly, this would provide strong support for its underlying assumptions about the cognitive processes used by subjects in arriving at judgments. However, when complete accuracy cannot be obtained, the likelihood that several different formulations are equal in accuracy is increased. It is conceivable in fact that the model that provides the closest empirical approximation is based upon assumptions that obviously conflict with the implications of theory and research concerning the nature of the processes it purports to describe. In such a case, should the model be accepted or rejected? The answer may depend largely upon the philosophical temperament of the investigator, and whether he is primarily interested in "prediction" or "explanation."

In the pages that follow, theory and research bearing upon a general additive model of information integration will be presented. Then, specific models that assume either a summative or an averaging process of integration will be described and evaluated. Finally, an alternative approach will be proposed, one based upon the interpretation of category ratings as subjective expected values, which can theoretically account for several of the effects of information described in Chapter 8. The models to be discussed in this chapter will be applied primarily to impression formation phenomena. However, this research and the theory underlying it have more general implications, as we shall see in later chapters.

II. THE GENERAL ADDITIVE MODEL

A. Methodological Considerations

1. *Summation vs. Averaging.* In most general terms, an additive model of information integration is described by the equation

$$E_o = \sum_{i=0}^{N} k_i V_i$$

$$(9.1)$$

where V_i is the value of the ith of N pieces of information along the scale used for recording judgments and k_i is a parameter indicating the contribution of this piece of information to E_o. Note that if $N = 0$, $E_o = k_o V_o$; this value presumably represents the evaluation of O when no information about it is available.

As we have noted, there are two basic types of additive models. One, a *summative* model, assumes that each piece of information has an absolute weight (w_i), the value of which is unrestricted; that is, $k_i = w_i$, or

$$E_o = \sum_{i=0}^{N} w_i V_i \qquad (9.2)$$

The second, an *averaging* model, also assumes that each piece of information has an absolute weight w_i, but further assumes that the contribution of each piece of information to E_o depends upon its *relative* weight; that is,

$$k_i = w_i / \sum_{i=0}^{N} w_i,$$

or

$$E_o = \frac{\sum_{i=0}^{N} w_i V_i}{\sum_{i=0}^{N} w_i} \qquad (9.3)$$

The fundamental difference between a summative and an averaging model is, therefore, that in the latter model $\Sigma k_i = 1$, while in the former no such restriction is made. For either type of model to be useful, the absolute weight (w_i) and scale value (V_i) of each piece of information either must remain constant over all sets in which the piece is contained, or else must be specifiable functions of measurable characteristics of the information presented (e.g., redundancy or inconsistency, shifts in meaning, etc.)

The distinction between Eq. (9.2) and Eq. (9.3) is often not as clear as the above discussion suggests. For example, suppose two pieces of information, A and B, are presented both separately and in combination. If Eq. (9.3) is valid, the evaluations based upon these sets of information would be

$$E_A = \frac{w_A V_A + w_o V_o}{w_A + w_o},$$

$$E_B = \frac{w_B V_B + w_o V_o}{w_B + w_o},$$

and
$$E_{AB} = \frac{w_A V_A + w_B V_B + w_o V_o}{w_A + w_B + w_o}$$

Solving for $w_A V_A$ and $w_B V_B$ in the first two equations and substituting in the third:

$$E_{AB} = \frac{(w_A + w_o')E_A + (w_B + w_o)E_B - w_o V_o}{w_A + w_B + w_o}$$

$$= (w_{A'} + w_{o'})E_A + (w_{B'} + w_{o'})E_B - w_{o'} V_o$$

$$= (1 - w_{B'})E_A + (1 - w_{A'})E_B - w_{o'} V_o , \qquad (9.4)$$

where $w_{A'} + w_{B'} + w_{o'} = 1$.

Note, however, that in this case, the sum of the weights attached to E_A and E_B may often be greater than 1. (This is necessarily the case if $w_o' > 0$.) Thus Eq. (9.4) is not clearly distinguishable from a summative model of the form of Eq. (9.2). On the other hand, the weights attached to E_A and E_B in Eq. (9.4), while they do not sum to unity, are theoretically not independent. There are statistical procedures that help to determine whether the nature of their dependence is consistent with Eq. (9.3). These procedures are based upon the theory of functional measurement developed by Norman Anderson. The theoretical foundations of functional measurement, and its use in assessing the validity of several alternative assumptions underlying additive models, have been described in detail in an important theoretical paper by Anderson (1970) and thus do not require great elaboration here. However, since goodness-of-fit tests based upon functional measurement theory have been used extensively in research on impression formation, and since they can be used more generally in the study of attitude formation and change (see Anderson, 1971b), some of their more relevant aspects are worth reviewing.

2. *Implications of an Additive Model.* Consider for simplicity two sets of information, A and B, each composed of three adjectives. Assume that each adjective in set A is paired with each adjective in set B and that subjects make judgments based upon all such pairs along an equal interval scale. Suppose we perform an analysis of variance of these judgments as a function of A and B. If the attributes described by the adjectives within each set differ in favorableness, the main effects of A and B should be significant. However, what about the A × B interaction? If the interaction is not significant, this would indicate that the effects of adjectives in set A are completely independent of the effects of the adjectives in set B. This is of course what is predicted by a summative model of the form of Eq. (9.2), that is:

$$E_{AiBj} = w_{Ai} V_{Ai} + w_{Bj} V_{Bj} + w_o V_o .$$

TABLE 9.1

Predictions Generated by Summative and Averaging Models
for Three Hypothetical Groups of Data

| | | Parameter values | | | Collective values predicted by | | | | | |
					Summative model			Averaging model		
A.		w	V							
	Set A: A_1	2	−2		B_1	B_2	B_3	B_1	B_2	B_3
				A_1	−7	−4	−1	−1.4	−.8	−.2
	A_2	2	0	A_2	−3	0	+3	−.6	0	+.6
	A_3	2	+2	A_3	+1	+4	+7	+.2	+.8	+1.4
	Set B: B_1	3	−1							
	B_2	3	0							
	B_3	3	+1							
B.										
	Set A: A_1	2	−2	A_1	−5	−4	−1	−1.67	−1.0	−.2
	A_2	2	0	A_2	−1	0	+3	−.33	0	+.6
	A_3	2	+2	A_3	+3	+4	+7	+1.0	+1.0	+1.4
	Set B: B_1	1	−1							
	B_2	2	0							
	B_3	3	+1							
C.										
	Set A: A_1	4	−2	A_1	−10	−8	−6	−1.67	−1.60	−1.00
	A_2	1	0	A_2	−2	0	+2	−.67	0	+.67
	A_3	4	+2	A_3	+6	+8	+10	+1.00	+1.60	+1.67
	Set B: B_1	2	−1							
	B_2	1	0							
	B_3	2	+1							

Note—Predicted values based upon each model assume that $w_o = 0$.

Predictions made by such a model for three sets of sample data are tabulated in Table 9.1 and plotted in Fig. 9.1. Note that the effects of A adjective favorableness at each level of B adjective favorableness are parallel, regardless of whether or not adjective weights vary within each set. An averaging model of the form of Eq. (9.3) would also predict no interaction if the same absolute weight is attached to each piece of information in a given

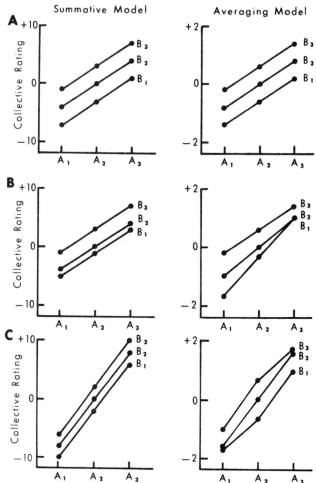

Fig. 9.1. Category ratings as a function of component likeableness, based upon data in Table 9.1.

set (that is, if $w_{Ai} = w_A$ for all i, and $w_{Bj} = w_B$ for all j); in this event,

$$E_{AiBj} = \frac{w_o V_o}{w_o + w_A + w_B} + \frac{w_A V_{Ai}}{w_o + w_A + w_B} + \frac{w_B V_{Bj}}{w_o + w_A + w_B}$$

$$= w_o' V_o + w_A' V_{Ai} + w_B' V_{Bj} ,$$

and the relative weights attached to A and B adjectives, w_A' and w_B', remain constant over adjective pairs (see Table 9.1 and Fig. 9.1).

Suppose on the other hand that the A × B interaction is significant. This would indicate either that a summative model of the form of Eq. (9.2) is invalid, or that a summative model is valid but the absolute weight attached to each adjective is not constant over the pairs in which the adjective is contained. On the other hand, it would not necessarily invalidate an averaging model. Consider the sample data shown in Table 9.1(B), where the absolute weight of each A adjective is the same ($w_{Ai} = w_A$ for all i) but the absolute weights of B adjectives differ ($w_{Bi} \neq w_{Bj}$). In such a case, the effect of A adjectives at each level of B will be related negatively to the absolute weight of the B adjective. However, the effect of A adjectives when paired with one B adjective is a constant multiple of the effect of these adjectives when paired with any other B adjective. Values predicted by an averaging model under such conditions, based upon the same data shown in Table 9.1(B), are plotted in Fig. 9.1(B), which shows that the effects of A at each level of B differ only in slope. A statistical test of this type of interaction is possible. Specifically, the A $\times$ B interaction should be concentrated in its Linear $\times$ Linear component. If variance due to this component is eliminated, the residual interaction should be zero. (For a fuller discussion of this procedure, see Anderson, 1970, 1971b.)[1]

Unless precautions are taken, characteristics of the information contained in *both* set A and set B are likely to vary unsystematically. If certain of these characteristics (novelty, ambiguity, etc.) affect the absolute weights attached to this information, these weights would then vary within both sets (that is, $w_{Ai} \neq w_{Aj}$ and $w_{Bi} \neq w_{Bj}$), and the A $\times$ B interaction could appear quite unsystematic. However, when the information in each set is ordered with respect to the absolute weight attached to it, the interaction implied by an averaging model has a predictable form. For example, suppose that the absolute weight attached to a piece of information increases with the extremity of its scale value. Sample data pertaining to such a condition are shown in Table 9.1(C); collective ratings predicted by Eq. (9.3), based upon these data, are plotted in Fig. 9.1(C). Note that the family of curves converges as the extremity of B information increases. This simply indicates that as the absolute weight of one component increases, the effect of the other component becomes less, which is of course consistent with an averaging model. A summative model could not account for an interaction of this form unless the absolute weight attached to each piece of information varied systematically as a function of the type of information accompanying it. In the particular example given above, it could be argued that when a piece of information is very favorable, a second piece that is also favorable is likely to be redundant, while a piece that is very unfavorable is apt to be inconsistent and therefore discounted. The second piece of information might therefore have a smaller *absolute* weight in both instances than if it were presented with more neutrally polarized information. When the first piece of information is unfavorable, analogous arguments could be made. This interpretation, which is consistent with the empirical effects of redundancy and inconsistency described in Chapter 8, also implies the convergence

---

[1] Such a test is of course meaningless unless there are more than two levels of each factor. In many of the studies in which interactions have occurred, only two levels of each factor were used.

pattern shown in Fig. 9.1(C). However, when there is less *a priori* basis for assuming that the absolute weight of a piece of information is *systematically* affected by the information accompanying it, the general convergence pattern described in this figure provides reasonably strong support for an averaging formulation. In any event, the combination rule suggested by such an interaction is additive.

Another reason why the convergence pattern shown in Fig. 9.1(C) might emerge is that the response scale is not equal interval. That is, if more extreme response categories include wider ranges of stimulus values, such a pattern might emerge even if the subjective judgments of A and B combine summatively. In this regard, Bogartz and Wackwitz (1970) have shown that interactions of the sort described in Fig. 9.1(C) can often be eliminated by appropriate *post hoc* transformations of the response scale. In contrast, note that the absence of an A × B interaction supports *both* the validity of Eq. (9.2) *and* the scaling assumptions underlying the measurement of collective and component ratings.

Now suppose that despite attempts to order information according to its absolute weight, the convergence pattern shown in Fig. 9.1(C) does not emerge. This could indicate one of two things. First, Eq. (9.3) may be an invalid description of information integration processes. Second, Eq. (9.3) may be valid but either the absolute weight or the scale value of each piece of information presented is idiosyncratic to the collective in which it is contained.

While the above discussion pertains to judgments based upon only two pieces of information, the procedures involved can of course be used to investigate the manner in which any number of pieces combine to affect judgments. With these considerations in mind, let us turn to some of the research bearing upon the validity of an additive model of information integration and evaluate the support for such a model.

B. Tests of Additivity in Impression Formation

Most rigorous investigations of impression formation processes have been performed within the framework of "information integration theory," as elaborated in an excellent and important paper by Anderson (1971b). The label used by Anderson to describe his formulation is somewhat overinclusive; in fact, there are several different theories of information integration, as we shall see. However, Anderson's formulation has undoubtedly had greater impact than any other theory proposed to date, and many of the ideas in this chapter have been stimulated, directly, or indirectly, by his model.

One general hypothesis based upon Anderson's formulation has been that the evaluative implications of information combine additively to affect judgments of the object described by it, and much research has been devoted to a test of this general hypothesis. As we have implied in our previous discussion, tests of additivity are extremely difficult if the effects of different pieces of information depend upon their redundancy or inconsistency, or if the information presented is interpreted differently in different contexts. The combined effects of these factors could produce idiosyncratic differences in both the absolute weight and the scale value of each piece of information as a function of the other information presented with it and thus prevent an exact statistical test of the general model. To eliminate these problems, Anderson has typically given subjects detailed instructions about how to treat the information they receive. For example, subjects are often told that each adjective used to describe a given stimulus person is equally important and should be given equal attention, that each adjective was contributed by a different acquaintance of the person, and that some apparent inconsistencies may be expected since each acquaintance may see a different aspect of the person's personality (cf. Anderson, 1965a, 1965b, 1967, 1968a, 1971a). The timing of stimulus presentations, and the interval between stimulus presentation and subjects' ratings, are also often controlled. These procedures may decrease the tendency for subjects to give the presented adjectives different weights and therefore may justify the assumption that these weights remain constant over stimulus combinations. Such procedures may also predispose subjects to interpret each adjective as an independent indication of the characteristic that is most representative of the person's personality, and therefore of his likeableness; this may increase the tendency to use an averaging rule, for reasons suggested earlier in this chapter.

Under the experimental conditions described above, Anderson has obtained very strong support for additivity, although small but significant discrepancies have often been found. In an early study (Anderson, 1962) subjects estimated how well they liked persons described by 27 sets of three adjectives each. These sets were formed by first choosing three groups (A, B, and C) of three adjectives each. The adjectives in each group represented three different levels of likeableness. All possible ABC combinations were then formed. Twelve subjects, run individually, were exposed to these stimuli on five successive days, the first two days being used for practice. When presenting stimuli, precautions were taken to minimize the effects of order and to encourage the subjects to pay equal attention to each adjective. (This was done by having the experimenter read the adjectives aloud and having the subject repeat them immediately in the reverse order.) Separate analyses of variance were performed on each subject's judgments as a function of the three adjective sets and session. Significant deviations from additivity (estimated from the pooled interactions involving various combinations of A, B, and C) occurred in only three of twelve cases, and these deviations were very small. On the average, 93.5% of the total variance in collective ratings was accounted for by the additive effects of A, B, and C.

Data collected by Anderson in two later studies (1965a, 1968b) indicate that deviations from an additive model in which adjectives are assumed to receive equal weight may be due primarily to the fact that unfavorable attributes, unlike favorable ones, become more influential as their scale values become more polarized. Stimulus adjectives in the first study (Anderson, 1965a) were selected from four levels of normative likeableness: H (high), $M+$ (moderately high), $M-$ (moderately low), and L (low). These adjectives were divided into two groups, A and B, each containing two adjectives at each likeableness level. Collectives of four adjectives were then constructed by combining two adjectives in A with two adjectives in B to form the following sets: $4H$ (i.e., $HHHH$), $2HM+$, $2M+2H$, $4M+$, $4M-$, $2M-2L$,-$2L2M-$, and $4L$. (Several stimulus replications were constructed according to this procedure.) Adjectives in each set were presented simultaneously. Evaluations based upon each set were made along an unbounded response scale with 50 representing neutrality.

Assume that the adjectives contained in these sets have equal and additive effects upon evaluations. Then, the sum of the evaluations based upon $4H$ and $4M+$ sets should equal the sum of the evaluations based upon $2H2M+$ and $2M+2H$ sets. Similarly, the sum of the evaluations based upon $4L$ and $4M-$ sets should equal the sum of the evaluations based upon $2M-2L$ and $2L2M-$ sets. The mean evaluations based upon each type of set, defined in relation to neutrality (50), and the relevant sums to be compared are as follows:

$$E_{4H} + E_{4M+} \quad = 29.39 + 13.20 = 42.59$$
$$E_{2H2M+} + E_{2M+2H} = 21.11 + 21.11 = 42.22$$
$$E_{4L} + E_{4M-} \quad = -32.36 + -10.50 = -42.86$$
$$E_{2M-2L} + E_{2L2M-} = -24.33 + -24.33 = -48.66$$

The first two sums are nearly identical and therefore support the assumption that H and $M+$ information had equal and additive effects. However, the difference between the second two sums, while not large, was statistically significant. The nature of this difference suggests that L adjectives have relatively greater influence than $M-$ adjectives when these two types of information are combined.

The second study (Anderson, 1968b) was similar except that sets of six adjectives ($6H$, $3H3M+$, $3M+3H$, $6M+$, $6M-$, $3M-3L$, $3L3M-$, and $6L$) were formed and presented to subjects sequentially rather than simultaneously. Evaluations were recorded by placing a check along a 2-inch unlabeled line that was later divided into 20 equal parts for scoring purposes. Mean evaluations based upon each set, defined in relation to the center of the response scale, and the relevant sums to be compared, were:

$$E_{6H} + E_{6M+} \quad = 7.53 + 1.83 = 9.36$$
$$E_{3H3M+} + E_{3M+3H} = 4.33 + 4.66 = 8.99$$
$$E_{6L} + E_{6M-} \quad = -8.94 + -4.84 = -13.76$$
$$E_{3M-3L} + E_{3L3M-} = -7.56 + -6.90 = -14.46.$$

The difference between the first two sums is again small and nonsignificant. However, the fourth sum is just significantly more negative than the third. Thus these results are completely consistent with those of the earlier study.

While Anderson's data suggest that the criteria for assigning weights to favorable adjectives differ from those for assigning weights to unfavorable ones, this difference may be illusory. As suggested in Chapter 8, information has more influence if its implications are either more extreme or are more negative. In $M-L$ sets, the L adjective is *both* more extreme and more negative than the $M-$ adjective and therefore should receive relatively greater weight. However, in $M+H$ sets, the H adjective is the more extreme but the $M+$ adjective is the more negative. If the effects of negativity and extremity upon the absolute weight of information are about equal, their effects upon the *relative* weights attached to H and $M+$ adjectives may cancel when they are presented in combination, leading to no apparent difference in their influence. Anderson's results are quite consistent with this interpretation.

The data pertaining to unfavorable adjectives in the above two studies call into question the validity of a summative model. However, they are not necessarily inconsistent with an averaging model; they only invalidate the assumption that the absolute weight attached to each piece of information is the same. Results of several other studies also call this assumption into question, although these results are not always as clearly interpretable as those described above. In a study primarily designed to investigate context effects, Anderson (1966) constructed sixteen sets of three adjectives by combining pairs of context adjectives at each of four levels of likeableness (HH, $M+M+$, $M-M-$, and LL) with a "test" adjective at each of the same four levels (H, $M+$, $M-$, and L). He analyzed evaluations of persons described by these triads as a function of context likeableness and test adjective likeableness and found the interaction of these two variables, described in Fig. 9.2, to be significant. Test × context interactions have also been reported by Anderson (1971a), Wyer and Dermer (1968), and Wyer and Watson (1969). These interactions are shown in Figs. 9.3 and 9.4. These findings contradict both a summative model of the form of Eq. (9.2), and an averaging model in which component adjectives receive equal weight. The interaction obtained by Anderson (1971a) is of the sort expected if more polarized adjectives (H and L) have greater absolute weight than less polarized ($M+$ and $M-$) adjectives. However, interactions obtained in our studies are less systematic and suggest that component weights are not a function of their normative likeableness alone. As Anderson (1966) points out, these interactions could be due in part to changes in the scale values of the components once they are presented in the context of others. Whether such changes would result from meaning shift or from other factors, however, is not completely clear (for a detailed discussion of the possible effects of context on meaning, see Chapter 8).

When the information presented is inconsistent, deviations from a simple additive model may occur because one or more pieces are discounted. That

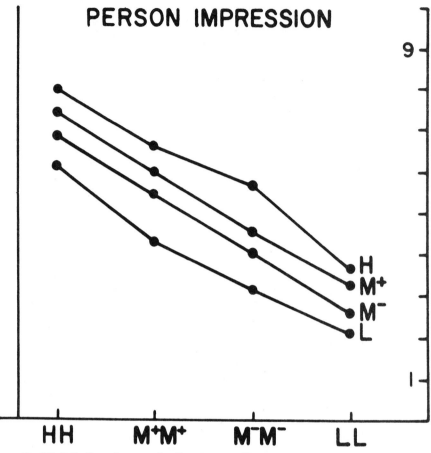

Fig. 9.2. Collective ratings as a function of context likeableness and test adjective likeableness (reprinted from Anderson, 1966, p. 279).

is, an adjective may have a relatively smaller absolute weight when it is inconsistent with the adjectives accompanying it. Evidence of discounting was reported by Anderson and Jacobson (1965) in a study described in Chapter 8. These authors formed sets of three adjectives such that two (A and B) were either high or low in likeableness while the third (C) was always low. If there is no discounting and adjectives receive equal weight, all interactions involving A, B, and C would be zero. However, suppose that the "odd" adjective in each set (that is, the adjective that differs in scale value from the other two) is discounted. This adjective would be either from set A or from set B. Therefore, if discounting occurs, the A × B interaction should be significant, while the remaining interactions should remain at zero.[2]

---

[2]The fact that interactions involving C remain zero under the discounting assumption may not be intuitively obvious. The reader is referred to Anderson and Jacobson (1965) for a detailed explanation of this prediction.

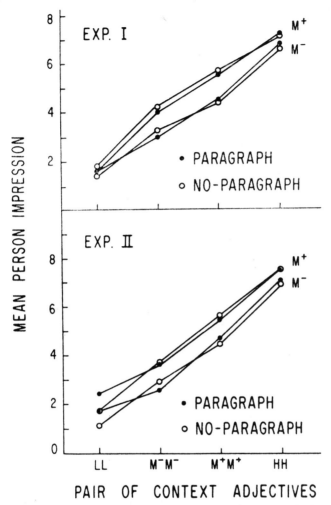

Fig. 9.3. Collective ratings as a function of context likeableness and test adjective likeableness under conditions in which subjects did and did not write a paragraph describing their impression before making each rating (reprinted from Anderson, 1971a, p. 80).

Subjects were run under three instructional conditions. In no case were interactions involving C significant, indicating that the effects of C adjectives always combined additively with those of the other two adjectives. The A × B interaction was highly significant when subjects were instructed that the adjectives might not be equally important and that they might need to pay more attention to some adjectives than to others. However, the magnitude of this interaction was greatly reduced when subjects were instructed to treat each adjective as equally important. The assumption that the absolute weight of information remains constant over the collectives in which it is contained may therefore be valid only when subjects are specifically instructed to weight

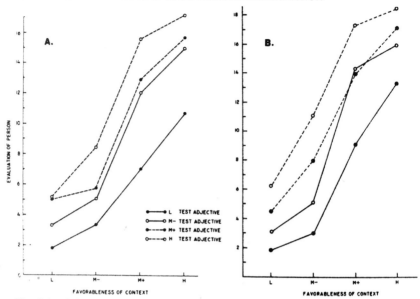

Fig. 9.4.   Collective evaluations as a function of context likeableness and test adjective likeableness, (a) reprinted from Wyer and Dermer (1968, p. 10) and (b) based upon data from Wyer and Watson (1969).

each piece of information equally. In less well-controlled situations, provision must be made for changes in the weight attached to components as a function of their context. If these changes cannot be specified *a priori,* the usefulness of an additive model in describing the effects of information in such situations may be somewhat limited.

C. Tests of Additivity in Other Stimulus Domains

The stimulus materials used in each of the experiments cited above consisted of personality trait adjectives. An additive model has also been applied, with varying degrees of success, to the integration of other types of information. These studies generally imply that unfavorable information has greater influence than favorable information. For example, Anderson and Norman (1964) investigated the effects of four different types of stimulus materials: adjectives (which were presented with instructions to estimate how well a person described by them would be liked), foods (judged in terms of the desirability of a meal composed of them), life events (judged in terms of the desirability of a week in which the events occurred), and headlines (judged in terms of the interest of a newspaper containing them). Sets of six stimuli of four general types were constructed: 6H, 6L, 3H3L, and 3L3H. In three of the four stimulus domains (adjectives, foods, and life events), the sum of the mean evaluations of 6H and 6L sets was greater than the sum of the mean ratings of 3H3L and 3L3H sets (8.87 vs. 7.93, 9.10 vs. 8.66, and 8.97 vs. 8.37, respectively); these differences are consistent with an averaging model in which unfavorable information receives a greater absolute weight. In the domain of headlines, the direction of this difference was reversed (9.13 vs. 9.91), indicating that interesting (H) headlines were more influential than uninteresting (L) ones. However, judgments of interest value and judgments of desirability should probably be distinguished; interesting headlines, while labeled H in Anderson and Norman's study, could actually pertain to more unfavorable situations than uninteresting, or L, headlines. In this event, all four sets of data would have similar implications.

In later studies, Anderson and his colleagues have considered the effects of presenting different types of information simultaneously. In one study (Lampel & Anderson, 1968), college females rated males in terms of their desirability as dates. These ratings were based on both visual information (photographs) and verbal information (adjectives). Two pairs of adjectives were selected: One pair (A) consisted of one H and one L adjective; the other (B), of one H and one M+ (moderately likeable) adjective. All possible AB combinations were then combined with a photograph (C) that was either low, medium, or high in attractiveness. Analysis of variance of ratings as a function of A, B, C, and stimulus replications indicated that the A × C and B × C interactions were both significant, while the A × B interaction was not. Mean ratings as a function of type of photograph and the four AB adjective combinations are shown in Fig. 9.5. These data indicate clearly that the effect of verbal information varies directly with the attractiveness of the photograph accompanying it. (In other words, the personality characteristics of stimulus persons substantially affected their desirability as dates if they were physically attractive but had relatively little influence if they were unattractive.) Moreover, the effects of verbal information at each level of photograph attractiveness differ by a fairly constant slope. These data would be consistent with an averaging model such as Eq. (9.3), if a constant weight is attached to a different pieces of verbal information but the absolute weight of visual information is related negatively to its favorableness. A summative model of the form of Eq. (9.2) could not as easily account for these results.

The differential influence of photographs in the above experiment is consistent with the general hypothesis that unfavorable information has greater weight. However, it is somewhat curious that L adjectives did not receive greater weight than H adjectives in this study, thus producing a significant A × B interaction. These results do not replicate the earlier findings reported by Anderson and Norman when H and L adjectives were combined.

In two experiments, Sidowski and Anderson (1967) asked subjects to estimate their preferences for working as a doctor, lawyer, teacher, or accountant in each of four cities. The cities chosen were either high, moderately high, neutral, or moderately low in attractiveness as a place to live. Analyses of variance of preference ratings were performed as a function

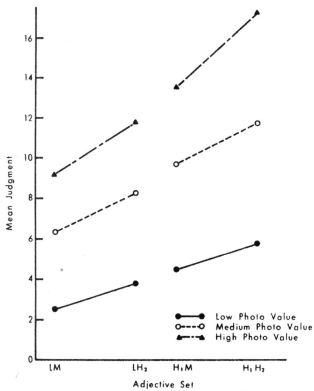

Fig. 9.5. Mean stimulus ratings as a function of adjective likeableness and attractiveness of photographs (based upon data from Lampel & Anderson, 1968).

of occupation and city. Although the interaction of these two types of information was significant, the source of this interaction appeared to lie in the effect of location on preferences for working as a teacher. As Fig. 9.6 indicates, the effects of location on preferences for working in other vocations were virtually identical. The authors reasonably attribute the greater effect of location on preferences for working as a teacher to the greater influence that socioeconomic conditions of the locale were expected to have on teachers' jobs. In contrast to the Lampel and Anderson study, however, the interaction of the two types of information presented cannot be attributed simply to differences in the *absolute* weight attached to pieces with different scale values. That is, the effect of location upon preferences for jobs as a teacher is not a constant multiple of its effect upon preferences for other vocations.

A study of impression formation that used more complex stimulus materials than personality adjectives was reported by Sawyers and Anderson (1971). Subjects evaluated presidents of the United States after reading two paragraphs describing their actions. In making their ratings, subjects were asked to attach equal importance to the implications of each paragraph. The paragraphs presented were either very favorable to the president de-

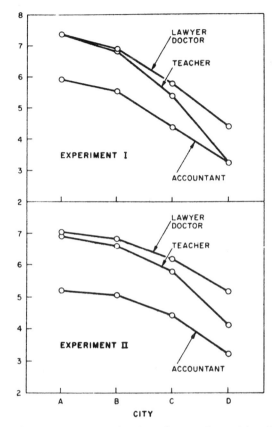

Fig. 9.6. Mean job preferences as a function of occupation and location (reprinted from Sidowski & Anderson, 1967, p. 279).

scribed (H), moderately favorable (M+), moderately unfavorable (M−), or very unfavorable (L). Paragraphs were combined in such a way that several separate test of an additive model were possible. Mean evaluations are plotted in Fig. 9.7 as a function of the favorableness of the first paragraph presented for each of two levels of favorableness of the second paragraph. If either a summative model or an averaging model in which components receive equal weight is valid, the two curves in each cell of this figure should be parallel. In fact, they are significantly nonparallel in only one instance (shown in the center figure in the top row).

Sawyers and Anderson's study is particularly interesting, since the situations constructed were similar to those used in traditional studies of attitude change. That is, each president was the object toward which subjects' attitudes were to be changed, and the paragraphs describing him were "persuasive communications." The evidence for additivity in this study would be very important if the effects reported are independent of subjects' initial attitudes toward the objects being judged. However, this seems

TEST OF INTEGRATION THEORY IN ATTITUDE CHANGE

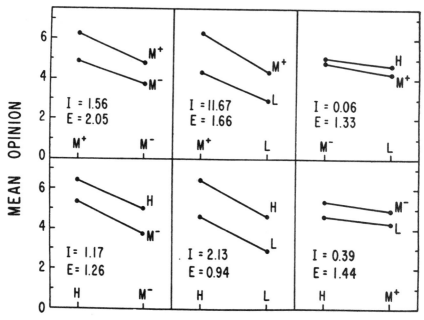

Fig. 9.7. Mean opinion ratings of U.S. Presidents as a function of the favorableness of component persuasive communications (reported from Sawyers & Anderson, 1971, p. 232).

unlikely. Subjects may normally be more likely to accept the validity of information supporting their initial opinion than information opposing it, as suggested in Chapter 7. On the other hand, the results of McGuire and Papageorgis's (1961) study, discussed in Chapter 8, suggest that subjects are relatively more influenced by a supporting communication if it is presented after a refutational message. These factors would produce interactions of the two communication favorableness variables plotted in Fig. 9.7, the nature of which depends upon the initial attitude toward the objects being evaluated. Sawyers and Anderson do not report the extent to which the relations described depend upon the particular president to which communications pertained, some of whom (Andrew Jackson, Woodrow Wilson, etc.) may initially have been regarded favorably, and others of whom (e.g., Rutherford B. Hayes, James K. Polk) may initially have been regarded unfavorably. The procedure of pooling over attitude objects (and thus over differences in initial attitude) may have prevented interactive effects of the communications from being detected. (Instructions to attach equal weight to each piece of information may also have decreased the magnitude of these effects.)

When the initial evaluation of the attitude object is relatively neutral, these concerns may be less serious. Indeed, the additive effects of information under such conditions are clearly demonstrated in the study by Tannenbaum (1967) discussed in detail in Chapter 6. In this study, subjects read two communications about teaching machines, one from a favorable source and one from an unfavorable source. Communications attributed to these sources either supported or opposed the use of teaching machines. In effect, the four conditions of the study represented all cells of a 2 × 2 design in which one factor pertained to information (positive or negative) from a favorable source and the second to information from an unfavorable source. Although the interactive effects of these factors were not tested, data described in Table 6.8 show that the effect of information from the favorable source was nearly the same, regardless of the type of information from the unfavorable source that was paired with it. In other words, the effects of the two pieces of information were independent and additive.

The above summary does not begin to cover all of the research on information integration that bears upon the hypothesis that information has additive effects on judgments. Indeed, much relevant research has not been specifically designed to investigate this hypothesis. (Tannenbaum's study is a case in point.) As we shall see in Chapter 10, the results of research intended to test the implications of cognitive balance theory for social inference processes are often more consistent with an additive formulation of information integration than with a consistency model. An additive model, regardless of its validity as a description of the underlying process used by subjects in arriving at judgments, may therefore be a very useful tool for predicting social inferences in fairly complex situations.

D. Conclusions

What do the studies reported in this section imply about the validity of an additive (summative or averaging) model? Tests of such a model were based upon two fundamental assumptions: first, that the response scale is equal interval; second, that each piece of information in a collective has a natural absolute weight that is independent of the characteristics of the other information presented with it. If these assumptions are valid, the interactions obtained in several studies of information integration clearly invalidate a summative model of the type described by Eq. (9.2). For such a model to be given serious consideration, it must provide for changes either in the weights attached to different pieces of information or in the evaluative implications of this information. Both types of changes are conceivable. For example, the weight of a given piece of information may depend upon its redundancy or inconsistency with the information accompanying it, while its scale value may depend upon the particular interpretation given to it when it is presented in the context of other information. Nevertheless, if the nature of these changes cannot be determined *a priori* and incorporated into a summative model, such a model has limited predictive utility even if theoretically valid.

The research described in this section also tends to invalidate an averaging model that assumes that each piece of information presented has the same absolute weight. A more appropriate assumption is that the absolute weight of information increases with both the extremity and the negativity of its scale value. However, these differences in weighting cannot account for the interactive effects of information reported in all studies (cf. Sidowski & Anderson, 1967; Wyer & Dermer, 1968).

The support of an additive model appears to increase when the instructions given subjects are designed (a) to eliminate many of the idiosyncratic effects of information described in Chapter 8 and (b) to minimize tendencies to discount information that appears inconsistent. This could indicate that the basic process underlying information integration is additive, and that an additive model would be perfectly accurate if idiosyncratic characteristics of the information being combined could be identified a priori and their effects incorporated into such a model. Another possibility is that detailed instructions about how to treat the information presented actually affect the integration process itself, and that as a result the procedure used by subjects to arrive at judgments under such instructional conditions differs qualitatively from that used in less well-controlled situations. But more about this later. First, let us consider some of the specific models of information integration that have been proposed in recent years and evaluate the empirical support for each.

III. SPECIFIC ADDITIVE MODELS OF INFORMATION INTEGRATION

Aside from its ability to generate accurate quantitative predictions about the manner in which information combines to affect judgments, a model of information integration must be able to account for two well-established and apparently contradictory findings. First, evaluations become more extreme as the number of equally favorable pieces of information presented becomes greater (Anderson, 1965a, 1967; Fishbein & Hunter, 1964). Thus, the evaluation based upon several pieces of equally favorable information is often more polarized than the evaluation based upon any single piece considered in isolation. The magnitude of this "set size effect" is greater when the pieces of information in the set are less redundant (Wyer, 1968). The second finding is that evaluations based upon highly polarized and moderately polarized information in combination are often less extreme than evaluations based upon the highly polarized information alone (Anderson, 1965a, 1968a). While the first set of findings seems to imply that the evaluation of an object is a function of the sum of the evaluative implications of the information presented about it, the second set suggests that the implications of each piece of information are averaged in arriving at a collective judgment.

The apparent inconsistency of the above findings may be made more salient by considering the implications of each for the construction of persuasive communications. Suppose that one person wishes to convey a maximally favorable impression of an object and has the opportunity to describe either one or several equally favorable attributes of the object. Should he describe as many of these attributes as possible, or should he concentrate only on a single attribute? Suppose that a second person has the opportunity to describe both highly favorable and moderately favorable attributes of the object. Would he be better off describing only the very favorable attributes, ignoring the moderately favorable ones, or should he describe as many favorable attributes as he can, regardless of the magnitude of their favorableness? Apparently, the first person should describe as many attributes as possible, while the second would be well-advised to concentrate only on the most favorable attributes.

Can the same additive model theoretically account for both sets of findings? Let us consider a number of specific summative and averaging models that have been proposed in recent years and not only evaluate the empirical support for each but also see how it might potentially explain both "set size" and "averaging-like" effects. Then, we will return again to the general question of summation vs. averaging and discuss in more detail the evidence for each type of process.

A. The Congruity Model of Information Integration

The congruity principle of information integration (Osgood et al., 1957) states that the evaluation of an object described by several pieces of information is an average of the evaluations based upon each piece considered separately, each evaluation weighted by its relative polarity. In general form, the model is described by the equation:

$$E_o = \frac{\Sigma |E_i| \, (E_i)}{\Sigma |E_i|} \tag{9.5}$$

where E_o is the evaluation of an object O, E_i is the evaluation based upon the ith piece of information about O (defined in relation to a point of affective neutrality), and $|E_i|$ is the absolute magnitude of E_i.

This formulation is appealing since if valid it would generate exact predictions of E_o without the introduction of *ad hoc* parameters to be established empirically. Unfortunately, tests of the fit of this model (e.g., L. Anderson & Fishbein, 1965; Rokeach & Rotham, 1965; Wyer, 1969b) have shown it to be inaccurate. A good example is provided by data from a study by the author (Wyer, 1973a) described in Chapter 2. Subjects evaluated persons described by each of eight single adjectives and also persons described by each of the 28 possible pairs formed from these adjectives. By using Eq. (9.5), predicted ratings of each pair along a scale from −5 to +5 were calculated for each subject separately on the basis of his ratings of single adjectives. Collective ratings, averaged over subjects, are plotted as a function of mean predicted ratings in Fig. 9.8(A). Predicted and obtained ratings were correlated .955; more important, the standard error of

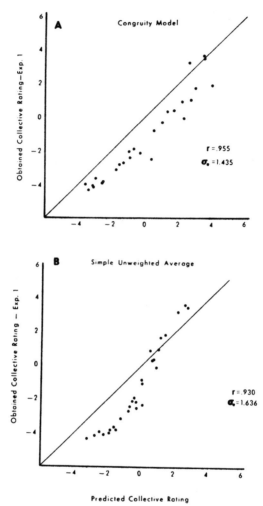

Fig. 9.8. Mean obtained collective ratings as a function of mean predicted ratings based upon (a) congruity theory [Eq. (9.5)] and (b) the simple unweighted average of the component ratings (reprinted from Wyer, 1973a).

estimating obtained from predicted values was 1.435.[3] To provide a basis for comparison, collective evaluations are plotted in Fig. 9.8(B) as a function of the simple unweighted average of component evaluations. In this case, the correlation between mean collective ratings and the unweighted average of the components was .930, and the standard error of estimate was 1.636. Thus, weighting each component by its relative extremity increases the predictive accuracy of an averaging model. However, there are obviously

---

[3] $\sigma = \sqrt{\dfrac{\Sigma(O_i - P_i)^2}{N}}$ where O_i and P_i are the obtained and predicted values of the ith of N stimuli.

major errors in predictions based upon Eq. (9.5). In calculating predicted values, component evaluations were defined in relation to a value of O along the bipolar category rating scale used in reporting judgments. The assumption that the scale origin is located at the midpoint of the rating scale may often be invalid. However, it seems unlikely that the invalidity of this assumption could account for the gross inaccuracy of Eq. (9.5) in this study. In an earlier study (Wyer, 1969b), magnitude estimation procedures were used, and the position of the scale origin was estimated empirically by using curve-fitting procedures. Nevertheless, the discrepancies from prediction obtained in this study were similar to those shown in Fig. 9.8(A).

Actual collective evaluations appear to be both more extreme and more negative than those predicted by congruity theory. Thus, the fit of the model is poor at the negative end of the scale, where negativitiy and extremity have additive effects, but is relatively better at the positive end, where these factors have compensating effects. Indirect evidence that negativity has an effect independent of extremity was obtained by Wyer and Watson (1969). In their study, sets of three adjectives were evaluated. The unweighted average of the normative likeableness ratings of the adjectives contained in these sets was either moderately high ($M+$) or moderately low ($M-$); however, at each level of mean component likeableness, the difference in likeableness of two of the adjectives was varied. For example, the mean likeableness of adjectives in $M+$ sets was approximately $+3$ along a scale from -10 to $+10$; however, the range of likeableness values of adjectives contained in these sets was either low ($+3$, $+3$, $+3$), moderate (0, $+3$, $+6$), or high (-3, $+3$, $+9$). Adjectives contained in $M-$ sets were selected according to analogous criteria. According to Eq. (9.5), the collective ratings of $M+$ sets should be about $+3$, $+5$, and $+5.4$ when the range of likeableness values of the adjectives in these sets was low, moderate, and high, respectively, while the predicted collective ratings of $M-$ sets should be about -3, -5, and -5.4 at these levels. In other words, the collective evaluations at each level of mean component likeableness should become more extreme as range increases, but the *rate* of increase should become less. However, suppose negativity as well as extremity determines the relative influence of components. Sets of high range adjectives contain more negative as well as more extreme adjectives. Thus, these negative adjectives should make ratings of $M-$ sets more extreme than values predicted by Eq. (9.5) but should make ratings of $M+$ sets less extreme than values predicted by this equation. Results, summarized previously in Table 6.4(A) support these hypothesis. As range increased from low to moderate, collective evaluations became more extreme, as expected. However, when range increased from moderate to high, the rate of increase in extremity of evaluations of $M-$ sets became greater, while the extremity of evaluations of $M+$ sets actually decreased. Note also that actual collective ratings were generally more favorable than predicted ratings, suggesting the existence of a positivity bias. Such a bias could also decrease the predictive accuracy of Eq. (9.3).

It may be recalled from Chapter 8 that both more polarized and more unfavorable pieces of information are less ambiguous, and that less ambiguous information appears to have greater influence. Perhaps the greater influence of extreme and/or unfavorable information is due to the lower ambiguity of this information. To this extent, the predictive accuracy of a model of the form of Eq. (9.5) might be increased by weighting each component by an inverse function of its relative ambiguity rather than by its relative extremity.

Prediction of "set size effects". Equation (9.5) obviously predicts that moderately favorable information, if added to highly favorable information, will decrease the evaluation of the object being described. However, the congruity principle has often been rejected out of hand because of its apparent inability to account for the fact that evaluations based upon two equally favorable pieces of information are often greater than evaluations based upon each piece considered separately. This particular criticism may be unjustified. Set size effects are typically inferred on the basis of mean evaluations of both components and collectives. An averaging model that gives greater weight to more extreme components can predict that set size effects will occur *on the average.* To see this, consider two adjectives A and B. Assume for simplicity that 50% of all evaluations based upon A alone are $+1$ and that the other 50% of the evaluations based upon this adjective are $+3$. Assume that the distribution of evaluations based upon B alone is similar. According to Eq. (9.5), the four possible combinations of ratings of A and B $(E_A = E_B = +3, E_A = E_B = +1, E_A = +1$ and $E_B = +3, E_A = +3$ and $E_B = +1)$ should generate four different collective ratings $(+3, +1, +2.5,$ and $+2.5,$ respectively). If A and B are independent, these ratings should occur with equal frequency. The *mean* evaluation would then be $+2.25,$ which is greater than the *mean* evaluation of either component considered separately $(+2.0)$. In other words, there would be an apparent set size effect despite the fact that the collective rating made by any individual subject lies between his two component ratings. Moreover, suppose that when a subject is uncertain about his evaluation of each component in isolation, he combines his alternative evaluations of one component (e.g., $+3$ and $+1$) with his alternative ratings of the other ($+3$ and $+1$) in all possible ways according to Eq. (9.5), and his collective rating represents the mean of these possible combinations. Then, set size effects would be detected in ratings made by individual subjects as well as in grouped data. To this extent, the congruity model could theoretically predict both of the effects often assumed to differentiate summative and averaging models.

An interesting implication of the above interpretation may be worth mentioning. If the unweighted average of component evaluations is held constant, Eq. (9.5) generates more extreme collective evaluations when the component values are more dispersed. For example, the predicted evaluation based upon three adjectives with the scale values $+5$, $+3$, and 0 is greater (4.25) than that based upon three adjectives with the values $+4$, $+3$, and $+1$ (3.63). Therefore, the preceding analysis implies that set size effects will be greater when there is substantial disagreement among subjects about the evaluation based upon each component when considered separately, or when individual subjects are more uncertain about their evaluations based upon each component in isolation (that is, when the information presented is more ambiguous). Data are not available concerning the validity of this hypothesis.

B. Fishbein's Summative Model

The interactive effects of information obtained in tests of a general additive model do not necessarily rule out a summative model that takes into account changes in the weight of an adjective when it is combined with other information. Such a model has been proposed by Fishbein (1963). His formulation, described in detail in Chapter 6, is given by the equation:

$$E_o = \Sigma P_i E_i \qquad (9.6)$$

where E_o is the evaluation of an object O, P_i is the subjective probability that O possesses an attribute i, and E_i is the evaluative implication of this attribute.

As we have seen in Chapter 8, this formulation is useful in describing and predicting the differential effects of information that varies with respect to such characteristics as ambiguity, novelty, and redundancy. However, adequate tests of the formulation are difficult for several reasons discussed in Chapter 6. For example, the appropriate scaling of P_i and E_i is not clear. Moreover, evaluations of O may be based not only upon attributes described in the information presented about it, but also upon other, unspecified attributes of O that are not known to the investigator. Despite these difficulties, correlational studies have provided qualified support for the formulation. L. Anderson and Fishbein (1965) asked subjects to read one of five brief communications about a person, "Mrs. Williams," and then to evaluate her along a series of semantic differentials similar to the A scales described in Chapter 6 (page 147). In one communication, no adjectives were used to describe Mrs. Williams; in a second, she was described as "honest;" in a third, as both "honest" and "friendly"; and in a fourth, as "honest," "friendly" and "helpful." A fifth communication was like the fourth except that Mrs. Williams was described as "honest" at two different points in the communication. After reading the communication and rating Mrs. Williams, subjects also estimated, along a set of semantic differentials similar to the B scales described previously, the likelihood that she possessed each of the three attributes and evaluated each of the attributes separately along the A scales. These latter data provided values of P_i and E_i for each attribute.

Predicted evaluations of E_o were estimated from Eq. (9.6) for each subject separately. Beliefs associated with all three attributes were used, regardless of whether or not they were described in the information presented. Predicted and obtained estimates of E_o were correlated .66 ($p < .001$). For purposes of comparison, Anderson and Fishbein also calculated predicted values of E_o based upon the congruity principle, in this case considering only the evaluations of the particular attributes specified in the information. These values were correlated only .38 with obtained values. (The magnitude of this latter correlation was apparently similar, regardless of the number of attributes mentioned in the communication.) Thus it seems reasonable to conclude that Fishbein's model is more accurate than Osgood's in predicting the *relative* magnitudes of evaluations based upon different pieces of information. This of course does not mean that it can generate more exact quantitative predictions of these evaluations without introducing empirically estimated slope and intercept parameters. Unfortunately, standard errors of estimating obtained values of E_o from predicted values were not reported.

A modification of Fishbein's model, which partially takes into account differences in the redundancy of the information presented, was tested by Wyer (1969b). In this study, the evaluation based upon two adjectives A and B (E_{AB}) was predicted on the basis of the equation:

$$E_{AB} = (1 - \frac{P_{A/B}}{2}) E_A + (1 - \frac{P_{B/A}}{2}) E_B - (1 - \frac{P_{B/A}}{2} - \frac{P_{A/B}}{2}) O_r \qquad (9.7)$$

where E_A and E_B are the evaluations of A alone and B alone, $P_{A/B}$ and $P_{B/A}$ are the conditional probabilities that an object described by B would be described by A and that an object described by A would be described by B, respectively, and O_r is the scale origin.[4] Stimuli for this study consisted in part of 49 adjective pairs which were formed by combining each of seven adjectives in one set (A) with each of seven adjectives in a second (B). Adjectives in each set varied over a wide range of normative likeableness. Estimates of $P_{A/B}$ and $P_{B/A}$ were obtained from normative data used in other studies of redundancy effects (see Chapter 8). Subjects evaluated persons described by both single adjectives and adjective pairs by using a magnitude estimation

---

[4] To derive this equation, Wyer assumed that if A is considered before B, the evaluation of O would be equal to the evaluation based upon A plus the proportion of the evaluation based upon B that was not redundant with A; thus,

$$E_{A1B2} = (E_A - O_r) + (1 - P_{B/A})(E_B - O_r) + O_r.$$

Similarly, if B is considered before A,

$$E_{A2B1} = (E_B - O_r) + (1 - P_{A/B})(E_A - O_r) + O_r.$$

If an equal number of subjects consider A and B in each order when they are presented simultaneously, the average evaluation based upon these adjectives would be the average of the two predicted values which, after simplifying, becomes the expression in Eq. (9.7).

REDUNDANCY MODEL   CONGRUITY MODEL

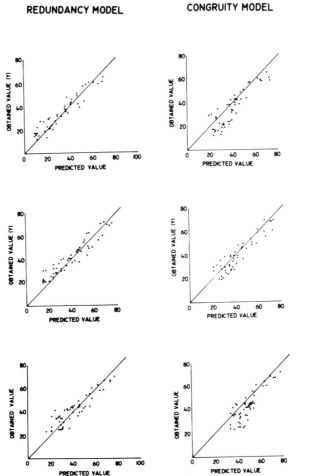

Fig. 9.9. Mean collective ratings (E_{AB}) as a function of predicted ratings based upon Eqs. (9.7) and (9.5) (reprinted from Wyer, 1969, p. 36).

procedure in which the modulus stimulus was assigned a value of 50. The modulus used was either high ("agreeable"), neutral ("near-sighted"), or low ("ill-tempered") in likeableness. Values of O_r were estimated under each modulus condition by using curve-fitting procedures. For purposes of comparison, we also calculated predicted values of E_{AB} using a modification of Eq. (9.5) which allows scale origin to be estimated empirically. Mean obtained values of E_{AB} are plotted in Fig. 9.9 as a function of mean predicted values based upon each formulation. The standard error of estimating E_{AB} from Eq. (9.7) was 5.35, 5.64, and 5.79 under positive, neutral, and negative modulus conditions, respectively, while the standard error of estimating E_{AB} from the extension of Eq. (9.5) was 8.05, 6.11, and 9.25, respectively. Since tests of both formulations require that one parameter, scale origin, be estimated empirically, a comparison of the fit of these models seems legitimate. On the basis of this comparison, the extension of Fishbein's formulation is the more accurate.

"Set size" vs. "averaging" effects. Equation (9.6) can obviously account for set size effects. The first clear evidence of such effects was in fact reported by Fishbein and Hunter (1964), who found that evaluations of hypothetical persons increased with the total favorableness of the information recalled about these persons, although the average favorableness of this information decreased slightly over the conditions being compared. However, how could Eq. (9.6) account for the fact that the addition of moderately favorable adjectives to highly favorable adjectives *decreases* the evaluation of objects described by this information? To explain this finding, one would have to assume that although the additional information increases beliefs that the object O possesses moderately favorable attributes, it also increases beliefs that O possesses unfavorable attributes not specified in the information presented. Similarly, the addition of moderately unfavorable information to extremely unfavorable information would have to increase beliefs that O possesses favorable attributes. While such effects probably occur, it is unclear whether they are of sufficient magnitude to account for the "averaging" effects obtained in studies such as Anderson's (1965a, 1968b).

C. Anderson's Averaging Model

While we have shown that even a simple weighted average model can potentially account for set size effects, these effects are more easily predicted by a formulation proposed by Anderson (1965a). This model assumes that the effect of a relatively neutral "initial impression" of O (I_o) is averaged in with the effects of new information about O. That is,

$$E_o = \frac{w_o I_o + \Sigma w_i V_i}{w_o + \Sigma w_i} \tag{9.8}$$

where V_i is the scale value of the ith piece of information presented, w_i is the weight attached to this piece of information, and w_o is the weight attached to the initial impression I_o. To see more clearly how the formulation may apply, consider three pieces of information, A, B, and C, which have scale values of 8, 8, and 2, respectively. If the weights attached to each piece of information and to I_o are equal ($w_o = w_i = w$), and if the scale value of I_o is 0, then the evaluations based upon each piece of information separately are:

$$E_A = E_B = \frac{w(0) + w(8)}{2w} = 4$$

$$E_C = \frac{w(0) + w(2)}{2w} = 1.$$

However, the evaluations based upon A and B in combination would be:

$$E_{AB} = \frac{w(0) + w(8) + w(8)}{3w} = 5.33,$$

and the evaluation based upon A and C in combination would be:

$$E_{AC} = \frac{w(0) + w(8) + w(2)}{3w} = 3.33.$$

Thus the evaluation based upon both A and B is greater than the evaluation based upon either component in isolation, while the evaluation based upon both A and C lies between the evaluations of the two components.

Anderson (1967) showed that Eq. (9.8) can provide a very good quantitative description of set size effects as well as a qualitative one. Stimuli for this study consisted of sets of 1, 2, 3, 4, 6, and 9 adjectives that were either all highly favorable (H) or all highly unfavorable (L). To insure that set size effects would not be attributable to differences in the specific adjectives involved, each adjective was used the same proportion of times in forming sets of each size. As expected, the extremity of evaluations increased consistently with set size. Moreover, this increase was proportionately less as each additional piece of information was added. This is also consistent with Eq. (9.8), which predicts that as the amount of information increases, evaluations will asymptote to a level equal to the scale value of the adjectives being presented.

In applying Eq. (9.8), Anderson assumed that the weight attached to each component adjective is the same ($w_i = w$). Therefore, since in the above study all adjectives in each set had the same scale value ($V_i = V$ for all i), Eq. (9.8) may be rewritten

$$E_o = \frac{w_o I_o + kwV}{w_o + kw}$$

where k is the number of adjectives in the set. To simplify matters further, Anderson normalized weights so that $w_o = 1-w$ and assumed that $I_o = 0$. Substituting these values into the above equation and solving for w yields the expression

$$w = \frac{E_o}{kV - (k-1)E_o}$$

This value should be constant regardless of set size. To test this hypothesis, Anderson also assumed that V, the only unknown on the right side of the equation, was equal to the maximum or minimum value along the response scale used, depending upon whether the set was composed of H or L adjectives, and then calculated w for each set size based upon estimates of E_o made by each subject separately. Averaged over subjects, w was remarkably similar at each combination of set size and likeableness (H or L). Pooled over likeableness levels, the mean values of w in one study were .46, .44, .44, .47, and .57 for sets of 1, 2, 3, 4, and 6 adjectives, respectively, and in a second study were .42, .38, .40, .38, .40, and .54 for set sizes of 1, 2, 3, 4, 6, and 9, respectively. The relatively high estimate of w for the largest set size in each study was attributed to a tendency of subjects to overuse extreme response categories when rating sets of the largest size. The similarity of w over the other set size conditions, in combination with the increase in extremity of evaluations with increasing set size, provides impressive support for Anderson's formulation of information integration processes.

1. Effects of Difference in Initial Impression. In testing the validity of Eq. (9.8), Anderson typically assumes that the evaluation of a person before information about him is presented is affectively neutral, and therefore that $I_o = 0$. This may not always be the case. If subjects differ in their predispositions to evaluate persons favorably or unfavorably before they know anything about them, then according to Eq. (9.8), they should also differ in their evaluations of these persons *after* information about them becomes available. However, the effect of such initial differences should be relatively less when the amount of information presented is large, and thus $kw >> w_o$. To test these hypotheses, Kaplan (1971b) inferred subjects' predispositions to evaluate persons positively or negatively from the favorableness of the adjectives they selected for describing "people in general." Subjects with each predisposition evaluated persons described by sets of 2, 4, or 6 adjectives. Adjectives in each set were either high or low in likeableness. Pooled over set size and likeableness levels, subjects with positive predispositions made more positive evaluations than those with negative predispositions. Moreover, these differences, while they occurred regardless of the number of traits presented, decreased consistently as set size increased. Unfortunately, a second experiment performed by Kaplan did not consistently replicate these findings; moreover, decreases in the effect of predisposition with increasing set size occurred only when the adjectives presented were low in redundancy. Since an increase in set size produced a more extreme evaluation even when adjectives were highly redundant, which suggests that this additional information had some effect, this contingency would not be expected and is difficult to explain.

Kaplan's findings could be attributed at least in part to the combined effects of response bias and ceiling effects. For example, subjects who have positive response biases are more likely to use extremely positive scale categories for evaluating persons described by relatively little information and therefore are unable to increase the extremity of these ratings once more information becomes available. Subjects with negative response bias are less apt to use extremely positive categories in rating persons and thus have more room to increase their category ratings as set size increases. For similar reasons, ceiling effects at the negative end of the scale would be greater, and thus set size effects would be less, for subjects with negative response biases. These effects could explain the convergence of ratings by subjects with different predispositions as set size increases. Nevertheless, the consistency of Kaplan's results with the implications of Eq. (9.8) is worth noting.

2. *Empirical Estimation of* I_o. For Eq. (9.8) to predict set size effects, the scale value of the initial impression must be less polarized than the scale values of the information being presented. While this assumption seems intuitively reasonable, it has seldom been tested. As we noted earlier in this chapter (p. 270), when Eq. (9.8) is applied to evaluations based upon two pieces of information, A and B, it reduces to the expression

$$E_{AB} = (1-w'_B)E_A + (1-w'_A)E_B - w'_o\, I_o,$$

where E_A and E_B are the evaluations based upon A and B separately, w'_A and w'_B are the relative weights attached to the *scale values* of A and B, and w'_o is the relative weight attached to the scale value of the initial impression (I_o). This expression is equivalent to the best fitting function relating E_A and E_B to E_{AB}:

$$E_{AB} = k_i E_A + k_2 E_B + k_3.$$

One way of estimating empirically the parameters in Eq. (9.8) is first to solve for k_1, k_2, and k_3 with standard regression procedures, and then to solve for w'_A, w'_B, w'_o, and I_o in terms of these constants. An indication of whether Eq. (9.8) is preferable to other models that reduce to the best linear fit relating component ratings to collective ratings is whether the values of these parameters are psychologically meaningful.

Limited evidence concerning this issue is available. Wyer (1969b) obtained data on evaluations based upon both single adjectives and adjective pairs, by using magnitude estimation procedures in which the modulus (positive, neutral, or negative) was given a value of 50. He assumed that the weights attached to E_A and E_B were equal and found that the best fitting functions relating E_{AB} to the sum of E_A and E_B under the modulus conditions were:

$$E_{AB} = .60(E_A + E_B) - 17.4$$
$$E_{AB} = .59(E_A + E_B) - 15.0$$

and
$$E_{AB} = .60(E_A + E_B) - 20.8.$$

These equations yield values of w_A' and w_B' equal to about .40 and a value of w_o' equal to about .20. These values seem reasonable. However, the estimates of I_o derived from these equations were 87, 87, and 108 respectively. These values were higher in each case than the rating of the most favorable single adjective presented. (Specifically, "understanding," which had a normative likeableness rating of +9.64 along a scale from −10 to +10, was rated only 82, 84, and 96 under the three modulus conditions.) Such values of I_o, while they would not necessarily invalidate the model, would prevent it from accounting for "set size" effects when the information presented is favorable. However, some caution should be taken in generalizing the results of this study to conditions in which category rating procedures are used. In fact, regression analyses of category ratings have provided much more meaningful estimates of I_o (see Footnote 6, p. 316).

D. Warr's Two-Process Formulation

Each of the formulations we have discussed so far assumes that the underlying process of information integration is *either* summative *or* averaging, and that the same process is used by subjects regardless of the nature of the information presented. While it would indeed simplify matters if this were the case, there is no *a priori* reason to believe that it is. It is equally reasonable to suppose that both processes may be involved at different times, depending upon the type of stimulus to be evaluated and the type of information presented about it. It is also conceivable that the process used depends in part upon the particular set of information being presented. Such a hypothesis has been made by Warr (1973b). He proposes that when two pieces of information have different evaluative implications, their implications are averaged, with the more extreme implication having the greater influence. However, when the two pieces of information have similar implications, their effects summate. Thus, the "set size" effects and the "averaging" effects discussed at the beginning of this section are the result of two different integration processes.

More specifically, Warr hypothesizes that when a subject is asked to make a judgment based upon a pair of adjectives, he focuses upon the one he believes to have the more extreme implications when considered in isolation (that is, H) and then modifies the judgment based upon this adjective alone according to the implications of the remaining adjective (L). If the two adjectives have similar implications, the second adjective strengthens the inference based upon the first, resulting in a more extreme judgment than that based upon H in isolation. However, when the two adjectives have different implications, the less extreme adjective weakens the inference based upon H and therefore "pulls back" this inference toward that implied by L.

Warr has obtained preliminary evidence to support his hypothesis. Unlike most of the studies we have described, Warr did not restrict his attention to inferences about likeableness but instead investigated the effects of information upon inferences about several different attributes. Stimulus adjectives were presented both separately and in pairs; in each case, subjects estimated how likely it was that a person described by the stimulus information would possess each of a set of 16 response traits. These estimates were made along a scale from -5 (certainly would not) to $+5$ (certainly would). Consider two pieces of information, H and L, the first of which has more extreme judgmental implications than the second. If a simple averaging process is involved, the judgment based upon H and L in combination (J_C) would be described by the expression

$$J_C = w J_L + (1-w) J_H \tag{9.9a}$$

where J_H and J_L are the judgments based upon H and L in isolation and w is the relative weight attached to the least extreme of these judgments (J_L). Solving for w in this equation,

$$w = \frac{J_H - J_C}{J_H - J_L} = \frac{J_H - J_C}{R} \tag{9.9b}$$

where R is the range of the two component judgments. In principle, w should lie between 0 and 1. A value of w that empirically exceeds these limits is not psychologically meaningful and would indicate that Eq. (9.9a) is an invalid description of the integration process being used.

Warr calculated the value of w associated with each collective evaluation on the basis of data from each subject separately. He then plotted these values, averaged over both subjects and response dimensions, as a function of the difference in magnitude between the two component judgments. Two aspects of his data are important. First, when $R > 1$, w was between 0 and 1; moreover, w appeared to be constant over values of R. In other words, a simple averaging model accurately described the manner in which components combined to affect collective judgments. However, when $R < 1$, the value of w increased abruptly and ultimately exceeded 1. This discontinuity in the function relating w to component range suggests a difference between the integration process used when component pieces of information have similar scale values and the process used when components have different scale values. This finding is of particular interest, since none of the other models considered in this section would predict such a discontinuity.

While w may be independent of component range when $R > 1$, it may nevertheless vary with other characteristics of the information presented. In fact, further analyses of Warr's data indicated that when L and H adjectives differed in the direction of their implications (that is, when one implied the presence of the response trait while the other implied the absence of the trait), w was greater when J_L was negative (that is, when L implied the absence of the trait) than when it was positive.

Warr hypothesizes that when larger sets of information are presented, inference processes are similar to those involved when only two pieces are considered. That is, the subject initially focuses upon the piece of information with the most extreme implications and then will modify the judgment based upon this piece according to the information with the least extreme implications. To this extent, Eq. (9.9a) should describe these inferences when $R > 1$. Warr goes on to hypothesize that the modifying power of the information with the least extreme implications depends in part upon the similarity of its implications to those of the other pieces of information presented. Specifically, consider a set of three adjectives, H, L, and M, where H leads to the most extreme judgment when considered in isolation (J_H), L to the least extreme judgment (J_L), and M to a judgment (J_M) that lies somewhere between J_H and J_L. Warr proposes that the weight attached to J_L is in part a function of the position of J_M in relation to J_H and J_L. This position, w_M, can be described by the ratio

$$w_M = \frac{J_H - J_M}{J_H - J_L}$$

Thus, w_M, and therefore w in Eq. (9.9a), decreases as J_M approaches J_H.

Warr investigated the support for this interpretation in a second study (Warr, 1973a). Sets of three adjectives, and the single adjectives comprising these sets, were each rated along a set of 13 response dimensions according to a procedure similar to that used in the first experiment. In analyzing his data, Warr considered only responses to adjective sets in which J_H and J_L differed in direction and in which $R > 1$. Estimates of w, calculated on the basis of Eq. (9.9b), were affected, as hypothesized, both by the sign of J_L and by w_M. That is, w was greater when J_L was negative than when it was positive, but w was not correlated with R, thus replicating the results of the first experiment. However, w decreased as J_M approached J_H. The fact that the effects of J_L positivity and the position of J_M were independent suggests that that value of w when three adjectives are judged can be described as a linear function of (a) the value of w when J_H and J_L are presented as a pair and (b) the relative position of J_M; that is

$$w_{triplet} = k_1 w_{pair} + k_2 w_M + k_3$$

where k_1 - k_3 are regression weights, and w_{pair} is a function of the sign of J_L. This possibility may warrant further consideration.

IV. THE CASE AGAINST AVERAGING

It is undoubtedly clear by now that "critical" tests of summative and averaging models, and the identification of the psychological processes to which they pertain, are very difficult to construct. The data usually interpreted as evidence for a summative process (e.g., the "set size" effect) can be accounted for by an averaging model such as Anderson's. On the other hand, the "averaging-like" effects when moderately polarized information is added to highly polarized information could in principle be predicted by a summative model, such as Fishbein's, which takes into account the influence of attributes other than those specified in the information presented.

Certain differences between the models may be tested, however. Consider the following two alternative descriptions of an evaluation based upon adjectives A and B, as a function of the scale values of these adjectives when considered separately (S_A and S_B), and an initial impression (I_o):

$$E_{AB} = w_A S_A + w_B S_B + w_o I_o \qquad (9.10)$$

and

$$E_{AB} = \frac{w_A S_A + w_B S_B + w_o I_o}{w_A + w_B + w_o} \qquad (9.11)$$

where w_A, w_B, and w_o are the absolute weights attached to A, B, and the initial impression. Suppose that w_A and w_B are allowed to vary independently of one another, and also of S_A and S_B. Suppose further that S_A and S_B are similar in direction (both positive or both negative), but that S_B is less polarized than S_A. Then, holding w_A constant, the summative model [Eq. (9.10)] predicts that E_{AB} will increase with the value of w_B under all conditions. However, the averaging model [Eq. (9.11)] predicts that the direction of change in E_{AB} resulting from an increase in w_B will depend upon the difference between S_A and S_B. To see this, assume that $I_o = 0$, and that the weight of S_B is either high (w_{BH}) or low (w_{BL}). Then, an increase in the weight assigned to S_B can be shown to increase E_{AB}, so that

$$\frac{w_A S_A + w_{BL} S_B}{w_A + w_{BL} + w_o} < \frac{w_A S_A + w_{BH} S_B}{w_A + w_{BH} + w_o},$$

only under conditions in which

$$\frac{S_B}{S_A} < \frac{w_A}{w_o + w_A}.$$

When $I_o = 0$, the ratio of the scale values of A and B is theoretically equal to the ratio of the evaluations of persons described by these adjectives considered separately (obtained under conditions in which $w_A = w_B$). Therefore, Eq. (9.11) implies that an increase in w_B will increase the extremity of E_{AB} only when

$$\frac{E_B}{E_A} < \frac{w_A}{w_o + w_A},$$

where E_A and E_B are the normative evaluations of persons described by A alone and by B alone, respectively. In any event, the equations imply that for a given set of values of w_A and w_o, the likelihood of "summation-like" effects should decrease as the difference between E_A and E_B increases.

To construct stimuli for investigating this possibility, the author selected two sets of adjectives (A and B), each of which contained one adjective at each

TABLE 9.2

Evaluations [a] of Positive Pairs
as a Function of E_A, E_B, w_A, and w_B

E_A	w_A	w_B	E_B			
			H_{3+}	H_{2+}	H_+	H
H_{3+}	High	High	6.50	7.61	5.36	5.25
	High	Low	7.43	6.82	4.57	5.11
	Low	High	6.61	4.53	4.71	3.54
	Low	Low	5.21	4.68	4.00	3.43
H_{2+}	High	High	6.93	6.93	4.86	4.11
	High	Low	6.50	5.64	5.29	1.71
	Low	High	5.89	5.75	4.04	3.93
	Low	Low	5.43	4.82	3.89	3.50
H_+	High	High	5.89	4.46	3.57	2.57
	High	Low	6.43	2.96	3.07	1.18
	Low	High	3.18	3.18	2.07	2.18
	Low	Low	4.46	2.57	2.92	1.00
H	High	High	5.04	3.11	2.07	.25
	High	Low	3.89	4.21	3.04	.46
	Low	High	5.14	2.11	2.14	.29
	Low	Low	3.14	2.46	1.36	.32

[a] $N = 28$ subjects per cell.

of four levels of positive normative likeableness: H_{3+}, H_{2+}, H_+, and H; pooled over two stimulus replications, the mean likeableness of the adjectives at these levels (along a scale from −10 to +10) was 9.00, 6.36, 3.50, and 1.28, respectively. Each A adjective was then paired with each B adjective to form 16 pairs within each stimulus replication. An analogous procedure was used to construct pairs of adjectives selected from four levels of negative likeableness: L_{3-}, L_{2-}, L_-, and L; averaged over A and B sets and replications, the mean likeableness of adjectives representing these levels was −8.81, −6.31, −3.70, and −1.20, respectively. Subjects were presented stimuli on slides, with instructions that each adjective in a pair had been used by one of four different judges to describe a person on the basis of a job interview. Two judges were each described as having a record of 95% accuracy in their

TABLE 9.3

Evaluations [a] of Negative Adjective Pairs
as a Function of E_A, E_B, w_A, and w_B

E_A	w_A	w_B	E_B			
			L	L-	L₂-	L₃-
L	High	High	−4.18	−5.25	−5.43	−6.50
	High	Low	−1.32	−1.39	−4.18	−3.68
	Low	High	−1.14	−1.64	−3.36	−6.43
	Low	Low	−1.53	−1.86	−2.46	−4.78
L-	High	High	−5.10	−5.21	−5.43	−5.61
	High	Low	−4.11	−3.89	−4.64	−6.32
	Low	High	−2.68	−2.61	−4.71	−3.79
	Low	Low	−2.71	−3.14	−4.14	−4.46
L₂-	High	High	−7.07	−7.14	−7.71	−8.50
	High	Low	−4.67	−4.82	−5.54	−7.00
	Low	High	−5.64	−5.00	−6.64	−7.21
	Low	Low	−3.86	−4.89	−4.57	−5.82
L₃-	High	High	−6.39	−8.00	−7.89	−8.54
	High	Low	−5.86	−5.07	−6.07	−6.96
	Low	High	−3.68	−5.78	−6.50	−7.04
	Low	Low	−4.00	−4.96	−5.11	−5.50

[a] $N = 28$ subjects per cell.

descriptions, as borne out by "later experiences with the interviewee," and the other two were described as accurate only about 55% of the time, or "slightly better than chance." The likeableness of A and B adjectives (E_A and E_B) and the reliability of the source of these adjectives (w_A and w_B) were varied independently. (No subject received the same pair of adjectives under more than one combination of w_A and w_B).

Mean evaluations (E_{AB}) as a function of E_A, E_B, w_A and w_B are shown in Tables 9.2 and 9.3 for the two groups of adjective pairs described above. In each table, there are 24 possible comparisons between evaluations made when the less polarized adjective in a pair has a low weight and those made when this adjective has a high weight. These comparisons are indicated by brackets. When component ratings were both positive, an increase in the weight of the less polarized adjective increased E_{AB} in 20 of the 24 cases.

TABLE 9.4

Mean Evaluations of Adjective Pairs as a Function of the Ratio of Their Normative Scale Values and the Weight of the Less Polarized Adjective

Pair		Positive Adjective Pairs			Pair		Negative Adjective Pairs		
	E_A/E_B	Evaluation of Pair		Difference		E_A/E_B	Evaluation of Pair		Difference
		low w_B	high w_B				low w_B	high w_B	
$H_{3+}H_{2+}$	1.42	5.70	6.39	.69	$L_{3-}L_{2-}$	1.40	-2.58	-3.60	-1.02
$H_{2+}H_+$	1.82	3.73	4.08	.35	$L_{2-}L_-$	1.70	-4.64	-5.55	-.91
$H_{3+}H_+, H_+H$	2.65	2.87	4.32	1.44	$L_{3-}L_-, L_-L$	2.73	-4.67	-6.45	-1.78
$H_{2+}H$	4.97	2.45	3.84	1.39	$L_{2-}L$	5.26	-4.57	-6.43	-1.86
$H_{3+}H$	7.03	4.20	4.43	.23	$L_{3-}L$	7.34	-5.27	-5.06	.21

Note—In each case, B refers to the less polarized adjective in the pair.

When the component ratings were both negative, an increase in the weight of the less polarized adjective decreased E_{AB} in 20 of 24 cases. To explore further the implications of Eq. (9.11), adjective pairs were divided into five groups on the basis of the ratio of the scale values of the adjectives comprising them. The pairs comprising groups, and the approximate ratio of the scale values of the adjectives involved, are shown in Table 9.4. Mean evaluations based upon these pairs are also shown in this table as a function of the credibility of the source of the less polarized adjective. There seems to be no systematic difference in the effect of the weight of the less polarized adjective as a function of the ratio of the two component adjectives.

There is only one way in which an averaging model could account for the data described above. If the absolute ("natural") weight attached to the "initial impression" [that is, w_O in Eq. (9.11)] is substantially greater when the source of one of the adjectives presented has low credibility, this factor might be sufficient to offset the effect of a decrease in the absolute weight attached to the adjective itself, and it might bring the predicted rating below that based upon the same information from highly credible sources. While this is conceivable, it would contradict the assumption usually made in testing averaging models, that the "natural" weight of each component (presumably including I_O) does not depend upon the type of information accompanying it. Thus, all things considered, it seems reasonable to conclude that the preceding data support a summative model of information integration over an averaging model.

Data consistent with the conclusion drawn from the above study have been reported in two other experiments which were not specifically designed to investigate the summation versus averaging controversy. Rosenbaum and Levin (1969) manipulated source credibility by ascribing information to persons occupying different social roles. Subjects rated persons described by sets of adjectives that had normative scale values that were similar in direction (positive or negative) but different in magnitude. In three of four cases for which data were reported, evaluations became more extreme (relative to the midpoint of a 0-7 scale) as the source of the less polarized information became more credible. In a study of novelty effects, described in detail in Chapter 8, the author (Wyer, 1970a) found that when the normative likeableness ratings of adjectives presented were similar in direction, but different in magnitude, evaluations of the persons described became more extreme as the novelty of the less polarized adjective increased.

While the results of the preceding studies are fairly consistent with the implications of a summative model, they do not necessarily demonstrate that such a model is a valid description of the psychological processes of information integration; they simply indicate that an averaging model is invalid. Several tests of an additive model, described earlier in this chapter, have shown significant interactive effects of the information presented. These interactions rule out a summative model that assumes that the absolute weight attached to each piece of information remains constant over the sets in which it is contained. It is possible, if not probable, that the absolute weight of a piece of information depends upon its context. However, it is also possible that *neither* a summative nor an averaging model is a valid description of information integration processes, except under very restricted conditions.

As we have noted, there are also theoretical reasons to believe that neither a summative nor an averaging model provides an exact description of information integration. That is, if the evaluation of an object along a category scale reflects the expected value of an underlying distribution of subjective probabilities that O belongs to each of the scale categories, quantitative predictions based upon either type of model are at best approximate. Moreover, the integration of information about O may be a quite different process than that implied by either type of additive model. In light of the questionable validity of additive models of information integration on both theoretical and empirical grounds, it may be worthwhile to consider the implications of this interpretation of category ratings in more detail, and to identify the assumptions that must be made in order to generate quantitative descriptions of integration processes based upon this interpretation.

V. A CONCEPT IDENTIFICATION FORMULATION OF INFORMATION INTEGRATION

A complete theoretical model of information integration must take into account characteristics of information, other than favorableness, that determine the magnitude of its influence. Certainly two pieces of information with similar scale values do not always have the same effect when combined with other information. Moreover, two pieces of information that lead to different evaluations when presented in isolation may have similar effects when combined with a third piece of information. The occurrence of such instances usually appears unsystematic and is often attributed to errors of measurement. Such a conclusion may be premature, however. In this section, an alternative formulation of information integration is proposed, one based upon the interpretation of cognitive processes described in Chapter 2. While this formulation is not completely developed, it can in principle account for many idiosyncratic effects of information. Moreover, it can potentially account for both set size effects and "averaging-like" effects.

A. Some Initial Assumptions

The formulation to be proposed was described generally at the beginning of this chapter. Some specific examples may help to clarify the nature of the assumptions required to generate quantitative predictions based upon this formulation. First, consider two adjectives, A and B. Theoretically, there is a subjective distribution of objects described by each adjective along the category scale used to record evaluations, and the evaluations based upon this adjective alone is estimated by the expected value of the distribution of objects described by it. The group of objects described by both A and B is the conjunction of these distributions, and therefore the evaluation of a single object described by both A and B is the expected value of this conjunction. Unfortunately, the exact nature of the conjunctive distribution cannot be inferred from the expected values of the component distributions alone. Nor can it be determined *a priori* from the component distributions themselves without making some simplifying assumptions. Suppose that the probability that an object described by A is in category i is $P_{i/A}$, and that the probability that an object described by B is in i is $P_{i/B}$. If A and B were independent *for all i*, the probability that an object described by both A and B is in i would be given by the equation.[5]

$$P_{i/AB} = \frac{P_{i/A}P_{i/B}}{P_i}$$

However, the assumption that A and B are independent is most tenuous, as research on redundancy and inconsistency effects imply. The subjective probability that a person is "warm," for example, is clearly greater if he is known to be "friendly" than if he is not. Other assumptions, while still questionable, may be less obviously invalid. Consider the first two hypothetical distributions shown in Table 9.5, which pertain to a sample of 100 persons described by adjective A alone and a sample of 100 persons from the same population described by adjective B alone. The expected value for the first distribution, and thus the predicted evaluation based upon A (E_A), is

$$E_A = \Sigma P_{iA} V_i = .2(0) + .2(1) + .3(2) + .3(3) = 1.70$$

and the expected value of the second distribution (E_B) is

$$E_B = \Sigma P_{iB} V_i = .1(-1) + .1(0) + .1(1) + .3(2) = .4(3) = 1.80$$

It is likely, but *not necessary*, that a certain proportion of the persons in the sample of those described by A are also in the sample of persons described by B, and that these persons are distributed over the scale categories. Although the actual number of people in category i that are common to both samples cannot be determined, the *maximum* number of such people is the smaller of the two frequencies with which people described by A and people described by B are in the category. For example, the maximum number of persons in both samples who are in category "−1" (the smaller of 0 and 10) is 0; the maximum number of persons in both samples who are in category "0" (the smaller of 20 and 10) is 10, and so on. The distribution of the maximum number of persons in each scale category who are described by both A and B

---

[5] This can be derived from Eq. (10.1) if it is assumed that $P_{AB} = P_A P_B$ and that $P_{A/iB} = P_{A/i}$.

TABLE 9.5

Hypothetical Frequency Distributions and Predicted
Category Ratings for Alternative Sets of Information

Descriptive information		Category Rating							Expected Value
		−3	−2	−1	0	1	2	3	
A	n	0	0	0	20	20	30	30	
	P	0	0	0	.2	.2	.3	.3	1.70
B	n	0	0	10	10	10	30	40	
	P	0	0	.1	.1	.1	.3	.4	1.80
C	n	5	10	20	30	20	10	5	
	P	.05	.1	.2	.3	.2	.1	.05	0
D	n	0	0	30	40	30	0	0	
	P	0	0	.3	.4	.3	0	0	0
E	n	10	10	30	30	20	0	0	
	P	.1	.1	.3	.3	.2	0	0	−.60
F	n	0	0	0	10	40	20	30	
	P	0	0	0	.1	.4	.2	.3	1.70
G	n	10	30	10	5	5	30	10	
	P	.1	.3	.1	.05	.05	.3	.1	−.05
H	n	0	0	0	10	20	60	10	
	P	0	0	0	.1	.2	.6	.1	1.70
A and B	n	0	0	0	10	10	30	30	
	P	0	0	0	.125	.125	.375	.375	2.00
A and C	n	0	0	0	20	20	10	5	
	P	0	0	0	.36	.36	.18	.09	1.00
A and D	n	0	0	0	20	20	0	0	
	P	0	0	0	.5	.5	0	0	.50
A and E	n	0	0	0	20	20	0	0	
	P	0	0	0	.5	.5	0	0	.50
E and G	n	10	10	10	5	5	0	0	
	P	.25	.25	.25	.125	.125	0	0	−1.325
F and G	n	0	0	0	5	5	20	10	
	P	0	0	0	.125	.125	.50	.25	1.875
A and F	n	0	0	0	10	20	20	30	
	P	0	0	0	.125	.25	.25	.375	1.875
A and H	n	0	0	0	10	20	30	10	
	P	0	0	0	.143	.286	.429	.143	1.573

is shown in Table 9.5. Now, assume that the *actual* number of persons in each category who are described by both A and B is a constant proportion of the maximum number in the category who are described by both adjectives. Then, the expected value of the actual distribution of persons in the scale categories (E_{AB}) would be identical to the expected value of the distribution of maxima; that is,

$$E_{AB} = \Sigma\, P_{iAB} V_i = .125(0) + .125(1) + .375(2) + .375(3) = 2.00,$$

as shown in Table 9.5.

.While the assumption described above is undoubtedly incorrect, it may nevertheless provide a reasonably good approximation of the conjunctive probability distribution and therefore may generate fairly accurate predictions of collective ratings. We will present empirical evidence bearing upon this possibility later in this chapter. First, however, let us consider several phenomena reported in the research literature on impression formation and attempt to interpret them within the general framework we are proposing. For purposes of demonstration, we will use the procedure described above in predicting collective ratings from component probability distributions. However, the basic points to be made do not depend upon the validity of the specific assumptions underlying this procedure.

B. Implications for Impression Formation Phenomena

Set Size and "Averaging-like" Effects. Note that in the preceding example the predicted evaluation based upon both A and B is greater than the evaluation based upon either A or B separately. In contrast, consider the predicted evaluation based upon both A and C, also described in Table 9.5. This evaluation lies between the evaluation based upon A alone and the evaluation based upon C alone. Thus, both "set size" and "averaging-like" effects can be predicted. In general, set size effects are most likely (although not necessary) when the expected values of the component distributions are similar, while "averaging-like" effects are more likely as these expected values become more discrepant. This is also a prediction of Anderson's model (see page 301).

Idiosyncratic Effects of Information. In general, the effect of a given piece of information depends not only upon the expected value of the distribution underlying it, but also upon other characteristics of the distribution that may be idiosyncratic to the piece of information involved. Thus, adjectives that have similar scale values when considered in isolation may have different effects when combined with another adjective, while adjectives with different scale values may produce similar evaluations when combined. For example, in Table 9.5, adjectives C and D both have theoretical ratings of 0 in isolation but lead to theoretical collective ratings of 1.00 and .50 respectively when combined with A. On the other hand, adjectives D and E, which have different ratings in isolation (0 and −.6), both produce the same collective rating (.50) when combined with A; similarly, adjectives A and G, which theoretically produce evaluations of 1.70 and −.05 respectively when considered in isolation, lead to the same evaluation (1.875) when combined with F. In general, the effect of a given piece of information depends not only upon the expected value of the distribution underlying it, but also upon other characteristics of the distribution that may be idiosyncratic to the piece of information involved. Thus the formulation can in principle account for many differences that cannot be easily interpreted on the basis of the additive models described earlier in this chapter.

It is conceivable that the effects of information in different contexts will vary not only in magnitude but also in direction. For example, Aronson, et al. (1966) found that information that a competent person spilled coffee over himself increased his likeableness, while information that an incompetent person committed this blunder decreased his likeableness. These results would be extremely difficult to explain on the basis of an additive model of information integration, unless it is assumed that the attribute "spills coffee over oneself" has a different scale value when applied to competent persons than when applied to incompetent ones. These results could be explained on the basis of the proposed formulation if the distribution of persons described by the attribute "spills coffee over oneself" is bimodal along the evaluative scale involved. To see this, consider the distributions E, F, and G in Table 9.5. The evaluation based upon G alone is −.05. However, the addition of G to E decreases the predicted evaluation from −.60 to −1.325, while the addition of G to F increases the predicted evaluation from 1.7 to 1.875. If the distributions underlying E, F, and G are similar to those underlying evaluations based upon the attributes "incompetent," "competent," and "spills coffee over oneself," Aronson et al.'s findings could be explained.

Context Effects. The proposed formulation is consistent with Ostrom's change-of-meaning interpretation of context effects (see Chapter 8, page 237). The range of possible meanings assigned to an adjective is reflected by the distribution of its evaluative implications, and therefore by the distribution of subjective probabilities that objects described by it belong to each of the categories along an evaluative scale. Ostrom hypothesizes that when one adjective is associated with another, certain of its alternative interpretations are rendered improbable. These interpretations are most apt to be those with evaluative implications that differ from those of the "context" adjective. For example in Table 9.5, if B is presented in the context of A, interpretations that imply membership in the category "−1" are most likely to be discounted. The evaluation of B in the context of A would be a function of the evaluative implications that remain, and therefore would be greater than the evaluation of B when considered in isolation. Note that as normative evaluations of "test" and "context" adjectives become more discrepant, the distributions underlying these evaluations typically overlap less. More evaluative implications of the test adjective should be rejected under such conditions, producing a greater shift in the evaluation of this adjective. This implies that relatively unfavorable test adjectives will be rated more positively as their context becomes more favorable, and that relatively favorable test adjectives will be rated more negatively as their context becomes more unfavorable. In both cases, ratings of the test adjective involved would increase with the favorableness of its context. This has been found to be true empirically (e.g., Anderson, 1966; Wyer & Dermer, 1968).

Uncertainty, Negativity, and Extremity. The example showing that A and D produce a lower predicted collective rating than A and C is of additional interest. Although the distributions of persons described by C and of persons described by D have the same expected value, the distribution of persons described by D has a lower dispersion; that is, there is less subjective uncertainty associated with ratings based upon D than with ratings based upon C. In general, the region of overlap of two distributions is displaced toward the expected value of the one with the lower dispersion. Since the expected value of the conjunctive distribution falls within this region of overlap, this implies that less ambiguous pieces of information will have relatively greater influence, as suggested in Chapter 8. To this extent, the formulation can also account for the effects of negativity and extremity. That is, information that produces more unfavorable or more extreme ratings when presented in isolation tends to be less ambiguous, as inferred from the distributions underlying these ratings. Therefore, this type of information should have relatively more influence when it is combined with other information. Furthermore, to the extent that situational factors such as source credibility also affect the probability distribution underlying a judgment based upon a piece of information, the influence of these factors may also potentially be accounted for.

Redundancy. The redundancy of two adjectives, as defined in Chapter 8, cannot generally be determined from the probability distributions underlying their evaluations when considered separately. However, two adjectives are more likely to be redundant when the distributions underlying their ratings overlap than when they do not. When two distributions are identical, the predicted collective evaluation is the same as the evaluation of either component in isolation. If two component distributions have the same expected value but are not identical (as in the case of distributions A and F in Table 9.5), and therefore are less redundant, the predicted collective rating may often be greater than the evaluation based upon each component in isolation. To this extent, the proposed formulation can account for redundancy effects of the sort found empirically (Wyer, 1968, 1970a). On the other hand, in some cases the predicted evaluation based upon two equally favorable but nonredundant pieces of information can be less extreme than either component evaluation. (An example of this is provided by combining distributions A and H in Table 9.5.) Whether such cases occur empirically is unclear.

Inconsistency. For the proposed formulation to account for inconsistency effects, some additional assumptions are required. Two pieces of information are inconsistent if the probability distributions underlying evaluations based upon them do not overlap or, in other words, if it is theoretically impossible for an object to be described by both pieces simultaneously. This is most likely to occur when the expected values of the two distributions differ greatly. If a subject is asked to evaluate a person described by two adjectives and believes that such a person could not exist in actuality, how is he likely to respond? One possibility, suggested by research on the effects of inconsistency, is that he will discount one of the adjectives. If this occurs, it seems reasonable to expect that the adjective discounted will be the one with the less clear evaluative implications (i.e., the more ambiguous). A second possibility is that the subject will arrive at an evaluation based upon each adjective separately and then average these evaluations. Which possibility is more likely is an empirical question.

C. An Empirical Test of the Formulation

Although exact quantitative predictions based upon the concept identification formulation theoretically cannot be made, preliminary research has indicated that the simplifying assumptions described above generate surprisingly accurate descriptions of the manner in which information combines to affect evaluations. Before describing this research, however, it may be worthwhile to restate more formally the information integration procedure used and the assumptions underlying it.

1. Assume that N random samples, each consisting of objects described by a different one of N pieces of information, are drawn from a given population and that each sample is distributed along a scale of ordered categories. Then, the number of objects contained in all N samples and in category i (n_i) is given by the equation:

$$n_i = C(\min [n_{ik}, k = 1, N])$$

where n_{ik} is the number of objects in i that are described by piece k, and C is a constant of proportionality. The subjective probability that an object described by all N pieces of information is in i, or P_i, is then:

$$P_i = \frac{n_i}{\Sigma n_i} = \frac{\min [n_{ik}, k = 1, N]}{\Sigma(\min [n_{ik}, k = 1, N])} \tag{9.12a}$$

If the same number of persons is described by each component distribution, the predicted value of P_i can also be expressed in terms of probabilities; that is,

$$P_i = \frac{\min [P_{ik}, k = 1, N]}{\Sigma(\min [P_{ik}, k = 1, N])} \tag{9.12b}$$

where P_{ik} is the probability that a person is in i and is described by k.

2. When $\Sigma(\min [n_{ik}, K = 1, N] \neq 0$ (that is, when the distribution described in Assumption 1 partially overlap) the evaluation of an object described by all N pieces of information (E_o) is predictable from Eq. (2.1), that is,

$$E_o = \Sigma P_i V_i,$$

where V_i is the value of the ith scale category and P_i is defined by Eq. (9.12).

3. When $\Sigma(\min [n_{ik}, k = 1, N]) = 0$ (when the distributions described in Assumption 1 do not overlap), one of two things will occur:

    a.   *Discounting assumption.* The more ambiguous piece of information will be discounted. In this case, E_o will equal the expected value of the distribution that has the lowest uncertainty associated with it, as inferred from Eq. (2.2).

    b.   *Averaging assumption.* The evaluation based upon each piece of information considered separately will be averaged; that is, E_o will be the simple average of the expected values of the N component distributions described in Assumption 1.

The predictive validity of these assumptions was tested with the use of data collected by the author (Wyer, 1973a), described in Chapter 2 (page 27). These data consisted in part of both actual ratings and subjective frequency distributions associated with eight single adjectives and all 28 possible pairs formed from these adjectives. The accuracy of the formulation in predicting actual collective ratings from the frequency distributions underlying component ratings was determined separately for conditions in which the run. The distributions generated by these subjects overlapped in at least 14 of 42 instances for each of the 28 pairs, and they did not overlap in at least 3 instances for each of these pairs.)

When distributions overlapped, predicted collective evaluations were calculated by applying the procedure described under Assumption 2 above. Mean obtained category ratings based upon adjective pairs are plotted in Fig. 9.10(A) as a function of mean predicted values, considering in each case only data from subjects whose component distribution overlapped. While predicted and obtained ratings were highly correlated, predicted ratings underestimated obtained ratings when the categories involved were negative. This could indicate a basic flaw in the formulation. However, it could also indicate that Assumption 1 is invalid. That is, the actual number of persons in each category who are described by both adjectives may not be a constant proportion of the maximum possible; rather, this proportion (C) may be greater when categories are negative than when they are positive. If this were the case, it could also account for evidence that adjectives with negative scale values have more influence when combined with other information than do

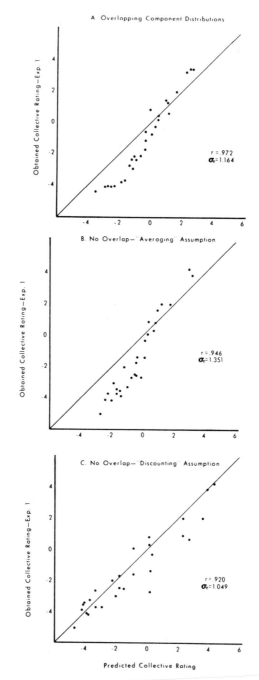

Fig. 9.10. Obtained category ratings as a function of predicted ratings (a) when component distributions overlap, and when component distributions do not overlap, based upon (b) an "averaging" assumption and (c) a "discounting" assumption (reprinted from Wyer, 1973a).

adjectives with positive scale values (Anderson & Norman, 1964; Wyer & Watson, 1969).

When component distributions did not overlap, the predictive validity of the "discounting" and "averaging" assumptions was investigated separately. Predicted evaluations were calculated for each subject according to each of the criteria described under Assumption 3 above, and these values were then averaged over subjects. Mean obtained collective ratings are plotted as a function of mean predicted values under each assumption in Figs. 9.10(B) and 9.10(C), in each case considering only those instances in which the component distributions involved did not overlap. While the predicted ratings based upon the averaging assumption were more highly correlated with obtained values, they generally underestimated these values. Deviations from predictions based upon the discounting assumptions were less systematic and on the whole were smaller than those based upon the averaging assumption. Since the slope and intercept parameters required to produce a good fit for the averaging assumption have questionable psychological significance, the discounting assumption may be more valid. Mean obtained ratings, pooled over overlapping and nonoverlapping conditions, are plotted in Fig. 9.11(A) as a function of mean predicted ratings, employing the discounting assumption under conditions of nonoverlap. The correlation between mean predicted and mean obtained ratings, and the standard error of estimates obtained from predicted values, both suggest a better fit when these conditions are combined than when each is considered separately.

1. *Comparison with Other Models.* For purposes of comparison, the accuracy of three alternative predictors was determined: the simple average of the actual component evaluations, the congruity formulation described by Eq. (9.5), and the best fitting linear function relating collective evaluations to component evaluations. Data pertaining to the first two predictors have already been discussed (see Fig. 9.8); neither was as accurate in estimating collective ratings as the concept identification formulation. To determine the best fitting linear function, the more and less favorable adjectives in each pair were weighted separately. This function, obtained by using standard regression procedures, was

$$E_{AB} = .525E_A + .84E_B - .574,$$

where E_A is the more favorable component evaluation. Obtained ratings are plotted in Fig. 9.11(B) as a function of predicted ratings based upon this equation. While the standard error in estimating obtained collective ratings from this equation was much lower than the error in estimating these ratings with the concept identification model, the correlation between obtained and predicted values was virtually identical in the two cases. Since Anderson's weighted averaged formulation (Eq. 9.8) is equivalent to the best linear fit of

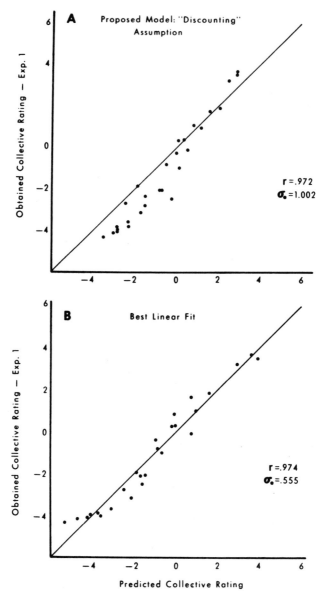

Fig. 9.11. Obtained collective ratings as a function of predicted ratings based upon (a) the concept identification model, and (b) the best fitting linear function relating component ratings to collective ratings (reprinted from Wyer, 1973a).

component ratings to collective ratings,[6], the proposed formulation is as

---

[6]If the parameters relevant to Eq. (9.8) are solved for in the above regression equation, the relative weights attached to the more and less favorable components (w_A' and w_B') are .155 and .475, respectively, the relative weight attached to the initial impression (w_o') is .370; and the scale value of the initial impression (I_o) is +1.61.

accurate as Anderson's if slope and intercept parameters in each model are estimated empirically by using curve-fitting procedures. In the case of the concept identification model, however, the psychological meaning of such parameters is unclear.

The stimulus pairs used in the above study were constructed from a small number of adjectives, each with different evaluative implications. Therefore, the ability of the proposed formulation to account empirically for phenomena such as set size effects, and for instances in which two adjectives with similar ratings in isolation have different effects when combined with others, can unfortunately not be evaluated on the basis of the data obtained.

2. *Prediction of Uncertainty Associated with Collective Ratings.* If the subjective uncertainty associated with a category rating can be inferred by applying Eq. (2.2) to the probability distribution underlying it, a subject's uncertainty about his rating of a collective, as well as the rating itself, should be predictable from the distributions underlying his component evaluations. A problem again arises when these distributions do not overlap, indicating that the information presented is inconsistent. Under such conditions, the uncertainty of the collective rating would intuitively be expected to be greater than that of the evaluation based upon either component considered separately. Thus, under nonoverlapping conditions, an approximate estimate of uncertainty might be obtained by summing the two component distributions and applying Eq. (2.2) to this pooled distribution.

This last assumption was made in predicting the uncertainty associated with collective ratings in the study described above. That is, when component distributions overlapped, the uncertainty associated with collective ratings was estimated by applying Eq. (2.2) to the theoretical conjunctive distribution derived according to the procedure outlined under Assumption 1. Under nonoverlapping conditions, Eq. (2.2) was applied to the sum of the two component distributions. The mean predicted uncertainty, calculated according to these procedures, was correlated .819 ($p < .001$) with the mean uncertainty of the actual collective distributions generated by subjects and .768 ($p < .001$) with the mean of subjects' actual estimates of their uncertainty about their collective ratings as reported along a category scale. Data relevant to these correlations are plotted in Fig. 9.12.

While the data described above suggest that the concept identification model does a reasonably good job of predicting subjects' uncertainty about their evaluations of persons described by several pieces of information, an additional implication of the formulation should be noted. As long as two adjectives are at least partially consistent (that is, as long as the distributions of objects described by them overlap), the uncertainty associated with ratings based upon both adjectives in combination should generally be less than the uncertainty about ratings based upon either adjective alone. Furthermore, uncertainty should be relatively less when the evaluative implications of the two components differ (and thus the component distributions do not overlap

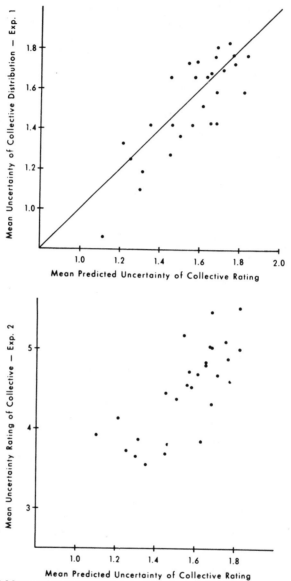

Fig. 9.12. (a) Mean uncertainty associated with collective distributions and (b) the mean of subjects' actual estimates of their uncertainty about their category ratings, as a function of predicted uncertainty based upon the concept identification formulation (reprinted from Wyer, 1973a).

greatly) than when their implications are similar. This would make sense if in fact subjects use the information presented to identify the category to which the object belongs; as the overlap of two distributions become less, or, in other words, as the number of possible categories to which the object belongs decreases, certainty about the object's category membership should be greater. However, this prediction was not supported. If anything, uncertainty about collective ratings increased as component evaluations became more discrepant, even when the only cases considered were those in which the distributions underlying these evaluations overlapped. This finding creates problems for the theoretical formulation being proposed. Perhaps the uncertainty associated with collective evaluations is a function of the degree of nonoverlap of the two component evaluations as well as the degree of overlap. In other words, one's uncertainty about the evaluation of an object may depend not only upon the distribution of evaluative categories to which the object could belong if the information about it is valid, but also upon differences in the evaluative implications of this information.

D. Concluding Remarks

The model of information integration proposed in this section may be evaluated on both theoretical and practical grounds. Theoretically, it is of course only as valid as the major basic assumption: The evaluation of O along a rating scale is the expected value of an underlying distribution of subjective probabilities that O belongs to each of the scale categories. Moreover, if this assumption is valid, the formulation can at best provide only an approximate quantitative description of integration processes. However, given the somewhat arbitrary nature of the assumptions made in the initial test of the model, the results of this test are promising.

An important feature of the formulation is its ability to account theoretically for several of the phenomena reported in empirical studies of information integration. Among these are set size and "averaging" effects, and also the effects of information ambiguity, extremity, negativity, and perhaps even redundancy and inconsistency. Changes in the meaning of information in different contexts, and the effects of these changes upon judgments of the favorableness of this information, can also be interpreted. While these effects can be incorporated *post hoc* into other models described in this chapter, through differential weighting of the information presented, few if any of these models can generate *a priori* predictions about the nature of these effects and the conditions under which they will occur. Of course, if the present formulation is to be taken seriously as a quantitative description of information integration, its *empirical* effectiveness in predicting set size effects and the idiosyncratic effects of information when presented in different contexts must ultimately be determined.

Although in this section the formulation has been applied to inferences based upon a restricted type of information, the general principles described have implications for less esoteric and therefore perhaps more interesting phenomena. For example, suppose a subject receives a persuasive communication. If the subject is already familiar with the object of the communication, he may already have formed certain beliefs about it before receiving the message, and thus he may be able to assign it to a category along an ordinal scale of favorableness. This estimate, or his "initial attitude," may represent the expected value of the distribution of probabilities that the object belongs to each of the scale categories available. The communication may also have several possible evaluative implications; that is, it may imply that the object belongs with some probability to several different scale categories. In general, the distribution of these probabilities will differ from the distribution underlying the subject's initial attitude. Now, after the subject receives the communication, his "final attitude" may be a reflection of the conjunction of the distributions associated with his initial attitude and the position advocated in the persuasive communication; thus it may be predictable in much the same manner that evaluations based upon two pieces of information are predicted in impression formation research. To this extent, the influence of a communication should theoretically be a function of the relative uncertainty of the position advocated by the communication and the subject's initial attitude. That is, a communication should have greater influence to the extent that its implications are clear, and to the extent that the subject is uncertain about this attitude toward the object before the communication is presented. It is interesting to speculate what would occur in the above situation if the probability distributions associated with the communication and with the subject's initial attitude do not overlap. The range of the distribution underlying the subject's initial attitude may be roughly equivalent to his "latitude of acceptance" as defined by Sherif and Hovland (1961), that is, the range of judgments of the issue that the subject considers acceptable. Sherif and Hovland hypothesized that if the position advocated by a communication is outside one's latitude of acceptance, it will have little or no influence upon his judgment. This would be predicted by the proposed formulation if a subject is more certain about his initial attitude than about the implications of the communication and if the discounting assumption is valid. On the other hand, if a subject is more certain about the implications of the communication than about his initial attitude, the discounting assumption implies that the communication will be maximally effective, and that his initial attitude will have little if any effect. Thus, the proposed formulation suggests a contingency in the predictions of "assimilation-contrast" theory.

Despite its theoretical interest, the approach described in this section is cumbersome to use in practice. Even if the formulation is refined to increase its predictive accuracy, it is questionable whether the accuracy attained would be sufficient to outweigh the practical difficulties of acquiring the data needed to apply it. And at best, this formulation can theoretically generate only approximate descriptions of integration processes. The approximations obtained through the use of additive models may be nearly as good for all practical purposes. Unfortunately, most additive models proposed to date require the *post hoc* estimation of one or more parameters through curve-fitting procedures in order to describe information integration accurately. However, a linear model in which slope and intercept parameters can be determined *a priori* would certainly be of great practical value for generating reasonably accurate quantitative predictions of the combined effects of information upon judgments, regardless of the theoretical validity of the model as a description of the actual process used by subjects in arriving at these judgments. This will become increasingly clear in the next chapter, where cognitive balance implications for social inference phenomena are discussed and evaluated.

10
COGNITIVE BALANCE APPLICATIONS TO SOCIAL INFERENCE PHENOMENA

The principles of cognitive balance and their validity in describing the manner in which cognitions are organized have been discussed extensively in Chapter 5. These principles have additional implications for the manner in which pieces of information combine to affect judgments. If information is given about two sentiment or unit relations among a set of three elements, inferences about the quality of the third relation may be predicted by applying these laws. In this chapter, the role of cognitive balance in social inference processes will be considered in some detail.

Balance principles pertain to four basic types of inference. Consider a configuration consisting of a person, P, and two other elements, A and B. Then, these types of inferences may be described as follows:

1. $Pr_1A \supset Ar_2P$, or $Ar_1P \supset Pr_2A$
   where r: is any of the three
   relations p, o, or n
2. $Pr_1B \cap Ar_2B \supset Pr_3A$
3. $Pr_1A \cap Ar_2B \supset Pr_3B$
4. $Pr_1A \cap Pr_2B \supset Ar_3B$

These types are shown graphically in Fig. 10.1, where solid lines indicate known relations and dotted lines indicate the relation to be inferred. In the case of Type 1 inferences, balance theory predicts that r_1 and r_2 are the same (both p, both o, or both n). In each of the other types of inference, r_3 should be p if r_1 and r_2 are either both p or both n; r_3 should be n if r_1 is p and r_2 is n, or if r_1 is n and r_2 is p; finally, r_3 should be o if either r_1 or r_2 is o. These rules, which as stated pertain to sentiment relations, would also pertain to unit relations if positive (u) and negative (u') relations are interpretable as p and o, respectively.

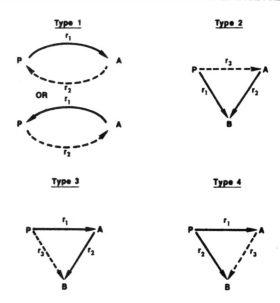

Fig. 10.1. Balance diagrams describing inference Types 1-4.

The applicability of balance principles to social inference phenomena may be evaluated on the basis of two somewhat different criteria. One criterion is whether cognitive balance is actually one of the factors governing inferences, and whether balance principles, if they predict inferences accurately, do so for the reasons implied by the theory. The assumptions underlying balance principles differ substantially from those underlying the information integration models discussed in Chapter 9. According to balance theory, imbalance creates cognitive tension; therefore, such tension will be avoided by forming new cognitions that are maximally balanced with other cognitions about the same elements. However, as we noted in Chapter 5, there is little evidence to support the assumption that imbalanced sets of cognitions *per se* are aversive or, for that matter, that balanced sets are particularly pleasant. Thus, if balance principles describe social inferences accurately, the reasons for their accuracy may differ from those implied by balance theory as it was originally formulated.

The second and more practical criterion is simply the accuracy and reliability of balance principles in predicting inferences, regardless of their theoretical basis. As we shall see, balance principles can be applied in several quite different situations. If these principles predict inferences accurately in all of these situations, they would be an extremely powerful tool. However, balance is undoubtedly not the only factor that governs social inferences, and its effects may often be overriden by those of other, more situation-specific factors that are not taken into account by the theory. The utility of balance principles in predicting inference phenomena may therefore be limited, even if the principles are theoretically valid.

If the social inference processes to which balance principles theoretically pertain are considered from the information-processing perspective we have attempted to develop in earlier chapters, two general hypotheses are suggested about the conditions in which balance principles are most apt to apply. The first is based upon the assumption that when subjects are called upon to infer a particular relation between two persons or objects from information about other relations involving these elements, they reflect upon their previous experience with elements similar to those described in the information and predict the relation that they believe to be most representative, or typical, based upon this pool of subjective experience. Thus, suppose subjects believe that persons who disagree on matters of concern to them are generally less apt to like one another than are persons who agree about such matters. Then, in the absence of any other information about two hypothetical persons, P and A, and an issue B, they may predict that P's relation to A is positive when they are told that P and A have similar sentiments toward B, and that it is negative when they are told that P's and A's sentiments differ. However, suppose that P, A, and B are more specifically described. (For example, suppose P and A are salesmen, and B is a sales contract.) Then, subjects may not base their inference upon their previous experience with persons and objects "in general" but rather upon their experience with members of the particular classes of elements to which A and B belong. The relations among these elements in these classes may often differ from those among elements in general.

While the above interpretation seems obvious, it of course puts quite a different perspective upon the role of balance in social inference processes. That is, these principles may describe inferences accurately *only insofar as they summarize subjects' previous experience with the types of objects about which inferences are made.* A corollary of this hypothesis is based upon the possibility that the sets of relations implied by balance principles are in fact believed to be most representative of those subjects have found to exist among persons and objects in general. If this is the case, it follows that the less information a subject has about the nature of the elements being related, the more likely it is that his inferences will be predictable from balance principles.

A second hypothesis about the conditions in which balance principles describe inferences accurately is suggested by the theory and research on information integration cited in Chapters 8 and 9. Note that one person's (P's) sentiment toward a second (A) is interpretable as an evaluation of A along a dimension of "likeableness." This evaluation is presumably a function of the type of attributes A is believed to have. To this extent, information should affect estimates of P's sentiment relation to A only insofar as it has implications for these attributes. In some instances, these implications are fairly clear. For example, A's liking for P and the similarity between A's and P's attitudes toward B may both function as attributes of A that affect evaluations of him in much the same manner as other attributes ("intelligent," "kind," etc.). The favorableness and relevance of these attributes may depend upon the nature of A and B. However, if these attributes are favorable, their effects should theoretically be predicted by integration models of the sort described in Chapter 9, as well as by balance principles. On the other hand, in many situations to which balance theory applies, the implications of the information presented for attributes of the object to be judged are less clear; these implications often may depend upon the particular type of objects involved and upon characteristics of the specific situation in which the judgment is made. In these conditions, balance principles may be less apt to describe inference processes accurately.

If either or both of the above hypotheses are valid, the objectives of social inference research should be to identify the classes of elements that subjects believe are and are not typically related in the manner implied by balance principles, and to understand the nature of the assumptions made by subjects under conditions in which these principles do and do not appear to apply. While the nature of these boundary conditions is difficult to predict *a priori,* some hypotheses may emerge from a review and analysis of previous research that bears upon each of the four types of inference described above. Let us therefore turn to a consideration of this research.

I. TYPE I INFERENCES: $Pr_1 A \supset Ar_2 P$ or $Ar_1 P \supset Pr_2 A$

A. Inferences Based upon Sentiment Relations

When the subject is not an element of the configuration, the question to which this type of inference is most obviously relevant is whether persons are expected to like others who like them or to dislike others who dislike them. Intuitively, this question would be answered in the affirmative, and there is empirical support for this prediction. Feather (1967) asked subjects to infer a hypothetical person's (P's) liking for another person (A) on the basis of information that A's sentiment toward P was either strongly positive, mildly positive, mildly negative, or strongly negative. Mean estimates of P's liking of A under these four conditions, defined in relation to the midpoint of a 7-point scale, were 1.49, 1.04, −1.25, and −1.61, respectively.

While Feather's results are hardly surprising, it is important to note that no information about P and A was available, other than P's relation to A. These data may therefore indicate that subjects, based upon their previous experience, believe that persons in general tend to like others who like them. However, suppose that subjects were asked to predict whether an Iowa schoolboy's feelings about a female French sex symbol are reciprocated by her. This inference seems less likely to be described by balance principles. One reason for this is that subjects are apt to believe that internationally known sex symbols are unlikely to know or even to have heard of youngsters from a small town in the American midwest; even if they have, they may not be expected to attach much importance to the sentiments of such persons. More generally, when the classes of objects represented by P and A are more circumscribed, inferences about their relationship may be less likely to be predicted by balance theory.

Other conditions in which reciprocal sentiments between persons may not be inferred are suggested by the information integration research described in Chapters 8 and 9. If a subject is told that A likes P, he may expect A's sentiment to be regarded by P as a favorable attribute and thus may increase his belief that P evaluates A positively. However, the magnitude of this increase may depend upon whether A is believed to have other attributes and the effect of *these* attributes upon likeableness. Thus, in the above example, information that the international sex symbol adores an Iowa schoolboy is apt to lead subjects to infer that the schoolboy likes her. On the other hand, since the sex symbol may have other well-known attributes relevant to like-ableness, subjects are likely to infer that his sentiments toward her are favorable, independently of this information. In any event, the above ex-amples indicate the importance of clarifying the assumptions made by subjects under conditions in which reciprocal sentiment relations are inferred and of circumscribing the conditions under which these assumptions are made.

The preceding discussion has been restricted to conditions in which the subject himself was not an element in the relation to be inferred. While similar considerations may often arise when P is the subject himself, in-ferences under such conditions may not strictly be Type 1. As we will see, a distinction should be made between the subject as judge or observer (P) and the subject as an object of evaluation. Thus, information that A likes the sub-ject establishes a sentiment relation, not between A and P, but rather be-tween A and a third element, P's "Self." Presumably P also has a sentiment relation to "Self," which can be either positive or negative. Interpreted in this manner, a subject's inference about A, based upon information that A likes him is really an instance of a Type 2 inference (that is, Pr_1 "Self" $\cap$ Ar_2 "Self" $\supset$ Pr_3A). Similarly, P's inference that A likes him based upon in-formation that establishes a sentiment relation between P and A is in-terpretable as a Type 4 inference (Pr_1 "Self" $\cap$ Pr_2A $\supset$ Ar_3 "Self").

B. Inferences Based upon Unit Relations

A unit relation between P and A is often assumed when P and A are both members of the same group or class (cf. Feather, 1967). However, in-formation to this effect could be interpreted as bearing upon *two* unit relations, one between P and a group B and the other between A and B. To this extent, inferences based upon this information would be classified as Type 2 rather than Type 1. Better examples of Type 1 inferences based upon unit relations may be inferences of P's evaluation of a group A based upon information about P's membership in A, or inferences about P's evaluation of an object A, given that P owns it.

No systematic studies have been done on Type 1 inferences involving unit relations, perhaps because, like similar inferences involving sentiment relations, they are usually believed to be trivial. However, there are undoubtedly many limitations to the generality of the hypothesis that balance principles describe these inferences accurately. Certain of these contingencies are suggested by applying the probabilistic formulation proposed in Chapter 4. Consider the equation

$$P_L = P_A \, P_{L/A} + (1 - P_A) \, P_{L/A'} \tag{10.1}$$

where P_L is the belief that a group A is liked, P_A is the belief that P belongs to A, and $P_{L/A}$ and $P_{L/A'}$ are beliefs that A is liked by persons who do and do not belong to it, respectively.

If Eq. (10.1) is valid, balance principles should describe the effects of information about P's membership in A to the extent that $P_{L/A} > P_{L/A'}$. In the absence of information about the nature of P and A, subjects are likely to assume this to be the case. However, $P_{L/A}$ is apt to be low when P's membership in A is believed to be involuntary (e.g., if A is the "U.S. Army"); alternatively, $P_{L/A'}$ is apt to be high if A has high social status (e.g., the "U.S. Supreme Court"). To the extent that subjects make either of these assumptions, the difference between $P_{L/A}$ and $P_{L/A'}$ should be less, and therefore information that P belongs to A should have less positive effect upon their beliefs that P likes A. While these hypotheses are fairly obvious, the application of this equation has the combined advantages of both circumscribing conceptually the conditions in which Type 1 inferences are described by balance principles and providing a quantitative description of the magnitude of these inferences.

A similar equation may be useful in describing the effects of information about P's sentiment toward A upon beliefs that P has a unit relation to A, specifically,

$$P_A = P_L \, P_{A/L} + (1 - P_L) P_{A/L'}$$

where $P_{A/L}$ and $P_{A/L'}$ are the beliefs that P belongs to (or owns) A given that he likes and does not like it, respectively. According to this equation, information that P likes A will increase beliefs that P has a unit relation to A as long as $P_{A/L} > P_{A/L'}$. Again, contingencies in this relation are fairly obvious. For example, $P_{A/L}$ is likely to be less if A is "the Playboy Club" than if it is a phonograph record; to this extent, P's liking for A is less apt to affect beliefs that P owns (or belongs to) A in the former conditions than in the latter.

II. TYPE 2 INFERENCES: $Pr_1B \cap Ar_2B \supset PrA$

A Type 2 inference is one in which P's relation to A is inferred from information about P's and A's relations to B. Although this type of inference is common in research on attitude change and social inference, balance principles have often not been used to interpret the results of this research. For example, the impression formation task described in Chapters 8 and 9 may be viewed as a Type 2 inference about P's (the subject's) sentiment relation to a person A, based upon P's sentiment relation to a set of personality attributes (B) and a unit relation between A and B. Byrne's (1971) paradigm for studying the effects of similarity in attitudes upon attraction involves a Type 2 inference of P's sentiment toward a person A, based upon information about P's and A's sentiment relations to a third object B. The effects of favorable and unfavorable evaluations by another upon evaluations of the source (cf. Harvey et al., 1957; Steiner, 1968) can be interpreted as the result of a Type 2 inference of P's (the subject's) sentiment relation to A from P's and A's sentiments toward P's "self" (B). Several other situations may be constructed which exemplify this general type of inference, the nature of which depends upon whether r_1 and r_2 are sentiment or unit relations and whether P is the subject himself or is a third party whose relation to A is to be predicted. If balance principles are used by subjects to avoid cognitive tension that would result from imbalanced sets of cognitions, these principles should apply equally well in all of these situations. On the other hand, if they apply only to the extent that they reflect subjects' previous experiences with the type of elements about which information is presented and inferences are made, they are less apt to be universally applicable. To evaluate the merits of these alternative hypotheses, let us turn to some of the empirical research that bears, directly or indirectly, on the role of balance in Type 2 inferences.

A. Research on Type 2 Inferences about Others' Attitudes

Two fairly comprehensive studies of Type 2 inferences about other persons' attitudes have been reported. One study, by Wyer and Lyon (1970), determined whether the accuracy of balance principles in predicting Type 2 inferences was greater than chance, and also whether this accuracy depended upon the type of elements (persons or objects) to which the inferences pertained. In this study, all relations among elements were sentiment relations. Data from a second study, by Feather (1967), bear upon the influence of information about both unit and sentiment relations, and also upon the manner in which information about different types of relations combines to affect judgments.

1. *Effects of Type of Element.* The basic materials used in Wyer and Lyon's study are described in Chapter 5. Subjects first read a short paragraph about three elements (P, A, and B) which did not contain any

information about their relations to one another. Three types of configurations were described. In one (POO), P, A, and B were all persons; in a second (POX), P and A were persons but B was an object (a type of drug or a charity); in the third (PXX), A and B were both inanimate objects (either governmental policies or cleaning establishments).

Immediately after reading each paragraph, subjects under control conditions indicated which of three statements was most likely to describe the relation between a given pair of elements. One of these statements described a positive sentiment relation (p), a second an affectively neutral (o) relation, and the third a negative (n) relation between the elements, as indicated by normative data. The proportion of subjects who inferred each type of relation under those conditions was used as the unconditional probability of inferring this relation.

Under experimental conditions involving Type 2 inferences, subjects read two context statements, one suggesting that P's sentiment toward B (r_1) was either p (positive) or n (negative), and the other suggesting that A's sentiment toward B (r_2) was either p or n. These statements provided one of four different contexts: C_{pp}, C_{np}, C_{pn}, and C_{nn}. Subjects then predicted which one of three statements was most likely to describe P's sentiment toward A (p, o, or n). The difference between the proportion of subjects who selected a given statement in a given context condition and the proportion who selected this statement under control conditions was assumed to indicate the effect of the context information itself, over and above the effects of general response biases or of idiosyncratic characteristics of the persons and objects involved. These differences are shown graphically in Fig. 10.2.

According to balance principles, the probability of inferring a given relation between P and A should increase with the positivity of this relation when r_1 and r_2 are similar in direction (that is, under C_{pp} and C_{nn} context conditions) but should decrease with its positivity when r_1 and r_2 differ in direction (under C_{np} and C_{pn} conditions). These predictions were supported when A and B were both objects but not when A was another person. Moreover, the relation between the proportion of relations inferred and their positivity was frequently nonmonotonic; that is, relative to control conditions, o relations were predicted sometimes more often and sometimes less often than either p or n relations. These latter deviations from balance theory predictions are difficult to interpret.

When A was another person, beliefs that P liked A were consistently decreased by information that P and A had different sentiments toward B, as balance theory would predict. However, information that both P and A disliked B increased inferences that P liked A only when B was another person, while information that P and A both liked B did not affect these inferences, regardless of the nature of B. Thus, while persons with similar attitudes were more often believed to like one another than were persons with dissimilar attitudes, as balance principles suggest, this difference ap-

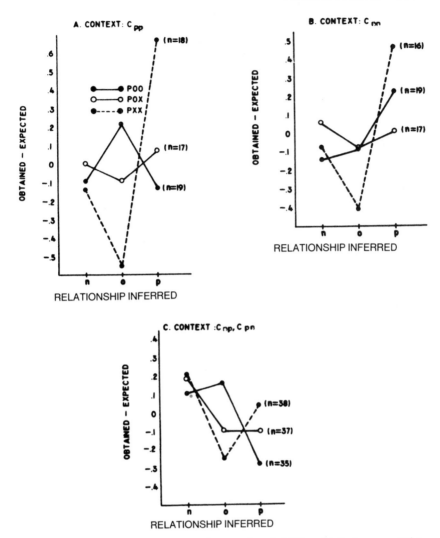

Fig. 10.2. Difference between obtained and expected probabilities of inferring p, o, and n relations as a function of context—Type 2 inferences (reprinted from Wyer & Lyon, 1970, p. 609).

pears primarily attributable to a decrease in inferred liking resulting from disagreement rather than to an increase in liking resulting from agreement. Perhaps disagreement in atitudes, which may lead to open conflict among the persons involved, is considered to be a sufficient condition for disliking, while agreement in attitudes is not regarded as sufficient for liking.

The above conclusion of course does not imply that persons are *not* expected to like those who agree with them; it only implies that information that they agree does not *increase* these expectations. When P and A were both persons, positive relations between P and A were inferred more frequently than negative ones (although less frequently than neutral ones) even when no information about their sentiments toward B was available (under control conditions). Since P's and A's relations to B were also inferred to be p more often than n under control conditions, this difference is probably due to a general positivity bias when inferring relations involving persons (see Chapter 5, page 119).

Implications for balance theory. Wyer and Lyon's data provide indirect support for the hypothesis that balance principles are valid only insofar as they reflect subjects' previous experience with the types of elements involved. Subjects appear to assume that "persons in general" have negative sentiment relations toward other persons and groups who disagree with them. On the other hand, they assume that agreement is a determinant of a positive sentiment relation only if this sentiment is directed toward an organization or an institution (that is, under PXX conditions; see Fig. 10.2). Unfortunately, only a few sets of elements were used in the configurations studied by Wyer and Lyon, and therefore the generality of this conclusion over all types of organizations is unclear.

2. *Effects of Type and Intensity of Relation.* Feather (1967) investigated the effects of two additional factors upon Type 2 inferences: the type of relations involving B (sentiment or unit relations) and the intensity of these relations. Subjects estimated the magnitude of one person's (P's) liking for another (A) on the basis of different sets of information about A's liking of P, P's and A's group membership, and P's and A's attitude toward "the present immigration policy" (B_1). Each relation was either positive (p) or negative (n) and was either weak (W) or strong (S). For example, information about A's liking of P described this relation as "Likes a lot" (p_s), "rather likes" (p_w), "rather dislikes" (n_w), and "dislikes a lot" (n_s). Information about P's and A's sentiment relations to the immigration policy (B_1) described their feelings as "strongly in favor" (p_s), "mildly in favor" (p_w), "mildly opposed" (n_w), or "strongly opposed" (n_s). P's and A's unit relations to a third element (B_2) were conveyed through information that they "belong to the same tightly knit group," "belong to the same loosely knit group," "belong to different groups that are rather inclined to remain separate and avoid much contact with each other," or "belong to different groups that are strongly inclined to remain separate and avoid contact with each other." Feather assumed that this latter information affected a single unit relation between P and A rather than P's and A's unit relations with a third element B_2. However, according to the present interpretation, the first two pieces of information described above would indicate that P's and A's unit relations to B_2 are *similar* and are either both intense ($p_s \cap p_s$) or both weak ($p_w \cap p_w$). The second two pieces suggest that P's and A's relations with B_2 are *different* and are either both weak ($p_w \cap n_w$) or both intense ($p_s \cap n_s$). Feather also appears to have assumed that a "negative unit relation" functions as a negative sentiment (n) relation rather than as the absence of a relation (o). However, note that the

TABLE 10.1

Mean Estimates of P's Liking for A as a Function
of Disagreement between A and B

Units of disagreement	Relevant sets of information	Mean estimate
0 (strong)	$p_s \cap p_s$; $n_s \cap n_s$	1.28
0 (weak)	$p_w \cap p_w$; $n_w \cap n_w$	.95
1	$p_s \cap p_w$; $p_w \cap p_s$;	.91
	$n_s \cap n_w$; $n_w \cap n_s$	
2	$p_w \cap n_w$; $n_w \cap p_w$	−.07
3	$p_s \cap n_w$; $p_w \cap n_s$;	−.42
	$n_w \cap p_s$; $n_s \cap p_w$	
4	$p_s \cap n_s$; $n_s \cap p_s$	−1.04

information used to describe the $p_s \cap n_s$ and $p_w \cap n_w$ combinations of relations suggest antagonism between members of B_2 and members of the other group involved. This possible confounding of unit and sentiment relations may justify Feather's interpretation. In any event, estimates of P's liking for A, given information about unit relations with B_2, and defined in relation to the midpoint of a 7-category scale, were 1.43, .55, −.90, and −1.31, respectively. In other words, inferences were more favorable when P's and A's unit relations to B_2 were similar than when they were dissimilar, and they were more extreme when these relations were strong than when they were weak.

Feather manipulated P's and A's sentiment relations to B_1 independently. The 16 possible combinations of information about P's and A's attitudes toward B_1 can be placed into six different groups, each represented by a different amount of disagreement. The sets of information comprising these groups are shown in Table 10.1, where the first symbol describing each set pertains to P's relation to B_1, and the second pertains to A's relation To B_1. Estimates of P's liking for A, averaged over relevant sets of information, are also shown in Table 10.1. These estimates decrease monotonically as disagreement increases. Moreover, agreement leads to more favorable inferences when the attitudes involved are intense rather than weak. These results essentially parallel those involving unit relations.

3. *Combined Effects of Different Sets of Information.* Since Feather studied the effects of different types of information presented both separately

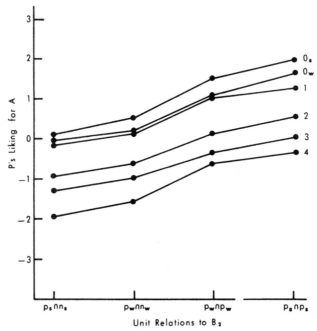

Fig. 10.3. P's liking for A as a function of P's and A's similarity in attitude toward B, and in the unit relations to B_2 (based upon data from Feather, 1967).

and in combination, it is possible to determine from these data the manner in which different types of information combine to affect Type 2 inferences. To investigate this question, mean estimates of P's liking for A were calculated for each combination of level of disagreement about B_1 and difference in unit relation to B_2. These data are plotted in Fig. 10.3. The statistical significance of the interaction of the two types of information in question was not determined by Feather. However, the curves shown in Fig. 10.3 are remarkably parallel, suggesting that the effects of the two types of information are nearly additive. A regression analysis of mean evaluations based upon the two types of information in combination (E_{UD}) was performed as a function of mean evaluations based upon information about unit relations in isolation (E_U) and evaluations based upon different levels of disagreement in isolation (E_D). This analysis yielded the equation:

$$E_{UD} = .574E_U + .926E_D - 2.356. \tag{10.2}$$

Obtained and predicted values of E_{UD}, plotted in Fig. 10.4, are correlated .993, indicating that .986 of the variance in E_{UD} can be accounted for by an additive function of evaluations based upon each type of information when presented separately.

To examine further the additive effects of the two types of information, a comparison similar to that suggested by Anderson (1965) and described in

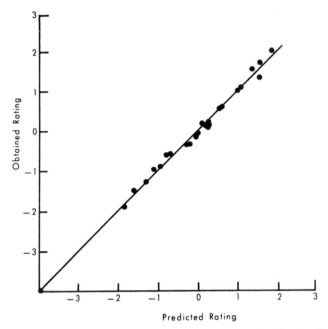

Fig. 10.4. Obtained inferences of P's liking for A as a function of predicted estimates based upon Eq. (10.2) based upon data from Feather, 1967).

Chapter 9 was made. Let p represent agreement in unit relations with B_1 ($p_s \cap p_s$ and $p_w \cap p_w$) and let n represent disagreement ($p_s \cap n_s$ and $p_w \cap n_w$). Similarly, let p represent the three lowest levels of disagreement in attitudes toward B_2 and let n represent the remaining levels. If the effects of these types of information are additive,

$$E_{pp} + E_{nn} = E_{pn} + E_{np} \qquad (10.3)$$

where the first subscript pertains to unit relations with B_1 and the second to sentiment relations with B_2. Averaged over appropriate conditions, the sum of E_{pp} ($M = 5.44$) and E_{nn} ($M = 2.78$) was 8.22, while the sum of E_{pn} ($M = 3.91$) and E_{np} ($M = 4.13$) was 8.04. These values are sufficiently close to suggest additivity.

Feather's data also provide an indication of how Type 1 and Type 2 inferences combined to affect judgments. Consider first the effects of information relevant to Type 1 inferences: information about A's liking for P and information about P's and A's sentiments toward B_1. Mean evaluations are plotted in Fig. 10.5 as a function of these two types of information. The influence of information about A's liking for P is fairly similar at each level of agreement. The curves converge slightly as A's sentiment toward P becomes more negative. This convergence would be consistent with a weighted average model of information integration in which negative sentiment relations

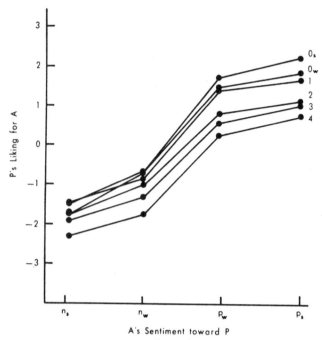

Fig. 10.5. P's liking for A as a function of A's sentiment toward P and the similarity between P's and A's attitudes toward B_1 (based upon data from Feather, 1967).

have greater absolute weight than positive sentiment relations. A regression analysis of collective evaluations (E_{SD}) as a function of evaluations based upon A's sentiment relation to P (E_S) and disagreement in attitudes toward B_1 (E_D) yields the equation

$$E_{SD} = .992E_S + .479E_D - 2.031. \qquad (10.4)$$

Obtained and predicted values of E_{SD} based upon this equation, plotted in Fig. 10.6, were correlated .984; thus .968 of the variance in E_{SD} can be accounted for.

An indication of the additivity of the effects of the two types of information can be obtained by applying Eq. (10.3). Assume that the first subscript of each component refers to the sign of A's sentiment toward P, and that the second subscript refers to agreement about B_1 as defined previously. Averaged over appropriate conditions, the sum of E_{pp} ($M = 5.71$) and E_{nn} ($M = 2.33$) is 8.04, while the sum of E_{pn} ($M = 4.74$) and E_{np} ($M = 2.93$) is 7.67.

Estimates of P's liking for A as a function of information about A's liking for P and information about P's and A's unit relations to B_2 are plotted in Fig. 10.7. Additivity is again suggested. A regression analysis of these evaluations (E_{SU}) as a function of E_S and E_U yielded the equation

$$E_{SU} = .918E_S + .273E_U - 1.017 . \qquad (10.5)$$

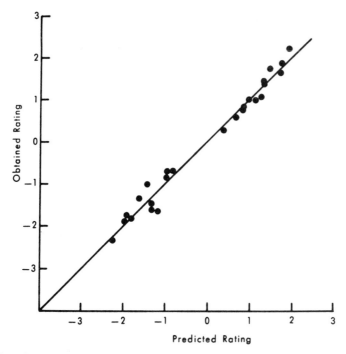

Fig. 10.6. Obtained inferences of P's liking for A as a function of predicted ratings based upon Eq. (10.4) based upon data from Feather, 1967).

Obtained and predicted values of E_{SU} based upon this equation, plotted in Fig. 10.8, are correlated .980; thus .961 of the variance in E_{SU} is accounted for by the additive model. If Eq. (10.3) is applied, the sum of E_{pp} ($M = 5.49$) and E_{nn} ($M = 1.98$) is 7.47, and the sum of E_{pn} ($M = 4.38$) and E_{np} ($M = 2.77$) is 7.15.

The preceding analyses considered separately do not indicate whether the effects of different types of information summate or average. However, certain conclusions can be drawn from a comparison of Eqs. (10.2), (10.4), and (10.5). First, note that in each case the intercept is not 0, and furthermore the sum of the weights attached to the two types of information exceeds unity. This rules out a simple averaging model that does not allow for the effects of initial impression. Note further that the weight attached to each type of information is different in each equation. Thus a summative model [Eq. (9.10)] would be applicable only if the absolute weight attached to each piece of information depends upon its context. While it is less apparent, an averaging model such as Anderson's [Eq. (9.12)] also requires such an assumption. As demonstrated previously (page 270), Anderson's model may be rewritten in the general form

$$E_o = (1-w_{B'})E_A + (1-w_{A'})E_B - w_{o'}I_o$$

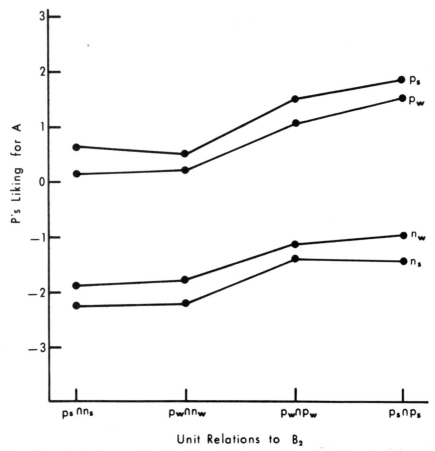

Fig. 10.7. P's liking for A as a function of A's sentiment toward P and the similarity between P's and A's unit relation of B_2 (based upon data from Feather, 1967).

where E_A and E_B are evaluations based upon two pieces of information A and B, and w_A', w_B', and w_o' are the relative weights attached to the *scale values* of A, B, and the initial impression I_o. Since the three relative weights sum to 1, these weights and also I_o may be calculated for each of the three regression equations generated by Feather's data. These values are shown in Table 10.2. Now suppose that the absolute weight of I_o remains constant, regardless of the type of information presented, and that this weight has a normalized value of 1. Then, the normalized weight attached to each other type of information can be calculated. These data, shown in Table 10.2, also suggest that the absolute weight attached to each type of information depends upon what type of information accompanies it.

It is important to note that each of the three types of information considered by Feather has substantial influence upon estimates of P's liking

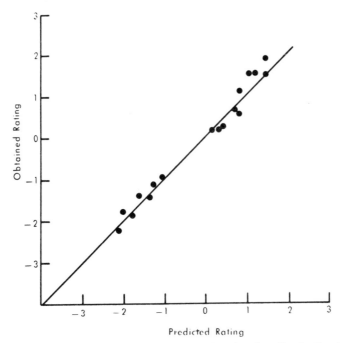

Fig. 10.8. Obtained inferences of P's liking for A as a function of predicted ratings based upon Eq. (10.5) (based upon data from Feather, 1967).

for A when this information is presented alone. However, when information about A's liking for P is available, it is given far greater weight than the other two types of information. When A's liking for P is not known, information about the similarity of P's and A's attitudes is more influential than information about P's and A's group membership. Information about the similarity of P's and A's group membership, while it has nearly as much influence as information about A's liking for P when there is no other basis for making a prediction, contributes very little to inferences when other information *is* available. Perhaps subjects think that each type of information bears upon the probability that P likes A but regard this information as differentially reliable. Thus, when more than one type of information is available, subjects may focus on the type they believe is most reliable and discount the implications of the less reliable information.

The particular order of importance of the three types of information considered in Feather's study may have limited generality. This ordering may depend upon the particular object or issue toward which attitudes are expressed, and the particular groups to which P and A belong. For example, if the attitude object were banana nut bread and the "closely knit group" were the Ku Klux Klan, the relative emphasis placed upon similarity in attitude and similarity in group membership might be reversed.

TABLE 10.2

Weights Attached to Scales Values of Component Pieces of
Information Required for Best Fit of Anderson's (1965)
Model of Information Integration

Equation	I_o	Relative weights				Absolute (normalized) weights			
		$w_{S'}$	$w_{U'}$	$w_{D'}$	$w_{o'}$	w_S	w_U	w_D	w_o
Eq. (10.2)	4.31	—	.074	.426	.500	—	.148	.952	1
Eq. (10.4)	4.31	.521	—	.008	.471	1.11	—	.017	1
Eq. (10.5)	5.32	.727	.082	—	.191	3.81	.424	—	1

Implications for balance theory. To the extent that subjects' inferences about hypothetical persons and objects are based upon "cognitive summaries" of their previous experiences with such elements, balance principles appear to be accurate representations of these summaries when the persons and objects involved are described very generally. That is, subjects appear to assume that "persons in general" are more apt to like another if (*a*) the other likes them, (*b*) the other's attitudes are similar to theirs, or (*c*) the other belongs to the same group, than if these conditions are not met. However, the tendency to draw inferences from one or another of these assumptions depends substantially on the availability of other information that has implications for the relation to be inferred.

Some general implications for cognitive balance theory should be noted. If balance principles are used in order to avoid the creation of unpleasant cognitive states, the cognitive processes underlying inferences based on imbalanced sets of relations (e.g., on information that A likes P but that P and A have different sentiments toward B) should differ from those based on balanced sets of relations. (In the former case, subjects should tend to discount or misinterpret the information, in order to produce a completely balanced set of cognitions, and this should affect their inferences about P's sentiment toward A.) However, the parallellism of the curves shown in Figs. 10.3, 10.5, and 10.7 indicates that the inference processes under conditions in which information has "inconsistent" implications do not differ from those under conditions in which information has "consistent" implications; in each case, the implications of the information appear to combine additively to affect the inference to be made. Thus there is no evidence that the processes underlying inference based upon imbalanced sets of relations differ from those based upon balanced sets.

B. Research on Inferences About One's Own Attitudes

A substantial body of research on attitude formation and change can be interpreted as Type 2 inference processes. Most of this research is concerned with the manner in which a subject's (P's) own attitude toward another person (A) is affected by information that P and A agree or disagree in their sentiments toward a third object (B). This research differs primarily in the nature of the object B; that is, in some cases B is a third person; in others, an issue or institution; and in still others, P's "Self." Balance principles imply that the fundamental inference process involved is the same in each case.

1. *Effects of Similarity in Attitudes Toward Another Person.* One of the most interesting demonstrations of the use of balance principles in predicting Type 2 inferences is provided in a study by Aronson and Cope (1968). These authors were concerned with the effect that one person's (A's) evaluation of a second (B) would have upon P's evaluation of A. Balance theory of course predicts that P will tend to evaluate favorably those who either like the persons he likes or dislike the persons he dislikes. Aronson and Cope eliminated several alternative hypotheses about why such effects might occur and also eliminated experimental demand characteristics. A quite innovative procedure was used to accomplish these objectives. Each subject (P) ostensibly participated in a study on creativity in which he was required to write a story about each of three pictures. Subsequently, the experimenter (B) evaluated P in one of two ways. Under "Harsh" conditions, intended to lead P to dislike B (PnB), B told P "starkly and brutally" that his stories were unimaginative and uncreative; according to the authors, B "acted as if he enjoyed making these negative statements." Under "Pleasant" (PpB) conditions, P was also told that his stories were poor but was administered this feedback "gently," being told not to worry about his performance. Following his evaluation of P, B was called outside the experimental room by a supervisor (A) who either praised him for his outstanding work in writing a report (ApB) or berated him for work described as "virtually worthless," "sloppy," and "somewhat stupid" (AnB). Although A and B were out of sight, P could hear A's comments clearly.

Upon reentering the experimental room, B instructed P to go upstairs to an office where a secretary would give him credit for the entire experiment. On a pretense, the secretary told P that the supervisor was involved in a different project and badly needed help in telephoning persons from outside the university to participate. She then asked P if he would volunteer to call potential subjects. The number of calls P agreed to make was assumed to indicate the favorableness of his attitude toward A. The results were unequivocal. When P's sentiment toward B was presumably favorable, he volunteered to make more phone calls when A's relation to B was favorable ($M = 18.2$) than when it was unfavorable ($M = 6.2$); when P's sentiment toward B was presumably unfavorable, he volunteered to make more calls when A's relation to B was unfavorable ($M = 12.1$) than when it was favorable ($M = 6.3$). These results are completely consistent with predictions based upon balance principles.

At a more mundane level, however, Aronson and Cope's findings may simply provide evidence that similarity in attitudes toward another person is in fact an attribute relevant to liking. In interpreting their findings, it is worth bearing in mind that the data obtained reflect the *relative* favorableness of evaluations of A resulting from different types of information, and they do not indicate the absolute favorableness of P's attitude under the various experimental conditions. It is interesting to compare Aronson and Cope's results with those obtained by Wyer and Lyon when Type inferences about other persons' sentiments toward A were made on the basis of similar information. Figure 10.2 shows that in POO configurations, subjects were less likely to infer a positive relation between P and A when P's and A's attitudes toward B were dissimilar (C_{pn} and C_{np}) than when they were similar (C_{pp}) and (C_{nn}). This finding is consistent with Aronson and Cope's results. However, when P's and A's attitudes were similar, p relations were no more likely to be inferred (relative to control conditions) than were n relations. In other words, although information that P and A disagreed about B decreased beliefs that P liked A, information that P and A agreed did not increase these beliefs. If these results generalize to conditions in which P is the subject himself, they do not necessarily suggest that the enemy of one's enemy (or the friend of one's friend) is a friend, as Aronson and Cope conclude, but rather suggest that the enemy of one's friend (or the friend of one's enemy) is an enemy.

2. *Effects of Similarity in More than One Attitude.*

a. *The similarity-attraction hypothesis.* The most extensive research on the relation between similarity in attitudes and interpersonal attraction has been conducted by Byrne and his colleagues (Byrne, 1971). Although Byrne has interpreted his research in the context of a social reinforcement model of attraction, its relevance to balance theory is obvious. His research is of additional interest since it bears upon the question of how information about similarity in attitudes toward several different objects combines to affect inferences. The latter question is of practical as well as theoretical importance. In everyday life, P's liking of A is unlikely to depend upon his agreement with A about just one issue. More frequently, P finds that he agrees with A about some things and disagrees with him about others. To this extent, any given sentiment toward A is balanced with certain sets of relations and imbalanced with other sets. Under such circumstances, how can P's attitude toward A be predicted?

This question was investigated empirically by Byrne and Nelson (1965a). They considered two possibilities: first, that P's liking for A is a positive function of the *number* of similar attitudes that P and A have in common; second, that it was a positive function of the *proportion* of similar attitudes.

TABLE 10.3

Mean Attraction Toward Strangers as a Function of
the Number and Proportion of Similar Attitudes
(after Byrne and Nelson, 1965a, p. 660)

| Proportion of similar attitudes | Number of similar attitudes | | | Total |
	4	8	16	
1.00	11.14(0)[a]	12.79(0)	10.93(0)	11.62
.67	10.79(2)	9.36(4)	9.50(8)	9.88
.50	9.36(4)	9.57(8)	7.93(16)	8.95
.33	8.14(8)	6.64(16)	6.57(32)	7.12
Total	9.86	9.59	8.73	

[a]Number of dissimilar attitudes are given in parentheses.

To determine the relative validity of these two hypotheses, the authors gave each subject (P) fictitious feedback that another (A) agreed with his responses to several different opinion statements. This feedback was constructed in such a way that both the number of agreements (4, 8, or 16) and the proportion of agreements (.33, .50, .67, and 1.00) varied independently over experimental treatments. Each subject participated in only one treatment. After receiving feedback, P estimated his attraction to A. Mean attraction is shown in Table 10.3 as a function of both number and proportion of similar attitudes. Analysis of variance of these data indicated that attraction increased with the proportion of agreements but was not a function of the number of agreements.[1]

Based upon these data and the results of other studies, Byrne and Nelson hypothesized that P's attraction to A is a simple linear function of the proportion of similar attitudes. Mean estimates of attraction in a number of Byrne's experiments are plotted in Fig. 10.9 as a function of mean proportion of agreements. In light of the fact that situational differences among the

---

[1]To vary number and proportion of agreements independently, it was necessary to confound both variables with the total number of pieces of information presented. Thus the effect of proportion of agreements could be interpreted as an effect of total number of pieces of information presented, or alternatively, as an effect of the number of disagreements. If this interpretation were correct, however, there should also be an effect of the number of agreements, which is also confounded with both of these variables. The fact that the effect of number of similar attitudes was not significant argues against this interpretation.

ATTITUDES AND ATTRACTION

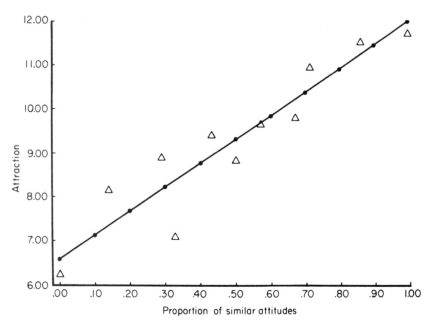

Fig. 10.9. Attraction as a function of proportion of similar attitudes (reprinted from Byrne & Nelson, 1965a, p. 661).

experiments considered may have produced unsystematic discrepancies from prediction, the linearity of this relation is impressive.

b. Some interpretative ambiguities. The above data appear to suggest an "averaging" rather than a "summative" process of information integration. However, several considerations raise questions about such a conclusion. Perhaps the most important consideration is methodological. As we just noted in footnote 1, in order to manipulate the proportion of agreements and the number of agreements independently, both variables were confounded with the total number of pieces of information presented. That is, in holding the proportion of agreements constant, the number of attitude statements about which P received feedback increased with the number of agreements; in holding the number of agreements constant, the number of feedback items was related negatively to the proportion of agreements. It is conceivable that the amount of feedback affected the manner in which subjects positioned the response scales they used to report their judgments of attraction. If this is the case, Byrne and Nelson's results may have been an artifact of differences in response language.

To see more clearly the nature of this artifact, assume that, contrary to Byrne and Nelson's hypothesis, subjective judgments of attraction are a linear function of the *number* of agreements. However, suppose that when P

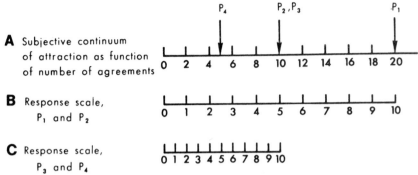

A Subjective continuum of attraction as function of number of agreements

B Response scale, P_1 and P_2

C Response scale, P_3 and P_4

Fig. 10.10. Subjective judgments and response scale position of hypothetical person receiving 20 pieces of information (P_1 and P_2) and persons receiving 10 pieces of information (P_3 and P_4).

is asked to evaluate A along a rating scale based upon information about A's attitudes, he positions this scale so that the most extreme category corresponds to the most extreme subjective judgment he believes he might make of A, based upon the amount of information he expects to receive. (For an elaboration of the rationale underlying such an assumption and its general implications, see Chapter 3.) The position of this category along the subjective continuum of attraction would then increase with maximum *possible* number of agreements between P and A, and therefore with the number of items about which P receives information. The effects of this can be demonstrated by an example. Suppose that the subjective judgments of A corresponding to different numbers of similar attitudes are positioned as shown along the continuum in Fig. 10.10(A). Assume that two subjects, P_1 and P_2, receive information about 20 attributes of A and are asked to rate A along a 10-category scale. Since the maximum possible attraction to A is that implied by 20 similar attitudes, both subjects would position their response scale as shown in Fig. 10.10(B). Assume that two other subjects, P_3 and P_4, receive information about 10 of A's attitudes. The response scale of these subjects would be positioned as in Fig. 10.10(C). Now, suppose that the information given P_1, P_2, P_3, and P_4 indicates that A agrees with 20, 10, 10, and 5 of their responses, respectively. The subjective judgments of A made by these subjects are shown by the positions of the arrows along the first continuum in Fig. 10.10. The category ratings of A by these subjects can be predicted by projecting their subjective judgments upon the appropriate rating scale. The number of attitudes similar to A's, the proportion of attitudes similar to A's, and the predicted category rating of A are shown in Table 10.4 for each hypothetical subject. The actual subjective judgments of A correspond to the *number* of similar attitudes. That is, P_1 is most attracted to A, and P_4 is least attracted to A, while P_2's and P_3's attraction to A is the same and lies between these values. However, the *category ratings* of A appear to be a function of the *proportion* of similar attitudes. That is, P_1 and P_3 rate A equally high, while P_2 and P_4 rate A equally low. Moreover, holding

TABLE 10.4

Attraction Ratings by Four Hypothetical Subjects
Along Response Scales Shown in Fig. 10.6

Subject	Proportion of agreements	Number of agreements	Scale used	Predicted rating
P_1	1.0	20	I	10
P_2	.5	10	I	5
P_3	1.0	10	II	10
P_4	.5	5	II	5

the proportion of similar attitudes constant, the number of agreements does not affect ratings of A. These predictions are identical to the results reported by Byrne and Nelson. To this extent, Byrne and Nelson's findings could be due to differences in the language used to report attractions along a category scale, and the conclusion that proportion rather than number of agreements determines attraction could be exactly opposite to that implied by differences in the subjective judgments made by subjects!

The above interpretation of Byrne and Nelson's results is of course speculative. Furthermore, note that this interpretation would be applicable only when different subjects make judgments at each combination of variables shown in Table 10.3. An alternative procedure would be to use a within-subject design in which P receives information about 12 different persons, each set corresponding to a different one of the cells of Byrne and Nelson's design (see Table 10.3). In this case, P would be more likely to position his rating scale similarly when evaluating all 12 persons, and the contribution of response language differences to these judgments should therefore be reduced.

Two other ambiguities arise in interpreting Byrne and Nelson's data. The first is suggested by Wyer and Lyon's finding that while information that P and A had dissimilar sentiments toward B substantially decreased subjects' beliefs that P's attitude toward A was favorable, information that P and A had similar sentiments toward B did not strengthen these beliefs. If these results generalize to conditions in which P is the subject himself, they would imply that P's attraction to A is more likely to be a function of the extent of A's disagreement with P than a function of the proportion of times that A agrees with him. In Byrne and Nelson's study, the proportion of agreements and the number of disagreements were negatively correlated (see Table 10.3 and footnote 1); thus it is impossible to test this interpretation directly.

Its credibility is somewhat weakened by the fact that the number of disagreements was correlated positively with the number of agreements (see Table 10.3), and yet the effect of this latter variable, although in the direction expected from the above line of reasoning, was not significant. However, it is worth noting that the mean attraction to A was 11.62, 10.79, 9.36, 9.07, 7.28, and 6.57 when the number of disagreements was 0, 2, 4, 6, 8, 16, and 32, respectively. To clarify this ambiguity, one would of course need to manipulate the proportion of similar attitudes and the number of dissimilar attitudes independently and compare the effects of each.

The second ambiguity is more conceptual than methodological. It is conceivable that P's attitude toward A is based upon of some index of A's agreement with him about issues in the entire population of those about which he is concerned. When, as in Byrne and Nelson's study, P is told that A agrees with him about issues in a sample selected from this population, he may use some characteristic of this sample as a basis for estimating the relevant population characteristic. If P's attraction is based upon the proportion of times A agrees with him in the population, he may assume, correctly, that the proportion of agreements in the sample is a better estimate of this population parameter than is the number of agreements in the sample. However, suppose that P's attraction to A is based instead upon the number of times A agrees with him in the population. If the sample is representative, the proportion of agreements in the sample is linearly related to the number of agreements in the population as well as to the proportion of agreements. In contrast, the number of agreements in the sample *per se* provides little indication of the number of agreements in the population, particularly if the population size is not known to P. In other words, regardless of whether the number or the proportion of agreements in the population is the basis for attraction, the proportion of agreements in the sample is a better index of this population characteristic than is the number of agreements in the sample. Considered in this light, Byrne and Nelson's data suggest that the effects of information about agreement on different issues are additive, but their data do not indicate whether these effects summate or average. To answer this last question, the size of the entire population of issues of concern to P and A, rather than the size of the sample of issues drawn from this population, must be systematically varied.

    c. *Effects of Issue Importance.* The effect of agreement between P and A depends upon the importance to P of the issues involved. However, the contribution of importance may not always be detected. For example, information that A agrees with P on a certain proportion of important issues has no greater effect upon P's attraction to him than information that he agrees with P on the same proportion of unimportant issues (Byrne & Nelson, 1964, 1965b). In the absence of any other information, each proportion may be used as an estimate of the proportion (or number) of times that P and A agree about issues in the population of those relevant to P. The effect of importance should be more apparent when the issues about which A agrees and disagrees vary systematically in their relevance to P. Byrne, London, and Griffitt (1968) found that agreement on important issues and disagreement on unimportant ones had more positive effects on attraction than agreement on unimportant issues and disagreement on important ones. In fact, under these conditions differential weighting of attitude items on the basis of their importance is necessary in order to detect a linear relation between attraction and proportion of agreements (see Byrne, 1971, p. 73).

 d. Concluding remarks. While Byrne has successfully demonstrated that similarity in attitudes affects attraction, this in itself is not particularly surprising. As we have noted, A's similarity in attitude toward B may function as an attribute of A that affects P's evaluations of him in much the same manner as do other attributes such as "friendly" or "intelligent." To this extent, the manner in which information about several of A's attitudes combines to affect evaluations should be described by one or more of the general models of information integration cited in Chapter 9. Moreover, the effect of information about A's similarity to P with respect to any particular attitude may be contingent upon factors similar to those described in Chapter 8 (i.e., its redundancy or inconsistency with other pieces of information about A, its novelty, etc.). Byrne's data and its implications should perhaps be considered within the context of this more general theoretical and empirical analysis of information integration, as well as from the standpoint of balance theory.

 3. Effect of Information About Oneself Upon Evaluations of the Source. One of the more interesting examples of Type 2 inferences occurs when P is asked to evaluate A after receiving information about A's evaluation of him. In this situation, B is interpreted as P's "Self." The predictions of balance theory under such conditions are somewhat unclear. On one hand, a positive unit relation exists between P and Self; as a result, P's sentiment relation to A should always be positive when A evaluates him favorably and always negative when A evaluates him unfavorably. On the other hand, P may also have a sentiment relation to Self which is either positive or negative, depending upon the favorableness of P's self-concept. If P's self-concept is favorable, predictions would be identical to those made on the basis of a positive unit relation between P and Self. However, if P has an unfavorable self-concept, balance principles imply that P should like a person who dislikes him (and thus agrees with him about Self) and dislike a person who likes him (and thus disagrees with his attitude toward Self).

 Let us consider this situation from a somewhat different point of view. We have previously argued that "liking of P" and "agreement with P" may function as attributes of A that combine to affect his evaluation in much the same way as other attributes. To this extent the favorableness of A's evaluation of P and the similarity between this evaluation and P's self-

TABLE 10.5

P's Judgment of A as a Function of A's Evaluation of
P's Self and Agreement between P's and A's Evaluation
of Self (from Deutsch & Solomon, 1959)

Agreement/disagreement	A's evaluation of P's Self	
	Negative	Positive
A. P's overall evaluation of A		
P and A agree	5.7	6.6
P and A disagree	4.5	5.7
B. P's liking of A		
P and A agree	5.2	6.0
P and A disagree	3.3	4.8

Note—Estimates, made along a 7-point scale, have been reverse scored so that high scores indicate more favorable judgments.

evaluation may contribute independently to P's liking for A. Adequate tests of the independent effects of these variables are difficult, since it is usually hard to find persons who dislike themselves with any degree of intensity, and it is equally hard to induce a high degree of general self-contempt through information provided in the laboratory. However, Self is a multidimensional construct, and it may indeed be possible to manipulate self-evaluations experimentally along a particular dimension. This approach was taken by Deutsch and Solomon (1959). Subjects first performed an achievement task on which they appeared to do either very well (PpSelf) or very badly (PnSelf) according to ostensibly objective criteria. They also received information that an anonymous judge had evaluated them either very favorably (ApSelf) or very unfavorably (AnSelf) on the basis of this performance. They then rated the judge along a set of evaluative dimensions and also estimated how well they would like the judge. All four combinations of levels of these variables were run. Although Deutsch and Solomon report their data as a function of P's self-evaluation and A's evaluation, these data are rearranged in Table 10.5 to show P's judgments of A as a function of A's evaluation of Self and the agreement between P's and A's evaluations of Self. Both variables had a positive influence upon both P's general evaluation of A and his liking for A. Moreover, the interaction of these two variables (or the main effect of P's self-evaluation, as tested by Deutsch and Solomon) was not significant, indicating that the favorableness of A's evaluation of P and his agreement with P had additive effects. These results are consistent with results reported by Feather when subjects inferred other persons' attitudes on the basis of similar information.

There are some problems with the interpretation of these data. Since P's evaluation of Self is based on ostensibly objective criteria, A's agreement with this evaluation may reflect his general competence as a judge of ability. If P's liking for A is based in part on A's competence, this could account for the effect of similarity shown in Table 10.5. Alternatively, P may expect the experimenter to approve of competent persons more than incompetent ones, and may bias his own evaluations of A in the direction of these expectancies. In either event, P's and A's agreement about Self *per se* would not be the critical factor underlying evaluations of A; rather, agreement would have an effect only insofar as it has implications for A's ability as a judge.

Gerard (1965) attempted to manipulate experimentally P's sentiment toward Self by using a procedure similar to that described above. In this study, two successive Type 2 inferences may have been used to arrive at an evaluation of A. Each subject (P) was told that he had performed either poorly or well on the initial trials of a discrimination task, and then, on later trials, he was given the impression, irrespective of his *actual* behavior, that his predisposition to respond was either similar or dissimilar to that of another participant (A). (To accomplish this, P was told that his "initial impulse" to choose one or the other stimulus could be detected by electrodes attached to his forearm. He was then given fictitious feedback about his own and A's initial impulses which indicated that these impulses were either similar or dissimilar.) After performing the discrimination task, P completed a projective test, on the basis of which his approach and avoidance reactions to A were inferred.

Assume that feedback about P's initial performance established either a positive (p) or negative (n) relation between P and Self, while information about P's and A's initial impulses indicated that the relations of Self and A to a particular judgment (X) were either similar (Self$p$X $\cap$ ApX or Self$n$X $\cap$ AnX) or dissimilar (Self$p$X $\cap$ AnX or Self$n$X $\cap$ ApX). These relations involve Self and X rather than P and X, since P is observing Self elicit the initial impulses.) By applying the laws of psycho-logic, P's relation to A can be predicted for each combination of P's ability (high or low) and similarity in initial impulses:

High ability P, initial impulses similar:
PpSelf $\cap$ (ApX $\cap$ Self$p$X) $\supset$ PpSelf $\cap$ ApSelf $\supset$ PpA
High ability P, initial impulses dissimilar:
PpSelf $\cap$ (AnX $\cap$ Self$p$X) $\supset$ PpSelf $\cap$ AnSelf $\supset$ PnA
Low ability P, initial impulses similar:
PnSelf $\cap$ (ApX $\cap$ Self$p$X) $\supset$ PnSelf $\cap$ ApSelf $\supset$ PnA
Low ability P, initial impulses dissimilar:
PnSelf $\cap$ (AnX $\cap$ Self$p$X) $\supset$ PnSelf $\cap$ AnSelf $\supset$ PpA

Estimates of P's attraction to A, based upon the projective test used by Gerard, clearly supported these predictions. However, there is an alternative interpretation of the results of this imaginative study, which is similar to that given to Deutsch and Solomon's experiment. First, note that we have assumed P's judgment of A to result from two successive Type 2 inferences. However, one could as easily assume that P's relation to X is initially inferred from P's relation to Self and Self's relation to X (a Type 3 inference), and that this is then followed by a Type 2 inference about P's relation to A on the basis of P's and A's relations to X. Of the two interpretations, the latter may be the more plausible. The information P receives about his own ability and his initial impulse to choose X may in combination indicate whether X is valid or invalid. Once this is established, P may infer A's ability from his support for or opposition to X. If P considers competence to be a favorable attribute relevant to liking, Gerard's results could be explained without recourse to balance theory.

C. Other applications of Balance Principles

The preceding discussion has been restricted to conditions in which P's and A's relations to B were either both sentiment relations or both unit relations. Balance principles have rarely been applied directly to conditions in which these two relations are of different types. It seems intuitively reasonable to expect that balance principles will often describe inferences accurately under these conditions, although not necessarily for the reasons that balance theory suggests. For example, if P is told that A has a unit relation to an object B (that A belongs to a certain group, that he owns a certain object, or has a certain personality characteristic), and if P knows nothing else about A, his evaluation of A is likely to be similar in direction to his sentiment toward B. In effect, A's unit relation to B may function as an attribute of A, and P's judgment may be determined by his belief about the favorableness of this attribute.

The above interpretation, while straightforward, suggests some specific conditions in which balance principles will *not* apply. For example, suppose A's unit relation to B (e.g., his ownership to B) prevents P from having it. If P has a favorable sentiment toward B, he may regard A's positive unit relation to B as an unfavorable attribute of A, and therefore may dislike A. The resulting set of relations would be imbalanced. Balance principles are also hard to apply when information is presented about A's unit relation to more than one element. This is particularly the case when P's sentiment relations to these two elements differ, and thus they have opposite implications for P's sentiment toward A. Theoretically, this condition should create "ambivalence" (cf. Abelson & Rosenberg, 1958) which would be resolved through cognitive reorganization in the manner described in Chapter 5. However, it seems more likely, based upon research cited in this and earlier chapters, that the effects of these pieces of information are nearly additive, and therefore can be described by models such as those discussed in Chapter 9.

D. A Quantification of Type 2 Inference Processes

Differences in the magnitude and direction of inferences about P's sentiment toward A may theoretically be predicted by using an extension of the subjective probability model described in Chapter 4, that is,

$$E_A = P_{S_B} E_{S_B} + (1 - P_{SB}) E_{S'_B} \qquad (10.6)$$

where P_{S_S} is the belief that P and A have similar attitudes toward B, and E_{SB} and $E_{S'}$ are P's evaluations of persons whose attitudes toward B are known to be similar or dissimilar to his, respectively. This equation could also be used to describe the effects of similarity in group membership; in this case P_{S_B} would pertain to P's belief that he and A share membership (or nonmembership) in a group B, and E_{S_B} and E_{S_B} would represent P's evaluations of persons who were and were not similar to him with respect to membership in B.

In addition to its potential value in describing quantitatively the effects that information about P's similarity to A has on P's evaluation of A, the above equation is a useful conceptual tool for circumscribing the conditions in which balance principles will and will not predict these effects. Note that the effects of information that P and A are similar depend upon the magnitude of the difference between E_{S_B} and $E_{S'_B}$. This information should increase P's evaluation of A, as balance principles imply, only when this difference is positive. One can conceive of instances in which this is not the case. For example, if B is the characteristic "dominant" or "likes to dominate others," E_{S_B} (P's evaluation of persons who are similar to him in this characteristic) is likely to be low. Or, if B is the category "male," it is conceivable that $E_{S'_B}$ (in effect, the evaluation of females) may be relatively high. In each of these cases, information that P and A are similar with respect to B would have relatively little positive effect. More generally, P may be more apt to like A if they share extreme sentiments toward B than if they share moderate or neutral sentiments, as Feather's data show. Equation 10.6 could account for this difference only if the quantity $E_{SB} - E_{S'_B}$ increases with the intensity of the attitudes involved, that is, if strongly held attitudes are more "relevant" to liking than moderate ones.

E. Summary and Evaluation

With the exception of data reported by Wyer and Lyon, none of the research described in this section directly contradicts predictions based upon balance theory. Nevertheless, the utility of applying balance principles to Type 1 and Type 2 inferences may be limited. As implied by balance theory, estimates of P's liking for A are a positive function of three factors: A's liking of P, the similarity between P's and A's attitudes, and the similarity of P's and A's group membership. However, these three factors appear to function as attributes of A, and the laws governing their influence, both separately and in combination, appear to be similar to those that govern the effects of information about other characteristics of A (e.g., his honesty, intelligence, etc.). To this extent, the information integration models described in Chapter 9 may be more useful than balance principles in predicting the effects of information concerning these attributes. Data obtained both when P is the subject himself (e.g., Deutsch & Solomon, 1959) and when other persons' evaluations of A are predicted (Feather, 1967) support this conclusion.

Balance principles can of course be used to predict whether the three attributes described above are regarded as favorable or unfavorable; however, the magnitude of their favorableness may depend upon the type of attitude object, or the type of groups to which P and A belong. Such sources of variance cannot be accounted for on the basis of balance theory alone and must be investigated empirically.

III. TYPE 3 INFERENCES: $Pr_1A \cap Ar_2B \supset Pr_3B$

Type 3 inferences occur when subjects are asked to estimate P's (their own or another's) sentiment toward B on the basis of information about P's relation to A and A's relation to B. There are many empirical examples of this sort of inference in the literature, only a subset of which have been traditionally interpreted within the theoretical framework of cognitive balance. Again, let us consider some of this research and evaluate its implications for the conditions in which balance principles describe these inferences.

A. Research on Type 3 Inferences about Other Persons' Attitudes

Although data bearing directly upon Type 3 inferences about other persons' attitudes are limited, Wyer and Lyon's study is again relevant. In certain conditions of this study (described in detail on page 329), subjects read two context statements describing P's sentiment relation to A (p or n) and A's sentiment relation to B (p or n) and then chose which of three statements describing P's sentiment toward B (p, o, or n) was most likely to be valid. The elements in each configuration consisted either of three persons (POO), two persons and an object (POX), or one person and two objects (PXX). The proportion of times that each type of relation was inferred in each context, defined relative to the proportion of times it was inferred in the absence of context information, is shown in Fig. 10.11. These results are similar in several respects to analogous data pertaining to Type 2 inferences (see Fig. 10.2). In PXX configurations, p relations were inferred more frequently than n relations when the two context relations were similar (C_{pp} and C_{nn}) but were inferred less often than n relations when the context

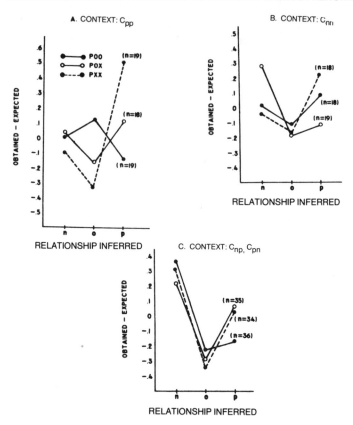

Fig. 10.11. Difference between obtained and expected probabilities of inferring p, o, and n relations as a function of context–Type 3 inferences (reprinted from Wyer & Lyon,   1970, 609).

relations differed (C_{np} and C_{pn}). However, when A was another person rather than ain institution or organization, inferences were consistent with balance theory only when the context consisted for one n and one p relation. In other words, P was expected to dislike things (objects or other persons) that were either liked by persons he disliked or were disliked by persons he liked. However, he was generally not expected to like things more when they were disliked by disliked persons or were liked by liked persons. (This does not mean P was expected to dislike B in these latter conditions; in fact, the expectancy that P would like B in the absence of any context information was moderately high. However, this expectancy was not appreciably *increased* by the context material.)

These data raise questions concerning the usefulness of balance principles in predicting Type 3 inferences about others' attitudes. Certainly there is no evidence that these inferences minimize cognitive inconsistency, as defined by these principles. However, what general conclusions may be drawn about the factors that *do* affect inferences of this type? Subjects may make one of two basic assumptions when inferring P's relation to B. First, they may assume that P's tendency to adopt A's attitude toward B is determined by his regard for A. In this event, our data indicate that P is expected to be more influenced, either positively or negatively, by an institution or organization than by a single person. Second, subjects may assume that P's liking for A depends upon whether or not P and A agree about B. To this extent, they would not actually be making a Type 3 inference but rather would be making a Type 2 inference in reverse; that is, they would be inferring a "premise" (that P and A agree about B) from a "conclusion" (that P likes A). In this case, our results would suggest that attitudes toward an organization are more often assumed to be based upon its support for one's own views than are attitudes toward another person. In either case, these data reinforce our position that balance principles are not applied universally but rather describe inference processes only when they reflect subjects' general experience with the types of persons and objects involved.

Inferences based upon unit relations. Wyer and Lyon's study pertains only to conditions in which the information presented described sentiment relations. Different considerations arise when one of the two relations described is a unit relation. For example, suppose subjects are asked to infer P's sentiment toward B on the basis of information about P's membership in a group A and A's sentiment toward B. In such a case, predictions based upon balance principles are consistent with the laws of formal logic. That is, if P belongs to A and if members of A are likely to support (or oppose) B, then P is likely to support (or oppose) B. On the other hand, if P does not belong to A, P's sentiment toward B could not logically be inferred from A's sentiment toward B. This is also an implication of balance theory if nonmembership in A is interpreted as the *absence* of a relation $(Pu'A)$ rather than as a negative (n) relation.

B. Research on Type 3 Inferences about One's Own Attitude

1. *Effects of Source Attractiveness upon Communication Impact.* A common example of a Type 3 inference occurs in research on the effects of source prestige upon the impact of a persuasive communication. These effects have already been discussed at some length in Chapter 6. At that time, however, we considered changes in evaluations of both a source and an object that were produced by a communication associating them. The present focus will be upon the manner in which two pieces of information, one intended to affect P's sentiment relation to a source A, and the other describing A's relation to an object B, combine to affect P's judgment of B.

Effects of different criteria for judging source attractiveness. According to balance principles, information that a source (A) is favorable should increase P's tendency to adopt attitudes similar to A's, while information that A is unfavorable will increase P's tendency to adopt positions that are diametrically opposed to A's. As we have suggested, however, the magnitude of these effects, and why they occur, may depend in part upon the reasons that A is judged favorably. The results of a study by Kelman (1958) suggest the nature of certain of these contigencies. Students at an all-Black university listened to a recorded message advocating segregation of colleges, a concept generally opposed by students at the time the study was run. In one condition, the source (A) was described as a wealthy alumnus who was in a position to award money both to the University and to individual students. In a second, A was described as a student-body president of a neighboring all-Black university. In a third, A was described as an eminent scholar specializing in Black history. In all conditions, subjects reported their own opinions about the desirability of segregated colleges both immediately after hearing the speech and again some time later. An additional factor considered by Kelman was the source's apparent access to subject's initial questionnaire responses.

What would balance theory predict under such conditions? All three sources may be evaluated favorably by subjects, and therefore each should have a positive influence on subjects' attitudes. However, the basis for the favorable source evaluation differs substantially in the three conditions. That is, A may be regarded positively in the first case because he can deliver rewards to P; in the second, because he has high status among P's peers; and in the third, because he is an authority in an area of interest to P. Kelman found that communications attributed to the wealthy alumnus had an influence on opinions expressed immediately after receiving the communication, but only when subjects believed that A would learn of their responses. Communications attributed to the student-body president affected the opinions reported even when the source did not have access to these responses; however, this influence was not maintained over time. The communication had an enduring influence on opinion only when A was described as an expert in Black history. While A may not have been regarded equally favorably under these three conditions, this fact alone could not account for these fairly complex findings. In the first two conditions, P may change his *responses* to conform to what he believes is expected of him by others, but he may not change his actual opinions. When A is a potential donor of rewards, P may report an opinion similar to A's when A has access to these reports, but P may otherwise respond in a manner that he believes is more generally considered to be socially desirable. When A is a highly respected peer, P may temporarily believe that a pro-segregation view is socially desirable and may respond accordingly, pending verification of this belief through his discussions with other peers. Once this belief is invalidated, however, P's response may revert to its original, pre-communication position. In any event, the communication seems to have affected P's actual opinion (as opposed to his report of this opinion) only when A was ostensibly knowledgeable about the issue. These findings place some implicit qualifications on the conditions in which balance principles apply to Type 3 inferences. Clearly, positive regard for A is not enough to insure that A has an enduring influence on judgments. This influence may occur only when regard for A is based upon his expertise in the area.

Some other contingencies. Further evidence that liking is not in itself a determinant of influence is provided in a study of conformity by Wyer (1966), to be discussed in detail in the next section. Briefly, we found that in the absence of an incentive to perform well on a judgmental task, subjects conformed appreciably to others' (A's) judgments only if they liked A *and* they were informed that A probably did not like them; conformity was low when P was told he was liked by A, regardless of his personal liking for A. In contrast, when an incentive to perform well was provided, subjects conformed to judgments of a liked A, regardless of information about A's liking for them, but *also* conformed to judgments of a *disliked* A who liked them. In other words, P's tendencies to accept the judgment of a liked A, and to reject the judgment of a disliked A, depended both upon information about A's liking for him and upon the importance P attached to being correct.

The magnitude of a source's influence may also depend upon his apparent prejudice or bias toward the object or issue to be evaluated. Consider, for example, an early study by Kelman and Hovland (1953). In this experiment, subjects listened to a tape recorded communication that advocated leniency toward juvenile offenders (B). Some subjects were told that the source of the communication (A) was a respected juvenile court judge, while others were told that the source was an exconvict suspected of peddling dope. Kelman and Hovland argued that the judge would be more highly regarded than the exconvict and therefore should have more influence upon subjects' own attitudes toward leniency. This, of course, is what balance theory predicts and what the results showed to be the case. However, another interpretation of these results is possible. This latter interpretation is based on the hypothesis that A's influence is not a function of his favorableness but instead depends on his credibility or the extent to which he is believed to be free from bias in reporting his personal views. Suspicions of bias may often be affected by the consistency of a person's responses with those expected of him by virtue of his actual or desired social role. In a study by Jones, Davis, and Gergen (1961), subjects heard a recorded interview with a job candidate who described himself as having characteristics that were either consistent or inconsistent with the requirements of the job for which he was applying. Then they rated the candidate in terms of what he was "really like." Applicants whose responses implied attributes required by the job were judged to have only moderate amounts of these attributes, while applicants whose responses indicated they were unfit for the job were judged to have extreme amounts of the attributes implied by these responses. In other words, subjects attached relatively little credibility to responses that were consistent with role demands but attached high credibility to responses that deviated from role expectancies.

What implications do these findings have for Kelman and Hovland's experiment? It seems reasonable to assume that juvenile court judges are believed to be fairly severe in their treatment of juvenile delinquents, while criminals, particularly dope pushers, have a vested interest in leniency. Therefore, advocacy of leniency for juvenile delinquents may be regarded as a less biased opinion when attributed to the judge than when attributed to the dope pusher. Perhaps if the communication had advocated *severe* treatment of juvenile delinquents, the judge might have been regarded as more biased than the dope pusher, and thus his opinion might have had *less* influence than that of the "unfavorable" source. Such results would of course be directly opposite to those predicted by balance principles.

In evaluating the conclusion that source favorableness is not a sufficient condition for source influence, it should be noted that Aronson and Golden (1962) found racially prejudiced subjects to be more influenced by white sources than by black sources who were judged to be equally intelligent. This finding could indicate that source favorableness *does* have an effect independent of source expertise. However, other explanations of this finding are possible. For example, prejudiced subjects may believe that opinions advocated by whites are more socially desirable than those advocated by blacks, independent of their validity. To this extent, the sources used by Aronson and Golden may have differentially affected subjects' *reports* of their attitudes but not the attitudes themselves.

Effects of disliked sources. Balance theory implies that when P's relation to A is negative, P's evaluation of B should be opposite in direction to A's. Support for this prediction is quite limited. Sampson and Insko (1964) found that information that presumably induced P to dislike another (A) led P to change estimates of a physical stimulus that were initially similar to A's. However, as we noted in Chapter 1, there are alternative interpretations of these results that call into question the strength of their support for balance theory. More commonly, it is found that positions advocated by another have small but positive effects even when the source is disliked or is regarded as not credible (e.g., Weiss, 1957). There may be several reasons for this. One, suggested by Osgood and Tannenbaum (1955), is that an assertion supporting a particular position may have a positive influence upon a subject's judgment, regardless of the source to which it is attributed. This effect, which is presumably due to the content of the information contained in the assertion, may often be sufficient to overcome the negative effects of the source. The second reason is that although the source is unfavorable, his judgments are not believed to be more often incorrect than correct. This point will be elaborated presently.

2. *Effects of Group Membership upon Conformity.* Let us now briefly consider the effects of a positive *unit* relation between P and A upon P's adoption of A's judgments or, more simply, the effect that P's membership in a group A will have on P's conformity to A's opinions. This effect has been

the subject of substantial research, most of which has not been considered in the context of balance theory. It seems reasonable to suppose that subjects are more apt to conform to positions advocated by a group if they belong to the group than if they do not. However, there are problems in testing this hypothesis. First, outside the laboratory, subjects may belong to several different groups simultaneously, and it is sometimes difficult to determine which group is influencing him at any given time. In such conditions, it is reasonable to suppose that a subject will be most influenced by the opinions of whichever group is most salient to him at the time he reports his opinions. Thus, if P is asked his attitude toward the use of marijuana on college campuses, he may respond differently when he is interviewed in his office at a large university than when he is interviewed at a meeting of a radical off-campus organization. However, such a phenomenon, if it occurs, would be difficult to interpret. For example, P's responses under the above conditions might not be a consequence of his group membership *per se*, but rather of tendencies to conform to expectancies of the interviewer or of external pressures to adopt the positions held by other group members. Moreover, it may be unclear whether the effect is due to the *unit* relation between P and his membership group or to his sentiment relation toward this group.

Perhaps the strongest support for the hypothesis that group membership *per se* affects P's adoption of group judgments was obtained in a rather ingenious study by Kelley (1955). Subjects who without their knowledge had been identified by the experimenter as Catholics or non-Catholics were administered a questionnaire concerning their religious beliefs in a large lecture room. Each questionnaire item was accompanied by a fictitious normative rating that was attributed to an unselected group of college students. Several of these ratings were deviant from those implied by traditional Catholic dogma. Before completing the questionnaire, some members of each religious group read a communication about the life of a Pope, while others read a short biography of a person not associated with any particular religion. Neither communication contained any information relevant to the items in the questionnaire. Since subjects ostensibly responded anonymously, and since they were not identified publically as Catholics or non-Catholics, tendencies to comply with the expectations held for them by others were probably minimal in this situation. Non-Catholics conformed equally to college student norms regardless of the previous communication they received. However, Catholics were much more resistant to influence (that is, they conformed more to the norms of their *membership* group) when they had read the communication about the Pope. These results do not bear directly upon the question of how *new* information about a group to which P belongs affects P's judgments. However, they do suggest that group membership *per se* may exert the sort of influence predicted by balance theory.

Other studies, while more directly relevant to information integration, provide more equivocal support for balance theory. For example, Jackson and Saltzstein (1958) formed experimental groups of subjects and then on a pretext excluded one member of each group from full participation. Both members and nonmembers performed a judgmental task and received feedback that the average judgment of group members differed substantially from their own. Group members subsequently conformed more to these norms than did nonmembers. While this result is consistent with balance theory, it may not have occurred for the reasons balance theory suggests. In the conditions constructed by the authors, a reward for good group performance was offered to members but not to nonmembers. This incentive may have generated greater implicit pressure upon members to make judgments similar to others and thus to share equally the responsibility for the group's success or failure. In other words, the results reported may not have been attributable to group membership vs. nonmembership *per se*.

P's conformity to group judgments may also depend upon the extent to which he believes that deviations from group norms will endanger his membership in the group or affect his group status. Hollander (1958) has argued that very high status members are less vulnerable to group pressure than intermediate status members, because their position is more secure. In support of this, Harvey and Consalvi (1960) found that both group leaders and low status members (who presumably have little to lose by not conforming) were less influenced by group judgments than were members of intermediate status. Wyer (1966) also reported evidence that conformity to group norms may be low unless members believe their acceptance in the group to be contingent upon their conformity. In both cases, group membership may have been necessary but not sufficient to lead subjects to adopt group judgments.

In this regard several authors (e.g., Kelley, 1952; Newcomb, 1943) have distinguished between *membership* groups and *reference* groups. P's reference group, or the group in relation to which he evaluates himself, may not always be one to which he actually belongs. In such cases, the relatively greater influence of the reference group may be due to P's stronger sentiment relation to this group.

C. Combined Effects of Information on Type 3 Inferences

Consider the four diagrams shown in Fig. 10.12, which describe the relations between P, B, and two sources, A_1 and A_2. In each case, the solid lines refer to the relations described in information being presented, and the dotted line to the relation to be inferred. Diagrams "b" and "c" would be balanced if P's inferred relation to B was p and n, respectively. In the other two diagrams, however, the relation between P and B that would balance the set of relations involving A_1 would produce imbalance among the relations involving A_2. What relation would be inferred under such conditions? While

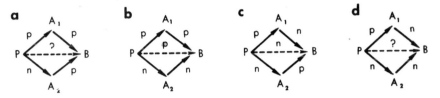

Fig. 10.12. Balance diagrams describing Type 3 inferences based upon information about B from two sources (A_1 and A_2).

few studies bear directly upon this question, the study by Tannenbaum (1967), described in detail in Chapter 6, is quite relevant. In effect, Tannenbaum constructed four conditions, each comparable to one of those described in Fig. 10.12. That is, in one case P received information that a favorable source (A_1) and an unfavroable source (A_2) both expressed a favorable opinion about an issue (B); in a second, P was told that A_1 opposed B but A_2 favored it, and so on. Tannenbaum found that the information from the favorable source and the information from the unfavorable source had independent effects. If generalizable, these results suggest that Type 3 inferences, like Type 1 and Type 2 inferences, combine additively to affect judgments of objects to which they pertain.

D. A Quantitative Description of Type 3 Inferences

The studies summarized above indicate that the applicability of balance principles to Type 3 inferences depends upon several additional factors that are not predictable from balance theory *per se*. While a general classification of these factors is difficult to obtain, an approach to investigating this question is suggested by applying the subjective probability model described in Chapter 4. For example, consider the equation,

$$P_B = P_A\, P_{B/A} + (1 - P_A)\, P_{B/A'} \tag{10.7}$$

where P_B is the belief that B is favorable, P_A is the belief that A regards B as favorable, and $P_{B/A}$ and $P_{B/A'}$ are the conditional beliefs that B is favorable, given that A does and does not advocate this position. According to this equation, there will be a positive relation between A's evaluation of B and P's evaluation as long as $P_{B/A} > P_{B/A'}$. On the other hand, when $P_{B/A} = P_{B/A'}$ there should be no relation between P's and A's judgments of B, and when $P_{B/A} < P_{B/A'}$ the relation should be negative.

For the implications of balance theory to be consistent with those of Eq. (10.7), $P_{B/A}$ would have to be greater than $P_{B/A}$ whenever A is liked but less than $P_{B/A'}$ whenever A is disliked. However, the magnitude of these inequalities would seem intuitively to depend upon the particular reasons for liking or disliking A. If a disliked person is simply believed to be unreliable, his opinions should simply be irrelevant to P's attitudes (that is, $P_{B/A} = P_{B/A'}$), and therefore information about them should have no effect at all. To have a negative effect, as balance principles predict, the source must be regarded as "negatively reliable," that is, as more often incorrect in his judgments than correct. While this may sometimes be the case, it is by no means universal, as Weiss's (1957) study suggests.

Contingencies in the influence of liked and disliked sources may be interpreted in terms of this equation. P's liking for A may often be based upon his judgment of A's competence, and therefore may reflect his belief that A's opinions are valid. To this extent, $P_{B/A} > P_{B/A'}$, as balance theory assumes. However, suppose A is described as "warm, friendly, generous, sympathetic, and undiscriminating in his praise of and regard for others." In such a case, P may like A but regard his evaluation of a third person (B) as totally unreliable, and thus $P_{B/A} = P_{B/A'}$. It is of course possible that P will adopt the opinions of a liked other (A), at least in public, even when he considers these opinions to be invalid. For example, he may not want to hurt A's feelings or to lose A's friendship by disagreeing with him. Or, A's opinions may be interpreted as a popular or socially desirable response and thus as an indication of how P should respond in order to be regarded favorably by others. Note that if the components of Eq. (10.7) are estimates of subjects' underlying beliefs, as distinct from their report of these beliefs, the effects of the latter factor would not be taken into account by this equation. However, if the equation is a valid description of the relations among subjective beliefs about A and B, the difference between obtained and predicted values of P_B, based upon this equation, would indicate the extent to which demand characteristics and other factors contribute to subjects' reported estimates of P_B, over and above the effects of the information presented.

Equation (10.7) may also be applied to conditions in which P's association with A is a unit relation. In this case, P_A would represent the belief that P belongs to A, and $P_{B/A}$ and $P_{B/A'}$ would be the respective probabilities that members and nonmembers of A support B. Some additional considerations are suggested by this description. For example, information that P belongs to A will generally increase P_A, while information that members of A support B will increase $P_{B/A}$. However, this information should have a positive effect upon beliefs that P supports B only if $P_{B/A'}$ is lower than $P_{B/A}$. As a simple example, suppose that in the absence of other information, subjects believe that $P_A = P_{B/A} = .1$ and that $P_{B/A'} = .9$. Then, applying Eq. (10.7), $P_B = .1(.1) + .9(.9) = .82$; that is, even in the absence of information subjects would predict that P is likely to support B. Now, suppose they are told that P belongs to A and that members of A generally support B. While this information may increase P_A to unity, it may not increase $P_{B/A}$ to an equal extent unless the information implies that *nearly every member* of A supports B. If $P_{B/A}$ increases only to .7, then P_B would actually decrease (to .7) after receiving this information. This possibility in no way implies that balance theory is invalid; the final relation between P and B is positive, as balance theory predicts. However, this belief would be less strong than in a control condition in which no information is presented. Moreover, if the *change* in inferences produced by new information is used to assess the validity of balance principles in describing these inferences, the conclusions drawn could be misleading. These problems may, of course, only be serious when subjects have strong preconceptions about P's membership in A and A's support of B, before these subjects receive information about these relations. If A and B are unfamiliar, each relation involving them may initially be believed to be equally likely (that is, $P_A = P_{B/A} = P_{B/A'} = .50$), and the effects of information bearing upon these beliefs may more obviously correspond to those predicted by balance theory. These contingencies may be worth exploring empirically.

E. Summary and Evaluation

The results of research on Type 3 inferences indicate that balance principles do not apply universally to these inferences. While Wyer and Lyon's data help to circumscribe the conditions in which these principles are most likely to apply, at least to inferences about other persons' attitudes, further research is clearly necessary in order to obtain a complete understanding of these conditions. It may be helpful to collect survey data to determine (*a*) the types of persons and objects that (in subjects' previous experiences) have typically been related in a manner consistent with balance principles and (*b*) the situational conditions in which these relations have typically occurred.

In less controlled situations in which P is the subject himself, several factors in addition to balance must typically be taken into account in order to predict inferences. While this does not necessarily mean that balance principles are invalid in such situations, it suggests that they are not particularly useful in either predicting or explaining the type of judgments made. These inferences appear to be more easily understood by simply considering the implications of the information presented for attributes of the object being evaluated, and the external incentives for P to conform to opinions expressed by another, regardless of their validity. That is, P will adopt A's judgment to the extent that information about A suggests that his opinions are valid, or to the extent that agreement with A appears to increase the likelihood of P's attaining an objective he desires (social approval, monetary reward, etc.). Whether cognitive balance principles *per se* are employed in arriving at these judgments is presently unclear.

IV. TYPE 4 INFERENCES: $Pr_1A \cap Pr_2B \supset Ar_3B$

This type of inference occurs when A's sentiment toward B is inferred on the basis of information about P's relations to both A and B. These inferences are less common than the other types described in this chapter, and there is relatively little research bearing upon them. Moreover, it is less intuitively obvious that balance principles apply to this type of inference than to other types we have considered.

A. Inferences When the Subject is not an Element of the Configuration.

1. *Inferences Based upon Sentiment Relations.* Before describing the research on inferences when P is not the subject but a third party, let us consider these inferences from the general information-processing point of view we have espoused in previous chapters and use this approach to identify the assumptions that subjects may make in arriving at these judgments. When r_1 and r_2 are both sentiment relations, the question to be asked is what information about P's liking for A and B has to do with A's liking for B. Presumably, liking for a person or object depends upon beliefs about the favorableness of its attributes. Thus, information about P's sentiments toward A and B may have implications for A's and B's attributes, which, in turn, may have implications for A's sentiment toward B. However, the nature of these implications may depend upon the particular attributes of A and B that are inferred from the information presented. When A and B are people, there are at least three possibilities:

a. Subjects may assume that liking is based upon similarity in attitudes toward certain basic issues. To this extent, A and B may be assumed to have similar attitudes if both are liked by P (and therefore both agree with *him*) or if both are disliked by P (and therefore disagree with him). However, A and B may be assumed to have dissimilar attitudes if P likes one but not the other. Therefore A and B should like one another more in the first two cases than in the third.

b. Popularity assumption. Subjects may assume that P's liking for B indicates that B has certain personality attributes that are generally regarded as favorable or unfavorable. For example, subjects who are told that P likes B may infer that B is warm, intelligent, and generous, while subjects told that P dislikes B may infer that B is stupid, loudmouthed, and mean. To this extent, it seems likely that A would also recognize these attributes in B, and his liking for B would be similar to P's, *regardless of P's liking for A.*

c. Congeniality assumption.[2] Subjects may assume that P's liking for A

---

[2] This assumption should not be confused with the friendliness bias identified by Rubin and Zajonc (1969). This bias pertains to a tendency to infer that if P likes (or dislikes) one person, he is apt to like (or dislike) another. While the choice of a similar term here is confusing, no more appropriate label is obvious.

indicates the extent to which A has certain attributes that affect his general tendency to like or dislike others. For example, subjects who are told that P likes A may infer that this is true because A usually responds favorably to other persons, and thus tends to like them, while subjects who are told that P dislikes A may infer that A usually behaves badly toward other persons, and thus generally dislikes them. To this extent, A's liking for B would be judged as similar to P's liking for A, *regardless of whether or not P likes B.*

Inferences about A's liking for B would generally be consistent with those predicted by balance principles only if the first of the above assumptions is the most commonly made by subjects. The assumptions are of course not mutually exclusive, and all three could contribute simultaneously to inferences.

The only known study that bears upon these questions was conducted by Wyer and Lyon (1970) and pertains only to sentiment relations among the objects involved. The materials and general procedure used in this study have already been described. In certain conditions, subjects were given statements describing a person's (P's) sentiment relations to both A (p or n) and B (p or n), and they then chose which of three additional statements (p, o, or n) was most likely to describe A's relation to B. Configurations consisted either of three persons (POO), two persons and an object (POX), or one person and two objects (PXX). The proportion of p, o, and n relations between P and A inferred under different context conditions and in different types of configurations, defined relative to the proportion of inferences made in the absence of context information, is shown in Fig. 10.13.

These data differ appreciably from analogous data pertaining to other types of inferences (see Fig. 10.2 and 10.11). When P's attitudes toward A and B differed, A's relation to B was predicted to be n more often then p, consistent with balance principles. However, information that P's sentiments toward A and B were both similar increased the probability of inferring a p relation only when B was not a person. Moreover, information that P disliked both A and B *decreased* the tendency to infer a p relation between A and B and increased the tendency to infer an n relation. These latter results, which were most pronounced when A was another person, are directly opposite to predictions based upon balance principles and suggest that either the congeniality or the popularity assumption, or both, might underlie inferences. To explore this possibility, data pertaining to C_{np} and C_{pn} conditions must of course be considered separately. The implications of these data are unclear. In C_{pn} conditions, n relations were inferred more often (.250) than p relations (.139), while in C_{np} conditions, p relations were inferred more often (.476) than n relations (.158). This would appear to provide evidence for the popularity assumption. However, relative to the proportion of inferences made in the *absence* of context information, n relations were inferred more often than were p relations under both conditions.

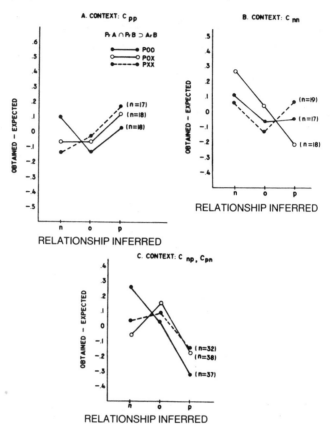

Fig. 10.13. Difference between obtained and expected probabilities of inferring p, o, and n relations as a function of context—Type 4 inferences (reprinted from Wyer & Lyon, 1970, p. 609).

2. *Inferences Based upon Unit Relations.* No research bears directly upon the nature of inferences about A's sentiment toward B from information about P's unit relations to A and B (e.g., from information that P is a member of groups A and B). It seems intuitively reasonable that balance principles will describe these inferences accurately when P's associations with A and B appear to stem from a common set of social or political values. For example, they should hold if A is the Ku Klux Klan and B is a political organization that supports a racist southern governor for President. However, a positive relation between A and B would seem less likely if A and B are dissimilar in function and objectives (e.g., the University Chess Club and the Democratic Party), or if they are groups to which P belongs through circumstances beyond his control (e.g., the Union of South Africa and the Negro race). Note that in each of these examples, subjects' beliefs about A's sentiment toward B might not be based upon information about P's membership in the groups *per se*, but rather upon subjects' prior knowledge

about characteristics of A and B, gained before this information was presented. Moreover, if subjects are not familiar with A and B before information about P's membership in them is communicated, their inferences may depend upon which of several arbitrary sets of assumptions they make about the nature of these groups and the basis for P's membership in them. That is, if balance principles *do* describe subjects' inferences under these latter conditions, they may do so because subjects typically assume that P's membership in the groups is voluntary and that membership in each stems from a common set of social interests and values. Similar considerations arise when one of the two given relations is a sentiment relation and the other is a unit relation.

B. Inferences When the Subject is an Element of the Configuration

Research on Type 4 inference processes when the subject himself is an element of the configuration is nearly as limited as research on such inferences when the subject is not personally involved. One particularly relevant study was recently reported by Gollob (1974a). Although we will discuss this study in greater detail in the context of Gollob's own theoretical approach to social inference phenomena, it is worth describing here briefly. In effect, Gollob presented subjects (P) with information that each of two persons (A and B) was described by a personality adjective. Each adjective was either high or low in normative likeableness and was thus assumed to produce either a positive or negative sentiment relation between P and the person described. After receiving this information, subjects were asked to estimate the likelihood that A reacted to B in a way that conveyed either a positive or a negative attitude toward B.

The design of the study allowed Gollob to determine the independent effects of three factors: the overall balance of the three relations involved, the similarity between A's relation to B and P's relation to A, and the similarity of A's and P's relations to B. The effects of the latter two factors may reflect the effects of the congeniality and popularity assumptions, respectively, on inferences. Gollob found that all three factors affected P's inferences about A's sentiment toward B. However, the magnitudes of these effects depended upon the particular verb used to describe A's relation to B. That is, balance was the major contributor to inferences only when A's relation to B was described as "admire" or "despise." In all other cases (for example, when these relations were described as "like" and "dislike"), the congeniality assumption appeared to contribute most to inferences. Possible reasons for these differences will be discussed in Chapter 12.

C. Effects of Group Acceptance Upon Conformity

An interesting application of balance theory to Type 4 inferences can be made in considering the effects of group acceptance on conformity. The inferences involved in this application differ from others discussed in this section. That is, if P, A, and B represent the subject, a group, and an object of judgment, respectively, these inferences would be generally described by the logical expression: $Ar_1P \cap Ar_2B \supset Pr_3B$. Balance principles predict that P will accept A's evaluation of B when A's sentiment toward B is favorable, or when P is "accepted" by A, but will adopt a position different from A's when A's sentiment toward P is unfavorable. Whether P's evaluation of B and A's evaluation of B would actually be opposite in direction under these latter conditions is unclear; as we have noted previously, factors such as the "assertion constant" may lead to A's judgment having a positive influence under all conditions. However, balance theory clearly predicts that P will tend more to adopt A's judgments of B when he is told that A likes him than when he is told that A dislikes him.

The study by Sampson and Insko (1964), discussed in detail in Chapter 1, bears upon the validity of these predictions. In effect, subjects were given information that another (A) either liked or disliked them and were then told that A's judgment of a physical stimulus was either similar or dissimilar to their own. P changed his judgments to agree with A's when A ostensibly liked him, but P changed his judgments to disagree with A's when A ostensibly disliked him. While these results are quite consistent with the implications of balance principles, there are alternative interpretations of these results that should be noted (see p. 5).

Other research on Type 4 inferences of this nature is less consistent with predictions based upon balance theory. In general, this research seems to indicate that the effect of group acceptance on conformity depends upon (a) whether acceptance is important to the subject, and (b) whether he feels that his acceptance depends upon his conformity. A theoretical analysis of the effects of acceptance has been made by Hollander (1958), who concludes that persons who are highly accepted have accumulated more "idiosyncrasy credits" and thus are less likely to lose status by deviating from group norms than are persons whose acceptance is more uncertain. The implication of this analysis, that conformity is low when acceptance is high, is opposite to that of balance theory.

A study of conformity by Wyer (1966) tends to support Hollander's formulation but demonstrates that the effect of acceptance on conformity depends both upon group attractiveness and the incentive provided to make accurate judgments of the object B. This study has additional interest, since it provides evidence of the manner in which information bearing upon Type 3 and Type 4 inferences combines to affect judgments. On the basis of sociometric data, groups of 10 high school students were formed such that half of the subjects in each group liked at least 7 other members of the group, while the other half liked no more than 3 other members. Upon arriving for the experiment, subjects received feedback that they were either well-liked or disliked by most other members of the group. They then judged the number

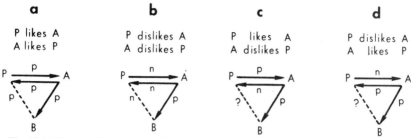

Fig. 10.14. Balance diagrams describing experimental conditions used in Wyer's (1966) study of conformity.

of dots on a slide, both before and after receiving fictitious feedback that other members' judgments were 30% larger than theirs.

Assume that the group (A) initially advocates a judgment B that deviates from P's original judgment. Then, the four experimental conditions may be described by the four balance diagrams in Fig. 10.14. Note that P's relation to B can be the result of either a Type 3 inference ($Pr_1A \cap Ar_2B \supset Pr_3B$) or a Type 4 inference ($Ar_1P \cap Ar_2B \supset Pr_3B$). In the situations described in diagrams *a* and *b*, balance theory makes similar predictions, regardless of which type of inference is involved. In the other two situations, however, the judgments based upon the two types of inferences would differ.

An additional variable in this study was the incentive provided to make accurate judgments. In one condition (low incentive), subjects were asked to perform the judgmental task to help test the adequacy of the apparatus and procedure for future experiments. In the second condition (high incentive), subjects were told that the task was a measure of leadership ability, and that persons who performed well might be selected to participate in future experiments for pay. Conformity, measured by the percentage change in judgments of B, is shown in Table 10.7 as a function of incentive, attraction to A, and acceptance by A. Under low incentive conditions, conformity was high only among subjects who were told they were disliked by persons they liked. These results suggest that under these conditions P tends to adopt A's judgments only when he both cares about whether or not A accepts him and has reason to believe that his acceptance is in doubt. If P is told that A likes him, he may feel that his acceptance is not contingent upon his agreement with A and thus may not be influenced. In any event, these results do not support the validity of balance principles in describing Type 4 inferences, and indicate that Type 3 inferences are predictable from balance theory only when P believes that A may not like him.

Under high incentive conditions, both acceptance by A and attraction to A increased the tendency to adopt A's judgment of B. Balance principles thus appear to be more applicable to inferences made under these conditions. However, the fact that conformity under high attraction, high acceptance conditions was no greater than under other conditions suggests that the effect

TABLE 10.7

Mean Conformity as a Function of Group Acceptance,
Group Attraction (Att) and Incentive to Perform Well (Inc)
(adapted from Wyer, 1966)

Acceptance	Low Inc		High Inc	
	Low Att	High Att	Low Att	High Att
High	10.8	9.9	15.2	15.6
Low	11.5	16.5	9.7	14.4

of these variables, and thus the effects of Type 3 and Type 4 inferences, are not additive. Since the conformity of subjects who were told they were not accepted by persons they liked was similar under both incentive conditions, it seems reasonable to conclude that the high incentive served primarily to increase the positive effect of information that A liked P. Perhaps such information increases P's belief that A is a good judge of social stimuli and therefore of physical stimuli as well. If this interpretation is valid, one could conclude that (a) Type 3 inferences underlie judgments made under low acceptance conditions, regardless of the incentive to make accurate judgments, and that (b) Type 4 inferences underlie judgments only when an incentive to perform well is provided, regardless of P's liking for A. If this were the case, balance principles could account for the results obtained. However, it seems equally legitimate to conclude that balance theory is not particularly helpful in either predicting judgmental behavior under the conditions of this study or in describing this behavior after the fact.

V. CONCLUDING REMARKS

In this chapter we have considered a wide range of conditions in which the relation between two objects is inferred from information about these objects' relations to a third. It is clear from the research bearing upon these inferences that the applicability of balance principles depends greatly upon both (a) the type of objects about which information is presented and inferences are made, and (b) the situational context surrounding these inferences. At the beginning of the chapter we speculated that balance principles are likely to describe social inference processes to the extent that the sets of relations implied by these principles provide a cognitive summary of previous experience with the type of objects involved in the relations. To this extent, it is not surprising that the predictive accuracy of balance principles is highly contingent upon the types of elements about which information is provided. Several general and specific contingencies have been noted in this chapter, and many others have undoubtedly been suggested to the reader in the course of this discussion. Unfortunately, the present state of our knowledge makes it difficult to develop a general conceptual understanding of these contingencies.

In analyzing the inference processes described in this chapter, we have often suggested various alternative assumptions that subjects may make when evaluating an object or when predicting others' evaluations of the object. These assumptions have generally pertained to the implications of the information presented for various favorable and unfavorable attributes of the object to be evaluated. To the extent that these implications can be identified, they appear to have approximately additive effects on the inferences being made, and thus these effects can potentially be described by general models of information integration such as those discussed in Chapter 9. However, the contribution of any given piece of information may depend greatly upon the type of information presented with it. Moreover, as we suggested in our analysis of Type 4 inferences, the same piece of information may have different implications, depending upon which of several criteria a subject bases his inference. Similar considerations of course apply to other types of inferences. For example, a subject who is told that P dislikes A and that A likes B may infer that B is "popular," and therefore that P likes B; or, he may infer that P dislikes A *because* A likes B, and therefore that P dislikes B. Or, he may believe that people who dislike one person (A) are apt to dislike others, and thus he may predict that P dislikes B for this reason. Inferences based upon either of the last two assumptions would conform to predictions based upon balance principles, while inferences based upon the first assumption would not. The likelihood that subjects made these assumptions, and thus the conditions under which balance principles are likely to apply, may depend greatly upon the type of objects involved. This example raises again a point that we have belabored before, particularly in discussing inferences when the subject himself is an element in the configuration. That is, balance principles may describe inferences accurately in some situations, but not for the reasons that balance theory implies. Even if balance principles generated accurate predictions of social inference phenomena in a given set of situations, their theoretical significance would be limited unless they could be closely tied to assumptions that subjects typically make in arriving at these inferences.

In our discussion, we have tended to focus upon the contribution of only one inference criterion at any given time. In fact, several criteria may be used simultaneously by subjects in arriving at their judgments. Thus, the more appropriate question may be not whether one or another criterion is used, but rather what factors determine the relative contributions of these criteria.

If the above conclusions are valid, there appear to be two related objectives for further research on the kind of inference processes described in this chapter. First, the set of alternative assumptions that subjects make in arriving at different types of inferences must be circumscribed, and a method for identifying the magnitude of their contributions must be developed. Second, the characteristics of persons and objects about which information is presented and inferences are made must be classified conceptually, and their effects upon the assumptions used by subjects in making inferences must be investigated systematically. While the attainment of these goals may seem formidable, an approach suggested by the work of Robert Abelson and his students may greatly facilitate this task. We will discuss this work in Chapter 12. First, however, let us consider a somewhat different issue that we have thus far ignored, and to which the approach to be described in Chapter 12 is also relevant, namely, the effect of behavior upon inferences about oneself and others.

11
EFFECTS OF ONE'S OWN BEHAVIOR UPON JUDGMENTS OF SELF AND OTHERS

Thus far we have carefully ignored a large body of theory and research on the effect that a person's own behavior may have upon his beliefs and attitudes. In light of the substantial interest in this question in recent years, a separate consideration of this question is justified.

Two general theoretical approaches to information processing have been discussed in this book, both of which have implications for the effects of behavior-related cognitions upon other cognitions. The first approach is based upon the assumption that the coexistence of inconsistent cognitions is aversive and, therefore, gives rise to cognitive reorganization. Thus, if a person's (P's) belief that he has recently behaved in a certain way is inconsistent with other, previously formed cognitions, these latter cognitions may be changed in order to eliminate this inconsistency. This approach has been formalized by Festinger (1957) as cognitive dissonance theory.

A second general approach assumes that P's judgment of an object O is based upon attributes that have implications for this judgment. When new information about O is presented, its implications are integrated with those of previous information about O, and therefore P's judgment of O may change. One source of information may be P's own behavior toward O. For example, friendly responses to O suggests that O has favorable attributes, or that P's attitude toward O is favorable. Note that P's behavior may provide information not only about O's attributes, but also about P's own attributes. In a simple case, if P has observed himself decide to go without eating for a period of time, he may infer that he is "not hungry." This hypothesis is similar in its implications to the James-Lange theory of emotion. That is, a person does not run because he is afraid; rather, he is afraid because he runs. A formalization of this approach has been proposed by Bem (1965).

A third formulation, which incorporates aspects of both dissonance theory and Bem's self-perception theory, has been outlined by Secord and Backman (1961). These authors assume that the attributes used by P to describe himself depend upon both the implications of his own behavior toward others and the implications of others' behaviors toward him. A state of congruence exists when the implications of information from both sources are consistent with P's self-perception. When these implications differ, incongruence exists, which P tends to eliminate by changing his interpretation of the information to make it internally consistent or, alternatively, by changing his self-perception.

Predictions based upon all three approaches are often similar. In the pages that follow, we will first state as clearly as possible the assumptions underlying each formulation and how it is used to generate predictions, and we will then consider the implications of representative research that bears upon the formulation.

I. COGNITIVE DISSONANCE THEORY

No other theoretical formulation has generated the amount of research that cognitive dissonance theory has inspired over the past decade and a half. This fact alone testifies to its importance in the area of attitude and belief change. While both the theory and the research bearing upon it have been amply criticized (e.g., Chapanis & Chapanis, 1964; Zajonc, 1968), the diversity of its implications and its ability to generate predictions that are not intuitively obvious continue to capture the imagination of a large number of researchers. The basic tenets of the theory, and the research generated by them, are well summarized by Zajonc (1968) and perhaps do not need extensive elaboration here. However, the approach we will take below may help to formalize the theory and to provide a mechanism for discussing certain basic theoretical points that deserve attention.

A. Theoretical Considerations

1. *Definition and Measurement of Dissonance.* According to Festinger (1957, p. 13), two cognitions are *dissonant* if, considering these two cognitions alone, the opposite of one follows from the other. More simply, two cognitions X and Y are dissonant if X implies Y′ (not-Y). Similarly, two cognitions are *consonant* if one follows from the other; that is, X and Z are consonant if X implies Z. Thus, a particular cognition, in this case X, may be dissonant with some cognitions and consonant with others.

It is important to note at the outset that the "implications" used to define consonant and dissonant elements are not necessarily logical. For example, consider the two cognitions "I believe in God" and "I do not go to church." If a subject thinks that belief in God implies going to church, these two cognitions would be dissonant. And yet there is no logical necessity that belief in God implies going to church. It just so happens that this particular subject, for whatever reason, assumes this to be the case. For others, who do not agree that belief in God implies going to church, the two cognitions in question would not be dissonant.

The above observation suggests an elaboration of the definition of dissonance proposed by Festinger. That is, X and Y are dissonant cognitions to a subject P if P simultaneously holds the *three* beliefs comprising the illogical syllogism [X; X implies not-Y; Y]. Alternatively, X and Z are consonant to the extent that P simultaneously holds the cognitions comprising the logically valid syllogism [X; X implies Z; Z]. Considered in this light, the construct of dissonance is conceptually identical to a condition of cognitive inconsistency as postulated by McGuire (1960) and described in Chapter 4, that is, a condition in which P's belief in a conclusion Y is not logically consistent with his beliefs in logically related premises.

In most laboratory studies designed to test dissonance theory, direct evidence of the existence of beliefs necessary to establish a condition of dissonance is not obtained. Typically, the cognition corresponding to Y in the above example is manipulated, and the cognition corresponding to X is assessed. However, the cognition *X implies not-Y* is *neither* manipulated *nor* assessed. Instead, it is generally assumed *a priori* that there is general agreement among subjects, and between subjects and the experimenter, that two cognitions imply the opposite of one another and therefore are dissonant. As we shall see, the need to make this assumption can often create problems in interpreting the results of such studies.

Many different beliefs may be related to a given cognition, some of which are consonant with it and others of which are dissonant. Moreover, certain of these beliefs may be strongly held, while others are relatively weak. Under these conditions, is it possible to obtain an index of the overall dissonance associated with the cognitions involved? To consider this possibility, let's take a specific example. Suppose P is confronted with a decision about whether to continue or to stop smoking cigarettes. P may have certain beliefs that "imply" he should smoke. For example, he may believe that cigarettes taste good, that they calm his nerves, or that they make him look socially sophisticated. Other beliefs may imply that he should not smoke. For example, P may believe that smoking is bad for one's health, that it costs too much, and that advertisements for cigarettes are obnoxious. The beliefs consonant and dissonant with the cognition "I smoke" (X) may be tabulated as follows:

$$X \text{ (``I Smoke'')}$$

Cognitions consonant with X (c_x)	Cognitions dissonant with X (d_x)
Cigarettes taste good (5)	Smoking is bad for one's health (10)
Smoking calms the nerves (4)	Cigarettes cost too much (3)
Smoking makes me seem sophisticated (1)	Cigarette advertisements are obnoxious (2)

The cognitions consonant and dissonant with the cognition associated with the alternative choice of behavior, "I do not smoke" (X'), can also be tabulated:

X' ("I do not smoke")

$c_{x'}$	$d_{x'}$
Smoking is bad for one's health (10)	Cigarettes taste good (5)
	Smoking calms the nerves (4)
Cigarettes cost too much (3)	Smoking makes me seem
Cigarette advertisements are obnoxious (2)	sophisticated (1)

Festinger defined the overall dissonance associated with a cognition X (D_x) to be some function of the proportion of all relevant cognitions that are dissonant with X, each weighted by its importance or intensity. The need to take into account differences in the importance of the cognitions involved is intuitively obvious. For example, in the situation being considered, P would experience more cognitive conflict by deciding to smoke if he both believes that smoking is bad for his health and is extremely concerned about his health than if he either believes that smoking is unlikely to be dangerous or is not concerned about his health. Dissonance theory is not explicit about how the weights attached to different cognitions are determined. However, it seems reasonable to assume that the weight attached to a cognition pertaining to X is a function of both the strength of P's belief that the statement involved is true and the strength of his belief that the statement, if true, implies he should or should not engage in the behavior described by X. (Thus, the weight attached to the cognition "Smoking is bad for my health" would be determined by both P's belief that smoking is in fact bad for his health and his belief that if it is bad for his health, he shouldn't smoke.) The strength of this latter belief may be reflected by P's judgment of the desirability of the behavioral outcome involved (in this case, "bad health"). In any event, if the relative weights attached to the various cognitions in our example are those shown in parentheses in the above schemata, the proportion of dissonance associated with the cognition X could be estimated from the proportion of all cognitions that are dissonant with X, each weighted by its relative importance. That is,

$$D_X = \frac{\Sigma d_x}{\Sigma c_x + \Sigma d_x} = \frac{10 + 3 + 2}{(5 + 4 + 1) + (10 + 3 + 2)} = .60 \qquad (11.1)$$

Similarly, the proportion of dissonance associated with the cognition X' would be

$$D_{X'} = \frac{\Sigma d_{x'}}{\Sigma c_{x'} + \Sigma d_{x'}} = .40$$

In this case, of course, $D_x + D_{x'} = 1$.

In the above example and also those to follow, the cognitions X and X′ describe alternative behaviors or choices. Most experiments designed to test dissonance theory are constructed on the basis of this assumption. That is, a subject P becomes committed to a given behavioral alternative, and changes are predicted in beliefs and attitudes, based upon their assumed consonance or dissonance with P's cognition that he has made this commitment. In principle, any cognition (e.g., "smoking is bad for one's health") could be identified as X. The reason for choosing a behavior-related cognition may be more practical than theoretical. It is difficult under normal circumstances to change a subject's belief that he is or has been engaging in a behavior. This is particularly true if the behavior, or the decision to behave in a certain way, has already occurred. Thus, when one of the cognitions of concern is related to a behavior, dissonance is most likely to be reduced by changing one or more of the other cognitions associated with the behavior-relevant cognition. The tabulating procedure described above helps to predict the nature of these changes, as we shall see.

2. *Basic Principles.* We are now ready to state the two basic principles of dissonance theory that will allow us to generate specific predictions of cognitive change. These principles are simply stated, but are extremely powerful.

1. Dissonance, as defined in the manner described above[1], is aversive. Thus, a subject will tend to avoid situations that give rise to dissonance. Moreover. he will tend to reduce any dissonance that exists by changing one or more of the beliefs that contribute to it.

2. The greater the proportion of dissonance (D_x) that exists at any given time, the more aversive it is, and thus the greater will be the tendency to reduce it by changing relevant beliefs.

Let us apply these principles to the hypothetical subject described previously. First, what choice of behavior would P make? Since dissonance is aversive and tends to be avoided, P should choose the alternative that produces the least proportion of dissonance. In other words, since $D_{x'} < D_x$, he should decide not to smoke. However, having made this decision, P still experiences dissonance $(= D_{x'})$ and thus should attempt to reduce it. From Eq. (11.1) it is clear that there are two general ways of doing this:

---

[1]Here and subsequently in this discussion, when applied to a situation or to an entire set of cognitions, the term "dissonance" refers to the *proportion* of dissonance existing within the set of beliefs, or D_x as defined in Eq. (11.1). This use of the term, which is consistent with common usage, should be distinguished from its use in referring to specific cognitions that are consistent or inconsistent in their implications.

a.   P may reduce the magnitude of $\Sigma d_x'$ by decreasing the subjective weights of the cognitions contributing to this sum. That is, he may decrease his beliefs that cigarettes taste good, that they calm his nerves, or that they make him appear sophisticated. Alternatively, he may decrease his beliefs that these attributes of cigarettes imply that he should smoke. These latter changes may often be reflected by decreases in the beliefs that the attributes are desirable.

b.   P may increase the magnitude of $\Sigma c_x'$ by increasing the weights of cognitions consonant with X'. That is, P may increase his belief that smoking is bad for his health, that cigarettes cost too much, or that cigarette ads are obnoxious. Alternatively, he may increase his beliefs that these factors imply not smoking. Another way of increasing $\Sigma c_x'$ is to increase the *number* of consonant elements. This could be done in several ways. For example, P may seek and read new information supporting his decision not to smoke. Alternatively, if he believes that *other* persons' not smoking is consonant with his own decision not to smoke, P may proselytize and attempt to convince others to stop smoking.

Since there are a variety of ways of reducing dissonance in a situation, it may often be difficult to predict which avenue will be chosen at any given time. Presumably several avenues are used simultaneously, since the only way to eliminate dissonance entirely is to reduce Σd_x to 0. However, this may be done by either changing beliefs that the dissonant assertions are true or by changing beliefs that if they are true, they imply the opposite of X. Thus, for example, P could decrease to zero the weight attached to the cognition "smoking calms the nerves" by either decreasing his belief that smoking does in fact calm the nerves, or by decreasing his belief that even if it does calm the nerves, he should not smoke. The latter change might be reflected by a decrease in P's belief that "calm nerves" is a desirable state of affairs. Which type of change is more likely in any given instance is not predictable from dissonance theory.

Certain types of predictions are reasonable, however. For instance, suppose in our hypothetical example that an eccentric uncle now offers P $10,000 to stop smoking. Presumably this would add an element (e.g., "I will receive $10,000 by not smoking") to those that are already consonant with the cognition "I am not smoking" and thus would reduce the value of $D_{x'}$ below its original value. Assuming that P would have stopped smoking even without this additional inducement, would he change his beliefs more or less as a result of this incentive? According to Principle 2 of dissonance theory, the answer is clear. Since a lower proportion of dissonance is associated with not smoking when the incentive is offered, there should be less tendency to reduce dissonance under this condition, and therefore there should be less change in beliefs associated with the behavior-related cognition.

B. Methodological and Conceptual Ambiguities in Interpreting Research on Dissonance Phenomena

In the pages that follow we shall consider the implications of dissonance theory for attitude and belief change in several different types of situations and shall discuss representative research bearing upon these implications. Before we embark on this task, however, it is worthwhile to mention some general difficulties encountered in interpreting this research.

1. *Operational versus Subjective Measures of Dissonance.* Most tests of dissonance theory follow a similar pattern. That is, a subject is required to decide how to behave in a situation where certain factors argue in favor of a given choice and other factors argue against this choice. Several experimental conditions are run, which presumably differ with respect to the amount of dissonance experienced by the subject. These differences are typically induced by providing differential justification for one of the choices (for example, by varying the money offered for making the choice, the severity of sanctions against it, the attractiveness of alternative choices, etc.). Changes in cognitions assumed to be relevant to the choice (e.g., beliefs that the choice was correct, that the outcomes of the choice are desirable, etc.) are then observed.

While the procedure described above is straightforward, the results are sometimes hard to interpret. While the proportion of dissonance in a situation is defined operationally in terms of situational variables, the actual determinant of attitude change is of course the dissonance subjectively experienced by P in these situations. Though this is fine, a problem arises in interpreting negative results. That is, suppose that in a particular case belief change does not occur in the direction predicted by dissonance theory, or that the conditions intended to produce different amounts of dissonance do not produce different amounts of belief change. What is one to conclude? One conclusion is simply that the theory is wrong; that is, although subjects experience dissonance, they do not reduce it by altering dissonance-producing cognitions. A second conclusion may be that dissonance was not in fact induced by the experimental procedure, or that the manipulation performed did not in fact produce different amounts of dissonance. To distinguish between these alternative interpretations, one must have an indication of the amount of dissonance experienced by subjects that is independent of their belief change. Such a measure is difficult to obtain and therefore is rarely if ever attempted. Without such an index, however, it becomes effectively impossible to disprove the theory. If results do not come out in the direction predicted by the theory, one can always argue that dissonance was not really present. It is of course tautological to use a demonstration of the phenomenon being predicted as a criterion for validating the existence of the conditions hypothesized to produce the phenomenon. This point, while obvious, may be worth making explicit in light of the substantial discussion in the literature of the "conditions that produce dissonance" (cf., Brehm & Cohen, 1962; Collins & Hoyt, 1972). In nearly all such discussions, the ultimate criterion for determining whether or not P experiences dissonance is whether or not he behaves as the theory predicts he should.

2. *Tolerance for Dissonance: The Need to Postulate a "Dissonance Threshold."* The critical reader may have already identified a logical inconsistency between the implications of Principles 1 and 2 as we have stated them. That is, without introducing some further assumptions, the hypothesis that the tendency to reduce dissonance through belief change increases with the magnitude of the dissonance experienced is partially contradictory to the hypothesis that *any* cognitive dissonance tends to be reduced. To see this more clearly, let us return to our earlier example in which P decides to stop smoking, and in one case receives a large monetary reward for doing so, but in the other case makes his decision without being promised a reward. Presumably the proportion of dissonance is less in the first case than in the second. However, if dissonance is aversive, why should not P reduce dissonance to *zero*, regardless of the magnitude of this proportion, and thus decrease equally in both conditions his beliefs that smoking tastes good, calms the nerves, and makes him seem sophisticated?

There are at least two answers to this question, neither of which is made explicit in typical discussions of the theory and its applications. One is suggested by the possibility that the cognitive reorganization necessary to reduce dissonance, which takes time to occur, proceeds more rapidly when the initial proportion of dissonance is high. Thus, at any point in time, cognitive reorganization is more apt to be detected when the proportion of dissonance is high than when it is low. A second possibility is that subjects actually do *not* reduce dissonance to zero but rather reduce it only to below a certain level, or *threshold,* that they can tolerate. For example, suppose in our example that P's tolerance threshold is a level of dissonance (D_x) of .1. Then, in the absence of the large reward, $D_x{}'$, which is initially .40 (see p. 377), will decrease by .3. However, suppose that when P is offered a substantial reward to stop smoking, the consonant cognition associated with this reward has a weight of 25. Then, the proportion of dissonance experienced by P under this condition would have an initial value of 10/50 or .20 and thus must be reduced by only .10 in order to reach P's tolerance level. The weights attached to dissonant cognitions would have to change less to reach this level in the second condition than in the first. Thus, *if* dissonance is not reduced any further once threshold is reached, greater change in beliefs would be predicted in the former condition than in the latter, consistent with Principle 2.

Unfortunately, while the assumption that dissonance below a certain minimum level is tolerated (and not reduced) eliminates conceptual ambiguities surrounding Principle 2, it creates problems when applying the theory empirically. That is, unless the dissonance threshold of the majority of subjects can be determined *a priori,* it is impossible to tell whether the absence of belief change in a particular experimental condition indicates that the theory is invalid or whether the proportion of dissonance induced was simply below most subjects' thresholds. This reemphasizes the need for a quantitative measure of the amount of dissonance experienced by subjects—a measure that can be obtained independently of the experimenta' manipulations assumed to produce this dissonance.

3. *Individual Differences in Dissonance Reduction.* A related problem concerns the interpretation of individual differences in the tendency to reduce dissonance. In most situations, some subjects will change their beliefs in the direction predicted by dissonance theory while others will not. At least, subjects will differ in the amount of change they manifest. Such differences could in part be the result of measurement error. However, they could also result from two additional factors: individual differences in the amount of dissonance experienced, or differences in the "tolerance" for dissonance (the tendency to reduce a given amount of dissonance; cf., Glass, 1968; Harvey, 1965). While either factor could empirically create differences in belief changes in a given experimental condition, the assumption of individual differences in tolerance for dissonance would be *theoretically* justified only if one postulates that *in general* dissonance below a certain threshold is not reduced, and that persons vary with respect to the magnitude of this threshold. Otherwise, to argue that only certain types of persons reduce dissonance would, in effect, be to question the validity of the general assumption that a state of dissonance is aversive and tends to be reduced. While this argument could empirically be valid, it would be embarrassing to the original formulation of dissonance theory and would also decrease its usefulness.

Subjects may often appear to differ in their "tolerance" for dissonance because they use alternative procedures for reducing it, some of which are not detected by the measurement procedures used in the experiment. For example, if subjects are induced to stop smoking they should reduce dissonance by decreasing the weight attached to the dissonant cognition "cigarettes taste good." They may accomplish this either by changing their beliefs that cigarettes do in fact taste good, or by changing their beliefs that "good taste" is desirable. Thus, if only one of these latter beliefs is assessed, subjects who reduce dissonance by the alternative method will not appear to be affected by it or will appear to "tolerate" it.

4. *Informational Aspects of Experimental Manipulations: An Alternative Interpretation of Dissonance Phenomena.* An additional and important difficulty in interpreting many empirical tests of dissonance theory should be noted. That is, while in experiments the changes in beliefs predicted by dissonance theory are usually straightforward, these changes are often identical to those one would expect if subjects use the situational characteristics assumed to affect dissonance as cues to the beliefs and expectations held by the experimenter and comply with these implicit

"demands." Although this possibility is elaborated in Chapter 1, let us reconsider it briefly in the present context.

As an example, suppose an experimenter either offers a subject P a reward for engaging in a certain behavior or threatens him with punishment for not engaging in it. This could mean two things. First, it could indicate that the experimenter personally considers the behavior to be important or desirable. Second, it could indicate that the experimenter believes that P dislikes the behavior and would normally not engage in it. If P interprets the incentive in the first way and attempts to respond in a manner the experimenter considers appropriate, he should report his attitude toward the behavior (or toward behavior-related objects) as more favorable when the incentive is high than when it is low. However, if he interprets the incentive in the second way, he should report his attitude toward the behavior as relatively less favorable when the incentive for manifesting it is high. This latter prediction is identical to that made by dissonance theory. Which interpretation is likely to be made by a subject, and thus the direction of the effects of different incentives upon the beliefs and attitudes he reports, undoubtedly depends upon the particular situational conditions in which the incentive is offered. Although certain of these contingencies were suggested in Chapter 1, a much clearer understanding of when a subject is likely to comply with an experimenter's implicit expectancies, and how these conditions differ from those in which the subject conforms to the experimenter's implicit values or attitudes, is necessary in order to place much confidence in a "demand compliance" formulation. As the above example suggests, without such an understanding it is often possible to interpret results after the fact as consistent with such a formulation, regardless of how they turn out. Ultimately, one must obtain independent evidence that subjects do in fact infer differences either in the experimenter's own attitude or in his expectancies for *their* attitudes from the information with which they are provided under different conditions. We also must be able to predict *a priori* when subjects are apt to respond in a manner that is consistent with one rather than the other.

Despite these problems, it is often instructive to reinterpret the experimental manipulations intended to affect dissonance as manipulations of what the experimenter desires or expects. It is also instructive to consider how well the actual effects of such manipulations support the hypothesis that subjects respond so as to conform to these expectancies and wishes. It should be noted that experimental manipulations of variables other than the incentive for engaging in an activity are often susceptible to such a reinterpretation. For example, consider two hypothetical situations in which an experimenter offers a child (P) a small reward to eat a vegetable that P dislikes. In one case, P is subsequently told that his parents would be informed about what vegetable he had eaten, and in the other case this information is not given. In both cases the experimenter may implicitly convey to P that he personally thinks the vegetable is desirable, simply by virtue of asking P to eat it. Alternatively, he may convey to P the hypothesis that "once you try a food, you often find it isn't as bad as you expected it to be." In any event, the additional information that P's parents will be told about it should further increase P's belief that the experimenter thinks the food is either good or important to eat, and that P should probably eat it at home. Thus, P should rate the food as more likeable in this condition than when P is not told that his parents will be informed. This is, of course, the same prediction made by dissonance theory and is consistent with results actually reported by Brehm (1959).

In the pages that follow, we will consider several representative studies designed to test one or another implication of dissonance theory, and we will assess both the support these studies provide for the theory and the extent to which they are consistent with the hypothesis that subjects respond in a way that they believe is consistent with experimental "demands." Finally, we will consider a few studies in which predictions based upon the two formulations differ and evaluate the relative support for each.

C. Effects of Reward and Punishment for Counterattitudinal Behavior

1. *Implications of Dissonance Theory.* Suppose P is offered an incentive to engage in a behavior B that he considers undesirable or that contradicts certain of his attitudes and values. This incentive may be in the form of either a reward for engaging in B or a threat of punishment for not doing so. Confronted with a choice, P will either decide to do B or not. First, suppose that P decides not to manifest the behavior. Then, a simplified dissonance table would be:

$$X \text{ (I am not doing B)}$$

c_x	d_x
B is bad	I would be rewarded for doing B (or punished for not doing it)

Clearly in this situation, D_x would be reduced by increasing the belief that B is bad. Now presumably the weight attached to the dissonant belief, and therefore D_x, increases with the amount of reward offered for doing B (or the amount of punishment for not doing it). Thus, the greater the magnitude of the incentive, the greater will be D_x, and therefore the greater will be the increase in P's belief that B is bad.

The above table is applicable only when the proportion of dissonance associated with not doing B is less than the proportion of dissonance associated with doing it. If the magnitude of the incentive continues to increase, a point will be reached at which the proportion of dissonance

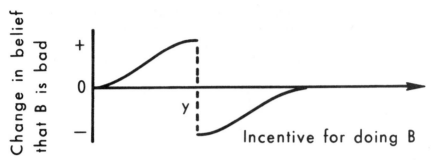

Fig. 11.1. Predicted change in belief that B is bad as a function of the amount of incentive for doing B, assuming that the minimal incentive required for B to occur is at point Y.

associated with not doing B is greater than that associated with doing it. At this point, P will presumably reverse his decision, resulting in the following:

$$X' \text{ (I am doing B)}$$

$c_{x'}$	$d_{x'}$
I am rewarded for B (or punished for not doing it)	B is bad

Under these conditions, P's beliefs that B is bad would decrease. However, as the incentive provided becomes still greater, the value of $D_{x'}$ should become less, and thus the belief that B is bad should decrease less.

These predictions, considered in combination, are interesting. Fig. 11.1 shows the theoretical amount of change in P's beliefs that B is bad as a function of the amount of incentive to do B, assuming that P does not do B when the incentive is low but decides to do B once the incentive reaches point Y. At Y, the proportion of dissonance associated with doing B and the proportion associated with not doing it are equal. The direction of change in P's belief is difficult to predict at this point, since it depends upon P's choice of behavior. However, the *magnitude* of change, in whichever direction, should be greater than that occurring when either more or less incentive is provided. This analysis has practical implications. Suppose a mother wishes to induce her child (P) to engage in some behavior (B) that she considers desirable but that P regards as unpleasant. She attempts to induce P to engage in B by punishing him for not doing so. How much punishment should she threaten to administer in order to produce the maximum increase in P's attitude toward B, and thus in his likelihood of doing B in the absence of surveillance? According to dissonance theory, the least amount of punishment necessary to induce P to do B will produce the greatest change in the desired direction. However, it is crucial that she be successful in her attempt to encourage P to do B. If P decides not to do B despite the anticipated punishment, his belief that B is bad will increase, and this increase will be greater when the punishment to be administered is greater. In other words, the mother is worse off by threatening to administer punishment that is ineffective than by not threatening to punish P at all. The moral of the story of course is that if one wishes to maximize an underlying change in another's belief through use of reward or punishment, one should be sure that the incentive offered is sufficient to produce the behavior desired, but that is not any greater than necessary to produce this behavior.

Effects of freedom of choice. An important theoretical issue, discussed at length by Brehm and Cohen (1962), should be noted in this context. These authors maintain that dissonance occurs only when the subject feels free to choose between two or more behavioral alternatives. If he feels that he has no alternative but to behave in a certain way, he should experience no dissonance, and therefore following the behavior he should not necessarily change his beliefs in either direction. While this point of view has been widely accepted, it implies a discontinuity between dissonance arousing and nondissonance arousing situations that seems illogical and is perhaps unnecessary. In principle, P *always* has a choice as to how he should behave; although he may be threatened with death or severe bodily harm unless he engages in a certain behavior, he technically must decide whether to engage in the behavior or not. The fact that in such a situation the arguments for choosing one alternative over the other are overwhelming is not to say that P has no choice.

In contrast, the analysis of dissonance phenomena described in this chapter treats the cognition associated with the amount of coercion (or amount of reward) as simply one element in a "cognitive summary table" of all beliefs that are consonant or dissonant with the cognition that P has chosen to engage in the behavior in question. Clearly, if the coercion is consonant with engaging in the behavior, and if this coercion is very great, a very low proportion of dissonance may be associated with the behavior. However, there would be *no* dissonance only if there were no existing cognitions that implied the opposite of the behavior manifested. As long as P maintains a belief that the behavior is "wrong," or is aware of any other reason why he should not manifest the behavior, *some* dissonance necessarily exists and, provided it is above subjects' "tolerance threshold," theoretically should be reduced through belief change.

With these considerations in mind, let us review some representative studies of the effects on behavior-related attitudes of incentives for choosing a behavior. Let us also assess the support for dissonance theory provided by this research.

2. *Effects of Positive Incentives.* To recapitulate, dissonance theory predicts that the greater the reward offered for engaging in an activity, the less effect the activity will have upon beliefs and attitudes to which it pertains. Two early studies support this hypothesis. In the first (Festinger & Carlsmith, 1959), each subject (P) after performing a tedious task was

induced for pay of either $1 or $20 to convince another that the task was actually interesting. Then, P reported his personal evaluation of the task. As predicted, P rated the task as more interesting under the low pay (high dissonance) condition. In a later study by Cohen (Brehm & Cohen, 1962), P was paid $.50, $1, $5, or $10 for writing an essay supporting a position with which he personally disagreed. As expected, beliefs in the position advocated generally increased, but they increased less as the magnitude of the incentive became greater.

Results of a study by Brehm and Crocker (Brehm & Cohen, 1962) are somewhat more difficult to account for on the basis of dissonance theory alone. In this study, subjects who had not eaten for several hours were asked not to eat for another 12 hours, under conditions of either no pay or pay of $5. In this case, P's belief that he is hungry is presumably dissonant with his decision not to eat, while his belief that he will receive pay for not eating is consonant with it. Thus, P's belief that he is hungry should theoretically decrease in both conditions, but the magnitude of this decrease should be relatively greater in the no-pay condition. In fact, hunger ratings decreased in the no-pay condition as expected. but *increased* in the high-pay condition. This latter change would presumably increase the proportion of dissonance in the situation.

While Brehm and Crocker's findings are partially contradictory to those predicted by dissonance theory, they are potentially consistent with the "demand compliance" interpretation described in Chapter 1 and reviewed briefly earlier in this chapter. That is, subjects who are offered high pay to continue without eating are likely to infer that the experimenter expects them to be very hungry, and thus they must be paid handsomely in order to continue without food. In contrast, subjects who are not offered pay may infer that the experimenter expects them not to be very hungry. Thus, the first group of subjects may report greater hunger after being asked to go without eating, while the second group of subjects may report less hunger. Results of the two studies by Cohen and by Festinger and Carlsmith are also consistent with an information-processing interpretation; the more pay a subject is offered to advocate a certain position, the more likely he is to infer that the experimenter expects him personally to disagree with the position, and thus to be unwilling to advocate it without some inducement. Therefore, he should report attitudes that are relatively less in agreement with the position he has advocated, as the aforementioned studies indicate.

"Dissonance" versus "Reinforcement" Effects. A controversial issue surrounding dissonance research on incentive effects, noted in Chapter 1, may be worth mentioning again here. That is, while studies such as those described above (see also Nuttin, 1966) have demonstrated a "dissonance" effect (a decrease in attitude change with an increase in the incentive offered for counterattitudinal behavior), others (Heslin & Amo, 1972; Rosenberg, 1965; Scott, 1957, 1959) have found a "reinforcement" effect (an increase in

attitude change with an increase in reward offered), and still others (Elms & Janis, 1965; Linder, et al., 1967) have found both. Many explanations have been offered for these apparently conflicting results, several of which are summarized by Zajonc (1968). It is worth noting that in most of the studies of counterattitudinal advocacy in which "reinforcement" effects have been reported, subjects either have agreed to advocate the position before they were informed of the reward they would receive (Linder et al., 1967; Scott, 1957, 1959) or have reported their attitudes to someone other than the person offering the reward (Rosenberg, 1965). In each of these conditions, subjects are less likely to interpret the size of the incentive as an indication that the person to whom attitudes are reported expects them not to believe in the position advocated, and thus the "dissonance" effect is less apt to be detected. (For an elaboration of this argument, see Chapter 1.)

Results that could be interpreted as an indication of compliance with both the expectancies and the wishes of the experimenter were reported by Heslin and Amo (1972) in a study designed to distinguish between dissonance reduction and reinforcement effects. Subjects were asked to prepare a counterattitudinal speech. After agreeing to do so, but before actually preparing the speech, their attitudes toward the position were assessed. Since the experimenter was ostensibly collecting speeches on both sides of the issue, his request to advocate the position is unlikely to have been interpreted as an indication of his own attitude toward it; however, subjects who agree to advocate a position and are subsequently asked for their attitudes may infer that the experimenter expects them personally to agree with the point of view they volunteered to express (or at least, not to oppose this position strongly). To this extent, they should report their attitudes as being more favorable toward the position following the decision to advocate it than before. After actually giving their speech, subjects were either praised or criticized for the manner in which they delivered it, and their attitudes toward the position were again assessed. If subjects interpret praise and criticism from the experimenter as indications that the experimenter personally likes and dislikes to hear them advocate the position, respectively, these reinforcers should have positive and negative effects upon their reported attitudes, and these effects should add to the earlier effects of conforming to the experimenter's expectancies. Heslin and Amo's results, shown in Fig. 11.2, are consistent with this interpretation. That is, subjects increased their attitudes toward the position after agreeing to advocate it, and then, relative to this postcommitment attitude, either increased or decreased their attitude again after delivering the speech, depending upon the type of reinforcement they received.

While the results of the above studies are consistent with a demand compliance hypothesis, those of other recent studies of incentive effects are more difficult to account for in this manner. For example, Sherman (1970) offered subjects either a choice or no choice about whether to write a counterattitudinal essay and paid them either nothing or $2.50 for doing so.

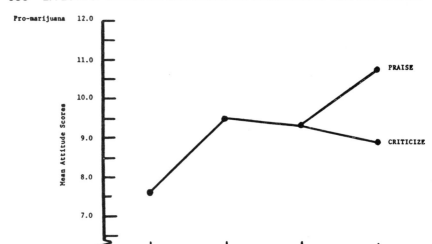

Fig. 11.2. Mean Attitude as a function of reinforcement and the point at which attitudes are assessed (reprinted from Heslin & Amo, 1972, p. 238).

This pay either was offered before subjects wrote the essay (prepay conditions) or was given to them "unexpectedly" after the essay was completed (postpay conditions). Since the pay was ostensibly being offered to participants regardless of which position they advocated in the essay, neither pay condition provided a reliable cue to the experimenter's personal attitude toward the position being advocated. Moreover, the postessay attitudes were reported to an experimenter other than the administrator of the task. Although apparently familiar with the essay-writing project, this new experimenter was ostensibly unaware of the position the subject advocated in his essay. Nevertheless, subjects who were given an opportunity to refuse to write the essay changed their attitudes in the direction advocated to a greater extent under no-pay conditions than under either pay condition. In contrast, subjects who were told to advocate the position, without being given an explicit opportunity to refuse, changed their attitudes less under the no-pay condition than under the two pay conditions. These findings, which imply that dissonance reduction occurs under free choice conditions but reinforcement effects occur under no (low) choice conditions, are hard to explain on the basis of a demand compliance formulation. However, attitude change was similar in magnitude under prepay and postpay conditions, in contrast to the substantial differences between analogous conditions in experiments where pay is more likely to be a cue to experimenter expectancies and wishes (e.g., Linder et al., 1967; see Chapter 1). This suggests that demand factors may have affected the results of these latter studies.

Contingencies of personal responsibility and behavioral consequences. Based upon a comprehensive review and analysis of the forced compliance literature, Collins and Hoyt (1972) hypothesized that monetary incentives

TABLE 11.1

Mean Attitude Change Based upon Responses to
Overlapping Items on Immediate Posttest and Pretest
(adapted from Collins and Hoyt, 1972, pp. 576-577)

Posttest	Low responsibility		High responsibility	
	$.50	$2.50	$.50	$2.50
A. Immediate				
High consequences	1.6	3.7	7.2	4.25
Low consequences	3.3	.9	2.45	2.8
B. Delayed				
High consequences	−1.2	−2.5	8.7	.8
Low consequences	2.6	1.8	−.7	2.5

have a negative effect upon attitude change only if subjects feel personally responsible for the attitude-related behavior they manifest and believe that their behavior has important consequences for either themselves or others. To test this hypothesis, subjects were offered either high or low pay to write a counterattitudinal essay (an essay opposing unchaperoned coed visiting in college dormitory rooms). They were told either that the essay would be used by administrators in deciding upon a visitation policy (high consequences), or that it would be used as a "historical report" and would not be considered by the administration (low consequences). Moreover, they were told explicitly by the experimenter that they were either responsible or not responsible for any effect the essay would have. After writing the essay, they completed an opinion questionnaire containing several items pertaining to the issue. Results appeared to depend upon whether the items on the posttest were the same as or different from those contained in the pretest (administered three weeks before as part of an anonymous survey). Results pertaining to "overlapping" items, summarized in Table 11.1A, showed that attitude change was greatest under the high responsibility, high consequences, low pay condition and least under the low responsibility, low consequences, high pay condition. While these results are consistent with the authors' predictions, other aspects of the data are difficult to explain. For example, no interactions of the three variables were significant in analyses of responses to overlapping items, while several interactions (the nature of which was not reported) occurred when both overlapping and nonoverlapping items were included. Moreover, the main effect of pay was significant when all items were included but was negligible when only overlapping items were included. The reason for these differences, and the extent of their consistency with dissonance theory, are unclear. Also, Table 11.1 shows that monetary incentive had a negative effect upon attitude change under high responsibility, high consequences conditions, but it *also* had a negative effect under low responsibility, low consequences conditions, and had a *positive* effect under low responsibility, high consequences conditions! The nature of the contingency of responsibility and consequences upon incentive effects is therefore somewhat confusing and inconsistent with the implications of dissonance theory. However, it should be noted that "anonymous" questionnaire data collected two weeks after the experiment showed that the effect of incentive under high responsibility, high consequences conditions increased, while its effect under the other two conditions described above diminished (see Table 11.1B). Thus, these latter data are more easily predictable from dissonance theory.

Summary. Although results obtained in early research on the effects of positive incentives are consistent with the hypothesis that subjects comply with experimental "demand" characteristics, as well as with dissonance theory, more recent studies have been less obviously consistent with a demand hypothesis. Nevertheless, the effects of incentives upon subjects' perceptions of these wishes and expectancies, and the role of these perceptions upon subjects' reported attitudes, cannot be completely ignored, as we shall continue to see in the discussion that follows.

3. *Effects of Noncompliance.* In the three studies of counterattitudinal advocacy described above, subjects invariably agreed to advocate the position requested, regardless of whether the incentive offered them was high or low. However, suppose subjects refuse to comply with the request, despite the incentive they are offered for doing so. According to dissonance theory, such subjects should change their attitudes away from the position they are asked to support. Moreover, the magnitude of this change should increase with the value of the incentive they give up by refusing to comply.

To test the above hypotheses, Darley and Cooper (1972) offered college freshmen either high ($1.50) or low ($.50) pay to write an essay advocating the enforcement of "proper" dress for high school students. To insure that subjects would typically refuse to comply with the request, despite the monetary incentive, the essay-writing task was purportedly unrelated to the experiment being conducted, the administrator of the task was ostensibly not enthusiastic about his job, and the task was attributed to a sponsor (a local parent association) that subjects were likely to regard unfavorably. After being asked to write the essay and refusing to do so, subjects returned to the "experiment" and completed an attitude questionnaire, one item of which pertained to the essay topic. Compared to control subjects who were not asked to write the essay, high-pay subjects changed their attitude away from the position they were requested to advocate, while low-pay subjects did not.

While Darley and Cooper's results are consistent with predictions of dissonance theory, a "demand compliance" interpretation cannot be discounted. The final attitude questionnaire was administered by a university faculty member who ostensibly had no association with the sponsor of the essay-writing task, and who had no knowledge of whether the subject did or did not comply with the request to write the essay. The question to be raised is therefore whether the implications of the monetary incentive being offered generalize from the sponsor of the essay-writing task to the university faculty member administering the attitude questionnaire. A large incentive in this study may indicate either that the sponsor's own attitude toward the position to be advocated is favorable, or that the sponsor expects subjects to be opposed to this position. However, subjects are unlikely to assume that the attitudes toward proper dress that are held by members of the parents' association are shared by the "liberal" social science faculty at a university. It is more likely that the parent group's expectation that subjects personally oppose the position is shared by university faculty. If subjects make this assumption and report their attitudes accordingly, Darley and Cooper's results would be predicted.

4. *Effects of Negative Incentives.* Two types of studies have been performed to test the effects of negative incentives for engaging in a behavior upon behavior-related attitudes and beliefs. In one type, subjects are induced not to engage in a behavior by threatening them with punishment. Under such conditions, dissonance theory predicts that attitudes toward the behavior will decrease following the decision to forego the behavior, but they will decrease less when the threat is severe than when it is mild. In the second type of study, subjects are induced to engage in an activity despite having to undergo an aversive experience (an "initiation"). Under these conditions, attitudes toward the activity should theoretically increase and should increase more when the initiation is more aversive. Let us consider a study representative of each type.

Devaluation of forbidden activity. The best known study of the first type described above was conducted by Aronson and Carlsmith (1963) using children as subjects. After ranking five attractive toys in order of preference, P was then forbidden to play with the second-ranked toy in one of three ways. In *mild threat* conditions, the experimenter told P that he would have to leave the room for a while and that he would appreciate it if P did not play with the toy during his absence. In *severe threat* conditions, the experimenter told P that he would be extremely angry if P played with the toys during his absence and would take all of the toys and go home. In a third, *control* condition, the experimenter took the second-ranked toy out of the room with him. After the experimenter returned, P again ranked the five toys in order of preference.

According to dissonance theory, the attractiveness of the forbidden toy should decrease under *both* threat conditions described above, but it should decrease relatively more when the threat is mild. As predicted, the proportion of subjects under mild threat conditions who decreased their ranking of the toy was greater (36%) than the proportion who increased their ranking of it (18%). However, under severe threat conditions the majority of the subjects (64%) *increased* their ranking of the toy, and *no* subjects decreased their ranking of it. These latter percentages were identical to those obtained under control conditions.

The increase in attractiveness of the toy under severe threat conditions is difficult to explain on the basis of dissonance theory alone. However, note that both under these conditions and under control conditions, the experimenter may be implicitly telling P that he (the experimenter) attaches considerable importance to the toy. If P conforms to the experimenter's implicit evaluation of the toy under these two conditions, an increase in his ranking of the toy would be expected. In this regard, while preparing a taped laboratory demonstration of Aronson and Carlsmith's study some years ago, the author had occasion to observe children's behavior when the experimenter was out of the room. Although the children exposed to mild threat typically seemed to forget completely about the forbidden toy and to play with the others, severely threatened children often appeared to be preoccupied with the forbidden toy, approaching it and looking it over, and making movements to touch it without actually doing so. While these observations were made of a limited number of subjects and thus must be considered "anecdotal," they are consistent with the assumption that the severe threat conveyed the impression that the toy was very important or desirable, and that the children increased their own preference for the toy as a result.

The behavior observed during the above mentioned demonstrations also provides a clue to the reasons that the forbidden toy may appear to decrease in attractiveness under mild threat conditions. Data collected during the course of the demonstrations suggested that under these conditions children increased their preferences for the particular toys they had played with during the experimenter's absence, and that the *relative* ranking of the forbidden toy decreased as a result. Whether the absolute magnitude of the toy's attractiveness decreased is unclear. Two additional studies should be considered in this regard. First, Freedman (1965) found that at least two months after an experiment comparable to Aronson and Carlsmith's, children exposed to mild threat tended less to play with the forbidden toy in a free choice situation than did children exposed to severe threat. However, if children do in fact adopt preferences for toys they are familiar with, and thus for the toys they originally played with under mild threat conditions, this finding is not too surprising. Second, Lepper (1973) found that decreases in the ranking of the forbidden toy under mild threat conditions were eliminated when subjects were told prior to the administration of threat that other children agreed with their initial ranking. This contingency supports the general hypothesis that when other persons' evaluations are known, subjects use this information as evidence of what is expected of them personally and report their own evaluations accordingly. It is of interest in this context to note that in Lepper's study, as in Aronson and Carlsmith's, attraction to the forbidden toy increased (nonsignificantly) under severe threat conditions, regardless of the information provided about other children's judgments. Information about the experimenter's implicit evaluation of the toy thus appears to have been more influential than explicit information about peers' evaluations. This is not too surprising if, indeed, subjects' responses are guided primarily by the tendency to respond in a manner that the experimenter desires or expects.

Effects of severity of initiation. The effects of undergoing adversity in order to engage in an activity upon evaluations of the activity were first demonstrated by Aronson and Mills (1959) in an experiment described in Chapter 1. In this study, female subjects who read aloud a vivid description of sexual behavior in order to join a discussion group subsequently rated the group discussion as more interesting than did subjects who were required to read only a short list of mildly sex-related words. Several alternative interpretations were offered for the results of this study, most of which have been shown to be invalid (cf., Gerard & Mathewson, 1966). However, the most plausible of these interpretations, suggested in Chapter 1, is that subjects attempted to evaluate the group discussion in a way that coincided with the experimenter's personal judgment of its desirability. That is, the more severe the initiation, the more the experimenter appeared to consider the group discussion important, and therefore the more favorably it was rated. Schopler and Bateson's (1962) demonstration—that the effect of severity of initiation is completely eliminated when the experimenter makes explicit his own views about the discussion to be rated—provides indirect but compelling support for this interpretation.

D. Effects of Choice between Attractive Alternatives

A second concern of dissonance research, the effects that choosing between attractive alternatives have on evaluations of these alternatives, is closely related to the research on incentive effects described above. In such a situation, the "aversive" consequence of choosing one of the alternatives does not derive from external punishment or threat, but instead from the loss of something desirable. For example, suppose P is confronted with a choice between two alternatives A and B. He chooses A. Presumably the belief that "A is attractive" is consonant with the cognition that P has chosen A, while the belief that "B is attractive" is dissonant with this cognition. Therefore, P should both increase his liking for A and decrease his liking for B.

The magnitude of the reevaluations described above may depend upon several situational factors, the effects of which are also predictable from dissonance theory. For example, suppose P's choice is among more than two alternatives. Since the attractiveness of *each* rejected alternative is dissonant with P's choice of A, the amount of dissonance experienced, and thus the reevaluation of both selected and rejected alternatives, should increase with the number of alternatives rejected. Second, consider the effects of differences in the physical and functional similarity between A and B. For example, suppose that A is a mystery novel and that B is either a second mystery novel or a sports shirt. If B is equally attractive in the two cases, in which case should there be greater reevaluation of alternatives following the choice of A? The answer becomes intuitively clear if we consider the extreme case in which A and B are two identical copies of the same novel. In this case, P loses nothing by choosing A over B and should experience no dissonance. Dissonance occurs only to the extent that something is lost by choosing A. Thus, in general, A and B should be reevaluated more when they have few characteristics in common than when they are similar.

The predictions described above were supported in an early study by Brehm and Cohen (1959). Children initially indicated their liking for each of a set of toys and then chose one of a subset of these toys to take home. This subset consisted of either two or four toys that were either functionally similar (bags of games, or pieces of baseball equipment) or dissimilar. After making their choices, subjects reevaluated the entire set of toys. Evaluations of selected and rejected alternatives both changed in the directions predicted by dissonance theory; moreover, the changes were greater in magnitude when the rejected alternatives were either greater in number than, or dissimilar to, the selected alternative.

1. *An Interpretative Difficulty: When Does Reevaluation Occur?* Perhaps the most important question to raise in interpreting Brehm and Cohen's study is whether the reevaluation of alternatives, although *measured* after P's choice was made, actually occurred after this decision. When P's choice has important consequences for him, he may consider the available alternatives more carefully than he did when he was first asked to evaluate them, and his decision may reflect the results of these additional considerations. (If the available alternatives were *equally* attractive initially, some reevaluation would presumably be necessary in order to make a decision.) Such reevaluations would be irrelevant to dissonance theory, which is concerned only with *post*decisional changes in beliefs and attitudes.

In practice, it is obviously difficult to pinpoint the time at which reevaluation occurs. However, it may be possible to identify variables that affect the magnitude of predecisional changes and variables that affect the magnitude of postdecisional changes, and determine the independent contributions of each. This strategy was used by Jecker (1964). He argued that the amount of predecision reevaluation should depend upon the importance of the decision. For example, if P is asked to choose between A and B but believes he has a good chance of getting both alternatives regardless of his choice, he may attach less importance to his decision. He may therefore tend less to reevaluate the alternatives in the course of his decision making than if he believes he has little chance of ultimately receiving the rejected alternative. In contrast, postdecision shifts should not depend upon the difficulty of making the original decision, but rather they should depend upon the actual consequences of this decision. Therefore, if P after making his choice learns that he will receive both alternatives anyway, he should experience no dissonance and no postdecision reevaluation should occur. On the other hand, if P does not receive the rejected alternative, dissonance should be generated and reevaluation should take place.

To explore this possibility, Jecker had subjects choose between two phonograph records. Before making their choice, some subjects were told that there was a .05 probability of receiving both records regardless of their decision, while others were told that there was a .95 probability of receiving both. After making their choice, half of the subjects in each initial probability condition were actually given both records, while the remaining subjects only received the one they had chosen. The amount of reevaluation did not depend upon the initial probability of receiving both records, suggesting that evaluations either did not change at all during the course of the decision or changed equally in both conditions. However, under both probability conditions, subjects who received only one record reevaluated the alternatives more in the predicted direction than did subjects who received both records. These data support the hypothesis that postdecisional reevaluation of the sort predicted by dissonance theory does in fact occur.

2. *Compliance with Experimenter Expectancies.* An additional question is whether alternatives are reevaluated because subjects tend to change their judgments to those they believe the experimenter expects or considers to be desirable. For example, suppose subjects believe they are expected to like things they choose more than things they reject, and attempt to conform to these expectancies. Gerard, Blevans, and Malcolm (1964) reported data bearing upon this possibility. P initially rank ordered a set of pictures and was then administered an art judgment test. In a second session, he was told that, based upon this test, his ability to judge art was either high, average, or low. Either before or after this feedback, he was asked to choose between two of the pictures he had rated during the first session. He then reranked the entire set of pictures. Note that information that P is a good judge of art implies that the alternative he has chosen is probably better than the one he has rejected, while information that he has low ability suggests that the chosen alternative may "objectively" not be as good as the rejected one. Thus, a "demand" hypothesis would imply that alternatives would be reevaluated in the direction predicted by dissonance theory when P is told he has high ability, but in the opposite direction when P is told he has low ability. This is in fact what Gerard et al. found: pooled over other conditions, the change in the relative ranking of chosen and rejected alternatives after making the choice was .92, −.55, and −.83 under high, average, and low ability conditions, respectively. (The negative change could also be predicted by dissonance theory if it is assumed that when P thinks he is a poor judge, his belief that the rejected alternative is good is consonant with this cognition.)

The effects of an additional variable considered by Gerard et al. also support the possibility that demand compliance contributed to the differences they report. Half of the subjects received feedback about their ability before making their choices, while the remaining subjects received feedback after making their choices. The effect of demand characteristics should be relatively more apparent in the latter condition, when subjects are in effect told more directly that the picture they have just chosen is probably either better (under high ability conditions) or worse (under low ability conditions) than the one they rejected. (When feedback is given before the choice, subjects may take this information into account in making their decision; that is, subjects who believe they are poor judges may select the picture they like least, under the assumption that it is actually a better one.) Results are consistent with this interpretation; the relative rankings of alternatives changed by +1.00, −1.60, and −1.18 units under high, average, and low ability conditions when feedback about ability was given after subjects had made their choices but changed by only +.75, +.33, and −.50 units when this feedback preceded their choices.

Two contingencies in the results reported by Gerard et al. should be mentioned. First, the effects of ability were greater when P chose between alternatives that were similar in their initial attractiveness than when he chose between alternatives that differed substantially in their initial attractiveness. Second, the effects of differences in ability were greater when P was told that he could keep the chosen alternative as a gift than when he was simply asked to state his preference for the two alternatives. These contingencies, although clearly predictable from dissonance theory, are not inconsistent with a "demand compliance" hypothesis.

Finally, it should be noted that Malewski (1962) obtained results similar to Gerard et al.'s by using a less direct index of self-esteem, namely, the mean evaluation made of each subject by his classmates. This finding is also not necessarily incompatible with a "demand compliance" interpretation. That is, persons who typically are evaluated favorably by others are more likely to believe that others expect them to make sound, rational decisions than are persons who typically are evaluated unfavorably; as a result, they may tend more to comply with experimenter expectancies that they like chosen alternatives better than nonchosen ones.

E. Dissonance Reduction versus Demand Compliance—Some "Critical" Comparisons

The above survey does not begin to cover the vast number of studies designed to test the implications of dissonance theory for the effects of behavior upon attitudes and beliefs. A more complete summary and evaluation of these studies is given by Zajonc (1968). While certain of these experiments may not be susceptible to the criticism that their results could be due to attempts by subjects to comply with experimental "demand" characteristics, this criticism seems applicable to the large majority. Although it is often difficult to separate the potential effects of attempts to reduce dissonance from the effects of compliance with implicit experimenter "demands," it is not impossible. Let us consider two alternative approaches and evaluate the implications of each for the alternative hypotheses we have raised.

1. *Compliance with the Requests of Liked and Disliked Sources.* Suppose P is asked to engage in counterattitudinal behavior by someone he either likes or dislikes. Compliance with the request of a disliked person should generate more dissonance, and thus should produce greater attitude change, than should compliance with the request of a liked person. On the other hand, P should try to agree more with someone he likes than with someone he dislikes. Thus, if P assumes that the source favors the position he wants P to advocate, P should express a relatively more favorable attitude toward this position when the source is liked, contrary to predictions of dissonance theory.

Janis and his colleagues performed two nearly identical experiments relevant to this issue. In one experiment (Janis & Gilmore, 1965), subjects wrote an essay favoring the requirement of an additional year of mathematics and physics in the undergraduate curriculum. The essay writing was ostensibly sponsored by either a commercial publishing company (a presumably unfavorable sponsor) or a national research organization (a favorable sponsor). In the second study (Elms & Janis, 1965), the issue involved was the advisability of allowing American students to go to Russia for their entire four-year college education, and the favorable and unfavorable sponsors were the U.S. government and an agency of the Soviet Union, respectively. Half of the subjects in each study reported their personal attitudes toward the issue immediately after deciding to write the essay but before they actually did so, while the remaining subjects did not report their own attitudes until after they wrote the essay. In both studies, subjects who had actually written the essay agreed more with the position advocated when the sponsor was favorable than when the sponsor was unfavorable. Elms and Janis also found a positive effect of sponsorship when subjects reported their attitudes before writing the essay, but this effect was not significant; in contrast, Janis and Gilmore found that under this condition subjects agreed more with the position they decided to advocate when the sponsor was unfavorable. The different effects of sponsorship obtained under the two order conditions are hard to explain. However, in only one of four cases were results in the direction predicted by a "dissonance redirection" hypothesis.

Zimbardo, Weisenberg, Firestone, and Levy (1965) found that in a different type of situation the effect of source favorableness was consistent with that predicted by dissonance theory. That is, subjects evaluated an unpleasant food more favorably when they had agreed to eat it for someone they liked. However, a closer scrutiny of the authors' manipulation of source favorableness suggests that in this particular situation compliance with the experimenter's "demands" as well as dissonance reduction may have been more pronounced in the unfavorable source condition. Subjects were told that the experimenter (a Brigadier Commander of the university ROTC) had been rated by ROTC members as very competent, but either as cold, bossy, and difficult to work for (under disliked source conditions) or as pleasant and nice to work for (under liked source conditions). In addition, while both experimenters were pleasant to the subjects while conducting the experiment, the dislikeable experimenter treated his assistant in a cold and authoritarian manner (ordering him about and criticizing him) while the likeable experimenter was very friendly to his assistant. While this manipulation may have affected attitudes toward the experimenter as intended, it could also have created the impression that the disliked source was more likely to be upset by failure to conform to his expectancies and wishes. In this regard, it is worth noting that the assistant rather than the experimenter administered the postexperiment questionnaire on which ratings of food were reported. While this procedure often helps to minimize the effects of experimental demand factors, in this case it may have had the opposite effect. That is, subjects may have tended to believe that the assistant would be abused by the disliked experimenter if things didn't go his way, and therefore may have attempted to decrease the probability of this occurring by responding as they thought the experimenter would like them to. While this interpretation is quite speculative, it suggests that the effect of compliance with expectancies cannot be discounted in Zimbardo et al.'s experiment.

2. *Effects of Threat Revisited: Some Direct Support for Demand Compliance.* A specific attempt to separate the effects of dissonance reduction from the effects of compliance with experimenter expectancies and wishes was made by the author. This was a study of the effect that sanctions against cheating on an achievement test had on reported attitudes toward honesty. First let us outline briefly the rationale for the study, and then describe the procedure used and the results obtained.

Theoretical rationale. Assume that P is confronted with a decision either to cheat or not to cheat on an achievement test under conditions in which the experimenter has either threatened him with severe punishment for cheating or has simply asked him not to cheat without threatening him. First, suppose P decides to cheat. If he has a favorable attitude toward honesty, this attitude would be dissonant with his decision, and therefore should decrease in favorableness. Moreover, since the severity of the anticipated threat is also dissonant, his attitude should decrease more when the threat is severe than when it is mild. On the other hand, suppose P decides not to cheat. Then, his attitude toward honesty would be consonant with his decision and should increase in favorableness. Moreover, since his belief that he would be punished for cheating is also consonant, his attitude should increase less when the severity of the anticipated punishment is greater. Thus, the direction of the attitude change predicted by dissonance theory depends upon the nature of P's decision. However, note that regardless of this decision, P's postdecision attitude toward honesty should be less favorable when the sanctions against cheating are severe than when they are mild or nonexistent.

In contrast, suppose P responds in a manner he believes is considered desirable by the experimenter. Since the experimenter appears to attach more importance to honesty when he threatens P with severe punishment for cheating than when he does not threaten him, P is apt to report his own attitude toward honesty as more favorable under the former conditions, regardless of whether he actually cheated on the achievement test. To this extent, the effect of severity of threat upon P's reported attitudes toward honesty would be directly opposite to that predicted by dissonance theory.

An alternative hypothesis should be noted at this point. It is conceivable that subjects interpret the severity of the threat as an indication of the extent to which the experimenter believes they are dishonest. For example, an experimenter who administers a severe threat may convey the impression that he expects subjects to be dishonest, and thus he must intimidate them in order to prevent them from cheating. If subjects make this interpretation and comply with experimenter expectancies, they should report less favorable attitudes toward honesty when the threat is more severe, as dissonance theory would also predict. Thus, a negative relation between attitudes toward honesty and severity of threat would be consistent with both dissonance theory and a "demand compliance" formulation, while a positive relation between these variables would support only the latter.

Method. Male subjects (P) participated in an experiment with an attractive female accomplice (O) who posed as another subject. After interacting informally, during which time O behaved in a friendly manner toward P, both subjects were asked to take an achievement test. Under *severe threat* conditions, the experimenter indicated that he had been authorized by the university to take severe action (e.g., suspension from the university) against persons who gave or received information on the task. Under *mild threat* conditions, the experimenter indicated that it was important that persons neither give nor receive information on the test, but he did not actually threaten them. In *no threat* conditions, the experimenter mentioned that there was really nothing wrong with giving or receiving information on the test, but that he wished they would not do so.

While subjects were engaged in the task, the experimenter left the room on a pretense. During his absence, O ostensibly experienced great difficulty with one of the problems, and according to a standardized procedure asked P for the answer (which he sometimes provided and sometimes refused to provide.)

Upon returning, the experimenter asked subjects to complete an attitude questionnaire, two items of which pertained to honesty.

Results. It is of course important to know whether or not dissonance was aroused in the study. Since the dissonance associated with a decision to cheat should increase with the severity of threat, fewer subjects should make this decision as threat increases. This was in fact the case; of 24 subjects exposed to each level of threat, 22 cheated under no-threat conditions, 12 cheated under mild threat conditions, and 4 cheated under severe threat conditions.

Unfortunately, while the effect of threat upon cheating behavior validates the assumption that dissonance was aroused in the study, it creates problems when analyzing the effects of experimental variables upon attitudes. However, these effects are clearly more consistent with a "demand compliance" hypothesis than with a "dissonance reduction" hypothesis. The final attitudes toward honesty reported by cheaters under no threat, mild threat, and severe threat conditions were 4.6 ($n = 22$), 10.7 ($n = 12$), and 9.6 ($n = 4$), respectively, and the final attitudes reported by noncheaters under these same conditions were 11.1 ($n = 2$), 10.5 ($n = 12$), and 12.6 ($n = 20$). Thus, pooled over both cheaters and noncheaters, the final attitudes toward honesty were 5.1, 10.6, and 12.1 under the three levels of threat. These results do not of course mean that dissonance reduction did not occur under the conditions of this study. However, if it did occur, its effects were apparently much less pronounced than the effects of attempts to comply with experimenter demands.

F. Motivating Effects of Dissonance

Dissonance theory assumes that cognitions change in order to eliminate an aversive motivational state produced by dissonant beliefs. The hypothesis that dissonance is drive-inducing is difficult to test directly. An indirect approach is to determine if manipulations of the dissonance in a situation produce differences in behavior on an unrelated task, and if these differences are similar to those that should result from manipulations of general drive level. Three studies have in fact taken this approach. In one (Zimbardo, Cohen, Weisenberg, Dworkin, & Firestone, 1966), subjects were paid different amounts of money to learn lists of words while intermittently receiving electric shock. Since the amount of pay was consonant with performing the task, there should be less dissonance, and thus less general arousal, in the high pay condition than in the low pay condition. The task was one that should theoretically be performed better under low arousal. However, learning was actually better under the high dissonance conditions. Moreover, high dissonance subjects also perceived the pain of the shocks to be less and showed lower GSRs to the electric shocks. The authors argued that the high dissonance subjects reduced dissonance more by decreasing the painfulness of the shocks and thus were actually at a *lower* drive level than the low dissonance subjects. However, there is a much simpler explanation for their findings. That is, subjects under low dissonance (high pay) conditions may have inferred that the experimenter expected the shocks to be painful. (Otherwise, why were they offered so much pay?) These subjects may therefore have been more frightened of the shocks than were the high dissonance (low pay) subjects. To this extent, their GSRs would have been greater, and their learning relatively more impaired, as Zimbardo et al.'s results suggest.

A more straightforward investigation of this issue is reported by Cottrell and Wack (1967). Subjects volunteered for this experiment in order to fulfill a laboratory requirement in introductory psychology. Upon arriving at the experiment, subjects run under high dissonance conditions were told that they unfortunately could not receive laboratory credit for the experiment, but they were asked to participate anyway. Subjects run under low dissonance conditions were told they would receive the expected amount of credit. Then, all subjects performed a paired-associates task intended to establish verbal habits of different strengths. This was done by pairing unfamiliar "training"words with photographs different numbers of times. Following this task, subjects were asked to identify the training words when they were presented tachistoscopically. On several "pseudorecognition" trials, the actual word presented differed from any of the training words and was effectively unrecognizable. The frequency with which subjects responded with training words on these trials should be a positive function of the strength of the verbal habits formed during training, which is in turn a positive function of the level of drive or arousal experienced during the training task. Cottrell and Wack therefore predicted that more training words would be reported under high dissonance conditions than under low dissonance conditions. Results supported this prediction.

In a similar study, Waterman and Katkin (1967) manipulated dissonance by having subjects write an essay either supporting or opposing their own view. Subsequently, subjects performed either a simple or a complex symbol manipulation task. It was assumed that drive level would be related positively to performance on the simple task but related negatively to performance on the complex task. Therefore, high dissonance subjects were expected to perform better than low dissonance subjects on the simple task but worse than low dissonance subjects on the complex task. In fact, high dissonance subjects performed better on both tasks. Perhaps the "complex" task was not as complex as the authors assumed, and thus general arousal facilitated performance on this task as well as on the simpler one.

Although these studies are ingenious attempts to demonstrate that dissonance has effects similar to that of general arousal, there are ambiguities in their interpretation. While subjects run under the various experimental conditions may have differed in arousal, it is unclear that this arousal was produced by dissonance *per se*. In Waterman and Katkin's study, for example, it could be argued that subjects who wrote an essay opposing their own view felt that they had performed more poorly on the essay-writing task than those who wrote an essay supporting their own view, and thus they were more interested in compensating for this "failure" by performing well on the symbol manipulation task. In Cottrell and Wack's study, subjects under high dissonance conditions were read a letter from the psychology department that implied that because the experimenter was not a psychologist (he was described as a member of the Department of Educational Research), he was not doing meaningful research and thus did not qualify to give experimental credit. He was further criticized in the letter for treating subjects as "guinea pigs" rather than people. While this information may have reflected negatively upon the experimenter, and thus induced dissonance with the decision to participate, it may also have engendered sympathy for the experimenter who had nerve enough to read the letter in its entirety to the subjects. In either event, it was clearly the sort of letter that would generate interest among the subjects. In contrast, subjects under low dissonance conditions were read a seven-minute essay on the history of California, presumably to hold constant the length of time spent in the experiment before performing the learning task. This essay may if anything have decreased subjects' interest in the experiment. Thus in both studies, high dissonance subjects may have had more interest in the experiment, and thus may have been more motivated to perform well, than did low dissonance subjects, but for reasons that were theoretically unrelated to the dissonance arousing aspect of the situation *per se*.

G. Evaluation

The research generated by cognitive dissonance theory is imaginative and has produced some extremely interesting findings. Many of the effects reported in the studies described in this section might not yet have been discovered had they not been implied by this theory. However, despite its heuristic value, there is little conclusive evidence that the theory itself is valid. The general assumption that subjects respond in a way that they believe is expected of them by the experimenter potentially accounts for many of the results reported in these studies.

The "demand compliance" interpretations we have given to the studies mentioned in this section have been generally *post hoc* and frequently very speculative. To have much confidence in their validity, one would need to obtain direct measures of subjects' perceptions of the experimenter's expectancies and values under the various experimental conditions being compared, and perhaps also an indication of whether subjects do in fact try to respond in a manner consistent with these expectancies and values. In any event, the existence of alternative explanations of dissonance phenomena does not in itself imply that the theory is invalid. Nevertheless, the frequency with which a "demand compliance" interpretation can be made of these phenomena decreases one's confidence in the theory's validity, or at least in its applicability to laboratory research on attitude and belief change.

With these considerations in mind, let us now turn to a quite different formulation of the effects of one's own behavior on one's beliefs and attitudes, a formulation applicable to most of the phenomena to which dissonance theory pertains, but one which may have even broader implications.

II. BEM'S THEORY OF SELF-PERCEPTION

A. General Considerations

A nonmotivational formulation of the effects of one's behavior upon one's beliefs and attitudes has been developed by Bem (1965, 1967). Bem's formal statement of his theory borrows heavily from the formulation of verbal behavior proposed by Skinner (1957). However, at the risk of some injustice to Bem, we shall consider this theory from the perspective of the general information-processing approach we have developed in previous chapters.

It seems reasonable to assume that inferences about oneself are governed by processes similar to those that govern inferences about others. These latter inferences may be based upon several types of information: personality adjectives used to describe the person himself and (if relevant) the attitude object, information about his typical reactions to other persons, objects, and events, and information about others' behavior toward him. Inferences about oneself may be based upon similar types of information. Thus, as an example, a subject's inference that P likes O may be based upon a general description of O as warm and outgoing, information that P himself has attributes that suggest he is generally friendly to others, information that P has often behaved in specific "friendly" ways toward O (that he has invited O home for drinks, or that he has gone out of his way to help O), or information that O typically behaves toward P as if P were a friendly person (for example, that he invites P to parties, or that he goes out of his way to talk to P). When more than one type of information is available, a subject's inference may be some weighted function of the implications of each type. Now suppose that P himself is asked whether he likes O. His judgment may be based upon information similar to that described above. That is, it may be based in part upon P's beliefs that O has favorable attributes relevant to liking; in part, upon P's perception of himself as *generally* friendly and outgoing, in part, upon P's recollection of how he has behaved toward O in the past; and in part, upon P's perception of how O has behaved toward him. In this case, as in the first, P's judgment may be a weighted function of the implications of these several pieces of evidence.

Without denying the relevance of other types of information, Bem has concentrated upon the implications of P's own behavior or reaction for the judgment to be made. He argues quite compellingly that persons in their everyday interactions with others do not usually ask themselves specifically about their personal feelings or motives. Often such a judgment is not made until one is asked for it by another. Thus, P may behave in either positive or negative ways toward O, seek his company or avoid him, laugh at his jokes or make biting remarks about him, all without formally making a judgment about whether he likes or dislikes O. Once he is asked for such a judgment, P may reflect upon his previous behavior toward O and the conditions under which it has occurred and may use this information as a basis for the judgment. Bem hypothesizes that this estimate is similar to that P would make about another person's liking for O, given comparable information about that person's behavior.

To apply the above hypothesis, one must understand the conditions in which the behavior of a person (oneself or another) is assumed to be a reliable indication of his beliefs, attitudes, or general personality. While this understanding must ultimately be gained empirically, some intuitive assumptions seem reasonable. For example, suppose P is observed performing a certain task. A possible implication of this behavior is that P enjoys the task. However, if P is being paid a substantial sum of money to perform the task, he might be doing it for the money and not because he likes it. More generally, it is reasonable to assume that one's behavior toward an object is less likely to be used as a reliable indication of one's underlying attitude toward the object when it can be attributed to other, external factors.

The relevance of Bem's approach to much of the research used to support dissonance theory now becomes clear. As an example, consider Festinger and Carlsmith's (1959) study in which P was offered either $1 or $20 to convince O that a task was interesting. P's agreement to convince O could indicate that he personally thinks the task is interesting. However, a disinterested observer is more likely to make this interpretation if P is paid only $1 than if he is paid $20. Similarly, if P himself is asked to report his attitude toward the task, he may also be more apt to infer his attitude toward the task to be favorable in the $1 condition. This is of course what dissonance theory also predicts and what Festinger and Carlsmith found. Note, however, that the inference that P favors the position he advocates under low pay conditions is more likely to be made if he is given a chance to refuse to advocate this position than if he is not given this opportunity. Thus, as Sherman (1970) found, an inverse relation between the magnitude of the pay for advocating a position and attitudes toward this position is more likely under "free choice" conditions than under "no choice" conditions.

Most if not all of the research on incentive effects upon attitude and belief change may be interpreted in a similar manner. For example, persons who are offered a large sum of money to write an essay but refuse to do so are more likely to oppose the position to be advocated in the essay than are persons who refuse to write the essay when less money is offered. Thus, as Darley and Cooper (1972) found, subjects who observe *themselves* refusing to write an essay under "high pay" conditions should infer that they are more opposed to the position they are asked to advocate, and thus should report less favorable attitudes toward this position, than subjects who observe themselves refusing to write the essay under "low pay" conditions. Also, persons who voluntarily avoid engaging in an activity are more likely to dislike the activity than persons who avoid the activity under threat of punishment. Thus, as Aronson and Carlsmith (1963) found, children who have observed themselves avoid playing with a toy should infer that they like the toy less when the threat of punishment for playing with it is mild than when it is severe.

In considering various applications of Bem's hypothesis, it should be noted that this hypothesis often has somewhat broader implications than does dissonance theory, since a person's behavior may be attributable to general characteristics of the person as well as to his attitude toward the particular behavior or object involved. For example, in the situation studied by Aronson and Carlsmith, children who are observed (by themselves or others) to avoid playing with an attractive toy voluntarily are more likely to be judged able to resist temptation than those who are observed to avoid playing with the toy under threat of punishment. If subjects who make such inferences about themselves subsequently behave in a manner consistent with these self-attributions, those subjects who are exposed to the mild threat conditions of Aronson and Carlsmith's study should subsequently be more resistant to temptation than subjects who are exposed to severe threat. In support of this hypothesis, Lepper (1973) found that the first group of subjects cheated less than the second group on an achievement task where rewards were given for success.

Self-perception vs. demand compliance.   Inferences of one's attitudes and beliefs from one's behavior, like dissonance reduction, may often be difficult to separate from tendencies to comply with experimental demand characteristics. Both self-perception theory and a demand compliance hypothesis are based upon the assumption that P's responses are determined by the implications of information he receives in the experimental situation. However, the source of the information is assumed to differ in the two cases. Specifically, Bem hypothesizes that the source of the information is P himself, while a demand interpretation assumes that the source is another person in the situation (generally, the experimenter).

There of course is no reason to believe that P's reported attitude is affected by information from only one of the two sources described above: Both experimental "demands" and the implications of P's own behavior may simultaneously influence his responses. However, the contributions of these factors are difficult to separate. For example, if P is asked to advocate publicly a position X and agrees to do so, the implications of information from both sources are the same. That is, P's own decision to advocate the position voluntarily implies that he agrees with the position, while the experimenter's request implies that the experimenter expects P to agree with it; thus, P should report a more favorable attitude toward X regardless of which informational cue he is using. A further problem is raised by the possibility that in many cases P may infer that the experimenter expects him to behave in a manner that is consistent with his (P's) underlying attitude toward X. In such cases, he may attempt to comply with this expectancy after the fact by reporting his attitude in a manner that he believes is consistent with the behavior the experimenter has observed him manifest. To this extent, the self-perception phenomena hypothesized by Bem would actually be the *result* of demand compliance and would not contribute to P's reported attitudes independently of this factor!

Leaving aside this last problem, certain strategies do seem feasible for determining the relative contributions of demand compliance and self-perception processes to reported attitudes. Note that a self-perception hypothesis would not apply unless the behavior that provides information about one's attitude or belief has in fact occurred. In contrast, a demand compliance interpretation requires only that the experimenter's request that P engage in the behavior, and the conditions surrounding this request, be communicated to P. Thus, suppose in the above example that subjects in one group are asked by the experimenter to advocate X voluntarily but to report their attitudes toward this position immediately after the request is made, before they decide whether or not to comply. Their responses at this time should be affected only by their inference that the experimenter expects them to comply (and thus to agree with X), and not by their own (as yet unmanifested) behavior. These responses, defined in relation to preexperiment attitudes, should indicate the effects of demand compliance. If the mean predecision attitude reported by these subjects is subtracted from the mean postdecision attitude reported by a second group of subjects, this difference should reflect the contribution of self-perception over and above the effects of demand compliance.

A recognition that both self-perception and demand compliance may contribute to inferences is necessary to explain several results reported earlier in this chapter. For example, consider again the severe threat condition of Aronson and Carlsmith's study. According to self-perception theory, P should view his decision not to play with the toy under threat of severe punishment as simply an unreliable indication of his attitude toward the toy, and therefore this decision should have no effect, either positive or negative, upon P's evaluation of it. In fact, however, evaluations of the toy increased under this condition. Brehm and Crocker's finding, that subjects increased estimates of their hunger following a decision to go without eating for high pay, is also hard to explain on the basis of self-perception theory alone. On the other hand, both findings are consistent with a demand compliance interpretation.

Since we have already belabored the contribution of experimental demand characteristics in previous sections of this chapter, the reader will be spared detailed analyses of their possible effects in research bearing upon self-perception theory. However, the need to identify these effects and to separate them from the effects of self-perception *per se* should be kept in mind in evaluating the implications of this research. An additional procedure for accomplishing this separation is suggested in the following section.

B.   Quantification of Self-Perception Phenomena

In effect, Bem's formulation is concerned with the manner in which a new piece of information (one's behavior) affects judgments. This is also the concern of Bayes' theorem (Edwards, 1968). Consider the following tautology in mathematical probability theory:

$$P_B\, P_{A/B} = P_A\, P_{B/A}$$

This can be rewritten in the form:

$$P_{A/B} = \frac{P_A P_{B/A}}{P_B} = \frac{P_A P_{B/A}}{P_A P_{B/A} + P_{A'} P_{B/A'}} \tag{11.2}$$

Now, assume that A is a particular attribute of a person and that B is a behavior related to this attribute. Then, P_A and $P_{A'}$ refer to the probabilities that the person does and does not have A, respectively, $P_{B/A}$ and $P_{B/A'}$ are the probabilities that the person would do B if he did and did not have A, and $P_{A/B}$ is the probability that the person has A given that he has decided to do B. If subjective probabilities obey the laws of mathematical probability, and if the terms of the above equation refer to a subject's (P's) beliefs about the events involved, the change in P's belief that he (or another) has A after receiving information that this person has done B $(P_{A/B} - P_A)$ could theoretically be predicted.

Equation 11.2 has several interesting implications. Predicted changes in P_A based upon this equation are tabulated in Table 11.2 as a function of initial values of P_A, $P_{B/A}$, and $P_{B/A'}$. Several things may be noted from these data. First, information that B has occurred will always increase the belief that P has A when $P_{B/A} > P_{B/A'}$, and will always decrease this belief when $P_{B/A} > P_{B/A'}$. Thus, if the behavior B is more likely to imply the presence of A than the absence of A, then the belief that A is present should increase following the behavior. Note also that at a given level of $P_{B/A}$, the magnitude of the change in P_A is inversely related to the value of $P_{B/A'}$. Since external incentives to perform B should normally increase $P_{B/A'}$, the predictions of Eq. (11.2) are generally consistent with those of dissonance theory.

Bayes' theorem, like dissonance theory, predicts that while a decision to manifest a certain behavior for a large incentive will have little effect upon

TABLE 11.2

Predicted Changes in P_A ($P_{A/B} - P_A$) as a Function of
P_A, $P_{B/A}$, and $P_{B/A'}$

$P_{B/A}$	$P_{B/A'}$	P_A				
		.1	.3	.5	.7	.9
.2	.2	0	0	0	0	0
	.4	−.047	−.124	−.167	−.162	−.072
	.6	−.064	−.175	−.250	−.263	−.150
	.8	−.073	−.203	−.300	−.332	−.208
.4	.2	.081	.162	.167	.124	.047
	.4	0	0	0	0	0
	.6	−.031	−.078	−.100	−.091	−.043
	.8	−.047	−.124	−.167	−.162	−.082
.6	.2	.150	.263	.250	.175	.064
	.4	.043	.091	.100	.078	.031
	.6	0	0	0	0	0
	.8	−.203	−.057	−.071	−.064	−.029
.8	.2	.208	.332	.300	.203	.073
	.4	.082	.162	.167	.124	.047
	.6	.029	.064	.071	.057	.023
	.8	0	0	0	0	0

beliefs that the behavior is desirable, a decison *not* to do so will greatly decrease beliefs that the behavior is desirable. To see this, suppose P is offered a large sum of money to manifest a behavior B. Although under such conditions P is likely to do B regardless of his own attitude toward it (A), his belief that he would do it if he regards it as desirable ($P_{B/A}$) may still be somewhat greater than his belief that he would do it if he does not consider it desirable ($P_{B/A'}$). To reflect these latter beliefs, assume that $P_{B/A} = .95$ and $P_{B/A'} = .90$. If P's initial belief that B is desirable (P_A) is .5, and if he decides to do B, his postdecision belief may be predicted from Eq. (11.2), that is,

$$P_{A/B} = \frac{.5(.95)}{.5(.95) + .5(.90)} = .514 .$$

Had P decided not to do B, the effect of this decision would be predicted by applying Eq. (11.2) to B' (a decision to *not* manifest B); that is,

$$P_{A/B'} = \frac{P_A P_{B'/A}}{P_A P_{B'/A} + P_{A'} P_{B'/A'}} \qquad (11.3)$$

$$= \frac{P_A (1 - P_{B/A})}{P_A (1 - P_{B/A}) + P_{A'} (1 - P_{B/A'})}$$

$$= \frac{.5(.05)}{.5(.05) + .5(.10)} = .33$$

Thus, P's belief that A is desirable should increase by only .01 (from .50 to .51) following a decision to do B, but it should decrease by .17 (from .50 to .33) following a decision not to do B.

The preceding analysis suggests that there is an inverse relation between the magnitude of change in P_A resulting from a decision to do B under a given set of circumstances and the magnitude of change resulting from a decision not to do B under the same circumstances. It may therefore seem paradoxical that if P's decision to do B has no effect whatsoever upon his belief that B is desirable, Bayes's theorem predicts that a decision *not* to do B will also have no effect. To see this, note that for $P_{A/B}$ to equal P_A in Eq. (11.2), $P_{B/A}$ must equal $P_{B/A'}$. But if this is true, $P_{B'/A} = P_{B'/A'}$, and thus, from Eq. (11.3), $P_{A/B'} = P_A$.

Other predictions of Bayes' theorem, while not inconsistent with dissonance theory, are not derivable from the theory. For example, holding the difference between $P_{B/A}$ and $P_{B/A'}$ constant, Table 11.2 shows that the predicted change in P_A becomes more positive (or less negative) as the values of these conditional probabilities increase. (Thus, a greater positive change in P_A resulting from B would be predicted if $P_{B/A}$ and $P_{B/A'}$ were .8 and .4, respectively, than if these probabilities were .6 and .2, respectively.) Another implication of Eq. (11.2) is that, for any given values of the conditional probabilities, the predicted change in P_A following the occurrence of B is nonmonotonically related to its initial value. That is, extreme initial beliefs about A should change less following the occurrence of B than do moderate beliefs. A general resistance to change of extreme attitudes and beliefs is, of course, a prediction of other theories (e.g., Osgood & Tannenbaum, 1955).

While Bayes' theorem has often been applied to decision-making and gambling behavior in physical stimulus domains (for reviews, see Edwards, 1968; Peterson & Beach, 1967; Slovic & Lichtenstein, 1971), it has not been applied in situations to which Bem's theory is directly relevant. As we noted in Chapter 4, Bayes' theorem generally provides too extreme estimates of subjects' beliefs in the occurrence of physical stimulus events (Edwards, 1968). Similar errors in prediction appear to occur when social stimuli are judged. A study by Ajzen (1971) is representative. Subjects received information about several hypothetical persons and a set of four alternative behaviors that each might manifest. In some cases, three of the four alternative behaviors had apparently desirable consequences, while in other cases three of the four alternatives had undesirable consequences. This manipulation was assumed to affect initial estimates of the likelihood that a person would choose a particular one of these behaviors. Subjects estimated the likelihood that a person would choose each of the four alternative behaviors (P_B), that a person had an attribute implied by the behavior (P_A), and that persons in general would choose the behavior, given that they had A $(P_{B/A})$. Then, they were told that a particular person did in fact decide to engage in the behavior, and they estimated the likelihood that this person possessed A $(P_{A/B})$. Averaged over eight experimental conditions, the correlation over subjects between predicted and obtained estimates of $P_{A/B}$ was only moderately high (.597). Moreover, obtained values were consistently less extreme (closer to .50) than predicted values. Ajzen's data also call into question some more general implications of the model. For example, beliefs that P possessed A changed more when initial values of P_A were relatively low than when they were moderate. This contradicts predictions suggested by the hypothetical data in Table 11.2. These results may place some limitations upon the general hypothesis that relations among subjective probabilities are described by the laws of mathematical probability.

Equation (11.2) does not take into account factors in addition to one's behavior (B) that affect self-judgments or, at least, the report of these judgments. However, if the equation is valid, it could be used to separate the effects of one's behavior from the influence of these other factors. For example, consider once again the finding of Aronson and Carlsmith, that attraction to a forbidden toy increased under severe threat conditions. If this result were attributable solely to self-perception processes, it could be predicted by Eq. (11.2) only if $P_{B/A}$ (the belief that one would avoid playing with the toy if he were attracted to it) were greater than $P_{B/A'}$ (the belief that one would avoid playing with the toy if he were *not* attracted to it). This is intuitively unlikely. However, if Eq. (11.2) provides a valid description of the contribution of B (one's avoidance of playing with the toy) to judgments of A, the difference between the observed postbehavior judgment of A and the value predicted by this equation $(P_{A/B})$ could be interpreted as the contribution of other factors, such as demand compliance, over and above the effect of B. This procedure of course requires an *a priori* demonstration that Eq. (11.2) is indeed valid. Nevertheless, a continued investigation of the usefulness of this equation in describing the effects of information about both one's own and others' behavior is warranted. Further implications of this equation, and some empirical data bearing upon them, will be discussed presently.

C. Similarity of Self-Perceptions to Perceptions of Others

Three fundamental empirical questions are raised by Bem's approach. First, are inferences based upon one's own behavior in specific situations actually similar to those based upon others' behavior under comparable conditions? Second, can subjects' own beliefs and attitudes be affected by manipulating situational variables that influence the interpretation they give to their behavior? Third and more generally, what factors determine when one's behavior in a given instance is inferred to be a reliable indicator of one's beliefs and attitudes? Let us consider these questions in turn, attending first to the conditions in which self-perceptions and perceptions of others are similar.

1. *Interpersonal Replications of Dissonance Studies.* If self-judgments and judgments of others are based upon similar types of information, the beliefs that subjects report after engaging in a behavior should be similar to the beliefs that these subjects are predicted to have by persons who observe this behavior. Bem (1965) obtained support for this hypothesis. The conditions used in two studies designed to test cognitive dissonance theory (Brehm & Cohen, 1962), described earlier in this chapter, were selected for consideration. In one study, subjects received either $1 or $5 to write a counterattitudinal essay. In the second, subjects who had not eaten for several hours agreed to go without eating for an additional 12 hours for pay of either $1 or $5. In each case, Bem presented his "observer" subjects with a paragraph that described as closely as possible the experimental situation in which the original "dissonance" subjects had found themselves. Some observers were told that the person described in the paragraph agreed to engage in the activity for the lower pay, while others were told that the person agreed to do so for the higher pay. The observers then predicted the person's judgment (that is, his attitude toward the issue described in the essay, or his estimate of how hungry he was) along a scale identical to that used by subjects in the original study. In each case, observers' predictions were nearly identical to the actual responses of subjects in the original study. These results are therefore quite consistent with Bem's hypotheses. Moreover, while they do not necessarily invalidate dissonance theory, they show that subjects' estimates of their own beliefs and attitudes under actual experimental conditions can often be predicted by persons who themselves are not personally involved in the experiment, and thus do not experience any "dissonance."

A better strategy for determining the similarity between subjects' inferences of other persons' attitudes and inferences of their own attitudes is to have observers witness "actor" subjects actually participate under different experimental conditions, and to compare their predictions of actors' attitudes with those actually reported by the actors under these conditions. This approach was taken by Calder, Ross, and Insko (1973) in an experiment

TABLE 11.3

Mean Enjoyableness Ratings as a Function of Experimental
Credit, Behavioral Consequences, and Freedom of
Choice (adapted from Calder et al., 1973, p. 91)

Subject	High Consequences		Low consequences	
	High choice	Low choice	High choice	Low choice
Actors				
½ hour	21.33	9.60	13.20	12.33
2 hours	14.80	16.20	16.40	9.40
Observers				
½ hour	11.70	11.00	5.40	9.50
2 hours	5.80	15.20	11.25	12.75

patterned after Festinger and Carlsmith's (1959). After engaging in a boring
task, subjects received either high or low "pay" (in this case, either 2 hours or
½ hour of experimental credit for trying to convince another (a confederate)
that the task was interesting. Two additional variables were considered: the
freedom of choice (manipulated by explicitly giving the subject a chance to
refuse to engage in the counterattitudinal activity, or by giving him no such
opportunity) and the consequences of the action (the subject's apparent
success in convincing the confederate that he thought the task would be
enjoyable). After participating under one of the eight combinations of
experimental variables, subjects reported their personal enjoyment of the
task along a 36-point scale. Each of these subjects ("actors") was observed
during the course of the experiment by another subject who was then asked
to predict the actor's estimate on the basis of the observations he had made.
Mean enjoyment ratings made by both actors and observers are shown in
Table 11.3. Observers tended to underestimate actors' ratings under high
choice conditions but not under low choice conditions, and their estimates
were less highly correlated with actors' estimates under the former conditions
($r = .11$) than under the latter ($r = .72$). However, while the triple interaction
of pay, choice, and consequences was significant ($F = 7.08$), the nature of
this interaction was not significantly different between actors and observers
($F = .35$); in other words, the combined effects of situational variables on
ratings by both groups were the same.

The results of the experiments described above are consistent with the hypothesis that the situational and behavioral cues used to infer the attitude of another are similar to those used to infer one's own attitude. One implication of this conclusion is of particular interest when applied to these studies. In the situation constructed by Calder et al., observers presumably made different attributions about actors under the two incentive conditions because they believed that persons would agree to advocate the position for a large incentive regardless of their personal attitude toward the position, but that persons would agree to advocate it for a low incentive only if they personally believed in it. In fact, however, actors were as likely to engage in the behavior when the incentive was low as when it was high; only one subject refused to do so in the entire experiment. In other words, although observers accurately predicted actors' attitudes under the two incentive conditions, these predictions were apparently the result of an *invalid* assumption they made about differences in the probability that persons opposed to the position would agree to advocate it under these conditions. However, this does not necessarily create a problem for the self-perception hypothesis; it is conceivable that actors' self-inferences, as well as observers' predictions, were based upon the same invalid assumption about the determinants of behavior in these situations.

2. *Effects of "Initial Attitudes" upon Self-Perceptions.* Note that in Bem's "interpersonal replications" of dissonance studies, "observer" subjects were not asked to predict the *change* in P's attitude resulting from his behavior, but only his final attitude. Conceivably, observers assumed that P's final attitude was also his initial attitude, before engaging in the behavior, and therefore might not have predicted any *change* in his beliefs resulting from the behavior. In fact, Jones, Linder, Kiesler, Zanna, and Brehm (1968) found that when subjects were told P's initial attitude as well as his behavior, they did not reproduce the results of dissonance studies. However, as Bem (1968) points out, this finding does not seem particularly relevant to a test of his hypothesis. Presumably, either P or an observer infers P's attitude on the basis of whatever information is available to him at the time he is asked to make his estimate. Jones et al., by *informing* observers of P's initial attitudes, may provide information that was not available to P himself, or at least was not salient to him, when participating in the original dissonance experiments. If P in the latter studies had also been informed of his initial attitude at the time he reported his final one, differences between these attitudes would undoubtedly be greatly reduced, perhaps to the extent reported by Jones et al. To provide an analog of the original dissonance studies, observers might be asked to *predict* P's judgment before learning of P's decision to engage in the judgment-related activity, and then to make a new prediction after receiving this information. These two predictions should be comparable to the "inferences" P himself makes before and after receiving this information, and therefore they may differ in a similar way.

The preceding argument would be less cogent if in fact subjects in the original dissonance studies, while not reminded of their initial attitudes, nevertheless recalled them at the time they reported their final judgments. However, a study by Bem and McConnell (1970) provides evidence against this possibility. Subjects initially completed an attitude questionnaire that included an item on whether university students should have control over the kinds of courses they are offered. Then, in a second session one week later, they were either asked if they would volunteer to write an essay advocating little control by students over course offerings (*Choice* conditions) or they were told to do so without being asked (*No Choice* conditions). After writing the essay, half the subjects under each condition estimated their attitudes toward student control over course offerings, while the remaining subjects were first asked to recall their original estimates of their attitudes (as reported the week before). The mean attitude change manifested by the first group of subjects, in the direction of the position advocated, was 9.3 and 2.8 under Choice and No Choice conditions, respectively. The mean errors made by the second group of subjects in recalling their initial attitudes were virtually identical (9.7 and 3.2 under Choice and No Choice conditions, respectively). Moreover, subjects' recollections of their initial attitudes were correlated .98 and .96 with their postbehavior attitudes under Choice and No Choice conditions but were correlated only .26 and .71 with their actual initial attitudes under these conditions. These data support the assumption that a subject's initial attitude is typically not very salient to him at the time he reports his final (postbehavior) attitude and, in fact, is often recalled erroneously as similar to his final attitude. It therefore may have minimal influence upon his postbehavior attitude. Jones et al.'s criticism of Bem's (1965) interpersonal replications of dissonance studies may thus be rejected on empirical as well as theoretical grounds.

There are of course circumstances in which a subject's initial attitude *is* salient to him at the time he reports his postbehavior attitude. Under such circumstances, his initial attitude may have greater influence, and his behavior may have relatively less effect. This possibility was investigated by Snyder and Ebbeson (1972). Subjects engaged in any essay-writing task under two choice conditions similar to those used by Bem and McConnell. However, the salience of initial attitudes was manipulated by asking some subjects before writing the essay to take some time to organize their thoughts and ideas on the issue to which the essay pertained, but not giving this opportunity to others. The salience of the counterattitudinal behavior was also manipulated by asking some subjects after writing their essays to rate the quality of the arguments contained in them. As expected, subjects changed their attitudes more under Choice conditions than under No Choice conditions only when their initial attitudes were not salient. The additional finding that increasing the salience of the behavior did not *increase* the effects of the choice manipulation is somewhat embarrassing to

Bem's theory. On the other hand, the results are even more embarrassing to dissonance theory. As Snyder and Ebbeson point out, dissonance is more likely to be experienced, and thus is *more* likely to be reduced through opinion change, when the cognitions involved (in this case, the initial attitude and the behavior-related cognition) are made salient. Thus the increase in the salience of initial attitude had an effect directly opposite to that predicted by a dissonance formulation.

3. *Some Additional Contingencies.* Snyder and Ebbeson's findings point out the unjustifiability of concluding that self-perceptions are determined *only* by the implications of one's immediately preceding behavior, and therefore that these perceptions will always be identical to judgments made of other persons who are observed in similar situations. Other research suggests that persons are likely to attribute their own behavior to situational factors, but tend to attribute others' behavior to stable, dispositional characteristics of the persons observed. For example, Jones, Rock, Shaver, Goethals, and Ward (1968) constructed a situation in which P observed O's performance either improve or deteriorate over a series of 30 problem tasks. P attributed more problem-solving ability to O when he first succeeded and subsequently failed than when he first failed and subsequently succeeded (a "primacy" effect). In contrast, when P himself performed the tasks and received similar feedback about his performance, he rated his own ability similarly under both of the conditions described above and attributed changes in his success rate to changes in task difficulty.

Two studies cited by Jones and Nisbett (1971) suggest similar differences between self-perceptions and perceptions of others. Nisbett and Caputo (1971) found that subjects attributed their own choices of course curricula, and of the girls they preferred to date most frequently, to characteristics of the objects chosen, but they attributed similar choices by their best friends to personal characteristics of the friend. In a second study (Nisbett, Legant, & Maracek, 1971), observers witnessed "real" subjects being asked to help administer an entertainment program to raise money for a university institute. Some subjects volunteered to assist while others did not. All subjects were then asked if they would be willing to canvass for the United Fund. Observers expected that those who volunteered to assist in the entertainment program would be more likely than nonvolunteers to help the United Fund. In fact, however, volunteers and nonvolunteers did not differ.

Some theoretical contingencies in the similarity between self-perceptions and perceptions of others can be identified by applying Eq. (11.2) to the inference processes involved. Suppose P and O have each chosen to engage in a behavior B, and P is subsequently asked to infer the likelihood that both he and O possess a behavior-related attribute A. These estimates are analogous to the subjective conditional probabilities P_{A_p/B_p} (the probability that P has A given that he has chosen B) and P_{A_o/B_o} (the probability that O has A given that he has chosen B). Applying Eq. (11.2),

$$P_{Ap/Bp} = \frac{P_{Ap}P_{Bp/Ap}}{P_{Ap}P_{Bp/A} + P_{A'p}P_{Bp/A'p}} \tag{11.4}$$

and

$$P_{Ao/Bo} = \frac{P_{Ao}P_{Bo/Ao}}{P_{Ao}P_{Bo/Ao} + P_{A'o}P_{Bo/A'}} \tag{11.5}$$

P's inference that he personally has A as a result of manifesting B will differ from his inference that O has A under comparable conditions if:

a. he believes himself to be more or less likely than O to have A before B is chosen $(P_{Ap} \neq P_{Ao})$; or
b. he believes himself more or less likely than O to choose B, given that each has A $(P_{Bp/Ap} \neq P_{Bo/Ao})$; or
c. he believes that he is more or less likely than O to choose B, given that each does not have A $(P_{Bp/A'p} \neq P_{Bo/A'o})$.

More generally, P's inference about himself will be similar to his inferences about O only when he perceives himself and O to be *initially* similar both with respect to the attribute being inferred and with respect to the likelihood that the behavior involved will be manifested.

The above formulation is useful in interpreting differences between self-attributions and attributions to others. For example, in the experiment by Calder et al. (1973), the fact that observers underestimated actors' estimates of the enjoyableness of a task after trying to persuade another that it was interesting $(P_{A/B})$ may be a result of the fact that the observers initially underestimated actors attitudes, *before* the actors had engaged in the counterattitudinal activity (P_A).

A study by Feather and Simon (1971) is also worth considering in this context. After P and O received feedback that they had either passed or failed an anagrams test, P estimated the extent to which both his own and O's performance was due to luck or ability. P attributed O's success more to ability than he did his own success, but he attributed O's failure less to ability than he did his own failure. These results would be predictable from Eq. (11.4) and Eq. (11.5) if P *initially* believed that O was more likely to have ability than he. To see this, assume that A is the attribute "has ability" and B is either the behavior "succeeds" or the behavior "fails." Then, if $P_{Ao} > P_{Ap}$ but if corresponding conditional probabilities in Eq. (11.4) and Eq. (11.5) are equal, these equations predict that $P_{Ao/Bo} > P_{Ap/Bp}$. If B is "succeeds," this inequality implies that P believes O is more likely than he to have ability, given that each has succeeded or, alternatively, P is more apt to attribute O's success to ability than his own success. On the other hand, if B is "fails," the inequality implies that P believes that O is more likely than he to have ability, given that each has failed or, alternatively, P is more apt to attribute O's failure to bad luck than his own failure. These predictions are consistent with Feather and Simon's findings.

Conclusion. The results of the above studies are hardly surprising. For example, the research reported by Nisbett and his colleagues simply indicates that the less one knows about a person (himself or another), the more likely he is to use this person's behavior in a single situation as an indication of a general attribute of the person. The results are important in the context of Bem's formulation, since they point out conditions in which a subject's self-perception is not determined exclusively by the implications of his immediately preceding behavior. However, it still seems justifiable to assume that one's immediately preceding behavior is *one,* if not the only, source of information he uses in making judgments of himself, and that it can substantially affect inferences about oneself in many experimental situations.

D. Situational Determinants of Self-Perception

If subjects infer their attitudes from their own behavior under various conditions, these inferences may be predictably affected by altering the situational context in which judgment-related behavior occurs. Several quite ingenious studies have been performed to demonstrate the validity of this hypothesis. In one (Bem, 1965), subjects were initially instructed to tell the truth or to lie in the presence of a green ("truth") light or amber ("lie") light. (The color of the two lights was counterbalanced over subjects.) Then, ostensibly as part of a different experiment, they made assertions that each of several cartoons was either funny or not funny in the presence of one of these lights, and finally they recorded the degree of funniness of the cartoons along a category scale. Although subjects were told that the lights were irrelevant to the cartoon judgment task and were flashing randomly, their category judgments of the cartoons were more extreme in the direction implied by their assertions when these assertions were accompanied by the "truth" light rather than the "lie" light.

In a second study (Bem, 1966), subjects who had told the truth and lied in the presence of the "truth" and "lie" lights, respectively, were then asked to make statements about their behavior on an earlier task (specifically, whether or not they had crossed out certain items in a word list). These statements were objectively either true or false; moreover, some statements of each type were accompanied by the "truth" light and others by the "lie" light. (Again, the lights in this part of the experiment allegedly flashed randomly.) When subjects were subsequently asked to recall whether their statements were true, they made more errors, and were less confident in the accuracy of their recall, when either objectively false assertions had been accompanied by the "truth" light or true assertions had been accompanied by the "lie" light than when their statements had been consistent with the implications of the light accompanying them. Bem discusses the potential practical implications of his findings for the extraction of false confessions. For example, if a person is induced to give a false confession under situational conditions in which he has previously told the truth, he may become less certain of whether or not his confession was a fabrication, and he may even come to believe that his confession was true. More generally, both this and the first study described above demonstrate that if situational cues become associated with certain types of behavior, they may affect the interpretation of later behavior that occurs in their presence.

A somewhat different study (Bandler, Madaras, & Bem, 1968) demonstrates that situational factors that induce subjects to respond differently to stimuli will affect the interpretations of these stimuli. In this study, P received a series of shocks and was asked to respond in one of two ways before judging its intensity. He was told that if a red light flashed while the shock was on (*Escape* conditions), he should turn off the shock by pressing a button; however, if a green light came on (*No Escape* conditions), he should *not* turn off the shock unless it was unbearable. P's behavior under Escape conditions implies that the shock being administered is intense, while his behavior under No Escape conditions implies that the shock is relatively mild. Thus, P should judge the shocks as more painful under Escape conditions than under No Escape conditions. This prediction was supported. Alternative explanations of these results are possible. For example, they are consistent with predictions of cognitive dissonance theory. Nevertheless, the study is an interesting application of Bem's formulation to attitude and belief processes.

E. Internal Cues to Self-Perceptions

The behavioral cues used by a subject to make inferences about himself may not always be observable. A second series of studies has focused on the effects of proprioceptive responses upon self-judgments. These effects, like the effects of more overt behavior, presumably depend in part on the situational conditions in which the responses occur. For example, these responses should be less likely to affect self-attributions if there are extrinsic reasons for making these responses.

The first direct test of this general hypothesis was made by Schachter and Singer (1962). Subjects ostensibly received an injection of a vitamin supplement called "suproxin" which in fact was either epinephrine (a drug that induces arousal similar to that experienced when one is emotionally excited) or salt water (a placebo). Subjects receiving the epinephrine were told one of three things. *Informed* subjects were told that the side effects of "suproxin" were those that typically accompany epinephrine (hand tremor, increased heart rate, and others), while *Misinformed* subjects were told that the injection would have side effects different from those resulting from epinephrine (that is, numbness, a slight headache, and itchiness).

Uninformed subjects and *Placebo* subjects were not given any information about possible side effects. Each subject was then asked to wait with another subject, actually an accomplice, until the injection took effect. During this period, the accomplice behaved in one of two ways. Under *Euphoria* conditions, he engaged in a series of behaviors inappropriate to the situation, such as animatedly tossing paper wads into a wastebasket, flying paper airplanes, and performing with a hula hoop. Under *Anger* conditions, each subject completed a questionnaire pertaining to rather personal details about himself and his family. While completing the questionnaire, the accomplice simulated first annoyance and finally anger, ultimately ripping up the questionnaire and tossing it into the waste-paper basket.

After being exposed to one of the above sets of conditions, each subject was administered a different questionnaire designed to measure his happiness or anger. Subjects who had received epinephrine but had been correctly informed about its side effects described themselves as substantially less happy (under Euphoria conditions) or angry (under Anger conditions) than did subjects under other conditions; they also manifested less general activity during the waiting period. Placebo subjects reported a moderate amount of emotion similar to that implied by the accomplice's behavior and showed a moderate amount of activity. Subjects who were either uninformed or misinformed about the effects of the drug reported the greatest emotion and manifested the greatest amount of activity.

A fairly simple-minded alternative explanation of these findings should be noted. A self-perception explanation assumes that the accomplice's behavior affected the interpretation subjects placed upon their own responses to the drug, and that this interpretation mediated the perception of their moods. However, subjects' moods may often be direct responses to the behavior of persons they are with and are not necessarily mediated by interpretations they place upon their own behavior. (That is, persons may be happy because their associates behave in "happy" ways, angry because their associates appear angry, etc.) These responses may generally occur (as suggested by the effects reported by Schachter and Singer under Placebo conditions) but may be heightened when subjects are aroused and thus more sensitive to external stimulation. However, a contingency in the influence of another's behavior may be whether the subject believes that this behavior genuinely reflects the other's mood; for example, a subject is less likely to feel happy when with persons who are only pretending to be happy than when with those he believes are genuinely happy. Thus, under the informed condition, subjects may have been less influenced because they believed that the accomplice's behavior did not reflect his actual mood, and not because they were better able to explain their *own* general arousal.

Other studies have focussed more directly upon the conditions in which subjects infer their beliefs about stimuli from their proprioceptive responses to these stimuli. Valins (1966) gave male subjects false feedback about their heart rate while they looked at photographs of nude females. Subjects' subsequent evaluations of the photographs were more favorable under conditions in which their heart had ostensibly beat faster. This finding seems to suggest that subjects used information about their heart rate as an indication of their attraction to the stimulus object and reported their attitudes accordingly. However, a later study (Valins, in press) showed that differences in evaluations as a function of heart rate were apparent even after subjects were told that the information they had received about their heart rate was false, and therefore was *not* a reliable index of their actual attraction to the stimuli. Valins concludes that internal responses to a stimulus do not simply have information value, but in addition they have a *directive* influence upon attention to the stimulus. In the present case, subjects who received feedback that their heart beat was rapid may have looked more critically at the stimulus being presented in order to "explain" their reaction, and thus they may have identified particularly favorable attributes of the stimulus that they would otherwise have overlooked. As a result, they may have made more favorable judgments of these stimuli and maintained them even after debriefing.

Subjects should be less apt to infer their beliefs about an object from their proprioceptive responses to it when they have reason to believe that these responses are due to other, extrinsic factors unrelated to the object. Implications of this general hypothesis were tested both by Nisbett and Schachter (1966) and by Davison and Valins (1969). In the first study, subjects received shocks of increasing intensity and were asked to indicate when the shock became intolerable. Before performing this task, subjects were given a drug (actually a placebo). Some subjects were told that the drug would increase their autonomic activity level, while others were told that it would have quite different effects. The authors hypothesized that the first group of subjects would attribute their arousal in part to the drug and would therefore tolerate a relatively more intense shock. Results supported this prediction.

Subjects in Davison and Valins' study, after reporting their tolerance for a series of shocks, received a placebo that allegedly reduced skin sensitivity. They then received a second series of shocks, which they believed were similar to those in the first series, but which in fact were much less intense. Thus, the level of shock tolerated by all subjects ostensibly increased in the second series. After exposure to the second series of shocks, some subjects were told that the drug they had received was actually a placebo, while others were not debriefed. All subjects, ostensibly after the "drug" had worn off, were then administered a third series of shocks. Davison and Valins reasoned that debriefed subjects would attribute their ostensibly higher tolerance for shock in the second series to their ability to withstand pain, while undebriefed subjects would attribute their higher tolerance to the effects of the drug. Thus, the former group of subjects should tolerate more intense shocks in the final series. Results showed this to be the case. Unfortunately, a "demand" interpretation of these results cannot be discounted; debriefed subjects are implicitly being told that they are expected to tolerate more intense shocks (by virtue of their past performance) and may therefore attempt to conform to these expectancies. Nevertheless, these results, like others cited in this section, are consistent with the hypothesis that subjects use both internal and external cues to infer their own attributes, and that their inferences can be modified by varying these cues.

F. Attributions About Other Persons

If Bem's general hypothesis is valid, further understanding of the conditions in which a subject will infer his personal characteristics from his own behavior may be gained by studying the conditions in which he will infer other persons' characteristics from their behavior. The identification of these latter conditions has been the concern of recent theory and research on attribution processes. There have been several theoretical treatments of attribution phenomena, initially by Heider (1958) and more recently by Jones and Davis (1965), Kelley (1967), Steiner (1970), and Anderson (1974). Rather than becoming too immersed in the details of this theory, it may be appropriate to summarize some of the research on factors that affect inferences of persons' attributes from their behavior.

1. *Generalizeability of Behavior over Persons, Objects, and Situations.* Suppose P benefits O. This behavior could have several implications:

1.   P is generally friendly and benevolent; that is, P's behavior reflects a general characteristic of P that is independent of the type of object toward which it is manifested.

2.   O is generally regarded favorably by people; that is, everyone behaves toward O in a benevolent manner.

3.   P has a uniquely favorable attitude toward O that is not generally shared by other persons.

4.   P is benevolent toward O for situation-specific reasons that are unrelated to his attitude toward O.

Kelley (1967) points out several factors that may determine which of these implications is likely to be valid. For example, if a number of people behave toward O as P does, P's behavior may not reflect an attribute of P, but rather a characteristic of O. On the other hand, if P responds to O as he does to a large number of other objects, it may reflect a general characteristic of P that has nothing to do with O *per se.* However, suppose P's behavior toward O is dissimilar to his behavior toward others, and that persons other than P do not behave in this way toward O. Unless P's behavior generalizes over situations, it is apt to be attributable to characteristics of the particular situation that exert an influence on P.

A study by McArthur (1972) bears upon the above hypotheses. Subjects estimated the likelihood that a hypothetical event (e.g., "John laughed at the comedian") was attributable to a characteristic of the actor ("John"), to a characteristic of the object ("the comedian"), or to situation-specific factors. The description of each event was accompanied by information that generalized the behavior over actors (e.g., "Almost everyone [hardly anyone] who hears the comedian laughs at him"), over objects (e.g., "John also laughs [does not laugh] at almost any other comedian"), and over situations (e.g., "In the past, John has almost always [almost never] laughed at the same comedian"). These types of information had interactive effects upon inferences; specifically, the behavior was judged more likely to reflect an attribute of the actor to the extent that it generalized over both objects and situations but did *not* generalize to other actors. Information about whether the behavior generalized over objects had the greatest effect, followed by information about whether it generalized over situations, and finally by information about its generalization over persons. In passing, note that these findings have implications for Eq. (11.2), which states that P's behavior (B) will affect inferences about one of his attributes (A) to the extent that $P_{B/A}$ differs from $P_{B/A'}$. McArthur's results indicate that this difference depends, to varying degrees, upon beliefs in the generality of this behavior over persons, situations, and objects.

2. *Situational Cues Affecting Attributions.* P's behavior is often observed in only one situation, and explicit information about its generalization over situations is not available. Nevertheless, characteristics of the situation may often suggest the extent of this generalization and therefore the likelihood that the behavior reflects an attribute of P. As suggested previously, P's behavior may be an unreliable indicator of P's underlying attributes if there are compelling external reasons for engaging in it, and therefore it may have little effect upon judgments of these attributes. On the other hand, a decision not to behave in this way, despite compelling external reasons for doing so, may be interpreted as extremely indicative of P's personal attributes and therefore may substantially affect judgments of these attributes. These predictions are intuitively reasonable, and moreover are consistent with Bayes' theorem, as we have shown earlier in this chapter. Although some of the situational factors that affect the interpretation of behavior are obvious, some representative studies bearing upon these factors may be worth reviewing briefly.

Relevance of behavior to external goal attainment. Jones et al. (1961) hypothesized that P's behavior is less apt to be attributed to an underlying personality characteristic if it appears to facilitate the attainment of a goal P desires than if it hinders him. Subjects listened to a person being interviewed for a position either as a submariner or as an astronaut. They were informed that the job of "submariner" required "other-directed" qualities (friendliness, cooperativeness, gregariousness), while the job of astronaut required "inner-directed" characteristics (self-reliance, independence of other people). During the course of the interview, the applicant's responses suggested he had attributes that were either consistent or inconsistent with the requirements of the job for which he was applying. Subjects subsequently rated candidates who presented themselves as having attributes required by the job as much less likely to have these attributes than candidates who presented themselves as having attributes opposite to those required by the job.

Compliance with expectancies of others.   Mills and Jellison (1967) asked college subjects to read a speech advocating an increase in the tax on trucks. Subjects were told that the speech had been made either to a group of truckers (who presumably were opposed to the position advocated) or to a group of railway men (who presumably favored this position). If subjects assume that people usually try to present themselves in a way that will be favored by others, a speech that deviates from the attitudes of the audience should be judged as a more reliable indication of the speaker's personal beliefs than a speech that conforms to the views of the audience. Consistent with this prediction, subjects rated the speaker as more honest, sincere, and impartial when the speech had allegedly been delivered to truckers rather than railway men. In addition to their potential relevance to self-perception processes, these results have implications for source effects upon attitude change. A speaker who is suspected of biasing his remarks in a way that his audience would favor should be less influential than a speaker whose remarks are obviously not intended to please his audience. In support of this hypothesis, Walster and Festinger (1962) found that subjects were more strongly influenced by messages from speakers who ostensibly were unaware that they were being overheard, and thus were not attempting either to ingratiate or to persuade these subjects, than by identical messages from speakers who were apparently aware that the subjects were listening.

Freedom of choice of behavioral alternatives.   Two studies (Steiner & Field, 1960; Jones & Harris, 1967) show directly that a person's behavior is more often inferred to reflect his underlying attitude if he chooses to engage in the behavior without any pressure to do so than if external demands are placed upon him. In Steiner and Field's study, a stooge (O) took part in a three-person discussion group on segregation. In one condition the experimenter assigned O the role of a prosegregationist, while in a second condition O volunteered to take the role. Subjects reported greater confidence that O actually favored segregation in the latter condition. Jones and Harris obtained fairly comparable results with a different attitude object (Fidel Castro). In the latter study, however, the direction of the position advocated by O had some effect upon subjects' judgments of O's attitude even under "low choice" conditions. It may be important to bear in mind the point we raised earlier in this chapter, that in principle a person *always* has some choice as to how to behave in the situations confronting him. In the present case, O could simply have refused to advocate the position he was assigned. To this extent, O's behavior may have been a relatively less reliable cue to his underlying attitude under "low choice" conditions than under "high choice" conditions, but a cue nonetheless.

A person's perceived freedom of choice may depend in part upon other attributes he is believed to have. For example, a person whose status and prestige is high in relation to the source of the request may be attributed greater freedom of choice about complying than a person whose status is relatively low (cf., Thibaut & Reicken, 1955). To this extent, the behavior of a high prestige source is more likely to be interpreted as a true reflection of his underlying attitudes.

Desirability of alternative behaviors. P's choice of a given behavior may of course depend not only upon his attitude toward this behavior and its consequences, but also upon his attitude toward alternative courses of action available to him. If these alternatives are undesirable, or if, in Thibaut and Kelley's (1959) terminology, his comparison level for alternatives (CL_{alt}) is low, P's choice may be attributed to his wanting to avoid undesirable alternatives rather than to a belief that the selected alternative is desirable. This prediction is consistent with Eq. (11.2). That is, when the alternatives to a particular behavior (B) are apparently aversive, the belief that P will choose this behavior even when he does not particularly enjoy it ($P_{B/A'}$) should increase, the difference between $P_{B/A}$ and $P_{B/A'}$ should be less, and the effect of information that he has chosen this behavior upon beliefs that he enjoys it ($P_{A/B} - P_A$) should be reduced. This hypothesis was tested directly by Ajzen (1971) in a study described earlier in this chapter. Briefly, subjects received information that a person P had chosen one of four alternatives. In one condition, three of the four alternatives had generally high utility, while in a second condition only one of the four had high utility. Beliefs that P had an attribute implied by his chosen behavior (one with high utility) were stronger when alternative behaviors also had high utility.

Implications for Self-Perception. If Bem's hypothesis is correct, the research summarized above has obvious implications for the effect of one's own behavior upon one's opinions. For example, a person who expresses an opinion that is consistent with his present or desired social role should believe himself less likely to hold this opinion than a person who expresses an opinion that deviates from role expectancies. Alternatively, a person who expresses a point of view to someone should be less apt to change his belief about this position if he thinks his audience agrees with him than if he thinks his audience disagrees with him. Moreover, such a person is less likely to change his belief toward the position advocated if he has been required to advocate this position than if he has volunteered to do so, and he is less likely to change his belief if he perceives himself to be of lower status than the source of the request than if he perceives himself to be of higher status.

An interesting application of this general line of reasoning can be made in predicting the effect of prior experience upon resistance to persuasion (cf. McGuire, 1964). That is, a subject who agrees to support a position for little or no monetary incentive will become more convinced of the validity of the position, and thus be more resistant to subsequent attacks upon this position, than a subject who supports the same position for a high incentive. To test this hypothesis, Kiesler and Sakumura (1966) initially paid subjects either $1 or $5 to read a speech supporting their own position on an issue. After this experience, all subjects read a communication attacking this view. As predicted, the subjects who were paid only $1 to read the supportive communication were less influenced by the subsequent attack than were those who read the same speech for $5.

G. Concluding Remarks

The hypothesis that subjects infer their own attributes from information about their own behavior, much as they infer the attributes of others from information about others' behavior, has extremely broad and important implications. It can account for the effects of behavior upon attitudes and beliefs at least as well as dissonance theory under conditions in which the latter formulation applies, and has implications for cognitive organization and change under conditions in which dissonance theory is not clearly relevant. Bem's "self-perception" theory is particularly attractive, since it requires no assumptions about an aversive internal state of arousal produced by "inconsistent" cognitions.

Bem's formulation is potentially consistent with the approaches to information integration described in earlier chapters. As we have noted, there is no necessary reason to believe that one's behavior is the *only* source of information that affects one's judgment of a stimulus. It is conceivable that the implications of one's own behavior combine with the implications of other types of information, perhaps in a manner similar to that described by the information integration models discussed in Chapter 9. This latter possibility has been explored in detail by Anderson (1974). Research designed to identify systematically the relative contributions of different types of information to attributions to oneself and others under different situational conditions may ultimately prove fruitful. A method for doing this has been proposed by Gollob (1974a, 1974b) and is described in Chapter 12.

III. SECOND AND BACKMAN'S THEORY OF INTERPERSONAL CONGRUENCE

A. Description of the Approach

In discussing Bem's formulation we noted that four general sources of information may bear upon judgments of a person's beliefs about an object: the general characteristics of the person himself, general attributes of the object, specific behaviors manifested by the person toward the object, and behaviors or reactions of the object toward the person. Bem was primarily concerned with the third source of information. In their theory of interpersonal congruence, Secord and Backman (1961) are concerned with all four sources.

Secord and Backman assume that the attributes a subject P ascribes to himself result both from P's observation of his own behavior toward other persons or objects and his interpretation of other persons' behavior toward him. For example, P's perception of himself as "intelligent" may in part be a consequence of P's observation of his performance on achievement tests, his perception that it is easy to get good grades in school, and his judgment that he can solve practical everyday problems quickly and easily. It may also be due to the fact that other people with whom he has contact tell him that he is intelligent, ask him for advice, ask him for help with their homework, and in other ways behave toward him as if he were bright.

Secord and Backman define a state of congruence as one in which P's self description is consistent with the implications of both his own behavior and others' behavior toward him. If incongruence arises, an unpleasant cognitive state is produced. This noxious condition can be eliminated in several ways, either separately or in combination. That is, P may change his self-perception. Or, he may try to interpret his behavior as being consistent with his self-perception. Or, he may try to interpret others' behavior toward him as being consistent with his self-perception. Moreover, he may attempt to disparage and avoid contact with others who behave toward him in a way that is inconsistent with his self-perception.

The interrelations of these possible effects may often be complex. For example, suppose P initially considers himself to be intelligent both because he has performed well in school and because others (O) respond to him as if he were bright. However, he then takes an intelligence test and learns that his IQ is only slightly above 100. How might P resolve this state of incongruence? One possibility would be to discount his performance on the IQ test; that is, he may attribute it to a "bad day," to lack of sleep the night before, or to lack of motivation to perform well. If such explanations are judged inadequate, however, P may have to conclude that his self-perception is incorrect and that he is in fact *not* intelligent. In this case, however, the state of incongruence is not yet eliminated, since O's behavior toward P is now inconsistent with this new self-judgment. To eliminate this inconsistency, P must now discredit O's behavior; that is, he must disparage O as someone who is either more stupid than he, or who is a bad judge of ability. Alternatively, he may attempt to avoid contact with O and thus prevent him from behaving toward P as if he were intelligent.

There are several general implications of Secord and Backman's formulation. For example, it implies that people prefer to interact with others whose judgments of them are similar to their self-judgments. This prediction, which is consistent with balance theory [2], is particularly interesting since it suggests that people who consider themselves to have unfavorable attributes should like, and prefer to interact more with, others who behave toward them as if they have these attributes than with those who behave toward them as if they have favorable attributes. This formulation also provides an explanation of the effectiveness of ingratiation. That is, suppose O wants P to respond to him in a friendly and helpful manner. If Secord and Backman's formulation is valid, an effective strategy for O would be to behave toward P *as if* he (P) were helpful and friendly. This may produce a state of incongruence which P could resolve by first changing his self-perception to "friendly and helpful to O," and then by actually behaving in a helpful and friendly way toward O. Note, however, that O's strategy would be effective only if P interprets his behavior as implying that P is friendly and helpful. If P is able to disparage O for his behavior, or to interpret it as an indication of O's stupidity or naivité, then P would not need to change his self-perception to retain congruence, and O's ingratiation strategy would backfire.

A weakness of Secord and Backman's theory is that it cannot predict *a priori* which of several alternatives will be used to retain congruence in any given situation. It is perhaps for this reason that the formulation has neither gained wider acceptance nor been exposed to an adequate empirical test. Nevertheless, it represents an interesting blend of the motivational assumptions underlying dissonance theory and the information integration approach taken by Bem. Both Bem and Secord and Backman assume that P's self-perception is a consequence of observations he makes of his own behavior. Secord and Backman go one step further in suggesting that the effects of P's self-perception and the interpretation he gives to his behavior are reciprocal; that is, P's self-perception may both affect and be affected by the interpretation he places upon his own behavior. Moreover, once P's self-perception is established, it may affect his interpretation of other persons' attitudes and behavior toward him. It should be noted that the phenomena predicted by Secord and Backman do not actually require the postulation of a noxious cognitive state. One need only assume that subjects interpret their own behavior in the context of others' behavior toward them, and interpret others' behavior in the context of their own beliefs about themselves. That is, if I believe myself to be intelligent, and someone behaves toward me as if I am stupid, this implies either that I am wrong in my belief or that the other doesn't know what he is talking about. The conclusion I come to depends in part upon other evidence bearing upon my intelligence, such as my own behavior in achievement and problem-solving situations. To this extent, then, Bem's formulation could be viewed as one component of the more general and comprehensive formulation of social inference proposed by Secord and Backman.

[2]This would be equivalent to a Type 2 inference ($Pr_1B \cap Ar_2B \supset Pr_3A$) where r_1 and r_2 are unit relations, r_3, is a sentiment relation, and B is a judgment of one of P's attributes.

B. Empirical Implications

While Secord and Backman have applied their theory to a substantial amount of research on social evaluation processes (Backman & Secord, 1959; Secord & Backman, 1964; Secord, et al., 1964), this research generally does not provide a critical test of their formulation. Indeed, most of their research can more easily be interpreted within the framework of cognitive balance theory. None of the research deals directly with the basic question of concern in this chapter, that is, the effects of one's own behavior upon one's beliefs. However, their formulation may often be applied to research performed within other theoretical frameworks, in which subjects' self-evaluations are considered to be a factor underlying the effects of behavior upon judgments. A good example of such an application is found in a study by Glass (1964). In this study, P initially took a personality test and then, in a second session, received feedback ostensibly based on this test. P was told either that he was mature, free of conflict, considerate, and sympathetic (*High Self-esteem* conditions) or was immature, inconsiderate, and had an unsatisfactory integration of motivations (*Low Self-esteem* conditions). This feedback presumably established P's perception of himself as either a "good guy" or a "bad guy." After receiving this feedback, P was introduced to a confederate (O) posing as another subject. P and O were given a chance to interact briefly, during which time O responded to P in a friendly manner. Then, the experimenter asked P and O to serve as "teacher" and "learner" respectively in a study of the effects of aversive stimulation on learning. In one (*Choice*) condition, P was explicitly told that he could refute to participate in the study and that continuing was his own responsibility. In a second (*No Choice*) condition, P's freedom to refuse was not made explicit. P's task was to administer a shock of 100 volts to O whenever he made an error. O ostensibly erred repeatedly, leading P to administer a substantial number of shocks to O during the course of the task. After completion of this task, P completed a questionnaire containing several items, some of which pertained to his liking for O.

What predictions would be made by the three formulations considered in this chapter? First, consider dissonance theory. The cognitions consonant and dissonant with the cognition "I am shocking O" may be tabulated as follows:

$$X \text{ (I am Shocking O)}$$

c_x	d_x
I am forced to shock O	I like O
	I am a good guy

Presumably, to reduce dissonance subjects should decrease their liking for O. Moreover, this decrease should be greater when P perceives himself to be a "good guy" (High Self-esteem conditions) than when he regards himself unfavorably (Low Self-esteem conditions), and greater when he is not forced to administer the shocks (Choice conditions) than when he feels required to do so (No Choice conditions).

Predictions based upon Bem's formulation are identical to those based upon dissonance theory. To apply this formulation, consider how a disinterested third party might interpret a subject's behavior under the various conditions of the study. Such a person is likely to assume that a subject who harms another is apt to dislike him. However, this assumption is more likely if the subject is not required to engage in this behavior, and it is also more likely if the subject himself is generally mature and considerate. Thus, if P applies similar reasoning in assessing the implications of his behavior for his attitude toward O, these attitudes should be affected more under High Self-esteem conditions than under Low Self-esteem conditions, and more under Choice conditions than under No Choice conditions.

To apply Secord and Backman's formulation, first consider the Low Self-esteem conditions. In this condition, P's behavior of harming O is congruent with his self-perception of a "bad guy." However, O's initial friendliness toward him (expressed during O's interaction with him before participating in the learning task) should be incongruent. Thus, P should tend to disparage O under this condition. In contrast, under High Self-esteem conditions, where P perceives himself to be a "good guy," his behavior of shocking O is incongruent with his self-perception, while his perception that O regards him favorably is congruent. In this case, P should not decrease the favorableness of his rating of O, at least as long as he maintains his self-perception. Thus, in summary, Secord and Backman's theory predicts that O will be derogated more in Low Self-esteem conditions than in High Self-esteem conditions, contrary to predictions of the other two theories.

The results obtained by Glass provide only partial support for any of the formulations, but they are most consistent with dissonance and self-perception theories. That is, when P was told he had freedom to refuse to participate, his evaluation of O decreased under High Self-esteem conditions ($M = -1.33$) but actually increased under Low Self-esteem conditions ($M = +.80$). However, when P was not told explicitly that he had a choice of participating or not, there was little change in his evaluation of O under either self-esteem condition.

Several aspects of Glass's data are embarrassing to dissonance theory. For example, although the absence of effects under No Choice conditions might be expected if indeed subjects felt they had absolutely no choice about participating in the study, supplementary data suggest that they did feel they had some choice ($M = 4.5$ along a scale from 1 to 7). Thus, while the effect of self-esteem should be less under No Choice than under Choice conditions, it should be in the same direction and significant under *both* conditions. Also, dissonance theory cannot easily predict an *increase* in evaluations of O under Low Self-esteem conditions. Finally, dissonance theory would predict a main effect of Choice versus No Choice, and this did not occur. On the other hand, the results obtained are clearly inconsistent with predictions based upon Secord and Backman's theory, which predicts that the devaluation of O should be greater under Low Self-esteem conditions than under High Self-esteem conditions—opposite to what actually occurred.

Glass's study provides a good mechanism for comparing predictions generated by Secord and Backman's formulation with those generated by other formulations of the relations between one's behavior and one's beliefs. One study, of course, does not make or break a theory. Unfortunately, sufficient research has not been performed to test the theory adequately. In its present form, the theory is often too vague to allow precise predictions of belief change. For example, it is difficult to determine *a priori* whether a particular type of self-relevant information will lead to a change in self-perception, or to a reinterpretation of one's own or another's behavior, in a manner that will reestablish congruence. However, in light of the potential generality of its application to the phenomena considered in this chapter, research designed to answer these questions is clearly warranted.

12
A CONCEPTUAL AND EMPIRICAL APPROACH TO THE INVESTIGATION OF COMPLEX INFERENCE PHENOMENA

As we have tried to point out in previous chapters, theoretical formulations of social inference phenomena typically oversimplify these phenomena in two ways. First, they implicitly assume that social inferences are governed by a single universal rule, rather than by several rules that may operate simultaneously and contribute differently to inferences under different conditions. Second, they often concentrate on only the evaluative or affective aspects of the information presented and the judgments being made, ignoring their descriptive or denotative aspects. Because of these factors, such formulations are of limited value in describing and predicting social inferences.

The frequent failure to take into account the descriptive implications of information is particularly unfortunate in light of direct evidence that their effects on judgments often override the effects of evaluative implications. Peabody (1967) asked subjects to infer attributes of persons under conditions in which the descriptive and evaluative implications of the information about these persons differed. For example, suppose P is asked to indicate whether a person is "generous" or "stingy," based upon information that he is "thrifty." "Generous" would be inferred on the basis of its affective similarity to the stimulus attribute, while "stingy" would be inferred on the basis of its descriptive (denotative) similarity to the stimulus. Peabody found that in every one of 70 different inference situations of this nature, judgments were governed more by descriptive similarity than by evaluative similarity.

The tendency to seek single universal rules of inference is understandable since until recently no general theoretical framework had been developed into which the complexities of social inference phenomena could be adequately incorporated, and no method had been developed for investigating systematically the different sets of assumptions that may underlie inferences based upon different types of information. However, Abelson (1973) has recently developed a general theoretical formulation of cognitive functioning that may satisfy the first of these needs, while Gollob (1974a, 1974b), a former student of Abelson, has developed a procedure for studying complex social inference phenomena that may satisfy the second. While these lines of work are still at an early stage of development, both are of sufficient importance to justify their detailed consideration. In this chapter, we will first discuss Abelson's and Gollob's theoretical formulations separately and summarize some of the research generated by each. Then, we will consider the two formulations in combination and attempt to show more directly the relevance of Gollob's work to Abelson's more general theory.

1. ABELSON'S THEORY OF IMPLICATIONAL MOLECULES

A. Theoretical Foundation

Although cognitive consistency may be a useful construct to use in the study of social inference phenomena, any single criterion for "consistency" is clearly inadequate. Perhaps no one has recognized this fact more than Robert Abelson, one of the original proponents of "symbolic psycho-logic" (see Chapter 5). In recent years, Abelson and his colleagues (Abelson, 1963, 1968, 1973; Abelson & Carroll, 1965; Abelson & Reich, 1969) have embarked upon a program of research that may lead to a much better understanding of the types of information that affects inferences in different situations, and of the contribution of cognitive consistency to these inferences.

The general theoretical approach taken by Abelson is described in detail by Abelson and Reich (1969) and has been elaborated by Abelson (1973). These authors postulate the existence of *implicational molecules,* or sets of sentences tnat are "bound together" by psychological implication. The nature of these molecules depends upon the general class of elements (subjects, verbs, and objects) to which they pertain. While such dependencies are matters for empirical investigation, certain hypothetical examples are given by Abelson and Reich. Consider three general classes of elements: an actor (A), an act or behavior (X), and an outcome (Y). Then, one molecule involving these elements might consist of the propositions [A does X; X causes Y, A wants Y]. Such a molecule may pertain to the general concept of purposive behavior; that is, persons do things to attain desired ends. It is important to note that the particular verbs in the proposition comprising the molecule, or the classes of elements involved, are not necessarily interchangeable. For example, the molecule [A wants X; X causes Y; A does Y] would not be sensible. On the other hand, a particular proposition may appear in more than one molecule. For example, a second plausible molecule containing the proposition "A does X" might be [B bosses A; B wants X; A does X]. An individual's cognitive structure may be composed of a number of such molecules, each pertaining to somewhat different classes of elements connected by various types of verbs.

Abelson and Reich hypothesize that if the relevant implicational molecules in a subject's cognitive structure can be identified, his inferences can be predicted on the basis of a "completion principle." This principle asserts that if all but one proposition of a molecule are known to be true, the remaining proposition will be inferred to be true. For example, suppose the molecule [A does X; X causes Y; A wants Y] exists in P's cognitive structure. Then, if P is told that a particular member of class A does X and that X causes some particular event of class Y, he will tend to infer that the member of A wants this event to occur. Or, if he is told that X causes Y and that a member of A wants Y, he will infer that the member of A is likely to do X.

In principle, many if not all of the inference rules described in previous chapters of this book would be candidates for implicational molecules. For example, balance principles could be viewed as molecules of the form [A likes B; B likes C; A likes C], [A likes B; B dislikes C; A dislikes C], etc. Self-perception phenomena (Bem, 1965) could be viewed as consequences of applying molecules of the form [I do X; persons who do X believe Y; I believe Y], etc. Beliefs that are organized according to the subjective probability model proposed in Chapter 4 [Eq. (4.6)] could be considered components of two molecules, [A; if A, then B; B] and [not A; if not A, then B; B]. It is also worth noting that the completion principle is consistent with assumptions of the theories to which the above molecules pertain. For example, balance theory assumes that any one of the three relations among elements of a triad can be inferred from information about the other two. Moreover, an application of the completion principle to the molecule [A; if A, then B; B] suggests that not only will beliefs in A affect beliefs in B, but beliefs in B will have reciprocal effects upon beliefs in A; this prediction is consistent with McGuire's (1960) hypothesis that beliefs in the conclusion of a syllogistically-related set of propositions will often have reciprocal effects upon beliefs in the premises.

B. Some Empirical Questions

It is nevertheless likely that the completion principle is not universally valid, or at least will often not apply equally well to each of the propositions contained in a molecule. For example, if the molecule [A causes B; B causes C; A causes C] were to exist, it would certainly be used less frequently to infer the validity of either the first or second premise than the validity of the third. In addition, any particular molecule is restricted to certain classes of objects and types of relations. The generality of the concepts to which any given molecule pertains, and the conditions under which the molecule is applied, must be able to be specified *a priori* before implicational molecule theory can be used to predict social inference phenomena effectively.

A second problem to be resolved concerns the extent to which one type of molecule has priority over another when each has different implications for the validity of a given proposition. For example, suppose P's cognitive system contains the two molecules [A does X; X causes Y; A wants Y] and [B bosses A; B does not like X; A does not do X]. If P is asked whether he believes that A does X, he might bring either or both of these molecules to bear upon this inference, and thus might arrive at different conclusions, depending upon which molecule he decides is more relevant. The factors that determine the relative contributions of implicational molecules to inferences under such conditions must ultimately be determined.

A third issue that must be investigated before Abelson's formulation can be used to generate accurate predictions concerns the conditions under which subjects will accept a general proposition on the basis of evidence about specific instances that support or oppose it. Molecules theoretically pertain to fairly broad conceptual categories and not to specific objects and events. To predict whether P will accept an assertion about specific objects, one must not only know the particular molecules P is likely to bring to bear upon this inference, but one must also know whether P believes that the information he has about these objects supports the general propositions contained in the molecules. For example, suppose P is told that Bob likes rock and roll and that Mary likes Beethoven sonatas, and P is then asked whether Bob likes Mary. The validity of the assertion "Bob likes Mary" might be determined on the basis of its consistency with the molecule [A likes X; B likes X; A likes B], where A and B are classes of persons to which Bob and Mary belong, respectively, and X is one of several general classes of objects to which the molecule is relevant. In the present case, assume that "music" is one of these general categories, and that it includes both "rock and roll" and "Beethoven sonatas." Then, if P believes that "Bob likes rock and roll" implies "A likes music," and that "Mary likes Beethoven sonatas" implies "B likes music," he would infer from this molecule that "A likes B" and therefore would accept as valid the assertion "Bob likes Mary." However, if P believes that the specific information about Bob and Mary is insufficient to accept the general propositions comprising the molecule, he would not apply the molecule and therefore might not accept the assertion.

All of the above questions may be investigated empirically. Once they are answered, implicational molecule theory may provide a general conceptual framework for integrating a broad range of phenomena related to cognitive organization and social inference. In fact, Gollob (1974a, 1974b) has developed a procedure for systematically identifying the criteria underlying social inferences and the extent to which the use of these criteria depends upon both the type of relation to be inferred and the type of objects being related. Since this procedure can be applied to many other general and specific issues we have raised in this book, it will be discussed in some detail. First, however, we will summarize some of the research concerning the third issue identified above, that is, the conditions in which subjects will accept a general proposition on the basis of limited information.

II. RESEARCH ON GENERALIZATION PROCESSES

As we have noted, the validity of a proposition about specific objects or events may be inferred in part on the basis of its consistency with previously-formed beliefs about more general categories of elements. For example, the statement that a particular Southern governor has vetoed a specific bill on open housing may be accepted as true because it is consistent with a more general belief that Southern politicians are opposed to civil rights legislation. Beliefs in these more general propositions may themselves be a result of information accumulated in the past about other specific instances of the general relation they describe. It is unclear, however, how much evidence is required before a general proposition is accepted as valid. Some propositions may be accepted on the basis of very little evidence, while others may require much more supporting evidence in order to be believed. Abelson and his colleagues have initiated a series of studies to explore some of the reasons for these differences.

In the first of these studies, Gilson and Abelson (1965) determined the acceptance of a general proposition as a function of the total amount of information bearing upon it, the proportion of statements that supported the proposition, and whether the verb connecting the subject and object of the proposition described a sentiment or a unit relation. Still another factor considered was whether the information supporting the proposition indicated that several members of the subject category were related in a particular way to a single member of the object category (*object-specific* information) or whether a single member of the subject category was related in this way to several members of the object category (*subject-specific* information). To give a concrete example, suppose that the general proposition to be validated was "People have gadgets." In one condition, nine pieces of information were presented, three in support of the proposition and six against it. In this condition, object-specific information consisted of the sentences:

A has X.	A does not have Y.	A does not have Z.
B has X.	B does not have Y.	B does not have Z.
C has X.	C does not have Y.	C does not have Z.

Subject-specific information consisted of the sentences:

A has X.	A has Y.	A has Z.
B does not have X.	B does not have Y.	B does not have Z.
C does not have X.	C does not have Y.	C does not have Z.

In a second condition, six of the nine sentences supported the proposition; in the object-specific case, all members of the subject class allegedly had Y as

TABLE 12.1

Proportion of Subsjects Giving "Yes" Response as a Function
of Evidence Form, Proportion of Supporting Instances, and Verb
(adapted from Gilson & Abelson, 1965)

Proportion and verb	Evidence Form	
	Object specific	Subject specific
.33 of instances positive		
Like	.375	.225
Have	.775	.300
.67 of instances positive		
Like	1.00	.975
Have	.975	.925

well as X, while in the subject-specific case, B as well as A allegedly had all three members of the object class. In still other conditions, only three pieces of information were presented, either one or two of which were positive instances. Finally, in some conditions the verb connecting people and gadgets was "have" (a unit relation) and in other cases it was "like" (a sentiment relation). Under each condition, P was asked, "Do people have (like) gadgets?" These judgments were investigated as a function of the type of information (subject-specific vs. object-specific), the amount of information supporting the proposition to be judged (1/3 vs. 2/3), and the type of relation described in the proposition (sentiment vs. unit).

Several aspects of Gilson and Abelson's results are of interest. First, the total amount of information presented, and thus the *number* of supporting instances, did not affect the proportion of times the general proposition was accepted. However, the *proportion* of supporting instances did have an effect. Table 12.1 summarizes the proportion of times the general proposition was accepted, averaged over different amounts of information, as a function of the type of relation involved (sentiment or unit), the proportion of supporting instances, and type of information (subject-specific vs. object-specific). When 2/3 of the information presented described supporting instances of the general proposition, the proposition was nearly universally accepted.

However, when only 1/3 of the information presented described supporting instances, the general proposition was accepted only when information was object-specific and the connecting verb was "have." In other words, the proposition "People have gadgets" was inferred from information that a person (or persons) have one gadget but not others; however, it was not inferred from information that one person has one (or more) gadgets but other persons do not. In contrast, the proposition "People like gadgets" was inferred neither from information that a particular person likes one gadget but not others, nor from information that a particular gadget is liked by one person but not others.

In a second experiment, Gilson and Abelson showed that their earlier findings generalize over several different subjects, verbs, and objects. In this study, 8 subjects, 8 verbs, and 8 objects were combined in all possible ways. P received either subject-specific or object-specific information that contained one supporting and two opposing instances. He then indicated whether he would accept a general proposition based upon this information. For example, in an object-specific case P was told: "There are three types of tribes—Southern, Central, and Northern. Southern tribes like sports magazines; Central tribes do not like sports magazines; Northern tribes do not like sports magazines." P then was asked, "Do tribes like sports magazines?" In a subject-specific case, P was told: "There are three types of magazines: sports, news, and fashion. Southern tribes like sports magazines, . . . do not like news magazines, . . . do not like fashion magazines." P was then asked, "Do Southern tribes like magazines?" The results of this study supported the conclusions drawn from the first experiment. That is, general propositions about unit relations ("produce," "buy," "have") were accepted much more frequently on the basis of object-specific information than on the basis of subject-specific information. However, general propositions about sentiment relations ("like," "understand," "avoid") were accepted infrequently, regardless of the type of evidence.

A series of studies by Abelson and Kanouse (Abelson & Kanouse, 1966; Kanouse & Abelson, 1967) provides further insight into the conditions in which subjects tend to infer general propositions from information about specific instances, and it shows the implications of this research for the construction of persuasive communications. In the first study, subjects received three pieces of information (assertions), either one or two of which were positive instances of a general proposition. In some cases, the object of each assertion was a concrete instance of the object of the general proposition; for example: "There are three kinds of bees: honey, bumble, and carpenter. Committees need honey bees. Committees do not need bumble bees. Committees do not need carpenter bees. Do Committees need bees?" In other cases, the object of each assertion pertained to a more abstract category than the object of the general proposition; for example: "Bees are flying, stinging, furry insects. Committees need flying insects.

Committees do not need stinging insects. Committees do not need furry insects. Do Committees need bees?''

In addition to the type of evidence and proportion of positive instances, Abelson and Kanouse varied the type of verb connecting subject and object. Two of their findings are of particular importance. First, general propositions that described positive unit relations were more readily accepted on the basis of concrete evidence than on the basis of equal amounts of abstract evidence. In contrast, propositions describing negative sentiment relations (e.g., "hate," "fear," or "avoid") were more readily accepted on the basis of abstract evidence than on the basis of concrete evidence. These differences make intuitive sense. A person who "has" one type of bee clearly can be said to have bees, while a person who "has" insects with one attribute similar to that of bees may not necessarily have bees. On the other hand, a person who "fears" only one type of bee may not fear bees in general, while a person who "fears" insects with a particular attribute possessed by bees would certainly be expected to "fear" bees.

Kanouse and Abelson (1967) applied the above findings in predicting the effectiveness of different types of persuasive communications. They constructed four communications on issues that subjects were unfamiliar with but were likely to perceive as meaningful (e.g., the effect of hunting regulations on the number of predatory birds). Each communication pertained to a core of two premises (e.g., "Hunting regulations produce increases in the number of legally protected birds" and "Farmers fear an increase in the number of legally protected birds") and a conclusion (e.g., "Laws against hunting legally protected birds are too strict"). In each case, the verb contained in one premise described a negative sentiment relation while the other conveyed a positive unit relation. The communication contained ostensibly factual information supporting each premise. This evidence was basically the same in all communications; however, in some conditions it pertained to concrete instances of the object of the premise (e.g., "Nebraskan crested hawks") and in other conditions it pertained to a more abstract category to which the object belonged (e.g., "Government-preserved wild life"). After reading these communications, subjects gave their own opinions about the conclusion and also rated how convincing the communication was. Results were clear. Regardless of the particular topic to which the communication pertained, messages containing concrete evidence supporting positive unit relations *and* abstract evidence supporting negative sentiment relations were more influential than messages containing either abstract evidence supporting positive unit relations *or* concrete evidence supporting negative sentiment relations.

Theoretical implications. To see the relevance of the research described above to implicational molecule theory, suppose that P is asked to judge the validity of the assertion "Bob likes Mary" and that his cognitive system contains the molecule [intellectuals like classical records; musicians have classical records; intellectuals like musicians], where "intellectuals" and "musicians" are classes to which Bob and Mary belong, respectively. If P applies this molecule, he would presumably accept the proposition "Bob likes Mary" to the extent he believes that "intellectuals like classical records" and "musicians have classical records" are both true. According to the results reported by Gilson and Abelson, P would accept the proposition "musicians have classical records" if he has evidence that several musicians have a particular classical record, but would *not* accept it if he has evidence that a particular musician has several classical records. Moreover, he would tend to accept the proposition "intellectuals like classical records" *only* if he has evidence that several intellectuals like several classical records. Therefore, P should be more apt to accept the proposition "Bob likes Mary" if (a) he is told that musicians typically own recordings of Beethoven's Fifth Symphony and that intellectuals typically like classical music than if (b) he is told that musicians typically own classical records and that intellectuals typically like Beethoven's Fifth Symphony.

Much more extensive research must be conducted to identify completely the sort of contingencies described above before implicational molecule theory can be rigorously applied. And as we have noted, this is only half of the battle. The other is to identify the type and generality of molecules that are likely to comprise a subject's cognitive system. Let us now consider a procedure that will be of substantial aid in attaining this goal.

III. GOLLOB'S "SUBJECT-VERB-OBJECT" FORMULATION OF SOCIAL INFERENCE

Gollob (1974a, 1974b) has developed a general procedure that can be used to identify the assumptions made by subjects in arriving at inferences about objects, and the extent to which these assumptions depend upon the particular type of information presented. Let us first describe this procedure in some detail and give several examples of its application to some of the theoretical and empirical issues raised in earlier chapters. We will then turn to some of the empirical research that has employed this procedure. Finally, we will draw upon certain aspects of this research in an attempt to demonstrate the value of Gollob's formulation in identifying the nature of implicational molecules and the conditions under which they are used.

A. Description of the Approach

Gollob (1974a, 1974b) has noted that the essential information contained in many triads of relations can be expressed in a single subject-verb-object sentence. Consider the three propositions "P likes A," "A dislikes B," and "P likes B." From P's point of view, the information in these propositions is contained in the single sentence "Likeable A dislikes likeable B." Such a sen-

TABLE 12.2

Presence (+1) and Absence (−1) of Sentence
Characteristics in Each Sentence Type

Sentence type	S-positivity	V-positivity	O-positivity	SV-balance	SO-balance	VO-balance	SVO-balance
ppp	1	1	1	1	1	1	1
ppn	1	1	−1	1	−1	−1	−1
pnp	1	−1	1	−1	1	−1	−1
pnn	1	−1	−1	−1	−1	1	1
npp	−1	1	1	−1	−1	1	−1
npn	−1	1	−1	−1	1	−1	1
nnp	−1	−1	1	1	−1	−1	1
nnn	−1	−1	−1	1	1	1	−1

tence would be representative of the general type *pnp*, where the first symbol refers to the valence of the subject ("likeable A"), the second to the valence of the relation implied by the verb ("dislikes"), and the third to the valence of the object ("likeable B"). Examples of other types of sentences *(ppp, ppn,* etc.) can also be easily generated.

Gollob has identified seven different characteristics of a subject-verb-object sentence that may potentially affect judgments based upon the sentence. These are subject (*S*), verb (*V*), and object (*O*) positivity, and four types of "balance": subject-verb (*SV*), verb-object (*VO*), subject-object (*SO*), and subject-verb-object (*SVO*). The criterion for determining balance in each case is an even number of negative valences (0 or 2). In the case of the first three types of balance, this simply means that the valences of the two sentence components involved are the same. The values of the characteristics in each of the eight sentence types are summarized in Table 12.2, where in each case +1 represents the presence of the characteristic (positivity or balance) and −1 represents the absence of the characteristic (or the presence of its opposite).

The summary shown in Table 12.2 has obvious but important implications. If judgments based upon all eight sentence types are available, the independent effect of each sentence characteristic upon these judgments may be inferred from the difference between the mean judgment of sentences designated as +1 in the column pertaining to the characteristic and the mean judgment of sentences designated as −1 in this column. Thus, the relative contributions of the seven characteristics may be reflected by the relative magnitudes of these differences. Statistical tests of the influence of the seven characteristics are in effect the seven orthogonal comparisons comprising a standard 2^3 analysis of variance. That is, if judgments are analyzed as a function of the valence *(p or n)* of the subject, verb, and object descriptions provided in the sentences being judged, the three main effects reflect the contributions of *S*-, *V*-, and *O*- positivity, and the four interactions of these variables reflect the contributions of the four types of balance.

Gollob postulates that inferences based upon the information contained in a sentence are a predictable function of some combination of the seven characteristics described above. Each of these characteristics pertains to a different assumption that subjects may make in arriving at a judgment. Thus, the contributions of sentence characteristics to a particular judgment may reflect the likelihood that each of these assumptions is made or, alternatively, the extent to which each of several different criteria is used by subjects as a basis for their judgments. The psychological interpretation of each sentence characteristic, and its potential role in inference processes, will become clear in the discussion that follows. Let us show how an *S-V-O* procedure can be applied to several theoretical and empirical problems discussed earlier in this book and attempt to demonstrate the value of this procedure in clarifying the psychological processes that govern social inference phenomena in these problem areas.

B. Applications of an S-V-O Analyses

1. *Sources of Cognitive "Bias."* In Chapters 5 and 10 we noted that several different factors may contribute to what subjects infer about the relation between two persons from information about these persons' relations to a third. These factors included a positivity bias (a result of the general assumption by subjects that relations among people are more likely to be positive than negative), a popularity bias (a result of the assumption that people who are liked by one person are apt to be liked by another), a friendliness bias (a result of the assumption that people who like one person are apt to like another), and a congeniality bias (a result of the assumption that a person who likes another is congenial, and thus is apt to be likeable himself). The contributions of these biases often appeared to override the contribution of cognitive balance principles to inferences about interpersonal relations. While there is some evidence for the existence of each of these biases, their relative contributions remain unclear. This latter question could be investigated by using an *S-V-O* procedure. For example, suppose judges were presented all eight combinations of sentiment relations among three persons P, A, and B (that is, "P likes A, A likes B, P likes B"; "P likes A, A likes B, P dislikes B"; etc.) and asked in each case to estimate the likelihood that the set of relations would actually occur. (In these triads, P could either be the judge himself or a third person.) As noted in the example at the beginning of the last section, these eight combinations of relations correspond to the eight sentence types shown in Table 12.2. If these judgments are analyzed as a function of *S*-positivity, *V*-positivity, and *O*-positivity, the relative contributions of the seven sentence characteristics would correspond to the relative magnitudes of the various biases described above.

a. The main effects of *S*-positivity, *V*-positivity, and *O*-positivity would indicate the magnitudes of *positivity* biases pertaining to P's relation to A, A's relation to B, and P's relation to B. The similarity in magnitude of these main effects would indicate the extent to which the positivity bias is independent of the type of persons involved in the relation. (This latter information would be of particular interest when P is the subject himself.)

b. A contribution of *VO*-balance would indicate the extent to which P's sentiment toward B is believed to be similar to A's sentiment toward B; the magnitude of this contribution would correspond to the magnitude of the *popularity* bias.

c. The contribution of *SO*-balance would indicate the extent to which P's sentiment toward A is believed to be similar to his sentiment toward B, and therefore the magnitude of the *friendliness* bias.

d. The contribution of SV-balance would indicate the extent to which P's sentiment toward A is believed to be similar to A's sentiment toward B. If this similarity is the result of an assumption that A's liking for B indicates that he (A) is congenial, and thus is likeable, this contribution would indicate the magnitude of the *congeniality* bias.

e. Finally, the positive contribution of SVO-balance would indicate the extent to which sets of relations implied by *ppp, pnn, npn,* and *nnp* sentence types are believed more likely to occur than sets of relations implied by *ppn, pnp, npp,* and *nnn* sentence types, and thus it would indicate the effect of *cognitive balance* on the inferences being made.

If the procedure described above is slightly modified, the contribution of various biases to inferences of the type identified in Chapter 10 can be investigated more directly. For example, to investigate the factors that contribute to Type 2 inferences ($Pr_1B \cap Ar_2B \supset Pr_3A$), judges could be given information about both P's relation to B (p or n) and A's relation to B (p or n) and then asked to estimate both the likelihood that P's relation to A is positive and the likelihood that it is negative. These data could be analyzed in a manner similar to that described in the first example, except that subjects' responses to the two items described above would comprise the two levels of S-positivity. Similar procedures could be used to infer the factors that govern Type 3 and Type 4 inferences. Empirical data obtained through these procedures will be discussed later in this chapter.

2. Source Characteristics that Affect Social Influence. Thus far in our discussion we have used p and n to refer to poles of a dimension with favorable and unfavorable evaluative implications, respectively. However, the general classification procedure proposed by Gollob can also be applied to sentence components that are not necessarily evaluative. For example, suppose one is interested in the extent to which males and females are believed to influence or be influenced by liberals and conservatives. To investigate this problem, one could arbitrarily designate one pole of each subject, verb, and object dimension (e.g., "male," "influence," and "liberals") by p and the opposite pole ("females," "are influenced by," and "conservative") by n. Thus, the sentence "Males are influenced by conservatives" would be of type *pnn*, and so on. If judgments of the validity of each of the eight possible combinations of S, V, and O are analyzed in this manner, the contribution of each of the seven sentence characteristics to the inferences could be determined and their relative magnitudes assessed. A positive contribution of SV-balance would indicate that males are believed more likely to influence O (or less likely to be influenced by O) than are females, regardless of O's liberalness or conservatism; a positive contribution of VO-balance would indicate that regardless of sex, people are believed more likely to influence liberals, and to be influenced by conservatives, than the reverse.

The preceding example suggests an application of S-V-O analysis to a rather practical problem. Suppose an experimenter wishes to know the conditions in which a source of information (S) is likely to induce attitude change. Intuitively, several factors may affect S's influence, including attributes of S himself (e.g., expertise, trustworthiness, friendliness, etc.), attributes of the person to be influenced (O), and the similarity between S and O. However, in any given situation the relative contributions of these factors to attitude change are often unclear. An initial step in investigating this problem systematically might be to ask judges to estimate both the likelihood that S would influence (p) O and the likelihood that S would be influenced by (n) O, where S is described by attributes that one might ultimately use to describe a "real" source, and O is described by attributes that are apt to characterize persons in the population of those one wishes to influence (for example, attributes relevant to O's self-concept, or descriptions of his social role). The relative contributions of SV-balance, VO-balance, and SVO-balance to these inferences, and the contingency of these contributions upon the type of dimensions used to describe S and O, may have implications for the conditions under which different sources of information will be effective. While these implications would need to be tested in actual social influence situations, the S-V-O formulation can help to generate initial hypotheses about the dynamics of these situations with a minimum investment of time and effort.

3. *A Comparison of Inferences about Self and Others.* We noted in Chapter 11 that subjects may often infer their own attributes from observations of their own behavior, much as they would infer attributes of others from observations of these others' behavior. However, we also pointed out that a person's behavior is unlikely to be the only determinant of his self-perceptions. Moreover, inferences about others and inferences about oneself may not always be identical. The S-V-O procedure can be used to investigate these possibilities and the conditions under which they are apt to arise. Suppose P is induced to help or to harm another (O) who is described as either kind or cruel, and P is subsequently asked to evaluate himself along a dimension of likeableness (that is, to estimate both the degree to which he is likeable and the degree to which he is dislikeable). These estimates are, in effect, inferences about an attribute of S in a subject-verb-object sentence where P himself is S. If these data are obtained under each combination of the experimental variables described above, an analysis of variance of estimates as a function of S (likeable vs. dislikeable), V (helps vs. harms), and O (kind vs. cruel) would enable the contributions of different sentence characteristics to be identified. The contribution of SV-balance would indicate the extent to which P infers his likeableness from his behavior, without considering the type of object toward which this behavior is directed. On the other hand, the contribution of SVO-balance would indicate the extent to which P's self-perception is based upon the implications of his

behavior towards different types of persons (that is, the extent to which he infers that he is likeable if he observes himself either helping kind persons or harming cruel ones). It is also conceivable that P's estimate of his likeableness is not based upon his behavior. If P has high self-esteem, he may judge himself to be more likeable than dislikeable, independent of other considerations. This tendency would be indicated by the contribution of S-positivity. On the other hand, P may infer his attributes to be similar in quality to those of others with whom he interacts. To this extent, SO-balance may contribute to his inference. The relative magnitudes of these contributions would indicate the priority given by P to these different considerations in arriving at his self-evaluation. Finally, if analogous information is obtained about evaluations of P by other persons who observe him under the various conditions described above, a direct comparison could be made between the contributions of these factors to P's self-perceptions and their contributions to "observers' " perceptions of P. For example, since "observers" are likely to have little information about S other than the behavior they have observed, while P himself has previously developed a fairly stable self-concept, it seems likely that S-positivity would contribute less to inferences about others than to self-inferences. However, other, perhaps more interesting differences, might also be detected.

A methodological point. To apply the S-V-O procedure in the situations described above, it was necessary to obtain separate judgments of the likelihood that S (the subject himself, or the person being observed) possessed the attribute representing each pole of a bipolar dimension (in this case, *likeable/dislikeable*). While these two judgments may appear to be redundant, they are essential in order to define the two levels of S-positivity and thus to perform an S-V-O analysis. If they are not obtained, main effects and interactions involving the attributes of S cannot be identified, and the contributions of S-positivity, SV-balance, and SVO-balance cannot be identified. This aspect of the data collection is the primary feature of the methodology that distinguishes the S-V-O procedure from more traditional approaches to the study of self-perception and social inference phenomena.

The preceding discussion only scratches the surface of many potential applications of an S-V-O procedure and the sort of conclusions that can potentially be drawn by applying it. Indeed, much of the existing research on social inference processes could be reanalyzed and reinterpreted in terms of the relative contributions of the seven sentence characteristics to the judgments made. In other cases, the S-V-O procedure cannot be applied only because, as noted in the preceding paragraph, separate judgments corresponding to each pole of one of the three dimensions describing S, V, and O have not been made. In these cases, a slight addition to the data collected could potentially increase substantially the amount of information obtained about the determinants of judgments in the situation being studied.

IV. EMPIRICAL STUDIES USING AN S-V-O PROCEDURE

Despite the value of applying an *S-V-O* procedure to fairly circumscribed problems in social perception and attribution, its primary contribution may ultimately lie in its ability to identify more general assumptions used by subjects in arriving at judgments of social stimuli, and to circumscribe the informational and situational conditions under which these assumptions are used. We pointed out in Chapters 8 and 9 that judgments of social stimuli of the sort typically studied in impression formation research may depend substantially upon the descriptive (denotative) implications of the information presented as well as its evaluative (connotative) implications. This fact was made even clearer in Chapter 10, where we showed that many situational factors not taken into account by balance principles contributed greatly to inferences.

Several studies performed by Gollob and others bear upon the above concerns. However, many of these studies (at least, those conducted by the present author) are preliminary in nature, and the results are often complex and difficult to digest. Although these data will be reported here in some detail for heuristic purposes, the average reader may wish to avoid becoming overly immersed in these details and concentrate instead on the more general implications of the results.

A. Social Evaluation Processes

Suppose P is asked to read a sentence describing A's behavior or feelings toward B and is then asked to evaluate A. This evaluation should be a function of the favorableness of A's attributes. Three characteristics of the sentence describing A may provide information about these attributes. One is of course the adjective used to describe A, and a second is A's behavior. To this extent, both *S*-positivity and *V*-positivity should affect evaluations. A third attribute may be the similarity between A's and P's attitudes toward B. This latter attribute may be reflected by the similarity between P's evaluation of B (suggested by the favorableness of the adjective describing B) and the evaluative implications of A's behavior toward B or, in other words, by *VO*-balance. Other sentence characteristics have less clear implications for the attributes of A and therefore would not be expected to have much effect upon evaluations.

A study by Gollob (1968) bears directly upon these predictions. Subjects read sentences of the form "The (*adjective*) man (*verb*) (*object*)" (for example, "The corrupt man reassures communists") and then evaluated the man. All eight combinations of subject, verb, and object favorableness were considered. Analysis of variance indicated that the main effects of adjective favorableness and verb favorableness (*S*- and *V*-positivity) each accounted for 37% of the variance in evaluations, while the verb by object interaction (*VO*-

balance) accounted for 22% of the variance; in other words, 96% of the variance was accounted for by these three factors. Moreover, the effects of these factors appeared to be additive. These results are therefore consistent with research reported in Chapters 9 and 10.

B. Subject Inferences

Suppose now that P is asked to infer a particular attribute of A on the basis of information about A's reactions to B and an attribute of B (for example, "A admires B. B is cruel. How likely is it that A is warm?"). Judgments of this sort and evaluations of A under the conditions described in the previous paragraph both pertain to an attribute of A. (In the latter case, the implicit attribute inferred is "likeable" or "dislikeable.") However, the definitions of the sentence characteristics assumed to affect these judgments may differ. In Gollob's (1968) study, S-positivity pertained to the quality of a *known* attribute of A upon which judgments of likeableness were partially based. In the present case, it pertains to the quality of the *unknown* attribute of A being inferred. The contribution of S-positivity, and also those of other informational factors, would be interpreted differently in the two cases.

The present author, in collaboration with Gollob, collected preliminary data that are relevant to these considerations. These data also help to identify contingencies in the use of different inference criteria upon the type of information presented. Since the design of this study, and the materials used, are similar to those in other studies to be reported in this chapter, they will be described in some detail.

Method. Judges were asked to estimate the likelihood that a person (S) possessed a given attribute on the basis of information about S's behavior or feelings (V) toward another (O) and an attribute of O. Each stimulus item was similar in form to the one described at the beginning of this section. The attribute used to describe O and the attribute of S to be inferred were each along one of the six bipolar dimensions shown in Table 12.3. These dimensions were of three types. Two types were clearly evaluative; however, one type (denoted S_{IR} and O_{IR} when applied to S and O, respectively) had implications for interpersonal relations, while the other (S_{St} and O_{St}) was more relevant to social status and prestige. The third type (S_P and O_P), which also had evaluative implications, consisted of two dimensions identified by Osgood et al. (1957) as relevant to "potency." In addition, six verb dimensions were used to describe S's reactions to O (See Table 12.3). These dimensions were also of three types; one type (V_A) described S's subjective feelings toward O, a second (V_B) described behavior with affective implications for O, and the third (V_C) described a relation of control by one party over the other.

The six dimensions associated with each sentence component were divided into two groups of three (one dimension of each type): S_1 and S_2, V_1 and V_2,

TABLE 12.3

Dimensions Used to Describe S, V, and O in Experiments
Pertaining to Subject, Verb, and Object Inferences

Types of dimensions	Group	Poles
Subject and object		
Interpersonal relations (S_{IR} and O_{IR})	S_1 and O_1	kind (p) vs. cruel (n)
	S_2 and O_2	warm (p) vs. cold (n)
Status (S_{St} and O_{St})	S_1 and O_1	successful (p) vs. unsuccessful (n)
	S_2 and O_2	beautiful (p) vs. ugly
Potency (S_P and O_P)	S_1 and O_1	strong (p) vs. weak (n)
	S_2 and O_2	hard (p) vs. soft (n)
Verb		
Feelings (V_A)	V_1	likes (p) vs. dislikes (n)
	V_2	admires (p) vs. despises (n)
Affect-related behavior (V_B)	V_1	helps (p) vs. harms (n)
	V_2	is friendly toward (p) vs. is unfriendly toward (n)
Control (V_C)	V_1	dominates (p) vs. is dominated by (n)
	V_2	influences (p) vs. is influenced by (n)

and O_1 and O_2. Eight different sets of stimulus materials were then formed, one for each combination of these groups (S_1 V_1 O_1, S_1 V_1 O_2, S_1 V_2 O_1, etc.). Twelve untrained judges (introductory psychology students) were then exposed to each set of materials; in each case, they estimated the likelihood that S possessed each of the six attributes along the dimensions pertaining to S on the basis of each of 36 sets of information describing V and O. These estimates were reported along an 11-point scale from 0 (not at all likely) to 10 (extremely likely). Therefore, considering all eight groups of judges, ratings along each of the six bipolar subject dimensions were made on the basis of each of the 144 possible combinations of information describing V and O.

Results. The poles of each dimension described above were designated p and n as shown in Table 12.3, and the contributions of the seven sentence characteristics to inferences were then calculated for each combination of subject, verb, and object dimensions. These contributions are shown in Table 12.4 as a function of the types of dimensions used to describe S, V, and O. (To make the primary contributors to inferences more salient, those with an absolute magnitude greater than 1.0 are underlined.) The effect of each sentence characteristic and its contingency upon the different types of information are evaluated statistically in Table 12.5.

As might be expected, V-positivity, O-positivity, and VO-balance did not appreciably affect subject inferences. While the contributions of V-positivity and VO-balance were statistically significant, the absolute magnitudes of their contributions were generally quite small $(M < .50)$. In contrast, the contributions of the other four sentence characteristics were often quite large and depended substantially upon both the dimensions along which information was presented and the type of attribute being inferred. A complete analysis of the nature of these contingencies is beyond the scope of the present discussion. However, some of the more salient aspects of these data may be worth summarizing.

SVO-balance contributed positively to inferences when V was along V_A or V_B and the attribute of S being inferred was along the same type of dimension as that used to describe O. More detailed analyses indicated that its contribution was greater when the attribute dimensions pertaining to S and O were identical $(M = 2.44)$ than when they differed but were of the same general type $(M = .82)$, and was greater when V pertained to S's feelings $(M = 2.08)$ than when it pertained to affect-related behavior $(M = 1.17)$. In other words, a person's similarity to O was more likely to be inferred from the favorableness of his feelings toward O than from the favorableness of his overt behavior toward O. While these findings are reasonably consistent with cognitive balance theory, others are less so. For instance, *SVO*-balance sometimes contributed negatively to inferences when the attributes of S and O were both evaluative but of different types (e.g., when S was inferred along S_{IR} and O was described along O_{St}). It contributed negatively to inferences along S_P when O was described along O_{IR}, and it also contributed negatively to inferences along S_{IR} when O was described along O_P; that is, an S who responded favorably to a kind (or warm) O was believed more to be weak (or soft) than strong (or hard), while an S who responded favorably to a strong (hard) O was believed more to be cruel (cold) than kind (warm). If "strong" and "weak" are regarded as favorable and unfavorable attributes, respectively, then these results, although intuitively plausible, are contrary to predictions based upon cognitive balance principles.

SV-balance was generally the major contributor to subject inferences, suggesting that judgments of an S's attributes are affected primarily by information about his behavior and attitudes toward O, regardless of the nature of O. However, the direction of this effect depended substantially

TABLE 12.4
Contributions of Sentence Characteristics to Subject Inferences

Sentence characteristic	Verb type	S_{IR}				Subject and Object types S_P				S_{St}				Average over subject types			
		O_{IR}	O_P	O_{St}	M	O_{IR}	O_P	O_{St}	M	O_{IR}	O_P	O_{St}	M	O_{IR}	O_P	O_{St}	M
A. S-positivity	V_A	-.21	-.44	-.52	-.39	.67	.30	.03	.33	.17	-.36	-.58	-.25	.21	-.17	-.36	-.10
	V_B	.32	.02	.00	.12	.71	1.19	.56	.82	.79	.72	.53	.68	.61	.64	.36	.54
	V_C	.12	.22	1.01	.45	.32	.16	-.53	-.02	.54	.34	.55	.48	.33	.24	.34	.30
	M	.08	-.07	.16	.06	.57	.55	.02	.38	.50	.24	.17	.30	.38	.24	.12	.24
B. V-positivity	V_A	-.04	.05	.15	.05	-.25	.07	-.00	-.06	-.04	.20	.05	.07	-.11	.11	.07	.02
	V_B	.05	.28	.05	.12	-.05	.23	-.11	.02	.14	.23	.12	.16	.04	.25	.02	.10
	V_C	.30	.23	.01	.18	.42	.30	.14	.29	.17	.03	.06	.09	.30	.19	.07	.19
	M	.10	.19	.07	.12	.04	.20	.01	.08	.09	.16	.08	.11	.07	.18	.05	.09
C. O-positivity	V_A	-.10	-.07	-.08	-.08	-.18	-.02	-.11	-.11	.05	-.21	.10	-.02	-.07	-.10	-.03	-.07
	V_B	-.06	-.07	-.17	-.10	.17	-.01	.09	.02	-.04	.04	-.18	-.06	.02	-.02	-.15	-.05
	V_C	-.08	.08	-.03	-.01	.06	.18	.08	.11	-.02	.01	.11	.03	-.01	.09	.05	.04
	M	-.08	-.02	-.10	-.07	.02	.05	-.04	.01	-.00	-.05	.01	-.02	-.02	-.01	-.04	-.02
D. SV-balance	V_A	1.40	2.15	3.53	2.36	-.77	-1.04	-1.30	-1.03	.15	.37	.88	.47	.26	.50	1.04	.60
	V_B	3.85	4.10	4.50	4.15	-1.38	-1.76	-1.30	-1.50	1.24	1.40	1.69	1.44	1.24	1.25	1.61	1.34
	V_C	-.85	-1.51	-.69	-1.02	2.82	3.58	2.42	2.94	1.13	1.34	1.56	1.34	1.04	1.14	1.10	1.09
	M	1.47	1.58	2.45	1.83	.22	.26	-.08	.13	.84	1.04	1.38	1.08	.84	.96	1.25	1.02
E. SO-balance	V_A	-.45	.43	-.10	-.04	.07	-.63	-.46	-.34	-.20	-.17	-.71	-.36	-.19	-.12	-.43	-.25
	V_B	-.63	-.07	-.37	-.36	-.31	.50	-.21	-.00	-.24	.06	-1.05	-.41	-.39	.16	-.54	-.26
	V_C	2.19	-.27	.35	.76	-.48	1.05	.52	.36	.72	.55	1.00	.76	.81	.44	.62	.62
	M	.37	.03	-.04	.12	-.24	.31	-.05	.01	.09	.14	-.25	-.01	.07	.16	-.11	.04

TABLE 12.4 (continued)

Sentence characteristic	Verb type	S_{IR}				Subject and Object types S_P				S_{St}				Average over subject types			
		O_{IR}	O_P	O_{St}	M	O_{IR}	O_P	O_{St}	M	O_{IR}	O_P	O_{St}	M	O_{IR}	O_P	O_{St}	M
F. VO-balance	V_A	.14	.09	.10	.11	.02	.07	.02	.04	.23	-.08	-.06	.03	.13	.03	.02	.06
	V_B	-.02	.22	.13	.11	-.23	.15	-.05	-.04	.09	.08	.09	.09	-.05	.15	.06	.05
	V_C	.10	-.12	-.09	-.04	.01	.06	.00	.02	.09	-.04	.17	.08	.07	-.03	.02	.02
	M	.07	.06	.04	.06	-.07	.09	.01	.00	.14	-.01	.07	.06	.05	.05	.03	.04
G. SVO-balance	V_A	3.36	-1.54	-.46	.45	-.92	1.69	.57	.45	1.24	.09	1.20	.84	1.22	.08	.44	.58
	V_B	1.91	-1.14	-.71	.02	-.27	.75	.31	.26	.55	-.23	.85	.38	.73	-.21	.15	.22
	V_C	.54	.46	.32	.44	-.80	.20	.06	-.18	-.31	.43	-.05	.12	-.19	.36	.21	.12
	M	1.94	-.74	-.29	.30	-.67	.88	.32	.18	.49	.09	.76	.45	.59	.08	.26	.31

TABLE 12.5

F-Ratios Pertaining to Contribution of Each Sentence Characteristic
and Its Contingency upon Informational Characteristics—Subject Inferences

	Sentence characteristic						
Effect**	S-positivity	V-positivity	O-positivity	SV-balance	SO-balance	VO-balance	SVO-balance
Mean	15.50*	15.87*	1.28	264.70*	1.08	4.28*	47.55*
Subject type (ST)	3.69*	.41	1.48	87.00*	1.60	1.25	4.46*
Verb type (VT)	18.11*	4.70*	2.43	20.74*	63.97*	.38	18.16*
Object type (OT)	5.97*	4.78*	.19	15.97*	4.20*	.05	12.66*
ST × VT	11.38*	2.72	1.08	194.93*	7.05*	1.87	7.62*
ST × OT	6.12*	.34	.59	14.79*	4.32*	2.40	84.98*
VT × OT	3.74*	3.35*	1.42	4.52*	8.62*	1.83	22.00*
ST × VT × OT	3.10*	.77	1.09	8.03*	21.39*	.74	24.92*

*$p < .05$

**For mean, $df = 1/88$; for ST, VT, and OT, $df = 2/176$; for ST × VT, ST × OT, and VT × OT interactions, $df = 4/352$; for ST × VT × OT interaction, $df = 8/704$.

upon both the dimensions along which information was presented and those along which attributes were inferred:

a. SV-balance contributed *positively* to inferences under two conditions: first, when V described feelings or affect-related behavior toward O and the attribute to be inferred was along S_{IR}; second, when V described control behavior and the attribute inferred was along either S_P or *successful/unsuccessful*. That is, S was believed more likely to be kind and warm, and less likely to be cruel and cold, if his reactions to O were favorable than if they were unfavorable; also, he was believed to be more hard, strong, and successful, and less soft, weak, and unsuccessful, if he controlled O than if he was controlled by O.

b. SV-balance contributed *negatively* to inferences when V described feelings or affect-related behavior and the attribute inferred was along *hard/soft*, and also when V described dominating behavior and the attribute inferred was along S_{IR}. That is, S was believed more likely to be soft than hard if his reactions to O were favorable rather than unfavorable; also, S was believed more apt to be cruel (or cold) and less apt to be kind (or cruel), if he dominated O than if he was dominated by O.

When V was described along a dimension pertaining to interpersonal relations (V_A or V_B), SV-balance contributed more positively to subject inferences when the attribute describing O was fairly irrelevant to the attribute of S being inferred. For example, this was true when the attribute to be inferred pertained to interpersonal relations (S_{IR}) and the attribute of O to status (O_{St}). This makes intuitive sense.

SO-balance. Table 12.4 shows that SO-balance contributed positively to inferences when S's response to O was described along V_C *and* the attribute of S being inferred was along the same type of dimension as that used to describe O. In fact, this relation held only when the verb dimension was *influences/is influenced by*. In other words, S was believed to have an attribute if he either influenced (or was influenced by) someone who possessed an attribute of the same type, but not if he influenced (or was influenced by) someone with a different type of attribute, even if its evaluative implications were similar.

S-positivity. The effect of S-positivity, like that of other characteristics, depended not only upon the type of dimension used to describe S, V, and O, but also upon the particular dimension representing each type. For example, it contributed positively to inferences along S_P and S_{St} when V pertained to helping or harming, but not when V pertained to friendly or unfriendly behavior. That is, S was believed more likely to be strong (hard) or successful (beautiful) than to be weak (soft) or unsuccessful (ugly) if he *either* helped *or* harmed O; however, this was not necessarily the case if he was described as friendly or unfriendly toward O. In addition, S was believed to be more kind than cruel if he either influenced or was influenced by O; this was particularly true when O was described along a dimension relevant to social status.

While the implications of these several contingencies are difficult to assimilate, they strongly suggest that the effects of sentence characteristics on subject inferences are principally determined by the descriptive rather than the evaluative implications of the information. This fact will become even more apparent in the following discussion of object and verb inferences.

C. Object Inferences.

Suppose P is asked to infer an attribute of B on the basis of information about an attribute of A and A's response to B (for example, "A is cruel. A admires B. How likely is it that B is warm?"). Such an inference differs from subject inferences primarily in the role of information about V (that is, about A's relation to B). Beliefs that B possesses a given attribute may depend in part upon the nature of the attribute itself (that is, upon O-positivity), and in part upon behavior toward B which was implications for this attribute (or upon VO-balance). Moreover, they may often be affected by the sort of reactions to B manifested by particular types of persons (or by SVO-balance).

To determine the conditions under which these and other criteria underlie object inferences, a study was conducted with the same basic materials used to investigate subject inferences. Judges received information about S and S's relation to O along a particular combination of the dimensions described in Table 12.3 and then estimated the likelihood that O possessed the polar attributes bounding three of the six object dimensions. (Stimulus items were similar in form to the example given in the preceding paragraph.) By using a design analogous to that described in the previous section, estimates were obtained of the likelihood that O possessed attributes along each of six dimensions based upon each of the 144 possible sets of information describing S and V. The contribution of each sentence characteristic to each inference, calculated in the manner described previously, is shown in Table 12.6 as a function of the types of dimensions used to describe S, V, and O. The statistical significance of these contributions is summarized in Table 12.7.

As might be expected, sentence characteristics that did not directly involve O (that is, V-positivity, S-positivity, and SV-balance) did not appreciably contribute to inferences about O. While a few significant effects occurred, the absolute magnitude of the contributions involved was small.

SVO-balance. SVO-balance contributed to object inferences in conditions similar but not identical to those in which it affected subject inferences. That is, it positively affected inferences when V described feelings or affect-related behavior (V_A or V_B) and the attribute of O being inferred was along the same type of dimension used to describe S. However, SVO-balance did not

TABLE 12.6

Contributions of Sentence Characteristics to Object Inferences

Sentence characteristic	Verb type	S_{IR}				S_P				S_{St}				Average over subject types			
		O_{LR}	O_P	O_{St}	M	O_{LR}	O_P	O_{St}	M	O_{LR}	O_P	O_{St}	M	O_{LR}	O_P	O_{St}	M
A. S-positivity	V_A	-.02	-.18	-.21	-.13	-.02	-.02	-.13	-.06	-.03	.04	.13	.05	-.02	-.05	-.07	-.05
	V_B	-.02	.03	-.09	-.03	-.18	-.02	.00	-.06	-.00	-.08	-.31	-.13	-.07	-.02	-.13	-.07
	V_C	-.04	-.14	.03	-.05	.03	.17	-.16	.01	.19	.13	.16	.16	.06	.05	.01	.04
	M	-.03	-.09	-.09	-.07	-.06	.04	-.10	-.04	.05	.03	-.01	.02	-.01	-.01	-.06	-.03
B. V-positivity	V_A	.03	-.05	.11	.03	-.10	-.25	.11	-.08	-.03	-.35	-.07	-.15	-.03	-.22	.05	-.06
	V_B	-.02	-.05	-.10	-.06	.13	.07	.05	.09	-.01	-.05	.12	.02	.04	-.01	.02	.02
	V_C	-.26	-.44	-.13	-.28	-.35	-.14	-.18	-.23	-.12	-.20	-.30	-.21	-.25	-.26	-.20	-.24
	M	-.08	-.18	-.04	-.10	-.10	-.11	-.01	-.07	-.05	-.20	-.08	-.11	-.08	-.16	-.04	-.10
C. O-positivity	V_A	.61	.52	1.55	.90	1.10	.67	2.04	1.26	1.80	.75	2.74	1.76	1.17	.65	2.11	1.31
	V_B	.63	-.73	.67	.19	1.39	-1.12	.69	.32	1.83	-.84	.92	.64	1.28	-.90	.76	.38
	V_C	.52	.51	.90	.64	.66	.30	.70	.55	1.06	.10	.67	.62	.75	.30	.76	.61
	M	.59	.10	1.04	.58	1.05	-.05	1.14	.71	1.57	.00	1.45	1.01	1.06	.02	1.21	.77
D. SV-balance	V_A	-.06	-.08	.19	.02	-.06	.06	-.04	-.01	.05	-.08	.10	.02	-.02	-.04	.09	.01
	V_B	.05	-.12	.18	.04	.21	.11	.22	.18	.17	.05	-.05	.06	.14	.01	.12	.09
	V_C	.07	.04	-.02	.03	.13	.04	.09	.09	-.21	-.18	-.03	-.14	-.00	-.03	.01	-.01
	M	.02	-.05	.12	.03	.09	.07	.09	.08	.00	-.07	.01	-.02	.04	-.02	.01	-.02
E. SO-balance	V_A	-.32	.16	-.07	-.07	.02	-.67	-.12	-.26	-.00	-.01	-.34	-.12	-.10	-.18	-.18	-.15
	V_B	-.76	.25	-.52	-.38	-.02	.12	.05	.05	.15	-.41	-.18	-.15	-.21	-.01	-.22	-.14
	V_C	1.76	-.36	.29	.57	-.15	1.09	.41	.45	.15	.43	.95	.51	.59	.39	.55	.51
	M	.23	.03	-.10	.05	-.05	.18	.11	.08	.10	.00	.14	.08	.09	.07	.05	.07

TABLE 12.6 (continued)

Sentence characteristic	Verb type	Subject and Object types												Average over subject types			
		S_{IR}				S_P				S_{St}							
		O_{IR}	O_P	O_{St}	M	O_{IR}	O_P	O_{St}	M	O_{IR}	O_P	O_{St}	M	O_{IR}	O_P	O_{St}	M
F. VO-balance	V_A	1.10	.13	.49	.48	1.05	.62	.48	.72	1.10	.04	.25	.46	1.08	.26	.41	.58
	V_B	.70	-.22	-.04	.15	.82	.11	.16	.36	.78	.03	-.29	.17	.77	-.02	-.06	.23
	V_C	1.49	-3.12	-.82	-.82	1.37	-3.73	-1.21	-1.19	.81	-2.73	-1.58	-1.17	1.22	-3.19	-1.20	-1.05
	M	1.10	-1.07	-.12	-.03	1.08	-1.00	-.19	-.04	.90	-.88	-.54	-.17	1.03	-.99	-.28	-.08
G. SVO-balance	V_A	3.97	-1.31	.97	1.21	-1.06	1.69	.30	.31	.03	.19	.84	.35	.98	.19	.71	.62
	V_B	2.54	-.95	.41	.67	-.62	.90	.43	.24	.14	.37	1.10	.54	.69	.10	.65	.48
	V_C	-.80	.85	-.08	-.01	.34	-.28	.09	.06	-.45	.24	-.25	-.16	-.30	.27	-.08	-.04
	M	1.90	-.47	.43	.62	-.45	.77	.28	.20	-.10	.27	.56	.25	.45	.19	.42	.35

TABLE 12.7

F-Ratios Pertaining to Contribution of Each Sentence Characteristic and its Contingencies to Informational Characteristics—Object Inferences

Effects**	Sentence characteristic						
	S-positivity	V-positivity	O-positivity	SV-balance	SO-balance	VO-balance	SVO-balance
Mean	.86	18.78*	73.24*	1.14	2.67	1.35	43.40*
Subject type (ST)	1.41	.24	10.91*	1.37	.04	1.71	12.74*
Verb type (VT)	1.73	6.40*	31.03*	1.53	25.72*	86.85*	23.11*
Object type (OT)	1.01	3.10*	34.94*	2.26	.07	64.04*	3.13*
ST × VT	1.36	1.30	3.31*	.76	1.89	2.13	5.22*
VT × OT	.17	.96	16.84*	.49	1.23	47.34*	10.80*
ST × VT × OT	1.60	1.29	1.00	1.22	14.05*	2.33	42.47*

* $p < .05$

** for the mean, $df = 1/72$; for ST, VT, and OT. $df = 2/144$; for $ST \times VT$, $ST \times OT$, and $VT \times OT$ interactions, $df = 4/288$; for $ST \times VT \times OT$ interactions, $df = 8/576$

contribute consistently to object inferences when the attributes describing S and O had evaluative implications but were of different types. Thus, the contribution of SVO (Heiderian) balance cannot be predicted on the basis of the affective implications of the information alone. SVO-balance contributed negatively to inferences about O when either S or O was described along a potency dimension and the other was described along a dimension pertaining to interpersonal relations. For example, O was inferred to be warm or kind if he was responded to favorably by a weak (soft) S or unfavorably by a strong (hard) S. Analogously, O was believed to be strong (or hard) if he was responded to favorably by a cold (cruel) S or unfavorably by a warm (kind) S. These results are similar to those obtained in analyses of subject inferences.

VO-balance. While the effects of *VO*-balance upon object inferences might be expected to parallel the effects of *SV*-balance upon subject inferences, a comparison of Tables 12.4 and 12.6 suggests that this was not the case. *VO*-balance contributed positively to inferences along O_{IR}; that is, O was believed more likely to be warm or kind, and less likely to be cold or cruel, when S's reactions to him were favorable or controlling than when these reactions were either unfavorable or subservient, regardless of the nature of S. However, *VO*-balance did not contribute to inferences along other types of dimensions when V was described along V_B, and it contributed negatively to these inferences when V was described along V_C. That is, O was believed more likely to be weak, soft, unsuccessful, or ugly (and less apt to be strong, hard, successful, or beautiful) when S controlled him than when he controlled S. The important theoretical aspect of these data arises when S's relation to O was along a control dimension. Then, *VO*-balance contributed positively to inferences when the attribute being inferred was evaluated and relevant to interpersonal relations, but it contributed negatively when the attribute inferred was evaluative but relevant to social status. Thus, the affective tone of the attributes inferred was not a sufficient basis for predicting the contribution of this sentence characteristic.

SO-balance. *SO*-balance contributed to object inferences under conditions similar to those in which it affected subject inferences. That is, it contributed positively to inferences only when S was described by an attribute along the same type of dimension as the attribute being inferred and V pertained to influence rather than domination. Put more simply, O was believed to have an attribute similar in type to that describing S if he either influenced or was influenced by S, but not if he dominated or was dominated by S.

O-positivity. Object inferences appear to be based upon O-positivity to the extent that S and V have unclear implications for the attribute being inferred. For example, when this attribute was relevant to interpersonal relations (along O_{IR}), O-positivity contributed relatively more when the attribute describing S was along dimensions *other* than S_{IR}; on the other hand, when the attribute to be inferred was not relevant to interpersonal relations, O-positivity was generally used only when V described S's feelings or attitude-related behavior toward O. Data in Table 12.6 also suggest that when V pertained to affect-related behavior, O was inferred to have more positive than negative attributes along evaluative dimensions (O_{IR} and O_{St}) but to have more negative than positive attributes along potency dimensions (O_P). Further analyses revealed that the second of these differences occurred only when the verb dimension was *helps/harms* ($M = -2.30$) rather than *is friendly/is unfriendly* ($M = .50$); for example, O was believed to be more weak than strong if S was described as either helping or harming him, but not if S was described as friendly or unfriendly toward him. Although this relation seems intuitively obvious, it is of interest since it exemplifies an instance in which the nature of V is clearly relevant to the inference about O, but its effect shows up in the contribution of O-positivity rather than VO-balance.

D. Verb Inferences

Of the three major types of inferences considered in this section, verb inferences may be the most complex. Suppose P is told that A possesses a certain attribute and is then asked to estimate the likelihood that A would behave or feel in a particular way toward a specific type of object (B). (For example, "A is generous (p). How probable is it that A has contempt for (n) intelligent people (p)?") In arriving at these estimates, P may conceivably make one or more of four different assumptions:

1. P may assume that when the adjective describing A is favorable, A is more likely to manifest favorable behavior and attitudes than unfavorable ones, regardless of the object toward whom the behavior is directed. In other words, P may employ the criterion of *SV-balance.*

2. P may believe that whether A will respond positively to a favorable object, and respond negatively to an unfavorable object, depends upon characteristics of A. To this extent, P's inferences may be predicted by using the criterion of *SVO-balance*; that is, if the adjective describing A is p, the verb and object would most likely be both p or both n, while if the adjective describing A is n, the verb and object would be most likely to differ in valence.

3. P may assume that favorable objects are responded to positively and unfavorable objects are responded to negatively, regardless of the charac-teristics of the person making these responses. This assumption would be similar in its effects to the "popularity bias" identified by Rubin and Zajonc (1969). If this is the case, P may apply a criterion of *VO-balance.*

4. P may assume that behavior toward an object is more likely to be positive than to be negative, regardless of the characteristics of either the object or the actor. This assumption, which in part could underlie the "positivity bias" reported in several studies of cognitive balance phenomena

TABLE 12.8

Mean Probability Estimates as a Function of
Description of B and Sentence Type—Experiment 1 (Gollob, 1974a)

Sentence	A. "Integration" sets	B. Other sets
ppp	4.60	5.01
ppn	−1.63	.49
pnp	−3.67	−4.78
pnn	− .02	−1.27
npp	−2.53	−1.85
npn	1.37	−2.51
nnp	1.92	.83
nnn	−1.43	1.42

(e.g., Wyer & Lyon, 1970; Zajonc & Burnstein, 1965), suggests that *V-positivity* will contribute to P's inference.

The likelihood of making each of these assumptions, and thus the contributions of the four sentence characteristics to which they pertain, may depend upon the particular information used to describe S, V, and O, as the studies described below suggest.

1. *Effects of Differences in Object Descriptions.* To demonstrate the usefulness of his formulation, Gollob (1974a) in one study presented information in the form described in the above example. Sixteen sets of stimulus items were selected which differed with respect to the particular verbs, adjectives, and nouns used to describe characteristics of S, V, and O. In each case, inferences were along a scale from −7 (extremely improbable) to +7 (extremely probable). Gollob found that the relative contributions of sentence characteristics depended upon the type of information used to describe O. In four sets of items, O was described as either approving (*p*) or disapproving (*n*) of integration. In the other 12 sets, O was described by either a favorable or an unfavorable personality adjective or social role (*intelligent/ignorant, considerate/inconsiderate,* or *physician/criminal*). Mean probability estimates based upon each of the eight sentence types are shown separately for "integration" sets and other sets in Table 12.8. The relative contributions of each of the seven sentence characteristics to these estimates, summarized in Table 12.9, suggest that when the object was described in terms of his attitude toward integration, *SVO*-balance contributed most to inferences, followed by *SV*-balance, and then *V*-positivity,

TABLE 12.9

Contributions of Sentence Characteristics on Probability
Ratings Shown in Table 12.8

Sentence characteristic	A. "Integration" items	B. Other items
S-positivity	−.01	.40
V-positivity	1.25	1.23
O-positivity	.51	.27
SV-balance	2.09	4.54
SO-balance	.79	.23
VO-balance	.65	2.32
SVO-balance	4.29	1.70

with VO-balance having very little effect. However, when O was described by a social role or personality adjective, SV-balance contributed most, followed by VO-balance, and then SVO-balance, with V-positivity contributing the least of the four characteristics pertaining directly to V. (In no case did a characteristic that did not pertain to V greatly affect inferences.)

While the above differences may be difficult to predict *a priori*, they are intuitively reasonable after the fact. First, consider data pertaining to "integration" items. S's reaction to a person with a certain attitude toward integration presumably depends upon his own attitude toward the issue. Although in Gollob's study S's attitude was not made explicit, it may have been suggested by the adjectives used to manipulate S-positivity (e.g., *generous/selfish, kind/cruel, sociable/unsociable,* and *optimistic/ pessimistic*). To this extent, the likelihood of a particular verb-object combination would depend upon S-positivity, or in other words, SVO-balance should be an important factor, while VO-balance alone should have little effect, as data in Table 12.9A suggest.

Now consider the other sets of items, in which O was described by a personality adjective or social role. Here, it makes more sense to expect that the effects of O's characteristics are independent of S's. That is, S may be believed to respond more favorably to an intelligent person than to an ignorant one, or more favorably to a physician than to a criminal, regardless of whether he personally is kind or cruel, or whether he is generous or selfish. Thus, the effect of VO-balance should be greater, and the effects of SVO-

TABLE 12.10

Mean Probability Ratings as a Function of Type of Verb
and Sentence Type—Experiment 2 (Gollob, 1974a)

Sentence type	A. Admires/despises	B. Other verbs
ppp	3.29	3.74
ppn	−4.01	− .15
pnp	−3.87	−3.66
pnn	.40	− .89
npp	−2.28	−2.17
npn	.21	−2.12
nnp	2.79	2.08
nnn	− .31	1.79

balance less, than when inferences are based upon the object's attitude toward integration. This in fact seems to be the case (see Table 12.9B).

2. *Effects of Differences in Verb Descriptions.* In a second study reported by Gollob (1974a), the relative contributions of sentence characteristics to verb influences were affected by fairly subtle differences in the verbs considered as well as the favorableness of the sentiments they described. Subjects received information about the subject and the object of a sentence and then estimated the probability that either a favorable or an unfavorable verb described S's relation to O. (For example, "A is friendly and B is unfriendly. How probable is it that A likes B?") In this study, S and O were typically described along attribute dimensions (e.g., *friendly/unfriendly, kind/cruel,* etc.). In all, eleven different sets of items were used. The results when the verb dimension involved was *admires/despises* differed from those obtained when other dimensions (*likes/dislikes, benefits/harms, often thinks about/rarely thinks about*) were involved.

Mean probability ratings for each sentence type are shown in Table 12.10 for (a) the three item sets in which *admires* and *despises* were the verbs to be inferred and (b) the eight sets in which other verbs were inferred. The effects of each sentence characteristic on each set of ratings are shown in Table 12.11. These data suggest that when the verbs inferred were *admires* and *despises, SVO*-balance was most important, followed by *SV*-balance and then *VO*-balance. When other verbs were inferred, however, *SV*-balance was most important, followed by *SVO*-balance and then *VO*-balance.

TABLE 12.11

Contributions of Sentence Characteristics to Probability
Ratings Shown in Table 12.10

	A. Admires/despises	B. Other Verbs
S-positivity	−1.15	− .13
V-positivity	− .45	− .01
O-positivity	.95	.34
SV-balance	1.72	4.07
SO-balance	.61	.22
VO-balance	1.50	1.58
SVO-balance	4.29	1.75

One can only speculate about the psychological significance of the differences in the relative influence of SV-balance and SVO-balance when different verbs were involved. However, feelings inspired by *admire* and *despise* may depend more upon the similarity in values of S and O than do feelings implied by verbs along dimensions such as *likes/dislikes* or *benefits/harms*. The latter verbs may be assumed to reflect general orientations of S which are implied by the adjectives used to describe him (in these cases, *friendly/unfriendly, kind/cruel*, etc.).

3. *Some Additional Contingencies.* Although Gollob's data demonstrate the importance of V-positivity, VO-balance, SV-balance, and SVO-balance to verb inferences, it is important to note that other characteristics may also contribute to these inferences. (Evidence for an effect of S-positivity was in fact obtained by Gollob; see Table 12.11A.) This would occur when a person is believed more likely to manifest responses described by both poles of the verb dimension involved than responses between these extremes. For example, a strong person may be more apt both to help and to harm another than is a weak person. Or, a successful person may be more likely both to be admired and to be despised than is an unsuccessful one. To this extent, verb inferences along *helps/harms* would appear to be a function of S-positivity, while inferences along *admires/despises* would be a function of O-positivity.

To explore these possibilities more fully, and to detect additional contingencies in the effects of different types of information upon the contributions of different inference criteria, we performed a study with materials and an experimental design similar to those used in the investigations of subject and object inferences. In this case, judges received information that S and O possessed attributes along different combinations of the dimensions described in Table 12.3. They then estimated the likelihood that S would respond to O in the manner indicated by the pole of one of the verb dimensions described in this table. Stimulus items were of the form "A is warm. B is cruel. How likely is it that A likes B?" The contributions of the seven sentence characteristics to these inferences, calculated in the manner described earlier in this chapter, are shown in Table 12.12 as a function of the general types of dimensions used to describe S, V, and O. The statistical significance of these contributions, and their dependence upon the types of dimensions involved, are shown in Table 12.13. All sentence characteristics affected verb inferences under some conditions. The major contingencies in these effects are summarized below.

SVO-balance. Of the three "balance" criteria expected to affect inferences, *SVO* (Heiderian)-balance was the least generally used. This characteristic, which reflects a tendency to assume that S's behavior toward O is contingent upon characteristics of O, did not contribute to inferences of control behavior and affected inferences of attitudes and attitude-related behavior only when S and O were both described along the same general type of dimension. The fact that it did *not* contribute to inferences when S was described along an evaluative dimension relevant to interpersonal relations and O was described along an evaluative dimension relevant to social status suggests that the influence of this characteristic is attributable to the descriptive implications of the information presented and not to its affective implications *per se.*

SV-balance. *SV*-balance generally contributed more to inferences than did any of the other six characteristics. This suggests that a person's behavior toward another is most often inferred from the nature of general attributes of this person, regardless of the attributes of the object toward whom the behavior is directed. When V pertained to feelings or affect-related behavior, *SV*-balance contributed more positively when S was described along evaluative dimensions relevant to interpersonal relations ($M = 3.83$) than when he was described along an evaluative dimension relevant to social status ($M = .60$) and contributed negatively when S was described along a potency dimension ($M = -1.08$). For example, beliefs that S would like (admire) or help (be friendly to) O were more strongly affected by information that S was warm (kind) or cold (cruel) than by information that he was successful (beautiful) or unsuccessful (ugly). Moreover, favorable feelings or behavior were believed less likely to be manifested by strong (hard) persons than by weak (soft) persons. These contingencies, which again are intuitively not very surprising, add still further support for the (by now, somewhat belabored) conclusion that the contributions of sentence characteristics to inferences are determined by the descriptive implications of the information presented and not by its evaluative implications *per se.*

TABLE 12.12
Contributions of Sentence Characteristics to Verb Inferences

Sentence characteristic	Verb type	S_{IR}				S_P (Subject and Object types)				S_{St}				Average over subject types			
		O_{IR}	O_P	O_{St}	M	O_{IR}	O_P	O_{St}	M	O_{IR}	O_P	O_{St}	M	O_{IR}	O_P	O_{St}	M
A. S-positivity	V_A	-.74	-.51	-.52	-.59	-.08	.00	.21	.04	-.66	-.65	-.74	-.68	-.49	-.38	-.34	-.41
	V_B	-.02	.15	.30	.12	.68	.82	.87	.79	.36	.11	.04	.17	.34	.36	.36	.36
	V_C	.24	.30	.88	.48	.11	.26	.11	.16	.36	.50	.52	.46	-.34	.38	.50	.37
	M	-.17	-.02	.20	.00	.24	.36	.40	.33	-.02	-.01	-.06	-.01	.03	.12	.18	.11
B. V-positivity	V_A	.50	.32	.38	.40	.07	.66	.55	.42	-.04	.47	.48	.30	.17	.48	.47	.38
	V_B	.73	.75	.42	.63	.56	1.16	.56	.76	.48	.49	1.16	.71	.59	.80	.71	.70
	V_C	.18	.85	.87	.63	-.45	-.10	.19	-.12	-.30	.22	.23	.05	-.19	.32	.43	.19
	M	.47	.64	.56	.55	.06	.58	.43	.36	.05	.39	.62	.35	.19	.53	.54	.42
C. O-positivity	V_A	.67	.28	1.05	.67	.74	.64	1.48	.95	.78	.85	1.50	1.04	.73	.59	1.34	.89
	V_B	.27	-.40	.25	.04	.62	-.47	.05	.07	.58	-.22	.15	.17	.49	-.36	.15	.09
	V_C	.15	-.06	.63	.24	.62	.28	.77	.55	.84	.21	.71	.59	.54	.14	.70	.46
	M	.36	-.06	.64	.31	.66	.15	.77	.53	.73	.28	.79	.60	.59	.12	.73	.48
D. SV-balance	V_A	2.63	3.02	3.14	2.93	-.95	-.50	-.78	-.74	.68	.05	.12	.28	.79	.86	.83	.82
	V_B	4.58	4.55	5.07	4.73	-1.56	-1.31	-1.41	-1.43	.98	1.09	.71	.93	1.33	1.44	1.45	1.41
	V_C	-.50	-.45	-.48	-.48	2.08	1.92	1.77	1.92	1.57	1.82	1.91	1.77	1.05	1.09	1.07	1.07
	M	2.23	2.37	2.58	2.39	-.14	.04	-.14	-.08	1.08	.99	.91	.99	1.05	1.13	1.12	1.11
E. SO-balance	V_A	.37	.12	.04	.18	-.15	-.42	.26	-.28	-.13	-.07	-.11	-.10	.03	-.12	-.11	-.07
	V_B	.31	.17	-.05	.14	.01	.03	.14	.06	-.02	.14	-.26	-.04	.10	.11	-.06	.05
	V_C	.66	.15	.34	.38	-.24	-.86	-.21	-.43	.28	.10	-.26	.04	.23	-.20	-.04	-.00
	M	.45	.15	.11	.24	-.12	-.41	-.11	-.21	.04	.06	-.21	-.04	.12	-.07	-.07	-.01

TABLE 12.12 (continued)

Sentence characteristic	Verb type	S_{IR}				S_P Subject and Object types				S_{St}				Average over subject types			
		O_{IR}	O_P	O_{St}	M	O_{IR}	O_P	O_{St}	M	O_{IR}	O_P	O_{St}	M	O_{IR}	O_P	O_{St}	M
F. VO-balance	V_A	1.27	-.04	1.54	.92	2.48	.31	1.94	1.57	2.70	.11	1.86	1.56	2.15	.13	1.78	1.35
	V_B	.01	.20	.21	.14	.87	.29	.80	.65	.95	.13	.46	.51	.61	.21	.49	.43
	V_C	.59	-1.95	-1.76	-1.03	-.01	-1.78	-1.91	-1.23	-.22	-1.74	-2.20	-1.39	.11	-1.82	-1.96	-1.22
	M	.62	-.60	-.01	.01	1.11	-.39	.28	.33	1.14	-.50	.04	.22	.96	-.50	.10	.19
G. SVO-balance	V_A	1.96	-.53	.34	.58	-.77	.80	.07	.03	.55	.04	.86	.48	.58	.10	.42	.37
	V_B	1.25	-.73	-.04	.16	-.20	.52	.35	.22	.59	.21	1.53	.78	.55	.00	.61	.39
	V_C	-.12	.50	-.10	.09	.01	-.13	.06	-.02	-.24	.10	-.08	-.08	-.11	.16	-.04	.00
	M	1.03	-.25	.07	.28	-.32	.40	.16	.08	.30	.12	.77	.40	.34	.09	.33	.25

TABLE 12.13

F-Ratios Pertaining to Contribution of Each Sentence Characteristic and Its Contingencies upon Information Characteristics—Verb Inferences

Effect**	S-positivity	V-positivity	O-positivity	SV-balance	SO-balance	VO-balance	SVO-balance
Mean	6.27*	23.64*	137.64*	209.86*	.01	13.06*	40.46*
Subject type (ST)	7.54*	2.64*	6.32*	121.74*	17.23*	7.92*	7.61*
Verb type (VT)	49.58*	5.32*	41.92*	12.44*	1.07	189.78*	11.69*
Object type (OT)	2.09	12.28*	13.64*	.60	3.35*	56.65*	5.49*
ST × VT	11.28*	5.48*	1.49	174.03*	6.81*	9.10*	7.11*
ST × OT	1.34	2.01	.37	1.84	1.88	1.16	23.46*
VT × OT	.64	1.91	6.18*	.11	2.35	18.28*	8.36*
ST × VT × OT	1.16	2.88*	1.54	2.41*	.59	4.19*	14.24*

*$p < .05$

**For mean, $df = 1/72$; for ST, VT, and OT, $df = 2/144$; for ST × VT, ST × OT, and VT × OT interactions, $df = 4/288$; for ST × VT × OT. interaction, $df = 8/576$.

SV-balance also contributed positively to inferences of control behavior, but only when S was described along S_P or S_{St}. For example, strong (hard) or successful (beautiful) persons were believed to exert influence or dominance, and weak (soft) or unsuccessful (ugly) persons were believed to be influenced or dominated, regardless of the nature of the other person involved in the relationship. (SVO-balance contributed negatively to inferences under these conditions.)

VO-balance. This characteristic presumably affects inferences to the extent that S's behavior toward O is believed to depend upon the nature of O, independently of the nature of S himself. It contributed positively to inferences of S's feelings about O (V_A) but had relatively little effect on inferences of behavior often assumed to reflect these feelings (V_B). Moreover, its contribution was pronounced only when O was described along an evaluative dimension $(O_{IR}$ or $O_{St})$. While information about O along potency dimensions did not affect beliefs about S's feelings or affect-related behavior toward him, both this information and indications of O's social status affected beliefs that S would control or be controlled by O. That is, O was expected to be less influenced by S if O was high in social status than if he was low. The negative contributions of VO-balance to these inferences are interesting to consider in the context of evidence that SV-balance contributed positively to these same inferences, while SVO-balance did not contribute to them at all. This suggests that inferences of control behavior are predictable as an additive function of characteristics of the controller and characteristics of the person being controlled, and do not depend upon the particular combination of persons involved in the relationship.

SO-balance. This was generally not a major contributor to verb inferences. More detailed analyses revealed that this characteristic contributed negatively to inferences of dominating behavior when S and O were described along the same type of dimension. That is, persons who were described differently along an evaluative dimension relevant to interpersonal relations (*kind/cruel* or *warm/cold*) were believed to be more apt to dominate one another than persons who were similar along these dimensions. This was not the case when V pertained to influence rather than dominance.

S-positivity. This contributed negatively to inferences of S's feelings toward O when S was described along either S_{IR} or O_{St}. Further analysis revealed that this relation was pronounced only when the verb dimension was *admires/despises* rather than *likes/dislikes*. That is, an S with a favorable attribute was believed less apt either to admire or to despise O, but was *not* believed less apt to like or dislike him, than was an S with an unfavorable attribute. This finding reemphasizes the conceptual difference between liking and admiration, which was suggested initially by Gollob's (1974a) research on verb inferences. When S was described along S_P, S-positivity contributed positively to inferences along V_B. Further analyses revealed that this contribution was large only when the potency dimension was *strong/weak* and the behavioral dimension was *helps/harms*. That is, strong persons were judged more likely both to help and to harm O than were weak persons but were not necessarily expected to be more or less friendly to him.

V-positivity. This generally contributed more to inferences of affect-related behavior toward O ($M = .70$) than to inferences of feelings ($M = .38$). Its contribution was greatest when S and O were both described along the same type of dimension.

O-positivity. When O was described along O_{st}, O-positivity contributed to inferences along V_A and, to a lesser extent, along V_C. This was primarily the case when the verb dimensions were *admires/despises* ($M = 2.13$) and *influences/is influenced by* ($M = 1.16$). In other words, successful or beautiful Os were believed to be both more admired and more despised, and were judged more apt both to influence and to be influenced by S, than were unsuccessful or ugly Os. In contrast, inferences of favorable or unfavorable behavior toward O were affected by *O*-positivity only when O was described along O_P and the behavior inferred was helping or harming. In this case, as might be expected, it contributed negatively; that is, strong (hard) Os were judged less apt to be either helped or harmed than were weak (soft) Os.

4. *Inferences about Idealized Events.* A study by Leaf, Kanouse, Jones, and Abelson (1968) provides further information about the factors that determine which sentence criteria are influential. Subjects in this experiment responded to questions about real situations (e.g., "Do considerate men harm cruel men?") and also idealized situations (e.g., "Should considerate men harm cruel men?"). When items pertained to real relations, the effect of *SV*-balance was greatest ($M_{diff} = 6.13$), followed by *SVO*-balance ($M_{diff} = 4.43$), and then *VO*-balance ($M_{diff} = 3.33$). These results are consistent with Gollob's findings under several conditions of his studies. However, when items pertained to idealized relations, *VO*-balance had the greatest effect ($M_{diff} = 4.57$), followed by *SV*-balance ($M_{diff} = 3.05$), and then *SVO*-balance ($M_{diff} = 1.97$). These data suggest that P believed that S *should* respond favorably to "good" persons, and unfavorably to "bad" persons, regardless of his personal characteristics. However, P believed that S's *actual* behavior toward O would depend more upon S's personal attributes than upon whether O was "good" or "bad."

E. General Implications

While each result described in the preceding sections seems straightforward, if not intuitively obvious, when considered in isolation, the implications of the data taken as a whole are complex and very difficult to digest. In light of the somewhat arbitrary selection of the dimensions along which information was presented and inferences were made, the primary value of these data at present may simply be to point out the complexities of social inference phenomena, and at the same time to show the potential value of Gollob's formulation in identifying the nature of these complexities.

It is clear that no single inference rule, or combination of rules, is applied in the same way to all types of inferences and in all situations. The contributions of sentence characteristics to inferences vary considerably with the general type of inference to be made, the type of attributes to be inferred, and the particular dimensions along which information bearing upon this inference are presented. Thus, if each sentence characteristic pertains to a different assumption about the implications of the information, then the likelihood that judges make these assumptions clearly depends greatly upon information content.

While the evaluative implications of the information presented may have some effect upon inferences, this effect appears to be generally small in relation to the effect of the descriptive or denotative implications of the information. Only occasionally did the contribution of a characteristic generalize over evaluative dimensions pertaining to interpersonal relations (*warm/cold* and *kind/cruel*) and those pertaining to social status (*successful/unsuccessful* and *beautiful/ugly*). While the attributes bounding the first type of dimension may differ in favorableness from those bounding the second type, this fact alone could not easily account for the many differences in inference rules used when these dimensions are involved. In many instances, the contributions of different sentence characteristics also varied over the dimensions *within* each general type being considered. This emphasizes the need to identify empirically the descriptive dimensions along which attributes and verb phrases vary. Some work on this issue has in fact been performed by Seymour Rosenberg and his colleagues (cf. Rosenberg, Nelson, & Vivekananthan, 1968; Rosenberg & Olshan, 1970; Rosenberg & Sedlak, 1972). Such research may be invaluable in ultimately understanding the descriptive effects of information upon inferences.

A distinction should be made between the difficulty an investigator may have in predicting the inferences made under different informational conditions and the complexity of the inference process itself, considered from the judge's point of view. The latter may in fact be quite simple. Despite considerable variation in the factors that contribute to inferences under different conditions, only one or two sentence characteristics contributed substantially to inferences at any one time. (Tables 12.4, 12.6, and 12.12 show that under no combination of subject, verb, and object dimensions did the absolute magnitude of more than three characteristics exceed 1.0.) Moreover, the contribution of the most influential characteristics was usually much greater in magnitude than the contributions of characteristics ranked second or third in importance. Perhaps judges do not take into account all possible factors that could conceivably have an effect upon the inference to be made. Rather, they may attend to only one or two factors that they feel are most relevant to this inference, based upon the particular type of information available, and give very little weight to other factors. This conclusion, if valid, is consistent with the implications of our analyses of Feather's (1967) data (see page 339)—that people base their inferences upon only those aspects of the available information that they believe to be most reliable, and ignore other relevant aspects which, under other conditions, might substantially affect their judgments.

V. AN ATTEMPT AT INTEGRATION

In light of the direct influence of Abelson on Gollob's early work, and their more recent collaboration (Gollob, Rossman, & Abelson, 1973), it is not surprising that the two major programs of research being conducted by these investigators are closely related. Indeed, it is perhaps more surprising that these investigators themselves have not yet established an explicit connection between their work. A preliminary attempt to do so will be made here in order to show more clearly the value of the S-V-O analysis in investigating fundamental questions raised by Abelson's more general theoretical formulation. These questions pertain primarily to two issues: first, the identification of implicational molecules and the generalization of these molecules over different classes of cognitive elements; second, the process of making inferences when more than one molecule is relevant to the inference being made.

A. The Identification of Implicational Molecules

Any sentence characteristic identified through S-V-O analyses which contributes to inferences under a given set of circumstances provides evidence for the existence of one or more implicational molecules. For example, suppose that *VO*-balance contributes negatively to both verb inferences and object inferences when O is described along the dimension *strong/weak* and V is described along *dominates/is dominated by*. This would suggest the existence of two implicational molecules: [B is strong; B dominates others] and [B is weak; B is dominated by others]. Or, suppose *SVO*-balance contributes positively to inferences of all three types when S, V, and O are described along the dimensions *warm/cold, helps/harms,* and *kind/cruel,* respectively. This contribution would provide evidence for the existence of four molecules: [A is warm; A helps B; B is kind], [A is warm; A harms B; B is cruel], [A is cold; A helps B; B is cruel], and [A is cold; A harms B; B is kind]. Note that a molecule suggested by *S-, V-,* or *O*-positivity would consist of only one proposition. For example, a positive contribution of *S*-positivity to subject inferences in the preceding example would indicate a molecule of the form [A is warm].

Unfortunately, not all types of molecules can be identified through the use of Gollob's formulation. For example, the molecules [A controls B; B controls C; A controls C] and [A wants C; B causes C; A does B] are not easily interpreted in terms of sentence characteristics, and thus their effects cannot be determined. Nevertheless, Gollob's approach is sufficiently general that it can potentially identify in a wide variety of situations the molecules that are relevant to inferences, as well as help to circumscribe the information characteristics that affect their use.

The data described in the preceding sections have some general implications for implicational molecule theory, and these may be worth mentioning. First and most obviously, the generalization of sentence characteristics over a set of informational conditions is an indication of the number of different molecules that are applied to inferences under these conditions. Specifically, a high degree of generalization would suggest that inferences are governed by a relatively small number of molecules, each of which pertains to relations among broad cognitive categories. On the other hand, if the effects of these characteristics are restricted to specific adjective and verb dimensions, this would indicate that a much larger number of molecules are involved, each of which pertains to small classes of elements. The S-V-O analyses reported in this chapter favor the second of the possibilities.

The validity of the "completion principle" postulated by Abelson and Reich may also be examined by using data obtained through an S-V-O analysis. This principle states that if a molecule consisting of two or more propositions exists in P's cognitive structure, P will infer the validity of any one of these propositions from information that the others are valid. Thus, if P's structure contains the molecule [A is cold; A harms B; B is kind], he should infer that each of the statements is true on the basis of information that the other two are true. Note that inferences of the validity of the three propositions in this molecule correspond to subject inferences, verb inferences, and object inferences, respectively, and the use of this molecule in making these inferences should be reflected by the contributions of SVO-balance.

An indication of the validity of the completion principle in specific instances may be obtained by comparing the data in Tables 12.4, 12.6, and 12.12. The principle should apply to an implicational molecule in the manner assumed by Abelson and Reich if the sentence characteristic to which the molecule pertains affects inferences about each sentence component (S, V, or O) involved in the characteristic. (For example, it would apply to a molecule pertaining to SVO-balance if this characteristic affects inferences of S, V, and O along the dimensions to which the molecule pertains; it would apply to a molecule pertaining to SV-balance if this characteristic affected inferences of both S and V along the dimensions specified in the molecule, and so on.) Data in the aforementioned tables show that the contributions of sentence characteristics to different types of inference vary considerably in magnitude. However, there are theoretical reasons to expect some degree of variation, which we will discuss presently. Considering only conditions in which the contributions of a characteristic to relevant inferences were all at least moderately high, the following sets of molecules appear to obey the completion principle:

1. [B is liked or admired by others; B is warm or kind], [B is disliked or despised by others; B is cold or cruel].

2. [A is warm or kind; A feels and behaves positively toward others], [A is cold or cruel; A feels and behaves negatively toward others].

3. [A is strong or hard; A harms and is unfriendly to others], [A is weak or soft; A helps and is friendly to others].

4. [A has high social status; A helps or is friendly to others], [A has low social status; A harms or is unfriendly to others].

5. [A is high in power or social status; A controls others], [A is low in power or social status; A is controlled by others].

6. [A and B are similar in social status (inferred from success or beauty); A feels or behaves positively toward B], [A and B are dissimilar in social status; A feels or behaves negatively toward B].

7. [A and B are similar along dimensions of warmth and kindness; A feels or behaves positively toward B], [A and B are dissimilar along dimensions of warmth and kindness; A feels or behaves negatively toward B].

8. [A is weak or soft; A feels positively toward B; B is kind or warm], [A is weak or soft; A feels negatively about B; B is cold or cruel], [A is strong or hard; A likes or admires B; B is cold or cruel], [A is strong or hard; A dislikes or despises B; B is warm or kind].

9. [A is similar to B along a particular attribute dimension; A both influences and is influenced by B], [A is dissimilar to B along a particular dimension; A neither influences nor is influenced by B].

The above list is only representative; further scrutiny of the data might reveal still other, and perhaps more interesting, molecules.

B. Multiple Determinants of Inferences

Abelson and Reich note that a particular proposition may often be contained in more than one implicational molecule. In such cases, several different molecules may be brought to bear upon the validity of the proposition. Since each proposition in a given molecule may be contained in a different number of other molecules, one consequence of this is that the relative contribution of a given molecule to inferences about each proposition contained in it may not be the same. To apply implicational molecule theory rigorously, one must not only be able to identify which molecules are relevant to any given inference, but must also determine the relative priority given to these molecules.

Fortunately, this task may not be as formidable as it first appears. Note from Tables 12.4, 12.6, and 12.12 that only a few sentence characteristics make appreciable contributions to an inference pertaining to any given combination of subject, verb, and object dimensions. This suggests that only a small number of molecules are brought to bear upon the validity of any given proposition. Gollob (1974a) has proposed a procedure for predicting the rank order of inferences pertaining to the eight possible sentence types (*ppp, ppn, pnp,* etc.) from knowledge of the relative contributions of the three characteristics that primarily affect these inferences. Let us describe this procedure by using an example. Data in Table 12.9A suggest that the three most important factors underlying inferences in this case were *SVO*-balance, *SV*-balance, and *V*-positivity. Following Gollob's notation, this priority ranking would be defined as an SVO/SV/V rule. Gollob hypothesizes that according to this rule, all sentences with *SVO*-balance should be ranked higher than sentences without *SVO*-balance. If sentences are similar in *SVO*-balance, those with *SV*-balance should be ranked higher than those without *SV*-balance. If two sentences are similar in both *SVO*- and *SV*-balance, the one that has *V*-positivity should be ranked higher. By referring to Table 12.2 and applying this rule, the rank order of the eight sentence types can be seen to be *ppp, nnp, npn, pnn, ppn, nnn, npp,* and *pnp.* Gollob postulates that if the rule is valid, the relative magnitudes of the inferences based upon these sentences should correspond to this rank order. In fact, the mean inferences based upon these sentences (see Table 12.8A) were 4.60, 1.92, 1.37, −.02, −1.63, −1.43, −2.53, and −3.67, respectively. Thus, with only one reversal, the magnitudes of the mean probability ratings are identical to the rank order implied by this rule. In other words, out of 28 possible paired comparisons of probability ratings, the SVO/SV/V rule predicts the higher rating correctly in 27 cases. This accuracy was substantially better than any alternative rule.

Now consider the data pertaining to other items. Here, the relative magnitudes of the effects of different sentence characteristics (Table 12.9B) suggest that an SV/VO/SVO rule might be most applicable. The rank order of sentences predicted according to this rule, and the actual mean inferences based upon these sentences, are: *ppp* (5.01), *nnn* (1.42), *nnp* (.83), *ppn* (.49), *pnn* (−1.27), *npp* (−1.85), *npn* (−2.51), and *pnp* (−4.78). Thus the rank order of the actual inferences based upon these sentences is exactly that predicted.

The results obtained in Gollob's second study are equally consistent with his procedure for forming inference rules. Since the rules used to generate the above predictions appear to be selected on a *post hoc* basis, their accuracy may seem less noteworthy. However, as Gollob points out, only 24 different rules can be formed from the four criteria primarily relevant to this type of inference (*SV*-, *VO*-, and *SVO*-balance and *V*-positivity), while there are 8! = 40,320 possible orders of the eight sentence types. Considered in this light, it is impressive for any one of the rules to predict accurately the rank order of inferences based upon these sentence types.

To the extent that each sentence characteristic pertains to a different implicational molecule, the procedure described above may be used to determine the relative priority given to different molecules under various conditions, and it can, therefore, predict the nature of the inference to be made on the basis of these molecules. Unfortunately, if the priority attached to different molecules is reflected by the relative magnitudes of the contributions of sentence characteristics corresponding to them, the determinants of these priorities are complex. Tables 12.4, 12.6, and 12.12 show that the *relative* magnitude as well as the absolute magnitude of the contributions of different characteristics vary not only with the type of information bearing upon the inferences but also with the type of inference to be made. Thus, in Abelson's terms, the order in which different molecules are brought to bear upon inferences of a given type may be hard to predict.

VI. CONCLUDING REMARKS

Despite the complexity of the data reported above, and the large amount of additional work that must obviously be done in order to develop a complete formulation of social inference phenomena, the approach suggested in this chapter is promising. Clearly we must dimensionalize the type of information used to describe objects and events to which inferences pertain. We must also come to a more general understanding of the effects that information along these dimensions has on the use of different inference criteria. The answers to these questions may not be easy to obtain. However, easy answers have never been guaranteed to investigators of phenomena in any area. Gollob's work suggests a mechanism for investigating the complexities of social inference phenomena; moreover, Abelson has provided a general theoretical framework within which these phenomena, regardless of their complexity, may be interpreted. At last, therefore, there is hope. It now remains for researchers to rise to the challenge that the complexities of these phenomena provide.

REFERENCES

Abelson, R.P.   Computer simulation of "hot" cognition. In S.S. Tomkins & S. Messick (Eds.), *Computer simulation of personality.* New York: Wiley, 1963.

Abelson, R.P.   Psychological implication. In R.P. Abelson, E. Aronson, W.J. McGuire, T.N. Newcomb, M.J. Rosenberg, & P. Tannenbaum (Eds.), *Theories of cognitive consistency: A sourcebook.* Chicago: Rand McNally, 1968.

Abelson, R.P.   The structure of belief systems. In K. Colby & R. Schank (Eds.), *Computer simulation of thought and language.* San Francisco: W.H. Freeman, 1973.

Abelson, R.P., Aronson, E., McGuire, W.J., Newcomb, T.N., Rosenberg, M.J., & Tannenbaum, P. (Eds.) *Theories of cognitive consistency: A sourcebook.* Chicago: Rand McNally, 1968.

Abelson, R.P., & Carroll, J.D.   Computer simulation of individual belief systems. *American Behavioral Scientist,* 1965, **8,** 24-30.

Abelson, R.P., & Kanouse, D.E.   The acceptance of generic assertions. In S. Feldman (Ed.), *Cognitive consistency: Motivational antecedents and behavioral consequents.* New York: Academic Press, 1966.

Abelson, R.P., & Reich, C.M.   Implicational molecules: A method for extracting meaning from input sentences. Paper presented at the International Joint Conference on Artificial Intelligence, Bedford, Mass., 1969.

Abelson, R.P., & Rosenberg, M.J. Symbolic psycho-logic: A model of attitudinal cognition. *Behavioral Science,* 1958, **3,** 1-13.

Ajzen, I.   Attribution of dispositions to an actor: Effects of perceived decision freedom and behavioral utilities. *Journal of Personality and Social Psychology,* 1971, **18,** 144-156.

Ajzen, I., & Fishbein, M.   Attitudes and normative beliefs as factors influencing behavioral intentions. *Journal of Personality and Social Psychology,* 1972, **21,** 1-9.

Allport, G.W.   Attitudes. In C. Murchison (Ed.), *A handbook of social psychology.* Worcester, Mass.: Clark University Press, 1935.

Allport, G.W., & Postman, L. *The psychology of rumor.* New York: Holt, 1947.

Anderson, L.R., & Fishbein, M.   Prediction of attitude from the number, strength, and evaluative aspect of beliefs about attitude objects: A comparison of summation and congruity theories. *Journal of Personality and Social Psychology,* 1965, **2,** 437-443.

Anderson, N.H.   Application of an additive model to impression formation. *Science,* 1962, **138,** 817-818.

Anderson, N.H.   Averaging versus adding as a stimulus-combination rule in impression formation. *Journal of Experimental Psychology,* 1965, **70,** 394-400. (a)

Anderson, N.H.   Primacy effects in impression formation using a generalized order effect paradigm. *Journal of Personality and Social Psychology,* 1965, **2,** 1-9. (b)

Anderson, N.H.   Component ratings in impression formation. *Psychonomic Science,* 1966, **6,** 279-280.

477

Anderson, N.H. Averaging model analysis of set size effect in impression formation. *Journal of Experimental Psychology,* 1967, **75,** 158-165.

Anderson, N.H. A simple model for information integration. In R.P. Abelson *et al.* (Eds.), *Theories of cognitive consistency: A sourcebook.* Chicago: Rand McNally, 1968. (a)

Anderson, N.H. Application of a linear-serial model to a personality impression task using serial presentation. *Journal of Personality and Social Psychology,* 1968, **10,** 354-362. (b)

Anderson, N.H. Likeableness ratings of 555 personality-trait words. *Journal of Personality and Social Psychology,* 1968, **9,** 272-279. (c)

Anderson, N.H. Functional measurement and psychophysical judgment. *Psychological Review,* 1970, **77,** 153-170.

Anderson, N.H. Two more tests against change of meaning in adjective combinations. *Journal of Verbal Learning and Verbal Behavior,* 1971, **10,** 75-85. (a)

Anderson, N.H. Integration theory and attitude change. *Psychological Review,* 1971, **78,** 171-206. (b)

Anderson, N.H. Cognitive algebra: Integration theory applied to social attribution. In L. Berkowitz (Ed.), *Advances in experimental social psychology.* Vol. 7. New York: Academic Press, 1974, 2-101.

Anderson, N.H., & Barrios, A.A. Primacy effects in personality impression formation. *Journal of Abnormal and Social Psychology,* 1961, **63,** 346-350.

Anderson, N.H., & Hubert, S. Effects of concomitant verbal recall on order effects in personality impression formation. *Journal of Verbal Learning and Verbal Behavior,* 1963, **2,** 379-391.

Anderson, N.H., & Jacobson, A. Effects of stimulus inconsistency and discounting instructions in personality impression formation. *Journal of Personality and Social Psychology,* 1965, **2,** 531-539.

Anderson, N.H., & Lampel, A.K. Effect of context on ratings of personality traits. *Psychonomic Science,* 1965, **3,** 433-434.

Anderson, N.H., & Norman, A. Order effects in impression formation in four classes of stimuli. *Journal of Abnormal and Social Psychology,* 1964, **69,** 467-471.

Aronson, E., & Carlsmith, J.M. Effect of the severity of threat on the devaluation of forbidden alternatives. *Journal of Abnormal and Social Psychology,* 1963, **66,** 584-588.

Aronson, E., & Cope, V. My enemy's enemy is my friend. *Journal of Personality and Social Psychology,* 1968, **8,** 8-12.

Aronson, E., & Golden, B.W. The effect of relevant and irrelevant aspects of credibility on attitude change. *Journal of Personality,* 1962, **30,** 135-146.

Aronson, E., & Mills, J. The effects of severity of initiation on liking for a group. *Journal of Abnormal and Social Psychology,* 1959, **59,** 177-181.

Aronson, E., Turner, J., & Carlsmith, J. Communicator credibility and communicator discrepancy as determinants of opinion change. *Journal of Abnormal and Social Psychology,* 1963, **67,** 31-36.

Aronson, E., Willerman, B., & Floyd, J. The effect of a pratfall on increasing interpersonal attraction. *Psychonomic Science,* 1966, **4,** 227-228.

Asch, S.E. Forming impressions of personality. *Journal of Abnormal and Social Psychology,* 1946, **41,** 258-290.

Attneave, F. *Applications of information theory to psychology.* New York: Holt, 1959.

Backman, C.W., & Secord, P.F. The effect of perceived liking on interpersonal attraction. *Human Relations,* 1959, **12,** 379-384.

Bandler, R.J., Madaras, G.R., & Bem, D.J. Self-observation as a source of pain perception. *Journal of Personality and Social Psychology,* 1968, **9,** 205-209.

Bandura, A., & Walters, R.H. *Social learning and personality development.* New York: Holt, Rinehart & Winston, 1963.

Bem, D.J. An experimental analysis of self-persuasion. *Journal of Experimental Social Psychology,* 1965, **1,** 199-218.

Bem, D.J. Inducing belief in false confessions. *Journal of Personality and Social Psychology,* 1966, **3,** 707-710.

Bem, D.J. Self-perception: An alternative interpretation of cognitive dissonance phenomena. *Psychological Review,* 1967, **74,** 183-200.

Bem, D.J. The epistomological status of interpersonal simulations: A reply to Jones, Linder, Kiesler, Zanna, and Brehm. *Journal of Experimental Social Psychology,* 1968, **4,** 270-274.

Bem, D.J., & McConnell, H.K. Testing the self-perception explanation of dissonance phenomena: On the salience of premanipulation attitudes. *Journal of Personality and Social Psychology, 1970,* **14,** 23-31.

Bergin, A.E. The effect of dissonant persuasive communications on changes in a self-referring attitude. *Journal of Personality,* 1962, **30,** 423-438.

Berkowitz, L., & Cottingham, D.R. The interest value and relevance of fear-arousing communications. *Journal of Abnormal and Social Psychology,* 1960, **60,** 37-43.

Bieri, J. Complexity-simplicity as a personality variable in cognitive preferential behavior. In D.W. Fiske & S.R. Maddi (Eds.), *Functions of varied experience.* Homewood, Ill.: Dorsey, 1961.

Bogartz, R.S., & Wackwitz, J.H. Transforming response measures to remove interactions or other sources of variance. *Psychonomic Science,* 1970, **19,** 87-89.

Brehm, J.W. Increasing cognitive dissonance by a *fait accompli. Journal of Abnormal and Social Psychology,* 1959, **58,** 379-382.

Brehm, J.W., & Cohen, A.R. Reevaluation of choice alternatives as a function of their number and qualitative similarity. *Journal of Abnormal and Social Psychology,* 1959, **58,** 373-378.

Brehm, J.W., & Cohen, A.R. *Explorations in cognitive dissonance.* New York: Wiley, 1962.

Byrne, D. *The attraction paradigm.* New York: Academic Press, 1971.

Byrne, D., London, O., & Griffitt, W. The effect of topic importance and attitude similarity-dissimilarity on attraction in an intrastranger design. *Psychonomic Science,* 1968, **11,** 303-304.

Byrne, D., & Nelson, D. Attraction as a function of attitude similarity-dissimilarity: The effect of topic importance. *Psychonomic Science,* 1964, **1,** 93-94.

Byrne, D., & Nelson, D. Attraction as a linear function of proportion of positive rein-forcements. *Journal of Personality and Social Psychology,* 1965, **1,** 659-663. (a)

Byrne, D., & Nelson, D. The effect of topic importance and attitude similarity-dissimilarity on attraction in a multistranger design. *Psychonomic Science, 1965,* **3,** 449-450. (b)

Calder, B., Ross, M., & Insko, C. Attitude change and attitude attribution: Effects of incentive, choice, and consequences. *Journal of Personality and Social Psychology,* 1973, **25,** 84-99.

Cartwright, D., & Harary, F. Structural balance: A generalization of Heider's theory. *Psychological Review,* 1956, **63,** 277-293.

Chalmers, D.K. Meanings, impressions, and attitudes: A model of the evaluation process. *Psychological Review,* 1969, **76,** 450-460.

Chapanis, N.P., & Chapanis, A. Cognitive dissonance: Five years later. *Psychological Bulletin,* 1964, **61,** 1-22.

Cofer, C.N., & Appley, M.H. *Motivation: Theory and research.* New York: Wiley, 1964.

Coleman, J.C. *Abnormal psychology and modern life.* Glenview, Ill.: Scott, Foresman, 1964.

Collins, B.E., & Hoyt, M.F. Personal responsibility-for-consequences: An integration and extension of the "forced compliance" literature. *Journal of Experimental Social Psychology,* 1972, **8,** 558-593.

Cooper, J., & Jones, R.A. Self-esteem and consistency as determinants of anticipatory opinion change. *Journal of Personality and Social Psychology,* 1970, **14,** 312-320.

Cottrell, N.B., & Wack, D.L. Energizing effects of cognitive dissonance upon dominant and subordinate responses. *Journal of Personality and Social Psychology,* 1967, **6,** 132-138.

Cromwell, H. The relative effect on audience attitude of the first versus the second argumentative speech of a series. *Speech Monographs,* 1950, **17,** 105-122.

Dabbs, J.M. Self-esteem, communicator characteristics and attitude change. *Journal of Abnormal and Social Psychology,* 1964, **69,** 173-181.

Dabbs, J.M., & Leventhal, H. Effects of varying the recommendations in a fear-arousing communication. *Journal of Personality and Social Psychology,* 1966, **4,** 525-531.

Darley, S.A., & Cooper, J. Cognitive consequences of forced noncompliance. *Journal of Personality and Social Psychology,* 1972, **24,** 321-326.

Davison, G.C., & Valins, S. Maintenance of self-attributed and drug-attributed behavior change. *Journal of Personality and Social Psychology,* 1969, **11,** 25-33.

Davol, S.H. An empirical test of structural balance in sociometric triads. *Journal of Abnormal and Social Psychology,* 1959, **59,** 393-398.

Deaux, K.K. Anticipatory attitude change: A direct test of the self-esteem hypothesis. *Journal of Experimental Social Psychology,* 1972, **8,** 143-155.

Deutsch, M., & Gerard, H.B. A study of normative and informational social in-fluences upon individual judgments. *Journal of Abnormal and Social Psychology,* 1955, **51,** 629-636.

Deutsch, M., & Solomon, L. Reactions to evaluations by others as influenced by self evaluations. *Sociometry,* 1959, **22,** 93-112.

Dillehay, R.C., Insko, C.A., & Smith, M.M. Logical consistency and attitude change. *Journal of Personality and Social Psychology,* 1966, **3,** 646-654.

Duke, J.D. Critique of the Janis and Feshbach study. *Journal of Social Psychology,* 1967, **72,** 71-80.

Dustin, D.S., & Baldwin, P.M. Redundancy in impression formation. *Journal of Personality and Social Psychology,* 1966, **3,** 500-506.

Ebbinghaus, H. *Memory: A contribution to experimental psychology.* (Trans. by H.A. Ruger & C.V. Bussenius) New York: Teachers College, 1913.

Edwards, A.L. *Technique of attitude scale construction.* New York: Appleton-Century-Crofts, 1957.

Edwards, W. Conservatism in human information processing. In B. Kleinmuntz (Ed.), *Formal representation of human judgment.* New York: Wiley, 1968.

Elms, A.C., & Janis, I.L. Counter-norm attitudes induced by consonant versus dissonant role playing. *Journal of Experimental Research in Personality,* 1965, **1,** 50-60.

Feather, N.T. A structural balance approach to the analysis of communication effects. In L. Berkowitz (Ed.), *Advances in experimental social psychology.* Vol 3. New York: Academic Press, 1967.

Feather, N.T., & Simon, J.G. Attribution of responsibility and valence of outcome in relation to initial confidence and success and failure of self and other. *Journal of Personality and Social Psychology,* 1971, **18,** 173-188.

Feldman, S. Motivational aspects of attitudinal elements and their place in cognitive interaction. In S. Feldman (Ed.), *Cognitive consistency: Motivational antecedents and behavioral consequents.* New York: Academic Press, 1966.

Festinger, L. *A theory of cognitive dissonance.* Stanford: Stanford University Press, 1957.

Festinger, L., & Carlsmith, J.M. Cognitive consequences of forced compliance. *Journal of Abnormal and Social Psychology,* 1959, **58,** 203-210.

Festinger, L., & Maccoby, E. On resistance to persuasive communications. *Journal of Abnormal and Social Psychology,* 1964, **68,** 359-366.

Fishbein, M. An investigation of the relationships between beliefs about an object and attitude toward that object. *Human Relations,* 1963, **16,** 233-239.

Fishbein, M. Prediction of interpersonal preferences and group member satisfaction from estimates of attitudes. *Journal of Personality and Social Psychology,* 1965, **1,** 663-667.

Fishbein, M. A behavior theory approach to the relations between beliefs about an object and the attitude toward that object. In M. Fishbein (Ed.), *Readings in attitude theory and measurement.* New York: Wiley, 1967.

Fishbein, M., & Hunter, R. Summation versus balance in attitude organization and change. *Journal of Abnormal and Social Psychology,* 1964, **69,** 505-510.

Freedman, J.L. Long-term behavioral effects of cognitive dissonance. *Journal of Experimental Social Psychology,* 1965, **1,** 145-155.

Freedman, J.L., & Sears, D. Warning, distraction and resistance to influence. *Journal of Personality and Social Psychology*, 1965, **1**, 262-266.

Gerard, H.B. Deviation, conformity, and commitment. In I.D. Steiner & M. Fishbein (Eds.), *Current studies in social psychology*. New York: Holt, Rinehart & Winston, 1965.

Gerard, H.B., Blevans, S.A., & Malcoim, T. Self-evaluation and the evaluation of choice alternatives. *Journal of Personality*, 1964, **32**, 395-410.

Gerard, H.B., & Fleischer, L. Recall and pleasantness of balanced and unbalanced cognitive structures. *Journal of Personality and Social Psychology*, 1967, **7**, 332-337.

Gerard, H.B., & Mathewson, G.C. The effects of severity of initiation on liking for a group: A replication. *Journal of Experimental Social Psychology*, 1966, **2**, 278-287.

Gewirtz, J.L., & Baer, D.M. The effect of brief social deprivation on behavior for a social reinforcer. *Journal of Abnormal and Social Psychology*, 1958, **56**, 49-56.

Gilson, C., & Abelson, R.P. The subjective use of inductive evidence. *Journal of Personality and Social Psychology*, 1965, **2**, 301-310.

Glass, D.C. Changes in liking as a means of reducing cognitive discrepancies between self-esteem and aggression. *Journal of Personality*, 1964, **32**, 531-549.

Glass, D.C. Theories of consistency and the study of personality. In E.F. Borgatta & W.W. Lambert (Eds.), *Handbook of personality theory and research*. Chicago: Rand McNally, 1968.

Glixman, A.F. Categorization behavior as a function of meaning domain. *Journal of Personality and Social Psychology*, 1965, **2**, 370-377.

Goldstein, M. The relationship between coping and avoiding behavior and response to fear arousing propaganda. *Journal of Abnormal and Social Psychology*, 1959, **58**, 247-252.

Gollob, H.F. Impression formation and word combination in sentences. *Journal of Personality and Social Psychology*, 1968, **10**, 341-353.

Gollob, H.F. Some tests of a social inference model. *Journal of Personality and Social Psychology*, 1974, **29**, 157-172.

Gollob, H.F. The Subject-Verb-Object approach to social cognition. *Psychological Review*, 1974, in press. (b)

Gollob, H.F., Rossman, B., & Abelson, R.P. Social judgment as a function of the number of instances, consistency, and relevance of information presented. *Journal of Personality and Social Psychology*, 1973, **27**, 19-33.

Haaland, C., & Venkatesan, M. Resistance to persuasive communications: An examination of the distraction hypothesis. *Journal of Personality and Social Psychology*, 1968, **9**, 167-170.

Hammond, K.R., & Householder, J.E. *Introduction to the statistical method*. New York: Knopf, 1962.

Harvey, O.J. Personality factors in resolution of conceptual incongruities. *Sociometry*, 1962, **25**, 336-352.

Harvey, O.J. Some situational and cognitive determinants of dissonance resolution. *Journal of Personality and Social Psychology*, 1965, **1**, 349-355.

Harvey, O.J., & Consalvi, C. Status and conformity to pressure in informal groups. *Journal of Abnormal and Social Psychology,* 1960, **60,** 182-187.

Harvey, O.J., Hunt, D.E., & Schroder, H.M. *Conceptual systems and personality organization.* New York: Wiley, 1961.

Harvey, O.J., Kelley, H.H., & Shapiro, M.M. Reactions to unfavorable evaluations of self made by other persons. *Journal of Personality,* 1957, **25,** 393-411.

Heider, F. Attitudes and cognitive organization. *Journal of Psychology,* 1946, **21,** 107-112.

Heider, F. *The psychology of interpersonal relations.* New York: Wiley, 1958.

Hendrick, C., & Costantini, A.F. Effects of varying trait inconsistency and response requirements on the primacy effect in impression formation. *Journal of Personality and Social Psychology,* 1970, **15,** 158-164.

Hendrick, C., & Jones, R.A. *The nature of theory and research in social psychology.* New York: Academic Press, 1972.

Hershkowitz, A. Interpersonal agreement and disagreement on objects and values: A preliminary study. Unpublished doctoral dissertation, University of Kansas, 1954.

Heslin, R., & Amo, M.F. Detailed test of the reinforcement-dissonance controversy in the counterattitudinal advocacy situation. *Journal of Personality and Social Psychology,* 1972, **23,** 234-242.

Hess, E.H. The pupil responds to changes in attitude as well as to changes in illumination. *Scientific American,* 1965, **212,** 46-54.

Himmelfarb, S., & Senn, D.J. Forming impressions of social class: Two tests of an averaging model. *Journal of Personality and Social Psychology,* 1969, **12,** 38-51.

Hinckley, E.D. The influence of individual opinion on the construction of an attitude scale. *Journal of Abnormal and Social Psychology,* 1932, **3,** 283-296.

Hollander, E.P. Conformity, status, and idiosyncrasy credit. *Psychological Review,* 1958, **65,** 117-127.

Hovland, C.I., Campbell, E.H., & Brock, T. The effects of "commitment" on opinion change following communication. In C.I. Hovland (Ed.), *The order of presentation in persuasion.* New Haven: Yale University Press, 1957.

Hovland, C.I., Harvey, O.J., & Sherif, M. Assimilation and contrast effects in reactions to communication and attitude change. *Journal of Abnormal and Social Psychology,* 1957, **55,** 244-252.

Hovland, C.I., Janis, I.L., & Kelley, H.H. *Communication and persuasion.* New Haven: Yale University Press, 1953.

Hovland, C.I., & Sherif, M. Judgmental phenomena and scales of attitude measurement: Item displacement in Thurstone scales. *Journal of Abnormal and Social Psychology,* 1952, **47,** 822-832.

Hovland, C.I., & Weiss, W. The influence of source credibility on communication effectiveness. *Public Opinion Quarterly,* 1951, **15,** 635-650.

Jackson, J.M., & Saltzstein, H.D. The effect of person-group relationships on conformity processes. *Journal of Abnormal and Social Psychology,* 1958, **57,** 17-24.

Janis, I.L. Effects of fear arousal on attitude change: Recent developments in theory and experimental research. In L. Berkowitz (Ed.), *Advances in experimental social psychology*. Vol. 3. New York: Academic Press, 1967.

Janis, I.L., & Feshbach, S. Effects of fear-arousing communications. *Journal of Abnormal and Social Psychology*, 1953, **48**, 78-92.

Janis, I.L., & Gilmore, B.J. The influence of incentive conditions on the success of role playing in modifying attitudes. *Journal of Personality and Social Psychology*, 1965, **1**, 17-27.

Janis, I.L., & Milholland, H.C. The influence of threat appeals on selective learning of the content of a persuasive communication. *Journal of Psychology*, 1954, **37**, 75-80.

Jecker, J.D. The cognitive effects of conflict and dissonance. In L. Festinger (Ed.), *Conflict, decision, and dissonance*. Stanford: Stanford University Press, 1964.

Johnson, D.M. *The psychology of thoughts and judgment*. New York: Harper, 1955.

Jones, E.E., & Davis, K.E. From acts to dispositions: The attribution process in person perception. In L. Berkowitz (Ed.), *Advances in experimental social psychology*. Vol. 2. New York: Academic Press, 1965.

Jones, E.E., Davis, K.E., & Gergen, K.J. Role playing variations and their informational value for person perception. *Journal of Abnormal and Social Psychology*, 1961, **63**, 302-310.

Jones, E.E., & Gerard, H.B. *Foundations of social psychology*. New York: Wiley, 1967.

Jones, E.E., & Harris, V.A. The attribution of attitudes. *Journal of Experimental Social Psychology*, 1967, **3**, 1-24.

Jones, E.E., & Nisbett, R.E. *The actor and the observer: Divergent perceptions of the causes of behavior*. New York: General Learning Press, 1971.

Jones, E.E., Rock, L., Shaver, K.G., Goethals, G.R., & Ward, L.M. Pattern of performance and ability attribution: An unexpected primacy effect. *Journal of Personality and Social Psychology*, 1968, **10**, 317-340.

Jones, R.A., Linder, D.W., Kiesler, C.A., Zanna, M., & Brehm, J.W. Internal states or external stimuli: Observers' attitude judgments and the dissonance-theory self-persuasion controversy. *Journal of Experimental Social Psychology*, 1968, **4**, 247-269.

Jordan, N. Behavioral forces that are a function of attitudes and of cognitive organization. *Human Relations*, 1953, **6**, 273-288.

Kanouse, D.E., & Abelson, R.P. Language variables affecting the persuasiveness of simple communications. *Journal of Personality and Social Psychology*, 1967, **7**, 158-163.

Kaplan, M.F. Context effects in impression formation: The weighted average versus the meaning change formulation. *Journal of Personality and Social Psychology*, 1971, **19**, 92-99. (a)

Kaplan, M.F. How response dispositions integrate with stimulus information. (Center for Human Information Processing, Technical Report No. 19.) La Jolla: University of California, San Diego, 1971. (b)

Kelley, H.H. The two functions of reference groups. In G.E. Swanson, T.M. Newcomb, & E.L. Hartley (Eds.), *Readings in social psychology.* New York: Holt, 1952.

Kelley, H.H. Salience of membership and resistance to change of group-anchored attitudes. *Human Relations,* 1955, **8**, 275-290.

Kelley, H.H. Attribution theory in social psychology. *Nebraska Symposium on Motivation,* 1967, **14**, 192-241.

Kelly, G.A. *The psychology of personal constructs.* New York: Norton, 1955.

Kelman, H.C. Compliance, identification, and internalization: Three processes of attitude change. *Journal of Conflict Resolution,* 1958, **2**, 51-60.

Kelman, H.C., & Hovland, C.I. "Reinstatement" of the communicator in delayed measurement of opinion change. *Journal of Abnormal and Social Psychology, 1953,* **48**, 327-335.

Kiesler, C.A., Nisbett, R.E., & Zanna, M.P. On inferring one's beliefs from one's behavior. *Journal of Personality and Social Psychology,* 1969, **11**, 321-327.

Kiesler, C.A., & Sakumura, J. A test of a model for commitment. *Journal of Personality,* 1966, **3**, 458-467.

Kogan, N., & Tagiuri, R. Interpersonal preference and cognitive organization. *Journal of Abnormal and Social Psychology,* 1958, **56**, 113-116.

Krantz, D.L., & Campbell, D.Y. Separating perceptual and linguistic effects of context shifts upon absolute judgments. *Journal of Experimental Psychology,* 1961, **62**, 35-42.

Lampel, A.K., & Anderson, N.H. Combining visual and verbal information in an impression-formation task. *Journal of Personality and Social Psychology,* 1968, **9**, 1-6.

Leaf, W.A., Kanouse, D.E., Jones, J.M., & Abelson, R.P. Balance, character expression, and the justice principle: An analysis of sentence evaluation. *Proceedings of the 76th Annual Convention of the American Psychological Association,* 1968, **76**, 423-424.

Lepper, M.R. Dissonance, self-perception, and honesty in children. *Journal of Personality and Social Psychology,* 1973, **25**, 65-74.

Leventhal, H. Findings and theory in the study of fear communications. In L. Berkowitz (Ed.), *Advances in experimental social psychology.* Vol. 5. New York: Academic Press, 1970.

Leventhal, H., & Trembly, G. Negative emotions and persuasion. *Journal of Personality,* 1968, **36**, 154-168.

Linder, D.E., Cooper, J., & Jones, E.E. Decision freedom as a determinant of the role of incentive magnitude in atttitude change. *Journal of Personality and Social Psychology,* 1967, **6**, 245-254.

Lund, F.H. The psychology of belief: IV. The law of primacy in persuasion. *Journal of Abnormal and Social Psychology,* 1925, **20**, 183-191.

Malewski, A. The influence of positive and negative self-evaluation on postdecisional dissonance. *Polish Sociological Bulletin,* 1962, **3-4**, 39-49.

Manis, M. The interpretation of opinion statements as a function of message ambiguity and recipient attitude. *Journal of Abnormal and Social Psychology,* 1961, **63,** 76-81.

McArthur, L.A. The how and what of why: Some determinants and consequences of causal attribution. *Journal of Personality and Social Psychology,* 1972, **22,** 171-193.

McFarland, S.G., & Thistlethwaite, D.L. An analysis of a logical consistency model of belief change. *Journal of Personality and Social Psychology,* 1970, **16,** 133-143.

McGuire, W.J. A syllogistic analysis of cognitive relationships. In M.J. Rosenberg, C.I. Hovland, W.J. McGuire, R.P. Abelson, & J.W. Brehm (Eds.), *Attitude organization and change.* New Haven: Yale University Press, 1960.

McGuire, W.J. Resistance to persuasion confirmed by active and passive prior refutation of the same and alternative counterarguments. *Journal of Abnormal and Social Psychology,* 1961, **63,** 326-332.

McGuire, W.J. Inducing resistance to persuasion: Some contemporary approaches. In L. Berkowitz (Ed.), *Advances in experimental social psychology.* Vol. 1. New York: Academic Press, 1964.

McGuire, W.J. Theory of the structure of human thought. In R.P. Abelson et al. (Eds.), *Theories of cognitive consistency: A sourcebook.* Chicago: Rand McNally, 1968. (a)

McGuire, W.J. Personality and susceptibility to social influence. In E.F. Borgatta & W.W. Lambert (Eds.), *Handbook of personality theory and research.* Chicago: Rand McNally, 1968. (b)

McGuire, W.J. The nature of attitudes and attitude change. In G. Lindzey & E. Aronson (Eds.), *Handbook of social psychology.* Vol. 3 (2nd ed.) Reading, Mass.: Addison-Wesley, 1968. (c)

McGuire, W.J., & Millman, S. Anticipatory belief lowering following forewarning of a persuasive attack. *Journal of Personality and Social Psychology,* 1965, **2,** 471-479.

McGuire, W.J., & Papageorgis, D. The relative efficacy of various types of prior belief-defense in producing immunity against persuasion. *Journal of Abnormal and Social Psychology,* 1961, **62,** 327-337.

McGuire, W.J., & Papageorgis, D. Effectiveness of forewarning in developing resistance to persuasion. *Public Opinion Quarterly,* 1962, **26,** 24-34.

Milgram, S. Liberating effects of group pressure. *Journal of Personality and Social Psychology,* 1965, **1,** 127-134. (a)

Milgram, S. Some conditions of obedience and disobedience to authority. *Human Relations,* 1965, **18,** 57-76. (b)

Miller, N.E., & Campbell, D.T. Recency and primacy in persuasion as a function of the timing of speeches and measurements. *Journal of Abnormal and Social Psychology,* 1959, **59,** 1-9.

Mills, J., & Jellison, J.M. Effect on opinion change of how desirable the communication is to the audience the communicator addressed. *Journal of Personality and Social Psychology,* 1967, **6,** 98-101.

Murdoch, P.H. The effects of categorization-style and cognitive risk upon judgment response language. Unpublished masters thesis, University of North Carolina at Chapel Hill, 1965.

Newcomb, T.M. *Personality and social change.* New York: Dryden, 1943.

Newcomb, T.M. Interpersonal balance. In R.P. Abelson et al.(Eds.), *Theories of cognitive consistency: A sourcebook.* Chicago: Rand McNally, 1968.

Niles, P. The relationship of susceptibility and anxiety to acceptance of fear-arousing communications. Unpublished doctoral dissertation, Yale University, 1964.

Nisbett, R.E., & Caputo, G.C. Personality traits: Why other people do the things they do. Unpublished manuscript, Yale University, 1971.

Nisbett, R.E., Legant, P., & Marecek, J. The causes of behavior as seen by actor and observer. Unpublished manuscript, Yale University, 1971.

Nisbett, R.E., & Schachter, S. Cognitive manipulation of pain. *Journal of Experimental Social Psychology,* 1966, **2,** 227-236.

Norris, E.L. Attitude change as a function of open or closed-mindedness. *Journalism Quarterly,* 1965, **42,** 571-575.

Nuttin, J.M., Jr. Attitude change after rewarded dissonant and consonant "forced compliance." *International Journal of Psychology,* 1966, **1,** 39-57.

Orne, M.T. On the social psychology of the psychological experiment: With particular reference to demand characteristics and their implications. *American Psychologist,* 1962, **17,** 776-783.

Osgood, C.E., Suci, G.J., & Tannenbaum, P.H. *The measurement of meaning.* Urbana: University of Illinois Press, 1957.

Osgood, C.E., & Tannenbaum, P.H. The principle of congruity in the prediction of attitude change. *Psychological Review,* 1955, **62,** 42-55.

Osterhouse, R.A., & Brock, T.C. Distraction increases yielding to propaganda by inhibiting counterarguing. *Journal of Personality and Social Psychology,* 1970, **15,** 344-358.

Ostrom, T.M. Perspective as an intervening construct in the judgment of attitude statements. *Journal of Personality and Social Psychology,* 1966, **3,** 135-144.

Ostrom, T.M. Meaning shift in the judgment of compound stimuli. Unpublished manuscript, Ohio State University, 1967.

Ostrom, T.M., & Upshaw, H.S. Psychological perspective and attitude change. In A.G. Greenwald, T.C. Brock, & T.M. Ostrom (Eds.), *Psychological foundations of attitudes.* New York: Academic Press, 1968.

Papageorgis, D. Anticipation of exposure to persuasive messages and belief change. *Journal of Personality and Social Psychology,* 1967, **5,** 490-496.

Papageorgis, D., & McGuire, W.J. The generality of immunity to persuasion produced by pre-exposure to weakened counterarguments. *Journal of Abnormal and Social Psychology,* 1961, **62,** 475-481.

Parducci, A. Category judgment: A range-frequency model. *Psychological Review,* 1965, **72,** 407-418.

Peabody, D. Trait inferences: Evaluative and descriptive aspects. *Journal of Personality and Social Psychology Monograph,* 1967, **7,** (4, Whole No. 644).

Peak, H. Attitude and motivation. *Nebraska Symposium on Motivation,* 1955, **3,** 149-188.

Peterson, C.R., & Beach, L.R. Man as an intuitive statistician. *Psychological Bulletin,* 1967, **68,** 29-46.

Peterson, C.R., Ulehla, L.J., Miller, A.J., Bourne, L.E., Jr., & Stilson, D.W. Internal consistency of subjective probabilities. *Journal of Experimental Psychology,* 1965, **70,** 526-533.

Pettigrew, T.F. The measurement and correlates of category width as a cognitive variable. *Journal of Personality,* 1958, **26,** 532-544.

Phillips, J.L. A model for cognitive balance. *Psychological Review,* 1967, **74,** 481-495.

Regan, D.T., & Cheng, J. Distraction and attitude change: A resolution. *Journal of Experimental Social Psychology,* 1973, **9,** 138-147.

Rodrigues, A. The psycho-logic of interpersonal relations. Unpublished doctoral dissertation, University of Michigan, 1966.

Rodrigues, A. Effects of balance, positivity, and agreement in triadic social relations. *Journal of Personality and Social Psychology,* 1967, **5,** 472-476.

Rokeach, M. *The open and closed mind.* New York: Basic Books, 1960.

Rokeach, M., & Rothman, G. The principle of belief congruence and the congruity principle as models of cognitive interaction. *Psychological Review,* 1965, **72,** 128-142.

Rosen, N.A., & Wyer, R.S. Some further evidence for the "Socratic effect" using a subjective probability model of cognitive organization. *Journal of Personality and Social Psychology,* 1972, **24,** 420-424.

Rosenbaum, M.E., & Levin, I.P. Impression formation as a function of source credibility and the polarity of information. *Journal of Personality and Social Psychology,* 1969, **12,** 34-37.

Rosenberg, M.J. An analysis of affective-cognitive consistency. In M.J. Rosenberg, C.I. Hovland, W.J. McGuire, R.P. Abelson, & J.W. Brehm (Eds.), *Attitude organization and change.* New Haven: Yale University Press, 1960.

Rosenberg, M.J. When dissonance fails: On eliminating evaluation apprehension from attitude measurement. *Journal of Personality and Social Psychology,* 1965, **1,** 28-42.

Rosenberg, M.J., & Abelson, R.P. An analysis of cognitive balancing. In M.J. Rosenberg, C.I. Hovland, W.J. McGuire, R.P. Abelson, & J.W. Brehm (Eds.), *Attitude organization and change.* New Haven: Yale University Press, 1960.

Rosenberg, S., Nelson, C., & Vivekananthan, P.S. A multidimensional approach to the structure of personality impressions. *Journal of Personality and Social Psychology,* 1968, **9,** 283-294.

Rosenberg, S., & Olshan, K. Evaluative and descriptive aspects in personality perception. *Journal of Personality and Social Psychology,* 1970, **16,** 619-626.

Rosenberg, S., & Sedlak, A. Structural representations of implicit personality theory. In L. Berkowitz (Ed.), *Advances in experimental social Psychology.* Vol. 6. New York: Academic Press, 1972.

Rubin, Z., & Zajonc, R.B.   Structural bias and generalization in the learning of social structures. *Journal of Personality,* 1969, **37,** 310-324.

Sampson, E.E., & Insko, C.A.   Cognitive consistency and performance in the autokinetic situation. *Journal of Abnormal and Social Psychology,* 1964, **68,** 184-192.

Sawyers, B.K., & Anderson, N.H.   Test of integration theory in attitude change. *Journal of Personality and Social Psychology,* 1971, **18,** 230-233.

Schacter, S., & Singer, J.E.   Cognitive, social, and physiological determinants of emotional state. *Psychological Review,* 1962, **69,** 379-399.

Schmidt, C.F.   Personality impression formation as a function of relatedness of information and length of set. *Journal of Personality and Social Psychology,* 1969, **12,** 6-11.

Schopler, J., & Bateson, N.   A dependence interpretations of the effects of a severe initiation. *Journal of Personality,* 1962, **30,** 633-649.

Scott, W.A.   Attitude change through reward of verbal behavior. *Journal of Abnormal and Social Psychology,* 1957, **55,** 72-75.

Scott, W.A.   Attitude change by response reinforcement: Replication and extension. *Sociometry,* 1959, **22,** 328-335.

Scott, W.A.   Conceptualizing and measuring structural properties of cognition. In O.J. Harvey (Ed.), *Motivation and social interaction.* New York: Ronald Press, 1963.

Scott, W:A.   Psychological and social correlates of international images. In H.C. Kelman (Ed.), *International behavior.* New York: Holt, Rinehart & Winston, 1965.

Scott,W.A.   Attitude measurement. In G. Lindzey & E. Aronson (Eds.), *Handbook of social psychology.* Vol. 2 (2nd ed.) Reading, Mass.: Addison-Wesley, 1968.

Secord, P.F., & Backman, C.W.   Personality theory and the problem of stability and change in individual behavior: An interpersonal approach. *Psychological Review,* 1961, **68,** 21-32.

Secord, P.F., & Backman, C.W.   Interpersonal congruency, perceived similarity, and friendship. *Sociometry,* 1964, **27,** 115-127.

Secord, P.F., Backman, C.W., & Eachus, H.T.   Effects of imbalance in the self-concept on the perception of persons. *Journal of Abnormal and Social Psychology,* 1964, **68,** 442-446.

Shannon, C.E., & Weaver, W.   *The mathematical theory of communication.* Urbana: University of Illinois Press, 1949.

Sherif, M., & Hovland, C.I.   *Social judgment.* New Haven: Yale University Press, 1961.

Sherman, S.J.   Attitudinal effects of unforseen consequences. *Journal of Personality and Social Psychology,* 1970, **16,** 510-521.

Sidowski, J.B., & Anderson, N.H.   Judgments of city-occupation combinations. *Psychonomic Science,* 1967, **7,** 279-280.

Skinner, B.F.   *Verbal behavior.* New York: Appleton-Century-Crofts, 1957.

Slovic, P., & Lichtenstein, S. Comparison of Bayesian and regression approaches to the study of information processing in judgment. *Organizational Behavior and Human Performance,* 1971, **6,** 649-744.

Snyder, M., & Ebbeson, E.B. Dissonance awareness: A test of dissonance theory versus self-perception theory. *Journal of Experimental Social Psychology,* 1972, **8,** 502-517.

Steiner, I.D. Reaction to adverse and favorable evaluation of one's self. *Journal of Personality,* 1968, **36,** 553-563.

Steiner, I.D. Perceived freedom. In L. Berkowitz (Ed.), *Advances in experimental social psychology.* Vol. 5. New York: Academic Press, 1970.

Steiner, I.D., & Field, W.L. Role assignment and interpersonal influence. *Journal of Abnormal and Social Psychology,* 1960, **61,** 239-246.

Steiner, I.D., & Spaulding, J. Preference for balanced situations. (Report No. 1, Department of Psychology) Urbana: University of Illinois, 1966.

Tannenbaum, P.H. Initial attitude toward source and concept as factors in attitude change through communication. *Public Opinion Quarterly,* 1956, **20,** 413-425.

Tannenbaum, P.H. Mediated generalization of attitude change via the principles of congruity. *Journal of Personality and Social Psychology,* 1966, **3,** 493-499.

Tannenbaum, P.H. The congruity principle revisited: Studies in the reduction, induction, and generalization of persuasion. In L. Berkowitz (Ed.), *Advances in experimental social psychology.* Vol. 3. New York: Academic Press, 1967.

Tannenbaum, P.H., & Gengel, R.W. Generalization of attitude change through congruity principle relationships. *Journal of Personality and Social Psychology,* 1966, **3,** 299-304.

Taylor, H.F. *Balance in small groups.* New York: Van Nostrand, 1970.

Thibaut, J.W., & Kelley, H.H. *The social psychology of groups.* New York: Wiley, 1959.

Thibaut, J.W., & Reicken, H. Some determinants and consequences of the perception of social causality. *Journal of Personality,* 1955, **24,** 113-133.

Thurstone, L.L. *The measurement of values.* Chicago: University of Chicago Press, 1959.

Upshaw, H.S. Own attitude as an anchor in equal-appearing intervals. *Journal of Abnormal and Social Psychology,* 1962, **64,** 85-96.

Upshaw, H.S. The effect of variable perspectives on judgments of opinion statements for Thurstone scales: Equal-appearing intervals. *Journal of Personality and Social Psychology,* 1965, **2,** 60-69.

Upshaw, H.S. The personal reference scale: An approach to social judgment. In L. Berkowitz (Ed.), *Advances in experimental social psychology.* Vol. 4. New York: Academic Press, 1969.

Valins, S. Cognitive effects of false heart-rate feedback. *Journal of Personality and Social Psychology,* 1966, **4,** 400-408.

Valins, S. Persistent effects of information about internal reaction: Ineffectiveness of debriefing. In H. London & R.E. Nisbett (Eds.), *The cognitive alteration of feeling states.* Chicago: Aldine, in press.

Volkman, J. Scales of judgment and their implications for social psychology. In J. H. Roher & M. Sherif (Eds.), *Social psychology at the crossroads.* New York: Harper, 1951.

Wallace, J. Role reward and dissonance reduction. *Journal of Personality and Social Psychology,* 1966, **3,** 305-312.

Walster, E., & Festinger, L. The effectiveness of "overheard" persuasive communications. *Journal of Abnormal and Social Psychology,* 1962, **65,** 395-402.

Walters, R.H., Marshall, W.E., & Shooter, J.R. Anxiety, isolation, and susceptibility to social influence. *Journal of Personality,* 1960, **28,** 518-529.

Warr, P. Combining three items of personal information. *British Journal of Psychology,* in press. (a)

Warr, P. Inference magnitude, range and evaluative direction as factors affecting relative importance of cues in impression formation. *Journal of Personality and Social Psychology,* in press. (b)

Waterman, C.K., & Katkin, E.S. Energizing (dynamogenic) effect of cognitive dissonance on task performance. *Journal of Personality and Social Psychology,* 1967, **6,** 126-131.

Watts, W.A., & Holt, L.E. Logical relationships among beliefs and timing as factors in persuasion. *Journal of Personality and Social Psychology,* 1970, **16,** 571-582.

Weiss, W. Opinion congruence with a negative source on one issue as a factor influencing agreement on another issue. *Journal of Abnormal and Social Psychology,* 1957, **54,** 180-186.

Wellens, R., & Thistlethwaite, D. An analysis of two theories of cognitive balance. *Psychological Review,* 1971, **78,** 141-151.

White, B.J., Alter, R.D., & Rardin, M. Authoritarianism, dogmatism, and usage of conceptual categories. *Journal of Personality and Social Psychology,* 1965, **2,** 293-295.

Wiest, W.M. A quantitative extension of Heider's theory of cognitive balance applied to interpersonal perception and self-esteem. *Psychological Monographs,* 1965, **79,** (14, Whole No. 607).

Wyer, R.S. The effects of incentive to perform well, group attractiveness, and group acceptance on conformity in a judgmental task. *Journal of Personality and Social Psychology,* 1966, **4,** 21-26.

Wyer, R.S. The effects of information redundancy on evaluations of social stimuli. *Psychonomic Science,* 1968, **13,** 245-246.

Wyer, R.S. Effects of general response style on own attitude and the interpretation of attitude-relevant messages. *British Journal of Social and Clinical Psychology,* 1969, **8,** 104-115. (a)

Wyer, R.S. A quantitative comparison of three models of impression formation. *Journal of Experimental Research in Personality,* 1969, **4,** 29-41. (b)

Wyer, R.S. Information, redundancy, inconsistency, and novelty and their role in impression formation. *Journal of Experimental Social Psychology,* 1970, **6,** 111-127. (a)

Wyer, R.S. The prediction of evaluations of social role occupants as a function of the favorableness, relevance, and probability associated with attributes of these occupants. *Sociometry,* 1970, **33,** 79-96. (b)

Wyer, R.S. The quantitative prediction of belief and opinion change: A further test of a subjective probability model. *Journal of Personality and Social Psychology,* 1970, **16,** 559-571. (c)

Wyer, R.S. Test of a subjective probability model of social evaluation processes. *Journal of Personality and Social Psychology,* 1972, **22,** 279-286.

Wyer, R.S. Category ratings as "subjective expected values": Implications for attitude formation and change. *Psychological Review,* 1973, **80,** 446-467. (a)

Wyer, R.S. The effects of information inconsistency and grammatical context upon evaluations of persons. *Journal of Personality and Social Psychology,* 1973, **25,** 45-49. (b)

Wyer, R.S. Further test of a subjective probability model of social inference processes. *Journal of Research in Personality,* 1973, **7,** 237-253.

Wyer, R.S. Changes in meaning and halo effects in personality impression formation. *Journal of Personality and Social Psychology,* 1974, in press. (a)

Wyer, R.S. Functional measurement analysis of a subjective probability model of cognitive functioning. *Journal of Personality and Social Psychology,* 1974, in press. (b)

Wyer, R.S. Some implications of the "Socratic effect" for alternative models of cognitive consistency. *Journal of Personality,* 1974, in press. (c)

Wyer, R.S., & Dermer, M. Effects of context and instructional set upon evaluations of personality-trait adjectives. *Journal of Personality and Social Psychology,* 1968, **9,** 7-14.

Wyer, R.S., & Goldberg, L. A probabilistic analysis of the relationships between beliefs and attitudes. *Psychological Review,* 1970, **77,** 100-120.

Wyer, R.S., & Lyon, J. A test of cognitive balance theory implications for social inference processes. *Journal of Personality and Social Psychology,* 1970, **16,** 598-618.

Wyer, R.S., & Polsky, H. Test of a subjective probability model for predicting receptiveness to alternative explanations of individual behavior. *Journal of Experimental Research in Personality,* 1972, **6,** 220-229.

Wyer, R.S., & Schwartz, S. Some contingencies in the effects of the source of a communication upon the evaluation of that communication. *Journal of Personality and Social Psychology,* 1969, **11,** 1-9.

Wyer, R.S., & Watson, S.F. Context effects in impression formation. *Journal of Personality and Social Psychology,* 1969, **12,** 22-33.

Zajonc, R.B. Cognitive theories in social psychology. In G. Lindzey & E. Aronson (Eds.), *Handbook of social psychology,* Vol. 1. (2nd ed.) Reading, Mass.: Addison-Wesley, 1968.

Zajonc, R.B., & Burnstein, E. The learning of balanced and unbalanced social structures. *Journal of Personality,* 1965, **33,** 153-163.

Zajonc, R.B., & Sherman, S.J. Structural balance and the induction of relations. *Journal of Personality,* 1967, **35,** 635-650.

Zimbardo, P.G., Cohen, A.R., Weisenberg, M., Dworkin, L., & Firestone, I. Control of pain motivation by cognitive dissonance. *Science,* 1966, **151,** 217-219.

Zimbardo, P., Snyder, M., Thomas, J., Gold, A., & Gurwitz, S. Modifying the impact of persuasive communications with external distraction. *Journal of Personality and Social Psychology,* 1970, **16,** 669-680.

Zimbardo, P.G., Weisenberg, M., Firestone, I., & Levy, B. Communicator effectiveness in producing public conformity and private attitude change. *Journal of Personality,* 1965, **33,** 233-255.

AUTHOR INDEX

Numbers in italics refer to the page on which the complete reference is listed.

494

SUBJECT INDEX

499